BRITTON ON FILM

BRITTON ON FILM
THE COMPLETE FILM CRITICISM OF ANDREW BRITTON

edited by Barry Keith Grant

with an Introduction by Robin Wood

WAYNE STATE UNIVERSITY PRESS

DETROIT

Library of Congress Cataloging-in-Publication Data

Britton, Andrew, 1952–1994.
Britton on film : the complete film criticism of Andrew Britton / edited
by Barry Keith Grant ; with an introduction by Robin Wood.
            p. cm. — (Contemporary approaches to film and television
series)
Includes bibliographical references and index.
ISBN 978-0-8143-3363-1 (pbk. : alk. paper)
1. Motion pictures. I. Grant, Barry Keith, 1947– II. Title.
PN1994.B68 2008

791.43—dc22
2008019046

To Art Efron, a mentor who taught me so much about criticism,
and Robin Wood, who first showed me how to be a critic of cinema

Andrew Britton was born in Salisbury, Wiltshire, in the United Kingdom in April 1952. He graduated in 1974 with a first-class degree in English and American Literature from King's College, London, and went on to study as a postgraduate at the University of Warwick with noted film critic Robin Wood.

Britton's career as a lecturer in Film Studies began at the same university in 1978, and he went on to teach at Essex University (1979–85), Trent University, Ontario, Canada (1985–88), York University, Ontario, Canada (1988–89), and Reading University, England (1992–93). He was also a guest lecturer at other universities in Britain, Canada, and the United States, including a term as a visiting professor at Queens University, Ontario, Canada in 1983.

Britton was a member of the editorial boards of the film magazines *Framework* and *Movie* and of the editorial collective of the Canadian magazine *CineAction*. In 1989–90, he was involved in program research at the National Film Theatre in London, and in 1991, he was editor of the official program of the London Film Festival. Britton was also a joint contributor to *The American Nightmare: Essays on the Horror Film* (1979) and the editor of *Talking Films* (1991). His book *Katharine Hepburn: The Thirties and After* (released in the United States as *Katharine Hepburn: Star as Feminist*) was nominated for the British Film Institute's Book of the Year Award in 1985.

Britton died of complications from AIDS in April 1994.

Contents

Part Four: Film and Cultural Theory

Preface

I met Andrew Britton only once, and that was just briefly. It must have been in late 1986 or early 1987, when I was visiting Robin Wood and Richard Lippe in their Toronto apartment to deliver (this was before the days of e-mail and the Internet) a final copy of my essay on Tobe Hooper's remake of *Invaders from Mars* for publication in their film journal, *CineAction*. Although at that time the journal still had the exclamation mark attached to its name, Certainly the moment had nothing of the drama that Wood describes in his introduction to this volume of his first meeting with Britton, whom he was taking on as a graduate student. In my case, I had been chatting amiably with Robin and the other members of the magazine's editorial collective when there was a knock at the door. It was Andrew, I believe just arriving or returning from the UK, for there was an intense and joyful connection that immediately arose between him and Robin when Andrew entered the room that implied a lengthy separation. I have a mental image of Andrew's face, politely saying hello to me when introduced but already looking beyond and then moving past me, his attention fixed on Robin. The connection between them was so strong, so palpable, that it seemed to exclude all else, certainly a stranger like myself. There was nothing for me but to depart, and as quickly as possible, I humbly took my leave.

Although Britton had hardly taken notice of me, I certainly had been aware of him for years through his writing. The horror film and the American Gothic had long been an interest of mine, and I remember the pleasure I took upon first reading "The Devil, Probably," his contribution to *The American Nightmare*, the landmark book on the horror film based around the retrospective that Wood programmed in 1979 for the Toronto International Film Festival (then known as the Festival of Festivals). Periodically, I would come across an essay by Britton, primarily through *CineAction* or *Movie*, and marvel at its erudition as well as the surgical precision with which he could critique a theoretical argument. Yes, he was merciless in his dissections, but he also was —there is no other word for it—funny. He possessed an inimitable ability to demolish a critical position while at the same time demonstrating a remarkably rich sense of humor. Coming to film studies with a background in literature, as I had—and suspected that Britton did as well—I particularly admired his ability to move with intellectual ease and assurance between cinema and prose fiction.

In the essay on *Invaders from Mars* that I discretely deposited on the table on my way out after meeting Britton, I compared the film to the 1953 original, directed by William Cameron Menzies, in order to tease out the implications of what I called "Science Fiction in the Age of Reagan." At the same time, Britton was publishing his much more ambitious and important piece "Blissing Out: The Politics of Reaganite Entertainment." His essay was astonishingly comprehensive in scope, monumental even, mine much more modest, but it was only one of a number of occasions when I took delight in discovering that this distinctive and always interesting critic was on a wavelength similar to mine.

Skeptical of theoretical trends, Britton was a critic who was remarkably attuned to the nuances of texts, whether cinema or literature. Consider his thorough readings of *Meet Me in St. Louis* and *Now, Voyager* as examples of his ability to provide fresh and compelling interpretations of canonical Hollywood films which have been the focus of much critical attention; by contrast, the essay on *Mandingo* shows how Britton managed to discover considerable value in a movie that otherwise had been completely overlooked by film scholars. Britton was able to question and resist the ideas of others because he was so persuasively detailed in his own analyses. Admirably, he did not shrink from exposing flaws even in important works by major artists, as he convincingly does, for example, in his discussion of Jean-Luc Godard's *Tout va bien*. Britton's grasp of theory, particularly Marxism and psychoanalysis, was extraordinary. His critiques of *Screen's* theoretical views and Wisconsin formalism are the most convincing I know. Yet, although he was adept with theory, he was less a theorist than a critic. By this I do not mean to suggest that theory and criticism are mutually exclusive, and Britton's work demonstrates as well as anyone's how they might work together.

I became involved in this book at Robin's suggestion. It was his initial idea to gather together his former student's essays on film and criticism, and he entrusted the task to me as an editor of some experience. Because of my familiarity with Britton's work and my shared opinion of its value, I agreed without hesitation to take on the job. Happily, my editorial labors, apart from the detective work involved in tracking down incomplete or missing references, have been a pleasure, for Britton's prose, for all its critical complexity, is at once remarkably elegant and supple. He left little for even the most assiduous editor to do beyond converting spelling and punctuation to American English, adding release dates to film titles, and the like. Occasionally I have added an endnote or parenthetical explanation of an unfamiliar term. In a way, my one personal encounter with Andrew Britton seems metaphoric of his place in the history of film studies. He was undeniably brilliant, but like all brilliant lights, he burned intensely and all too quickly. He produced this remarkable series of essays in just fifteen years, appearing for a brief moment on the critical horizon, and then he was gone. Although he seemed to have burst on the scene already a sophisticated and fully developed critical intelligence, he was not afforded the opportunity and time to grow as a film critic and produce the sustained body of work I have no doubt he would have. It is my hope, though, that the publication of this book will give to Britton's film criticism and theory the recognition it so clearly deserves.

Barry Keith Grant
St. Catharines, Ontario

Acknowledgments

As the volume editor, I am grateful to a number of people for helping to make this book happen. Annie Martin, Acquisitions Editor at Wayne State University Press, provided her unwavering support for this project from the beginning. Professors Hilary Radner and Alistair Fox of the Department of Media, Film and Communication at the University of Otago in Dunedin, New Zealand, were wonderful hosts during the summer of 2007 and generously allowed their graduate students to work on this project. Two of those students, Ph.D. candidates Bronwyn Polashek and Pamela Fossen, devoted their research skills to tracking down many of the incomplete references in the original essays. Kristin Harpster Lawrence at Wayne State University Press ably oversaw the book's production, David Alcorn of Alcorn Publication Design provided the excellent design and packaging of the book, and Linda O'Doughda was astonishingly diligent in her copyediting of the manuscript.

My own Department of Communication, Popular Culture and Film at Brock University in St. Catharines, Ontario, Canada, provided me with the necessary time to complete the manuscript. Justine Cotton, a Humanities and Social Sciences Reference Librarian at Brock, helped me track down some of the most mysterious references. Richard Lippe generously gave me access to his impressive stills collection, as did my colleague Jim Leach to his personal library. Andrew Britton's sister, Vanessa Fox, provided the information for her brother's biography. Dan Barnowski applied his technical expertise to digitally scan and prepare all the essays from their original sources. Finally, thank you to Robin Wood, at whose suggestion this book came to be and without whom it would have been impossible.

Thank you to the following journals for permission to reprint material which was originally published in their pages:

CineAction. "Cary Grant: Comedy and Male Desire," 7 (December 1986): 36–51; "A New Servitude: Bette Davis, *Now, Voyager* and the Radicalism of the Woman's Film," 26/27 (Winter 1992): 32–59; "*Meet Me in St. Louis*: Smith, or the Ambiguities," 35 (August 1994): 29–40; "Alfred Hitchcock's *Spellbound*: Text and Countertext," 3/4 (Winter 1986): 72–83; "Their Finest Hour: Humphrey Jennings and the British Imperial Myth of World War II," 18 (Fall 1989): 37–44; "In Defense of Criticism," 3/4 (January 1986): 3–5; "The Philosophy of the Pigeonhole: Wisconsin Formalism and 'The Classical Style,'" 15 (Winter 1988/89): 47–63; "The Myth of Postmodernism: The Bourgeois Intelligentsia in the Age of Reagan," 12/13 (August 1988): 3–17; "Consuming Culture: The Development of a Theoretical Orthodoxy," 19/20 (May 1990): 11–19.

Movie. "Sideshows: Hollywood in Vietnam," 27/28 (Winter 1980/Spring 1981): 2–23; "Blissing Out: The Politics of Reaganite Entertainment," 31/32 (Winter 1986): 1–42; "*The Exorcist*," 25

(Winter 1977–78): 16–20; *"Mandingo,"* 22 (Spring 1976): 1–22; *"10," "The Great Waldo Pepper,"* and *"The Other Side of Midnight,"* 27/28 (Winter 1980/Spring 1981): 105–8, 66–70, and 73–77, respectively; *"Metaphor and Mimesis: Madame de…,"* 29/30 (Summer 1982): 93–107; "Thinking about Father: Bernardo Bertolucci," 23 (Winter 1976–77): 9–22; "The Ideology of *Screen*," 26 (Winter 1978–79): 2–28.

Framework. "The Family in *The Reckless Moment,*" 4 (Autumn 1976): 17–24; "Sexuality and Power, or the Two Others," 6 (Autumn 1977): 7–11, 39; and 7/8 (Spring 1978): 4–11; "Living Historically: Two Films by Jean-Luc Godard," 3 (Spring 1976): 4–15.

"Detour" appeared originally in *The Movie Book of Film Noir*, ed. Ian Cameron (New York: Continuum, 1993), 174–83, and "Notes on *Pursued*" in *The Movie Book of the Western*, ed. Ian Cameron (London: Studio Vista, 1996), 196–205. "The Devil, Probably: The Symbolism of Evil" and *"Jaws"* appeared originally in *The American Nightmare*, ed. Robin Wood and Richard Lippe (Toronto: Festival of Festivals, 1979), 34–42 and 54–57, respectively. "Foxed: *Fox and His Friends*" appeared originally as part of "*Fox and His Friends*: An Exchange of Views by Bob Cant and Andrew Britton" in *Jump Cut* 16 (1977): 22–23. "For Interpretation: Notes Against Camp" appeared originally in *Gay Left* 7 (Winter 1978/79): 11–14.

Introduction: Andrew Britton and the Future of Film Criticism

by Robin Wood

"Our superior, gentlemen. Our superior in every way."
– Professor Carrington in Howard Hawks's *The Thing from Another World*

Andrew Britton was, and remains, quite simply, the greatest film critic in the English language. But he was not, like Hawks's monster from outer space, an "intellectual carrot." His greatness lies as much in his humanity as in his intelligence. His neglect (I am tempted to say "suppression") within most contemporary film studies programs is easily accounted for by that single word "humanity." Humanity has not seemed to enter very much, over the past two decades, in the academic world of film studies (an absence that, to my mind, partly discredits it, though it *has* come up with the occasional usable discovery). In its place we have had "theory." Theories can be useful (I have drawn on a number in my time), but when they become an end in themselves, they generally lose their utility. Over the last decade of academic film studies, we have witnessed many theories which come and go, the latest replacing the previous rather as in the fashion world. "Oh, Madam, we've just got this new theory in. *Everyone* will be wearing it soon. You really mustn't be seen without it." And of course, academics will simply *have* to keep up. I have never, at any stage in my career, considered myself an "academic" in this sense, and I'm fairly sure Andrew felt the same, although we both taught in universities.

I have received hints recently, from various sources, that "theory" is on the way out: a startling pronouncement. Could it mean that film studies teachers will have to start watching movies again? Or watching them as something more than "examples" illustrating the latest theory? If this is indeed the case, this is the ideal moment for the rediscovery (for many, no doubt, the discovery) of Andrew Britton. I want to say at once to any academic or nonacademic with a serious interest in the cinema—and I hope this will not be mistaken for "false modesty"—it is more important to read this book than to read my own collected writings. It is my hope that its publication will initiate no less than a new era in film studies.

There are a number of reasons for Andrew's neglect, which the present edition of his collected writings is intended to remedy. One reason is surely his quite devastating attacks on certain aspects of film theory: attacks which, to my knowledge, were never answered (because they couldn't be?) but were merely ignored, in the hope that they would go away or be forgotten.

(See the essays in part four of this book, "Film and Cultural Theory"). Another is that, in his relatively short life, he produced only one book, and his essays (spread over a number of different publications) have never before been collected. The book, ostensibly a study of Katharine Hepburn, has never been recognized for the major work it undoubtedly is. In my opinion, its release was mishandled, especially in its American edition published after Andrew's death, when, against my protests, its original title, *Katharine Hepburn: The 30s and After,* was changed to *Katharine Hepburn: Star as Feminist,* despite the fact that its author states very firmly that Hepburn could *not* be considered a "feminist" although her career is of interest to Feminism. It is, in fact, a book that should be compulsory reading for anyone seriously interested in the Hollywood cinema. It goes far beyond any narrow star study, with brilliant sections on genre, the "meanings" of stars, the phenomenon of cinematic partnerships (Tracy/Hepburn, Astaire/Rogers, Bogart/Bacall), along with detailed readings of Hepburn's major films.

Andrew and I

When I first met Andrew I had recently begun a new life. I had returned to England from three years at Queen's University in Kingston, Ontario, Canada, with a broken marriage and a new partner, John Anderson, who abandoned an extremely promising position with Universal Pictures in Toronto to live with me. I rapidly discovered that the world of film study had been transformed during my absence. Everything I stood for was passé, and semiotics (a word I had never encountered during my time in Canada) had taken over. I also discovered that I had in the meantime been set up as The Enemy (together, of course, with numerous others): I was branded an "anti-intellectual," a relic of a now discredited humanism. After a year of despair in London I applied (without much hope) for a new film studies position at Warwick University, to initiate its first film studies program.

To my amazement, I was accepted: my first real ego boost since returning to England. John and I moved to Coventry (the nearest city); John bought a house with his savings (my own income going largely for child support), and he and I started a new life. After a year or so there was another source of amazement: a graduate student from Australia, Tom Ryan, now a distinguished figure in the Australian film community, wanted to come and study under me. I couldn't understand why. Everything, then, was semiotics, the rudiments of which I was struggling to grasp, though more for the sake of understanding what was going on than from any sense that I might "join the club." Everyone who was progressive was into semiotics, and I had always thought of myself, in some sense, as "progressive." However, I readily (if with some trepidation) accepted my first graduate student guessing (correctly, apparently) that semiotics was as unfamiliar in Australia as it was in Canada. Tom moved in as our lodger. Another applicant soon turned up, however, this time British. I accepted him in fear and trembling, little knowing that he would transform my life.

I remember the morning I was to meet Andrew at Coventry station. It was very strange. I arrived early (I've always been afraid of keeping people waiting). I watched all the passengers emerge, scrutinizing all the faces to make out what I was letting myself in for. They dispersed, I waited. At last there was just one very tall, very dark-haired, slightly forbidding young man left. We looked at each other. We looked away. I looked at my watch. We looked at each other again. We looked away. I think I was the one who at last gave in to this mutually nervous exhibition of chronic shyness. I forced myself to go up to him and utter the momentous words, "Are you Andrew Britton?" And he was.

One of the first things I recall Andrew saying to me was that he had had to choose between me and Peter Wollen as his supervisor, and he had decided on me and Warwick. Peter's admirable *Signs and Meaning in the Cinema* was (quite rightly) one of the key texts of that time, the most accessible of the many texts on semiotics that were appearing. I recall that I didn't know how to respond; I just looked down at my feet and mumbled something about hoping Andrew had made the right choice, while actually feeling that he had made the wrong one. But at the same time, it came as the second great ego boost. Andrew, John, Tom, and I quickly bonded, together with a fifth member of what took on something of the closeness of a family, Deborah Thomas, who came over from America: another graduate student who chose Warwick and me because her thesis was on Ingmar Bergman, on whom I'd written a book and in whom the semioticians showed no interest. Deborah has since distinguished herself both as critic and as teacher in her admirable books (*Reading Hollywood, Beyond Genre*) with their meticulously detailed close readings, and she now lives permanently in England.

When (with the sponsorship of Peter Harcourt) I was offered a post at York University in Toronto, I leapt at it, largely because John, who had no legal status in Britain, wanted to return to Canada, where we separated while remaining close friends. Andrew followed, Richard Lippe became my new partner, and with occasional visits from Deborah, we continued as a kind of loose, mutually supportive family. In order to have legal status, Andrew entered into a marriage of convenience with a willing friend, but he never obtained more than a part-time and intermittent teaching position. Some years later he returned to England. Although it was never mentioned, I think we all knew that he had AIDS, at that time still a death sentence. He shut himself off from us completely, and died in his early forties. For a year afterward I frequently dreamed him alive, and woke up with a feeling of total desolation.

A Working Partnership

It didn't take long for me to recognize in Andrew a far finer mind than my own, at once broader and deeper, able (apparently with little effort) to encompass wider issues, to assimilate ideas and theories of which I would catch only uncertain and hesitant glimmers, able to probe deeper into the problems films raised, to uncover implications that I would often miss. To watch him read was a remarkable experience in itself: his eyes would travel swiftly down a page over which I would struggle for perhaps ten minutes and still have no great confidence that I had grasped its essentials, and he would be able to tell you what had been said. And so the student and the teacher exchanged roles. I learned a great deal from Andrew over the ensuing ten years, which resulted in what I now see clearly as my most fruitful, confident, and creative period—the period in which I wrote the new sections of *Hitchcock's Films Revisited* (1989), *Hollywood from Vietnam to Reagan* (1986), and what I regard as my best book, *Sexual Politics and Narrative Film* (1998).

There was no question here of "cribbing." I don't believe I stole Andrew's ideas, and I never tried to imitate him. It was a matter, rather, of his humility and my awareness that he genuinely respected my work. If he was aware, on some level, of its inferiority to his own, he never manifested this in any way, conscious or unconscious. Given the outspokenness—the outright and sometimes brutal contempt—that was released upon those critics and theorists he despised, "humility" may seem a strange word, yet there was nothing false about it; there was nothing false about Andrew. He was a great critic because he was a great human being, the greatness manifesting itself consistently in his writing. Of how many of our critics can this be said? I managed to remain very much myself. It was his support and encouragement that were so important to me. He never at any time made me *feel* my inferiority, and I am sure that his enthusiasm for my work was genuine.

We swiftly developed a great affection for each other, and a mutual respect, and I believe my support was as important to him as his to me. This would not have been possible, of course, without a shared basis in our interests and aims, in our attitudes and allegiances, both in art and, increasingly, in politics. My early work has no clear political basis. My political interests began prior to my relationship with Andrew, in my greatly overdue "coming out" as gay, my commitment to gay liberation and then, as a natural consequence, to radical feminism. It was Andrew who added Marxism (or, in my case, more precisely, a loose kind of socialism, as I've never read Marx) to my agenda. He was sometimes critical of my work and had no hesitation in attacking me in print (see, for example, his discussion of *The Deer Hunter* in the essay "Blissing Out: The Politics of Reaganite Entertainment"), clearly and rightly regarding such disagreements as beyond any personal relations. Above all, he was a person of innate and incorruptible goodness, the spirit of generosity very strong in him, however merciless to his professional enemies (for which see, again, the section on "Film and Cultural Theory" in this book).

Andrew was a great film critic because he was never "just" a film critic. Film has been with us for scarcely more than a hundred years; a great critic of *anything* should surely have a secure sense of belonging to a rich cultural tradition that goes back thousands. It is important for a critic to be grounded in (for example) Shakespeare and Tolstoy, Mozart and Mahler, Rembrandt and Klee. Andrew's intellectual and emotional roots were in literature, music, and the visual arts as much as in film, and the sense of value implicit in his writings is fed by that wider tradition. At the same time, his approach to criticism was by no means restricted to the search for masterpieces: he could find interest and a degree of value in films generally passed over (and in some cases already forgotten)—see his short pieces on *The Great Waldo Pepper* and *The Other Side of Midnight*.

We shared an admiration for the work of F. R. Leavis, the great literary critic, yet our relationship to his work was somewhat different. I had the great good fortune to be at Cambridge University during Leavis's tenure there, and I attended all his lectures religiously. To an extent, inexperienced and impressionable, I was swallowed up in the Leavis charisma, unable to distance myself or to achieve any independence of thought. Andrew had had no direct experience of Leavis, knowing him only from his books. For me, Leavis was for many years a kind of god figure, beyond doubt or question; to Andrew, he was one influence among many, though an important one, as I think is clear from Andrew's writings. We took over from Leavis a certain attitude to criticism, summed up by Leavis's familiar definition of the ideal critical exchange

("This is so, isn't it . . ."/"Yes, but . . ."), and to art in general (the notion that great art "is intelligent about Life"). But we also felt the necessity to move beyond Leavis into a more explicitly critical concern with the political (in the widest sense) implications of films, whether this was expressed openly or implicitly. This has become even more urgent since Andrew's death, though it consistently pervades his writings. We both knew that the serious critic can no longer (if s/he had ever wished to) pass down immaculate judgments from an ivory tower. Not only our civilization (or what is left of it) is at stake today but also the future of life itself, and our critical judgments must inevitably be affected by this condition. Andrew saw all this with admirable clarity, even in the years when global warming was little more than a scientific hypothesis. His work is always, implicitly, leftist and strongly committed.

Toward a Fully Responsible Criticism

Hopefully, the age of theory has not been wasted. Plausible theories of film should be available for reference, and theory classes should of course continue. However, certain points must be made. The theories with which I have come into (admittedly marginal) contact are not really "theories of film" but theories of mainstream cinema, and they should be designated as such. I have yet to hear of a theory that embraced (say) Howard Hawks, Yasujiro Ozu, Andrei Tarkovsky, Walt Disney, and Stan Brakhage, nor would such a thing be possible. In fact, one of the chief functions of film theory, from its roots in semiotics onward, seems in effect to have been to establish the proposition "Alternative cinema good, mainstream cinema bad," though this is sometimes misleading. When I first discovered the (in many ways admirable) texts of Raymond Bellour, for example, I assumed that he despised Hitchcock's films and was ruthlessly demolishing them. It was only when I met and talked with him that I abruptly realized, to my amazement, that he admired them perhaps even more than I did. It remains true, I think, that for many film students today a great film is not an emotional and intellectual experience that can change or modify one's sensibility, one's way of looking at the world; it's a piece of evidence to be slotted into the right pigeonhole. The lure of theory to the academic mind is obvious: the "truth" of a theory is alleged to be demonstrable (at least until the next one comes along and replaces it), whereas a value judgment, while it can be argued, cannot be proven. As soon as a theory is grasped, it can be manipulated by anyone, whereas a sense of value implies personal commitment and individual intelligence; it is not "there" to be applied to a given text. This is why theory is such a godsend to an all-too-common version of "the academic mind": mastering the theory requires a certain kind of intelligence (a kind I myself have never possessed, as abstract thought loses me rather quickly), but a kind that does not demand the personal and concentrated application, emotional as well as intellectual, of the whole human being. The familiar phrase "Oh, that's merely academic" is relevant here.

If the dominance of theory continues, at the expense of the detailed reading of actual films, their meaning and their value, there will be little left between the hermetic abstruseness of theory and the slick and superficial "entertainment" of most reviewers (who concern themselves only with the new releases). Academic film study will have closed itself off from any wider audience, and all continuity between academia and a wider public will be lost (it is fragile enough already).

Over the past few years, I have sensed a steadily rising disillusionment in academia generally, an increasingly widespread murmur that perhaps, after all, it has been a mistake to replace the study of films with the study of theories about them. The time seems ripe for Andrew Britton's posthumous comeback, and I look forward to seeing his work disseminated among film students. His sharp perceptions, often unanswerable judgments, and at times brilliant wit should certainly appeal to them. These readings of individual films and of the work of major directors are surely unsurpassable in their depth of insight, their attention to detail, their fluent sense of the relations among director, genre, star presence, and historical/political background. We are living in a progressively deteriorating and collapsing civilization on a planet that may already be doomed by human greed and obstinacy. We cannot afford to lose the voices of intelligence and integrity, in whatever field, in what may be the ultimate battle for life. Here is a voice that must not be lost.

BRITTON ON FILM

Part One
Hollywood Cinema

Cary Grant: Comedy and Male Desire (1986)

It should be said at the outset, in explanation of the method of this essay, that I wish to be concerned with the functions and thematic content of the Cary Grant persona. What follows is neither an account of Grant as a performer nor a biography or history of his career.

Obviously, much might be written on the subjects I have chosen to ignore. A theoretical interest in modes and traditions of performance could find no more complex and rewarding a theme than comic acting in the popular American cinema; and in Cary Grant, we have a striking, and highly specific, conjunction of diverse European and American comic conventions: British music hall, American vaudeville and variety, and the line of sophisticated comedy initiated by Ernst Lubitsch For a historian of the star system and its evolution, the details of Grant's career would have their significance. Grant was the first major star to go "independent": after his contract with Paramount expired in 1937, he was never again under exclusive contract to any studio, and he was centrally involved in the selection of his material and collaborating personnel.

The first of these subjects seemed to raise issues too large to be dealt with profitably in a short monograph on a single actor: the responsible discussion of performance (discussion, that is, radically unlike the familiar kind) would have demanded an attention to its contexts and lineage, and a range of comparative reference, which lie beyond the scope of this essay. The second, on the contrary, threatened either to narrow or to blur the focus: it acquired a secondary importance beside the things which it seemed to me most necessary to say about Grant.

These things concern definitions of masculinity, the use of comedy to criticize and transform traditional gender roles, and the extent to which characteristics assigned by those roles to women can be presented as being desirable and attractive in a man. I have chosen, accordingly, to concentrate on specific films and on Grant's meaning as the hero of them.[1]

There is a tendency to assume that the great stars are a known quantity. In an attempt to account for the appeal of Cary Grant, David Shipman writes:

> It is his elegance, his casualness, his unaccented charm; he is, as Tom Wolfe put it, "consummately romantic and consummately genteel"—"the old leathery charmer," in Alexander Walker's words (regretting his earlier, more interesting existence as a "hard-eyed cad"). It certainly isn't from acting ability: his range must be the most limited of all the great matinee idols. His gift for light comedy has been much touted, but it's been a mite heavy at times and one can think of half a dozen names who were sometimes better. (254)

That is probably representative. The "limited range" needn't detain us: the assumption involved is so clearly that which inspires Pauline Kael to remark that "one does not necessarily admire an icon, as one admires, say, Laurence Olivier, but it can be a wonderful object of contemplation," and to suggest that Grant "might have become a great actor" if he had "taken more risks like *None but the Lonely Heart.*" (Kael, "The Man from Dream City," 26)

But the "charm" and the "romantic" obviously call for comment, and it may be useful to begin by emphasizing an aspect of them which is habitually ignored. Consider the dialogue of the love scene on the train in *North by Northwest* (1959).

> EVE: This is ridiculous. You know that, don't you?
> THORNHILL: Yes.
> EVE: I mean, we've hardly met.
> THORNHILL: That's right.
> EVE: How do I know you aren't a murderer?
> THORNHILL: You don't.
> EVE: Maybe you're planning to murder me, right here, tonight.
> THORNHILL: Shall I?
> EVE: Please do. [They kiss.]
> THORNHILL: Beats flying, doesn't it?
> EVE: We should stop.
> THORNHILL: Immediately.
> EVE: I ought to know more about you.
> THORNHILL: Oh, what more could you know?
> EVE: You're an advertising man, that's all I know.
> THORNHILL: That's right. Oh, the train's a little unsteady.
> EVE: Who isn't?
> THORNHILL: What else do you know?
> EVE: You've got taste in clothes, taste in food.
> THORNHILL: Taste in women. I like your flavor.
> EVE: And you're very clever with words. You can probably
> make them do anything for you . . . sell people things they don't need
> . . . make women who don't know you fall in love with you.
> THORNHILL: I'm beginning to think I'm underpaid.

The sense of an ironic lack, or refusal, of intimacy which this communicates is an inflection of something which is, in fact, characteristic of Grant's love scenes, and of his playing of them. Alfred Hitchcock, characteristically, takes the exchange of sophisticated wit to the verge of the unpleasant: Thornhill's self-regarding self-possession is assimilated, on the one hand, to the economic values of Madison Avenue and, on the other, to an irresponsible male sexual consumerism. In retrospect, of course, the irony is complicated by our discovery of who Eve is, but the revelation that Thornhill's feeling of urbane mastery in the love scene is illusory doesn't alter the fact that it is there to be cultivated. Indeed, it is the crux of the irony that prior to Eve's deception of him (which, unlike his own sexual confidence, isn't inspired by egotism), Thornhill has told her, "honest women frighten [him]."

The use to which Hitchcock puts Grant here isn't unprecedented. In his fifth film, *Blonde Venus* (1932), Grant plays a wealthy businessman who uses the need of Helen Faraday (Marlene Dietrich) for money to make her become his mistress. Two films later, he was cast as Pinkerton in a version (nonmusical!) of *Madame Butterfly* (1933). In *Sylvia Scarlett* (1935), he plays a confidence trickster who appears, at the outset, to embody for Sylvia (Katharine Hepburn) the promise of liberating adventure but who is gradually revealed to be cynically exploitative. In *Indiscreet* (1958), Philip Adams pretends to Anna Kalman (Ingrid Bergman) that he is married and unable to obtain a divorce so as to keep her as his lover while avoiding a substantial commitment to her.

Suspicion (1941) and *Notorious* (1946), the first two of Grant's four films with Hitchcock, fully elaborate this aspect of the persona, subordinating it entirely to the director's thematic concern with the male need to possess and subjugate female sexuality. In the Devlin of *Notorious*, sexual egotism becomes an extraordinarily convoluted misogyny—Devlin seeks to turn Alicia (Ingrid Bergman) into a whore so that he can then despise her for being one—and imagery and narrative movement link the romantic hero directly to his antagonist, Sebastian (Claude Rains): the film begins with Alicia's relapse into alcoholism in response to Devlin's refusal to trust her and ends with Sebastian's attempt to poison her. Like his counterpart, Mark Rutland (Sean Connery), in *Marnie* (1964), Devlin can accept the heroine only when she has been reduced to a state of complete emotional and physical prostration. The long-take kissing sequence, with its disturbingly impersonal sensuality (it anticipates the train sequence in *North by Northwest*), is usefully emblematic of these things. Asked by Devlin to explain her remark that "this a very strange love affair," Alicia replies, "Perhaps because you don't love me."

It is not merely perverse to preface an account of Grant by noting a use of him which no one will argue to be fully characteristic. What these roles have in common is an urbane amoralism and irresponsibility, issuing in the exploitation of women; but "irresponsibility"—which turns out to be a key word in discussing Grant—can be defined in more than one way, and Grant is not only a lover figure but also a comedian. In *Notorious* and *Suspicion*, irresponsibility appears entirely negatively, as sexual opportunism, and Alicia and Lina (Joan Fontaine) are subtly complicit with their exploitation. Significantly, both women initially see the Grant character as a means of detaching themselves from, and rebelling against, fathers they hate, only to discover that they have become subject to another form of patriarchal oppression, to which they then succumb out of a masochistic fascination (Lina) or a self-contempt which the man relentlessly exacerbates (Alicia). The Hitchcock films are distinguished from, say, *Indiscreet* by the absence of the comedy of male chastisement. Stanley Donen's film really takes off, after its turgid exposition, when Anna discovers that she has been deceived and sets about exacting retribution. And it is in general true that when, in comedy, the Grant character is closest to the cynical emotional detachment and exploitativeness of Devlin, he is partnered by an active heroine who contests the terms of the relationship between them and undertakes his "spiritual education."

"The comedy of male chastisement": Grant's movies are full of scenes in which he is subjected to the most extreme discomfiture, humiliation, and loss of face by women. *Bringing Up*

Baby (1938) and *I Was a Male War Bride* (1949) are obviously the most excessive cases—Howard Hawks takes the persona as far in this direction as Hitchcock does in the other—but examples are multiple. Consider the magnificent sequence in *The Awful Truth* (1937) in which Lucy Warriner (Irene Dunne), masquerading as the sister of her ex-husband Jerry (Grant), discredits him in front of his new fiancée, Barbara Vance, and her upper-class family; or the sequence in *Mr. Lucky* (1943) in which Dorothy Bryant (Laraine Day) compels Joe Adams (Grant) to join a group of women war-relief workers and learn to knit while male passersby gradually gather, astounded, at the window; or the moment in *Houseboat* (1958) in which Tom Tinston (Grant), immaculately attired for work, finds the gangplank of the houseboat slowly subsiding beneath him, to the delight of Cinzia (Sophia Loren) and his children.

Given that the comedy of moments such as these is so often bound up with the undermining of masculinity—or, at the least, of male prestige and dignity—it is remarkable that the comedy is never hostile and that, since the Grant character is not ridiculed, the sense in which he appears ridiculous is a complex one. It is partly a matter of the loss of dignity being continuous with the loss of qualities which have no positive value whatever: the social world of the Vances in *The Awful Truth* and the diplomatic milieu of *Houseboat* are rejected by the films. At the same time, Grant's acting characteristically conveys an ironic distance from, or pleasurable complicity with, his degradation: at first appalled and embarrassed by Lucy's eruption into his fiancée's home, Jerry is more and more delighted by it; *Bringing Up Baby* ends with David Huxley (Grant) admitting that the day he spent with Susan (Katharine Hepburn) was the most wonderful of his life. Here, loss of dignity involves the acquisition of a kind of irresponsibility which is very different from the kind Grant embodies in *Suspicion*.

Discussion can be focused by referring in greater detail to the great comedies of the late '30s: the first of them, *The Awful Truth*, clinched Grant's status as a major star. Leo McCarey's film begins with Jerry Warriner stretched out under a sunlamp at his club, trying hastily to cultivate the tan which his wife will naturally expect him to have acquired during a supposed visit to Florida. Jerry's deceit of her is accompanied by the conviction (quite unfounded) that Lucy has been unfaithful to him, and in the ensuing recriminations the two agree to divorce. If Jerry's combination of possessive jealousy and duplicity is viewed negatively, his ebullience appears in a more favorable light in comparison with Lucy's new suitor, Daniel Leeson (Ralph Bellamy), who may be described, with every propriety, as "straight." Daniel offers Lucy a conventional respectability and probity and a conventional sexual role: he treats her with deeply felt but labored gallantry and deference, which will be her reward for uncomplaining acquiescence in the duties of a wife.

But while Jerry and Daniel are sharply distinguished from each other, they have in common a refusal to trust Lucy, which is rooted in two opposite but complementary forms of masculine complacency. Jerry takes for granted his own right to a life independent of his marriage, and to lie to Lucy about it, but he swells with proprietary indignation when Lucy claims the same right for herself. Daniel, in turn, assumes that Lucy can have no desire which life with him cannot satisfy. His sentimental chivalry is the counterpart of Jerry's insincerity, and each man conceals a possessiveness which denies any freedom or autonomy to Lucy herself and is all too ready to conclude that she has "broken her trust."

The action of the film consists in the comic correction of Jerry's insincerity and the comic confirmation of his energy: that is, the function of the comedy is to distinguish between, and evaluate, two forms of irresponsibility. The insincerity and the associated proprietorship express a conviction of male sexual right, and correction takes the form of loss of face. Consider the sequence in which Jerry, convinced yet again that Lucy is having an affair with her singing teacher, Armand Duvalle (Alexander D'Arcy), bursts into Duvalle's apartment only to discover that Lucy is singing, to Duvalle's accompaniment, before a large audience. Jerry attempts to save the situation by taking a seat at the back of the room, but he is further confounded when the chair collapses; and Lucy, delighted by his humiliation, converts the closing phrase of her song into a gentle laugh of triumph.

If *The Awful Truth* chastises male presumption and opportunism, the energies it affirms are energies Jerry shares with Lucy. Masculinity, as Ralph Bellamy invaluably embodies it, is presented—in that unadulterated form—as stolid, lumpish, and boring, and his peculiar relationship to energy is given to us in his performance on the dance floor and his rendering of "Home on the Range." The tone of the reference to the western is crucial, both to an understanding of screwball comedy and to the significance of its supreme male practitioner. The West, where definitions of masculinity are concerned, traditionally provides the norm of potency and derives its meaning from its opposition to settlement and "civilization"—the domesticity which, in American culture, is synonymous with the oppressive power of women and which threatens the male with emasculation. *The Awful Truth* retains one part of this opposition and reverses the other. Civilization is still associated with femininity, but it appropriates from the West the free play of anarchic energy, and the western hero appears as the spokesman of repression, propriety, and constraint.

To say no more would be, of course, to simplify. Civilization in *The Awful Truth* is also the Vances, just as in *Holiday* (1938) it is the Crams and in *Bringing Up Baby* it is the dinosaur. It is an essential characteristic of the couples created at the end of these films that they cannot exist in established bourgeois society: *The Awful Truth* ends in a snowbound ski lodge in the mountains, *Holiday* on a liner between America and Europe, and *Bringing Up Baby*, most drastically of all, on a rickety scaffolding with the dinosaur, the film's central image of bourgeois patriarchy, lying in ruins beneath it. If *The Awful Truth* recognizes the enabling possibilities of civilization, it also perceives that what is enabled is incompatible with civilization as it is and, indeed, expresses itself in defiance of it: Lucy's disruption of the Vances' dinner party, the departure of Linda (Katharine Hepburn) from her father's house (*Holiday*), and Susan's destruction of the skeleton (*Bringing Up Baby*) have obvious points in common.

"The enabled" is, in each case, a revision of bourgeois gender roles: it is the Grant character's commitment to, and acquisition of, a subversive "femininity," and the consequent redistribution of power within the couple, which makes the couple socially impossible. In each case, too, femininity partakes both of civilization and of the drives which civilization alienates. Femininity in *Bringing Up Baby* is not only the leopard but also Miss Katharine Hepburn, New England heiress, Bryn Mawr graduate, and notorious representative of high-toned culture. The anarchic energies released in these films do not subserve a fantasy of regression to a pre-cultural stage, and they have nothing in common with that model of the return of the repressed enacted by the Gothic, shared by Freud, and leading both, finally, to stalemate. We may feel that a return of the repressed is involved, but it doesn't have the suggestion of "dark primal forces" which so often accrues to the monster in the horror film and which allows the genre to rationalize the reinstatement of repression. If the femininity which erupts in *The Awful Truth*, *Holiday*, and *Bringing Up Baby* is inimical to the society it disturbs, it is also associated, as is usual in the American tradition, with sophistication and refinement. This dual character makes the repressed that returns not the monstrous inhabitant of the "seething cauldron of excitements" (Freud's own phrase) which precedes social life, and on whose containment social life depends, but the harbinger of a more free and pleasurable culture.

I have noted that, as regards Jerry, the comedy of *The Awful Truth* has two distinct functions, and it will be obvious that, throughout the film, he and Lucy visit humiliation on each other. Jerry's insincerity and negative irresponsibility are very much a part of the world of the Vances in which he figures as urbane and eligible male and in which the aspects of sophistication to which the film is opposed are concentrated. The scenes of which he is the butt serve to chasten his presumptuous possessiveness of Lucy (the concert) and to expose and detach Jerry from the ethos in which insincerity is a constituent of urbane form (Lucy's masquerade). Yet it is what Jerry and Lucy have in common that allows Jerry to function as he does in Lucy's relationship with Daniel Leeson and that makes the hilarious sequence in which, concealed from his rival behind a door, Jerry repeatedly makes Lucy laugh at Daniel's heartfelt recitation of his doggerel love poem by tickling her under the arm so unlike an exercise of power over her. It is always apparent that Daniel is Lucy's drastic overcompensation for what is at fault in Jerry and that she recognizes, and resists, from the outset the staid sexual decorum that Daniel brings with him. Jerry, in the scene just mentioned, evokes Lucy's own sense of absurdity: the scene would be distasteful rather than funny if we felt that anything more than politeness was involved in *not* laughing at Daniel's poem.

The substance of this point can be demonstrated by comparing *The Awful Truth* and *His Girl Friday* (1939), the thematic parallels being so close. Hawks's film is another comedy of remarriage in which, again, the marriage has broken up because of the Grant character's irresponsibility, and in which the alternative man is played once more by Ralph Bellamy. The astonishing brilliance of *His Girl Friday* is legendary, but merely to place it beside McCarey's film (or *Bringing Up Baby*) is enough to reveal the drastic limitations summed up neatly by Robin Wood: "Given the alternatives the film offers, the only morally acceptable ending would be to have Hildy walk out on both men; or to present her capitulation to Walter as tragic." (*Howard Hawks*, 77) Walter Burns, of all Grant's comic characters, is the closest to Devlin, but while in *Notorious* the loathsomeness of the character is clearly and consistently the issue, in *His Girl Friday* it isn't, and by the time we get to "Stick Hitler on the funny pages!" the confusion of attitude could hardly be greater. The confusion is generated both by the transportation of the asocial male group of the Hawksian adventure film into the bourgeois world of the comedies and by Hawks's inability to decide whether the group is implicated in that world or an answer to it. The indecision is reflected in the treatment of Hildy (Rosalind Russell). She is hardly a representative Hawks comic heroine: Bruce Baldwin would have to be played by Cary Grant rather than Ralph Bellamy to make that of her. At the same time, because Hawks does not really know what he thinks of the values of the group, he is unable fully to endorse the theme of the heroine's assimilation to it characteristic of the adventure films. Hildy's withering "Gentlemen of the Press!" in the aftermath of the journalists' brutal harassment of Mollie Malloy (Helen Mack) implies a definitive judgment on the group to which the film gives great weight, but from which it is entirely unable to follow through.

The particular material of *His Girl Friday* deprives the male group of its value as a positive alternative to bourgeois society while also demanding a reconceptualization of the comic function of the Hawks heroine which Hawks is unwilling, or unable, to undertake. For, if Walter Burns scarcely needs to have alienated energy liberated, he is very much a candidate for the correction of male arrogance and complacency. Walter is obviously exploiting Hildy, and *His Girl Friday* demands—uniquely in Hawks's comedies—an explicitly political and explicitly feminist development of the theme of the woman's education of the hero. Such a development is hardly conceivable, and Hawks responds by producing a Hawks comedy in reverse: the film traces the process by which Hildy is worn down into submission and ends—astonishingly, after she has been reduced to tears—with her following Walter out of the Press Room weighed down by baggage which he refuses to help her carry.

The process by which Lucy is detached from Daniel Leeson in *The Awful Truth* is, for all the structural similarity, very different. In effect, Lucy and Jerry function as the return of the repressed for each other: each intrudes in turn to prevent the other's entry into a world of family in the company of partners who respectively embody, in parodic form, the accumulated associations of "West" and "East." That much of the film's comedy consists in the dramatization of repression is particularly clear in McCarey's use of Mr. Smith, the Warriners' pet terrier. Mr. Smith, standing in for a child, clearly represents the marriage. The divorce hearing ends with a dispute over custody, and Mr. Smith is unable, when invited, to choose between the partners, though Lucy finally wins his preference by the underhanded stratagem of producing, surreptitiously, his favorite toy. In one of the film's most sustained comic set pieces, Lucy finds herself having to conceal from Jerry the fact that Armand is in the apartment, and then, surprised by a visit from Daniel, to conceal the presence of both men from him. Having hidden the men themselves, Lucy notices the compromising presence of their bowler hats. Throughout the sequence, Mr. Smith, with pertinacious insistence and to Lucy's increasing discomfiture, repeatedly retrieves the hats from their hiding place and returns with them, and the threat of scandal, to the parlor. The sequence ends with the eruption of Jerry and Armand from concealment and the besmirching of Lucy's reputation, which puts an end to her relationship with Daniel. The comedy is beautifully succinct: Mr. Smith, as emblem of the marriage, acts through the submerged logic of Lucy's "forgetting" of the hats and realizes her desire to check the onset of domesticity.

The use of Mr. Smith both as symbol of the Warriners' union and as focus of the comedy of repression is crucial to the significance of *The Awful Truth*. In not being a child, but replacing one, Mr. Smith dissociates the marriage from reproduction, or the prospect of it. (This function is fulfilled even more strikingly in Asta the dog's next incarnation—as George in *Bringing Up Baby*—where he actually deprives David of the phallus by burying his "old bone" in the garden, thus fulfilling David's unexpressed desire to stay at Susan's farm and to fail to complete the skeleton of the dinosaur. I will return to the sexual symbolism of Hawks's film in greater detail later.) Indeed, far from representing a child, Mr. Smith (again, like George) seems at once to express and to provide an occasion for a kind of childlikeness in the couple. Consider the sequence in which Jerry and Daniel first meet at Lucy's apartment. As Daniel and Lucy talk about the divorce, Jerry romps boisterously on the floor with Mr. Smith, and Lucy responds to Daniel's evident surprise at such behavior by remarking merely, with a marvelously offhanded drop of the wrist, that that is her husband. *Bringing Up Baby* gives us an exactly analogous moment. Susan's aunt, believing David to be a big game hunter, discovers him chasing after George through the shrubbery in a desperate search for the missing bone, and on asking Susan, in astonishment, if that is what David understands by big game hunting, receives the reply that "David is playing with George." Both incidents turn on a discrepancy between the behavior of the Grant character and a conventional paradigm of masculinity ("the West" and Hemingway machismo, respectively), and in both cases, the fact that the discrepancy also involves an opposition between the liberation of energy and its constraint gives to "playing with the dog" a strong positive connotation. Masculinity appears here as a code learned from the book of myth, and we are invited to laugh at the decorous inhibitedness of the student.

Juxtaposing the central couples of *The Awful Truth*, *Bringing Up Baby*, and *Holiday*, we see that ideas of "play" and the "childlike" are fundamental to all of them, and that in each case play is directly linked to a rebellion against patriarchal sexuality. I have analyzed *Holiday* at length in my book on Katharine Hepburn and will do no more here than point to the significance of the playroom, and its association, through Linda's mother (who died, Ned [Lew Ayres] tells us, trying to be a good wife), with oppressed and liberating non-phallic sexual energy. The principle of all three films is to identify play in the sense of recovered infantile polymorphousness (which is, effectively, the meaning of "screwball") with "sophistication," the apogee of cultivated adulthood. The sophisticated couple is the couple whose sexuality is no longer organized by the phallus. The characteristic co-presence in these works of the two apparently distinct comic modes of farce and wit is the expression of this thematic principle. The partners engage in roughhouse, epigram, and repartee; the anarchic consorts with the urbane; the infantile drives that precede maturity and civilization are suddenly definitive of them.[2]

The Grant characters in these films can be distinguished by virtue of their precise relation to these drives. In *Holiday*, they unite Linda and Johnny from the start: Linda's commitment to the playroom and Johnny's to his holiday represent two parallel forms of irresponsibility, the alignment of which, as the film progresses, gradually defines play equally as non-phallic desire and as the refusal of alienated labor. In *Bringing Up Baby*, Susan is David's liberator: the hero's polymorphous energies have been entirely repressed, and the male ego must be destroyed in order to release them. *The Awful Truth* embodies a kind of middle term in that the hero's education involves the correction rather than the liberation of energy. The films are united, remarkably, by their affirmation of a feminized hero and of a couple whose validity and vitality are continuous with his feminization. Hawks's film, as the most extreme of the three, demands closer consideration here: the way in which it redefines a process we might be tempted to describe as "emasculation" is fundamental to our sense of the value of the Grant persona.

Bringing Up Baby begins with Professor David Huxley on the verge of final and complete assimilation to a world of "order," which is defined in terms of three interdependent characteristics.

1. A particular concept of reason, logic, and rational inquiry, the sterility and obsolescence of which are already implied by its being dedicated to the reconstruction of the skeleton of a brontosaurus. As Susan later remarks of the intercostal clavicle, "It's only an old bone." As the film progresses, this model of reason is increasingly generalized so as to refer to a whole organization of the ego. David's consciousness and sense of self are entirely bound up with his status as a scientist.

2. Bourgeois marriage. David's imminent marriage to Alice Swallow (Virginia Walker) is immediately linked to the dinosaur through David's remark, on receiving the telegram announcing the discovery of the missing bone, that it's so marvelous that "two such important things should happen on the same day." Alice tells David their marriage will have "no domestic entanglements of any kind"; and while he goes on to mention having children, it is sufficiently clear, even if one doesn't know either Hawks's work or the genre, that what is at issue is not reproduction but sexual pleasure. The marriage will be "purely dedicated to your work"—that is, to the repression and alienation of sexual energy.

3. Capitalism. David's rational inquiry is to be funded by a million-dollar grant, which he must devote himself to extracting from the legal representative of Mrs. Carlton-Random (May Robson), the benefactor.

The brontosaurus is the film's inclusive image for this world. Later, casting round desperately for an incognito for David, Susan settles, with perfect accuracy, for "Mr. Bone." He is about to enter patriarchy, and his destiny will be to perpetuate it.

The whole meaning of *Bringing Up Baby* turns on the evidence, in the opening sequences, of David's resistance to this destiny. The resistance is, at this stage, unconscious and manifests itself in a series of Freudian slips. David has forgotten who Peabody is ("Peabody? What Peabody?"), and he also has to be reminded of Mrs. Carlton-Random and the prospective endowment. In the next sequence, on the golf course, he has again forgotten that Peabody is only Mrs. Carlton-Random's lawyer and does not actually have the money in his gift. When he arrives at the nightclub, David is unable to make up his mind whether to keep or to check his top hat, an item of the formal uniform he has put on to impress Peabody; a. few moments later, David's second meeting with Susan is marked by his slipping up and squashing the hat ("You throw an olive and I sit on my hat—it's all perfectly logical.").

Thereafter, the meaning of these "errors" is clarified: they cease merely to express an antagonism to what David thinks he wants and become explicitly the means of fulfilling a wish for what he thinks he doesn't want. After Susan has torn his coat, David tells her that he is going to count to ten with his eyes closed, and he wants her to have disappeared when he opens them. She promptly walks away, and it is revealed that David has been standing on the hem of her dress, thus causing the "accident" that forces them together again.

Two sequences later, David watches, appalled, as Susan tries to wake Peabody by hurling pebbles at his bedroom window, and, having virtually confessed his complicity ("I think we ought to go now, but somehow I can't move"), sees her fell with an enormous rock the man on whom his future depends.

One aspect of David's slips is especially important, given the film's thematic: that is, the forgetting or confusion of names and identities and—more generally—the breakdown of rational discourse. Much of the comedy of *Bringing Up Baby* is a matter of the disintegration, simultaneously, of the apparently stable male ego and its language. As David leaves the museum for the golf course, he is already saying, "Good-bye, Alice—I mean, professor": even at this stage, his slips are being connected with the mistaking of gender. Subsequently, Hawks uses this motif to link David and the film's other representative patriarchal figures: the agent of law, Constable Slocum (Walter Catlett); the adventurer, Major Applegate (Charles Ruggles); and the psychiatrist, Dr. Lehmann (Fritz Feld). Susan tells her aunt that David's name is Mr. Bone, without forewarning David himself. Aunt Elizabeth proceeds, in all innocence, to introduce David to Major Applegate as Mr. Bone, and David, attributing the unfamiliar name to the major, says, "Hello, Mr. Bone" at the same moment the major does. The scene ends with the major calling out, "Good-bye, Major Applegate" as David leaves.

Throughout the jail sequence, Constable Slocum persists in believing that the characters cannot be who they say they are and adheres tenaciously to Susan's fantastic misrepresentation of them. Having explained to Susan that psychiatrists do not believe that everyone who behaves strangely should be described as "crazy," Dr. Lehmann, the film's professional adjudicator of the rational, produces a massive, unconscious facial convulsion. In each case, the patriarch's assurance of competence and self-possession is shown to be illusory: the harmonious male ego is jangled by the slightest vibration.

The themes of language and repression are again interconnected during the amazingly dense expository sequence in the museum. When finally reminded of who Peabody is, David becomes wildly vivacious and enthusiastic and tells Alice, "I'll knock him for a loop," only to receive the stern admonition: "No slang, David! Remember who and what you are!" It is clearly important, given Susan's masquerade as Swinging-Door Susie in the jail sequence, that David's failure to remember who and what he is should express itself here in the use of slang.

Thus, Susan's sudden appearance on the golf course isn't arbitrary. As David's future lover, she is both a character in her own right and the embodiment of repressed impulses in David himself—impulses which he fears but to which he's sufficiently drawn to conjure them up so as to prevent his induction into patriarchy. Susan's value is defined through a series of reversals of the values of David's world. Consider, for example, Susan's language, which impedes rational discourse as strikingly as David's errors, but in an entirely different way. Both constitute a return of the repressed, but whereas in David's case the repressed appears merely as an interruption of language, in Susan's it has itself been organized *as* a language.

One incident must suffice for demonstration. Susan tricks David into coming to her apartment by pretending she is being mauled by her leopard (which, at this stage, David has never seen). Arriving breathless to find Susan in perfect health, David refuses to believe that the leopard exists, but when he discovers it in the bathroom, he panics at once and cries desperately to Susan, "You've got to get out of this apartment!" Unperturbed but bewildered, Susan replies, "But David, I have a lease."

In terms of rational discourse, Susan's reply is nonsense, but "there is sense behind joking nonsense such as this, and it is this sense that makes the nonsense into a joke." (Freud, *Jokes,* 57) The joke consists in the cryptic dramatization of two attitudes to the repressed: David's injunction makes no sense to Susan because she cannot conceive of the leopard's being an object of fear, though from David's point of view the fear is rational, and the comedy is produced by the collision between the two orders of logic. The source of Susan's power in the film is that while David's slips disturb his speech incoherently, Susan disturbs it coherently: her logic is the articulate expression of the forces internal to David's which his seeks, nevertheless, to disown. Elsewhere, of course, Susan's language is characterized by the kind of verbal play Freud sees as being essential to the pleasure of jokes and in which Susan indulges most freely as Swinging-Door Susie. The different use of language has its corollary in a different model of identity. David's rational discourse and rational ego, depending on repression, are constantly vulnerable to disturbance, but Susan is both stable and protean. Her constant metamorphoses embody a real consistency which instantly exposes the factitious wholeness of patriarchal order.

Susan is the antagonist not only of the linguistic order of the bourgeois world but also of its organization of property. On her first appearance she walks off with David's golf ball and responds to his attempt to establish the distinction between "mine" and "thine" by remarking that she's "not too particular about things like that." She proceeds at once to take his car and fails completely to understand a lengthy conversation in which David tries to tell her that the car is his. Later in the film she appropriates another car, in the course of evading a conviction for having parked in front of a fire hydrant, and agrees to return it not because of moral qualms but because "I don't like it anyway." The significance of Susan's lack of concern for private property is crystallized in her exasperated question to David in the parking lot: "Your ball? Your car? Does everything in the world belong to you?" Capitalist property is organized by men, and the second car Susan takes belongs not just to anyone but to Dr. Lehmann, from whose table, in the nightclub sequence, Susan has already removed a bowl of olives before creating the confusion in which David is accused of stealing Mrs. Lehmann's purse. The fact that the main violation of property rights in the film—the appropriation of David's bone—is performed by the dog George (the third, with Susan and Baby, of the agents of the return of the repressed) makes the significance fully explicit. The undermining of property is also the undermining of phallic power, and the phallus ("It's rare! It's precious!") the quintessential commodity.

To describe Susan as a thief would be inaccurate in that it would imply she knows what private property is. It is the case, rather, that she thinks of things in terms of their use value only and is unable to conceive of their belonging to anybody: having come to the golf course in a car, she will naturally leave in one. When, in the jail sequence, Susan pretends to be a notorious thief, she is not identifying with crimes against property (which can't have a meaning if property doesn't) but improvising a solution to the problem of the moment: the virtue of crime, from Susan's point of view, is that it will capture the imagination of Constable Slocum.

Her own imagination is fired by the idea of playing with the linguistic idiom of the film gangster (David tries in vain to convince the Constable that Susan is "making it all up out of movies that she's seen"), and Hawks extends the play, through an in-joke about Grant's previous role as "Jerry the Nipper" in *The Awful Truth*, to the conventions of his own film.

The appropriation of the phallus—it might be thought that what Susan does to David can be summed up as "castration." It is, in fact, the distinction of *Bringing Up Baby* to have dissociated the theme of a man's discovery of his "femininity" from the idea of loss—loss of dignity, loss of status, loss, ultimately, of the balls. What Hawks emphasizes is the gain; the losses are themselves felt to be positive. Indeed, it is the acquisition of the phallus which is associated with deprivation: *Bringing Up Baby* would be a completely different film if it were not so emphatically established that Susan enables the resurgence of a femininity which David already possesses and which, despite himself, he is unwilling to renounce. This premise makes of an action that might be rendered as castration an experience of release and pleasure, and the moment when David is at last prepared to admit that it was pleasure is the moment that the dinosaur collapses. Having hunted for the bone with desperate fervor, David refuses it when Susan brings it to him, and his refusal is the admission that the hunt had less to do than he thought it did with its ostensible object. For him, as for George and Susan, it was play, and in noting this we make a fundamental point about the Grant persona. If castration in *Bringing Up Baby* becomes something else, it is because Grant's acting conveys the enjoyment of incidents which are theoretically demeaning.

The extraordinary nature of the kind of hero embodied by Grant in his comedies of the late '30s has hardly been recognized, but in what other male star, classical or modern, is the realization of a man's femininity endorsed so specifically and explicitly? And what other male star is both romantic hero and farceur? There is clearly a relationship between the two propositions. Consider the moment in *Bringing Up Baby* when David, harassed, beleaguered, and attired in ill-fitting hunting pink (Susan having stolen his clothes), tries to get Susan to grasp how vital it is that her aunt should not find out that David is in fact the eminent Professor Huxley. Susan listens dutifully, with an expression of entranced abstraction, but when David has finished she betrays her real preoccupation by telling him, "You look so handsome without your glasses." David's comic indignity, which by this time has been very clearly equated with feminization (his previous costume was Susan's negligee), doesn't make him the less attractive, and the fact that it doesn't has a corresponding effect on the idea of "indignity"—David's glasses are part of the constraining uniform of Professor Huxley. Characteristically, we are asked to find Grant romantically attractive because, rather than in spite of, his being made to look "ridiculous."

It is significant that in order to transform Grant, in *Notorious*, into the most detestable leading man in the American popular cinema, Hitchcock has entirely to subdue the comedian. The point made by Hitchcock's casting, here and in *Suspicion*, is that being the romantic lover—self-consciously tall, dark, and handsome—is in itself to be in power. The situation in these films, and in the "persecuted wife" melodrama generally (think of the practice of casting famous lover figures—Charles Boyer in *Gaslight* [1944], Robert Taylor in *Undercurrent* [1946]—as the oppressive husband), is the reverse of that in film noir. It is because the heroines of *Notorious* and *Suspicion* desire the Grant character that they become vulnerable to him.

14

Cary Grant, as Devlin, with Ingrid Bergman, in *Notorious*. Personal collection of the editor.

To say no more than that Grant's being, generally, both romantic and comic removes the sexual threat won't quite do: though that is importantly part of it, the formula is too negative in suggestion. What we have in *The Awful Truth*, *Holiday,* and *Bringing Up Baby* is something like an image of a positive bisexuality: something with which we are familiar in the personae of many of the great female stars, but which it is difficult to parallel among the men. All three films are concerned with the elimination of the differential of social/sexual power within the heterosexual couple and use Grant to formulate a type of masculinity which is valuable and attractive by virtue of the sharing of gender characteristics with women. The particular beauty of Grant's collaboration with Katharine Hepburn consists (questions of acting apart) in the complementary bisexuality of the Hepburn persona. (I have made the case for the radical bearing of the partnership elsewhere [*Hepburn,* 98–99].)

Given the thematic content of the early Grant persona it is, perhaps, hardly surprising that Cary Grant the person sometimes became the object of antigay animus and innuendo. Kenneth Anger's book *Hollywood Babylon* reprints a '30s cartoon of Grant which bills him as the star of a film called "Who's a Fairy?" (177) In her biography of Grant, Lee Guthrie suggests that studio executives were at one time so worried about Grant's image—particularly after he began to share a house with Randolph Scott—that they set out expressly to manufacture publicity which would build up Grant's "virility" and quotes from a contemporary interview with

Scott which appeared beneath the caption, "Randy says the guy's regular." (104–5) For all their gratuitousness, such things have a marginal critical interest as evidence of a felt discrepancy between the Grant persona and the dominant social norms of masculinity.

The screwball comedies, in particular *The Awful Truth*, invite comparison with the romantic comedies of Grant's maturity—*An Affair to Remember* (1957), *Indiscreet* and *Houseboat* (1958), and *North by Northwest* (1959). The Grant characters in these later works have obvious points in common. Each is defined, at the outset, in terms of spiritual emptiness and aimlessness. Nickie's grandmother (Kathleen Nesbitt) tells Terry (Deborah Kerr) in *An Affair to Remember* that Nickie has abandoned his painting because "he has been too busy—'living,' as they call it," and adds that "everything came too easily to him." In *Houseboat*, Tom tells Cinzia that he is "one of the undomesticated animals," and that while adults admire him for being "suave and debonair," children "look right through me as if there was nothing there. Maybe there isn't." In *North by Northwest*, Thornhill tells Eve (Eva Marie Saint) that the middle initial of his monogram (R.O.T.) stands for "nothing." In each case, the emotional shallowness is associated with the Grant character's being sexually "unattached." Nickie is a playboy; Philip Adams in *Indiscreet* lies to Anna so as to avoid marrying her; Tom is a widower whose dedication to his profession has alienated him from his children; and when Thornhill, in response to Eve's charge that he "doesn't believe in marriage," tells her that he's been married twice, she replies, "See what I mean?" Shallowness is answered and corrected, in each case, by falling in love.

The schema is, of course, reductive: the limits of the present purpose should not be allowed to suggest that masterpieces (which I take McCarey's *An Affair to Remember* and Hitchcock's *North by Northwest* to be) can be exhausted in a formula. *An Affair to Remember* is one of the cinema's most poignant inquisitions of romanticism and the conditions of its realization. Terry's remark to Nickie's grandmother as the couple leaves her house ("It's a perfect world. Thank you for letting me trespass") establishes McCarey's theme. The "perfect world" is a walled flower garden, and the film is preoccupied with the way in which the impulse to return to it creates the conditions in which it is lost. It is while she is "looking up" to "the nearest thing to heaven" that Terry has her accident, and her obsession (we may compare her to Max Ophüls's Lisa) with refusing to contact Nickie until she is actually well enough to go to him in person almost succeeds in destroying the relationship. Terry's redemption of Nickie, then, has its irony, and the play between the demeaning idealization of women characteristic of Nickie's bachelorhood ("Every woman I meet I put up there") and Terry's romantic idealism has a greater complexity than might at first appear.[3]

North by Northwest is virtually unique in Hitchcock's work in that here male sexuality does not remain, at the end, unregenerate: it might be compared in this respect with *Notorious*, in which Devlin's "change of heart" is ironically undercut. Roger Thornhill, exemplary capitalist male, successful, urbane, and cynically confident of his secure possession of himself and his world, finds himself "by chance" the pawn of the ruling class of that world. For the Professor (Leo G. Carroll), the film's supreme patriarch and the guardian of democratic law, Thornhill's fate is a matter of pure contingency, and in being reduced to a mere agent for the preservation of the structure of power which the Professor represents, Thornhill is placed in a position like

Eve's: each is being used to "get Vandamm," the patriarchal challenger. On the first appearance of Vandamm (James Mason), he and Thornhill are paralleled to each other: Hitchcock's inter-cut panning shots as the two men circle each other establishing the one as the other's mirror image. (The casting of James Mason, whose persona shares with Grant's a suave urbanity which has often been identified with calculating sexual oppressiveness, is clearly relevant here.)[4] The Professor, Thornhill, and Vandamm have in common the exploitation of Eve: the Professor uses her to seduce Vandamm, who uses her in turn to seduce Thornhill, who, as the dialogue I quoted earlier indicates ("I'm beginning to think I'm underpaid"), sees her as an occasion for the demonstration of his sexual charisma.

The action can be defined in terms of Thornhill's gradual identification with and commitment to Eve, through an experience of powerlessness—of the woman's function in patriarchy—and an accompanying disengagement from the Professor and Vandamm, who, though political antagonists, are equally patriarchs. *North by Northwest* ends, famously, with one of Hitchcock's most brilliant images of patriarchal power, the presidential monoliths of Mount Rushmore, which impede the couple's escape. We note that while the statues embody, of course, a bombastic myth of the bourgeois democratic state, it is Vandamm's house which is concealed behind them. The final images—the cut from Thornhill lifting Eve to safety on the mountain to his lifting her into his berth on the train—are deeply ambiguous in suggestion, and the content of the ambiguity is enacted in the last shot of the train's disappearance into a tunnel. The phallic symbol ("But don't tell anyone") completes the partial reinstatement of male authority—Eve has been impassive about Thornhill's rescue, and to his renaming of her ("Come on, Mrs. Thornhill")—but it is also clear that the concluding image dramatizes a withdrawal from the world of patriarchal struggle in which the action has been set. The dissonance isn't resolved, but I think we feel it to be different in kind from the bleak, ironic dissonance on which *Notorious* ends: Devlin hasn't been separated from Sebastian as Thornhill has been from Vandamm and the Professor (who end up side by side on another peak of the mountain), and it is indeed of the essence that Devlin's "conversion" allows him, in taking over Sebastian's role, to assume power over Sebastian and Alicia at the same time.

Indiscreet and *Houseboat*, for all their charm, are very much simpler propositions. The Grant character's attractiveness and desirability consist in his being "one of the undomesticated animals," and the films seek to reconcile the contradiction between the allure characteristic of the sexual wanderer and domesticity. Grant hardly ever plays action heroes (he has never made, and is unimaginable in, a western), and when he does, we are primarily aware of how unlike an action hero he is. The unlikeness is brilliantly exploited by Hawks in *Only Angels Have Wings* (1939), in which Jeff's toughness—the insistently signaled "masculinity" of the leader of men—is analyzed as the camouflage of vulnerability. It is also significant, given the persona established by the screwball comedies, that the homoerotic component of Hawksian male friendship is more clearly focused in the relationship between Jeff and Kid (Thomas Mitchell) than in the equivalent relationships in *To Have and Have Not* (1944) and *Rio Bravo* (1959). Yet as my description will have implied, the use to which Grant is put in *Houseboat*, and elsewhere, can be discussed in terms of the opposition between settling and wandering so fundamental to the action hero.

The inflection, however, is unique. Wandering, as Grant embodies it, is urban (Ernie Mott in *None but the Lonely Heart* [1944] described himself as "a citizen of the Great Smoke—and I don't stay put!") and, whether Cockney or sophisticated, is associated not with male achievement in the adventurer's sense but with the pursuit of "idle pleasure"—a hedonistic commitment to ease and comfort which may survive on chicanery (*Sylvia Scarlett, Mr. Lucky*), and which is almost always at one with the bachelor's desire to "play the field." Ernie Mott calls his rags "the uniform of my independence," and Roger Thornhill might have said the same of his executive's suit. Even as a wanderer, Grant does not inhabit the world of male action, and we cannot conceive of the adventurer's wandering, whatever else it may come to mean (in, for example, James Stewart's work for Mann and Hitchcock), being equated with emotional shallowness. The project of *Houseboat* is to extricate from the shallow "the suave and the debonair," growth of the same soil, and transplant them into the home.

The strength of *Houseboat* and *Indiscreet* is clearly the comic education of male presumption, the comedy issuing in recognition and change, but it could hardly be maintained that the couples formed at the end of these films have anything like the radical suggestiveness of those produced by the screwball comedies. The difference consists in quite distinct conceptions of what "falling in love" means; or rather, in the absence in the screwball comedies of anything approximating to what falling in love conventionally denotes. The phrase hardly covers the experience of David and Susan in *Bringing Up Baby*, despite Susan's plangent cry, as she realizes that she is going to have to steal David's clothes again to prevent his getting away, that he is "the only man I've ever loved." As for the Warriners, long married and in the throes of divorce, the romantic belongs to the past: even when they return, at the end of *The Awful Truth*, to the mountain chalet they knew in happier days, it is not for the reenactment of a nostalgic yesterday but for the last act in the comedy of the reorganization of gender roles—comedy organized by one of the cinema's most delightful erotic metaphors (the large black cat that valiantly holds shut the door of Lucy's bedroom with its paw, frustrating Jerry's attempts at entry until Lucy herself permits it). Linda Seton and Johnny Case, in *Holiday*, do "fall in love" in something more like the familiar sense, and their doing so produces two of the film's most beautiful moments: the solitary waltz to the tune of the music box on New Year's Eve, and Linda's confession of her love to her father, Ned Seton. Yet here again, the film's very premise—Johnny has already fallen in love with, and become engaged to, Julia Seton (Doris Nolan) with exemplary romantic dispatch—makes something different of the Johnny/Linda relationship, which grows out of a mutual allegiance to the complex oppositional values embodied in play.

It may be said that the screwball couples don't fall in love because they learn to "have fun" instead, and that the beginning of "fun" is the end of "romance." To put the same thing in a different way, they don't fall in love because they dispense with the phallus, and with it the phallic organization of desire—the organization which may be sublimated as "love" and which entails an opposition between being in love and being "one of the undomesticated animals." In *Houseboat*, the hero's education is tied in with the theme of the domestication of the wanderer, the containment of male sexuality within the couple and the home. In *Bringing Up Baby*, David becomes "undomesticated," but not in any sense that can be easily grasped by the settling/wandering antinomy. Male sexuality is not "contained" but transformed; the screwball comedies are thinking toward a concept of sexual relations in which sexual energy is not of the kind that is either contained (in the interests of social reproduction) or dissipated. The films produce, in fact, a utopian resolution of the romantic and the polymorphous: a stable, monogamous couple in whom bourgeois gender identities, and their normative social function, no longer obtain.

The resolution is a difficult one, and the difficulty appears strikingly in the fact that Grant can be cast not only in films which seek to reconcile the charm of the bachelor and man-about-town with domesticity but also in comedies of the male's domestic repression. Compare *Houseboat* and *Room for One More* (1951), the subject of which is the impossibility, for "Poppy" Rose (the theme of the father's emasculation is sufficiently blatant), of having sex with his wife because of her obsessive impulse to adopt into the Rose home—swelling the ranks of the couple's own children—a succession of deserving orphans. It is characteristic of the Grant persona that the experience of domestic constraint should be as little a matter of the yearning for adventure as wandering was the pursuit of it: there is no hint in *Room for One More* of the desire of George Bailey (James Stewart) in *It's a Wonderful Life* (1946) to "lassoo the moon." Consider the sequence in which Poppy undertakes to give Jimmy-John (Clifford Tatum Jr.) a sex education lesson, illustrating his lecture by drawing the outline of a male and female figure in the sand with a stick. Anna (Betsy Drake), his wife, remarks on how badly the female figure is sketched, and Poppy replies cryptically that he has had to "draw from memory." In its commitment to the inestimable value for the orphans of a "good home," the film is also committed to the value of the hero's celibacy, and his patient, self-abnegating fulfillment of a father's responsibilities is rewarded in the final shot, but the comedy depends throughout (as it does, though with a very different emphasis, in *Houseboat*) on the contradiction between the Grant persona and domesticity.

A similar theme is implicit in *Mr. Blandings Builds His Dream House* (1948), in which the hero's dissatisfaction with settlement expresses itself, ironically, in the compulsiveness with which he pursues his ambition of constructing the perfect family home. That, at least, is potentially the theme. The film in fact submerges it and is left hesitating among the opinions that (1) the "dream house" represents a valid democratic aspiration; (2) it is "irresponsible," because the father's obsession with the dream house threatens to disrupt the family; and (3) Blandings is neurotic (see, for instance, his paranoid jealousy of Bill Cole [Melvyn Douglas]).

The themes from which *Mr. Blandings* withdraws are fully dramatized in Grant's last film for Howard Hawks, *Monkey Business* (1952), whose radical dissimilarity to *Bringing Up Baby*, magnified by the superficial resemblances, is eloquent of the completeness with which the synthesis of screwball comedy has disintegrated. There is nothing here of the reconciliation of alienated sexual energy and "refinement." The return of the repressed in *Monkey Business* is much closer to that characteristic of the Gothic: that is to say, there is no equivalent for Susan. The energies liberated by B-4 are no longer capable of transforming the ego which denies them but are instead refracted through it: they have the character at once of being "primal" and of having been generated by "necessary" social constraints that we associate with the horror film, and with its difficult impasse.

The completeness of Hawks's hostility to bourgeois society keeps *Monkey Business* a comedy, but it is clearly significant that it is the last of his comedies (if we set aside the attempt to remake *Bringing Up Baby* as *Man's Favorite Sport?* [1964]). In the period which produced Douglas Sirk's melodramas, the ability to conceive of any creative energies surviving the middle classes is already strained to the limit. Consider the extent of the distance between the discomfiture the Warriners inflict on each other in *The Awful Truth*, or the kind of play involved in the hunt for the bone in *Bringing Up Baby*, with the sequence in *Monkey Business* in which Barnaby (Grant) and Edwina Fulton (Ginger Rogers) bedaub each other with paint, or that astonishing climactic scene where Barnaby and the children, dressed as Indians, prepare to scalp Hank Entwhistle (Hugh Marlowe). Oppositional play has become retributive violence, and having fun has taken on a Hobbesian complexion. *Monkey Business* is an extraordinary work, but by 1952 the exhilaration of release in screwball comedy has lost, irretrievably, its utopian dimension.

Is pleasure democratic?

The word I first proposed for Grant was irresponsibility, but it will have been apparent that the transition is an easy one. "Pleasure," in fact, in bourgeois language is a profoundly dubious quantity. Bourgeois rhetoric promises "life, liberty, and the pursuit of happiness," but it turns out, when we read the representative documents, that "liberty" is the liberty of the free market and that these felicities are for the industrious. Pleasure involves a venal moral relaxation and a willingness, where the necessities of life are concerned, to have something for nothing. Moral relaxation expresses itself in, and conduces to, social parasitism, and pleasure is an addiction of all classes except the bourgeoisie.

The interplay between ideas of pleasure and irresponsibility in the Grant persona explain its peculiar class character. Grant can play, on the one hand, the working-class man as feckless Cockney, indigent, carefree, and work-shy: Ernie Mott in *None but the Lonely Heart* is representative ("You know me, ducky—tramp of the universe!"). He can also play the idle rich, executives and professionals of that level of attainment at which the notion of labor tends to acquire a theoretic air and we are primarily conscious of its rewards. The Grant persona is profoundly incompatible with industry, and this, of course, is an essential aspect of its attractiveness. Yet it also raises ideological problems, which appear in the fact that each class type can merge into the confidence trickster. Thus we have Jimmy Monkley in *Sylvia Scarlett*, the proletarian adventurer as charlatan and glib opportunist, or, in *Mr. Lucky*, Joe Adams, illegal gambler and draft dodger (and, though American underworld, still Cockney). Conversely, Johnny Aysgarth in *Suspicion* is an upper-class English playboy, who until the arbitrary happy ending, is living off and conspiring to murder his wife, and the Grant characters in *Indiscreet*, *Houseboat*, and *North by Northwest* all share a duplicity which is clearly correlated with class privilege.

The kind of issues raised by the conflict between a commitment to pleasure and a democratic life of moral probity and honest toil emerges very clearly in *Holiday*, which seeks to solve the problem by introducing a distinction, classically left-populist, between the spirit of "democracy" and its actual operations. Johnny embodies the ideals of the first insurgent bourgeoisie (the holiday is his "Declaration of Independence") and Mr. Seton a contemporary capitalism which is felt to have lost touch with those ideals through an obsession with accumulation: for Mr. Seton, Johnny's lack of interest in making money is "un-American." This hiving off of democratic principle from capitalist reality, as a thing distinct and superior in kind, allows *Holiday* to reclaim energies which express themselves in an aversion to profitable labor, and it does so in such a way as to restate the problem. As I noted earlier, the film is compelled to conclude that the American spirit cannot survive in America.

The representation of Grant as a viable democratic figure, then, depends upon the holding together of a standard of bourgeois-democratic responsibility and qualities which, by that same standard, can be construed as irresponsible. *Holiday* succeeds, insofar as it does, by arguing that bourgeois rhetoric—embodied by the aspirations of the Founding Fathers—and bourgeois practice have no connection with each other, and *People Will Talk* (1951) enacts a variant of the same strategy: the moral values and allegiances of Dr. Praetorius, while they incite the wrath of the hidebound petit bourgeois community, express a real, normative democratic feeling.

The case appears at its most fascinating, as we might expect, in Grant's appearances in the "commitment" film: that trans-generic cycle of the '40s in which the action turns on the winning for the democratic cause of a previously uncommitted, and thus irresponsible, figure. It is of the essence of the Grant persona that he can be cast both as the spokesman of democracy—*The Talk of the Town* (1942), *Once Upon a Honeymoon* (1942)—and as the commitment figure—*Mr. Lucky, None but the Lonely Heart.* Grant's penultimate film, *Father Goose* (1964), is still able to exploit this motif.

The peculiar success of *Once Upon a Honeymoon* (to which Robin Wood has devoted the splendid article "Democracy") lies in its closeness to the screwball tradition: a tradition which is still, at this point, artistically viable and from which the film derives a normative concept of the democratic couple in which the idea of "irresponsible" pleasure has great positive value. It is against this norm that the kind of irresponsibility represented by Katharine Butte-Smith (Ginger Rogers) is measured. She aspires, essentially, to the world of the Vances and the Setons, which means, here, not the American *haut bourgeoisie* but European fascism (though the possibility of the link was always there: see, for example, Frank Capra, or the emphasis in *Holiday* on the fact that Seton and Laura Cram are sympathetic to Hitler).

The persistence of this tradition allows the director of *The Awful Truth* to associate, in *Once Upon a Honeymoon*, Katie's progress toward commitment with the recovery of sexuality and pleasure: the couple can be politically responsible while continuing to occupy the outskirts of the realm of play. What is lost in the fusion is the sexual progressiveness of screwball comedy. The propaganda theme necessitates a conservative dramatization of gender—the couple must be, however "heightened," the normal American couple, associated in the film's imagery with reproduction, and play in *Once Upon a Honeymoon* (Grant's tape measure and saxophone) is phallic.

Yet the inner tensions of the Grant persona create an occasion for the most fascinating inflections of the "commitment" thematic. The persistent gender ambiguity of the persona manifests itself in *The Talk of the Town* in the way in which the Rogers part from *Honeymoon* comes to be played by a man. Nora Shelley (Jean Arthur), while being obviously necessary for appearance's sake, is no less conspicuously irrelevant to the relationship between Leopold Dilg (Grant) and Michael Lightcap (Ronald Colman), and her redundancy is nowhere more apparent than in the penultimate scene in which Lightcap renounces her to his "rival" at the very point at which, were Lightcap a woman, he would be united with Dilg himself. Indeed, the terms in which Lightcap describes Dilg, and Dilg's love, to Nora suggest unmistakably his own declaration of love, and the stolidity of *The Talk of the Town* is very much a matter, not merely of director George Stevens, but of the necessary impossibility of realizing the film's latent content.

In *Notorious*, Hitchcock continues to use Grant as the spokesman for democracy but deprives it of all positive significance by dissolving the absolute distinction between democracy and fascism on which the commitment film depends. This inflection or, more precisely, negation of the genre is of course characteristic. Three years before *Notorious*, in *Lifeboat* (1944), Hitchcock had argued that fascism rises to power with the connivance, and on the basis of the deadlocked class antagonisms, of bourgeois democracy, and as we have seen, the relationship between Devlin and Sebastian is taken up again, though with crucial new developments, in *North by Northwest*. The dominant popular reading of the Grant persona—"consummately romantic and consummately genteel"—is essential to Hitchcock's purpose in *Notorious*, and it is powerfully evoked in the sequence built round Alicia's party and the ensuing intoxicated car ride. The revelation that Devlin is an American agent and the first manifestation of brutality against Alicia (here, physical brutality—Devlin knocks her out) come together, though Hitchcock's imagery has already prepared us for it: from his first appearance, Devlin has been associated with the predatory oppressiveness of the male look at women which the film's opening shot has established as a crucial motif. It is a motif which links Devlin with Sebastian, and it is developed with astonishing power and complexity in the film's great central sequence at Sebastian's reception—the sequence that ends with Devlin's staging, for Sebastian's gaze, of the embrace which leads to the discovery that Alicia has been working for the Americans, and the attempt to murder her. The suave fascist male acts through the sexual impulses of the suave democratic male, it having always been clear that both Devlin and Sebastian see Alicia primarily as a means of consolidating their sense of their own potency. *Notorious* takes up the connection between the heroine's democratization and male tutelage from *Once Upon a Honeymoon* but inverts its meaning.

In *Mr. Lucky*, we have *Once Upon a Honeymoon* in reverse, with Grant in the Rogers part. Katie O'Hara, the Brooklyn burlesque queen, becomes Joe Adams, the Cockney/Brooklyn con man, and the film sets out to infuse the democratic with the trickster's acumen and ebullience while submitting its antisocial character to democratic correction. The mix produced a clear class character. In *The Talk of the Town*, where Grant plays the representative of democracy, Dilg's plebian origins carry no suggestion of the shady or the shiftless (though the film demonstrates its awareness that such a connotation is latent in Grant's working-class characters by making of Dilg an obstreperous worker who has been falsely accused of burning down a factory). In *Mr. Lucky*, where Grant plays the commitment figure, the link between the plebian and dishonesty is fully realized and must be dissolved in the course of the action. At the same time, Joe Adams, though the commitment figure, is also a man, and "education" is reciprocal in *Mr. Lucky* in a way that it isn't in *Once Upon a Honeymoon*: Dorothy Bryant must be democratized too, not in the sense of learning commitment but in that of surrendering, through her experience of Joe, the complacency of a daughter of the upper middle class.[5]

In the light of the persona developed by the screwball comedies, in which the tone and the content of the comedy of education are so very different, it is clearly crucial that the anarchic energy associated so strikingly in the earlier films with femininity should appear increasingly as "boyishness." The hero's phallic status is partially restored, and Grant's sexual charisma becomes that of the lover who is also a scapegrace son.

It is often brought against the screwball comedy—from a "left" position which it is certainly proper to call "vulgar"—that the genre is a celebration of wealth and of the wealthy. Nothing could be further from the truth: the hostility to wealth and the social/class privilege endowed by its accumulation could hardly be clearer than it is in *The Awful Truth* and *Holiday*. The wealth of the screwball couple, like its childlessness, is a means of detaching the partners from any social function: it is a precondition for the destruction of the gender roles which are defined by their social function. Wealth in its capitalist meaning becomes valueless. Its purpose is to eliminate the "realm of necessity" and permit the leap into the "realm of freedom"—or at the least, of "post-scarcity anarchism"—whose values, as I've indicated, are categorically non-bourgeois. In the nature of things, such a project is impossible in the commitment film, though the passage into the realm of bourgeois democracy may drive from it something of its élan.

In a sense, many of Grant's films are commitment films: comedies of the commitment of the errant male to marriage and settlement which celebrate the reconciliation of the pursuit of pleasure with social forms which may not at first appear to conduce to it. Of the later films, *North by Northwest* is, perhaps, the closest to the tendency and suggestion of the masterpieces of the late '30s. It is the value of Cary Grant to have embodied a male heterosexuality which is so different in tone from that of the action hero, and which is arrived at through a different kind of relationship with women: a relationship in which the woman appears so often as the educator of the male and of his pleasure. But it is in the screwball comedies, where that process takes on so radical a character and is distinguished most drastically from a concept of patriarchal "domesticity" and "domestication," that the value is completely realized. Here, uniquely in the popular cinema, Grant's acting creates the attractiveness of male femininity and of the relationships enabled by it.

If I have failed to take up the question I raised at the beginning—the question of Grant's imputed "limitations" as an actor—that is not only because I take the answer to the question to be obvious and see little point in addressing a failure to perceive it. The reasons which make the proposition that "Cary Grant is a great actor" the reverse of a commonplace require diagnosis, but not refutation. The more important fact is that the felicities of comic acting are more difficult to describe and discuss than acting usually is, and I have preferred to avoid the laboriousness involved in demonstrating that performance is "productive of meaning." How does one describe Grant's reaction, in *Bringing Up Baby*, to the news that his marriage is to have "no domestic entanglements of any kind"? The slight hesitation, the movement of the head (both brilliantly judged), the shift from incomprehension to startled inference, all of which contribute so much to the comic force of the payoff line, "I mean 'of any kind,' David." Yet, if the screwball comedies are the essence of the persona, they also provide the basis for an evaluation of the performer's skills. Here, surely, are imaginative and technical resources comparable to those of Laurel and Hardy and Keaton.

A New Servitude: Bette Davis, *Now, Voyager,* and the Radicalism of the Woman's Film (1992)

I wish to discuss *Now, Voyager* (1942) not only because I love it but also because it seems to me to raise a number of important critical issues in a particularly suggestive form. There is, in the first place, the question of the political status of popular culture. It is depressingly characteristic not only of the discourse of common sense but also of many supposedly theoretical discourses about the Hollywood cinema that they assume that Hollywood movies are mere inert deposits of "the dominant ideology"—at the best, of its internal contradictions. I wish to offer *Now, Voyager* as a representative case of a work which is explicitly and systematically critical—it is, in effect, an Oedipal fantasy about the expulsion of men from the family—and to provide an account of the conditions in which such a fantasy could be conceived, dramatized, and become "popular."

I will add here, parenthetically, that the reinstatement of a concept of intention ought to be recognized as axiomatic for a properly Marxist aesthetics. Marx's famous comparison of the bee and the architect is a comparison between "creative labor" which is instinctual and innocent of all intention, and purposive social activity undertaken by social agents in the context of a complex social present. Art, and indeed discourse itself, are such activities. Every discourse, even the simplest, is a social action which involves, by definition, the use of given conventional materials—and which may effect their transformation. The intentional fallacy, with which intention as such is so frequently and with such facility conflated, consists in the assumption either that an intention is definitive of the meaning of a discourse in some absolute sense or that the validity of an interpretation can be guaranteed by reference to an intention, expressed or imputed. I do not wish to use the word "deconstruction" again, but I will say that "what these gentlemen lack is dialectics." It ought to be possible to formulate a theory of discourse, and of art, which is sufficiently agile to grasp the fact that, on the one hand, discourse can only exist in social use as embodied intention and that, on the other, it can exist only within what Raymond Williams has a called a framework of "possibilities and constraints" which are in principle prior to any given speaker and of which s/he need not be aware. (*Marxism and Literature*, 65) Thus, works of art embody, or enact, a historical project: they are not tabulae rasae, infinitely available for promiscuous free association and "text-construction." But at the same time the project does not exhaust the work, which may very well be divided against itself in more or less complicated ways and which may very well generate meanings that exceed, resist, or elude its own intention.

Secondly, I want to argue that *Now, Voyager* exemplifies the complexity of the Hollywood tradition. I was once taken to task in print for referring to nineteenth-century American fiction in an article which was supposed to be about *Mandingo*—the objection being (as I recall) that I had allowed my "background in High Culture" to intrude where it had no place. I am sure I am at least as strenuously opposed to the notion of "high culture" as my critic was, but I am equally sure, when I look at *Now, Voyager*, that high culture is most certainly not a category to which (let us say) the novels of Henry James and Charlotte Brontë automatically belong but a category which has been imposed upon them. Dr. Samuel Johnson once wrote journalism, Charles Dickens once wrote best sellers, and Mozart and Verdi once wrote hit tunes. If the works of these and other persons have now become high culture, that is not because of some intrinsic property of "highness" which they have in common. High culture represents nothing more than the bourgeoisie's misuse of its own, and other people's, artifacts, and if we exclude the products of the various "modernisms" (which the bourgeoisie was never much interested in consuming in any case), we may state it as something of a general rule that today's high culture is the "entertainment" of yesterday and the day before, fetishized and surrounded by barbed wire. Classical Hollywood, of course, is in danger of becoming high culture itself, after the usual fifty-year time lag, and it is therefore all the more important to bear in mind that classical Hollywood was important because it produced a large number of works in which the contents of high culture were released from their ideological quarantine, and in which the great gulf fixed (itself a bourgeois invention) between "high" and "plebeian" culture was effectively abolished. These works, of which I will argue that *Now, Voyager* is one, were immediately enjoyed by a large and extremely diverse popular audience, but they were also in direct and intimate contact with the contemporary avant-garde, and they restored and renewed major traditions from the past which would otherwise have been consigned to the museum and the academy. Brontë is as crucial an influence on 1940s Hollywood as *Citizen Kane* (1941), and to find a creative use for *Jane Eyre* in the middle of the twentieth century is in itself a major achievement.[1] I wish, therefore, to locate *Now, Voyager* and its genre and star not only in their immediate historical situation but also in a tradition of works about the position of women which Hollywood inherits from the nineteenth-century novel: a tradition in which Brontë and James are key moments; which has, obviously, a feminist tendency; and from which *Now, Voyager* derives its central metaphors —Woman as governess, Woman as foundling, Woman as heiress.

Finally, in that I have described *Now, Voyager* as an "Oedipal fantasy," I want to address the matter of psychoanalysis and its role in textual criticism and to argue that the specific ways in which a work articulates the material of the primal fantasies generated by the Oedipus must themselves be located historically—in terms of the particular situation of a work, a genre, and a culture.

The Woman's Film and World War II

It is a commonplace that the astonishing efflorescence of the woman's film in the early '40s had something to do with the war. The economic facts, as they pertain to Hollywood, are pretty generally known, I suppose; they are dutifully detailed by all the standard histories—which, however (predictably), mystify their significance by construing them from an economic point of view. What the war did was to impose an extraordinary hiatus in the development of American capitalism: it postponed by about ten years that general social process in terms of which the

Hollywood studio system was already becoming archaic and anomalous even as its character-istic institutions were being consolidated. We may describe this process—of which commer-cial radio, inaugurated in 1922, was the premonitory cultural form—as a movement toward an economy based on individual consumption and social relations characterized by the dispersal and atomization of persons who are located in "the home" and constructed as "consumers" by a variety of discourses and practices: a form of "mobile privatization," in Raymond Williams's phrase. (*Television*, 26)

Culturally, commercial television is the key institution of this phase of American capital-ism. Funded as it is by advertising (that is, by the selling of audiences to capital), American commercial television reciprocally defines the spectator as consumer of commodities and entertainment as promotion for the promotion, and it creates artistic forms which are at every level directly determined as forms by the marketing of the viewer. The principles of fragmen-tation and flow entailed on television form by the capital structure of the medium preempt intensities and complexities of emotional engagement, and reduce the spectacle to an arbitrary background which perpetually foregrounds, celebrates, and seductively fetishizes consump-tion while mystifying its conditions.

The war created a kind of time lock in which the emerging social forms of "mobile priva-tization" were abruptly suspended and in which the public, social pleasures of "movie-going," and the hegemony of an entertainment medium whose capital structure was internal to itself, were granted an unlooked-for and, as it were, accidental reprieve. But even more than this was at stake. After 1941, the domestic American audience was dominated by women: women, moreover, who were being encouraged to feel that their natural place was not in the home but outside it. That the proletarianization of American women had a radicalizing effect we know: it has been admirably documented, and even if it hadn't been, it is deducible from the films that they enjoyed. Suddenly the home, which serves at once to desocialize women and to separate them from each other, no longer existed as such. Bette Davis's audience was defined by the workplace on the one hand and the cinema on the other.

The European Emigration

This radical restructuring of American social relations, and thus of the composition and the orientation of Hollywood's audience, took place in the context of another momentous cultural change—the European emigration. The tendency for the great European directors to gravitate toward Hollywood had, of course, become apparent much earlier: Ernst Lubitsch arrived in 1924, Victor Sjöstrom in 1926, and F. W. Murnau in 1927. The motivation in these cases, how-ever—although Lubitsch was Jewish and Murnau both Jewish and gay—was not primarily political: here, the attraction of Hollywood was a matter of technical and economic resources superior to any available in Europe, even in Germany, and the assurance of artistic freedom in deploying them. The mass emigration began in earnest in 1933 after Hitler became chancellor; by 1941 the Weimar Republic had moved to California, and Hollywood had become the last bastion of European high modernism.

The influence of the emigration on the Hollywood cinema is not susceptible to precise calculation: clearly, there can be no question of many of the most illustrious exile names having made a direct contribution to studio productions as individuals (though some of them did). What we can say—for it is demonstrably true—is that the emigration impinged on a society in a state of absolutely fundamental structural upheaval (economic, political, and ideological) and that under these conditions an extraordinary fusion took place between the already existing conventional languages of the American genres and the forms, idioms, and preoccupations of the European avant-garde. "Under these conditions" is the crucial phrase: if we try to discuss "the European influence" independently of the historical situation in which it had its effect, we will find ourselves talking, in the usual way, about "Expressionist lighting," "the demonic city," and "Germanic camera angles"—which is what most accounts of the "influence" boil down to. It would be more to the point to remind ourselves that from 1941 to 1945 the United States was an ally of the Soviet Union; that throughout the same period the traditional social functions of the home, and traditional discourses about it, were in crisis; and that if the melodrama, the Gothic, and the thriller took so readily to psychoanalysis and proved to be so congenial to directors who had worked with, or absorbed the dramatic theory of, Bertolt Brecht, that is because these genres were in fact amenable to radical appropriation and development.

German modernism had the impact on Hollywood that it did because it caught the world's leading capitalist power at a peculiarly vulnerable, contradictory, and anomalous moment in its history—a moment in which the goal of world hegemony necessitated an *entente cordiale* with an anticapitalist state in which women were pouring into factories and shipyards in droves, in which the economy was booming but there was little to be bought except movies, and in which hundreds of radical intellectuals, perceived as signifiers of prestige and victims of fascist tyranny, could be welcomed to the homeland of democracy and let loose upon a film industry with an autonomous capital structure and a virtual monopoly of artistic production. In these circumstances, and under cover of the usual alibi of entertainment, the American cinema could quietly incorporate, with every appearance of legitimacy, what the modern movement had to give and assimilate it to its own sufficiently complex traditions.

The influences which hold most decisively for the Hollywood melodrama were those of Brecht and Freud. I have argued elsewhere that the anti-naturalism of the melodramatic tradition, and its tendency to conceive of characters as exemplary embodiments of objective social forces and contradictions in an implicitly didactic and polemical mode, were very readily available for Brechtian inflection. (*Hepburn*, 102–3) In the work of Fritz Lang, Otto Preminger, Vincente Minnelli, Douglas Sirk, and the Max Ophüls of *Caught* and *The Reckless Moment* (both 1949), we see the melodrama turning into a form of American epic theater which is frequently very much more complex and profound than the plays of Brecht himself. If Brecht's influence has passed virtually without notice (except in the case of Sirk), no one will need to be reminded of the standard line on Hollywood's enthusiastic reception of Freud, which has been an object of facetious jocularity for decades. It is not necessary to deny that we can point to numbers of movies in which psychoanalysis is indeed reduced to a glib, knowing pop psychology, but the fact that *Lady in the Dark* (1944) is ridiculous (and Mitchell Leisen's film, it is worth pointing out, was adapted from an arty, middle-brow Broadway play) is hardly a good reason to traduce the analysis of male heterosexuality in *Gaslight* (1944), or of romantic love in *Letter from an Unknown Woman* (1948), or of mother/daughter relations in *Now, Voyager*.

The use of Freudian theory in the great 1940s melodramas is not especially assertive or explicit, and indeed the phrase "the use of" may be thought to be unfortunate in its implications: there is nothing in *Letter* or *Random Harvest* (1942) or *Rebecca* (1940) which reminds us of the kind of "applied" psychoanalysis (applied for the delectation of *l'homme sensuel moyen*) which we find in, say, *Blue Velvet* (1986) or *Riddles of the Sphinx* (1977). We have the impression, rather, both that Freud has become a part of the common discursive currency and that he has been included in it in a remarkably creative way: it is not for the credulousness or the superficiality or the schematic nature of their appropriation of Freud that *Notorious* (1946), *The Locket* (1946), and *Angel Face* (1952) are exemplary. We may argue, on the contrary, that if psychoanalysis enabled a radical deepening and clarification of the material and preoccupations of the genre, these in their turn encouraged an exceptionally partial, and a uniquely political, engagement with psychoanalysis. Freud (and the emigration) did not fall like a bolt from the blue on a culture hitherto disingenuous and naively affirmative. The genres in which their influence was most keenly felt—the melodrama, the woman's film, the Gothic, the urban thriller—had already generated distinguished critical work addressed to the contradictory realities, material and symbolic, of a specific historical culture. For the present purpose, it will be sufficient to add that the conventions of the woman's film were not a stranger to concepts of "masculine dominance" and "gender oppression"; that the genre's tradition included one of the most radical bodies of work in the cinema (the films of Josef von Sternberg and Marlene Dietrich); and that Freud's influence on it was inseparable from the outset from that of the key nineteenth-century feminist novel. If we add to this complex of factors the wartime experience of the woman's film's audience, we are perhaps in a position to suggest that the moment at which Freud "arrived" favored, or at least allowed for, a progressive interest in him. Certainly, psychoanalysis became something rather different in the hands of the melodrama from what it notoriously became in the hands of the American medical profession—a fact of which the abrasive attitude toward therapy in, say, *Kings Row* (1942) and *The Locket* is a telling and piquant illustration.

The Woman's Film

There is no such thing as an intrinsically radical genre: the woman's film is no more progressive per se than the western is conservative per se. A genre is produced in historical circumstances in which a cluster of related values, practices, and discourses on the maintenance and reproduction of which a given culture absolutely depends undergoes a crisis of consent, such that the values and practices in question are experienced at once as necessary, unavoidable, even natural, but also as a source of conflict, friction, unhappiness, and disharmony. Genres presuppose an ambivalence and uncertainty about a set of dominant values and institutions which is sufficiently profound and sufficiently generalized so as to create an audience for narratives in which the crisis of these values is repeatedly acted through, with the most minute variations and inflections, and in which the terms of the status quo whose institutions are at stake are continually renegotiated and resecured. If general consent could unproblematically be won for the proposition that women ought to love and be defined by men, there would be no woman's film. The condition of existence of the genre is the fact that this proposition is both emphatically dominant and potentially at risk and that it is historically possible to respond to it by asserting either that it is perhaps not woman's destiny to love and be defined by men at all, or that even if it is, the consequences and ramifications of this destiny are in substance unacceptable. Of course, if general consent could be won for these counterarguments, there would be no woman's film either. It is the very impossibility practically of resolving the conflict of interpretations and evaluations and emotional allegiances which the genre articulates that gives rise to the genre—that promotes, in other words, a correspondingly intense investment in the constant reenactment, redescription, and resolution of the conflict as dramatic fantasy. Needless to say, such conflicts can be defined and followed through in ways which are more or less subversive of the priorities of the dominant culture, and in ways which are not subversive of them at all. The materials of a genre are always culturally explosive, virtually by definition, but the nature of the treatment of these materials is determined by other factors. The two most important factors are the artists involved and, above all, the specificities of the historical situation in which genre, artist, and audience intersect with each other.

While I will be mainly concerned here with the films about motherhood which Bette Davis made in the late 1930s and early '40s—and with *Now, Voyager* as the greatest of them—I wish first to consider the contemporary cycle of woman's films about the domestic persecution of married women by their husbands which Thomas Elsaesser has called the "Freudian-feminist melodrama." (11) These two groups of works, though utterly different, have one essential feature in common—their implacable hostility to the social institutions of, in Adrienne Rich's phrase, compulsory heterosexuality and to the organization of desire which answers to those institutions—and they illuminate each other in extremely important ways. I should make it quite clear at the outset that I am perfectly well aware that there are many wartime woman's films which, far from proposing a hostile critique of bourgeois heterosexuality, undertake massively to reaffirm the role of wife-and-mother as heroic guardian of the "unconquerable fortress" of the American home, or which concern themselves with women's experience of loss, bereavement, and emotional frustration or deprivation. It is no part of my purpose to demonstrate that the complex American wartime situation guaranteed the exclusive production of anti-patriarchal woman's movies. I claim merely that it enabled them, and on an impressively substantial scale. Works of art are made by persons, and it would be the most ludicrous determinism to suggest that persons who find themselves in a given historical conjuncture must react to it in one particular kind of way. The war, and Hollywood's institutions, allowed for the celebration of the norms as well as their contestation, and I am interested here in the fact that the contestation took place and that it has been almost completely ignored. We may assume, I take it, that the audience which enjoyed *Now, Voyager* and *Rebecca* also enjoyed, say, *The White Cliffs of Dover* (1944), and I am equally far from suggesting that the spectators of wartime woman's movies were bound together by a univocal revolutionary consciousness. Fantasy life, after all, is extraordinarily complex and contradictory, and a great deal is at stake, emotionally and psychologically, in deriving pleasure from a narrative about the abolition of sexual arrangements in which one is at the same time deeply implicated. That this is the pleasure *Now, Voyager* offers I have no doubt, but it hardly follows that such pleasure is incompatible with enjoyment of another narrative in which the same arrangements are affirmed. Indeed, the conservative fantasy may well serve to create an emotional space for the fantasy of resistance and repudiation, and it is implicit in what I have already said about genre that the pleasure of generic art has its roots in the most extreme imaginative ambivalence.

Having said this, it is only proper to add that films like *Mrs. Miniver* (1942) and *Since You Went Away* (1944) are far from being as simple, as unproblematic, or as contemptible as they might seem to be on the evidence of memory, hearsay, or the scholarship of Hollywood historians and TV guides. It would be hard to advance higher claims for masculine dominance and American domesticity than *Since You Went Away*, which goes so far as to identify its absent patriarch with God, yet his very absence involves the film in difficult contradictions. When we come to a masterpiece like *Random Harvest*, which passionately commits itself to the projection and realization of a utopian heterosexual ideal, we find on inspection that the ideal is remarkable for its radical perversity. Like a number of other wartime woman's films about "lost loves," *Random Harvest* turns out to be a celebration of the primal crime and the mother/son incest which follows from it. Here, too, although heterosexuality is deliriously reconstituted, the film draws its energy from a fantasy of the negation of the Oedipus.

The Freudian-Feminist Melodrama

The Freudian feminist cycle was initiated by Alfred Hitchcock in his first American film, *Rebecca*, which now seems more and more to be the seminal 1940s work: from the point of view of the present discussion, it is the work in which psychoanalysis, Brontë, and the American Gothic are articulated with each other on the ground of the woman's film. The cycle proceeds through Hitchcock's *Suspicion* (1941), George Cukor's *Gaslight*, Jacques Tourneur's *I Walked with a Zombie* (1943), Minnelli's *Undercurrent* (1946), Lang's *Secret Beyond the Door* (1948), Sirk's *Sleep, My Love* (1948), Preminger's *Whirlpool*, (1949), and Ophüls's *Caught*; it is also a decisive influence on two more major Hitchcock films, *Notorious* (1946) and *Under Capricorn* (1949). At the risk of schematizing these works—which are extremely complex and diverse, and a number of which are masterpieces—I would like to outline their recurrent structural features: not all the films have all the features in common, but when we consider the cycle in its totality, the insistence of a dominant thematic pattern is very striking.

1. A heroine who is defined as socially inexperienced, naive, sexually innocent—above all, as "romantic" in the conventional, colloquial sense.
2. She meets and falls in love with a charismatic stranger played by an actor who is inscribed in convention as "ideal romantic lover"—a Cary Grant, a Charles Boyer, a Laurence Olivier, a Robert Taylor, a Don Ameche. (This pattern persists in derivatives and pastiches of the Freudian-feminist melodrama which long postdate the end of the cycle proper: consider, for instance, the casting of Rex Harrison in *Midnight Lace* [1960]). In some cases, though not in all, the film emphasizes the Oedipal aspect of the heroine's love by indicating that the husband is older than she is and/or her superior in social rank: in *Rebecca*, de Winter (Olivier) both replaces and is, as it were, symbolically summoned by the heroine's father who, when she was a little girl, gave her a picture postcard of the de Winter mansion, Manderley.

The crucial point, however, is that the heroine's motive for falling in love invariably derives from a fantasy of release, fulfillment, and liberation which she projects onto the man—liberation from a traumatic past (*Gaslight*), from an oppressive family (*Suspicion*), from the demeaning social role of "old maid" (*Undercurrent*), from economic dependency and exploitation (*Rebecca, Caught*), and from the sense that she is sexually unattractive, and thus that she is "not the sort of girl men marry," as Joan Fontaine puts it in *Rebecca*. The heroine perceives her husband as the guarantee (dashing, urbane, and glamorous as he is) of a completely unanticipated, and virtually fabulous, new life of freedom and sexual pleasure, and she happily commits herself to the "normal" destiny of woman in the belief that marriage is the condition of her own self-realization. The marriage takes place at the beginning of the narrative, the rest of which is concerned with the bloody aftermath of "the happy ending."

A number of these elements persist in *Notorious* and *Under Capricorn*, in which, of course, the heroine is very different from the generic type and in which the Freudian-feminist convention is only one of the materials in play. The Ingrid Bergman character in both works is sexual and transgressive; she is subject not to one man but to two, both of whom, for different reasons, have an investment in gaining power over her, and the figure in whom she glimpses the chance of a "new life" is not her husband. Nevertheless, the Freudian-feminist theme of the heroine's subjugation through romantic love remains: she is drawn to her lover in the first place because he seems to embody the promise of redemption. Devlin's (Cary Grant) power over Alicia (Bergman) in *Notorious* is the power of guilt about her own and her father's past—guilt which she hopes she can assuage through him but which, in fact, he relentlessly (and neurotically) exacerbates, eventually drawing her into a helpless complicity with her own victimization. Hatty (Bergman) in *Under Capricorn* also believes, at the outset, that she can transform and redeem herself through Adair (Michael Wilding), but here, magnificently, the film moves toward a spiritual recovery in which this investment in the lover is abandoned.

3. Enter "the house"—archaic, marmoreal, labyrinthine, patriarchal. It is here, of course, that *Jane Eyre* and the American Gothic tradition intersect: the prototypes are Brontë's Thornfield Hall on the one hand and Edgar Allan Poe's House of Usher on the other. "The house" embodies the masculine secret—the secret of the husband's castration. For it rapidly transpires that the heroine, too, unbeknownst to herself, has been constructed as the object of a fantasy which bears no relation whatever to hers, and which requires her to expiate her husband's profound conviction of his impotence by submitting to a corresponding project of domination. In *Jane Eyre* and *Rebecca*, the husband's fear of "being castrated" is inspired by a first wife who appears in the work as the symbolic embodiment of female sexual energy which has refused patriarchal regulation and which is experienced by the husband (though not by the text) as demonic. In *Gaslight*, the emblem of intimidating female power is the heroine's guardian and surrogate mother, whom the husband has murdered years before, and his obsession with her is an obsession with finding and appropriating her missing jewels, the ownership of

which, in principle, has passed to the heroine by matrilineal descent. *Gaslight* defines the jewels as fetishes and dramatizes the husband's compulsion to steal them (which he himself, it's made clear, does not understand) in terms of a need to put the phallus back in its rightful place: she doesn't have it, I have it. The metaphorical content of the husband's pathology in these films is invariably of this kind. Masculinity, as the Freudian-feminist melodrama perceives it, is driven by an obsessional horror of lack, which has been aroused by a figure from the husband's past (usually, but not always, female) who represents for the husband the troubling or negation of sexual difference, and which can only be exorcized by "the making of a lady"—by the demonstration that the heroine is, incontrovertibly, "feminine," as in castrated, powerless.

4. From the heroine's point of view, the theme of the Freudian-feminist cycle can be expressed in the formula "compulsory heterosexuality as nightmare." The husband—as is, of course, "normal"—aspires to impose the patriarchal organization of sexual difference around the phallus as the signifier of that difference, and the films use the metaphor of persecution to identify the husband's project with a process of systematic, socially organized, and socially legitimated disempowerment. The effect of the process is the heroine's confinement to the house, where a wife ought naturally to be and where her predicament is therefore invisible: *Gaslight, Caught,* and *Notorious* in particular lay great stress on the fact that it is precisely the identification of women with "the private sphere" that allows the persecution of the heroine to proceed. The power relations, and the division of labor, which sustain bourgeois privacy are in any case naturalized, and because a woman's place is in the home it becomes exceedingly difficult to tell whether or not she is there of her own volition or to contest her husband's account of the matter. The point is brilliantly made in the excruciating sequence in *Gaslight* in which Gregory Anton (Charles Boyer) causes Paula Alquist (Ingrid Bergman) to have a nervous breakdown at a concert with the express purpose of demonstrating "in public" that his wife's condition necessitates her incarceration in the "private" home—as opposed to being a consequence of it. The very notion of the domestic privacy of socially unequal partners serves in itself to mystify or rationalize the real conditions of the heroine's privatization, and it is their perception of this fact which gives the Freudian-feminist films their extraordinary intensity. The possibility of the heroine's persecution is objectively entailed by the social form of the institution of marriage.

5. The heart of bourgeois privacy is the marital bedroom, and its privacy is sanctioned in the name of the act of love. In the Freudian-feminist melodrama, with magnificent symbolic logic, the marriage bed becomes the site of the heroine's ultimate terror and humiliation and of the displacement of her sexuality into hysteria. In *Caught* she becomes literally bedridden, and in *Notorious* and *Under Capricorn* the inviolable seclusion of the bedchamber facilitates an attempt to murder her. It is *Gaslight,* again, however, which produces the cycle's most extraordinary metaphor for the power relations of the boudoir. Here, the master bedroom is directly below the attic, and every evening, while Anton plunders his wife's property in his desperate search

for the purloined phallus, Paula, prostrate on the bed, cowers in horror beneath him. The symbolic geography of the patriarchal home has rarely been mapped with such exquisite precision.

6. The sexual drives repressed in the marriage bed for the greater glory of masculine dominance accumulate elsewhere—in the West Wing, at the houmfort,* on the third floor, in the cellar, the attic, the boathouse, the stables—in a space of taboo within or adjacent to the house; many of the films move inexorably toward their spectacular and momentous return. In *Jane Eyre*, *Rebecca*, and *Secret Beyond the Door* (and, of course, "The Fall of the House of Usher") the powerful female energies which the male protagonist has sought to disavow erupt, the house is destroyed, and the patriarchal line is extinguished. In *Undercurrent*, the husband is trampled to death by his brother's stallion, whose stables correspond to the boathouse in *Rebecca* (both of them are guarded by a Faulknerian idiot who is privy to, but who cannot articulate, the house's secret). In the great climactic scene of *Gaslight* the heroine recovers her powers, takes control of her mother's house, and she herself expels her husband from it, instructing the police (in words which seem to sum up the meaning of the Freudian-feminist melodrama in a phrase) to "take this man away."

It is hardly surprising, given the cycle's thematic, that Freudian-feminist melodramas find it exceptionally difficult to negotiate an ending: the interpretation of the final scene of *Suspicion* remains controversial to this day. Narrative closure in Hollywood movies very regularly means "the formation of the heterosexual couple," but it is fairly clear that at the end of these astonishing Gothic visions of the cost of male-dominated heterosexuality for women such closure cannot carry much conviction. The films may well be obliged, in the last five minutes, either to redeem the husband or to wheel on an acceptable alternative—rather as the good king is wheeled on at the end of Jacobean tragedy—but they are committed by the logic of their narratives to undercut their own resolution, sometimes inadvertently, usually with deliberate irony. The "restoration of the couple" in *I Walked with a Zombie* is so perfunctory that it can scarcely be said to take place. In *Rebecca*, Hitchcock suggests that the newly found sexual maturity and self-confidence of the second Mrs. De Winter (Fontaine)—she is, in effect, about to become Rebecca—disqualify her as a possible love object for the husband to whom she appears to have been reconciled and who instructed her, in the days of their courtship, "never to be thirty-six years old." In *Gaslight*, Cukor brutally dispels any confidence we might have been tempted to have in Brian Cameron (Joseph Cotten) by associating him, through the image of the gloves, with Gregory Anton's fetishism; and in *Caught*, Ophüls also uses imagery of clothing (in this case, the gift of a coat to the heroine) to establish a connection between the film's ostensibly antithetical representatives of masculinity.

The objection has sometimes been made that the Freudian-feminist melodrama defines women as, in essence, victims and explains the heroine's persecution in terms of the intrinsically passive and masochistic nature of the feminine character. This objection seems to me to

---

*The place on the Caribbean island where the local voodoo worshippers gather in *I Walked with a Zombie*.

be almost incredibly perverse. The Freudian-feminist heroine is indeed offered as exemplary, but the point of the entire cycle is that she is exemplary for the passion and intensity with which she has internalized the desires, fantasies, and ambitions which the culture encourages her to have. If she is her husband's victim it is because she has been schooled to be his good and dutiful wife, and if she becomes the object of his violence it is because she is supposed to think of herself as the object of his love. The films are concerned, in the best Gothic manner, with the horror of the normal, and while they clearly invite us to "identify" (it might be better to say "empathize") with the heroine, they are very far from being in the business of selling the female spectator a delicious shudder at the spectacle of her own helplessness. *Rebecca* and *Gaslight* and *Notorious* are so distressing because our involvement with the heroine is so complex. We identify with her very closely, but we are also the spectators of a symbolic drama which makes critically present to us the determinants and the conditions of existence of the experience with which we are identifying. The currently dominant "theories" (if they can be called that) of narrative identification induce blindness to the very possibility of such complexities of point of view—from which, nevertheless, the Freudian-feminist melodrama derives its political force. The films neither present women as born masochists nor solicit the spectator (construed as female) to immerse herself in the predicament of the damsel in distress who stands in urgent need of rescue by the good man from the turpitude of the bad. They offer an account of the feelings they insist that we share, and their representative distinction (representative of the greatness of the great melodramas) is to have achieved a form of spectatorial involvement in which the most intense kind of participation in the subjectivity of a particular character coexists with a heightened awareness of the objective social forces in relation to which that subjectivity is organized. The foolish dualism of "involvement" and "detachment" can only mislead: for the spectator of the Freudian-feminist melodrama, the heroine's experience exists at one and the same time as feeling and as object.

It is certainly the case, however, that—with the crucial exception of *Under Capricorn*—the Freudian-feminist melodrama confines itself to the negative critique of patriarchy. Without Brontë's *Jane Eyre* the films could hardly exist, but they nevertheless leave out of the account those central aspects of the novel which can be fairly represented by this excerpt:

> It is vain to say human beings ought to be satisfied with tranquillity: they must have action; and they will make it if they cannot find it. Millions are condemned to a stiller doom than mine, and millions are in silent revolt against their lot. Nobody knows how many rebellions besides political rebellions ferment in the masses of life which people earth. Women are supposed to be very calm generally: but women feel just as men feel; they need exercise for their faculties, and a field for their efforts as much as their brothers do; they suffer from too rigid a restraint, too absolute a stagnation, precisely as men would suffer; and it is narrow-minded in their more privileged fellow-creatures to say that they ought to confine themselves to making puddings and knitting stockings, to playing on the piano and embroidering bags. It is thoughtless to condemn them, or laugh at them, if they seem to do more or learn more than custom has pronounced necessary for their sex. (105–6)

The central theme of *Jane Eyre* is Jane's struggle to define her own destiny, and Brontë's interest in heterosexuality is subordinate to this theme. The Freudian-feminist melodrama has absorbed the influence of Brontë's critique of heterosexuality, but it largely ignores her over-riding preoccupation with the heroine's self-making: at the end of *Rebecca* and *Gaslight*, the positive work of feeling one's way toward new norms and new possibilities remains to be done. I will argue here that this is the work which *Now, Voyager* undertakes—through an appropriation of the work of Brontë of quite extraordinary radicalism.

Now, Voyager and Jane Eyre

My title, "a new servitude," is taken from one of the most famous and beautiful passages in *Jane Eyre*. Jane has been teaching at Lowood for eight years. "I had given allegiance to duty and order," she says; "I was quiet, I believed I was content." The departure from the school of Miss Temple, Jane's colleague and only friend (who marries a man described, with wonderful Brontë-esque astringency, as "an excellent man, almost worthy of such a wife"), convinces Jane that she no longer has a reason, as she puts it, to "be tranquil": ". . . now I remembered that the real world was wide, and that a varied field of hopes and fears, of sensations and excitements, awaited those who had courage to go forth into its expanse, to seek real knowledge of life amidst its perils." She goes to the window, opens it, and looks out—as women in nineteenth-century novels and Hollywood melodramas so often find themselves doing: "I desired liberty; for liberty I gasped; for liberty I uttered a prayer; it seemed scattered on the wind then faintly blowing. I abandoned it and framed a humbler supplication. For change, stimulus. That petition, too, seemed swept off into vague space. 'Then,' I cried, half desperate, 'grant me at least a new servitude!'" Jane considers the phrase, and concludes that there must be "something in it" because

> . . . it does not sound too sweet. It is not like such words as Liberty, Excitement, Enjoyment: delightful sounds, truly, but no more than sounds for me, and so hollow and fleeting that it is mere waste of time to listen to them. But Servitude! That must be a matter of fact. Any one may serve. I have served here eight years; now all I want is to serve elsewhere. Can I not get so much of my own will! Is not the thing feasible! Yes—yes—the end is not so difficult, if I had only a brain active to ferret out the means of attaining it. (83)

Jane, in other words, cannot overthrow patriarchy single-handed. Given, then, the fact of masculine dominance, what are the possibilities? To what extent, under these onerous and intractable conditions, can the heroine ask the question "what do I want?" profitably?—in such a way, that is, as to act on it.

Both *Jane Eyre* and *Now, Voyager* are about women for whom the question of political action does not arise, for obvious historical reasons, and who are correspondingly preoccupied with the task of negotiating between the promptings of their own will and an actually existing social world which is in every way inimical to them. Both works, too, have an obviously similar narrative movement. At the outset, the heroine is located in a position of humiliating and embattled dependency in a home ruled, in the Name of the Father, by an intensely neurotic widowed woman whose oppression of the heroine is traced by the work to her own self-oppression. The main body of the narrative is concerned with the heroine's attempt to discover what her will is, and what she wants, in relation to the things that a succession of representative men want for her. We end in both cases with the setting up of another "home" governed by conventions and constraints which we are invited to read, not as having been simply imposed on the heroine by patriarchy, but as having been determined by her through a strategic compromise with it. This is what the "new servitude" means: it is "neither free absolutely nor constrained absolutely"; while we are certainly to feel that the heroine remains subject to the demands of a culture whose interests are essentially opposed to hers, we are also to feel that she has got, in Jane's phrase, "so much of her own will" as possible under the given conditions. The subject, then, can be expressed in the form of a question: how can the heroine make a history for herself in circumstances which conduce to her not having one at all?

The implications of posing this question as the subject of an American film are foregrounded by the film itself through another reference, this time explicit, to literature—to the lines of Walt Whitman from which the film takes its title: "Untold want by life and land ne'er granted/Now, Voyager, sail thou forth to seek and find." It is Dr. Jacquith (Claude Rains)who introduces the quotation, and who goes on to say that "If Old Walt didn't have you in mind when he wrote those lines, he had somebody very like you." The *film*'s point, of course (and it is one of its many points against the doctor) is that "old Walt" most certainly did not have Charlotte (Bette Davis) or anyone like *her* in mind for the simple reason that in American culture the persons who sail forth to seek and find, who take to the open road, who "light out for the territory"—are men. If the film so elaborately invokes the poet of the "dear love of comrades," it is precisely to stress the anomalousness of doing so in a narrative about a woman. The opposition between heterosexual settlement and homosexual mobility so fundamental to American culture is premised on the assumption that women do, and want to, stay at home, and that they do, and want to, impose on men the domestic shackles which are so congenial to themselves—thus driving men out into the wilderness to bond with each other. An American Jane Eyre is a paradox, and it is the function of the film's title to present this paradox as an essential component of the theme.

The Erasure of the Phallus

In order to understand *Now, Voyager* (and indeed, the woman's film as a genre), we need to understand its conventions, and the most radical and—to 1980s audiences—the least familiar of these conventions is that which governs the representation of the "romantic lover."

It will be immediately apparent that the casting of woman's films tends to be jarringly asymmetrical: the heroine is radiant, passionate, vivid, brilliant, and played by an actress of genius (a Davis, a Garbo, a Hepburn, a Bergman, a Stanwyck); the hero can scarcely be said to exist. This structural inequality is especially striking, perhaps, in such cases as the two Greta Garbo versions of *Anna Karenina* (1927, 1935), where the films derive from a novel in which the lover is as complex and profoundly realized a character as the heroine herself. Anna remains, as Garbo embodies her, Tolstoyan, but Vronsky has been reduced to stage machinery. The automatic explanation, to the effect that the lover is "badly played," is tempting but inadequate: while it is certainly true that the acting of John Gilbert and Fredric March is, in the worst sense of the word, "conventional," their feebleness is evidently a function of the films' total lack of interest in them, and this lack of interest indicates in its turn that the films find it impossible from the outset to offer Vronsky as a viable alternative to Karenin. Even when "the lover" is played by an actor who is in principle a powerful and distinctive presence, the actor's charisma is negated by the narrative type he is playing: Robert Mitchum's role in *Undercurrent*, or Clark Gable's in *Susan Lenox (Her Fall and Rise)* (1931) are exemplary in this respect. The same rule by no means applies to the "bad husband" (or his equivalent): Basil Rathbone's glacial Karenin is substantial enough, and Boyer's staggering performance in *Gaslight* only emphasizes the significance of the casting of Joseph Cotten as his replacement. The heroine's passion, and the unacceptable heterosexual male who is responsible for her suffering, are felt to be dramatically real, but the man whom she loves, or whom the text seems to thrust upon her as the solution to all her problems, is not.

It is all too easy for the sophisticated modern spectator (who has got as far, after all, as Steven Spielberg) to fail to recognize this convention as a convention, and to smile knowingly at what s/he takes to be the susceptibility and simplemindedness of a primitive female audience which (it is happily assumed) went weak at the knees every time Paul Henreid appeared on the screen. The films themselves provide no evidence whatever for this assumption, which is based entirely on a pejorative psychology of women reinforced by the habitual tendency, where Hollywood movies are concerned, to read narrative events independently of their realization. Because woman's films are about "romance," it follows as the night the day that they are, and were in that distant and more innocent age enjoyed for being, "romantic"—and they are therefore "camp" now for the inhabitants of a culture which loses no opportunity to flatter us all on our ability to see through everything. But alas, Paul Henreid is a strategy—and the works in which he and his ilk are vaguely on hand were made for an audience very much more cultivated, and incomparably more political, than any imaginable popular audience today.

The best way to define the lover convention is through an analogy with a proposition of Jacques Lacan's in his seminar on female sexuality, *Encore*.[2] Lacan suggests that the status of the concept of Woman in a phallocentric Symbolic order can be expressed as the formula Woman, under erasure: patriarchal language includes Woman, but only as that which is at the same time excluded "by the nature of words." ("God," 144) The formula for "the lover" in woman's films is Phallus. In himself, the lover is not of the slightest importance: he is merely a logical abstraction entailed in the undertaking to dramatize the heroine's experience of heterosexuality. It is this experience which matters, and the lover is a conventional function of its representation: that is to say, he is the catalyst required in order to motivate the complex social/emotional predicament in which the heroine finds herself as a result of "being in love." The Symbolic of the woman's film includes the lover as signifier of the phallus, but it includes him only as a precondition for the enactment of the woman's desires, sufferings, and struggles, which the genre defines as dramatic objects independent, and visibly in excess, of the phallus as the lover signifies it. This excess of the heroine's intensity over the object which seems to generate it is articulated by the star system and is registered as an excess of the dramatic reality

Bette Davis (Charlotte Vale) and Paul Henreid (Jerry Durrance) in *Now, Voyager*. Personal collection of the editor.

of the star actress over that of the leading man. Indeed, the woman's film produces an entire repertory of actors, as innumerable as the progeny of Banquo in *Macbeth*, whose sole purpose in life is to embody (if that's the word) the erasure of the phallic signifier. The most exquisitely null, the most thoroughly and systematically erased, of these standard items of male furniture is no doubt George Brent, but it seems peculiarly fitting that another of them, Herbert Marshall, actually had a wooden leg.

This extraordinary convention has a striking precedent in the symbolic language of a nineteenth-century form which is literally "melodramatic"—the woman-centered tragic opera. Vicenzo Bellini's and Gaetano Donizetti's treatment of their tenors in *Anna Bolena, Norma, Il Pirata, I Puritani, Maria Stuarda*, and their other *opera seria* corresponds exactly to the treatment of the lover in the woman's film, and it is legitimate to assume that the main reason that these magnificent works are so seldom performed (the fiendish difficulty of the soprano roles apart) is that few competent tenors can be found who are prepared regularly to take on the thankless task of singing in them. Even when the composer is kind, or canny, enough to placate his tenor with one or two good arias, the important role in the prima donna opera (where there is one) is always the baritone, just as the important male role in the woman's film is always the father, the husband, or the doctor. *Norma* and Donizetti's historical operas subordinate the male characters to a central relationship between women in the same way, and for the same reasons, as the films of Davis and 1930s Katharine Hepburn. Even more remarkably, there is an intimate connection between the metaphor of persecution in the Freudian-feminist melodrama and the classical operatic theme of the heroine's decline into madness and delusion—a connection of which Cukor, at any rate, is aware: the Bergman/Boyer relationship in *Gaslight* begins under the distinctively unfavorable auspices of a quotation from *Lucia di Lammermoor*. As we might expect, the echoes of the convention of the "mad scene" are especially pronounced in D. W. Griffith's melodramas with Lillian Gish, which are in themselves one of Hollywood's main links to the nineteenth century. Gish's hysteria in the closet in *Broken Blossoms* (1919) and the baptism of the dying child in *Way Down East* (1920) are, in effect, mad scenes, and in the famous sequence with the bouquet of flowers in *A Woman of Affairs* (1928), the convention passes from Gish to Garbo.

The woman's film, in fact, has drawn the conclusions of Italian woman-centered tragic opera from the dramatic material the two forms have in common. The basis of the convention of the erased phallus, in both cases, is the fact that while the man is theoretically necessary in order for heterosexuality to take place, he is also curiously marginal, and even irrelevant, to the general cultural issues which it raises. There is no question of love being his destiny—and no question, therefore, of the existing structure of the social order being at stake in his unhappiness with, yearning for, ambivalence about, or rejection of heterosexual relations. Thus, when he has said "I love you, love me in return," his dramatic interest is exhausted; the fate of patriarchy itself, however, hangs on the woman's response. If she says "yes," all is well: the affirmative reply secures her in her subordinate social position and is as intrinsically undramatic as the "I love you" it answers. But if she then withdraws her consent, or if she says "perhaps," "yes, but," "on condition that," "couldn't we wait?" "*mai più* ["never again"]" (the operatic variant), or plainly "no," then the seamless fabric of masculine dominance begins to unravel and a thousand narratives instantly materialize. The woman's film dramatizes heterosexuality, from the woman's point-of-view, as a site of struggle and conflict, oppression, and potential resistance, in which the heroine is subjected to radically contradictory pressures, imperatives, drives, obligations, and sympathies. In the presence of this critical turmoil, on the outcome of which the heroine's well-being and the dominant social arrangements diversely and incompatibly depend, the lover himself is effaced. He is merely required to unleash it.

A great many woman's films of the 1930s and late '20s create the distinct impression that although they habitually make use of the convention of the erased phallus, they do not quite understand its consequences and implications—or that they understand them only in an essentially pragmatic manner. (The exception, of course, is von Sternberg, who understands it perfectly, as the performances of Victor McLaglen in *Dishonored* [1931], Clive Brook in *Shanghai Express* [1932], and Cary Grant in *Blonde Venus* [1932] very sufficiently attest.) Thus, if Garbo is in love with Conrad Nagel, Ramon Novarro, and even Gavin Gordon, that is because it is Garbo whom people go to see, and they would continue to go to see her if she were in love with Joe Schmo—as, to all intents and purposes, she usually is. The effect of this pragmatism, however, is to expose compulsory heterosexuality to attack on its weakest flank: the reality of the sexual promise of the male is irretrievably undermined. That *Queen Christina* (1933), for example, wishes us to believe in that promise there can be no doubt. The film's insistent theme is the tragic conflict, for a woman, between heterosexual love (identified with fulfillment) and power (identified with self-abnegation), and we are invited to feel that Christina (Garbo) has discovered, through her love for Antonio (John Gilbert), the authentic sexual identity which her duties as a monarch have always required her to suppress. And yet in that legendary bedroom sequence—legendary, precisely, as a locus classicus of Garbo's art—Antonio becomes a mere bemused spectator ("What are you doing?") of the *jouissance* which he is alleged to have caused and which Christina herself goes on to compare to the experience which God must have had when He created the world and beheld "all His creatures breathing, living." The male is as completely superfluous to the privileged moment of heterosexual awakening as he will be to the privileged moment of heterosexual loss enshrined in the final shot, where Antonio's death at last provides the film with a cast-iron alibi for the ecstatic annihilation of its own manifest content. Finally, at the very moment of closure, and protected by the mask of tragedy, *Queen Christina* can confess with impunity the secret of which it both is and is not in possession—the secret of Garbo's (the woman's) power and self-sufficiency. The paradox of *Queen Christina* is that although it could not exist in the form that it does without the convention of heterosexual romantic tragedy, the film shows no real interest in this convention and at all points uses it opportunistically so as to realize meanings and feelings which are in contradiction with it.

The woman's film stumbles upon this secret unawares: its discovery is the inevitable but (we may assume) accidental result of the mediation of the genre's thematic by the star system. The secret was shared (that is, known and not known) by Garbo's audience.

> Female, 17, white, high-school senior: "I imagined myself caressing the heroes with great passion and kissing them so they would stay osculated forever . . . I practiced love scenes either with myself or with a girlfriend. We sometimes think we could beat Greta Garbo, but I doubt it." (Durgnat, 59)

These extraordinary remarks are quoted by one Herbert Blumer in his book *Movies and Conduct* (published in 1933 in apology for the Hays Code) as evidence of the appalling effects of Garbo movies on the morals of America's youth, and I think we are entitled to claim that they are representative. In saying this I do not mean to imply, of course, that all Garbo's female fans, if asked, would have expressed themselves in the same way: Blumer's candid interviewee strikes us as representative because the fantasy she describes (and, it would seem, wholeheartedly acts out) corresponds so exactly to the treatment of heterosexuality in *Queen Christina* itself. The fantasy has three components: a lesbian identification with Garbo; a lesbian identification with "the hero" in his capacity as Garbo's love object; and an active heterosexual identification with Garbo which reverses the power relations of compulsory heterosexuality and assigns to the erased phallus the task of confirming the speaker's sense of her own sexual potency. The conventional "feminine" heterosexual identification is the only one of the various possibilities which has been excluded, and its exclusion is obviously the point of the fantasy. It would be a very serious error to assume that the speaker has merely allowed her erotic imagination to run riot and that in doing so she has left Garbo's work far behind her. On the contrary, the significance of the fantasy is precisely that the movies which inspired it allow for, and even encourage, the kind of imaginative investment which the fantasy represents, for the conventions which the woman's film employs to dramatize compulsory heterosexuality have the curious effect of undermining its rationale. It ceases to be possible to think of the man as naturally causing, justifying, and potentially gratifying the woman's desire, and the extraordinary excess of the heroine's reality and energy over her lover's makes her available both for identifications and for forms of object choice which are subversive and perverse.

Since the appearance of Laura Mulvey's famous and much-reprinted essay on "Visual Pleasure and Narrative Cinema," it seems to have become one of film theory's articles of faith that Hollywood movies construct a masculine identification. The blatant inaccuracy, the tendentiousness, and the cavalier indifference of the "readings" of Sternberg, Howard Hawks, and Hitchcock with which Mulvey substantiates her thesis do not seem to have diminished its popularity in the slightest, so nothing that is said about it here will be found at all convincing by those whose desire to be told what Mulvey tells them considerably exceeds their interest in the works she purports to discuss. I will risk the suggestion, nevertheless, that a great many woman's films give us grounds for inquiring whether they allow for a masculine identification at all. Confronted by *Queen Christina*, *Stage Door* (1937), or *Now, Voyager*, what can the masculine (that is, male-identified) heterosexual male spectator possibly do? He can, I suppose, in principle, identify himself with the erased phallus and desire the heroine. Quite apart from the fact that the films neither incite nor reward such an imaginative exercise (it must be both a staggeringly difficult and an exceptionally thankless task to identify with George Brent), however, the male spectator who, in defiance of the obstacles, undertakes it will inevitably find himself identifying with a person and a position which the film he is watching has more or less abrasively placed. In that the erasure of the phallus is something which the woman's film does but to which it seldom refers, it is just conceivable that a male-identified man might find some means of inserting himself into the symbolic field of the work: not all woman's films actually announce that they are erasing the phallus as Sternberg's and many of Davis's do, and works which are more reticent on this point may perhaps allow a certain leeway for masculine appropriation. The price to be paid is the misreading of the film—and (it may be imagined) a nagging sense of being left out even as one insists on being included. The masculine spectator who approaches *Queen Christina* from John Gilbert's direction must fail to see what is going on, and he can hardly be spared the suspicion (at whatever level of consciousness) that he has himself been placed under the sign of erasure. His only alternative is to be bored; and I gather from such conversations as I have had with women who saw the films at the time of their release that men either did not go to woman's films at all or went to them under duress. It is very easy to see why.

For the female spectator, however, the woman's film invites to a positive festival of perverse affects. As we learned from Herbert Blumer's shameless interviewee, the erasure of the phallic signifier which creates such difficulties of access for the masculine spectator works wonderfully for the women in the audience, in that the lover's very vacancy opens up a quite extraordinarily diverse and complex range of imaginative options in relation to the female star. The woman's film derives its emotional power from the realization of these options, which survive—which exist, indeed, independently of—the operation of the narrative laws which sometimes seem to foreclose them. The fact that Garbo or Davis or Stanwyck are killed or married off at the end does not matter. The restoration of the patriarchal order, when it takes place, is purely conventional and is usually presented as being so.

World War II crystallized the significance of the woman's film in rather the same way that, thirty years later, the war in Indochina and its domestic ramifications crystallized the significance of the horror movie. Suddenly, under the conjoint impact of German modernism, psychoanalysis, Hitchcock's recovery of *Jane Eyre*, and the revolutionary transformation of the social position of American women, the generic secret which *Queen Christina* does and does not know becomes available for systematic articulation. The Freudian-feminist melodrama and Davis's films about motherhood explore this secret and its implications in very different ways, but one's sense of the interrelatedness of two bodies of work is strikingly confirmed by the casting of George Brent in *The Spiral Staircase* (1945), where the exemplary fetishistic psychopath of the one group of films coincides with the exemplary erased phallus of the other.[3]

The Mother as Governess

The treatment of the lover in *Now, Voyager* (and the group of Davis movies with which it belongs) is inseparable from the film's preoccupation with motherhood. Here, as in *The Old Maid* (1939) and *The Great Lie* (1941), the important relationships are not relationships of heterosexual love but relationships between women and children—in particular, of course, between mothers and daughters—and men appear in the films only as functions of these relationships. This concern with motherhood is, again, strategic. It represents an attempt to negotiate a fundamental narrative problem which works that analyze the vicissitudes of heterosexuality from a woman's point-of-view have repeatedly encountered and which is classically exemplified in *Jane Eyre* itself. Brontë wishes to criticize male-dominated heterosexual love as an institution, and she does so with incomparable power and intensity. She has no alternative at the end of her great novel, however, but to imagine the heroine's "new servitude" in terms of the institution she has rejected. The final chapter of *Jane Eyre* begins, famously, with the portentous and inexorable sentence—"Reader, I married him" (426)—and while it may certainly be argued that this sentence presents, rather than simply reproduces, the laws of closure, the fact remains that these laws weigh heavily on the last quarter of the novel, after Jane's discovery of the mad wife and her departure from Thornfield. Brontë is imaginatively obliged at this point to introduce a second heterosexual man, the pastor and aspiring missionary St. John Rivers, and although the sequences dealing with Jane's struggle for spiritual survival against Rivers's egotism and possessiveness are magnificently done in themselves, Rivers's primary function at the level of structure is to offer Jane access to the public world in which things are done and history is made on terms which are plainly unacceptable, and thus to rationalize the narrative's obligation to affirm a reformed heterosexual domesticity at the close. Jane is perfectly willing to go with Rivers to India, but she refuses the offer of marriage on the acceptance of which he insists as an absolute condition of her accompanying him; while his intransigence on this point is eminently credible psychologically (his domination of Jane will only be complete when he is in a position to deny her sexual gratification), it has the practical effect of foreclosing the range of options open to the heroine. Jane is no longer faced with the task of defining herself autonomously in the social world, in relation to constraints of her own choosing, but with an exclusive alternative which consists of two men, both of whom propose marriage but only one of whom can be thought of as "needing" her.

Jane's return to Rochester is necessary because Brontë can only imagine the total rejection of masculine dominance as the madwoman—that is, as self-immolation—and indeed, the madwoman is the kind of embodiment of female rage and rebellion which appears in a work where the necessity of reinstating bourgeois marriage in some form or other is unavoidable. Jane and Bertha Mason are linked throughout the novel by fire imagery, but it is not Jane who burns down the patriarchal house and blinds Rochester—and the madwoman's paradoxical role, as a surrogate embodiment of Jane's own fury, is to collaborate with Rivers in the engineering of the narrative conditions for Rochester's redemption and Jane's incorporation in the status quo as wife and mother. The madwoman creates that "need" of Rochester's for Jane which allows the novel to suggest that the new servitude can be realized in the form of Jane's marriage to him, and Brontë proceeds dutifully to tell us that the bad patriarchal home (Thornfield) has been replaced by a good one (Ferndean) and that Jane is happy. But she does not believe a word of it, and she leaves us, in her final paragraph, not with the happy family and the happy couple but with St. John Rivers, who has labored mightily for his race and who, when he dies, "will stand without fault before the throne of God." (429) Brontë knows well enough that this is the only place to be, but in order to stand there herself she is obliged to shift her own, and her reader's, identification, not only from the heroine to a man but also to a man who embodies values to which her novel is implacably opposed. Rivers derives his power over Brontë's imagination from one fact, and from one fact only: we are told—in a phrase which clearly corresponds to "Reader, I married him"—that "St. John is unmarried: he never will marry now." (429) Because he is a man, Rivers can make his new servitude for himself, and in the context of Jane's domestication at Ferndean, his vices suddenly appear as heroic virtues: "his is the sternness of the warrior Greatheart, who guards his pilgrim convoy from the onslaught of Apollyon." (429)

If the Freudian-feminist melodrama derives its inspiration from Jane's relationship with Rochester, the Davis motherhood cycle ignores Rochester completely and concentrates instead on the latent possibilities of the relationship to children entailed by Jane's profession. Brontë indicates the nature of these possibilities herself in that extraordinary passage of the novel's final chapter in which the memory of Adele, Rochester's ward and Jane's pupil, emerges from the textual unconscious to haunt the corridors of the happy heterosexual home.

You have not quite forgotten little Adele, have you reader? I had not; I soon asked and obtained leave of Mr. Rochester, to go and see her at the school where he had placed her. Her frantic joy at beholding me again moved me much. She looked pale and thin: she said she was not happy. I found the rules of the establishment were too strict, its course of study too severe, for a child of her age: I took her home with me. I meant to become her governess once more, but I soon found this impracticable; my time and cares were now required by another—my husband needed them all. So I sought out a school conducted on a more indulgent system, and near enough to permit of my visiting her often, and bringing her home sometimes. (427)

Here, it might be said, we have the germ of *Now, Voyager*: even as the walls of patriarchy close in upon her, Brontë envisages another ending from which Rochester has been excluded and in which Jane's "times and cares" can be devoted to another object.

The role of the governess is, understandably, one of the nineteenth century's dominant metaphors for the position of women. The point of the metaphor is the indeterminacy of the governess's place in the structure of patriarchal domesticity: she is neither properly a servant nor properly a part of the family. Although the governess can in some sense be thought of as occupying the role of a parent, there is no question of her being anything other than a menial and an inferior: in her biography of Brontë, Elizabeth Gaskell records an incident in which the mother of one of Brontë's pupils, having overheard her child tell Brontë that he loved her, promptly exclaimed—in Brontë's presence, and in front of all the children—"Love the *governess*, my dear!" At the same time, her intimate contact with the children of her employers places the governess in a position curiously different from that of the other servants—with whom she unquestionably belongs but from whom she is also separated by her functions in relation to bourgeois private life. Her status in the home is fundamentally contradictory, and in one of the key governess narratives, *The Turn of the Screw*, Henry James defines these objective contradictions as the material basis of the narrator's hysteria. The governess becomes exemplary of the destiny of women because she is included in the family as that necessary nonperson whose task it is to reproduce, through her education of children who are and are not hers, the norms and values of the social order which oppresses her. "I see more clearly than I have ever done before," wrote Brontë, "that a private governess has no existence, is not considered as a living rational being, except as connected with the wearisome duties she has to fulfil." (Gaskell, 115)

The equivalent metaphor for girlhood is the metaphor of the foundling—initiated, like so much else, by Jane Austen in *Mansfield Park*. Like the governess, the foundling is in, but very definitely not of, the patriarchal family. She associates and she is educated with the other children, but she is also inferior to the servants, and she is continually reminded of her difference and her dependency and of her obligation continually to express her gratitude for the privilege of being permitted to remain in the home at all. As the young Jane Eyre is dragged off for punishment in the red room, she is told by Abbot the maid: "And you ought not to think of yourself on an equality with the Misses Reed and Master Reed, because Missis kindly allows you to be brought up with them. They will have a great deal of money and you will have none: it is your place to be humble, and to try to make yourself agreeable to them." (Brontë, 13)

We are now in a position to define more precisely the nature of *Now, Voyager*'s appropriation of *Jane Eyre*. Charlotte begins life as a foundling: the Masters Vale have a great deal of money and she has none, and it is her place "to repay a mother's love and kindness" by being a dutiful and obliging daughter. She then becomes the madwoman in the attic, but instead of channeling her energy into burning the house down, she invests it in the project of transforming the social functions of the governess. The governess brings up another person's child within the patriarchal family, and in doing so she is condemned to perpetuate the social conditions of her own subordination. Charlotte takes another person's child out of the patriarchal family, and in doing so she creates the social conditions in which both her own subordination and that of another foundling are eliminated. The formula for *Now, Voyager* is "the governess conquers the house," and in the final scene the new servitude which, because of Rochester, is "impracticable" for Jane Eyre is successfully negotiated.

The Davis motherhood cycle begins with two films which use the governess metaphor quite explicitly. Davis plays a governess in *All This and Heaven Too* (1940), and the position in which the "Aunt Charlotte" of *The Old Maid* is eventually included in bourgeois domesticity, while not literally that of a governess, is plainly analogous to it. *The Old Maid*, of course, is a tragedy: the first Charlotte's attempt to remove her child from the family is thwarted near the beginning of the film, and she is subsequently trapped in the social role which the heroine of *Now, Voyager* is able to transform. The difference between the two Charlottes is primarily a difference of consciousness: I have argued elsewhere that the protagonist of *The Old Maid* is defeated because she never questions in principle the social/sexual values which are the cause of her own suffering (*Hepburn*, 71–79), and it is useful to think of *Now, Voyager* as a remake of, or sequel to, the earlier work in which the heroine's ability critically to disengage herself from patriarchal femininity allows her to resist and overcome the social forces which destroy her predecessor. *The Great Lie* represents a point of transition between the two works. There is no space here for the detailed analysis which this extraordinary (and rather difficult) film deserves. It will be sufficient to say that *The Great Lie* takes the crucial step—crucial, that is, for the radical reinvention of the governess metaphor—of suggesting that the total elimination of the phallic signifier from the child-rearing process is not only possible but also desirable.[4]

The shift of emphasis in the Davis motherhood cycle from Jane Eyre's relationship with Rochester to her relationship with Adele is accompanied, quite logically, by the most drastic and systematic campaign of phallus erasure in the history of the woman's film: with brutal and unrepentant frankness, the lover is reduced to a device for the production of children. Indeed, to father a child in these films is more or less to accept a passport to narrative oblivion. As soon as George Brent and James Stephenson have performed the function of providing Bette Davis and Miriam Hopkins with offspring in *The Old Maid*, they are simply killed off—James Stephenson in a horse-riding accident and George Brent in an extraordinarily peremptory version of the American Civil War which consists of fifteen seconds of stock footage. George is even more cruelly exposed in *The Great Lie*, where he is set up against not only Davis but also Mary Astor at her most glittering and astringent, and once he has made her pregnant with the child that Davis will adopt, his plane instantly crashes in a region of the Amazon rain forest which is presented as being peculiarly and unnaturally difficult to find. He is rescued from it for the purposes of the film's astonishing last movement, the theme of which is the spoiling of the happy ending by the renaissance of a phallus who has been rendered completely redundant and who only serves to reawaken the archaic social and emotional conflicts which have been overcome in his absence. As Jerry Durrance, Paul Henreid's only real purpose in *Now, Voyager* is to be the father of Tina and (as I will argue later) the agent of Charlotte's discovery that she does not actually want the romantic satisfactions with the interdiction of which, by her mother, she has previously identified her oppression. In both *The Old Maid* and *The Great Lie*, the critique of the phallic function as the lover enacts it is both confirmed and amplified by a critique of the imagery and conventions of male-dominated generic narratives: the invocation of the war film in *The Old Maid* and, in particular, of the western in *The Great Lie* is absolutely fundamental to each film's meaning.

The signifier of the erasure of the phallus in *Now, Voyager* is, of course, the cigarette. Jerry's famous cigarette trick may well be a phallic symbol, but those who giggle at it and enjoy their imaginary superiority to the simple 1940s souls who didn't would be better employed in asking themselves what exactly it is about the phallus that is being symbolized. Jerry lights up for the first time, it will be recalled, in the cafe sequence at the beginning of the second voyage, and his instant reaction to Charlotte's expression as she smokes the cigarette he has given her is to declare that he wishes he "understood" her. His presumption is immediately placed by Charlotte's reply; it is crucial that the male offer of the cigarette is explicitly associated at the outset with the attitude to women of which Freud's famous question—"*Was will das Weib?*" (What does Woman want?)—is the classical expression. *Now, Voyager* goes out of its way to be clear both that Jerry, in giving Charlotte the cigarette, is assigning her the position of Woman and that Charlotte sees this and refuses to adopt the position ("He wishes he understood me!"). This resistance is, if anything, even more pronounced in the balcony sequence in Rio, where (as I will argue in greater detail later) Charlotte openly questions the value of the pleasures of heterosexual romance with which the offer of the cigarette is again associated. In the final sequence, when for the first time Charlotte hands the cigarettes to Jerry herself, the meaning of the cigarette motif is reversed—and that its meaning should be so reversed is the point of the motif. The image, which on its first appearance, signifies the erasure of Woman by patriarchal heterosexuality and the romantic discourses with which it is encrusted now marks the erasure of the phallic signifier itself; the cigarette is the consolation prize which Jerry wins after he has submitted to Charlotte's decision that Phallus should be excluded from the house.

How to Look after a Doctor

Charlotte's three lovers, then, are all types of the erased phallus, but there is a fourth man in the film—psychiatrist Dr. Jacquith—who presents us with a rather different set of issues.

There are two kinds of doctor in American texts. The good doctor is a secular priest or deity who exercises the divinity's powers of life and death through his control of an impersonal therapeutic technology. The good doctor's religious affiliations are crucial, and it is hardly surprising that he has often found occasion to manifest himself as the Father and the Son—in Dr. Kildare, in the significantly titled *All Creatures Great and Small*, and in *Welcome Stranger* (1947), where Bing Crosby and Barry Fitzgerald reenact, as country doctors, their earlier partnership as Catholic priests in *Going My Way* (1944). The power of life and death is the power of reward and punishment ("The Lord giveth and The Lord taketh away," as Jacquith puts it). Accordingly, "the hospital" is that lofty seat of social judgment (*St. Elsewhere*) to which metaphysical emergencies are admitted for remedial surgery and intercession, and for the tallying of the pros and cons of their reinstatement in the culture. Those of the good doctor's patients whose relationship to patriarchy is terminally contradictory expire under a cloud of pathos, but those who show promising signs of becoming normal at some future date are literally recuperated.

Even when his goodness is unimpeachable, the good doctor arouses ambivalent feelings. James Kildare, after all, is an interesting name for a physician whose ministrations are supposed to be redemptive (*ça parle?*), and while there can be no doubt of the benevolence either of Kildare himself or of his mentor, Dr. Leonard Gillespie, the very splitting of the good doctor into the Gods of the Old and New Testament bespeaks a certain disquiet about the implications of a secular figure who has usurped the prerogatives of the Creator. The Lord who giveth and taketh away is a God of wrath, and his adjudication of questions of morality has sometimes seemed excessively harsh: the critical role which "the agonizing decision" so often plays in medical narratives is evidence in itself that ideas of illness, cure, and death are potentially troublesome metaphors for a process of normative social control.

The goodness of the good doctor absolutely depends on the enforcement of a rigorous distinction between "the hospital" and "the home." The culture's ills are taken to a saintly shaman who is, precisely, elsewhere—outside and above them. The place of cure is in, but not of, the social world whose spiritual casualties pass through the good doctor's hands, and his otherness in relation to that world at once legitimates his power and guarantees the appropriateness and impartiality of medical justice. Characteristically, the good doctor is celibate, like the priest: he must not be seen to have any personal investment in the social/sexual arrangements whose costs and contradictions are inscribed in the bodies of his patients. However, as soon as the power structure of the hospital is in some way implicated in the power structure of actually existing society, and it begins to appear that the physician has some sort of stake in maintaining the order of things which generate illness, then the laws of ideological contradiction assert themselves and the good doctor turns immediately into the bad one.

The bad American doctor himself comes in two varieties: the doctor as charlatan and the doctor as killer. The former is a professional trickster who peddles confidence in, or passive resignation to, American capitalism by offering a fake ideal cure for its miseries. Herman Melville's *The Confidence-Man*, with his "Protean easy-chair" and his "omni-balsamic reinvigorator," is the classical example of this type, who rubs shoulders with the charlatan priest (both in Melville and in, for example, *Elmer Gantry*) and who is invariably identified with the Devil. The doctor as killer, by contrast, takes his science with the utmost seriousness, and he is continuous, not with the priest, but with another secular god, the Promethean scientist. Poe, as we might expect, is especially sensitive to this connection ("The Facts in the Case of M. Valdemar"). The murderous doctor represents a patriarchal authority which legitimates, and mystifies, itself through a discourse of objective rationality and which derives from this discourse an impersonal warrant for the enforcement of the dominant power structures at the level of the family. For the bad doctor does not kill just anybody: Henry James makes the point with his characteristic precision at the very beginning of *Washington Square*, in the course of introducing us to Dr. Austin Sloper, the most appalling father in the history of fiction: "For a man whose job it was to keep people alive he had certainly done poorly in his own family; and a bright doctor who within three years loses his wife and his little boy should perhaps be prepared to see either his skill or his affection impugned." (83) Of the bad doctor's skill there can be no doubt, but his affection is another matter. Sloper is a misogynist, and it is logical enough that the exercise of the skill in the bourgeois home should be primarily associated with the oppression and destruction of women. In Melville's extraordinary short story "The Paradise of Bachelors and the Tartarus of Maids," male control and exploitation of women's labor in capitalist production is explicitly analogized with male control of women's fertility through gynecology. In *King's Row* (1942) we find not merely one misogynistic doctor but two, both of whom confine their daughters to the house and drive them mad. For the present purpose it is much to the point that the screenplay of *King's Row* was written by Casey Robinson and that one of the doctors is played by Claude Rains.

Of course, neither the good doctor nor the bad is an exclusively American type. Molière took note of the fact that the ideologies of bourgeois medicine were spurious as soon as they had been invented, and many nineteenth-century novels draw attention to the role of the medical profession in the subjugation of women: *Dombey and Son* by Dickens is an obvious example. Nevertheless, the idea of the doctor has a peculiar resonance in American culture: Henry James, again, hits the nail on the head with devastating accuracy.

> This profession in America has constantly been held in honor, and more successfully than elsewhere has put forward a claim to the epithet of "liberal." In a country in which, to play a social part, you must either earn your income or make believe that you earn it, the healing art has appeared in a high degree to combine two recognized sources of credit. It belongs to the realm of the practical, which in the United States is a great recommendation; and it is touched by the light of science—a merit appreciated in a community in which the love of knowledge has not always been accompanied by leisure and opportunity. (*Washington Square*, 80)

"The healing art" is the perfectly mystified bourgeois business, and the doctor—who is able to make a great deal of money from activities which contribute at the same time to the general sum of human wisdom—is the perfect culture-hero for a "community" which is single-mindedly but uneasily dedicated to "the realm of the practical" in which profits are realized. Both the avatars of the bad physician—confidence man and lethal guardian of patriarchal privilege—follow naturally from James's observations.

In *King's Row*, *Spellbound* (1945), *The Locket*, *Guest in the House* (1944), *Hilda Crane* (1956), and *The Cobweb* (1955), bourgeois therapy comes into the inheritance of bourgeois medicine. The critique of the institution of psychoanalysis so central to this melodramatic tradition culminates magnificently in *Marnie* (1964), where Hitchcock explicitly identifies the analytic cure with male-dominated marriage as the two approved "houses of correction" for intransigent female sexuality. The famous free association sequence in which Marnie (Tippi Hedren) exposes the authority structure of the therapeutic session takes place, with exemplary logic, in Marnie's bedroom, and Mark's (Sean Connery) deployment of analytic technique to reassert his power is equated with the rape to which he has subjected his wife a little earlier in the narrative.

Inasmuch as they use analytic categories while deploring bourgeois therapeutic practice, these films define such practice as a reactionary appropriation of psychoanalysis. The analyst appears in the work, not as an agent of enlightenment but as a powerful representative of the social order whose disastrous emotional consequences the work has explored, and the films foreground this contradiction between two very different uses of Freudian ideas by incorporating it in their thematic through the recurrent motif of the male analyst's lack of self-knowledge. The patriarchal therapists of *King's Row*, *Spellbound*, and *The Cobweb* understand neither their objective social role nor the nature of their own investment in it, and they are driven by a fear of the loss of power which they seek to expiate through the spiritual conquest of their patients and their families.

The extraordinary intelligence of *Now, Voyager* nowhere reveals itself more clearly than in the film's perception that the good doctor and the bad doctor are the same person, and that the heroine must exercise constant vigilance in order to prevent the one of them turning into the other. Jacquith, in fact, is placed from the outset: in a work in which the erasure of the phallus is signified by the smoking of cigarettes, it is clearly significant that the surrogate Father's brusque intrusion into the female space of the Vale home should be announced by the sound of his discharging the contents of his pipe into a strategically situated urn. It is no less significant, given the symbolic status of the American doctor as a type, that throughout the opening sequence Jacquith should be at pains to win the confidence both of Charlotte and of Mrs. Vale (Gladys Cooper) by denying, or at least camouflaging, the fact that he is the American doctor at all. Both women insist, for their different reasons, that he is, and while we are left in no doubt that her mother is the main agent of Charlotte's oppression, the film goes out of its way to register the contradictoriness of Mrs. Vale's position (as the enforcer of a patriarchal law of which she is herself the victim) by allowing her a number of tellingly abrasive points against the medical profession in general and Jacquith's homespun rhetoric of nurture ("Are we flowers, doctor?") in particular.

Crucially, the film lays great stress on the fact that Charlotte herself, even in the depths of her prostration, is more than capable of subjecting the well-oiled bedside manner to exacting ironical scrutiny. Her very first line of dialogue—"Introverted, doctor"—cuts through the tracery of disarming euphemism with which Jacquith has just decorated his account of the social and emotional world in which Charlotte, after all, has had to live. In addition, while Jacquith deftly parries this tactless reference to the vocabulary of his profession with a further display of rough readiness ("I don't put much faith in scientific terms: I leave that to the fakers and the writers of books"), it is plainly suggested that some of Charlotte's irony passes over his head. The admiration which, deprecating his own "clumsiness," he lavishes on Charlotte's ivory work provokes a response ("I should think *you* were the *least* clumsy person I ever met") the tone of which he fails to note, and the function of this tone is to offer to the spectator the critical distance from Jacquith's urbanity which the heroine is shown spontaneously to fix on for herself.

The import of these things is clinched at the very end of the sequence in Charlotte's bedroom when Charlotte, reduced to hysteria, asks for Jacquith's help and he denies that she needs it. Charlotte knows as well as Jacquith that she does, but the film establishes categorically that more is at stake in the woman patient's being "helped" by the male doctor than the golden opportunity of learning how (in Jacquith's terms) to "bloom." Jacquith tells Charlotte that "a woman's home is her castle," yet Charlotte insists that he "came to pry"—as indeed he did. Later, while he contemptuously dismisses Mrs. Vale's defense of a "mother's rights" with the claim that "a *person* has rights, a *child* has rights," he emphatically does not refer to the rights of a *woman*. For Jacquith, Charlotte is simply a case of the disempowered *individual*, and the failure of this diagnosis to make contact with the thematic of *Now, Voyager* is subsequently confirmed by Jacquith's corresponding failure to grasp the implications of the film's title. For Charlotte, on the other hand, the relation with Jacquith is a relation of power, and her refusal to countenance any polite mitigation either of the desperateness of her own predicament or of the reality of Jacquith's authority as "doctor" inaugurates one of the film's major thematic motifs: at every point, Charlotte takes care to define the terms on which she will accept male "help" by making the nature of her own situation and her own needs transparently clear, whatever the cost in embarrassment and loss of face. Charlotte's insistence that Jacquith should do the prying he came to do is of the same order as her insistence in the aftermath of the Camille Beauchamp episode, that Jerry should know she is in the throes of a nervous breakdown and that Elliott Livingstone (John Loder) should be keenly and uncomfortably aware ("You must think me very depraved") of the demands to which he must accede before Charlotte will accept his proposal of marriage. It is not only at the end of the narrative that Charlotte imposes conditions on the men who wish to have access to her. On the contrary, *Now, Voyager* defines her early confessions of anxiety, disempowerment, and thwarted need as decisive and enabling moments of self-assertion within the existing structures of social/sexual power which Charlotte will abolish at the close. In that she is intensely conscious of her own position in relation to those structures, and in that she forces those around her to become aware of the objective, independent interests of a person so situated, Charlotte is able to constitute herself as the agent who transforms them.

Thus, Charlotte's acknowledgment of the real inequalities of power between herself and Jacquith embodies a logic, not of retreat and submission, but of resistance. Jacquith's "a woman's home is her castle" and his bluff disavowal both of his status and of the role which this status assigns to Charlotte are, in the circumstances, considerably worse than patronizing: they actively obscure the twin realities of Charlotte's present subordination as servant/daughter to the mother in the home and her potential subordination as patient to the doctor in the hospital. Charlotte confronts Jacquith now, indeed, as she will later confront Mrs. Vale: Jehovah and Elizabeth Tudor, respectively, they are figures of imperial stature who must be negotiated with, faced down, propitiated, and outflanked. *Now, Voyager*, of course, is keenly aware of the difference between them. Mrs. Vale is an exemplary victim of the paternal power which she wields by proxy, and her resentment of Charlotte ("the child of my old age") is directly traced to her resentment of the wifely duties which have obliged her to have a late child in the first place. As a girl, Charlotte both presents Mrs. Vale with an image of her own real powerlessness and provides her with a legitimate object for retrospective symbolic vengeance and self-assertion, and the animosity between the two women follows inevitably from this fact.

Jacquith, by contrast, is the Father *tout court*, and the film begins, as it will end, with the staging of the Oedipal scene in which an ingratiating patriarch enters the "woman's castle" in order to separate the daughter from the mother. It is crucial for the whole subsequent trajectory of the narrative that while Charlotte agrees provisionally to leave the home she repudiates the father's seduction by announcing that she sees the seduction for what it is and that she is, in any case, already a subject who is capable, despite her diminished resources, of demanding recognition on her terms rather than his. If, in particular, she compels Jacquith to "pry" into her erotic life, it is precisely to establish that she is already acquainted with the arcane mysteries of heterosexuality, and that to this extent initiation and enlightenment from the father will not be called for. The origins of the "Free Will Bill"—to the passing of which Jacquith later refers—go back to this moment. He does not have "enough power" to prevent Charlotte taking Tina away from both Jerry and himself because Charlotte has determined the foundations of his authority at their very first meeting. Appropriately, *Now, Voyager* leaves it to Tina, in the final scene, to deliver the coup de grâce. Before going off to dispose of Jerry, Charlotte asks Tina to "look after Doctor Jacquith" in her absence. "What a funny thing to say," Tina remarks as Charlotte walks away; "I thought a doctor was supposed to look after you!"

We may note, in conclusion, that this reading of Jacquith is confirmed by the treatment of the healing art in three earlier Davis films, all of them directed by Edmund Goulding and two written by Casey Robinson. In *The Old Maid,* Dr. Lanskell (Donald Crisp) hovers on such margins of the text as men are permitted to occupy to sympathize with the custodian of the bourgeois family, Delia (Miriam Hopkins), at the expense of another Aunt Charlotte, and to propose first castration and then murder as the obvious remedy for the contradictions of patriarchy. The sole function of the doctor who officiates at Sandra's (Mary Astor) confinement in *The Great Lie* is not to deliver the baby but to tell Maggie (Davis) how much he misses the presence of the anxious father and to fail to notice that she has usurped this prerogative herself. In *Dark Victory,* Judith Traherne (Davis) is besieged with the importunate claims of innumerable physicians, one of whom (Henry Travers) feels obliged to inform all who will listen that he "brought that little girl into the world," another of whom (George Brent) proposes to mastermind her departure from it, and none of whom can cure the mysterious, terminal feminine affliction which will allow her in the end to elude their grasp. Uniquely in the cycle of films about women with fatal diseases produced in the late 1930s and early '40s (part of the point of which, as a rule, is the very absence—the superannuation—of doctors), *Dark Victory* takes the regime of male medicine as its subject matter and records the necessary failure of its interminable quest to know and to eradicate the portentous symbolic thing which constitutes the woman's difference. The object, from birth to death, of fascinated scrutiny and therapeutic intervention, Judith nevertheless cannot be saved; the prognosis is, and must be, negative. In the film's magisterial final sequence, Judith leaves her lover with nothing but the masquerade of "wife" by means of which, at last, she claims the house for herself. The decisive difference between *Dark Victory* and *Now, Voyager* is that in the former the cost and condition of the heroine's "victory over the dark" is one of the cinema's few authentically tragic endings. Like Charlotte Vale, Judith finally makes her own history, conquers the home, and sends the man away, but unlike Charlotte, she must die in order to do it.

These four great masterpieces (the peak of Davis's incomparable achievement in the woman's film) form a tetralogy in which medicine and compulsory heterosexuality figure as the two repressive disciplines which seek to organize the heroine's desire, her fertility, and her relationships with other women in the interests of patriarchy. The films may be said to move from the heroine's defeat and containment (*The Old Maid*), through various fantasies of temporary, provisional, or Pyrrhic resistance and disengagement, to the successful achievement of practical self-emancipation in *Now, Voyager*, where the heroine reorganizes the social and symbolic fields in her own interest, and lover and doctor alike are expelled from the text.

One small, but striking and endlessly delightful, detail in *Now, Voyager* seems to sum up the significance of this development. In a work in which the male bourgeois doctor figures so prominently as a representative of the social forces which separate mother from daughter, and women in general from each other, it is especially appropriate that the working-class woman nurse Pickford ("Dora, not Mary") should be Charlotte's first ally and accomplice in the early stages of her campaign to reinvent the power structures of the patriarchal home. There is no equivalent for Pickford (the wonderful Mary Wickes) in the earlier films, and her meaning in the structure of *Now, Voyager* is reinforced by an implicit contrast with Jacquith's woman assistant at Cascades (Katharine Alexander), who invokes the authority of the absent patriarch to protest against Charlotte's first expedition with Tina. (Jacquith actually calls her "the chief of my police forces.") Pickford practices, not the healing art, but the art of symbolic guerilla warfare, and the film honors her contribution to the struggle against the ancien régime of "Queen Elizabeth" with a quintessential Davis line ("Dora, I suspect you're a treasure") which quotes the traditional term of approbation for the invaluable female domestic with a critically placing irony, and which could not conceivably have been addressed to a male member of the medical profession.

From Veil to Vale: The Renunciation of the Masquerade

Charlotte's experience of heterosexuality in *Now, Voyager* is very carefully and lucidly sequenced. Her surname is "Vale," and the pun on the name is crucial to the film's meaning. If the very word "psychiatry" should fill her daughter with shame (as Mrs. Vale tells her that it should), that is because Charlotte has dishonored the Name of the Father by being the first member of the Vale family to have a nervous breakdown. It will later transpire, however, in the course of Charlotte's last conversation with her mother, that she dishonors it even more by refusing to give it up; for the paradox of the female child's relation to the Name of the Father is that she can become worthy of it only by exchanging it, at the earliest possible opportunity, for the name of the Father's replacement. Where girls are concerned, to go through life with the Father's name is automatically to transgress the Father's law, which enjoins the daughter to put on, with a view to recruiting a husband, the mask of womanliness, which is symbolized in *Now, Voyager* by the wearing of a veil. Charlotte's discarding of the veil and her refusal to reproduce the patriarchal law by discarding her name go together, and by the end of the film "Vale" is no longer the Name of the Father at all but the signifier of the Father's exclusion. Hitchcock's *Rebecca* takes over the name de Winter in rather the same way, and this shared female crime against the Name of the Father expresses to perfection the nature of the relationship between Davis's motherhood films and the Freudian-feminist melodrama. If *Rebecca*'s attempt to live both within and against the laws of patriarchy is doomed to defeat, Charlotte's transcending negation of them is the corresponding normative victory.

The youthful Charlotte of the flashback defines herself single-mindedly in terms of conventional notions of femininity which she has derived from romantic fiction. "I only had novels to go on," she tells Jacquith. It naturally follows that she also defines herself in terms of what she thinks will be attractive to Leslie Trotter (Charles Drake): she dutifully immerses herself in his spiritual world by reading a manual on wireless telegraphy, and above all she makes herself available to him sexually because she "thought men didn't like girls who were prudes." While the feminine position which Charlotte quite consciously adopts in fact entails constant deference on her part to a set of imaginary obligations to the male, her investment in that position is plainly motivated by an impulse to rebel. She experiences her desire for Leslie as a means of asserting and liberating herself, and if she is never aware of her self-abnegation as such, that is because she receives a sense of her own supreme worth as a gift from the man she has flattered: her "moment of triumph" is the moment in which "he placed me on a throne." The woman's reward for forgoing her own desire—or rather, for never discovering what it is—is the homage of the man for whose sake she has forgotten herself. The film stresses that Charlotte's instinctive tendency at this stage to assert herself by proxy through a romantically overvalued man not only neutralizes her rebellion but also conduces to its practical failure. The very mother against whom Charlotte is struggling has been "placed on a throne" by a man, with the results that we see. In that the success of Charlotte's resistance is entirely contingent on the readiness of the man to play the heroic role which corresponds to her own assumption of womanliness, she has nowhere to go when he balks—which he promptly does at the mere sight of his superior officer.

The difference between this Charlotte and the Charlotte who embarks on the second voyage is marked by the fact that the masquerade as "Camille Beauchamp" provokes feelings not of pride, empowerment, and emancipation but of anxiety and discomfort: we may compare the young Charlotte's eagerness to make herself prettier for Leslie by getting rid of her glasses with the sense of physical inhibition and constraint which Davis conveys so brilliantly in the scenes with Jerry which precede the revelation of her imposture. Before she left the Vale house Charlotte had seemed to be quite clear that the knowledge that she was unattractive to men was a major, if not the sole, cause of her misery ("What man would look at me and say 'I want you'?"). The actual experience of being looked at and wanted is very different, however, and Camille Beauchamp is the object of an inquisitive male attention from which Charlotte withdraws even as she incites it. Indeed, the main effect of the masquerade is to tempt Charlotte continually to disclose what it conceals, and while there is no doubt an element of self-laceration and self-contempt in her disparaging references to "Miss Charlotte Vale," they also express Charlotte's resistance to the expectations which her image creates in its male audience. It is even possible to read the faux pas that finally blows her cover as a Freudian slip which frees her both of the false appearance of urbane and sophisticated self-possession and of the need to undermine the success of her own performance through constant displays of abrasive irony. The enigmatic "veil" of womanliness generates a self-consciousness and, above all, a sense of inferiority as acute and as painful as the clothes Charlotte wore in her mother's house, and it serves no better purpose than to impose on her the new obligation of "living up" to the requirements of a persona which, by this point, she does not even wish to adopt.

Mrs. Vale herself is the key to this development: it is of fundamental importance that Charlotte decides to permit Jerry to share her carriage not in the least because she is interested in him as such but in order to defy, and retrospectively avenge herself on, the mother who blighted her relationship with Leslie Trotter and whose image she conjures up at the very moment of her first meeting with her future lover. For Charlotte's masquerade embodies a contradiction: it is only for the male gaze at all inasmuch as it is primarily for the absent maternal gaze which would be scandalized by it, and Jerry recommends himself in the first place as the pretext by means of which Charlotte can present herself to Mrs. Vale as rebellious, autonomous subject. The film traces Charlotte's distance from and dissatisfaction with not only the literal masquerade as Camille Beauchamp but also the experience of the second voyage as a whole to the fact that this experience is from the outset a function of an earlier conflict with the mother which it does nothing to resolve, and the losses and defeats of which it actually confirms. Charlotte was once a nonsubject for Mrs. Vale ("I am my mother's servant"), and the masquerade provides her with the golden opportunity to become a nonsubject for Jerry: the male recognition which Charlotte thought she wanted in fact perpetuates the objectification she was trying to escape. In one of the film's most extraordinary moments, Charlotte is shown to acknowledge this within hours of winning unrestricted access to the lover her mother had denied her. Contemplating both the reflected image of Camille Beauchamp and Jerry's desire to "understand" her which this image has excited, Charlotte repeats to herself, "*He* wishes *he* understood me! . . . *He* wishes. . . ." Charlotte no longer feels that the question of who she is and what she wants can properly be asked, let alone answered, by a man: coming from Jerry, the question is (in both senses of the word) impertinent. Heterosexual romanticism defines Charlotte as a privileged object for the male, yet being "placed on a throne" in the mother's absence only confirms that it was the mother's presence ("He defied my mother") which gave Trotter's action its emotional significance. Charlotte's investment in her first great love was already determined by a demand for Mrs. Vale's acknowledgment of her selfhood, and this makes Charlotte's return to the home inevitable.

If any doubt remains as to the film's attitude to heterosexual romanticism it can be settled, perhaps, by reference to the systematic conventionalization of romantic imagery: Sternberg's treatment of Dietrich's idyllic vacation with Cary Grant in *Blonde Venus* provides a useful point of comparison. *Now, Voyager* is very much more helpful than Sternberg would ever deign to be, and as we are actually told that Rio Harbor is one of the few sights which doesn't disappoint you after the picture postcards, we have only ourselves to blame if we overlook the fact that the "Rio" we are offered consists precisely of a collection of tourist views. The harbor is dominated by a crude back-projection of Sugarloaf Mountain, and the statue of Christ on top of it (which the film might reasonably have ignored altogether) serves expressly as a means of preempting any tendency we might have to interpret the Rio episode in the light of Charlotte's redemption and spiritual rebirth ("There's something to rejoice your architect's heart!"). "Reality" in *Now, Voyager* is the patriarchal home, and the film places the romantic fantasy of an escape from it in emphatic quotation marks. We have been prepared for the rhetoric of "exotic Rio" during the flashback to Charlotte's first voyage. The site of Charlotte's first "tryst" (her own word) with Leslie Trotter is a sparse, starkly lit, and very stagy set, and the flashback is introduced by a shot of the pages of a book being rapidly turned: the memory that follows is effectively indistinguishable from the contents of the romantic fiction which has taught Charlotte the pattern of the masquerade. While the stock shots and the backdrops to which Rio is reduced mark the second voyage too as an excursion into fantasy, Charlotte's discomfort inside the world to which she has previously surrendered herself is as marked as is her resistance to the assumed glamour of Camille Beauchamp. The shot of Charlotte and Jerry sitting side by side on the upper deck of an open-top bus, against a back-projected streetscape, is an especially striking instance of that tension between public professions of happiness and intimacy and unappeasable private disquiet which reverberates through the entire sequence. Charlotte is still caught up in a performance, and the film uses the unreality of Rio both to express the heroine's distance from her own former ideals and to communicate this distance to us.

The film's evident disbelief in everything that Rio represents provides us with a clue, perhaps, to the meaning of a sequence which most admirers of *Now, Voyager* (including myself) would probably prefer to forget. It can hardly be denied that the painfully protracted and embarrassing comic turn involving the Latin American taxi driver whose imbecility and incompetence create the narrative conditions in which Charlotte and Jerry are obliged to spend the night together points to a loss of control over both tone and material which is all the more jarring for the sureness of the touch elsewhere. The failure of realization can neither be overlooked nor excused, but it is certainly suggestive, nonetheless, that the film loses its poise at this particular moment. The inclusion of "the night alone" is thematically crucial, for it must be established beyond doubt that Charlotte and Jerry have had sex and that Charlotte has had the opportunity to sample the delights she will later refuse; the film's disbelief in the value of what Jerry has to offer, though, is so total that it is unable to approach the big romantic scene with even a semblance of conviction. In other social circumstances it might be possible to represent the same event, from Charlotte's point of view, as a pleasurable sexual encounter without permanent, traumatic emotional importance, but bourgeois proprieties which have long survived the Hays Code foreclose such an option: the cinema of the 1980s is not exactly remarkable for its commitment to heroines who opt for promiscuous erotic pleasure outside marriage. The taxi driver and the labored farce of lost ways, missed turns, car accidents, and language barriers are the film's spontaneous and inarticulate response to a fundamental narrative obligation which it can neither avoid nor affirm, and while the results may be grotesque, they are not exactly the film's fault, and they are even a tribute to its integrity. They testify, in their coarse and helpless way, to the completeness of the film's antipathy to the mystique of heterosexual love, and it would not be appropriate to take *Now, Voyager* itself to task for failing to find some way of endorsing female carnality without at the same time compromising its critique of the institutions in which (if at all) a woman's desire is allowed to have a certain notional legitimacy.

Still less is *Now, Voyager* to be held responsible for the fact that the balcony scene in which the Rio sequence culminates is universally remembered as a locus classicus of 1940s romanticism: the evidence to the contrary is surely explicit enough. By any standard of comparison, it is a curious romanticism which inspires the heroine to recall the glorious moment when the earth moved with the bald question, "Was that happiness?" The film is evidently convinced that it wasn't, and Jerry himself is unable to offer a more pressing case in his own defense than the reply, "A small part of it, perhaps." Like the Rio sequence as a whole, the balcony scene continually insists on Charlotte's *alienation* from the signifiers of romantic feeling, imported wholesale, in this case, by the lover: she counters the rhetorical abstractions of ideal love by pointing to its practical costs ("You'll get burned, we used to say."). It is above all crucial, given the subsequent development of the narrative, that Jerry's love should continue to exacerbate Charlotte's sense of her own inferiority and that the scene should move toward an outburst of hysterical self-laceration ("an old maid's tears of gratitude for the crumbs offered") which is hardly distinguishable from that which followed the flashback.

At the end of the second voyage, then, as at the end of the first, Charlotte is still embroiled in the contradictions of a traditional femininity which holds out the promise of "subject-hood" but which, in practice, revives the feelings of self-loss and humiliation it is supposed to assuage. Jerry has changed nothing: Charlotte was veiled when she met him and she is veiled again when she parts from him at the airport. But if the Rio sequence looks backward, it also explicitly projects the narrative's goal: when Jerry kisses her at the climax of the balcony scene, Charlotte is already saying, "Please let me go!" It is a fitting conclusion to this exemplary romantic encounter. At this stage Charlotte cannot act on her resistance, but the function of her second voyage is precisely to dramatize her final disengagement from the fantasies left over from the first and thus to lay the groundwork for the film's great last movement: the third voyage, back to the home where Charlotte will seek to restore and repair the primary relation of love and solidarity between mother and daughter.

The meaning of *Now, Voyager* is embodied in a condensed form in its use of the conventional trope of "the star entrance." Davis makes three entrances—as "Aunt Charlotte," as "Camille Beauchamp," and as Bette Davis (as it were)—and each entrance serves as a kind of tonic chord which announces the key of the movement that follows it. The entrances have a number of features in common: they are all organized as coups de théâtre; in every case, Charlotte is appearing for the first time before a major character in the narrative; and all of them place the spectator in this character's position so that we share his/her experience of Charlotte's metamorphosis. The third entrance, however, is decisively different from the first two. The observers of the debut of Aunt Charlotte and Camille Beauchamp are men: respectively, Jacquith (the only member of the assembled company who does not know what Charlotte looks like) and Jerry, the Father and the lover; though in the second case the male gaze is shared by the tour operator and Jerry's impatient fellow passengers. On both occasions we are made acutely aware of Charlotte's discomfort at being looked at, and the invitation to take note of and identify with her self-consciousness and vulnerability distances our look from the man's. Where Aunt Charlotte is concerned, this distance is produced by the thwarting of our expectations. Jacquith is waiting for Charlotte Vale but we are waiting for Bette Davis, and after elaborately preparing us for her with close shots of hands carving and feet descending the staircase, the film gives us "not–Bette Davis," pathetically isolated in long shot in a composition dominated by the supporting cast. Our shock derives from the fact that Aunt Charlotte is the negation of everything that Davis represents, and it creates the initial discrepancy between our point of view and Jacquith's which the film will later use to place Jacquith's complacent condescension. Our reaction to the entrance of Camille Beauchamp is also necessarily different from that of her male audience, which, unlike us, knows her neither as Davis nor as the "not-Davis" to which she has been reduced in this film. The pan from feet to head which marks Camille's appearance signifies her objectification by the men who are looking at her, but we have no sooner been implicated in this look than we are returned to the experience of the person who is being objectified. Far from cutting to long shots and thus confirming our position as subject of the gaze, director Irving Rapper holds the close-up of Davis's face as Camille descends the gangplank so that we see and share Charlotte's trepidation and embarrassment. If the men are looking at the masquerade, we are the sympathetic witnesses of the anxieties it generates.

Above all, of course, neither Aunt Charlotte nor Camille Beauchamp is an identity determined by Charlotte herself. Each is a persona which has been adopted under duress in response to social pressures and constraints which Charlotte can do nothing to effect or regulate, and each makes her entrance unwillingly, emerging from her retreat only in response to a summons she has no choice but to obey. Aunt Charlotte, as her mother's servant, is peremptorily instructed to appear for family tea; Camille spends the whole cruise shut up in a cabin which she leaves at the very last possible moment; and Charlotte is taken to task, in both cases, for keeping her prospective audience waiting. Rapper gives concrete form to this complex of thematic ideas by emphasizing Charlotte's visual subordination both to decor and to other characters within static compositions (as in the scene of her introduction to Jacquith), and by confining her movements to situations in which she is compelled to react to some form of external provocation. Thus, while the crane shot which follows Camille's descent of the gangplank is motivated by her movement, it represents the very opposite of a command of the visual space. Charlotte is moving because she is obliged to, and any sense of spatial freedom which the camera movement might convey is firmly undercut not only by Davis's demeanor but also by the tightness of the close-shot composition.

The extraordinary dramatic power of Charlotte's third entrance is generated by the systematic contradiction of the common features of its predecessors, and Rapper prepares us for it by recapitulating the "entrance motif" in the scene in which Charlotte is reunited with Mrs. Vale. Once again Charlotte is compelled to make an appearance which she dreads; once again her movement within the image is wholly determined by external coercion; and once again she is up for the inspection of an inquisitorial gaze which, if not itself male, has nonetheless been co-opted for the interests of patriarchy and before which Charlotte is ordered to display herself like a mannequin at a fashion parade. The sequence moves toward an acknowledgment of defeat ("You've thought of everything haven't you, Mother?") which is immediately canceled by the sequence set, not in Mrs. Vale's room (itself formerly occupied, we have been told, by the Father himself), but in the room Charlotte has marked out as her own, against her mother's wishes.

Just as Charlotte put on the mask for the male look, she now abandons it in the presence of, and for, the mother: the imaginary self-assertion of Camille Beauchamp ("I was thinking of my mother!") is at last realized in practice. In a breathtaking display of bravura 1940s mise-en-scène, the spectacle of Woman is literally abolished and the narrative itself grinds to a halt as Charlotte's two audiences—Mrs. Vale and ourselves—are left to await the pleasure of the subject who is not yet there. The equivalent, for us, of the "nothing" which Mrs. Vale sees is Mrs. Vale's back: Charlotte's self-making deprives the look of its object and suspends the flow of dramatic time. When Charlotte reappears she has become Bette Davis, and she is no longer on display for approval, judgment, or interrogation. The cut back to long shot which isolated Aunt Charlotte in the doorway of the drawing room and the vertical pan which scanned and fragmented the body of Camille Beauchamp are alike refused, and the camera simply follows Charlotte's movement as she comes back into the room, acknowledging her new control of the visual space. While Charlotte is obviously defying Mrs. Vale, the film takes great care to point out that she is not the least interested in overpowering her mother, whom she asks only to "meet [her] half way." She asks for recognition as a subject from another subject, and in doing so she is rejecting not only her earlier position as her mother's inferior but also the position of the classical Oedipal rebel who asserts a rival claim to the possession of the phallus, and who thus defers to patriarchal authority in the very act of challenging a specific representative of it. Mrs. Vale is more than equal to a struggle for phallic mastery, and indeed, she proceeds spectacularly to initiate one by throwing herself down the staircase. This is not the sort of battle that Charlotte is interested in fighting, though, and she repeatedly declines to participate in the kinds of resistance which the structures of the Oedipus themselves encourage. The Oedipal subject is defined in opposition to another who is *not* the subject, and in the scenes which follow, Mrs. Vale does everything in her power to involve Charlotte in a contest for dominance which one person can clearly win and the other can clearly lose. If Charlotte's demand for recognition explicitly distances itself from the Oedipal logic of castration, Mrs. Vale's counteroffensive takes the form of an attempt to reinstate it.

The contest very rapidly comes down to money: Charlotte's economic dependence on her is the highest card in Mrs. Vale's hand, and her use of the threat of disinheritance to exact Charlotte's obedience very obviously recalls *Washington Square*. Because she is a woman Charlotte, like James's Catherine Sloper, is in the anomalous position of having a legitimate title to money which she must at the same time earn by being a tractable and dutiful daughter. The source of the anomaly is the fact that bourgeois money is the economic basis of masculine dominance, and it follows that the inheritance of this money by a woman creates the possibility of a very serious crisis of reproduction. The problem which exercises both Mrs. Vale and Dr. Sloper is that after the Father or his representative is dead, the recalcitrant heiress has just as much right to do what she wants with the patriarchal cash as the obedient one, and both parents are therefore concerned to find some means of guaranteeing in the present, while they are still alive, that their daughters will not abuse their economic power in the future. For Henry James, the heiress figures in work after work as an exemplary symbol of the contradictory and paradoxical position of women in a society which is both capitalist and patriarchal. In that she has a legal right to inherit, the heiress is recognized in principle as an autonomous agent in that the practical realization of this principle endows a woman with the material power to determine her own destiny; however, she is a potential threat to the social order which has so liberally acknowledged her legal existence, and men close in on her from all directions in order to take her power away again.

Now, Voyager takes up James's great theme and proposes a utopian reworking of it. Like Catherine Sloper before her, Charlotte does not actually care about the money, and both women prefer to disinherit themselves than to accept the parent's ultimatum, which thus has the unintended effect of confirming the heroine's sense of her power and her capacity for resistance: Charlotte's discovery that she is "not afraid" is the crux of Davis's performance, and the turning point of the film. Like Catherine Sloper too, Charlotte continues to live in the house as her parent's companion, but the difference between the two cases (a difference for which the sex of the parent is clearly decisive) is that Charlotte's refusal either to succumb to economic blackmail or to consent to an ongoing struggle for the dominance of the home provides the basis for a fragile and precarious compromise between Mrs. Vale and herself. They establish a modus vivendi, the basic principle of which is Mrs. Vale's acceptance of the inevitable and her preparedness to relinquish a real for a theatrical authority: "She barks but she doesn't bite," as Charlotte puts it in a letter to Jacquith. Crucially, Charlotte has an option that Catherine Sloper doesn't. If necessary, she can work, and given the film's conjuncture, the importance of the fact that Charlotte's self-confidence is definitively secured in the context of a discussion about financial independence hardly needs to be stressed. In the event, of course, Charlotte does get the Father's money, and as she does not then lose it again through marriage, like many another Jamesian heiress, she is in a position to deprive patriarchy of its economic base in the final scene. The *symbolic* necessity of Charlotte's readiness to work remains. The film's entire project would have been compromised had it not been made clear both that Charlotte does not stay with Mrs. Vale for reasons of economic security and that Charlotte herself is aware that material independence is the precondition for other kinds of autonomy.

The limits of Charlotte's compromise with her mother are brutally exposed when it founders, as it must, on Charlotte's rejection of heterosexuality. Her refusal of Elliot Livingstone's proposal precipitates a fatal confrontation in the course of which it emerges that Mrs. Vale has only agreed to "meet Charlotte half way" at all because she assumes that she will be rewarded for her tolerance of her daughter's transformation with a prestigious (and lucrative) marriage. Charlotte has been free to do "exactly as she pleases" inasmuch as her doing so seems to please Livingstone as well, and her decision (as she marvelously expresses it) to "buy a cat and a parrot and live in single blessedness" can appear to Mrs. Vale only as incontrovertible evidence of the total uselessness of the female child. Charlotte's attempt to restore the mother/daughter bond through her relationship with her own mother is doomed to failure because Mrs. Vale has internalized the priorities of patriarchy according to which the autonomous woman, no less than the hysterical invalid, is mere waste, and Charlotte responds with an extraordinary diatribe against "mother love" in which the film's critique of the perversion of mother/daughter relations by the patriarchal family becomes explicit.

Charlotte has in fact refused Livingstone in an agony of ambivalence—not because she loves him but because she wants to have a child, and she has told him quite frankly that "when I marry you that will be one of the main reasons." It is not a sufficient reason to go through with the marriage, and at the end of the scene in which she turns Livingstone down (having first ensured his acquiescence in her decision through a calculated affront to his sense of decorum), she plainly states for the first time that she now defines herself as a woman who will never get married. Livingstone's function in the film is to be, unlike Jerry, available for matrimony and thus to offer to Charlotte the chance to become a mother on traditional terms—terms which she refuses before the new opportunity represented by Tina has materialized. Motherhood within the patriarchal family can only lead to a repetition of Charlotte's relationship with Mrs. Vale and Tina's with Mrs. Durrance, and *Now, Voyager* uses the Livingstone scenes to tell us that although it is aware that it could propose some ideal reform of the family as a solution to Charlotte's difficulties, it has no intention of doing so.

The Moon and the Stars

One of the terms which occurs most regularly in discussions of the woman's film is "self-sacrifice." The genre, we are told—ad infinitum ad nauseam—habitually imposes renunciation on its heroines, in particular the renunciation of sex, and advocates in general the nobility and moral beauty of giving pleasure up. There are indeed woman's films which answer to this description, but they are far from being representative.[5] When we examine the critical literature, we find that films which do not answer to the description at all (such as *Blonde Venus*, *Stella Dallas* (1937), *Camille*(1936), and *Now, Voyager*) are repeatedly cited as exemplary of the woman's film's reactionary tendency to celebrate the improving effects of self-abnegation. The "sacrifice" formula tends to be popular with the same critics who like to inform us that Lisa's death from typhus at the end of *Letter from an Unknown Woman* represents a punishment for her sexual transgression—though we are not told why it was that the women of America (and of Europe too) were so eager to see movies which propagandized for their chastisement and deprivation. That the heroines of *Camille* and *Blonde Venus* "make sacrifices" is obvious, but one's preconceptions about the intrinsic conservatism of "popular culture" must be exceptionally obstinate if one persists in the belief that the films in which these sacrifices occur define them as some form of moral ideal. It is hardly surprising, perhaps, that a genre whose subject matter is the experience of woman in a capitalist, male-dominated culture should sometimes have occasion to dramatize situations in which the protagonist finds herself obliged to abandon aspirations and desires which conflict with that culture's norms and priorities, and more often than not the woman's film heroine "sacrifices" herself in response to social pressures which she cannot resist and which the work itself deplores.

Charlotte's alleged sacrifice in *Now, Voyager* is the sacrifice of the erased phallus. What she really wants (it seems) is Jerry—but Jerry is, with invincible decency and gallantry, married, and Dr. Jacquith, in his capacity as God, has placed this adulterous liaison under an interdict. Charlotte is, as she herself puts it, "on probation," and if she allows her overwhelming desire for her lover to manifest itself she will be deprived both of the custody of Jerry's child and of those few opportunities for platonic congress with the father that Dr. Jacquith permits her. The film's famous closing line—according to this reading—signifies Charlotte's acknowledgment that she will be obliged to make do with second best. The moon is beyond her grasp: she cannot "be happy," that is, because she cannot have Jerry, but she can at least be married to him in fantasy and construct in her imagination the idyllic patriarchal family, and the ideal sexual gratification, which she has been denied in practice by the stern dictates of a great social law.

It is not the least of the disadvantages of this account of the ending of *Now, Voyager* that it takes for granted an evaluation of Jerry which is strikingly at odds with that implied by the film itself. As we have seen, Charlotte has already decided by the end of the Rio sequence that the pleasures offered by Jerry are very far from being synonymous with "happiness." Later, during the second sequence at Cascades, when she broaches the question of adopting Tina to Dr. Jacquith, she promptly tells him that her affair with Jerry is "over" without giving the slightest evidence of nostalgia, regret, ambivalence, or emotional disturbance, and without suggesting that she has any lingering yearning for Jerry to overcome. Indeed, she herself introduces the topic of their relationship in order to clarify to Jacquith the nature of her interest in Tina and declares that the relationship is a thing of the past before the doctor has had a chance to forbid it. The film is quite clear throughout that Charlotte cannot achieve fulfillment through heterosexuality and that she is perfectly aware of this; any reading of the ending which suggests that Charlotte is constrained, under external duress, to sacrifice the supreme good of a sexual relationship with a man and make do as best she can with lesser and inferior satisfactions makes nonsense of the whole narrative.

It is the burden of *Now, Voyager*, in fact, that a sexual relationship with a man is not the supreme good and that in the circumstances the stars, far from being an inadequate substitute for the moon, are distinctly to be preferred to it. Charlotte is saying, I take it: "There may well come a time when it is possible for a woman to enjoy complete social and economic autonomy, bring up a child which is not her own outside the family *and* conduct a sexual relationship without dwindling into marriage and renouncing all forms of activity except those which marriage entails. This time has not yet come, and for the present I have no doubt about the relative position of these things on my list of priorities. You may come and see us whenever you wish. Good-bye." *Now, Voyager* endorses this decision, which it offers as the only rational one, and the final scene moves triumphantly, not toward the heterosexual embrace, but toward Charlotte's refusal of it, celebrated on the soundtrack by Max Steiner with a delirious dissonant interval.

The ending derives its extraordinary emotional power (which remains undiminished after innumerable viewings) from its repudiation of those forms of narrative closure in which the heroine is forced to renounce her desire to transgress, or in which transgression leads inexorably to death and defeat. Madame Bovary is the prototype of the female protagonist who, trapped by bourgeois domesticity, nurses impotent and self-destructive fantasies of rebellion and resistance, and we know well enough that narratives organized around such protagonists may have a potent critical force. In *Now, Voyager*, however, it is bourgeois domesticity which is consigned to the realm of fantasy. Practical life is reorganized along lines determined by the heroine, and the erased phallus, the traditional destiny of Woman, and the patriarchal family are all shoved gently off into the Imaginary. This critical inversion of the archetypal melodramatic ending is one of the film's most remarkable achievements, and we are not invited to feel either that Charlotte is denying herself anything or that the new arrangements diverge in any way from the order of priorities which she has established. On the contrary, the source of dramatic tension in the final scene is the fact that Jerry represents a potentially serious threat to the realization of Charlotte's wishes, and it ought to be enough (surely) to dispose forever of the "sacrificial" reading of the end of *Now, Voyager* to point out that Charlotte explicitly disposes of it herself. It is *Jerry's* reading, and Jerry's role at the close is to articulate for the last time the moral and emotional claims of the patriarchal order which is about to be eliminated. Charlotte both meets and displaces these claims by offering Jerry—again, quite explicitly—

a ghostly paradigm of the old régime. Having first scornfully repudiated Jerry's suggestion that instead of devoting herself to Tina she ought to be looking for "some man who could make [her] happy," Charlotte then refuses to permit the actual *realization* of the imaginative satisfactions she is prepared to concede: the "Please let me go" with which she responds to his attempt to kiss her is defined unequivocally as a victory. Jerry will have a role in the new order—but only as that which is in practice absent from it.

The final shot beautifully sums up the narrative trajectory of the last section of the film in a single rhetorical gesture. The camera tilts up away from Charlotte and Jerry toward the stars in a movement which is usually read (no doubt) as a signifier of romantic exaltation. The shot derives its meaning, however, from the fact that it exactly reverses the direction of the camera movement in the shot which ends the sequence dealing with Charlotte and Tina's holiday: here, the camera tilts down from the stars to show us Charlotte and Tina in a long shot, asleep in one another's arms. The movement away from the heterosexual couple completes itself in the movement toward a new form of the relationship between woman and female child, and thus a new practice of socialization, in a world in which masculine dominance has been marginalized.

Conclusion

It might, perhaps, be objected that the last thirty minutes of *Now, Voyager* are flawed by a certain schematism and conventionality in the representation of Tina, and there is a sense in which this objection is valid. Charlotte's transformation from the woman who asks "What man would look at me and say 'I want you'?" at the beginning to the woman who says "Please let me go" at the end is dramatized with a power, a lucidity, and an inwardness which enforce our wholehearted consent and which leave no questions to be answered, but it is certainly true that Tina is conceived primarily as a function of this transformation, and that she is never very clearly or specifically grasped in her own right. The nature and content of her relationship with Charlotte, in particular, tend to be taken on trust. That it is meant to embody possibilities which are radically new there can be no doubt, but it amounts to little more in practice than a rather generalized kindness and attentiveness on Charlotte's part and an equally generalized readiness to respond to such kindness on Tina's. The clearest indication we have of what Charlotte's education of Tina will entail for the girl herself comes in the sequence at Cascades in which Charlotte comforts Tina's anxieties about the fact that she is not "pretty" by telling her that true beauty is not a matter of one's physical appearance but of an inner spiritual strength and self-confidence. The implications of this sequence are explored no further, however, and the film even seems to lay itself open to the charge of reneging on its own convictions and its own logic by producing, in the final sequence, a Tina who is indeed a "pretty little girl" in the most conventional sense. Could it not be argued that Charlotte herself has feminized Tina for Jerry, in the best maternal way and that therefore *Now, Voyager* has not only failed to substantiate its own claim that the new social arrangements are to be valued because they enable the abolition of patriarchal gender roles but also has come perilously close to contradicting it?

That the film invites these questions is in a sense a criticism of it, and analysis is accordingly faced with the problem of deciding what weight the criticism ought to carry. I myself would wish to argue that the uncertainties of realization in the film's handling of Tina are inevitable and that similar uncertainties are in fact very commonly to be found in works of art which have the courage and integrity to project a radical utopia beyond the existing reality principle. The uncertainty and the courage go together. *Now, Voyager* has demonstrated, after all, that the socialization of women in the patriarchal family is invariably and necessarily disastrous, and that the only hope for Tina is to place her in the care of a woman who has renounced compulsory heterosexuality and who refuses to conduct any aspect of her life on the assumption that the desire and activities of woman should be organized by, or subordinated to the interests of, the culture of masculine dominance. Such a conclusion is in itself sufficiently astonishing, but it should, I think, be obvious that the ideological impediments to it are more easily overcome (given the traditions and conventions of the genre) in the case of a mature adult woman played by Bette Davis than in that of the little girl she adopts. It is at the point at which the identity and destiny of Charlotte/Bette Davis become exemplary for Tina that the film's touch becomes equivocal. To suggest that they ought to be exemplary (as *Now, Voyager* explicitly does) is one thing, but actually to show them being so is quite another, and the film steers clear of the explosive cultural problems involved in representing what Tina's upbringing by the kind of woman that Charlotte has become would be like.

Its hesitation is eminently understandable: a film which *did* dramatize the education of a little girl, outside the family, by a woman who has renounced the claims of patriarchy in all their forms could not have been made.[6] It is surely a sufficient tribute to the greatness of *Now, Voyager* that it says, with unmistakable clarity, that this is the kind of education which Tina should and, for her own good, must have, and we may excuse the film for its failure to enact this education in convincing concrete detail. Where the final sequence is concerned, it is indeed the case that Tina is presented to Jerry by Charlotte as a "little woman" in a pretty party frock who asks her father whether he really likes her and who is promptly interpellated as "feminine" by the father's embrace. This is because the rejection of Jerry's Oedipal claims on Tina must—the dramatic imperative is absolute—be left to Charlotte: culturally, it would have been quite impossible to show Tina resisting, or in essence deviating from, Oedipal femininity herself. It can only be resisted for her, on her behalf, by a woman played by a star who embodies the values which Bette Davis embodies. Such procedures may look like failures of integrity or nerve, but they are in fact a part of what Gerard Manley Hopkins called "the sakes" of the work, and unless we are sympathetically attuned to the ideological problems which *Now, Voyager* faces, we will find ourselves criticizing it on inappropriate grounds. The film is fully aware of the problems itself, and it is immensely to its credit that it does what it can to address them through a strategic deployment of metaphor. Tina is emphatically left "looking after the doctor," and it is hardly reasonable to expect more than this.

The Devil, Probably: The Symbolism of Evil (1979)

"as one between desire and shame suspended . . ."
—Percy Bysshe Shelley, *The Triumph of Life*

Clearly, the concept of evil has always been crucial to the horror film, but its appearance in the form of the devil allows us to focus with a particular clarity the genre's relation to the Gothic tradition of Romanticism and—more specifically—to a number of cultural problems and contradictions which that tradition has been consistently unable to resolve. The development of the Gothic seems to me to involve a particular inflection of pre-occupations which are far more generally characteristic of the Romantic movement: (a) the relation between the subject and object of perception, and the role of the perceiver in the definition of his/her reality; and (b) the nature of, and the value to be ascribed to, fundamental, socially proscribed or inhibited human energies. Obviously, the two questions are interrelated; as soon as one conceives of perception in terms of the perceiver's activity, one comes up at once against the problem of the nature of that activity, and of its determinants. Equally obviously, the Gothic raises and explores, before the advent of psychoanalysis, the familiar Freudian concepts: desire, the social origins of sexual repression, the unconscious, and the death drive.

My purpose here is to examine, in a number of major works, an insistent tendency within Gothic romanticism to associate the return of repressed sexuality with the devil and to suggest that the repetitiveness of the association—the apparent impossibility of transcending it—can be taken to demonstrate both the real progressiveness of the Gothic and its final intractability. I shall approach the modern horror movie by way of William Blake, Nathaniel Hawthorne, and Herman Melville (and Sigmund Freud, of course). I wish to begin by considering two of Blake's lyrics. They're to be found side by side in the notebook of 1791–92 (the so-called Rossetti Manuscript): the first was subsequently included as "The Garden of Love" in *Songs of Experience* (1794).

> I went to the Garden of Love,
> And I saw what I never had seen:
> A chapel was built in the midst,
> Where I used to play on the green.

And the gates of this Chapel were shut,
And Thou shalt not writ over the door;
So I turn'd to the Garden of Love,
That so many sweet flowers bore,

And I saw it was filled with graves,
And tomb-stones where flowers should be:
And Priests in black gowns were walking their rounds,
And binding with briars, my joys & desires. (Erdman, 26)

The second poem follows at once:

I saw a chapel all of gold
That none did dare to enter in
And many weeping stood without,
Weeping mourning worshipping.

I saw a serpent rise between
The white pillars of the door;
And he forcd & forcd & forcd—
Down the golden hinges tore

And along the pavement sweet
Set with pearls & rubies bright
All his slimy length he drew
Till upon the altar white

Vomiting his poison out
On the bread & on the wine.
So I turnd into a sty
And laid me down among the swine (Erdman, 458)

The nature and significance of the chapel in the first poem don't present a problem while we consider the poem on its own: the chapel embodies the spirit of a Christianity defined by the repression of "energy"—that energy which is "eternal delight" and which is characteristically located, for Blake, in childhood ("Where I used to play . . ."). Indeed, "A Little Girl Lost," the final poem in *Experience*, makes the connection between play and infantile sexuality explicit, and it takes as theme its prohibition by a father whose Medusa-like gaze (he is associated with a look which petrifies and with "hoary hair," the "blossoms" of which recall, inversely, those of the garden in which his daughter and her lover have played) is assimilated by the poem to "the Holy Book." On a first reading, we might suppose that the second chapel announces its function with equal lucidity: its connotations seem fairly obviously positive—the simple antithesis of those of the sty which replaces it, in the final couplet, after the serpent's intrusion. We might go on to say that the clarity of the symbolism is strikingly enforced by the sentence structure: the first sentence (which is also the first stanza) gives us the chapel and an implied sense of its spiritual value ("all of gold"); the second, bridging three stanzas, the monstrous act of desecration by the archetypal Christian emblem of evil; and the third, the breakdown and degradation which follow from it. "It [is] clear," remark the editors of the Longman's edition, "that the 'chapel of gold' is the temple of innocent love, defiled by the repression described in the previous poem. Love is perverted into something monstrous, and the sight revolts the poet." (Stevenson and Erdman, vi)

It is clear to me, on the contrary, that the meaning of the chapel of gold is far from clear and that as soon as we try to divine from the poem any actually realized significance for it, we come across insuperable difficulties. We can't, for example, distinguish it as sharply from the chapel of the previous poem, as the editors want to suggest. The doors of the first chapel are shut, and the legend over the door—associated with death in what follows—refers us implicitly to Dante's *Inferno*: the assimilation of institutional Christianity to hell and death won't surprise the reader of Blake's *The Marriage of Heaven and Hell*, in which the affirmation of energy is placed in the mouth of the devil. The doors of the second chapel are also barred to those outside, though this time not by a physical impediment but by fear—and a fear, moreover, which isn't in any way specified. Is it the fear produced by a sense of moral unworthiness, of being unfit to enjoy the splendors within? Or is it the kind of fear experienced by the little girl lost in the face of "a loving look like the Holy Book," the fear engendered by an actual or anticipated "Thou shalt not"? The ambiguity isn't resolved in the following couplet: is the anguish of the excluded congregation attributable to "grief for sin" or to the pain and desperation which might follow from an arbitrary and oppressive exclusion? Indeed, the reiterated "weeping," and the immediately following "mourning," make the precise sense of "worshipping" practically indecipherable: how, exactly, are we to read it in relation to the emphasis on grief? What kind of supplication is involved? Does it suggest "Forgive me, I have sinned"? Or "Relent in your harshness and cruelty"? Or are we to infer a critical consciousness of the morbidity which necessarily attaches to worship in a context defined by fear, guilt, and sorrow?

The first stanza, in fact, seems to be unreadable—it's impossible to say what it means—and the particular way in which in the last three stanzas Blake undertakes to demonstrate the chapel's "positive value" only goes to confirm the ambiguities to which I've pointed. For the positive value isn't in any way substantiated: it is simply asserted in the elaborate insistence on "white," "gold," "sweet," and a general material splendor the spiritual implications of which we are left to infer. This merely verbal iteration may deceive us into believing that the chapel has been convincingly characterized in a way which Blake has failed to achieve: for it is only that the words *white* and *golden* in connection with a chapel evoke a number of conventional associations of purity and sanctity, and the poem falls back on them. Blake's equivocation here is profoundly revealing: on the one hand, the chapel's positive function is wholly unrealized, and on the other, it fails to register the distinctness from the chapel in "The Garden of Love" which the intention seems to require.

When we have taken note of this, we are struck at once by the remarkable difference in the role of the narrator in the two poems. In "The Garden of Love," the narrator's activity is limited to, and doesn't survive, the motion of turning away, in the second stanza, from the chapel to the garden. That apart, he does no more than transcribe a vision in relation to which he is passive, and in which the only freedom that remains to him is that of not looking. Indeed, the progress of the poem enforces the inescapability of the fact from which, at first, he attempts to avert himself: the contagion of "Thou shalt not" is unavoidable, and we feel that it has already contaminated the narrator—the tone of the poem implies neither the capacity for, nor the possibility of, resistance. Similarly, while we're left in no doubt as to what the significance of the narrator's experience is, it doesn't issue—as it does in the second poem—in action, and the corollary of this is the narrator's impotence. The priests are "binding with briars my joys and desires," and he can only watch helplessly and resignedly as they do so. What the narrator sees is something that is being done to himself, yet the metaphor—and the dream-vision convention—displaces the experience onto an inanimate nature which cannot resist in itself and which is wholly inaccessible to the narrator's intervention. The experience is subjective and yet "out there" in such a way that nothing can be done about it.

Turning back to the second poem, we see at once that the serpent is doing what the narrator in "The Garden of Love" can't do, and the three-sentence structure, which seemed at first to reinforce the clarity and simplicity of the allegory, suddenly takes on a richer and more complex meaning. The first and last sentence define the conditions of stasis which precede and follow from the serpent's appearance: the second, again bridging three stanzas, gives us the serpent itself, its dynamic energy enacted in the transgression of the poem's formal divisions. Thus, while the characteristics of the chapel are vaguely left to be inferred from a conventionally appropriate vocabulary, the serpent is dramatized, the discrepancy being nowhere more apparent than in the line in which the serpent appropriates the imagery of dazzling visual brilliance which has been used to present the chapel. In "All his shining length he drew," "shining" is brought marvelously to life in the pattern of stressed long vowels which enact the serpent's impulsive progress, and we note, by comparison, the inertness of "the white pillars of the door," in which "white" certainly doesn't function dramatically.

In another draft of the poem, Blake changed "shining" to "slimy." The emendation does more than make the disgust explicit: it's already explicit enough in the enjambment—the poem's most brilliant dramatic effect—at the transition from the third to the fourth stanza, and the juxtaposition of white and vomiting that Blake gets by it. What shining most radically and damagingly implies is not only the insubstantiality of the poem's dualism—chapel and serpent suddenly partake of a common reality—but also the fact that that reality is more vividly and concretely present in the serpent than in the object it desecrates. The chapel simply isn't there in the poem, and its absence makes the disgust curiously excessive in relation to its ostensible motive. It isn't the violation of the chapel that Blake is disgusted by; and the intensity of the loathing goes clearly enough with the intensity of imaginative identification. As soon as the serpent appears, the observing "I" and the accompanying tone of objective statement are displaced, and we find instead a startlingly sensuous collaboration of the language with the imagined event. The monosyllabic harshness of the final couplet is only readable as a reaction (identical—paradoxically enough, in an artist who might seem to be Jonathan Swift's antithesis—to Gulliver's recoil from the Yahoos) against that identification: disgust here is inseparable from self-disgust and self-punishment.

The reading together of the two poems produces an impression of stalemate. The negative commentary in "The Garden of Love" on the priests' repression of energy is contingent on the narrator's impotence and on the metaphorical transposition of energy into "play" or passive, nonanimal sensuous forms ("sweet flowers"). The poignant cry of protest positively requires the sublimation of energy and a sense of the invincible potency of the agents of repression. In the second poem, where the sexual nature of the repressed makes itself felt, energy is imagined as evil, and the positive connotations of Christianity, however feebly and unconvincingly, return. Despair turns now, not on the denial of energy, but on the recognition of its nature, and the impossibility (registered in the ambiguous tone of identification and disavowal) either of dissociating oneself from it or of conceiving it as anything other than innately and necessarily destructive.

Indeed, the two lyrics give ample evidence of the incorrigible persistence in Blake's own verse of the very contradiction which, elsewhere, he sets out to diagnose in John Milton. In *The Marriage of Heaven and Hell*, the voice of the devil, denouncing the dualism of soul and body, and the debasement of energy which follows from it, affirms the sanctity of desire in the teeth of a Christian tradition which identifies energy with evil. The history of this tradition is written in *Paradise Lost*, and the passage moves toward the famous dictum that Milton was "of the Devil's party without knowing it." The marriage, as its title implies, aims at dialectical synthesis, but the magnificent audacity of the intention, and the liberating vigor and passion of the achievement, shouldn't distract us from the perception that the aim is illusory—that the very concept of dialectical synthesis is a chimera. The best that Blake can achieve is a momentary reversal of terms, whereby the devil becomes the spokesman of a "true" Christianity and announces that "Jesus was all virtue." Jesus is now defined in terms of "impulse" rather than as Milton's "governor [or reason]," but the association of Jesus and impulse gives the latter a connotation which the most insistent redefinition can't obliterate. The Christian dualism presents an insurmountable obstacle to dialectics, and the cultural load of the language constantly insists on reimposing itself. The attempt to marry heaven and hell, to celebrate the holiness of energy within a language which remains Christian, is defeated by everything which that language has come to embody, and when we look for an ambiguously convinced affirmation of sexual energy in Blake, we look in vain. It seems to me significant that F. R. Leavis, attempting in his analysis of "The Sick Rose" to establish the flower as an embodiment of "the warm security of love," resorts to an interpellated quotation from John Donne ("She's all States, and all Princes, I, Nothing else is"), the relevance of which is neither argued nor demonstrated, but which works to introduce, by sleight of hand, the suggestions of mutual sexual love which the rose clearly doesn't have. (*Living Principle*, 89–93) The rose implies not mutuality or reciprocity or interdependence, but a perfectly enclosed singleness, a oneness of being which excludes any of the senses of sexuality as a relationship. It is the "invisible worm" which introduces eroticism, and, we might add, the worm is created with a dynamism and tactile vividness which make it the reverse of "invisible." The worm is the serpent, and while the positive significance of the rose is made present in a way which demonstrates, by contrast, the unreality of the golden chapel, it can't be read as a positiveness about any form of human sexuality—unless, perhaps, the autoerotic.

Blake, of course, isn't of the Gothic tradition in the sense in which Hawthorne or Melville are, but the poems I've discussed provide us with an admirable instance of the problems which the Gothic confronts, and with a sense of their general historical pertinence. In accounts of *The Exorcist* (1973) and *Meet Me in St. Louis* (1944), I've already recorded the conviction that we must look to the nineteenth-century American literary tradition (the only one, apart from the German, in which the Gothic isn't marginalized) for the progenitors of the American horror movie, and that it's possible to trace a line of descent from Milton's devils (Satan and Comus) through the Faustian hubris of the protagonists of the American Gothic (Melville being, in this respect, very consciously "Miltonic") to the representatives of the devil so characteristic of the contemporary cinema. The link is provided by Puritanism and its aftermath. The peculiar intensity of Puritanism in America consists in the fact that the eternal struggle of good and evil was, for the first settlers, not merely a matter of metaphysical conviction but, with an unparalleled immediacy, a condition of concrete life and practice. The spiritual dualisms assumed a tangible material form in every fact of their experience, and the material presence of evil conditioned material remedies and struggles. The American Gothic is inconceivable without the specific historical conditions in which good and evil could be experienced in this way: even as it strives to question, transcend, or resolve the dualism and—hence its progressiveness—the structures of social confidence and experience with which the dualism is involved, the Gothic tends continually to regress to the very terms against which it struggles.

If we accept John Jones's hypothesis in his admirable book on John Keats that a great deal of Romantic art is characterized by the attempt to negotiate the cultural opposition between the subjective and the objective, to resolve the Cartesian dualism of the ego and its objects with the concept of "feeling" (Lord Byron's "To me high mountains are a feeling" is exemplary) (270–95), then we can say that the Gothic at once inserts an impediment to the more familiar Wordsworthian exaltation. "The ennobling interchange from within and from without" has, as its corollary, the desperation of the Ancient Mariner before a universe which has become simply a colony of his imagination. The ecstatic sense of oneness with the object in the activity of perception becomes, for Samuel Taylor Coleridge (and later, at the masthead of the *Pequod* for Ishmael), the horror of the loss of the material: a horror which can take the contradictory forms either of the imagination's inability to grasp the real (the "Dejection" ode) or of an appalling confusion in which the imagination engulfs reality altogether and imposes itself, uncontrollably, from without ("The Rime of the Ancient Mariner"). The residue is the sterile isolation of an ego striving, in the first case, to grasp and realize its world and subjected, in the second, to the tyranny of its own projected energies, whose material embodiment testifies again, in its different way, to the elusiveness of the romantic synthesis.

From the start, then, the Gothic poses the problem of perception in an especially acute form: what is the relationship between the moral/metaphysical order of the world (if there be such) and the perceiver's articulation of it? The question is raised as a question in "The Ancient Mariner" by crime or, rather, by the sense of having committed crime—by a transgression which dissolves the habitual grounds of certainty—and the American Gothic, with its peculiarly intimate relation to Puritanism, is incessantly preoccupied with a related issue: is evil a principle in nature or a means of interpreting it? Consider, for example, the following (it is the final paragraph of chapter 5) from *The Scarlet Letter*:

> The vulgar, who, in those dreary old times, were always contributing a grotesque horror to what interested their imaginations, had a story about the scarlet letter which we might readily work up into a terrific legend. They averred, that the symbol was not mere scarlet cloth, tinged in an earthly dye-pot, but was red-hot with infernal fire, and could be seen glowing all alight, whenever Hester Prynne walked abroad in the night-time. And we must needs say, it seared Hester's bosom so deeply, that perhaps there was more truth in the rumor than our modern incredulity may be inclined to admit.

Immediately prior to this, Hawthorne has raised the analogous question from Hester's point of view: has the scarlet letter "endowed her with a new sense . . . a sympathetic knowledge of the hidden sin in other hearts"? Or are her suspicions of the most apparently respectable citizens prompted by "the insidious whispers of the bad angel, who would fain have persuaded the struggling woman, as yet only half his victim, that the outward guise of purity was but a lie"? Or are these "perceptions" produced by an imagination corrupted by "the strange and solitary anguish of her life" within the community that oppresses her? Hawthorne concludes: "O Fiend, whose talisman was that fatal symbol, wouldst thou leave nothing, whether in youth or age, for this poor sinner to revere?—Such loss of faith is ever one of the saddest results of sin. Be it accepted as proof that all was not corrupt in this poor victim of her own frailty, and man's hard law, that Hester Prynne yet struggled to believe that no fellow-mortal was guilty like herself." (65–66)

Hawthorne equivocates, and nothing that follows finally settles the equivocation, which isn't to be taken either as duplicity or as a "modernist" strategy to render the narrative world problematic. The novel hesitates between two systems of explanation: between what one might call an ideological analysis of Puritanism, which locates the origins of perception in a specifically characterized historical society, and in which the conflict of desire and law is a matter to be particularized and located; and a tendency to reiterate the metaphysical terms of Puritanism as a condition of existence, even when any commitment to the associated social forms has become untenable. It is precisely this hesitation which allows Hawthorne to raise, explicitly, the most radical questions—which produces the problem of interpretation as, in effect, the novel's substantial theme. Consider, for example, the extraordinary discussion of the oppression of women in chapter 13: is women's struggle to attain "a fair and suitable position" in society a struggle against a history of social oppression and the "long hereditary habit which has become like nature" produced by it, or is it a struggle against "the ethereal essence, wherein [a woman] has her truest life"? (120) It is the possibility of proposing the first interpretation which generates the principle of ambivalence in the novel: for even while the second reading, which automatically defines Hester in terms of absolute moral/spiritual transgression, doesn't negate or reject the first, it does acquire from it a connotation of superb hubris which makes of Hester, even if she is, after all, monstrous, the tragic heroine.

The Scarlet Letter, then, allows us to isolate the limitations of the concept of ambivalence, the operation of which, in a number of distinguished horror movies, has been demonstrated by Robin Wood. ("Introduction," 14–15) It is the symptom of a cultural deadlock, and while the American Gothic has always been concerned with the dramatization of that deadlock, its very language and conventions incessantly reimpose it. To say this isn't to countenance some banal conviction of the one-way determination of "works" by "genres" (the kind of banality involved in, say, *Screen*'s account of "realism"); it is to insist that genres are historical forms which structure and negotiate reality in ways which can't be separated from the pressures, possibilities, and requirements of their historical moment. There comes a point when one must ask whether the continued use of the conventions doesn't impose unacceptable limitations on the possibilities of analysis; whether, in fact, the conventions haven't come to entail in themselves a sort of misrecognition which the most progressive modifications can't resolve without moving outside them altogether. The Gothic of Hawthorne's novel enacts a hesitation, which can be very precisely located historically, in the face of the problem of evil: it is possible that Hester Prynne has transgressed an absolute spiritual law and is in league with the devil; it is likewise possible that she has transgressed a law which is the product of intolerably oppressive historical conditions of which she is also a product (she herself isn't sure whether or not she is evil). The greatness of Hawthorne's novel consists in the fact that it raises the doubt, but it can only do so, and in such a way that it almost endorses the radical reading, because the doubt is there. The ambivalence with which Hester is viewed embodies at once a historical uncertainty and a commitment to her in spite of it—the kind of commitment which takes the form, while doubt remains, of Huck Finn's "Alright, I'll go to hell." This remains a radical commitment as long as it is possible to believe (a) that there is and isn't a hell to go to; (b) if there is, individual hubris is magnificent; and (c) if there isn't, the transgressing protagonist has demonstrated the inadequacy of the laws transgressed. The ambivalence of the horror movie relates, on the contrary, to the monster *qua* monster: it defines an attitude of regret to an inevitable and forgone conclusion, inevitable because the vapidity and sterility of a particular set of norms is the only other available option. We rarely find in the horror movie, as we do in the American literary Gothic, the possibility that the transgressor may embody a positive critique of the norms. We don't because (a) the social pressures inhibiting the suggestion of such a possibility operate, in Hollywood, with infinitely greater stringency, and (b) the hesitation registered by the Gothic is so fragile.

The transition from Hester Prynne to Regan MacNeil in *The Exorcist* is governed by both factors. It is perfectly legitimate to elucidate Regan's possession by the devil as I've tried to do elsewhere in this book, but the film actively opposes any such process. The Gothic no longer registers a hesitation at the surface of the text but produces an esoteric subtext which is directly at odds with the offered significance. Metaphor, in this instance, engenders and is engendered by misrecognition: the return of the repressed isn't cleanly distinguishable from the return of repression, the very image which dramatizes the one enforcing the other. The great American horror movies—*I Walked with a Zombie* (1943), *Psycho* (1960), *The Birds* (1963),

Sisters (1973) (to which, one might add on a slightly lower level of achievement, *Son of Frankenstein* [1939], *Curse of the Cat People* [1944], Larry Cohen's *It's Alive* [1974] and its sequel, and George A. Romero's *Living Dead* films)—seem to me to be characterized not so much by ambivalence—a phenomenon discernible in such eminently mediocre and objectionable works as Tobe Hooper's *The Texas Chainsaw Massacre* (1974)—as by the use of the monster as the focus, or the catalyst, for the critical analysis of everything that normality represents: though even here the films can't move beyond a despairing capitulation to an order which has been implicitly rejected (with the ambiguous exceptions of Alfred Hitchcock's *The Birds* and Romero's *Dawn of the Dead* [1978], which postpone the issue). But it is precisely here that discriminations arise—discriminations which turn less on ambivalence as such (it seems to me a neutral phenomenon) than on the way it is articulated.

Hitchcock's *Psycho* is the classic instance of an actually realized and presented enactment of the continuity between the normal and the monstrous, and it is almost able to move beyond both categories: not quite because, as in all horror movies, nothing seems to survive their obliteration; almost because the film is concerned less with either the norms or the aberrations as such than with the institutions, values, and experiences which define them and give them their continuity. The cynical, sadistic opportunism of Hooper's film (its "unpleasantness" in the bad rather than the good sense) is directly attributable to the fact that its monstrous family infinitely exceeds any dramatic significance that could possibly be ascribed to it. It is simply indulged, as it were, for its own sake: as a metaphor for an oppressed working class it is risible (the metaphor is merely obscurantist), and while Marion Crane in *Psycho* isn't established with much greater psychological precision than the "normal" characters in *Massacre*, our attitude toward her is quite distinct. The response which Robin Wood deprecates in the audience with which he saw Hooper's film ("Introduction," 22) is wholly comprehensible: it is the response the film incites, for its concentrated negativity has the effect of transforming its supposed representatives of the ultimate degeneracy of the family into types of exhilarating, anarchistic energy. If Norman Bates's atrocities in *Psycho* are never "exciting," it is because of the relationship the film has demonstrated between, on the one hand, Marion and Norman, and on the other, both of them and us. The effect is to establish quite clearly that Norman doesn't—and can't—imply any positive significance whatever. The "ambivalence" we feel toward Norman and the covert identification with the family which Hooper's film attempts so insidiously to construct are diametrically opposed phenomena. Hitchcock's film may end in negativity and despair, but Hooper is simply fiddling while Rome burns, and it shouldn't detract from our sense of the nastiness of the offense because he is fiddling, in Orwell's phrase, "with his face towards the flames."

Ambivalence toward the monster in Hooper's way seems to me as dangerous, in fact, as the opposite tendency to designate it as absolute evil, and for the same reason: both tendencies focus with particular clarity the impossibility, within the Gothic, of conceiving of the transformation of energies. It's a failure which, significantly enough, is fully adumbrated in the case of Melville, who in *The Confidence-Man* (1859) takes the American Gothic to the impasse which still confronts it. The theme of Melville's novel is that, for the society he depicts, salvation is damnation: the confidence man is Christ, and his being so entails his being also the devil.

The novel ends with his extinction of the light of the Old and New Testaments: "The next moment, the waning light expired, and with it the waning flames of the horned altar, and the waning halo round the robed man's brow; while in the darkness which ensued, the cosmopolitan kindly led the old man away. Something further may follow from this masquerade." (217)

The "something further" is, of course, as Melville implicitly acknowledges, unimaginable and unspecifiable: the devil as savior cannot but embody negativity. In *The Marriage of Heaven and Hell*, the devil becomes Christ; in *The Confidence-Man*, Christ becomes the devil. The two works embody the opposed limits of the dialectical possibilities which that language makes available. The perilous flimsiness and inadequacy of Melville's synthesis is acted out in his last work, *Billy Budd* (1891), in which, having concluded that "order" and its annihilation represent the only options, he undertakes to demonstrate the tragic necessity of repression and of a return of the repressed. Captain Vere is most directly characterized for us in the remark which, quoted in the aftermath of Billy's execution, has clearly the significance of a moral code: "'with mankind', he would say, 'forms, measured forms, are everything; and this is the import couched in the story of Orpheus with his lyre spellbinding the wild denizens of the woods.'"(128) That a general political implication is intended is also made explicit—Vere "once applied [this principle] to the disruption of forms going on across the Channel [the French Revolution] and the consequences thereof"—and it's of the essence of the use of Orpheus that "measured forms" should imply at once both civil stability (the building of Thebes) and sexual restraint (the binding of "nature"). The efficacy of each, for Vere, is that it involves the other, and that involvement entails the clear sense that sublimation (social life in general) is impossible without repression. The two concepts are, of course, theoretically distinct, and the price of their conflation is an accompanying "tragic sense of life": a dualism of Nature and Culture which assumes that the existence of society is simply a matter of controlling the instincts, and that it is unnecessary (or impossible) to distinguish between the forms and conditions of different social structures. Melville is left, in relation to his character Claggart, with contradiction and ambivalence: on the one hand, Claggart is insistently the serpent-devil, the product of a malign principle in Nature; on the other, he is Vere's counterpart, the product and agent of repressive social forms.

Clearly, no contemporary horror movie could endorse Vere's tragic stoicism: the modern Gothic can mourn or celebrate the disintegration of order, acquiesce in its restoration, or trap itself (as in Romero's *Martin* [1977]) in an endless formalistic confrontation with the inadequacies of the genre's language. Melville's "something further," I think, both anticipates such a deadlock and infers that the way beyond it can't involve the terms and oppositions within which he himself has worked.

Sideshows: Hollywood in Vietnam (1981)

The lack of ideological cohesion (in the protest movement) was not accidental: the students' "common denominator is really a kind of alienation from, and opposition to, this self-satisfied, complacent, well-fed and yet stupid bourgeois society." Unflatteringly, Deutscher said to the middle-class students: "you express the mood of your class in opposition to your class . . .You really express nothing but your parents' . . . middle-class attitudes towards the workers."
—Steven Unger, "Deutscher and the New Left in America"

The domestic antiwar protest movement precipitated by the Johnson administration's decision, after the fall of the puppet regime in Saigon in 1965, to charge Hanoi with aggression and extend American bombing north of the 17th parallel, was unprecedented in its significance. For the first time, an active mass defeatism existed in a Western capitalist country during wartime. Within months of the first teach-in (March 24) and the first major demonstration (the March on Washington on April 17), the governor of New Jersey found himself in the distressing position of having to declare in public that an open Marxist, Eugene Genovese, had a right to participate in teach-ins, even to say that the Vietcong ought to win, and still remain a professor. Such a thing would have been inconceivable ten years earlier, and it would be impossible now. What, then, were the conditions and characteristics of this movement?

1. In its early stages, the antiwar movement had its roots in and its major strength on college campuses, which remained focuses of dissidence throughout.
2. While it emphasized direct action and propaganda, its tactics, language, and modes of organization were learned from the civil rights movement. Participation in this, over the previous five years, together with protests against both restrictions on campus and the antidemocratic nature of federal government, fueled the rapid student mobilization of 1965.
3. The movement was led neither by the traditional peace organizations nor by the Communist or Socialist parties. Indeed, its political composition was both unstable and extraordinarily heterogeneous. One of the enabling conditions of the movement was the evidence of substantial disagreements about the conduct of the war within the American ruling class itself. No section of this class, of course—as Paul Sweezy, Leo Huberman, and Harry Magdoff point out in a brilliant collection of essays—was

opposed "to the imposition of United States domination on the largest possible part of the world," but if there was unanimity in strategic thinking, there were also differences over tactics and timing and over the ideologies through which strategy was conceived. (95) The most significant of these differences concerned the role and function of the military: the fall of Robert McNamara in 1968 emerged from the conflict between a group of professional military commanders in the Pentagon who saw "the military establishment not merely as the servitor of capitalist-imperialist interests, but also as an autonomous entity with a life and goals of its own," and the "traditional view of the American bourgeoisie" which defined "the military machine as the instrument of the socio-economic system, to be used in furtherance of the interests of the beneficiaries of the system." (95) This conflict was a radically new factor in American politics. Precisely because the aims and ideology of the protest movement were never distinctively socialist, it was able to assimilate large sections of traditional "liberal-imperialist" opinion, which sought to make it unambiguously clear that it was in no way against the government, let alone in favor of the people of Vietnam.

The heterogeneity of the movement was at once its greatest strength and its crippling weakness as a political force. On the one hand, the political independence of the mass demonstrations helped to legitimize a general climate of protest, checking the development of a war hysteria and—crucially—of a recrudescence of McCarthyism. On the other, there was no basis in the movement for a coalition around a general political program. All the major disputes in the movement were based on the contradiction between its potentially anti-imperialist tendency and the pressures toward liberal and reformist politics which were constantly being exerted on it. All the attempts to transform the movement into a "multi-issue" campaign subordinated mass action to—in the words of the People's Coalition for Peace and Justice (stirring appellation!)—"changing the structure of American society so that the Pentagon is no longer the strongest single force in our society," a change which was to be effected, naturally enough, without the disappearance of capitalism and through the medium of "progressive" elements in the Democratic Party. The People's Coalition, and other similar groupings for whom the function of the mass movement was to provide a political atmosphere conducive to the election of liberal "peace" candidates, was supported by the American Communist Party, which actually succeeded in ignoring the mass actions of April 24, 1971, in Washington and San Francisco until three months after they were called.

4. The movement developed without any general radicalization of labor and never achieved that substantial basis of support in the working class which might have transformed its modes of struggle and extended the antiwar protest into a challenge to the apparatuses of the state itself. It is true that the antiwar movement was paralleled by an upsurge of militancy in the Black movement: every major black organization came out against the war, black GIs were central to GI antiwar protests, and the black riots of the late 1960s were clearly related intimately to these developments. Analogously, the organizations of other oppressed groups were momentarily consolidated around

the campaign: the United Women's Contingent, the Third World Task Force, and the Gay Task Force were active in the movement; and at some women's colleges, newly formed women's liberation groups initiated antiwar actions. But while "the war in Indochina cut deeply into this society, raising and accentuating a number of questions about racism, sexism, unemployment, inflation, political repression," there was no basis within the movement on which these questions could be brought into a radical political focus, precisely because its major victories were won without mobilizing the labor movement. (*The Militant* [1971]) The reasons for this are obvious enough: quite apart from the nature of the movement itself, the generally obtaining impediments to a radicalization of labor in America operated here—notably, the ideological legacies of white American supremacism and McCarthyism, and the structure of the organized labor movement, at once incomplete, fragmented, and inordinately bureaucratized, assimilated more successfully than elsewhere to the interests of capital. The union bureaucracy of the AFL-CIO staunchly supported the White House/Pentagon policies throughout the first major escalation of the war (1965–70), and while the killings at Kent State in 1970 opened a number of cracks (a demonstration, for example, called by an important section of the union movement in New York, including local affiliates of the AFL-CIO, mobilized 25,000 workers and students including, significantly enough, larger black and Puerto Rican contingents than in any previous antiwar action), these did not widen substantially. The one force capable of redefining the strategy of the movement in terms of general political goals which were other than reformist in character remained virtually untouched by it.

While the tactics of American imperialism have varied since the annunciation of the Truman Doctrine in 1947—and as we have seen have been, indeed, a source of some antagonism within the American ruling class—its aims have remained constant. Those aims have been to check the spread of revolution in the Third World and, in so doing, to construct "strong counter-revolutionary bases and poles of attraction" for the expansion of American capital. (Sweezy et al., 77) American imperialism does not take the colonial form of the older imperialisms it displaces; instead, it constructs "legitimate" regimes conducive to the interests of the "free world" and assists them in their struggle against communist expansion. The Diem regime in Saigon, hastily improvised amid the ruins of the previous puppet administration of Bao Dai (which the French, with American diplomatic, military, and economic aid, had trumped up in 1947), is a classic case of such a government. In the late 1940s and early '50s, McCarthyism defined the ideological field within which America's postwar role could be experienced and justified: revolution was never the struggle of the oppressed against exploitation but an insidious conspiracy originating in Moscow, which it was America's bounden duty to forestall.

The defeat in Vietnam was the greatest blow to this strategy since the loss of China in 1949, no small part of the defeat consisting in the partial and temporary disintegration of the grid of beliefs and assumptions through which, since the McCarthy period, reality had been filtered. If the antiwar movement was incapable of addressing the fundamental structures and functions of the American state or of generating an articulate, overall critique of American society in the majority of its participants, it became—with the international support and the sharpening of domestic social tensions which it precipitated—an important factor both in limiting the ability of the American ruling class to conduct the war as it would have liked and in arousing widespread skepticism of the language in which the war (and American foreign policy as a whole) had traditionally been explained. This atmosphere was intensified, at the very moment of debacle in Indochina, by the first inklings of Watergate. The most cherished institutions of American legality were, it seemed, riddled with corruption. We have now entered a period in which a deepening economic recession, the catastrophic Soviet invasion of Afghanistan, and a further series of setbacks and defeats (Iran, Nicaragua, the rising revolutionary struggle in El Salvador and Grenada) have contributed to the dispersal of the heavy vapors of disillusion before a hysterical national chauvinism of comparable virulence to that of the 1950s.

The representative American films, and film cycles, of the 1970s are primarily of interest for the various ways in which they seek to negotiate a historical moment which includes not only Vietnam and Watergate but also the critique of the family and the questioning of traditional gender roles developed by the women's and gay movements. To put it in that way is to already suggest something of the nature of the films' engagement with their defining context. Across their differences, they are the product of a period in which a profound exacerbation of social conflicts and corresponding ideological disharmonies has been radically blocked, issuing in not structural change but retrenchment. There is a general sense that we can no longer believe in the things in which we once believed, though it's not clear whether we can believe in anything else; disillusionment is not characteristically accompanied by any clear recognition that our former beliefs were mystificatory in the first place. "Vietnam," "Watergate," and "feminism" figure not so much as definite, objective historical forces and events but as ideological irritants that are at once portentous and vague.

The irritation is clearly registered even in the cases where its real sources are not, and the blockage which the films typically register is a question not simply of an external collocation of social forces but of the interaction of these forces with cinematic modes and conventions which have a relatively longer history. Consider, for example, the popularity in the '70s of the concept of evil, flamboyantly embodied in the astonishing recrudescence of the Gothic and a recurring theme—satanic possession. The convenience of evil is that while it manifests itself in particular circumstances, it is in principle external to them and is subject, as such, to a peculiar ambiguity whenever it is used as a metaphor for social or psychological forces. The Gothic remains a progressive genre for as long as it can register a hesitation between conflicting systems of explanation (historical and existential) or function as a means of evading a taboo. The American Gothic of Nathaniel Hawthorne and Herman Melville is a classical instance of the first condition: here, the Gothic is the form of an ideological struggle within and against the terms of Puritanism; it disturbs (without ever definitely refuting) the explanatory power of those terms by suggesting that evil is a social category imposed on disruptive forces which Puritanism itself engenders. The work of Edgar Allan Poe, in which the Gothic provides a language for dramatizing sexual themes which would be otherwise unnegotiable, is a type of the second. It is crucial, then, in comparing two works from different historical periods—which nevertheless employ similar generic conventions—to remain aware that those conventions may be serving objectively different functions. Hawthorne's and Melville's interminable prevarications over the question of whether or not Hester Prynne and John Claggart are "evil"—the explicit subject, as it were, of *The Scarlet Letter* and *Billy Budd*—are very different in kind from the explicit assertion in *The Omen* (1976) that Damien is the Antichrist. The literary texts both propose and contest a category which remains intractable; a reading of *The Omen* may, against the grain of the text, contest the category and argue (correctly enough) that it should be read metaphorically, but its function in the text remains unambiguously obscurantist.

We may return to the original point by saying that while the very existence of the devil-child cycle testifies to an encounter between a metaphorical dynamic internal to the Gothic as a genre (the association of evil with socially determined sexual repression) and a historical situation in which the norms of bourgeois sexuality are radically in question in the culture, the fact that the films remain Gothic, and reaffirm so virulently the explanatory power of evil, is itself an index of their reactionary character. And it is clearly because the norms are in crisis that the reaction is so virulent. The circumstances which enable the appearance of what Robin Wood has called the real meaning of the genre also insist on that meaning's assuming a deeply mystified and conservative form. If *Shadow of a Doubt*, in 1943, is able to establish a complex interrelationship between its "monster" and a realized "normal" social milieu—in a way which clearly isn't matched by anything in *The Omen* or *The Exorcist* (1973)—this possibility is very much a fact of the comparative safety, in the culture as a whole, of the norms which the film undermines. The "safety" of those norms is embodied in the viability, and the separateness, of the genres whose conventions interpenetrate so disturbingly in Hitchcock's film; this use of genre to dramatize the very conflicts and contradictions implicit in conventions which function dominantly to contain, regulate, and naturalize them is indeed contingent on their social invisibility. As soon as those conflicts acquire, within the culture as a whole, a substantial political expression, the genres, insofar as they continue to be used, can function only to recuperate them or to register a confusion and inadequacy which are directly determined by the undermining of the conventions' purchase on them. The prevailing sense, across a wide range of films, of external forces which are radically beyond control, seemingly absurd or irresistible, is the logical corollary of this process: the failure of the explanatory and cohesive power of the conventions appears, in the dramatic worlds they mediate, as a disorder objectively given.

Of all the major genres, the war film is typically the least problematical ideologically. It has three classical modalities:

1. The valorization of the armed forces as the guardian of the status quo and the embodiment of its finest ideals. The rightness of the particular cause is never in question since it is always, in essence, the protection of "democracy"—or at least the system of government of the film's country of origin; death ("sacrifice") is tragic, but it is ennobled by the end which it serves. The forces are frequently seen as the representatives of an impersonal tradition in which individuality is (or, through initiation, comes to be)

subsumed and which endows the "personal" with a peculiar grandeur and significance. War is always regrettable but as we wage it, equally necessary and disinterested, and its ultimate purpose is the creation of a uniformly "democratic" world in which war will have no place.

2. The "antiwar" film tends to protest against war as such from an abstractly moral point of view, in the name, frequently, of a humanist ideal (*Grand Illusion* [1937]). As in the first case, war is extrapolated from its socioeconomic causes and functions, and we are confronted with its "horrors"—horrors which, given the vague definition of their origins and the status of the protagonist(s) as victim(s), seem both intolerable and irremediable. The genre is a medium of liberal protest and may issue in an appeal to "men of good will," in despair (*All Quiet on the Western Front* [1930]), or in a nihilistic cynicism which is, in effect, a form of quietism (*M*A*S*H* [1972]).

3. The "home front" movie in which, in the absence of men, a wife defends and preserves the bourgeois home and the values (equivalent, in domestic terms, to those embodied in the "public" realm by men in arms) it represents. *Mrs. Miniver* (1942) and *Since You Went Away* (1944) are the archetypes of this mode; *Coming Home* (1978) is a fascinating inversion.

None of these types is in any way troubling: one and three are, by definition, ideologically unproblematical, and the mere fact that there is no such thing as a film which is overtly pro-war indicates the limitations of the second. Vietnam is objectively unnegotiable within any of them: types one and three would amount to a defense of American imperialism, and type two would be incapable of distinguishing between imperialist and revolutionary war, and thus of grasping Vietnam's political specificity. At the same time, the actual case renders the three types ideologically unsatisfactory: only *The Green Berets* (1968) dared to defend America unambiguously, and the extensive sense of the particular illegitimacy of America's involvement made it difficult to offer Vietnam as a type of the evils of war per se. The traditional generic forms for the representation of warfare aren't easily available here.

Similarly, any account of America's involvement in Vietnam (or in Chile or Nicaragua) which is based on moral condemnation alone is doomed to irrelevance, because the ethical objections to that involvement can only be formulated in terms of a political analysis of its objective determinants and aims. To say merely that America shouldn't have been there tends to foreclose the recognition that it could scarcely have chosen not to be and that a negative judgment of its presence must necessarily derive its coherence and appropriateness from a socialist position. The very existence of the American state is bound up with such "involvements," for the logic of imperialism is the logic of its own dynamic, and not of undesirable moral decisions which might otherwise (given, perhaps, less venal personnel) have been less undesirable. The judgment that America should not have been in Vietnam is the ethical corollary of the political judgment that America's presence in Vietnam was entailed in its function in contemporary imperialism. It can become intelligible and actively efficacious only on that basis.

The Hero

Vietnam, then, can't be explained because of what the explanation would involve. At the same time, the action genres were traditionally dependent on a given system of explanation, and the function of a hero was endowed by it with the dramatic potency and the moral status necessary to control and regulate the forces defined, in contradistinction to him, as undesirable and subversive. As the system and the hero were mutually guaranteeing, a crisis within the one endangers the intelligibility of the other. What are the consequences, then, for a narrative which preserves a hero-function but posits in relation to him a situation (Vietnam) which is not only radically inexplicable but also has destabilized the structure of values which support and justify the hero's agency? The upshot of the contradiction is a hero whose activity (still deemed of value) remains "tragically" unrealized; a hero who is passive—not acting, but acted on; or a hero whose assertion of agency appears as compulsive and psychotic.

Who'll Stop the Rain (1978) provides a useful starting point in that it actually sets out to articulate the problem of the hero rather than being simply deposited by the problem's insolubility. That action is crucially in question is clear from the outset in the juxtaposition, in Jonathan's (Michael Moriarty) narration, of "So I've taken action" and "I've started something here that I can't stop." Action, then, involves a conscious surrender to impotence, which is also a consciously cynical amoralism ("I desire to serve God and grow rich, like all men."). Such a choice is justified by the conclusion that the war is, in the philosophical sense, the absurd: "In a world where elephants are pursued by flying men, people will naturally want to get high." The absurdity renders all action, in any case, gratuitous, and the only alternative of which Jonathan can conceive is the reiteration of the "suitably outraged stories" (he is a war correspondent) that he can no longer bring himself to write. Vietnam acts as a solvent of morality: acquiescence for egotistic ends—drifting with the stream—need only be referred to the fact that the war itself gives evidence of the meaninglessness and ineffectuality of choice.

Where action, for Jonathan, is predicated on a situation in which its possibilities are determinate and thus its forms are essentially beyond his control, it appears for Ray (Nick Nolte) as the medium of triumphant self-assertion through which he can create himself as "the hero." The link between the two men is defined in the conversation between Ray and Marge (Tuesday Weld) in which Ray reads to her from Friedrich Nietzsche: "In danger, all that counts is going forward. By growing used to danger, a man can allow it to become part of him." Marge's immediate response—"Is that what happened to Jon?"—refers us back to the scene in which Jonathan has asked for Ray's help in smuggling the heroin, where we discover that Jonathan "taught [Ray] out of that book," as well as to the imagery which, at their first appearance, links the two men: both are introduced to us bedaubed with mud, Jonathan cowering fetus-like in a ditch while shells explode around him, and Ray playing football.

The complementary images establish the contrast and the essential likeness with great precision: whether "heroic" or "unheroic," whether experienced as magnificently indeterminate self-realization or as necessary complicity, action for both is wholly egotistic and self-referential. There is nothing left, indeed, but the self for it to refer to, and Ray's "I don't always have to have a reason for the shit I do" is only the clearest indication that for him the business with the heroin has no other function than to provide a setting in which he can appear to himself in the heroic mode. The advantage, for Ray, of the superman is that his actions do not acquire their value from the end to which they are addressed but from the superman's performing them. The built-in tautology is the hero's last refuge from the recognition that his role has lost its objective correlative. As the film progresses, Marge begins to provide one, and it is unrealizable romantic passion which allows him—as he prepares, at the climax, to go down in splendor—to experience his own grandeur, through her, with particular intensity: "Did you see the way she walked to her fate? Nothing but class! She's the love of my life, man—no shit!" As she leaves him for the last time, Ray sees Marge as himself: a love which can't be consummated at last provides a focus for action without disturbing its self-sufficient and self-aggrandizing character.

The film's main problem derives from the contradictions engendered by its central image. The narrative premise—heroin smuggling—proposes a theme of war profiteering, in which, as the action progresses, the institutions of the state are increasingly implicated. But the image of drug addiction has a complex metaphorical significance which associates Jonathan, Ray, and Marge in terms of various forms of escapism. Marge's dependence on barbiturates and heroin; the complementary forms of amoralism, with Vietnam as alibi, lived through by Ray and Jonathan; and the myth of Mexico ("That's a good place") and 1960s hippie culture which Ray seeks to reconstruct on the mountain, and to which Marge allows herself briefly, in full consciousness of its illusory nature, to succumb ("Fuck reality!")—all these strands intermesh to suggest a society which is characterized by the adoption of strategies for unawareness. Marge's father's (David Opatoshu) admonition to Jonathan that "a sense of unreality is not a legal defense," and the characterization and development of Marge herself, imply a criticism of this pattern, but there is no clear sense of what "facing reality" would involve, and the metaphorical function of the drug image remains out of true with the theme of the drug as a commodity the circulation of which defines a structure of politico-economic relationships. The discrepancy is most apparent in the final scene of the film, in which the satisfactory resolution of the metaphorical sequence (the protagonists' renunciation of illusion and resumption of responsibility) coexists with a spurious resolution of its counterpart, the loss of the commodity blurring the fact that the relations which support it remain intact. The ambiguity has its consequence for the tentative reaffirmation of the Marge/Jonathan relationship, and it is scarcely surprising that the film is unable to suggest where they are going or what they are going to do.

A similar problem manifests itself even more damagingly in *Coming Home*. In the pre-credits sequence, set in the amenities room of the hospital where Luke (Jon Voight) is a patient, the wounded veterans discuss why they went to Vietnam, and what they thought they were fighting for. One of them remarks, "Some of us need to justify to ourselves what we did . . . How many guys d'you know can make the reality?" The film cuts directly from a shot of Luke, listening meditatively, to Bob (Bruce Dern) jogging on a runway, and the ensuing credits sequence repeatedly cuts between Bob and shots of the veterans—learning to walk, swim, manipulate false limbs—to the accompaniment, on the soundtrack, of "You're out of touch, my baby" from "Out of Time," a song which recurs as a leitmotiv throughout.

The relationship between the two men is as schematic as the description implies: Luke is "the guy who can make the reality," and Bob—the real cripple—the guy who cannot. What "making the reality" means in the film is given, at the end, in Luke's address to the school students, the intercutting of which with Bob's suicide corresponds exactly to the parallelism of the beginning: "I'm here to tell you it's a lousy thing, man, and I don't see no reason for it." The war is bad, and what is more unreasonable, "reality" does not involve an understanding of the event but the personal maturity required to renounce the need to justify one's part in it. The film's critique of Vietnam, in other words, is confined within safely liberal terms, and the ending appeals to a certain chastened but judicious complacency.

The emotional intensity which *Coming Home* seeks to generate around this—after all, sufficiently bland—conclusion derives entirely from the arbitrary decision to make Luke a paraplegic: without the sense that his personal injuries, and the bitterness induced by them, constitute a substantial impediment to his enlightenment, the progress toward it might seem less impressive. At the same time, by correlating his spiritual education with his reintegration into "normal life," the film is able to suggest—in a way which would clearly not have been possible if Luke were not seriously wounded—that the discovery that the war was wrong is by no means incompatible with fitting back inside a society which has not perceptibly changed. The emphasis on the sheer mechanics of learning to function as a paraplegic, quite apart from its sentimental rewards, allows the film to present Luke's integration as a more or less privatized process, the success of which is to be attributed to his moral stature. The film is thus able to avoid the problem of the hero's alienation from a society which is seen as in some way corrupt (a problem which inevitably presents itself in the other "coming home" narratives) and to argue, under cover of Luke's specific physical difficulties, that coming home is bought at the cost of a few liberal provisos about "having gone." It is logical, then, that the whole development toward the final *prise de position* (including the gesture of padlocking himself to the gates) should be hived off from the mass movement, which is simply eliminated from the film, and presented as individual acts of moral faith necessitated by private motives.

The alienation theme is, of course, introduced through Bob, but in as carefully segregated and personalized a form as Luke's comforting reconciliation of integration and protest: Bob's anguished cry of "I don't belong in this house, and they're saying I don't belong over there" expresses, given the circumstances—both Sally's (Jane Fonda) affair with Luke and the humiliating story of Bob's wound—a specific quandary. If the film, in effect, splits the hero in two, it is in order to preserve the function while projecting on to Bob and disavowing the traditional elements of it which would embarrass the political project. We have no difficulty, if we are the informed spectators to whom *Coming Home* addresses itself, in recognizing in Bob a type of the straight male we have learned to abhor: patriotic, macho, anal, insensitive, inhibited—the symptoms are unmistakable. He is the kind of man who thinks Vietnam is a good thing and does see a reason for it. Luke, it's implied, represents the change of heart which will discourage future Vietnams; he is the mirror image of the ideal spectator who wishes to believe that social transformations are effected by the acquisition of "correct" attitudes. Since Vietnam has no objective existence in the film, and since the America which made the war is present only in the form of Bob's marriage to Sally, Bob can become the scapegoat for the values of the "old America" which, in their absolute autonomy of any material basis, can be simply dismissed as "out of touch." The bland adoption of feminist attitudes—as safely endorsed as comic-strip machismo is discountenanced—shouldn't forestall the recognition that we have here the familiar ploy of saving patriarchy by castrating the patriarch; nor should the beauty, in the love scene, of the emphasis on female pleasure and fulfillment distract us from the insidious process whereby Bob, whom the editing of the credit sequence has already established as the "real" cripple, is constructed as the "real" eunuch too. Not only is Bob the paradigm of that archaic virility which some poor devils (not we—hence the possibility of pathos) still need to assert but also the symbolism of the electric toaster which Bob is discovered mending after making love to Sally ("This damn thing wouldn't pop up") is there to assure us of the impotence of such potency. Subsequently, both imagery—the wound in the calf, and compensating phallus-substitutes (revolver and bayonet)—and an emphasis, in terms of theme and narrative, on an introversion, passivity, and helplessness in striking contrast to the recovery and assertion by Luke (the one just man) of a mature control, conduce to "feminize" Bob. He is eliminated, moreover, by suicide—a means, traditionally, of asserting, while deriving poignancy from, a heroine's inability to affect the structures which oppress her. The disgracefulness of the film's treatment of Bob is inseparable from its profound dishonesty, which is a fact, in its turn, of the objective incoherence of liberal remedies for an unquiet conscience. That Sally's "politicization" should involve no more than a change of lifestyle is all part of the same case. Instead of living in the officers' mess, she moved to the beach; instead of straightening her hair, she "stopped straightening it." Bob liked her first incarnation, and Luke likes her second. In both cases she is a function of the hero's function, which is, as it were, the moral corollary of the revised coiffure.

The function of the coming home structure in *Rolling Thunder* (1977) is to adduce a cause (Vietnam) to which effects can be ascribed and, in so doing, to permit identification with a heroic project which can be at once admired and thought of as a psychotic aberration. For how, in that year, does one reconcile a conviction of the bankruptcy and superannuation of the action hero with an emotional allegiance to the values he embodies and the end (the creation of order) which he subserves? One makes him a madman, and experiences apology and endorsement as diagnosis and condemnation. Vietnam is on hand to provide the madness with its psychological rationale, and the symptom of "social breakdown" he sets out to remedy—the gang, one of whose members is also an ex-GI—with its origin. The mirror relationship between the hunter and the object of his quest once functioned as the medium for a critique of the hero: in *Rolling Thunder*, it has become one of the alibis (he is really misrecognizing forces in himself) necessary for a covert affiliation to him. To this extent, the film is a remake of *The Searchers* (1956) without the contradictions; director John Ford's attitude toward Ethan Edwards (John Wayne) is far more complex and unresolved than writer Paul Schrader's is toward Charlie (William Devane). The import of Schrader's existentialism—he "reread," he tells us, Jean-Paul Sartre's *La Nausée* before writing *Taxi Driver* (1976)—appears to be its promise of an intellectual perspective on the protagonist: an obsessive emotional investment in the narrative of ritual revenge and purification is rationalized as rigorous disengagement, and right-wing anarchism as a critique of a hero who "is just not smart enough to understand his problem." (Thompson, 10–11)

The gang that murders Charlie's wife and son, and effects his own symbolic castration, erupts immediately after he has discovered that his wife has had a lover in his absence—a lover she now wishes to marry. As in *The Searchers*, then, the villain does what the hero wants to do. But the gang is also really there. While, inasmuch as it functions symbolically, it defines Charlie's subsequent actions as pathological, its intolerable existence in a contemporary America of which it seems, on the available evidence, to be representative confers on the re-creation of Vietnam in the Midwest a certain monstrous appropriateness. There is certainly no sense that any other action would be more appropriate, and its monstrosity is counterbalanced by the extremity of the motive and an elimination of other possibilities all the more effective for the introduction, through Linda, of a criticism of Charlie which is then negated by making her fall in love with him. To her "Why do I always get stuck with crazy men?" he replies, "Cause that's the only kind that's left." In the ensuing moral vacuum, Charlie's "craziness" appears as integrity, and we can conclude, in any case, that whereas his quarry is venal, Charlie's actions are tragically irresponsible ("They pulled out whatever it was inside of me"). If the metaphysical alibi ("I'm dead") exonerates the hero by referring him to his traumatic origin, then the justice of his cause ("They don't have any right to live") re-creates his social/ethical function. His ends are sound, and he is without volition as regards his means. Within this project, the film can realize its deeper sexual theme: his family disposed of, Charlie restores, in the guise of cleansing violence, his homoerotic comradeship with Johnny Vohden (Tommy Lee Jones)—"This here's John Vohden: we were together." The last line of the film is "Let's go home, John."

Go Tell the Spartans (1978) and *Apocalypse Now* (1979) are set in Vietnam itself, and their strategies of recuperation are correspondingly different. The tone of *Go Tell the Spartans* is established by an opening scene in which the major (Burt Lancaster) puts a stop to the brutal interrogation of a Vietcong prisoner by the South Vietnamese sergeant, Nu Yen, and throughout the film the elaborate insistence that "it's their war" is accompanied by a systematic attempt to dissociate the Americans from the excesses of the ally with whom they have some-how become involved. Hamilton's idealistic address to his South Vietnamese combat troops about building "a fortress for liberty and justice," to which they respond with laughter and a chant of "Kill Communists!" is exemplary: Hamilton's sentiments are inappropriate and dis-ingenuous, but the irony at their expense is only a critique of the ideals to the extent that it defines them as quixotic. No American in the film wants to kill communists, and the pretense that the war is a purely domestic matter effectively represses the fact that the southern regime is an imperialist puppet and endorses the myth of "aggression from the north" in the name of which the offensive was escalated in 1965.

Analogously, the extraordinary scene in which one of the soldiers, high on drugs, hys-terically declaims the Gettysburg Address while shells explode around him implies that degree of distance from bourgeois rhetoric which can register a discrepancy between ideal and real-ity—a discrepancy that can only be left, in the absence of other explanations, as "absurd." For the war, above all, is "crazy" (the major remarks that "Sometimes I get the feeling we're in a goddamn loony bin"), and it appears as a succession of grotesque and surreal impertinences. To explain the war would be to characterize it as American and imperialist: the refusal to do so produces it as "the inexplicable" and allows the film, while deflating the more obvious com-placencies ("We won't lose—'cause we're Americans"), to reaffirm, through Courcey (Craig Wasson) and the major, a personal heroism all the purer for the absurdity which makes of it an *acte gratuite*. "That," the major remarks, referring to World War II, "was a tour worth the money. This one's a sucker's tour—going nowhere, going round and round in circles. Get on with the job, corporal!" The stoicism required to act as consistently as if you were in World War II while knowing you are in Vietnam—that is the major's position, and it is a kind of militarist rider to *il faut cultiver le jardin*. Courcey renounces the sucker's tour, but the strategy to which the film resorts in allowing him to do so (he is symbolically resurrected after apparently dying with the major) reflects an impulse to let him have, along with his heroism, the merits of knowing he has suffered in a thankless cause.

Apocalypse Now

In the spring of that year, having completed his second *Godfather* film, Francis Coppola told an interviewer that his next movie would deal with Vietnam, "although it won't necessarily be political—it will be about war and the human soul."
—Lawrence Suid

How can one not come, finally, to the conclusion that the normal head of the educated philistine is a dustbin in which history, in passing, throws the shell and the husk of its various achievements? Here is the apocalypse—Voltaire and Darwin, and the psalm book, and comparative philology, and two times two, and the waxed candle. A shameful hash, much lower than the ignorance of the cave. Man, "the king of nature" who infallibly wants to "serve," wags his tail and sees in this the voice of his "immortal soul!"
—Leon Trotsky

There is no more characteristic feature of the 1970s Hollywood cinema than the invitation to purchase the bankruptcy of American capitalism as the ultimate spectacle: the end of the world is realized as an exchange value. Of course, the commodity is packaged in a variety of ways. Robert Altman's work, for example, in which we are encouraged to participate in the ritual immolation of an "Aunt Sally" (country-and-western festivals, bourgeois weddings, health farms, the films' own conventions), is the pessimistic converse of reformism. The liberal traditionally believes that society can be changed by the piecemeal 'adjustment' of institutions which, for the purpose of the argument, are extrapolated from the social relations which sustain them. When this belief is no longer available, the same institutions appear, as carefully isolated as before, and in an equal and opposite motion, as microcosms of society—though of a kind, in Altman's case, conducive to what Victor Perkins has called, apropos *One Flew Over the Cuckoo's Nest* (1975), "narcissistic defeatism." The institution is representative enough for hopelessness to be generalized, while remaining sufficiently offensive to liberal sensibilities to be safely disavowed. *A Wedding* (1978) caters to the feeling that the eclipse of civilization is a grotesque pageant in which one is somehow agonizingly implicated, but which is finally attributable to those limited people over there. *The Texas Chainsaw Massacre* (1974), by contrast, is the exemplary case of apocalypse as visceral "high" and offers the pleasures, not of complacent disavowal, but of vicarious collusion with triumphant barbarism.

Apocalypse Now, while it is closer in feeling to Tobe Hooper's film than Altman's, is a different case again, though the understanding of history which produces Colonel Kurtz (Marlon Brando) as a hero has its precedents.

> It is on this bleak scene that a phenomenon has appeared: the American existential-ist—the hipster, the man who knows that if our collective condition is to live with instant death by atomic war, relatively quick death by the State as *l'univers concen-trationnaire*, or with a slow death by conformity with every creative and rebellious instinct stifled . . . why then, the only life-giving answer is to accept the terms of death, to live with death as immediate danger, to divorce oneself from society, to exist without roots, to set out on that uncharted journey into the rebellious imperatives of the self. (Mailer, 27)

By a supremely satisfying irony, the last action available to the individualist is the will to experience acceptance of the status quo as self-assertion: "encourag[ing] the psychopath in himself," he feels complicity as rebellion, and impotence as hubris. Kurtz's "You must make a friend of horror" is very much of this order, and *Apocalypse Now* asks us to attribute to an American officer serving in Cambodia that kind of value and significance.

While the meretriciousness of Francis Ford Coppola's film is peculiarly that of the Hollywood "art" movie, it is equally clear that what is wrong with *Apocalypse Now* is a matter not of its betrayal of, but its fidelity to, *Heart of Darkness*. For Conrad's novella is in no real sense anti-imperialist, and we register the moments in which it seems to try to be so (Marlow's description, for example, of the "grove of death") as curiously irrelevant to the overall intention. The book is about the impossibility of controlling the "primitive" and "elemental" and the danger, in imagining the contrary, of succumbing to it. The value we are to ascribe to action in the book has little to do with its material effects, still less with its politics. Has the actor "gone under" and surrendered to the seductive influences of the environment, or has he "kept going"?—that is the requisite criterion. All action, *sub specie*, is futile except inasmuch as it becomes an arena for the exercise of the stoic virtues which alone raise it above the utilitarian. While the company accountant whom Marlow meets lacks the sense of irony which allows Marlow to perceive the discrepancy between what he actually contrives to achieve and his self-importance in achieving it, nevertheless "in the great demoralization of the land, he kept up his appearance. That's backbone. His starched collar and got-up shirt-fronts were achievements of character." (47) Kurtz, of course, has gone under, but his is an achievement of character too: "Kurtz was a remarkable man. He has something to say. He said it . . . It was an affirmation, a moral victory paid for by innumerable defeats, by abominable terrors, by abominable satisfactions. But it was a victory!" (97–98) This is the way in which the gangster-hero gets inflated, and while F. R. Leavis has analyzed in *The Great Tradition* the merely "adjectival insistence" of the prose in which Kurtz is created, he fails to conclude that it testifies to the unbridgeable gap between the proposition that Kurtz is a "remarkable man" and the fact that he embodies, more completely than anyone else in the hook, "the flabby, pretending, weak-eyed devil of a rapacious and pitiless folly" which has been criticized in less charismatic agents of imperialism. (196)

As it is, the worst that could be said of Kurtz is that he, too, lacks a sense of irony. Marlow is left with little else, and the central philosophical problem in the book is that of reconciling its possession with doing anything at all. Contact with the sources of energy brings with it the threat of engulfment, distance that of impotence; one of the conditions for reducing colonialism to a metaphor for a bland psychoanalytical schema is a radical incomprehension of the reality from which the metaphor is drawn.

The allegorical meaning of *Apocalypse Now* is announced by an American general in between mouthfuls of his lunch: "There is a conflict in every human heart between Good and Evil—and Good does not always win." Vietnam is to be the external form for a Manichean psychic dualism, and in the final hour, cartloads of cultural impedimenta are portentously wheeled on—Kurtz brings in "The Hollow Men," and Eliot, in his turn, James George Frazer and Jessie Weston—in order to suggest that the action points out toward vast cosmic and metaphysical processes. Clearly, it is from this aspect of the film that Coppola's sense of the seriousness and significance of his undertaking derives: he is familiar enough with the cachet which attends an ability to identify esoteric references in literature, and the confidence that the spectator will be familiar with it as well provides him with the kind of inspiration which doesn't need to concern itself with what the references are referring to. The importance is self-evident and couldn't but suffer by specification, for it only functions as camouflage: it allows Coppola's real interests and allegiances to appear under acceptable colors. What those interests are emerges from the story—which has no equivalent in Conrad—of the children whose arms are amputated by the Vietcong after they have been vaccinated by American doctors. While on the allegorical level, the degeneration of American disinterestedness and beneficence can be referred to their exposure to tactics of this kind, the incident also functions, conversely, to recuperate Kurtz's methods, which appear, in such circumstances, eminently justifiable. At the same time, the people of Cambodia are assimilated to Conrad's notion of "primeval savagery" and represented as having subordinated themselves to a charismatic white man. The whole is subsumed by the reconstruction of the war as elaborate and expensive spectacle, through which the film seeks to excite the very appetites that, at the same time, the allegory ostensibly denounces. The affirmation of Conrad's imperialist myth of imperialism—and Freud's of war as "the scene of primal man, not to be abolished" (Freud, "Thoughts" XIV: 299)—both conceals and provides the basis for an exaltation of the technology of destruction and an apology for its use.

Ford/Cimino/Peckinpah

The dedication of the church in *My Darling Clementine* (1946) is, by common consent, one of the great things in Ford's work—and in the American cinema; one might say that the sequence realizes Tombstone with a striking particularity and concreteness. "Realizes" here doesn't in the least imply that, as we watch the film, we believe that such a community exists or ever did exist: it testifies, rather, to the vivid reality and substance with which a mythic concept of the embryonic pioneering community is endowed. Ford does not demand our allegiance to an inert ideological datum, the value of which is taken as read; that value is the upshot of a dramatic process, in which mise-en-scène, editing, and the direction of the players act through the reconciliation of complex thematic and conceptual oppositions. In defining the nature of that process, one might adduce the terms in which Leavis discusses Henry James's *The Europeans*: the product of "the interplay of different traditions . . . as he presents it transcends the vindication of one side against the other, or the mere setting forth of the for and against on both sides in a comedy of implicit mutual criticism. The informing spirit of the drama is positive and constructive: James is unmistakably feeling towards an ideal possibility that is neither Europe nor America." (*Anna Karenina,* 59)   Thus, Tombstone is neither Nature nor Culture, neither law nor spontaneity, neither the perfume nor the cactus rose, but a new unity for which the oppositions it transcends are at once indispensibly prerequisite and yet—as oppositions—inadequate; one's vindication of the "greatness" of the sequence would involve an analysis of the particular discursive procedures through which the unity, and its creation, are made dramatically real.

What are the conditions of this activity of "making real"? One might begin with the truism that as a western *My Darling Clementine* has to do, not with the actually existing material dynamic of westward expansion, but with an ideological refraction of that dynamic: the very concept of the organic community as a product of the dialectic of Nature and Culture through which, also, sexuality (here, the sublimated secular marriage of Earp and Clementine) is ratified and contained, is irreducibly mythic—and by no means confined, of course, to myths of the American West. As a refraction of American history (compounded of omissions, reconstructions, misrepresentations), the western enables a particular kind of imaginative engagement with the past; it provides a set of conventions within which the conflicts and contradictions of that past can be articulated in certain ways. Clearly, by definition, the ideological conflicts and tensions embodied in the genre (by no means all of which can be reconciled within it) do not correspond to real historical conflicts, but there is, nevertheless, a nonsymmetrical fit between them such that the development of the one may conduce dangerously to the appearance of certain elements of the other. Thus, for example, the irreconcilable claims of "settling" and "wandering"—an ideological opposition—eventually reach a point of tension so extreme that the value of "settling," and the very terms by which it is justified and naturalized, themselves come into question, and settling begins to appear as imperialism. This curious process whereby the unfolding of ideological contradictions tends continually to readmit, in however fragmentary a form, the history which the genre functions to redefine must be referred, of course, to the ongoing social reality within which the genre is included.

If the "reality" of the Tombstone of the church sequence must be referred to the intensity of Ford's imaginative commitment to the myth which sustains it, then a determinant of that is the possibility of such a commitment—a possibility embodied in the currency and vitality of the genre, and the relation among artist, audience, and language which such currency implies. At the same time, the successful realization of Tombstone in this sequence is bought at the cost of eliminating Doc Holliday and Chihuahua: both characters threaten the achieved ideological harmony of the sequence, and the latter brings with her a material historical reality (the subjugation of the Indian) which is inadmissible on any terms. That way of putting it implies that here, as well, distinctions must be made: Holliday's absence—given his significance in the dramatic interplay between different forms of the ideological concept of "civilization"—is a fact the film can accommodate. We are to associate him, through Hamlet, with certain elements of European "civilization" which are to have no place in the new community but which, nevertheless, have a substance and grandeur, embodied in Shakespeare's verse, that cast him, in his decline and supersession, in the tragic mold. He is a fully realized and articulated component in the assessment of "culture." The problem with Chihuahua is of a different order, and the grotesque oscillations of tone and attitude so characteristic of the film's presentment of her testify clearly enough to the fact that she is "unrealizable" within the terms it sets itself and can be registered only as a disturbance of them. Certainly part of Holliday's resonance in the film is attributable to the sense that his destination may be that of "civilization" as such, but he doesn't, as Chihuahua does, strain the concept itself, and the structure of assumptions which support it, to the breaking point.

Successes and failures of realization, in other words, are historically determinate: in a very real sense, they are presupposed (which isn't to say guaranteed) by the language employed. Analogously, our judgment of them should be informed by a clear historical sense of the work's location: is the use of that language, at that point, historically viable, or does it presuppose an inability or refusal to move beyond its confines—that is, a need for them? It is certainly the case that the dramatic reality of Tombstone has the effect of mystifying the reality of American imperialism, but it could hardly be said that that is part of the film's project. On the contrary, while the language in 1946 was given for Ford, and Tombstone was a given fact in it, the particular tone of the church sequence and its place in the dramatic whole are readable only in terms of a project which, while it isn't aware of imperialism, is vividly conscious of the fragility of imperialism's sustaining ideological motifs—of the fact that these are rooted in the affirmation of a past which is irrecoverably gone and which may, in the nature of things, become a future which can't be affirmed. The unawareness entails, as a condition, the exploration of ideology in ideological terms which have to do with the problematic nature of "civilization," but within these terms, the film takes its exploration to the point at which its language ceases to function (Chihuahua). It is this tendency, in fact—which implies, in Ford, a systematic (though radically delimited) critical appraisal of his own modes—which imparts to the church sequence its peculiar, poised lucidity. A historical moment in which a certain distance from the emotional allegiances enabling affirmation isn't yet such as to preempt it entirely is, in general, the condition of the realized particularity of Tombstone, which couldn't subsist in that way if the fine balance involved in continuing to use a language whose presuppositions are already to a degree critically present were disturbed.

I take the cue for juxtaposing *The Deer Hunter* (1978) with Ford's work from a review of the Michael Cimino film by Robin Wood and Richard Lippe in *Body Politic*. While emphasizing in their opening sentence that "on the simplest political level, *The Deer Hunter* is clearly disgraceful," the writers conclude nevertheless that it is great—the greatness consisting in "Cimino's intense commitment to his material and themes, in its masterly sense of structure, in its grasp of essential issues and the degree of complexity with which they are treated." It is the commitment—primarily to the Ukrainian working-class community of the steel-mining town of Clairton, Pennsylvania—

. . . that links the film most obviously to Ford and provides its emotional center . . . The Vietnam of the film, in fact, exists not for itself but only in relation to a certain concept of America which, while localized in a particular richly created ethnic community, is also meant to carry the weight of generalization. The film is deeply rooted in a mainstream Hollywood tradition embodied most impressively and complexly in the work of Ford, whose central preoccupation is with the definition of America as an idea as much as a reality.

The "rich particularity" consists, presumably, in the elaborate preoccupation with religious and ethnic ceremonial demonstrated in the film's first hour; it can certainly be said that we are invited to take this amplification of specialized forms and keepings as the symptoms of particularization. But if we pause to ask even so elementary a question as why the film is set in this specific community at all, it transpires very quickly that the "rich creation" is confined entirely to externals. We see Mike, Nick, and the others working in a steel mill, which obviously establishes them as "working class": we are shown a detailed performance of the rituals of Russian Orthodoxy, which clearly establishes "tradition," "ethnicity," and so on. But that is all. For the assurance that these characters are indeed workers of Ukrainian extraction, we are to rely entirely on rhetorical announcements of this kind. Nothing the characters do or say—nothing in the way they are conceived as characters—supports the declarations: on the contrary, the film relies on its inert reiteration of the appearances of concreteness—its "naturalism"—to camouflage the fact that its community is an abstraction, which can only be arrived at, and come to serve the ends which it does serve, through systematic mystification.

The point is well made by Mike Westlake in his review in the journal *North by Northwest*: "No generation gap here, no teenage delinquency, no racial problems (because all are of the same stock), no decaying city center and prosperous suburbs, no nearby campus with protesting students . . . and interestingly, in the face of the evident poverty of the community, no urge to better themselves, no union, no bosses, no police, just folk." (Issue 8) The choice of community reflects a recognition, at some level, that the Fordian ethos cannot be represented as a contemporary reality without the introduction of certain restrictions, and the profound dishonesty is a matter of offering the restrictions which make the community unreal as the tokens of its striking realness. *The Deer Hunter* isn't a western, and Clairton isn't given for Cimino as Tombstone is for Ford, who is so clearly intent, from inside the myth, on the unstable equilibrium of the organic community within the terms of the myth itself. He doesn't have to delimit the field in which a Tombstone is realizable precisely because he is himself an inhabitant of it and has the restricted consciousness of its internal strains produced, in 1946, by an undertaking to assess and explore it. But then Cimino is interested in Clairton only inasmuch as it allows him to experience what he is interested in as something else.

If the essential American organic community is presented as Ukrainian as well as working class, it is because the working-up of a safely esoteric national culture functions so as to recuperate its class character: if class were to become a real presence in the film, a whole set of unpalatable data relating to the subjective consciousness of the characters and the objective lines of force acting on and within the community would insist on expression. If we ask why, then, the problem of class is introduced at all, we come upon the real source of inspiration—the sublimated homoerotic romance to which, in the usual way, a community associated with domesticity and the power of women is inimical. Working-class men, we know, are close to the earth (here, the mountains), and as such have many of the advantages of black men without the disadvantages attendant on being black. An emphasis on their ethnicity can also preclude the disadvantages attendant on being working class. The residue of this complex act of filtration is "maleness"—in naturalistically close proximity, it appears, to the organic rituals of male solidarity, with the sexual undertow of which the film is clearly obsessed. In terms of the only substantive social conflict admitted by the film, the concrete specification (Ukrainian, working class, 1960s) is deeply irrelevant, its only function being to naturalize, to the film's satisfaction, the presentation of this conflict as a modern reality. The "rich particularity" is a mystification, and nothing more.

The first hour established two antagonistic forms of ritual: asocial and male (the hunt), and traditional/communal and female (the wedding). The hunt gives expression to a male "authenticity" unrealizable within the community and mediated in the film by standard emblems of romantic uplift; the cost, for the man, of estrangement from it is vividly depicted at the outset in Linda's father—broken, drunk, humiliated, and reduced to ineffectual violence ("Fucking bitch! All bitches! I hate them!"). At the same time, the group is threatened from within by the emergence of the sexual feeling which, unacknowledged, is the condition of its stability. The disharmony erupts most clearly in Stan's (John Cazale) description of Mike's essentialist mysticism ("This is this") as "faggot-sounding bullshit"; but it is also latent in the relationship between Mike (Robert De Niro) and Nick (Christopher Walken) itself. Indeed, the wedding proper is followed by a secular marriage of the men ("Don't leave me—you've got to promise definitely"), the eroticism of which is embodied in the very gesture (Nick's chaste concealment of Mike's nakedness) that disavows it.

The transition to Vietnam allows the film to promote these tensions with the assurance that the community will be disrupted from the outside before their effects become manifest, while at the same time acting them through in a displaced form. Most obviously, Vietnam separates Nick from Linda (Meryl Streep) and Mike, thereby preempting the heterosexual romance (Nick and Linda are engaged) and channeling the homoerotic intensity into a quest in which the desired object is, by definition, absent. Indeed, the last quarter of the film, with its insistent "inferno" imagery, is a version of the Orpheus myth, with Saigon as the shades and Nick as Eurydice. At this level, the function of the war is to regulate the film's sexual tensions by fracturing the narrative continuity which would insist on their expression. But that this isn't sufficient is clear enough from the curious analogy between the hunt and the game of Russian roulette: each a form of ritualized male violence, expressing power and subordination and enacted in an area removed from social controls. What exactly does the parallel imply?

At an early stage, Mike has been described as a "control-freak," and the implicit negative connotation is developed in the first hunt scene by the suggestion that his authority has a repressive aspect which incites disaffection with it: Nick's "What's the matter with you?" conveys a criticism, which we seem to be invited to endorse, of Mike's uncompromising attitude to Stan. Similarly, as Wood and Lippe point out in *Body Politic*, "the 'one shot' of Mike's deer-hunting skills becomes the 'one shot' that Nick fires into his own brain at the Russian roulette table." In other words, the basic principle of the hero's code seems to become the condition of his failure to perform the heroic function of regeneration. Even in the privileged setting of the mountains, Mike's authority seems inorganic by virtue of the tension it induces and its roots in personal compulsion; in Vietnam, we are to believe, its inefficacy is tragically demonstrated.

While Wood and Lippe fail to mention the elements in the film which contradict this reading—how, for example, is one to square the critical placing of the "one shot" philosophy with the inflated cliché-rhetoric of the hunt itself—the point has its partial validity: even when protected by systematic abstraction, the Cowper hero, in the modern reality to which the film transposes him, can't but figure ambiguously. It is crucial, in any case, that the ambiguity is rooted in the nature of the film's interest in him: the obsession with control, appearing as authoritarian intransigence, is a matter of sexual repression. Stan's outburst ("Sometimes I think you're a fucking faggot!") both foregrounds this and, because it comes from a character whose own "virility" is constantly, and derogatorily, called into question, discounts it, but Mike's two roles as repressed lover in a subtextual gay romance and as an icon of organic authority are fatally at odds with one another.

The function of the Russian roulette game is to solve the problem of the American hero by transposing the dubious aspects of his authority to the Vietcong, whose role in the power structure of the game is analogous to Mike's in the hunt. By the very token of this symbolic link between them, the Vietcong also appear as displaced manifestations of repressed sexual desire, affecting the absolute control over the other men which is confined, in the hunt, to a (significantly phrased) contempt ("Fucking assholes!") and moral absolutism. Mike maneuvers the first game to the point at which he can say, to Nick, "That means we gotta play each other": it has the significance of a sadistic sexual consummation.

This reading is recoverable from the film, though hardly presented by it, and its extreme unpleasantness consists not simply in the implication, deposited by "naturalism," that such games actually took place but also in the use of the Vietcong as the medium of a resolution of difficulties about the hero of which the film is in some vague sense aware. The problematic nature of his authority is redescribed as a sadistic totalitarianism external to him, and while at a symbolic level the film continues to bear the marks of the displacement which has taken place and testifies to its functions, the systematic drive to overwhelm the audience so characteristic of the Russian roulette scene is clearly designed to induce a state of emotional prostration in which, through an enforced identification with victims, we are prepared to consent to the sentimental self-exoneration that follows.

My own spontaneous reaction to Sam Peckinpah's *Cross of Iron* (1977) is given in the article "Sexuality and Power," and while I would stand by what I said there, my remarks are limited by a tendency to extrapolate the homoerotic themes from their dramatic context in a way which seriously oversimplifies the film. What that dramatic context is becomes apparent only when one grasps that the film is about Vietnam, and that it can be so in the way it is only because it is ostensibly about the retreat of the German army from the Soviets in 1943. The occupying force, fleeing in disarray before a communist power is, literally, German and fascist

Mike (Robert De Niro) and Steven (John Savage) as POWs in *The Deer Hunter*. Personal collection of the editor.

("For many of us Germans, the exterminator is long overdue") and therefore susceptible to extensive criticism.

From the beginning, *Cross of Iron* posits a fundamental class antagonism between the officer corps and the rank-and-file soldier, and it suggests that the class interests of the latter are opposed to the aims of the war. At the same time, it is clear that the war is the necessary condition for the existence of the "world without women" which provides the male group with its basis; it is the film's central female character—Eva (Senta Berger)—who points out to Steiner (James Coburn) not only that he needs the war but also that he is "afraid of what [he'll] be without it." Her remark refers us to the extraordinary passage, earlier in the film, in which Peckinpah intercuts the birthday celebrations in the dugout, culminating in the passionate kiss with which one of the men at once subjugates and consoles another's outburst of hysteria, with the scene in which Stransky (Maximilian Schell) discovers Triebig's (Roger Fritz) homosexuality and establishes the power which will later be used to blackmail him. Steiner needs the war, Eva implies, because it provides a setting for, and justifies, the commitment to men which would otherwise be recognized as sexual; it is symptomatic of the film's confusions that while it recognizes the logic of assigning Eva's remark to a woman, she introduces a disturbance which must also, through the Russian women-soldiers, be exorcized.

The felt contradiction between a male comradeship within the war and a class unity in opposition to it, such that the one is bought at the cost of complicity with the interests of the ruling class, provides the film with its central tension, for of course, the group is also cannon fodder in the imperialist war, and the circumstances which construct its unity also contribute to its destruction in a project which thus becomes, in a double sense, inimical to it. The working through of this logic proceeds inexorably to the moment in which Steiner's platoon is mowed down by the guns of its own army, on orders issued by Stransky and mediated by Triebig. Within the one image, Peckinpah both enforces and seeks to deny and recuperate the narrative's significance; in Triebig, Steiner's effective collaboration with the German ruling class in the name of an allegiance to the male group which denies its sexual component and, paradoxically, supports relations which threaten the unity achieved, appears as the betrayal of the group by a gay Machiavel.

Steiner rationalizes his position in terms of a self-sufficient ethical imperative of loyalty to which political considerations are irrelevant: "I don't care what you believe. Your duty is to us, the platoon, to me." On one level, the film endorses this, which, while it is addressed to the member of the SAS who joins the platoon when Steiner returns from hospital, has obvious relevance for Steiner's own attempt to reconcile hatred of "this uniform and everything it stands for" with continuing to wear it. Indeed, the exact coincidence of the fascist's appearance in the group and Steiner's decision, in the face of a challenge from Eva which can neither be denied nor accepted, to return to combat, testifies again to the implications of Steiner's arguments, which are fully articulated in the parallel between himself and Stransky. Both are involved in the war for private, individualist ends, and both seek to disembarrass themselves of any commitment to its politics: "I am a Prussian aristocrat! I don't want to be put in the same category [as fascists]." This is equivalent, from the officer's position, of Steiner's "I hate all officers"—the personal commitment is felt to be independent of its enabling circumstances and establishes a moral distance from them.

The equivocations and contradictions which attend the film's treatment of the class nature of the war are determined by the interrelation of three factors: the impediments to the complete articulation of its sexual themes, the impossibility of a class analysis of the state the Germans are fighting, and the inability (itself a fact of these other blockages) to find a position to affirm which can be anything but nihilist and stoic. The film can endorse, through Steiner, Carl von Clausewitz's aphorism to the effect that "war is a continuation of state policy by other means," but the exact nature of state policy here can only be defined as an imperialist offensive against "actually existing socialism," and the class theme is diverted into an encounter which can easily be read as the opposition between the aristocrat and the common man. There are obviously objective factors which militate against the dramatization, in a Hollywood film, of class opposition to state policy, but it is equally the case that the "fear" to which Eva refers is very much the film's, and that its ultimate commitment to Steiner's use of the war enforces the subordination of class to desexualized homoerotic comradeship. It also leads, inevitably, to despair— a despair which, while a product of the film's own terms, is experienced and offered by it as the objective impossibility of change. "One extreme to another, and neither works, nor will—ever!" It is crucial to our sense of the film's significance that its political despair and its inability fully to confront its sexual themes are intimately related to one another.

The extremity of the film's incoherence, and the correspondingly drastic nature of its attempts to negotiate it, is manifested with the greatest clarity in the scene involving the Russian women-soldiers. Peckinpah introduces the theme of the opportunities provided by war for the male brutalization of women and exonerates the group by punishing the figure within it who has foregrounded its implication with fascism. "Now we're even," Steiner remarks, as he surrenders the sacrificial victim through which the film expiates both an aspect of its sexual guilt (a castration for a rape) and a sense of the inconsistency of affirming the platoon while dissociating it from the aims of the war in which it has fought. At the same time, the astonishing process by which women as castrators come to be identified with communism points up—in a form all the more lucid for being hysterical—the film's entrapment within a position where the value of the male group has become contingent on the repression of its sexuality and its imbrication with American institutions which are at once unaffirmable and necessary.

It would be hard to argue for a preference of *Cross of Iron* over *The Deer Hunter* on the basis of anything achieved: while the sublimated American male romance was once able to provide the basis for art of the highest order, its passionate affirmation was always premised on the possibility of reading in it the paradigm of that "divine equality" (the phrase is Melville's) which is the essence of American democracy—an essence to which, nevertheless, American democracy as it actually existed was fundamentally inimical, and which could only be maintained in flight from it. The paradox depends on the identification of really existing society with settlement, domesticity, feminization: the true America is the asocial comradeship of "the kingly commons." The inadequacy of this concept is already fully dramatized by Mark Twain and Herman Melville, yet without the sense that such comradeship (so conceived) embodies a radically critical moral norm (of the kind exemplified by Huck's decision to "go to hell" for Jim) against which, as against its ideal, the inadequacies of existing society can be measured, a continued commitment to it is threatened with incoherence. A new coherence could, of course, be formulated but at the price of acknowledging the sexuality of the comradeship and rearticulating its relation to the society which excludes it in political terms.

Yet while both films are located within a bankrupt thematic, they are distinguishable: the status of their contradictions is radically different. Contradiction in Cimino's film is produced by the failure of a strategy of recuperation, in Peckinpah's (as in Ford's) by the limitations that contain, confuse, and compromise a project which is in a very real sense critical and exploratory.

Twilight's Last Gleaming

Since I have seen the uncut print of Robert Aldrich's 1977 film only once, and that three years ago, there can be no question here of doing more than draw attention to this astonishing work, leaving a substantial account of it until later. Its distinction consists not simply in its presentation of Vietnam—through the discussion of what is, in effect, Dr. Henry Kissinger's "madman theory"—as an objective political reality, independent of the characters' sexual traumas, but in its uncompromising rejection of political individualism, whether liberal or "heroic," which is seen quite clearly to lead to catastrophe. Nothing, it is true, survives its defeat; the film has no concept of oppositional mass struggle or collective agency, and to that extent the consolidation, at the end, of a repressive and apparently immutable state apparatus recalls the extreme political pessimism of the "paranoia" movie (compare, say, *The Parallax View* [1974]). It is distinguished, however, both from that genre and other Vietnam movies by the political specification of forces which elsewhere remain inexplicable and undefinable, rejecting alike the "it's-all-crazy" position and the image of the demoniac state classically exemplified by the Deep Throat sequences in *All the President's Men* (1976). Thus, while there is no suggestion that any force might avail against the state, the film is wholly devoid of reformist or palliative illusions: the institutions it defines aren't susceptible to catharsis, as they are in Alan J. Pakula's Watergate film, where the narrative emphasis on purgation partially contradicts but is, in another sense, facilitated by the vague and mystified nature of the "corruption." It is clearly, in principle, a criticism of the film that it is available for nihilist conclusions, but that is hardly the point one would choose to emphasize; what is so remarkable is its refusal (through its definition of the nature of the state) to be available for evolutionary ones.

Blissing Out: The Politics of Reaganite Entertainment (1986)

> The escape from everyday drudgery which the whole culture industry promises may be compared to the daughter's abduction in the cartoon: the father is holding the ladder in the dark.
> —T.W. Adorno and M. Horkheimer, *The Dialectic of Enlightenment*

> This was clearly going to be the music of the future—that if people were but rich enough and furnished enough and fed enough, exercised and sanitated and manicured and generally advised and advertised and made "knowing" enough, *avertis* enough, as the term appeared to be nowadays in Paris, all they had to do for civility was to take the amused, ironic view of those who might be less initiated. In his time, when he was young or even when he was only but a little less middle-aged, the best manners had been the best kindness, and the best kindness had mostly been some art of not insisting on one's luxurious differences, of concealing rather, for common humanity, if not for common decency, a part at least of the intensity or the ferocity with which one might be "in the know."
> —Henry James, *Crapy Cornelia*

> "*E.T.* is a bliss-out."
> —Pauline Kael, *The New Yorker*

The phrase "Reaganite entertainment" in my title is not to be taken in a strictly literal way. My concern is with a general movement of reaction and conservative reassurance in the contemporary Hollywood cinema, and it will be apparent that the characteristic features of this movement—both formal and thematic—are already substantially developed in films which were made before the election of the current president: not only *Rocky* (1976) and *Star Wars* (1977) but also the disaster cycle, the prototypes of which preceded even the final debacle in Vietnam. The phrase, nevertheless, seems apt. When I offer to plot a line of development, no one should suppose me to mean that the tendencies in American society which have been consummated in the Reagan administration came into being with the man himself, who is as far from having that kind of decisive originality as anyone you could hit on.

The generic term entertainment presents itself in that the current period has seen the massive, and almost exclusive, predominance of a type of filmmaking which, during the 1970s, did not rule out the possibility of more interesting, contradictory, and disturbing work. The fact that the contradictions and disturbances in question always emerged in despair already indicated that there was nothing to positively answer the cinema of confidence building represented by *The Towering Inferno* (1974) and *Jaws* (1975)—conservative revivals tended to be sustained by the absence of viable alternatives—but it would have been difficult to feel certain in 1974 that *The Towering Inferno*, for all its phenomenal success, was a foretaste of what was about to become the main tradition. At the time, the disaster cycle appeared to be reactionary in a relatively simple sense: it was a desperate attempt—the desperation could be seen in the banality and explicitness of the films' project—showing up a value system which was obviously in ruin. What was less apparent was a potential cultural vitality. Who could have guessed, or been willing to concede, that conventions so debased could have the power to exercise a decisive influence on the development of a medium with traditions as rich and complex as those of the popular American cinema? In 1974, *The Towering Inferno* looked merely exhausted. Its retrospective interest consists in the state of things to which we can now see it as pointing forward.

I mentioned an almost exclusive predominance. Although the current period seems monolithic, mention should be made of the group of films which were released in America in the fall and winter of 1981 and the spring of 1982: *Cutter's Way* (1981), *Reds* (1981), *True Confessions* (1981), *Rich and Famous* (1981), *Ghost Story* (1981), *Rollover* (1981), *Pennies from Heaven* (1981), *I'm Dancing as Fast as I Can* (1982), and the brief gay cycle (*Making Love*, *Partners*, *Personal Best*, and *Victor/Victoria* [all 1982]). With these we may associate *Heaven's Gate* (1980) and *Blade Runner* (1982), which appear respectively as the prologue and the postscript to this group. The quality and value of these films varies enormously, and by no stretch of the imagination could all of them be described as "innovatory" or "progressive": indeed, that is part of the point about them. What they have in common is their attempt to ideologically dramatize problematical material and their (in most cases, catastrophic) commercial failure: of the films named, only *Victor/Victoria* could be described as a hit. With the exception of *Blade Runner*, *Six Weeks* (1982), and *King of Comedy* (1983), it is difficult to think of any mainstream American film released since the spring of 1982 which is of even moderate distinction or which has any other interest than as a document in the history of taste. The virtual disappearance of significant work from the Hollywood cinema over so long a period, and the audience's rejection of such significant work as there is, are phenomena of some importance.

A few years ago in Toronto, I attended a screening, in a packed auditorium, of a horror movie called *Hell Night* (1981), one of the innumerable progeny of *Halloween* (1978) and *Friday the 13th* (1980). The film itself was about as uninteresting as it is possible for a cultural product to be: the audience, which consisted largely of teenagers, was remarkable. It became obvious at a very early stage that every spectator knew exactly what the film was going to do at every point, even down to the order in which it would dispose of its various characters, and the screening was accompanied by something in the nature of a running commentary in which each dramatic move was excitedly broadcast some minutes before it was actually made. The film's total predictability did not create boredom or disappointment. On the contrary, the predictability was clearly the main source of pleasure, and the only occasion for disappointment would have been a modulation of the formula, not the repetition of it. Everyone had parted with his/her four bucks in the complete confidence that *Hell Night* was a known quantity and that it would do nothing essentially different from any of its predecessors. Everyone could guess what would happen, and it did happen. In the course of the evening, art had shrunk to its first cause, and on coming out of the theater, I had the incongruous sense of having been invited to participate in communion.

This highly ritualized and formulaic character is the most striking feature of the contemporary entertainment film. It may be observed that generic art forms tend inevitably to the elaboration of formulae, and the observation can be allowed as long as we do not attempt to give it an explanatory status and as long as we insist on some very careful discriminations. It should be obvious, for example, that the kind of relation which links *Friday the 13th* and *The Burning* (1981), or *The Poseidon Adventure* (1972) and *The Towering Inferno*, or *Porky's* (1982) and *Zapped!* (1982) is very different from that between, say, *Rebecca* (1940) and *Undercurrent* (1946). As "persecuted wife" melodramas these two films have much in common, and Vincente Minnelli's debts to Alfred Hitchcock (and to George Cukor's *Gaslight* [1944]) can be minutely itemized, but what we are primarily aware of is significant variation, inflection, and development. If *Rebecca* is, almost explicitly, Minnelli's point of departure, the work influenced is utterly different in meaning, tone, and movement. By contrast, the differences between *The Poseidon Adventure* and *The Towering Inferno* are primarily decorative, and when we turn to *Jaws* and *Jaws 2* (1978), or *Rocky* (1976) and *Rocky III* (1982), even the superficial gestures toward novelty involved in staging the purification and resurrection of capitalism in a burning skyscraper rather than a sinking ocean liner have been reduced to a minimum. The structure, narrative movement, pattern of character relationships, and ideological tendency of *Star Wars*, *Tron* (1982), and *Krull* (1983) are identical in every particular: the variations, if that is the word, are mechanical and external. No doubt a study of the old B-western or movie serial would reveal a maximum of repetition and a minimum of variation, but the conditions of production in the Hollywood of that period conduced largely to the complex inflection of standardized generic motifs, whereas the conditions of production in contemporary Hollywood do not. "Genre," in fact, seems an entirely inappropriate word to describe the disaster movie or post–*Star Wars* science fiction. Whether we think of the Jacobean theater or the Victorian novel or Hollywood in the 1940s and '50s, it is apparent that the conventions of a genre exist in a productive relationship to the essential conflicts and contradictions of a culture: that is, they are both determined as conventions by those conflicts while also acting as a medium in which cultural contradiction can be articulated, dramatized, worked through. The conventions of Reaganite entertainment exhibit the very opposite of such a relationship. They function, rather, to inhibit articulation, and the impediments to thematic development which they set up must be referred to this function.

To leave it there is not, of course, enough. The ritualized repetitiveness of Reaganite entertainment goes with its delirious, self-celebrating self-reference—its interminable solipsism. *Raiders of the Lost Ark* (1981) refers to Republic serials of the '40s and the timeless "Boy's Own" mode of imperialist tub-thumping, and the Superman films to decades of movies and comic strips. The walls of the children's bedrooms in *Poltergeist* (1982) are festooned with *Star Wars* memorabilia, and both *Poltergeist* and *E.T.: The Extraterrestrial* (1982) make knowing jokes about sharks. As the children cautiously approach the toolshed in *E.T.* one of them hums the theme tune from "The Twilight Zone," and now *Twilight Zone: the Movie* (1983) has laboriously re-created, for the edification of a new generation, four sententious *contes moraux* from one of the institutions of Cold War Midwestern adolescence. The hero of *Tron* finds himself trapped in a video game of the kind which boomed in the wake of *Star Wars*, and one reads that at the time, the Disney Corporation had already invested millions before the film's release in yet more video games based on this movie based on video games deriving from movies. It has become obligatory for the clones of *Friday the 13th* to include a reference to, or pastiche of, the shower murder in *Psycho* (1960). And so on. It is another factor distinguishing the conventions of these films from those of genre that they are primarily engaged in referring to themselves and other movies, and related media products, and in flattering the spectator with his/her familiarity with the forms and keepings of a hermetic entertainment "world." The invocation of "the western" in *Rio Bravo* (1959) or *The Man Who Shot Liberty Valance* (1962) subserves a critical investigation of the conditions of existence of the genre. Self-reference, in other words, is in this case a means to a more rigorous reference outwards to the culture in which the western has been a significant form. Reaganite entertainment refers to itself in order to persuade us that it doesn't refer outwards at all. It is, purely and simply, "entertainment"—and we all know what that is.

We have become accustomed in recent years to the proposition that this kind of solipsism (not known as such, of course) is a property of the progressive, modernist text, and that bourgeois art naturalizes itself by suppressing the activity of its own writing. The proposition was always the most ludicrous kind of self-serving academic fiction, and I have discussed it in *Movie* on a number of previous occasions, but the present subject allows me to approach it from another angle. It is precisely characteristic of the bourgeois forms in which the ideology of entertainment is most relentlessly celebrated—show business and the musical—to be in essence solipsistic. And if bourgeois art suppresses or (a subtle nuance) contains the production of its own discourse, what are we to make of television?: the late capitalist medium par excellence, which can be virtually defined as a medium in terms of its self-referential foregrounding, endlessly reiterated, of its own forms.

I have used the phrase "the ideology of entertainment," and before proceeding, I should clarify it. In a sense, all popular cultural products appear as entertainment—*Psycho* as well as *Hell Night*, *The Pirate* (1948) as well as *There's No Business Like Show Business* (1954), *Written on the Wind* (1956) as well as the television series *Dallas*. The notion of entertainment corresponds to film's commodity form: to present something as entertainment is to define it as a commodity to be consumed rather than as a text to be read. This is precisely the condition on which we have been able to have *Psycho*, *The Pirate*, and *Written on the Wind*, which "pass" by a process of structural assimilation. Not all popular cultural products, however, actively articulate and embody the ideology of entertainment as show business and the musical classically do.

Artifacts which tell us that we are being entertained (the requisite feature of the kind of product I have in mind) also tell us that they are promoting "escape," and this is the most significant thing about them. They tell us that we are "off duty" and that nothing is required of us but to sit back, relax, and enjoy. Entertainment, that is, defines itself in opposition to labor, or, more generally, to the large category "the rest of life," as inhabitants of which we work for others, do not, in the vast majority of cases, enjoy our labor, and are subject to tensions and pressures that the world of entertainment excludes. It is of the essence that entertainment defines itself thus while appearing, at the same time, as a world unto itself. It does relate to "the rest of life," but only by way of its absolute otherness, and when the rest of life puts in an appearance, it is governed by laws which we are explicitly asked to read as being different from the laws which operate elsewhere. The explicitness of these strategies—the fact that they are always mediated by some form of direct address—is the crucial point. It is a condition of the function of entertainment that it should admit that the rest of life is profoundly unsatisfying, but lest the impulse to escape get out, it must be felt both that entertainment offers satisfaction that life does not and that it would not be reasonable—it would even be absurd—to look for them elsewhere. They belong to a special world on the margins of an existence which is in the nature of things largely unpleasurable. Entertainment tells us to forget our troubles and to get happy, but it also tells us that in order to do so we must agree deliberately to switch life off. The feeling that reality is intolerable is rapturously invoked but in such a way as to suggest that reality is immutable and that the desire to escape or transcend it is appropriate only to scheduled moments of consciously indulgent fantasy for which the existing organization of reality makes room. The ideology of entertainment is one of the many means by which late capitalism renders the idea of transforming the real unavailable for serious consideration.

"*Just* entertainment"—the word is often qualified in that way, and it is in its nature to connote something which is both gratifying and trivial. One has heard the phrase used so often in extenuation of a taste of which people are a little ashamed and which they assume others will despise. Ideologically, entertainment yokes together, with invisible violence, the ideas of pleasure and of the superficial, the anodyne, the unimportant. We are to enjoy it but we are also to feel that it doesn't matter, that it can't be taken seriously. We are invited deliberately to forget our troubles, but forgetting them *deliberately*, we never quite do. The success of any work offering itself as entertainment depends on its ability to achieve an acceptable balance between a yield of pleasure—a sense that one's escape has been valuable—and a feeling that, because it is escape, the experience bears no serious relation to the real business of life. Entertainment asks us to believe that it is supremely wonderful, as it must do if its claim to represent one of the capitalist system's rewards, one of the tokens of that system's superiority to other systems, is to carry weight. But the continual reinforcement of the otherness of entertainment intimates that however wonderful it is, and however wonderful we are too, all this wonderfulness is somehow insubstantial and peripheral when it comes to any matter of actual moment. The real perniciousness of entertainment in the sense I've described is that it cultivates a taste for pleasure while simultaneously demeaning the pleasure as an evasion of the realm of necessity. The product is marvelous, but it's also insignificant. You are sitting back and enjoying yourself and so you should, you've earned it—but none of it really counts.

The construction of the otherness of entertainment is inseparable from its solipsism: the active mobilization of the ideology of entertainment absolutely requires the active presentation of its conventions. The spectator is invited to become aware of those conventions and to think of them as defining a hermetic, autonomous world which has no bearing and no tendency and which relates to other social practices only by being different from them. The inscription of this difference—"there's no business like show business"—is the very stuff of entertainment, which does nothing that is not filtered through a besotted allusion to itself. The effect of this narcissistic self-reference, one form of which is the banal repetitiveness of entertainment formulae, is to produce a certain kind of complicity with the spectator, a knowing sense of familiarity with the terms of the discourse. This cultivated knowingness has effects in its turn. It is, on the one hand, a form of flattery. Nothing is more ingratiating than entertainment, which will go leagues out of its way to avoid anything which the spectator might find surprising. One does not need to watch television sitcoms or star specials for long to detect that one is being asked to feel that one is "in" on something. Entertainment addresses us individually, as special persons, but it suggests as well that "we all know, don't we?" and makes of the pleasures of communal feeling a cozy conspiracy of self-congratulation and spurious familiarity.

On the other hand, the more we are encouraged to feel that we know in advance what the discourse is doing, the less attention the discourse requires. The solipsism of entertainment, and its refusal ever to challenge the spectator, conduce to a kind of instinctive formalism, such that one's fixation on the unchanging rhetoric of the doing makes it extremely difficult to perceive that anything is being done. Works which tell us that we are being entertained present themselves as forms without a significance—or without any significance beyond that which is grasped by the self-explanatory term *entertainment*. We are not told not to think, but we are told, over and over again, that there is nothing here to think about. It is this fact that makes it possible for entertainment to engineer structures of feeling which cannot be examined. The feelings we have when we are being entertained are simply that: they elude any other kind of description and imply, indeed, that no other description can be given.

Anyone who has watched *Return of the Jedi* (1983) or *E.T.* with a large audience will agree that it is not strictly true that all works which articulate the ideology of entertainment prohibit intensities of feeling and involvement. It is clearly the case, however, that such intensities, when they occur, are absolutely determined by entertainment's solipsism. We are invited to bawl our eyes out when E.T. comes back to life, but it is virtually impossible to define what our response to this narrative event might mean because the film has already assigned it to a category germane to the experience of being entertained. What director Steven Spielberg says, in effect, via the reference to Peter Pan, is that in stories our wishes really can come true, and here is another story in which they do. *E.T.* sends out elaborate signals to the effect that the emotions it is inciting have to do with wish fulfillment, and it is precisely the foregrounding of wish fulfillment as a fictional category which inhibits our recognition of the content of the wishes to which the film is appealing. We are left with the proposition that "it all has to do with make-believe," and as a result, we are unable to refer the intensities on which *E.T.* has worked to anything outside the text or the species of text within which *E.T.* has classified itself.

In an article in a recent issue of *Screen*, Noel Burch has some interesting things to say which are immediately relevant to my present theme.

E.T.: Reaganite entertainment as wish fulfillment. Personal collection of the editor.

> For years we have assumed that the alienation effect was necessarily enlightening, liberating, that anything which undercut the empathetic power of the diegetic process was progressive. To be reminded that the scenes unfolding on stage or screen were artifice, to experience any mode of distancing was to be enabled to reflect upon a text and its production of meaning, etc., etc. It is beginning to appear to me today that United States television, more advanced in this respect than any other, save perhaps that of Japan, mobilizes a number of strategies whose cumulative effect is to induce a certain disengagement, a certain feeling that what we see—no matter what it is—does not really count. Distancing, in short, has been co-opted. (32)

What Burch says about television seems to me perfectly correct, but it is less that "distancing has been co-opted" than that distancing never actually had the magical properties that were attributed to it in the first place. The suggestion that it had, or could have, is derived from a formalist corruption of Bertolt Brecht, in whose work one may search in vain for any indication that distancing has any value, or any meaning, in and of itself. The theory Burch describes is curious because it assumes that an emotional involvement in a fiction entails an inability to perceive that the fiction is a discourse: if you are involved, you cannot possibly be aware of "the production of meaning." It follows that we can have two kinds of relation to a fiction: we are either "involved," in which case we are impervious to the fact that the fiction is written, or we are "distanced" and alert to it.

These alternatives are plainly inadequate. In an account of *Madame de . . .* (1953), I argued that the great mimetic fictions generate a continuous interplay between the deepest kind of emotional engagement and an analytical "out-sideness" to the dramatic world—an interplay in which each term is a component of the other and determines its specific character. Unless we are clinically certifiable, we are always aware that fictions are discourses: our understanding of the significance of this fact is variously defined by particular works. The words *involvement* and *distance*, as we are supposed to have understood them, can have no possible meaning for the simple reason that our involvement in a fiction is and can only be our relationship to it as a text, as a process of the production of meaning. The dualism of involvement and distance only makes sense on the basis of an older and, one had assumed, thoroughly disreputable, dualism of feeling and cognition, conceived of as being mutually incompatible. But the very phenomenon of art, in which the organization of feeling is the same thing as the activity of thought involved, makes such a dualism untenable.

The project of reminding the spectator "that the scenes unfolding on stage or screen [are] artifice" has given rise to many turgid and boring films and has been validated in much turgid and boring criticism. Such films and such criticism miss the point and make it difficult, as Burch points out, to distinguish between Jean-Luc Godard and George Lucas or an ad for Levi's. The question with which any fiction confronts us is not whether the text presents itself as a text but how it does. Each text defines in itself the conditions on which it is readable, but our relation to a text is never a relation to a thing in itself. Texts organize attitudes and feelings, and because they do they inevitably refer outside themselves, whether they tell us they are doing so or not, to the network of social relations and social practices within which, as texts, they are produced, and in relation to which the attitudes and feelings organized have their pertinence. Significant art—art of the most valuable kind—not only tells us that that is what it is doing but also transforms, or reinvents, the possibilities of reference. Such a transformation is effected through form (though it is not, by definition, "purely" formal, whatever such a phrase may mean): a new relation to language is a new relation to that which language articulates, and each is perceived through the other.

As I have said, in the great mimetic fictions our emotional involvement in and our observation of the text are not two separate things but aspects of a single process in which each of the theoretically separable abstract terms is defined by the other. This dialectic is realized in language, and to read such a work is to be engaged with a dramatic world which we see being created by language outside us. We are involved in the text, and we follow our involvement, as it were, as we follow the text. "Involvement" here is not unconsciousness any more than "detachment" is in the surgeon's attitude to the patient. Rather, the work's organization of attitudes to and feelings about a textual world which invokes a social world external to it is constantly present to the reader as an incitement to formulate anew the conditions of his/her general social experience. In the great narratives, there is no contradiction between the text's being about the text and the act of reading and the text's transforming the ways in which we are able to conceive of a social reality external to it, which is why it has proved to be so easy in recent years to discover so many "classical" texts with "modernist" tendencies. The function of Brechtian dramatic theory is not, as Brecht's formalist epigones asserted, to remind the poor benighted spectator that fictions are fictions, but to mobilize the dialectic I have described for explicitly revolutionary purposes: here, the incitement to reformulate the conditions of experience is intended to issue in a commitment to change them. Like the other great modernists of the early twentieth century (Arnold Schönberg remains the classical example), and unlike the cultural theorists of Althusserianism, Brecht felt no need to dismiss the art of the past as, in Burch's phrase, a "bad object" and was quite clear about the continuity of his own practices with those which he transformed so radically.

In this context, the meaning of the solipsism of entertainment becomes clearer. Consider, as a representative case, the moment in *The Road to Utopia* (1946) where Bob Hope and Bing Crosby, trudging through the Alaskan wastes, come upon a snowcapped mountain which is suddenly transformed into the Paramount logo, and Hope remarks, "There's our bread and butter." Are we to say that *The Road to Utopia* foregrounds the capitalist structure of the Hollywood film industry? Obviously not. The moment is exactly equivalent to that in *The Road to Bali* (1952) where a shot of Humphrey Bogart hauling the *African Queen* through a swamp is cut into Hope and Crosby's journey through another swamp in which Hope will shortly stumble across Bogart's Oscar, thus providing an occasion for a series of familiar gags about the fact that Hope himself has never won one.

It is not enough to say that this kind of ironic self-reference, in which works embodying the ideology of entertainment endlessly delight, draws our attention to the conventions. The irony is utterly different from that with which Fritz Lang or Hitchcock, Douglas Sirk or Minnelli "present" the happy ending. The function of the ironic happy ending is to make visible the ideological obligations that constrain the text by creating a felt contradiction between the dynamic of an actual narrative and the inertness of its resolution. The function of the irony of entertainment is to celebrate entertainment as a special practice with its own unique forms and keepings which we all know all about and which have no significance whatever. The feeling that entertainment is just entertainment and that nothing else can possibly be said about it is perhaps so very widespread because it is essential to the project of entertainment to define itself in terms of tautology. The way it presents itself is the most perfect form of self-mystification ever developed by a popular art form. It tells us that it is not doing anything except what we already know it to be doing, and because we know there is, of course, no need to find out.

To address the spectator in this way is, as Burch points out, to "induce a certain disengagement": the disengagement that comes from an imputed familiarity with a discourse the keynote of whose utterance is an appeal not to be taken seriously. (31) The most obvious form of this construction of distractedness is that which we associate with television, and which Burch describes so tellingly (though at the cost of the coherence of his article as a whole). It is obvious because the fragmentariness of commercial television is such as to forbid a concentration span of much longer than five or six minutes; the average, whether we think of the length of a commercial or the length of a sequence in a television movie or the time allotted to any one item in a news bulletin, is much shorter than this. This fragmentation, and the principle of cyclic repetition which governs it at every level, reduces everything on television to a particle of form. We know, of course, that the episode of *Dynasty* is fiction and the footage from El Salvador isn't, but there is a crucial sense in which neither matters more than the other

(Burch's point) and moreover that neither is more real than the other. One image of guerrillas in a rain forest or the remnants of a dynamited bridge, one shot of a townscape in the Middle East with the plumes of explosions in the background and gunfire on the soundtrack, is very much the same as another. It is authentic and immediate (immediacy, after all, is what television is about), but today's footage from the Middle East is hardly distinguishable from yesterday's, or, for that matter, from that which we saw ten years ago. (Or is it fifteen? When *did* that business start?) The history of the world becomes a cliché, as familiar and predictable as the latest sitcom about another petit bourgeois couple or the latest commercial for the newest video recorder, each interrupting the other in an endless stream that defines everything as already known.

Because it refers to and celebrates itself in the way that it does, entertainment is engaged at the same time in referring to and celebrating the spectator as the consumer of the spectacle. We are not, of course, to *feel* like consumers: we confront the text or the performer, and even commercials themselves, on terms of intimate mutual equality; each of us knows everything there is to be known about the other. A work governed by the ideology of entertainment never asks us to feel anything without sending up a signal that tells us the species of feeling involved and without congratulating us for recognizing the signal and having the feeling made to order already. Entertainment's self-reference and its flattering reference to the appropriateness of the spectator's response are part of the same process, and it is their mutuality which makes the process transparent. To respond inappropriately is to find oneself excluded from the human community, for it is essential to the entertainment emotion that one should feel that others are responding appropriately elsewhere. The most obvious case, of course, is the canned audience of television comedy, but the mobilization of the ideology of entertainment always depends on intimations of some such form of choral support. It is this fact which gives the emotions generated by entertainment their characteristically unrealized and sentimental quality. The criterion for the substance and validity of a feeling is supplied by the feeling's being one that is natural and inevitable on the given occasion, and part of the evidence of inevitability is the fact that, it is implied, the feeling is spontaneously shared: everyone is having it. Entertainment helps one to feel normal.

Consider the moment when, near the end of *E.T.*, during the final attempt to rescue E.T. from the "authorities" and return him to his spaceship, one of the boys asks Elliott, "Why doesn't he just beam up?" and receives the reply, "This is reality, stupid!" or words to that effect. This gives us the whole syndrome very clearly. There, characteristically, is the ironic invocation of entertainment and the invitation to read the film as "pure fantasy," and there is the gratifying reference to the spectator's knowledge of the convention. We are "disengaged"—to exactly the extent that we feel our involvement to come under the heading of common sense. At the same time, *E.T.* is appealing to needs and anxieties of and creating intensities in the spectator—needs, anxieties, and intensities with real historical sources and determinants—and resolving them in an intensely reactionary manner which never becomes visible. When Superman (Christopher Reeve) says that he stands for "truth, justice, and the American way," we all laugh because no one says that kind of thing any more—except, of course, in the context of a lighthearted escapist entertainment.

Reaganite cinema affirms through metaphors of disavowal and, when it maps the real, it most emphatically insists that we are exploring the land of make-believe. It generalizes and makes its value judgments under the guise of being esoteric and trivial, and if it works us up and makes us feel intense, it must also make us feel, from time to time, a little jaded. Reaganite entertainment is, in fact, the quintessence of entertainment: it creates the pleasurable obviousness of feelings that it tells us are untenable.

The Utopian Imagination

In *The Aesthetic Dimension*, Herbert Marcuse writes:

> The *nomos* which art obeys is not that of the established reality principle but of its negation. But mere negation would be abstract, the "bad" utopia. The utopia in great art is never the simple negation of the reality principle but its transcending preservation (*Aufhebung*) in which past and present cast their shadow on fulfillment. The authentic utopia is grounded in recollection. (73)

The significance of this important formulation becomes clearer in the light of something Marcuse says earlier: "Authentic art preserves [the memory of Auschwitz] in spite of and against Auschwitz; this memory is the ground in which art has always originated—this memory and the need to create images of the possible 'other.'" (56) He concludes: "Inasmuch as art preserves, with the promise of happiness, the memory of the goals that failed, it can enter, as a 'regulative idea', the desperate struggle for changing the world." (69) The argument is, of course, political: "The truth of art lies in its power to break the monopoly of established reality [that is, of those who established it] to define what is real." (9) To challenge a definition of the real is to challenge a definition of what it is possible to desire and what it is possible to do, and it is in the continuous reformulation of this challenge that the utopianism of significant art consists.

If Marcuse's use of the idea of utopianism seems odd, it is because it disturbs in a number of ways the meanings which the word has acquired in conventional usage. We tend to assume, firstly, whether or not we approve of the idea, that utopianism projects a state which is finished, that it implies a teleology, and secondly, that utopias are pleasant dreamworlds from which the disagreeable has been eliminated, in which the conflicts and problems that complicate actual living have been resolved, and which are primarily characterized by plenitude. They represent, in other words, what Marcuse describes as "the negation of the established reality principle." From this definition it is but a short step to the fascinating pejorative use of the word *utopian* which is so familiar a feature of a certain kind of right-wing polemic. It will be maintained, for example, that the ideal of socialism is a very good thing, but that it is utopian, that in practice it gives rise to a bad thing, and further, that the nonutopian elements of the ideal can be realized only under capitalism. Here, "utopian" and "idealistic" connote "unrealistic" and "impracticable," and it is only apparently a paradox that the mere negation of the established reality principle infallibly makes itself available for arguments which naturalize the status quo. The relation between a thesis and its antithesis only becomes productive when there is a significant (that is, dialectical) tension between them, and because the utopia founded in negation is only absolutely antithetical to the real it rejects, it is actually parasitic on it and succeeds in repressing any sense of alternative possibility. As we shall see, under certain circumstances this tendency of the negative utopia to rationalize an existing social order may provide the basis for artistic strategies of the most reactionary kind.

It will be apparent from the passages I have quoted that Marcuse's definition of authentic utopian feeling is bound up with an argument about the cognitive function of art. This argument is very much out of fashion today, but it is nonetheless crucial. For Marcuse, "the utopia in great art" is continuous with that art's concern for what it is legitimate to think of as being real. The negative utopia takes the claim of the established reality principle to be the definitively real for granted, and the satisfactions that such utopias afford are thoroughly permeated by this tacit acceptance of the authoritative nature of the world from which they offer a holiday. Any work that makes itself felt as significant, on the contrary, reconstitutes the real and, in giving it a new content and a new value, recreates our sense of what it may become. It is not enough to validate the utopias of art that they should enact a wish for the world to be different or better or more satisfying, for the fact that the wish originates within the world in which satisfaction is denied provides not the slightest guarantee that it will be essentially opposed to the values of that world, or even be substantially aware of what they are. It is only when the "promise of fulfillment" and the imagery of the world transformed are dramatized in relation to the forces that act against them and conduce to their defeat that utopia acquires a concrete cognitive content and becomes a means of conceptualizing reality rather than escaping from it.

It follows from this that authentic utopian feeling is not incompatible with a feeling of tragic loss or a context of struggle and protest. Indeed, the authenticity of the great utopian works—whether Shakespeare's *The Winter's Tale* or Bunyan's *The Pilgrim's Progress*, Mahler's "Das Lied von der Erde" or Blake's "The Marriage of Heaven and Hell," Marvell's "Horatian Ode," or Beethoven's "Choral Symphony"—is determined precisely by their presence. Of these works, which are obviously utterly different from each other, it may be said, in Blake's phrase, that "without contraries is no progression." The contraries are not willed away, for the concrete nature of the authentic utopia—the quality it has of being realized—depends on its including and accounting for its contradiction, which is thus deprived of the power it had to constrain and inhibit, to impose its stamp of closure on the real, even as it retains the character of a specific negative force which is virulently opposed to the achievement of fulfillment, and which continues to be armed against it. "Das Lied von der Erde" ends with death and parting as well as with rebirth and reunion, and to place *The Winter's Tale* or *Pericles* beside *King Lear* is both to perceive how close the great utopia is to the great tragedy and to grasp the utopian dimension of the tragic experience. To define the authentic utopia as an averted tragedy is not enough. In that it might be taken to imply an evasion or softening of dramatic logic in the interests of wish fulfillment, the description is too negative in suggestion, and it depends, in any case, on a mistaken understanding of the tragic, for tragedy absolutely depends on a vision of conditions which do not conduce to tragedy, and which the particular tragic process helps to define. Just as a word other than "tragedy" is needed to describe works in which the significance of waste, defeat, and loss is not positively articulated, so there can be no viable utopian feeling in which the tragic is not an active, defining presence which endows the "imagery of liberation" with its form.

Part of the reason for the enormous contemporary potency of the radical right in America and Britain lies in the skill with which the right has mobilized the utopian imagination. The success is, inevitably, temporary—the utopia cannot be realized, not least because the policies which the right actually pursues are inimical to it. In any case, the "success" is curious in itself, the conditions for it being so exacting: Reaganite entertainment could hardly work if it did not allow for its own fatuousness. The utopia it defines is, in William Morris's phrase, a "cockney paradise," and there can be very few indeed who do not in some sense know it.

The utopianism of the new radical right has two dimensions. On the one hand, it looks back from a position of geriatric postimperial decrepitude (Great Britain) or of recently humiliated and increasingly embattled hegemony (the United States) to a vanished golden age in which the nation was great and the patriarchal family flourished in happy ignorance of the scourges of abortion and a soaring divorce rate, gay rights, and the women's movement. On the other hand, it anticipates a gorgeous re-flowering of capitalism in which the good things will be born again under the aegis of the microchip once a flabby body politic has been slimmed down and its cancerous growths excised.

One of the central images of this rhetoric is that of the late nineteenth-century bourgeois family embalmed in late twentieth-century domestic software—the Victorian hearth in which the household gods are celebrated not around the pianoforte but around the computer. This image, with its cunning mixture of the idyllic serenity of antiquity and the benign and prodigal inventiveness of the modern, is a crucial one for the present purpose. Its allure is a matter of its proposing an asylum from a harsh and disagreeable public world which is at the same time positively accounted for. The world is shut out, but the wall is composed of materials which testify eloquently to the world's benefits. As with all reactionary utopias, the discourse of computerized Victoriana offers both an escape from the real and an accommodation with it. A second industrial revolution organized by capitalism can mean nothing but mass pauperization, a drastic exacerbation of inequality and, correspondingly, a strengthening of the coercive apparatuses of the state in an attempt to negotiate contradictions between the forces and relations of production whose immunity to the traditional palliatives is becoming increasingly evident.

Yet while the evidence is there, there is nothing in the discourse of social democracy (where it exists) to suggest a future prospect or a source of confidence in any way radically different from those offered by the right, with whose priorities social democracy is extensively complicit. It fails, above all, to address itself to the general experience of powerlessness which is one of the most characteristic features of this phase of late capitalism. Its representatives assert that they can run capitalism more efficiently, profitably, and humanely than the right does, but far from affirming that it is possible for the mass of people to intervene on the public world to change it, their attitude to popular mass action is consistently ambivalent, opportunistic, or hostile. It is this experience of the intractability of the social world which provides the basis on which the right can appeal to the value of well-appointed privacy as both a refuge from late capitalism and an embodiment of its advantages—all the more plausibly because the advantages, for those who can afford them, are real. "The family with a computer," in which the interpersonal harmony of a mythical past is re-created amid the commodities which guarantee the vitality and plenitude of a mythical future, is one of the key images of our time.

There could be no clearer indication of the value and significance of this image than the hysteria that is currently being generated, in Britain at least, around the "video nasty." No other culture but the British could have come up with quite that phrase, which deserves an essay in itself and which is already exercising the kind of hypnotic power which accrued, in a previous conjuncture, to the terms "mugging" and "welfare scrounger." The salacious charisma of the video nasty consists, as one might expect, in its enactment of the ideological contradictions which inevitably beset conservative reassurance. It has devolved upon the video nasty to represent the point at which the seamless whole of Victorian domesticity and the age of software exhibits tell-tale signs of shoddy manufacture. Alan Wolfe has pointed out that "the right, which introduces a critique emphasizing spiritual emptiness, liberal bankruptcy, the disruption of community and flagrant materialism, is tied to forces that cause most of its lament." (23)[1]

The moral panic which is now being generated around the dystopian vision of a generation brutalized in the cradle by its exposure to *The Driller Killer* (1979) and *I Spit on Your Grave* (1978) has the function of mystifying yet again, even as the contradiction is exposed, the necessary discrepancy between the right's appeal to the family as the repository of the good old values and its objective priorities, in the light of which the family is merely one market among other markets. The video nasty points to a fascinating cultural rupture, in which the two distinct services performed by the image of the technologized family (the economic function of stimulating consumption and the ideological function of embodying a utopia) have come into conflict. The moral panic—the lurid images of blasé middle-class and feckless working-class parents subjecting their helpless tots to irremediable trauma and psychic damage—redescribes the conflict, predictably enough, in terms of the spiritual dereliction of certain irresponsible consumers, but the impulse behind the need for redescription is clear enough. The family that provides a market for the new technology and a site for the valorization of capital is very much not the family in which the new technology goes hand in hand with traditional sanctity and loveliness.

One is tempted to call *Star Wars* a "video goody": it is certainly an exemplary negative utopia in Marcuse's sense. It leaves out everything about the existing reality principle that we would prefer to forget, redescribes other things which are scarcely forgettable in such a way that we can remember them without discomfort (and even with uplift), and anticipates rejection of the result by defining itself as a joke. Thus, Reaganite entertainment plays a game with our desire. It invites us to take pleasure in the worlds it creates and the values they embody, but because it is also ironic about them, it confirms our sense of what reality is and leaves us with the anxieties and dissatisfactions which leave a space for Reaganite entertainment. The films continually reproduce the terms of "the world as it is" while also a yearning for something different; if people go back to them again and again, it is perhaps because of the lack of satisfaction the films build into the pleasure: they regenerate the need for escape which they seem to satisfy and provide confidence of a kind which leaves us unconfident. By at once celebrating and debunking the "good old values," and addressing them both as viable norms and the conventions of a fantasy, Reaganite entertainment perpetuates a paralyzed anxiety and institutionalizes itself.

The Born-Again Comic Strip

Since the early '70s at least, evil has been a central element in the popular American cinema. The interest of evil here consists in the decisive ambiguities which arise when it comes to the attribution of agency. Evil describes the defective choice or desire of a person and his/her consequent actions, but it refers at the same time to an eternal metaphysical principle which is logically prior to all persons and which solicits them to ill doing. The idea of possession exposes the problem with particular clarity. Undoubtedly, *persons* are doing the wicked things, but if their wickedness proceeds from their being possessed by the devil, how are we to understand the relation between their actions and their will?

The significance of Hollywood Gothic in the '70s absolutely depends on this ambiguity. It is a staple feature of the "devil-child" cycle that the child is defined as the progeny of, or as being taken over by, an evil power which is absolutely external to the culture in which the child has been raised. At this level, which is dominant inasmuch as it embodies the insistence of the narrative, evil is associated with ideas of invasion and infiltration. Correspondingly, American bourgeois culture is exonerated from any responsibility for the monster it discovers in its midst, and the child itself is construed as the innocent victim of a hideous destiny. The internal tension, and thus the interest, of the films is a matter of the submerged discourse within which the child's possession appears as the decision of the classical American protagonist to "go to hell," as a conscious act of rebellion against the values of a bankrupt culture of which the child's parents are the immediate representatives. Of course, the two levels of meaning have the concept of evil in common: whether we read the child as victim or rebel, and America as blameless or derelict, there can be no question of the child's monstrousness. It is the subtext, however, which generates the films' intensity. The fear of children in the devil-child cycle is occasioned by a profound anxiety about the capacity of the bourgeois family to reproduce itself in social circumstances in which the young are extensively critical of, and even mobilized against, a status quo whose appearance of legitimacy has been seriously, though not fatally, undermined. Because the status quo must, of course, be reaffirmed, the decision to go to hell can never acquire the kind of positive value which it has in Mark Twain's *Adventures of Huckleberry Finn*. Nevertheless, because the conjuncture of Vietnam and Watergate is such as to expose the status quo to very damaging criticism, the child's rebellion emerges as a genuine and powerful threat. The rebellion can by no means be countenanced, but the security and credibility of the positions from which it might be resisted have been eroded.

Good and Evil, of course, are necessarily mystified concepts, and under late capitalism they cannot but serve a conservative function. Yet, if they are conceived as, say, *The Exorcist* (1973) conceives them, their conservatism is troubled and controversial. To take the terms seriously, as 1970 Gothic in general does, is to imply that the outcome of the struggle between them is seriously in doubt, and that it is so because there is something about Good which gives Evil a chance—even a raison d'être. Evil appears, correspondingly, as a dangerously subversive energy which is almost triumphant and which is only contained with great difficulty and at great cost, part of the cost being the feeling that the triumph of Good is temporary, provisional, and possibly meaningless: what content can the triumph have if it is not accompanied by a renewed sense of positive value?

To use the terms "successfully," it is necessary to foreground and capitalize on their banality—that is, to find some means of preserving the value judgments that the terms embody while at the same time subduing as completely as possible the sense that anything of real value is at stake in the contest between them. They must appear to be usable terms, with real weight and substance, but they must also seem specialized, esoteric, and conventional. We must be able to believe in and consent to them, but we must feel, too, that nothing of what is involved in the important kinds of conviction is involved here.

Luke Skywalker in *Star Wars*, like Damien in *The Omen* (1976), is the son of the devil: the lineage is as crucial as the glaring differences which may make the association of the two trilogies seem odd. The differences are determined by Lucas's simplification of the major ideological conflicts: Luke remains a rebel against the establishment, but his rebellion is dissociated from a commitment to Evil and redescribed as a crusade against it. The rebellion thus ceases to be dangerous while retaining the charisma of strenuous opposition. Luke's paternity bears no relation whatever to his desire—having been Darth Vader's antagonist, Luke becomes his redeemer. It is the fact that, in general, the confrontation of Good and Evil has been entirely purged of any hint of conflicts of ideological allegiance and any suspicion that desire might have its vicissitudes that gives the narrative of the *Star Wars* trilogy its reassuring quality. There is a struggle, but there is no dialectic. We are clearly supposed to feel, in *Return of the Jedi*, that there is a real danger of Luke's succumbing to the "dark side" of the Force, but it would go against the grain of the text to give this danger any real dramatic life: there is no fiend hid in this cloud. On the contrary, the cloud is hid in the fiend: Luke's supposed ambivalence is a mere narrative ploy which has the function of providing an occasion for the climactic revelation that the father is not ambivalent either.

The Reaganite horror movie adopts a strategy which is the complementary opposite of that of Reaganite space fiction. The Gothic has always depended on the fear that the repressed cannot be contained because it is in fact produced by the culture which seeks to contain it. The modern horror film (from *Halloween* and *Friday the 13th* onward) abandons the identification of the monster with the return of the repressed while institutionalizing the monster's indestructibility, thus inoculating the Gothic at a stroke.

This strategy has a number of corollaries. In those cases in which the monster cannot be killed, or has to be killed repeatedly, its resilience no longer means anything—except that we are continually in danger of persecution by a nameless, ineliminable, and motivelessly malignant principle of Evil. It has become customary to conceive of the monster in punitive terms, as the scourge of sexual license, sexual transgression, and female self-assertion. When this is the case, as in the "teenie-kill pic," the genre's new solipsism serves to mystify the monster's function by focusing our attention on narrative procedure in the abstract and by systematically trivializing character so as to preempt any complex emotional involvement in the action— indeed, to promote indifference to it. The prevailing suggestion that the monster is absolutely external to the culture it threatens allows those films which do permit the spectator to engage with the victims of a horror (when this is not also a punishment) unproblematically to reaffirm the norms the characters embody, as in *Poltergeist*. It is always possible, of course, to modify these various features so as to make them compatible. The rabid dog in *Cujo* (1983), for example, functions clearly as a punishment for sexual transgression, but *Cujo* is very unlike the teenie-kill pic in encouraging us to identify passionately with a heroine who, though an adulteress, is also a sympathetic, individuated person, so that we may share her realization that if her husband had been around to pronounce (as only husbands can) the "magic words" that keep Evil away, she and her child would not have been exposed to the depredations of working-class male sexuality in the first place. This is about the most complex modulation that we can expect in a contemporary horror film.

The Reaganite space and horror cycles, then, answer to one another. In the one case, Good is affirmed through the spectacle of its robustness and its pre-given triumph, and in the other through the spectacle of its terrible vulnerability to appalling alien forces or the punishment of deviations from it. The banality of the films derives from the undialectical conception of Good and Evil and the reduction to the level of routine of the contest between them, which conduces in itself to an estranged involvement: we are to be excited or horrified or gripped, but we are also to take the fundamental thematic categories of the text completely for granted.

Technology

Throughout the history of its rule, the bourgeoisie has sought consistently to rationalize and depoliticize its own technical priorities by reference to the concept of "progress." The usefulness of the concept for such a purpose is its apparent neutrality and the sense of inevitability which it embodies. The very word seems both to account for the general interest and to "assert Eternal Providence" in its own definition: to set oneself against progress is to appear as an opponent not only of the betterment of the human race but also of the necessity of history. In fact, of course, progress is never interest free, and its agents are far from being impersonal: in class societies, progress always relates in some way to an acceleration of the rate and scope of surplus extraction by the ruling class.

The function of the ideology of progress is to describe human history in terms of the improvement of techniques and to assert that this improvement brings with it an ever-greater degree of material and spiritual well-being to ever-larger numbers of people. The ideology's coherence and utility depends, obviously enough, on the fact that it does indeed make contact with the experience of substantial sections of the exploited groups and classes in the advanced capitalist countries, where, after all, the wealth produced by progress has been concentrated. It is a good thing to have a car and a stereo and a washing machine; a life in which they are available is distinctly preferable to a life in which they are not. It is on the basis of this important fact that the ideology of progress undertakes to mystify the conditions of their availability—and of opportunities for consuming them—as evidence of an objective tendency toward greater and greater equity in class society. For the purposes of the ideology, technology is technology: the spinning-jenny and the electric toaster, the nuclear generator and the telephone, the microchip and the refrigerator—all these are familiar milestones along the forward march of progress. In effect, the ideology conflates the status of the commodity and that of the means of production: because we can own and derive pleasure and benefit from objects which our parents could not have dreamed of owning, it is obviously the case that the wealth of capitalist society is being distributed more equally than it was and that the refinement of the techniques of production operates in the interests of all. The fact that the bourgeoisie's progress—that is, the unprecedented expansion of the forces of production which the rule of capital has produced—has actually to be recovered for the general interest by political means is suppressed, and history is seen as being borne toward equality by the sheer momentum of human inventiveness.

The ideology of progress obscures the conditions of the availability of commodities, not just through their proliferation but by attributing the comparative material well-being of certain sectors of the white working class in the West to the beneficence of capitalism rather than to the struggle of the working class itself. It goes without saying that the development of capitalist technique is motivated by the desire to increase the rate of profit, and each stage of this development, starting with the proletarianization of the peasantry during the Industrial Revolution, has provoked the most violent resistance from the exploited. Insofar as progress has brought with it an improvement in the economic and political condition of the classes that produce the wealth of capital, this improvement has been won through class struggle—though it is extremely important that the bourgeois parliamentary state operates in such a way as to produce the appearance that the rights of the exploited have been "granted." The ideology of progress underwrites this operation by suppressing the history of the class struggle and replacing it with a comfortable account of an inexorable and pacific voyage toward universal affluence.

As capitalism's second industrial revolution gets under way, talk of progress is naturally much in the air, and scarcely a day can be allowed to pass without a jeremiad against its enemies. The occasion for this talk is the fact that under the conditions of late capitalism, the only means by which the rate of profit can be secured, let alone increased, conflict directly and inescapably with the structure of social relations created by mature capitalism. The mass working class which was prerequisite for the primitive accumulation of capital and for its rapid expansion during the imperialist phase is now both economically unfeasible and, potentially, a serious political threat, and we are now entering a period in which the actual process of surplus extraction in general is becoming the focus of class confrontation. During the postwar boom—the period when, according to Mr. Harold Macmillan, the class struggle ended—it was elaborately maintained that the fruits of progress were for all. Now, when the working class seeks to protect itself against the effects of a recession, the function of which is to pauperize it and destroy it as an effective political force, it is construed once more as Luddite—as a fractious impediment to the great stride forward represented by the microchip.

It is hardly surprising, in a period in which the contradiction between the general interest and the interests served by modern capitalist technique is being exposed with relentless clarity, that capitalist popular culture should be so fundamentally preoccupied with the ecstatic celebration of technology. It is still less remarkable that this hymn to the spectacular glamour and excitement of high-tech future worlds should turn out to be written in two-part harmony—the other voice being given over to an ecstatic celebration of the good old family values and structures which the progress of capitalist production is flattening in its path. Reaganite space fiction is there to tell us that the future will be a thrilling replay of the past—with special effects.

The celebration of technology in these films is not only theme but form: it is, in the usual way, solipsistic; the dazzling mechanical accoutrements of the dramatic world are inseparable from the dazzling accomplishment of the text, which becomes the evidence, as it were, of its own vision. The six-Dolby sound, the 70mm, the trick work, the much-vaunted profligate expensiveness all testify in themselves to the magical potency and dynamic robustness of contemporary capitalism even as they realize a future state which represents the apotheosis of the same technology.

No one would be so foolish as to argue that the special effects are never stirring or impressive, or even that they are incapable of attaining a certain kind of simple grandeur. It would be hard not to be impressed, for example, by the appearance of the spaceship in *Close Encounters of the Third Kind* (1977), or by the opening shot of *Star Wars*, in which (in an effect that has been, understandably, much repeated, with diminishing returns) the space station seems to glide with massive and imperturbable serenity from behind and above the camera. The audiences that enjoy these films do not enjoy them for nothing, and there is indeed a pleasure involved both in the recognition of extreme technical mastery and in the experience of the excitements produced by it. The films also appeal—and this seems to me the fundamental point—to a sense of awe and wonder. This sense, or the need for it, may properly be described as an essential human characteristic—at any rate, as something which has been produced as such by the social history of the "political animal"—and it is more complex than it may seem: more is involved than going "ooh!" and "ah!" Behind the sense of awe lies the feeling which F. R. Leavis calls "impersonality," which is given classical expression, in his view, in a favorite and oft-quoted passage from the opening chapter of *The Rainbow* where the hero, Tom Brangwen, discovers that he does "not belong to himself." (*D. H. Lawrence*, 131) This sense of being intimately related with, and responsible to, ends and values which transcend the personal but in terms of which the personal achieves significance has been realized historically through the structures of feeling associated with two interrelated, if often contradictory, institutions— religion and the state. It seems plain that at the decisive moments of human history, the moments when the deepest logic of specific structural conflicts and contradictions is acted through, some such feeling is fiercely mobilized in the combatants, and that, equally, when we talk about certain structures of feeling being hegemonic—the feeling, say, of being "British" or "Christian" or "working class"—we are referring to the predominance of a certain sense of personality.

We do not need to be reminded of the iniquities which have been committed in the name of "impersonal feeling," but the fact that it is also definitive of the most valuable kind of cultural production should be sufficient in itself to warn against the assumption that this feeling is incompatible with or inimical to the socialist project. On the contrary, socialist internationalism should be seen as the condition of its final demystification—of the recovery for the collaborative enterprise of human production as a whole of sentiments which have been realized hitherto in conditions of scarcity and inequality, and which have been consistently embodied in works which survive and point outside those conditions only in the realm of art.

The curious mixture in Reaganite space fiction of the awe-inspiring and the banal, of the marvelous and the trivial, is determined by the attempt to generate a sense of wonder around values and feelings which everyone in some sense knows to be dead, and which can only exist under modern conditions as the most inert and empty kind of rhetoric. The emptiness cannot be concealed: indeed, as we have seen, its foregrounding is now the only condition on which the grandiose inflation of the same values can take place. The simple but at times genuine splendor and inventiveness of the films' technique is the means by which they recover the ground that is lost through the pressing need to confess to their own fatuousness, and by which the culture's most threadbare garments are passed off nevertheless as imperial raiment.

I have argued that the development of capitalist technique subserves the interests of capital, that it is developed and introduced without regard to other interests, and that it has been in the past, and is now becoming again, a focus of class struggle in which the question of the interests served by the mode of production as a whole is directly posed. If the technical wizardry of *Star Wars* and its ilk both asserts the dynamic energy of modern capital and surrounds the "traditional" values of mature capital with a mystical grandeur, what of the function of technology in the texts? The functions overlap, of course: the spectacle of the technique of the future defending the values of the past seals up the contradiction between the forces and relations of production and reaffirms the indivisibility and universality of capitalism, tireless in its promotion of the general interest as it was, is, and ever will be.

Yet there is an obvious sense in which the space cycle includes the problem of the political content of the development of the productive forces, albeit in a mystified form—includes it in order to dispel it. Thematically, the concern with technology and the idea of the eternal struggle of Good and Evil blend together so as to produce a vision of universal history in which the criterion appropriate to the judgment of technique is not political (this technology serves these class interests) but metaphysical (this technology is controlled by representatives of one or other of the eternal moral absolutes).

In most of the space films, Evil is more or less clearly the Soviet Union, as I will try to show in a moment, but it may also be projected on to a "bad" capitalist: the Gene Hackman and Robert Vaughn characters in the *Superman* films are the most obvious examples. In the extraordinary sequence in *Superman III* (1983) in which Ross Webster (Vaughn) uses a captured weather satellite to transform the climatic conditions and destroy the crops of a small South American state, the villain is even associated with an imperialist intervention in the Latin American revolution. The strategy of producing an aberrant wicked businessman to act as a scapegoat for those features of "truth, justice, and the American way" which we would prefer to forget as we celebrate their victory is a familiar one, for whose value in the contemporary currency we have the disaster cycle (*Earthquake* [1974], *The Towering Inferno*, *Jaws*) to thank, and the only interest of *Superman III* consists in the fact that the film finds it necessary to adapt this strategy to the character of the hero himself. In the course of the action, Superman is briefly taken over by the villain, loses his power, and abandons himself to cynical dissipation, but he is finally born again out of himself, as it were, after a titanic struggle with his corrupted alter ego. One might compare the sequence depicting Superman's degeneration and his effective complicity with Evil with Frank Capra's use of the opposition between George Bailey

(James Stewart) and Bedford Falls, and Mr. Potter (Lionel Barrymore) and Pottersville, in *It's a Wonderful Life* (1946). Capra's film has a real commitment to the ideal values of American democracy which shows up for what it is the slick and shallow opportunism, cynical and sentimental by turns, of Reaganite entertainment; its theme is the perilously close proximity between those ideal values and practical realities which are evidently monstrous. The very attempt to maintain the ideals may create the circumstances which demonstrate their contradictoriness and their unrealizability. There is no attempt to submerge or mystify this theme: it is, explicitly, what the film is about, and it is explored with a rigor and complexity which no work addressing that subject has surpassed. When Reaganite entertainment tells us that the same technology or the same Force may be used for good or ill, or shows us the hero gravitating toward the status of the villain, it is only to establish all the more clearly how utterly unlike and how completely unrelated the uses and the persons are.

It is also clearly significant that in the Superman films, where villainy and the destructive deployment of technology are associated with an American, the villain is played desperately, and with considerable strain, for grotesque comedy and is safely reduced to a comic strip nutter. His lack of any real ideological substance is blatantly exposed in *Superman II* (1980)—the most interesting of the trilogy—in which he is merely the puppet of the rival superpower whose representatives install him, as if to demonstrate the Reaganite way with *The Omen* and 1970s Gothic, as president of the United States. The bad American is either a joke or a Soviet pawn.

It is the distinction of *Blade Runner* to have proposed a counterblast to the discourse of Reaganite science fiction, and one may interpret the decision of the producers of Ridley Scott's film to tack on the ludicrous first-person narration before the film's release as an attempt not only to provide a reading aid for spectators who are now incapable of following any but the simplest narrative line but also to construct the text, through the pastiche of film noir, as yet another solipsistic disquisition on itself. The impulse is understandable. The future created in *Blade Runner*, with such amazingly imaginative vividness and consistency, is that of a decadent, authoritarian, amorphously polyglot capitalism, at once technically sophisticated and culturally debased. The exploitation and oppositional struggle of the replicants—a race of humanoid workers designed with a built-in terminal malfunction which causes them to die before their closeness to human beings asserts itself in a demand for social rights—are conceived, moreover, in class terms. There is no question here of Good and Evil: the development of the productive forces is dramatized in its relation to the expropriation of wealth and the exploitation of labor, in the context of a dramatic world where even formal democracy has been abandoned and the state appears openly as an instrument of class coercion. *Blade Runner's* reinstatement of the sublimated political content of the categories of the space cycle goes with a sustained inquisition of the cycle's forms and the simple pleasures they provide. The narrative audacities, and the complex and disturbing patterns of sympathy and identification, constitute in themselves an implicit commentary on the idiom they reject, as Scott more or less announces in the casting and use of Harrison Ford. "This film," we are virtually told, "is unreadable in terms of the expectations you bring to it." To invite the spectator to engage in a political criticism of the culture and its most popular texts is a risky business in the 1980s, and whatever its confusions and limitations may be, *Blade Runner* deserves our respect for having undertaken it.

Nuclear Anxiety

Earlier, [President Reagan] said video-game whizzes may make red-hot fighter pilots.

Speaking to a group of mathematics and science students at Walt Disney's futuristic Epcot Center, Reagan said today's video-game players are developing "incredible hand, eye and brain co-ordination."

"Watch a 12-year-old take evasive action and score multiple hits while playing 'Space Invaders' and you will appreciate the skills of tomorrow's pilot," the President said. But Reagan quickly added that "homework, sports and friends still come first."

—*Toronto Star,* March 9, 1983

The banal Christian dualism and the obsession with technology in Reaganite science fiction are most interestingly articulated in the films' attempts to deal with a form of technology by which everyone is now rather worried—nuclear weapons.

In a brilliant paper entitled "The Threat of Nuclear War and the Struggle for Socialism," by far the most inclusive and systematic account yet produced of the politics of nuclear armaments, Ernest Mandel remarks:

> Unlike the intensification of the nuclear arms race in the 1950s and 1960s, the present trend corresponds to an *intrinsic economic need* of the imperialist economy, linked to a long-term decline of the economic situation of capitalism. In conditions of stagnation of the rate of profit and of the "normal outlets," arms production is more and more "the substitute market" *par excellence* that stimulates a resumption of capital accumulation.
>
> The greater the long-term impasse for enlarged capital accumulation, the greater is the temptation to challenge the present division of the world between the capitalist and the post-capitalist sector (i.e., to try to reintroduce capitalism by war in those countries where it has already been abolished); and the greater is the temptation to prevent, through the use of nuclear weapons, any new victory of revolution in the imperialist countries or the "Third World." (33)

It is necessary to draw attention here to one of the most important political contradictions of the Reagan period. The most reactionary government in American history came to power in the context of a series of disastrous and humiliating defeats for American imperialism: the loss of Vietnam, the loss of Iran, the success of the Sandinista revolution in Nicaragua, and an upsurge of revolutionary struggle in El Salvador and Grenada, bringing with it the appalling prospect of a federation of socialist states in Latin America. At the same time, as Mandel points out, the "new factor" in the situation of imperialism is that while America was and is perfectly capable materially of intervening in Iran and Nicaragua, the domestic and international repercussions of the war in Vietnam have made it politically extremely difficult to do so. (24–25) The essential project of the Reagan administration is to recoup the recent losses of imperialism as rapidly as possible and to inhibit the further spread of world revolution, but the only means by which this project can be realized entail the twin risks of provoking massive popular opposition at home (and we should recall that less than a quarter of those eligible to vote actually did vote for President Reagan in 1980) and of undermining the viability of the ideologies through which, throughout the postwar period, the imperialist intention has been refracted. The cred- ibility of American foreign policy depends on its being defined as a defense of the Free World against an insidious conspiracy originating in the Kremlin, and it is now becoming difficult, even in the House of Representatives, to maintain a consistent majority for the proposition that the Latin American revolution can be construed in that light. The invasion of Grenada and the military presence in Beirut are clearly experiments, designed to discover the extent to which the ideological camouflage remains convincing in practice and the degree of the loss which is "acceptable" to the American people. But the very need for such experiments only emphasizes the difficulty of a ruling class which is hard-pressed at one and the same time to secure its real interests, come up to the level of its rhetorical triumphalism, and capture the support, or at least the indifference, of its domestic and international audience.

Given this political quandary on the one hand and on the other the objective logic and necessity, as Mandel describes them, of imperialism's investment in the production of nuclear weapons, the absolutely decisive significance of the American and European peace movements is self-explanatory. It might be said that these movements, at present, have all the strengths and weaknesses of the anti-Vietnam movement. The fact that they are popular fronts, in which eminent members of the Church and the liberal establishment are prominent and whose mass base includes huge numbers of the middle classes, makes it difficult to present them convinc- ingly as Bolshevik plots—though, of course, such descriptions have been and will continue to be given—but it also militates against their unification around a general political program with a socialist tendency. However, the peace movement is distinguished from the protest against Vietnam in one crucial respect: an antinuclear movement implicates the totality of the social relations of late capitalism inescapably and directly in a way which the opposition to the war in Indochina did not. It is being increasingly recognized that the only way in which imperial- ism can now conduct itself puts the very possibility of life at risk. While we can expect that what Mandel calls "the absurd and dangerous myth" of the Soviet design on western Europe will continue, in the short term, to exert its reactionary force, it is equally clear that the peace movement is already a serious material threat to imperialism and that the objective conditions of capitalism's decline are such as to increase that threat rather than diminish it.

The deep structure of Reaganite science fiction is determined by the existence of anxiety about nuclear weapons, and the function of the "escape" the films offer is to assuage it. The message is cogent and succinct: the bomb is a good thing in the hands of Americans and a bad thing in the hands of the Soviet Union. It is significant that not even Clint Eastwood's *Firefox* (1982), in which the message is to all intents and purposes explicit, goes quite so far as to discard the seventh veil: we are emphatically not told that the ultimate superweapon which the wicked Soviets have stolen and which Clint is struggling to recover is a nuclear weapon. Conversely, in *Never Say Never Again* (1983), which has the same basic plot (derived directly, in this case, from the earlier James Bond film *Thunderball* [1965]) and in which the captured weapons are Cruise missiles, the thief is not explicitly the Soviet Union but, as usual, SPECTRE.

There is a curious moment in *Never Say Never Again* which is usefully representative of the residual modesty and tact of even the most brazen of these works. It is the moment at which the chief villain, played by one of the era's favorite signifiers of implacable un-American activity, Max von Sydow (he performs a similar service for *Flash Gordon* [1980] and *Conan the Barbarian* [1982]), announces that SPECTRE is arming and financing the Latin American revolution, going on at once to add that it is supporting the counterrevolution too, since SPECTRE "makes no distinctions in questions of death." The equivocation (and it is worth pointing out that there is nothing equivalent to this moment in *Thunderball*) is all the more remarkable for the fact that the opening of *Never Say Never Again* shows James Bond undertaking a training program for counterinsurgency in Latin America.

We may be tempted to explain this fleeting reference to SPECTRE's political evenhandedness by noting that *Never Say Never Again* is, after all, a British film and James Bond a British hero, and indeed the film's attitude to SPECTRE is refracted through the characteristic national chauvinism of the Bond cycle, expressing itself here in a certain reticent but unmistakable asperity of tone at the expense of the United States. SPECTRE may be the Soviet Union, and its leading scientist may have a Russian accent, but the Cruise missiles *are* American weapons, and the ingenious ploy by which they are stolen not only emphasizes the fact that they are under American political control but also intimates that the safeguards against their "appropriation" (read "use") are inadequate. While *Never Say Never Again* is directed by the ostensible author of *The Empire Strikes Back* (1980), it reflects, as a Bond film, a specific national anxiety and asserts, in recompense, a specific national complacency all the more pronounced for the evidence of the nation's dependency. The British ruling-class superhero is required both to defeat the villains and to make up for the un-coolness and ineptitude of the allies. But one can take the point too simply. It is certainly possible to read the equivocation over SPECTRE's role in Latin America in terms of a feeling that the Yanks are as crass as the Reds are villainous and that Her Majesty's Government will be left, as usual, to clean up the mess. That equivocation, however, also tells us something important about the subliminal disquiet of even the most hawkish American movies and about why it is that *Raiders of the Lost Ark*, *Star Trek II: The Wrath of Khan* (1982), and the *Star Wars* trilogy are written entirely in code. In the first place, whether or not the political meanings are consciously intended and openly articulated by its maker, as in *Firefox* they clearly are, the film must remain "entertainment," and some means must be found of signaling to the spectator that in the last instance that is "just" what it is.

In illustration of this point, consider the commercial failure, after a promising start, of John Milius's *Red Dawn* (released in the United States, by some freak of chance, the week before the 1984 Democratic Convention and publicly endorsed by Reagan and Haig) and the corresponding triumph of what is perhaps, to date, the definitive Reaganite text—*Ghostbusters* (1984), which appeared a little earlier.

Red Dawn requires us literally to believe that World War III will be a remake of World War II, staged in the Midwest rather than in Europe, with the aid of advanced but nonnuclear technology. Yet even to imagine that such a premise can be taken seriously in 1984 is grossly to misconstrue the audience's sensibility. It is not merely that the only conditions on which the premise can be dramatized are such as to expose its unintelligibility (as Powers Boothe's memorable account of the logistics of the Soviet invasion is there to demonstrate); the film fails even to address the anxieties it is trying to mobilize. Milius's mistake is to have assumed that his own fervid and nostalgic sensibility, in which warfare is little more than an alibi for sentimental male bonding in the wilderness, is representative. The contemporary American audience can be seen, in fact, to be both less and more complacent: less in that the satisfactions *Red Dawn* offers as to the nature of any conceivable international conflict will persuade no one, and more in that the film's failure is obviously attributable to its not being satisfying enough. There is no market in Reagan's America for a "terrible warning" in the course of which all the major American characters die and which can offer nothing better in the way of a happy ending than a painfully arbitrary conjuring trick.

The subject of *Ghostbusters* is exactly the same as that of *Red Dawn*—the defeat of a Soviet invasion of America by the male group (armed, we are actually told in one of the film's most extraordinary moments, with illegal nuclear weapons)—and it should hardly be necessary at this stage to analyze the procedures to which Ivan Reitman's movie owes its sensational success. Once the significance of the ghost metaphor has been grasped, the terms of the nuclear project (the virtue and necessity of deterrence, the disastrous consequences of disarmament, the holocaust as catharsis of the powers of Evil) are self-evident. I will only add here that *Ghostbusters* confirms my account of the traditions of Reaganite entertainment. The theme and imagery of possession, and above all the association of the powers of darkness with active female sexuality (Sigourney Weaver), come directly from the 1970s horror film, and they provide further evidence for the contention that the reactionary degeneration of the Gothic is both a premonitory symptom of, and one of the enabling conditions for, the contemporary cinema of reassurance. As in *The Exorcist* (and, of course, *Indiana Jones and the Temple of Doom* [1984]), the supreme figure of Evil in *Ghostbusters* is an androgynous goddess associated with pre-Christian "Third World" religious cults, and at the film's climax she is subjected to a kind of nuclear gang rape by the three heroes ("Let's show this prehistoric bitch how we do things downtown!"). Inevitably, the potency of the threats she represents to American culture is linked to the presence within it, in position of power, of defective, emasculated men: Walter Peck (William Atherton), the film's spokesman for the antinuclear lobby, is repeatedly referred to as "dickless." At the same time, the comic modes which *Ghostbusters* employs, and the personas of Bill Murray and Dan Aykroyd, allow us to relate the film to those traditions in American entertainment of which, at an earlier stage in the argument, I offered the *Road* movies as representative. In Murray's incorrigibly cynical insouciance, from which a contemptuous indifference to everything (including the narrative by which we are being entertained) emerges as the ideal human characteristic, we have a specifically 1980s development out of Bob Hope.

If, as in *Firefox*, the Soviet Union is "only" Max von Sydow being dastardly again, and if the bomb is "only" a wonderful plane which provides an occasion for thrilling chases and special effects, the discomfort induced by referring to the real can be suspended, and we are at liberty to enjoy and subscribe to the text in perfect safety—which is what escape means in Reaganite entertainment. It may be ventured that the corollary of this point is that the mode the films employ is objectively entailed in their project in that the Reaganite worldview cannot be sustained in any other way. To dramatize the politics of the new right seriously would be to run the risk, under present conditions, either of exposing their incoherence or of stimulating the very anxieties which it is the films' function to lay to rest. The nature and success of John

Badham's *WarGames* (1983) vindicates such a hypothesis: the only contemporary Hollywood film at the time of writing which is actually about the outbreak of nuclear war is not about an attack by the Soviet Union but about the accidental launching of American missiles.

Since this article was first written, we have had Lynne Littman's *Testament* and David Cronenberg's *The Dead Zone* (both 1983). The general tacit agreement, uniting both the bourgeois press and those critical circles passing as "alternative," to see Littman's grotesquely reactionary film as something other than what it patently is can be attributed with something like confidence to the fact that the director is a woman; had *Testament* been signed by a man, would anyone have felt obliged not to notice that the nuclear holocaust, as Littman conceives it, is merely a pretext for feeling elegiac about the patriarchal nuclear family? The donnée is, in fact, gratuitous, as the ad line which offers the film as an account of "how one family living in a small California town handles a crisis" succinctly intimates: substitute terminal cancer for terminal war, as *Terms of Endearment* (1983) does, and the argument would remain unaffected. *Testament* sets itself single-mindedly, and with a sincerity which Steven Spielberg might envy, to extract pathos from the spectacle of the disintegration of affluent bourgeois privacy. Of the conditions of that affluence and that privacy Littman knows, complacently, nothing, just as she knows nothing of the "terrible forces" which disrupt them. Nobody in the film understands why the holocaust has occurred, and there is no sense either that they ought to have understood or that anything might have been done about it. Nor is there a sense that the "Why?" is a question to which a work purporting to dramatize this subject should or could address itself. Incredible as it may seem, given the material, the world is synonymous for all practical purposes—except (of course) its destruction—with the well-heeled Californian suburb, and *Testament* calls on the apocalypse to give a spurious atmosphere of tragedy to a selfish and self-serving vision of the dissolution of the suburban lifestyle. This lifestyle includes the gender roles assigned by it, and Littman's being a woman doesn't alter the fact that the discourse of *Testament*, quite apart from its addiction to noble helplessness, is inertly complicit in patriarchal ideologies to a degree that would have been found obviously ludicrous (and odious) in a less emotive context. The film's parti pris is most damagingly exposed in its complete inability to give any realized dramatic substance, within the realist terms that Littman sets up, to the aftermath of war, which seems to consist of the abrupt cessation of middle-class amenities: there is dust on the dinner service, no one is collecting the garbage, and the workers are raiding the pantry. As Littman also spares us the disagreeable details of human decay, all of which (a little incontinence apart) take place off screen, it is possible to imagine that she experienced the film's imaginative poverty as "tact"—but it is a betraying decorum. The war, for *Testament*, is merely a surrogate, portentous and vague, for everything "out there" which threatens the emotional equilibrium and material well-being of ourselves "in here," and it is entirely fitting that the film should display a serene indifference to the fate of anyone or anything that cannot be construed as belonging to, or as being a satellite of, the bourgeois family.

Though it is very seriously flawed, *The Dead Zone*, on the other hand, can be added to the small group of really interesting and distinguished contemporary American films. Its premise, like that of *Blade Runner*, engages directly with the thematics of Reaganite utopianism: the function of Johnny's (Christopher Walken) ability to decipher the past and foretell the future is to define, through his dystopian vision, the various ways in which masculine dominance organize the real, and to indicate universal destruction as the logical outcome of this organization. The film's theme is magnificently enacted in its structure, which juxtaposes a succession of disparate but complementary patriarchal monsters, each of whom asserts his potency through mass murder. The last of them, the aspiring senator Stillson (Martin Sheen) who, as president, inaugurates the holocaust, is used to link the radical populism of the American New Right to fascism and is associated by the casting with Kennedy (and thus the Bay of Pigs) and by theme and imagery with Reagan. In the scene in which Stillson successfully blackmails the editor of a country newspaper into withholding a hostile editorial, Cronenberg even goes so far as to frame Stillson next to Reagan's photograph. Most remarkably, *The Dead Zone* implicitly recognizes the thematic connection between the celebration of technology and the celebration of phallic power with which we are familiar from the *Star Wars* trilogy, *The Right Stuff* (1983), and the rest, and gives a devastating critical account of it. Correspondingly, Johnny's ability first to perceive and finally to contest the forces which his visions reveal derives from the loss of the phallus represented by his accident, and Cronenberg makes brilliantly expressive use of the "femininity" of the Christopher Walken persona. *The Dead Zone* has substantial weaknesses. Most damagingly, Sarah Bracknell, the Brooke Adams character, is never integrated into the film's thematic and remains, indeed, a mere cipher; the ending, moving as it is, radically compromises the dramatic argument by suddenly isolating Stillson as an aberrant case whose fortuitous destruction both purges the future of its dangerousness and fulfills a latent tendency to view Johnny as a messianic (male) redeemer ("It is finished"). These confusions and failures of realization undoubtedly compromise the film's achievement, but like *Blade Runner*, which is equally contradictory, it remains a remarkable intervention in the culture—not least because of the intelligence with which it confronts, through the tacit invocation of the theme of possession, the impasse of the Hollywood Gothic.

WarGames calculates brilliantly on the assumption that while we are always being told—and may like to believe—that nuclear war is really just a game of "Space Invaders" for grown-ups, none of us is for a moment convinced by this, and the calculation provides the film with its narrative premise: the weapons are launched by a schoolboy, a home computer and video games freak who tunes in by chance to the Pentagon computer. *WarGames* recognizes implicitly that the understanding of the relation between America and the Soviet Union as a relation between the powers of Good and Evil can only survive in the thin and rarefied atmosphere of the comic book, and that in other contexts American innocence has to be demonstrated rather than assumed. The demonstration is, of course, easy: the launching of the missiles *was* an accident, which bears no relation to the intentions of the American government and its military and which refers us not to the interests of those who control the weapons but to the regrettable fact that technology (which is itself interest free) has, briefly, escaped human control altogether.

Badham's other "nuclear" film, *Blue Thunder* (1983), works in a similar way, though here his perception that nuclear anxiety is only partially and imperfectly contained by anxiety about the Soviet Union involves him in more contentious, and correspondingly more interesting, material. The superweapon in *Blue Thunder* is a helicopter which has been developed by the American military for use in the suppression of a *domestic* insurrection, and the narrative is motivated by the discovery of a conspiracy to test the weapon and win public consent to its use by provoking black rioting which the helicopter can then be used to crush. The decision to cast as the leading villain a British actor, Malcolm McDowell, who clearly needed only the slightest encouragement to play for all they were worth the odious conventions of undemocratic upper-class privilege and to behave as if he were a member of the Gestapo (complete with black leather overcoat), instantly re-creates the external enemy left out by the narrative donnée, and this strategy reinforces the conservative tendencies of the theme, familiar from other conspiracy movies, of the one just American man fighting a system whose personnel have somehow become corrupted.

Yet the very fact that the film is obliged to resort to such strategies (and the introduction of the Darth Vader surrogate is only effected at the cost of a notably jarring shift of tone) confirms one's feeling about the nature of the need for them. *Blue Thunder* requires McDowell and *Raiders of the Lost Ark* and *The Wrath of Khan* require their elaborate camouflage of mystifying metaphor because they actually have to give form to the anxieties they address, even as they work to dissipate them. The interest of *WarGames* and *Blue Thunder* is that they demonstrate what is at stake in a set of texts which operate very differently. For, before *Raiders of the Lost Ark* can say "Don't worry about the bomb," it has to say "You are, of course, worried about the bomb because the Soviets have it." The Badham films, in admitting in their premise to the existence of disquiet about the policies and institutions of the *American* state, alert us to the mistake involved in forgetting that the films which don't are compelled to propose the terms of the fears they are designed to allay. Those terms are obviously hegemonic; consent can be won for them, but it is in the nature of the hegemony to be more vulnerable than the films' irrepressible air of robust and assertive confidence might suggest, and the limits within which they operate are not entirely advantageous to them.

The hegemony is vulnerable because there is a latent discrepancy, deducible as much from the texts themselves as from the culture in general, between the kinds of reassurance the films provide and the kinds of uncertainty the audience actually feels. If faith in "the American way" could be assumed a priori, it would not be necessary to be ironic about the liturgy, and while irony allows the service to proceed, it cannot but provide an unstable and unreliable basis for an ideological consensus. The irony allows for the deeper sources of disquiet, but it is precisely these that the films, by definition, cannot take seriously, let alone eliminate. At the moment, this may be fairly cold comfort. Reaganite entertainment has already had a decisive effect on the Hollywood cinema and its audience, and it can hardly be denied that *Raiders of the Lost Ark* can presuppose at least a massive desire to feel confident in the ways it suggests that one ought. Yet, while we may wish to behave as if the last fifteen years of American political and cultural history did not exist, we cannot spirit them away, and the films' negation or recuperation of history has the effect of a potential weakness as well as a potential strength. It is a tacit admission that the absence cannot be properly accounted for, and to stake everything on easy confidence is to run the risk of having the confidence exposed as easy. It would be ludicrously complacent to deduce from this that a concerted popular repudiation of the discourse of the right is inevitable or even likely in the immediate future, or that, even if it were, it would take the radical form. Nevertheless, the triumphant success of the banal cryptograms with which we are concerned and the cultural debasement to which they point are entirely bad enough without help from the assumption that the same audiences would give the same reception to "serious" or decoded expositions of the same sentiments.

Certainly, the success and the banality of *Raiders of the Lost Ark* and *The Wrath of Khan* are such as to challenge the most chastened optimism. *The Wrath of Khan* is again concerned with the theft by the powers of Evil of a technique developed by the "progress" of the powers of Good. The technique here is known, blatantly enough, as Genesis, the code name of a device which is able, by means of an explosion, to transform the molecular structure of dead and inorganic matter so as to produce living matter. The goodies plan to use the Genesis project to turn barren, lifeless, uninhabitable planets into garden paradises of back-projected fertility and abundance (the exceptional tackiness of the special effects is expressive in the most unfortunate way). However, if Genesis is exploded on a planet where life already exists, the result is a holocaust. This is the fell design of the wicked Khan, and the plot turns on the attempt by the crew of the *Enterprise* to prevent his capturing the Genesis mechanism and using it to destroy life as we know it.

The structure and thematic of *The Wrath of Khan* recapitulate those of *Raiders of the Lost Ark*, the key Reaganite nuclear film. "An army which carries the Ark before it is invincible": the ark is the bomb, and the astonishing denouement of Spielberg's movie enacts the most perfect representation of the conditions of American confidence that one could possibly imagine. The Ark of the Covenant is not, of course, a technique. It is the outward and visible form of a moral power which is superior to us all: a power which is not the product of human agency but which acts in our interests and which it is an act of hubris to aspire to control. By the mere expedient of averting our eyes (the last of Harrison Ford's many instructions to Karen Allen), we can be sure that this superhuman power will do everything that we want it to do without any cost to ourselves. Nuclear explosions (and the imagery of firestorm and mushroom cloud is clear enough) can take place within inches of right-minded American citizens who have the *nous* [common sense] to look away in time without the least deleterious effect. Satan, it is true, may have the Wehrmacht—or the Red Army—but God has the ultimate deterrent.

Raiders of the Lost Ark and *The Wrath of Khan* are parables of the redemptive and regenerative properties of the weaponry of annihilation in American hands, or in the hands of a deity whose Providence is exercised on America's behalf. Both parables are realized by means of simple but effective metaphors of disavowal. The importance of Nazism for *Raiders of the Lost Ark* is that it has come to represent something which can be experienced automatically as (a) adversary and (b) Evil, and which, Evil being a universal force, is easily construed as manifestation of the "same kind of thing" which possessed the inhabitants of the Cities of the Plains, from whose well-known fate the finale derives its inspiration. But Nazis can also be "Jerry" and "the Hun" and as such are fair game for pukka escapades. But whether we think of them as comic strip villains or agents of the devil, there can be no doubt either that we ought to be fighting them or that we will win, since the defeat of European fascism and God's revenge on Sodom and Gomorrah are both inscribed in the past. The film draws alternately on both bodies of myth, and its representative triumph is to have found a means of reconciling the discrepant forms of confidence and righteousness they embody and making them available to the present. As a result, the prospect of death with which nuclear war confronts us is dissolved and becomes, indeed as it does in *Star Wars*, a part of the definition of the Other. It is either what happens to the dark-skinned wogs at the hands of the white "Boy's Own" hero or the momentous theater of retribution in which the only performers are the enemies of the Lord. In the end, the message of *Raiders of the Lost Ark* is that if you are American you cannot die, and it is of the essence of this message that it is both a joke—something to do with comics and trick work—and an oracular pronouncement from the Old Testament.

The Wrath of Khan is more adventurous and wide-ranging in its cultural reference. Certainly, Spock is Christ, whose sacrifice redeems the world (and he is duly resurrected for *Star Trek III: The Search for Spock* [1984]), but the authors of *The Wrath of Khan* know that the Messiah is a Christian reinterpretation of classical fertility mythology and make full use of their knowledge in the imagery of the Genesis project. Even more significantly, Spock is associated not only with Christian salvation and the rebirth of Nature effected through the death of the pre-Christian fertility god but also with the kind of redemption undertaken by the counterrevolutionary martyr. He is explicitly identified with Sidney Carton, the hero of *A Tale of Two Cities*, who gives up his life to save an aristocrat and his family from the eighteenth-century equivalent of Bolshevism, and at the beginning of the film, the legendary opening words of Charles Dickens's novel ("It was the best of times, it was the worst of times. . . ") are virtually set up as an epigraph by Captain Kirk. The "spring of Hope" which revives around Spock's coffin in the final shots is defined firmly, if discreetly, in political terms. The case appears at its most fascinating, however, in the use to which *The Wrath of Khan* puts *Moby Dick*. Khan is identified with Ahab to the extent of being given his greatest lines, including his dying anathema ("From Hell's heart I spit at thee!"), and we are shown in passing that Khan's bookshelves boast copies of Dante and Milton, both of whom, in conjunction with Egyptian and Assyrian fertility myths, were crucially influential in the conception of Herman Melville's novel.

It is not enough simply to write this off as vulgar and pretentious, if only because vulgarity and pretentiousness are in fact characteristic of Reaganite entertainment at moments of maximum spiritual uplift and moral earnestness. They are generated in the yawning gulf between the grandeur of the rhetoric which the films pillage and the banality of the uses to which it is put. The banalization of *Moby Dick* in *The Wrath of Khan* is inseparable from a reactionary travesty of it. For Melville's Ahab is not the diabolical, un-American Other but precisely (among other things) a representative of white, Puritan, imperialist civilization. While, for the purposes of *Star Trek*, the whale may be indistinguishable from the starship *Enterprise*, it embodied for Melville everything which the commanders of such vessels, past and present, have sought to destroy, whether in the world or in themselves. It is not the least troubling aspect of this facile film that it manages to transform its culture's classical analysis of the content, functions, and determinants of American Otherness into a paradigm of the very categories which Melville wrote his "wicked book" (the phrase is his) to confute. *The Wrath of Khan* expels Ahab from the culture of its enemy and adopts the white whale as an emblem of the culture's innocence. In so doing, it exemplifies the kind of relation to the richest traditions of American bourgeois culture—a relation at once conservative, parasitic, and profoundly uncomprehending—which is characteristic of contemporary Hollywood as a whole.

Enough has been said to make an equivalently detailed account of other variants of the "nuclear" project unnecessary: the significance of the Death Star in *Star Wars*; of the fire-storms left in the wake of the marauding dragon in *Dragonslayer* (1981, which also inherits from *Raiders of the Lost Ark* the speeded-up cloud effects which now appear to be de rigueur in representation of the final conflict); of the association of General Zod (Terence Stamp) and his cronies with military dictatorship, an attempt to nuke the Eiffel Tower, and the infliction of a scaled-down version of the holocaust on Metropolis in *Superman II*. The nature of these things should, by now, be self-evident. There are three films, however, which seem to demand separate consideration: two of them—*Modern Problems* (1980) and *The Final Countdown* (1981)—because they approach the theme of nuclear power from a position quite distinct from any yet considered, and the third—*An Officer and a Gentleman* (1982)—because, although nei-ther "nuclear anxiety" nor science fiction, it commits itself to a defense of American militarism which announces itself as such with a directness and virulence unprecedented in the period.

Modern Problems is the first nuclear anxiety comedy, as opposed to nuclear satire: clearly, the difference between the contemporary idiom of reassurance and the idiom of "protest," whether or not satiric, adopted by films made in the aftermath of the Bay of Pigs represents a historical shift of momentous importance. The facetious insouciance of the title is suggestive in itself, but the film finds it as difficult as one would expect to be consistently humorous, or consistently anything, on the subject of a man who acquires miraculous powers as a result of having been exposed to radioactive waste. The difficulty is of the interesting kind that expresses itself in an uncontrollable tendency to become Gothic, and by its midway point, *Modern Problems* finds itself with no alternative but to construe its theme in terms of a parody of *The Exorcist*, complete with levitations and vomiting. Given the premise, it is impossible for the film to attribute Max Fielder's (Chevy Chase's) misfortune and the physical deterioration pro-duced by it to a malignant power external to the culture, both because they obviously can't be and because to take the Gothic metaphor seriously would be to preempt the comedy of confi-dence in which the project consists. Given the same premise, however, it is impossible to do anything else without indicating the institutions and technical/political priorities of the society which the comedy is intended to recuperate. The Gothic, the only discourse which would allow the film to talk about the unpleasant constitutional facts which the culture disowns with-out at the same time putting the culture at risk, is not available here, and *Modern Problems* has nothing left to do but parody the convention it cannot use. The grotesque comedy of posses-sion is a specific variant of the Reaganite solipsism: the flattering invitation to recognize the mechanics of what the text is doing is designed to cover the fact that it's doing it at all only goes to demonstrate how completely unviable the Gothic and the comic modes are in relation to this material. The calamitous box office failure of *Modern Problems* indicates that the only way to reassure a 1980s audience about power stations is to ignore them completely.

The interest of *The Final Countdown* is a matter of the tacit reference in its premise—an American nuclear battleship transported by a time warp to the Pacific Ocean on the eve of Pearl Harbor—to the beginning of the one conflict in which nuclear weapons were actually employed. The film does not embarrass itself by actually adverting to this, but it is the function of its theme to accommodate it. *The Final Countdown* argues that even when persons with foreknowledge of a past event find themselves in a situation in which the event has not yet taken place, they cannot prevent its happening. It draws the conclusion that History has an ineluctable necessity of its own which is not susceptible to human control. The proposition that any historical event was in essence inevitable is already mystified, of course, but it is impossible to imagine that anyone in 1983 can have the slightest interest in being told anything of the kind about Pearl Harbor. The function of Pearl Harbor in *The Final Countdown* is to be a type of the recurrent phenomenon of "unprovoked aggression against the United States," and the function of the time warp is to show us that the latter-day American establishment is just as assiduously bent on preventing the outbreak of hostilities as was its predecessor in 1941. However, if other countries will insist on attacking America, it cannot but respond: the real, unspoken subject of the film is Hiroshima, though the fact that the American vessel is a *nuclear* warship makes the existence and the content of the repressed apparent enough. *The Final Countdown* is only interested in the historical necessity of the treacherous "surprise attack" on Pearl Harbor inasmuch as it wishes to assert that such things will always happen in the teeth of all our efforts to keep the peace and that when they do, we will find it historically necessary to nuke the foreign power responsible. It is important that one of the first of the current spate of nuclear films should not only give that kind of gloss to one of the great unmentionable subjects of the Hollywood cinema but also carry the rider that nuclear war, when it comes, will be "over there" in the same painless kind of way.

If *An Officer and a Gentleman* is the most troubling Reaganite fiction, it is not just because it is by far the most loathsome; on this score, indeed, it can have few rivals in the history of Hollywood. It is primarily disturbing because it has become, quite unexpectedly, one of the biggest commercial successes of the period without disguising its sentiments in the least. It is, explicitly, a celebration of the American military which is blatantly concerned to recuperate Vietnam and which goes out of its way to be clear about the connection of these projects to the crudest and most reactionary ideologies of male dominance. The film does not require analysis. The present purpose is sufficiently served by indicating that it exists, and that the nature of its reception is such as to demonstrate that a text which can be defined quite properly as propaganda for the extreme right can become a triumphantly successful commodity without resorting to metaphorical camouflage. There is as yet only one *An Officer and a Gentleman*, but the fact that so large an audience exists for it invites a more pessimistic understanding of the enthusiasm for films whose strategies are in general considerably more circumspect.

Patriarchy

In one sense, at least, *An Officer and a Gentleman* is already fully representative: like the vast majority of contemporary Hollywood films, it is an unabashed apology for patriarchy. The term "patriarchy" is now a controversial one. A number of feminist writers have argued that it has come to be used too loosely, that the idea of paternal rule embodied in it is appropriate only to certain specific historical forms (in the main precapitalist) of the organization of women's oppression, and that the general sense in which patriarchy is synonymous with "masculine dominance" tends dangerously to homogenize and dehistoricize the relations of inequality between the sexes. Whatever one's position on this issue may be, it seems to me that patriarchy is very much the term to describe what gets reaffirmed in Reaganite entertainment: with unremitting insistence and stridency, it is the status and function of the father and their inheritance by the son that are at stake.

One may begin with the father/son cycle in contemporary melodrama: the cycle inaugurated by *Kramer vs. Kramer* (1979) and proceeding through *Ordinary People* (1980), *The Great Santini* (1979), *Tribute* (1980), *Middle-Aged Crazy* (1980), *Author! Author!* (1982), and *Tender Mercies* (1983). *On Golden Pond* (1981) also belongs in this group, though here the "son" becomes a grandson. The films may be subdivided into two categories, according to whether the main impediment to the formation of the patrilineal bond is created by the father or the mother. It is a question of nuance, of course, inasmuch as the exclusion of the mother is always of the essence of the project, but the nuance is an important one: there is a social basis for it.

In *Kramer vs. Kramer* and *Ordinary People*, which are fairly representative of the first group, the patriarchal family is threatened with dissolution by the mother's dereliction of duty. She ought to devote herself to providing love and support for her husband and son, but she fails to do so, and the films move toward the formation of an all-male family from which she is expelled. Both works are antifeminist in the strict sense that they articulate a conservative riposte to the critique of the domestic role developed by the women's movement. They argue, in effect, that if women wish to abandon that role, all well and good: they performed it badly, in any case, and succeeded only in causing general trauma and distress and preventing the emergence of the deep male intimacy which blossoms in their absence. In *Kramer vs. Kramer* and *Ordinary People*, we have a specific variant of the traditional American theme of male comradeship, from which they derive their latent misogynistic homoeroticism. The variant consists in the fact that whereas the traditional male bond came into being in the act of rejecting the home and entering the wilderness, it is consummated here in the conquest of the home and the exclusion of the woman from it. The result is that the woman, the value of whose independence has already been undermined, is denied as well even her traditional sphere of competence and is left, as the endings of both works make very clear, with absolutely nowhere to go.

Naturally, the antifeminism is contained. As respectable liberal works, which are obliged to see every side of every question, *Kramer vs. Kramer* and *Ordinary People* are fully aware of the need to cover their tracks; or, if that way of putting it suggests a degree and a grossness of calculation which works so tasteful could not permit themselves, let us say that they demonstrate the characteristic duplicity of liberal "sympathy." The tastefulness and the sympathy go together. Of course, Joanna Kramer (Meryl Streep) needed to go off and find herself, and of course, Beth Jarrett (Mary Tyler Moore) suffered bitterly from the death of her first son; the "understanding" and "compassion" so lavishly displayed by male characters within the text or implied by the narrative discourse itself are indispensable prerequisites for the moment when the accused is condemned in the most effective way possible—out of her own mouth. The climax of *Kramer vs. Kramer* is the moment at which Meryl Streep admits on the witness stand, in reply to a challenge from the prosecution that she has been a "bad mother," even as Ted

Kramer (Dustin Hoffman) generously signals to her his deepest conviction that she hasn't; Beth is unable to reply to the charges brought against her by her husband, more in sorrow than in anger, in the penultimate scene of *Ordinary People*. It may certainly be argued that the personas and the remarkable performances of the two actresses create a serious disturbance with which neither work is properly equipped to deal, but the nature of the properly dramatic intention is plain enough. Whether we are to understand them as running out on their responsibilities only to discover that they want the best of both worlds (*Kramer vs. Kramer*), or as being constitutionally incapable of affection (*Ordinary People*), women are responsible for the crisis of the patriarchal family, and their punishment is to discover that it can dispense with them. The dear love of comrades between father and son accounts for femininity and makes its official representative superfluous. It has been left to the horror film, however, to exact the sternest kind of retribution; consider the astonishing Gothic vision of an America, and an American boyhood, deprived of the father by the mother's ingratitude which is conjured up in *Cujo*.

The problem addressed in *The Great Santini* is quite different and potentially, given the patriarchal nature of the society, far more contentious. Sublimated homoeroticism has always been available in American culture as a means of dealing with a perceived threat from women, but it is a precondition of this function that homoeroticism should be rigorously dissociated from one of the most obvious determinants of homosexual feeling—that is, a "feminine" identification. (Herman Melville, characteristically, comes nearest to flouting the constraints, and to defining their nature, in that very seriously flawed yet magnificent novel *Pierre, or The Ambiguities*.) Even when the homoerotic sentiment is at its most lachrymose and sentimental, it must retain its connection with the certified offices and professions of maleness (the unction about paternity in *Kramer vs. Kramer* and *Ordinary People* is a relevant fact here): the misogyny endemic in the tradition, whatever else it may do, serves to project on to, and devalue in, women the feminine content of the intensity between the men. In psychoanalytic terms, this reading of the male bond censors the refusal of the male position through an identification with the mother against the father, which is one of the possible determinants of male homosexuality, and attempts to represent emotion which is plainly homosexual as the most incontrovertible evidence of a properly "masculine" ego.

The second group of father/son melodramas is concerned with sons who reject the social/sexual identity represented by their fathers: the stake here is the potential "failure" of the male Oedipus complex. The films proceed to demonstrate that a father who might appear to be unacceptably, and even viciously, exploitative and reactionary is in fact deeply vulnerable and troubled, and that if his family could only grasp that his vile behavior is an inarticulate means of compensating for a sense of alienation and failing powers, it would be immediately obvious that he is lovable and admirable after all. Obviously, the saving of the father is a theme with which melodrama has often been concerned, but these films are remarkable for the absence, or at least the marginalization, of the two major strategies by which salvation has been traditionally achieved: the melodramatic "change of heart," or the replacement of a "bad" father by a "good" one in whom the socially disruptive elements of the former have been eliminated but who continues to exercise the patriarchal function. The emphasis in *Tribute*, *The Great Santini*, and *On Golden Pond* falls on the acceptance of the father as he is. Far from being an oppressive anachronism, he is heroic and grand, the grandeur appearing all the more clearly in that he is condemned to cope with the prospect of imminent dissolution or the feeling that he has outlived his time. These films assume in their premise that the traditional patriarch is no longer a viable norm, and they go on to assert that there is a right reading of the evidence which points to the opposite of the obvious conclusion. The narrative movement traces the making of this reading by the son and ends with the successful transmission of the patriarchal role.

In retrospect from the *Star Wars* trilogy and *An Officer and a Gentleman*, *The Great Santini* emerges as the most significant work in this group, in that the father (played by Robert Duvall) is a leading member of the American armed forces: the values of patriarchy, as the film affirms them, are supremely embodied in the traditions of the imperialist military. *The Great Santini* is carefully set in the early 1960s, before the escalation of the Indochinese war, and we are at liberty to believe, if we wish, that the film has nothing to do with Vietnam: "Bull" Meecham became a hero long ago in the vague, unfocused distance of Korea. Nevertheless, the nature of the film's understanding of its own conjuncture could hardly be plainer. It takes as given the existence of a generation of men who have lived through Vietnam, whether or not as combatants, and for whom the masculine virtues have been pretty thoroughly discredited. Meecham represents both man-as-warrior and a brutal sexual chauvinism; in the family conflict which he generates, his son has identified himself with the position and the claims of his mother. *Home from the Hill* (1960), one thinks, and the thematic material is indeed sufficiently similar to invite detailed comparison; the findings it would yield can be summed up by juxtaposing the endings. Minnelli's film does indeed affirm a "family," but it is a family in which the essential functions of the bourgeois patriarchal family, the transmission of private property and of the gender roles corresponding to masculine dominance, have ceased to exist. It is an ad hoc gathering of the characters for whom patriarchy has no place, and in which both "father" and "son" are illegitimate. *The Great Santini* takes its ending wholesale from *Fort Apache* (1948, though there is nothing here of the effect of irony or disturbance produced by the massive contradiction between Ford's conclusion and everything that has preceded it): after his father's death, the son becomes the father he has fought, acquiring his bearing, language, and gestures, taking up a position of proprietary dominance toward his mother and sisters, and committing himself without reserve to the preservation of everything implied by his father's traditions. In its use of Minnelli and Ford, *The Great Santini* is again exemplary of the reactionary relation to the past that is a characteristic of the period.

The problem of effecting the son's identification with a father who is perceived to be bad is strikingly present in the *Star Wars* trilogy: how on earth, if one's father is Darth Vader, can one wish to inherit the phallus? *Return of the Jedi* neatly solves the problem by conjoining the symbolic repudiation of the mother typical of the one group of father/son melodramas with the redemption of the father typical of the other. I am indebted to Robin Wood for pointing out to me that the image of the Emperor (who plays a significant part in the narrative only in the last film of the trilogy) derives from that of the wicked witch in the Disney cartoon version of *Snow White and the Seven Dwarfs* (1937), and at the climax of *Return of the Jedi*, it is the phallic mother who is called upon to assume and expiate the father's guilt. Conversely, Darth

Vader, monstrous patriarch and leading representative of the ruling class of a brutally oppressive and rapacious imperial regime, turns out to be good after all, and while the irresistible surge of family feeling to which he finally succumbs may suggest the "change of heart," its dominant function is clearly to imply that when the chips are down, the paternal heart is fine just as it is. There is nothing in the least paradoxical in the proposition that the Empire represents both the Soviets and a "bad" American imperialism. On the contrary, if it is the essence of the project to affirm a "good" America by identifying the rebellion with the democratic self-assertion of the oppressed, the ambiguous signification of the Empire is a necessary precondition of the project's coherence and success. Insofar as the Empire is the Soviet Union, it is, of course, irredeemable and must be destroyed. As regards the Emperor, the association of communism with aberrations of gender and crimes against the family is easy in American culture (the various 1950s remakes of *Ninotchka* [1939], in which Bolshevism and the phallic woman consort naturally with each other, are representative). However, because the American father is implicated in the imperial design, he must be saved, and in the final shots of *Return of the Jedi*, Darth Vader joins Yoda and Obi-Wan Kenobe to make up the trinity of ghostly fathers which presides benignly over the formation of Luke Skywalker's superego.

In *The Great Santini* and the *Star Wars* trilogy, then, we have the documents of a cultural moment in which the saving of the father and the saving of imperialism attract each other. To these may be added *An Officer and a Gentleman* and *The Lords of Discipline* (1983), the significance of which is to have dramatized these themes in the context of a modern, postbellum America and in terms, explicitly, of the exemplary moral education of a new generation of male youth. *The Lords of Discipline* does for West Point what *All the President's Men* (1976) did for the American state, taking a symbolic catharsis of unrepresentative monsters as an occasion for demonstrating the viability of the institution as a whole, its virtue guaranteed by the purging of its detritus. In *An Officer and a Gentleman*, no such remedial purgation is necessary, and the film concentrates with relentless single-mindedness on the "making of a man" through trial by combat with, and reconciliation to, a symbolic father who is in this case literally "black," but who, like the hero's real father, cannot himself become a gentleman. His function, like Darth Vader's, is to be an officiant in the rite of passage through which the son attains the phallus, and his status as antagonist is likewise ultimately gestural. In each case, the conflict with the father is merely the prelude to acceptance of him, and the films are able to construct a dramatic "logic" whereby the feelings appropriate to the rejection of the culture are found, once acted through, to conduce to the reproduction of it.

In both *The Lords of Discipline* and *An Officer and a Gentleman*, the hero who becomes the guardian and representative of the honorable imperial code is most emphatically not a member of the privileged upper classes, which are indeed, in the manner of right-wing populism, the source of the corruption which the protagonist of *The Lords of Discipline* is required to purge. In this respect, both films, and *An Officer and a Gentleman* in particular, can be associated with the theme of male success and self-advancement within the capitalist system of which it has been the peculiar destiny of Sylvester Stallone to be the poet laureate, in the *Rocky* films and *Staying Alive* (1983). In spite of the recession, opportunities still exist in the 1980s for a man with balls: Stallone's discourse is a simple one, but the affirmation of stardom and exceptional prowess which is implicit in it has at least the virtue of demonstrating the quite extraordinary limits within which such a discourse is now compelled to operate. Part of the importance of recent Scorsese—*Raging Bull* (1980) and *King of Comedy* (1983)—consists in the films' acute critical interrogation of this whole set of themes.

If we are to ask what place is left for women in the new patriarchy, there can be no better answer than that provided by *Tender Mercies*. The hero of Bruce Beresford's film is another fallen patriarch, a superannuated country-and-western composer who is helped by his new wife to regain his creative powers and thus his former eminence, and who expresses his gratitude to her by writing a ballad with the touching refrain, "If you hold the ladder, baby, I'll climb to the top." This is particularly bald, but it is fully representative. Women who do not hold the ladder, or who try to shake it, or even climb up it themselves, are subjected to merciless ritual punishment, the most virulent and hysterical examples of which are to be found in *An Officer and a Gentleman* and *Staying Alive*. In both works, the bad woman is distinguished from the good woman, the hero's "girl," by virtue of a self-assertive impulse which she shares with the hero. In the former, this impulse leads her to cause the suicide of the nicest, most sensitive man in the film with the exception of the hero, who is left alive to call his friend's destroyer "a cunt." The equivalent figure in *Staying Alive* not only regards herself and her career as being more important than Tony Manero (John Travolta) but also makes the mistake of trying to treat him as a sex object, thus obliging him to hurl her bodily off the stage in the big climactic number in which he becomes a star, before pulling her back on again in a gesture supremely expressive of the extent of his own physical powers. The point is, if anything, even clearer in *Flashdance* (1983), with which *Staying Alive* invites comparison and which sets out, pathetically, to take note of the existence of sexual politics: a woman may work in a steel mill and even become a star, but only if she falls in love too.

What "holding the ladder" means in psychoanalytic terms appears in the fact that while Princess Leia, as Luke's sister, is supposed to have the Force, she cannot possibly have the phallus or internalize the father. The *Star Wars* trilogy shows not the slightest interest in the ambivalence of the Force as it pertains to her, and there is no question of her paternity becoming a dramatic issue. As a result, her having the Force at all, a role in the odd battle apart, begins to seem increasingly inconsequent: it is a fact in the plot, when the plot needs it, but it makes no contact at all with the trilogy's thematic, and it does not prevent Leia's functioning primarily as someone who will have to be married.

It is *E.T.*, however, which remains the ultimate Reaganite movie about patriarchy, and there is more to *E.T.* than either the film itself or the usual proliferation of video games, jigsaw puzzles, T-shirts, candy, Halloween masks, cuddly toys, and memorial literature. When *E.T.* appeared, Andrew Sarris remarked cryptically that the film had "garnered *Gone with the Wind* grosses in tandem with *Citizen Kane* reviews." There is little to be said about the grosses, but the reviews are another matter, and it is to them that I now turn.

E.T., Spielberg, and the Critics

The range of titles that turn up in individual lists is probably greater than ever. But when the votes are totted up, it appears that astonishingly little has changed . . .

All the same, there are undoubted pointers, such as a vote for Hitchcock, which reflects the hard work of the Hitchcock critical industry in the last two decades.
—Adair, "Critical Faculty"

[Ian Cameron] went on: "We know we can't have a *L'Avventura* or an *A Bout de souffle* under the present system. We are much more disturbed by the fact that we are not getting equivalents for *Psycho, Elmer Gantry* and *Written on the Wind*." Who knows, *Movie* may yet endorse the Campari School of British film-making—Alan Parker, Ridley Scott, Hugh Hudson.
—Adair, "Critical Faculty"

Students of the process by which tastes are formed could do worse than ponder those sentences, and should they persist in the hope that there is a reading of the phrase "the Hitchcock critical industry" apart from the obvious one, they might recall that Adair (for whom *Vertigo* [1958] is also one of the ten greats—obviously an equal of *Limelight* [1952] and *Le Testament d'Orphée* [1960]) believes that Alan Parker and Ridley Scott belong to a "school" and that *Midnight Express* (1978) meets *Movie*'s demands for a British equivalent of *Psycho*. "Astonishingly little has changed," and the little that has provides the evidence. If the nature of the greatness of *Vertigo*, and of the conditions for it, were at all generally recognized, could the following have appeared in the pages of "the best film magazine in the world" (I quote the encomium on the back cover of the same issue) on the occasion of *Sight and Sound's* fiftieth anniversary?

The sad truth was that the British auteurists had imported the glorious politique duty-free, so to speak, omitting to pay their dues to film history. What in Paris had been primarily a manoeuvre to revitalise a moribund national cinema was jellified into a dewy-eyed reactionary nostalgia for Hollywood's battery farm—(on Richard Fleischer's *Barabbas*, a pseudo-Biblical blockbuster: "Perhaps Fleischer had too much freedom . . .")—which, if you believed them, was alone capable of laying boxfuls of golden eggs, stamped with Leo the Lion. (Adair, "Critical," 253)

The writer who has come to enjoy this kind of fluency has paid far more than his dues to film history (as *Sight and Sound* understands it) and is less interested than he would have us suppose in refuting the auteur theory. If only the critics of the early *Movie* could have developed a materialist account of the cultural situation in which the theory was produced, they might have perceived, as Adair now perceives, that the revaluation of the Hollywood cinema was never at issue at all! Whatever was said about "Hitchcock and Hawks" in the course of an occasional polemic with "Delannoy and Decoin" had no more than an occasional significance, and while the revolution had its "excesses" as revolutions will, we are not to suppose that the judgment of the Hollywood cinema by the future directors of the New Wave differed in any essential respect from Adair's judgment of it. ("Critical," 252) No doubt a revolution was necessary, the French establishment being what it is, but if anyone had bothered to ask them at the time, Jean-Luc Godard and Jacques Rivette would have agreed that the undertaking to follow through from it on British soil—and in defiance of the British customs—was "reactionary." For the right reader (the reader to whom Adair's attitude to *Barabbas* [1962] comes naturally), it will no more be necessary to inquire how it was that the "battery farm" produced *Vertigo* than it will be to suspect that thirty years ago, when the film came out, Adair would have been unable to distinguish it from a hundred other products of the same farm. Such a reader (an Adair, if you like—he is very much his own audience) will find a high valuation of *Vertigo* perfectly compatible with self-promotion at the expense of the writers whose work made the judgment available, and will pass without difficulty from this:

> But then, like most of the cinephilic race, the *Movie* brats had a producer's cast of mind. Ideas were anathema to them. A mere idea would have smudged the smooth transparent sheen of so idiotically perfect an artefact as *The Four Horsemen of the Apocalypse*. Only when they were fashioned out of a hundred per cent genuine sow's ear, not out of silk, was the magazine interested in silk purses. (Minnelli, of course, could make a Gucci bag out of a sow's ear, and usually did.) (Adair, "Critical," 252–53)

to this:

> However . . . like the ineffable in general, it [*E.T.*] defies criticism. No, let me rephrase that: *E.T.* can of course be criticized, indeed it all but invites an unholy alliance of impressionistic, genre, sociological, auteurist and structuralist analyses. Except that, as we are dealing with a film to which one shamelessly capitulates, or does not, which draws laughter and tears as "naturally" as hot and cold water can be drawn from the corresponding taps, or does not, subjecting it to a close analysis would be like performing upon it the same operation as threatens E.T. himself. (Adair, "E.T.cetera," 63)

It would come as a surprise to Adair if he were told that one of the things to be said about *E.T.* is that it is the exemplary product of a state of affairs which is inimical to the making of a *Vertigo*, and that consequently the critic who admires, or thinks he admires, Hitchcock's film has his obligations to fulfill. But then it is possible for the critic to cultivate a sense of obligation which is incompatible with the writing of criticism, and when he has done so he will be surprised to be reminded of any of the rudiments of critical practices. The critic's duty, as Adair understands it, is most congenially realized in the refusal to be a critic. There are ideas in the world ("impressionistic, genre, sociological . . ."—the list is nothing if not exhaustive), though to pronounce an anathema on them is not quite the thing, unfortunately, and one "would have to have got into training a long time ago" in order to put them to use oneself. (Adair, "Critical," 256) In any case, the critic can do without them, for he is only called upon to reproduce a certain tone whose function is to assert, for himself and the right reader, a sense of effortless superiority which demands no more than the adoption of the tone to be enjoyed and which exempts one from the responsibility for relevant thought. The tone implies a taste and a set of values, and no more needs to be said about them than that they come ready-made and that they are to that extent anti-critical. Adair does not know that a contradiction is involved in placing *Vertigo* (and F. W. Murnau's *Sunrise* [1927]) on one's ten-best list and referring to Hollywood as a "battery farm," and he could not explain what an "idiotically perfect artefact" is if the question were put to him: given the tone, the question doesn't arise. And as an exemplary representative of the tradition he perpetuates, Adair is capable of absorbing the judgment that *Vertigo* is great, but he remains wholly unconscious of the grounds for it. The critic who is mindful of the danger of falling into debt to film history has one or two more names to cope with nowadays than he once did. The addition of the names makes no essential difference: the principles of evaluation according to which the names were once excluded remain intact, but the "critical faculty" has been sufficiently refreshed to feel secure in its indictment of the inertia of others.

"And the prize item of bad news is that, the odd exception apart, film reviewing in Britain has hardly budged in over three decades." (Adair, "Critical,"16) The right reader will feel as little embarrassment in assenting to that as Adair felt in writing it, in spite of what he goes on to say about every significant development in film studies during the same period—with such betraying equivocation. It is, indeed, the essence of the deplorable and too-familiar case that Adair should feel entitled to chastise his colleagues in Fleet Street for their "amateurism"—he adjures them to become critics "in the real sense of the word" ("Critical," 250)—and to rebuke Lindsay Anderson for his "aversion to any critical method requiring more than individual taste and discernment." ("Critical," 256) Even Adair can hardly suppose that the stagnation of British film reviewing and the intransigence of *l'homme sensuel moyen* are to be explained by a failure to perceive that Minnelli is a manufacturer of Gucci bags, or by anyone's needing to be told that it is "so horribly unfair" to be expected to have read Jacques Lacan. We may assume that Adair has found a means of satisfying himself that he and the "Fleet Street odd-job man" belong in a different category, and that his own attitude to structuralism and to Hollywood are profoundly different from that advanced by Lindsay Anderson in his notorious article. For the rest of us it will continue to seem that he is a symptom of the malady he purports to diagnose, and that he is primarily engaged in persuading his readership that facetious irony is sufficient in itself to constitute a point of view. If Adair is to be distinguished from the average reviewer in the "quality" press, it is only by virtue of the fact that the latter, having a less specialized audience, is naturally not called upon to persuade the right reader that his/her judgments about the cinema are more acute than those of the average reader of *The Sunday Times* or that the understanding of the history of film criticism that s/he may be presumed to have is correct. It is one of the curses of specialization that we are "supposed to have had the time," and even the inclination, to do so much more than the laity. Adair's purpose in the world seems to teach us to rejoice in the spirit of expertise without the least intellectual exertion.

The case is a familiar one. Given the fact that *Movie* figures largely among Adair's targets, there is an easy explanation to hand, for those who need it, of the motive which leads one to draw attention to the case again. I should insist, then, that I am only interested in what Adair has written to the extent that as it displays a kind of unconsciousness about "film history" and what is of value in it, this entails a radical irresponsibility in the assessment of the present. The critic who fails to see the point of saying what ought to be said about *E. T.* will not see the point of that last sentence. However, if one takes it to be part of the business of the critic to try to be particularly clear about what a given artifact is and does, and about the relation it adopts to the prevailing tendencies of a society to which a number of relations is possible, then one can only feel that the underwriting of the art of Steven Spielberg by fashionable metropolitan taste on both sides of the Atlantic is irresponsible in the worst kind of way. The significance of Adair's reflections on the critical faculty is that they exhibit with extravagant clarity the values and priorities of the tradition of thinking about the cinema which is implicit in the review of *E.T.* The review, it might be said, is where that tradition gets us—comment enough on a tradition in which an incapacity for discrimination has become a constituent of urbane good form.

The incapacity presents itself starkly in Adair's quite unjustified confidence that he knows the "kind of thing" that *E.T.* is and that he is responding appropriately for the kind. For the critic who affiliates to the same tradition, this is what the act of reading amounts to in any case: one assigns the text to its category and applies the learned criteria. By some freak of chance, the category which Adair brings to the Hollywood cinema happens to coincide with the commodity form of the films: Hollywood movies appear as entertainment and Adair, unless he receives an alternative signal from the tradition—to the effect that *Vertigo*, say, though not *Psycho*, is now "art"—proceeds dutifully to tell us that that is exactly what they are. He has no means whatever of interrogating the category or of making any other distinctions within it than those traditionally allowed for (the list, on page 254, of the sanctioned representatives of such High Seriousness as is to be found in America is numbingly conventional). So when Adair announces that "no purpose could possibly be served by analyzing *E.T.*," he is doing what has always been done. It is worth taking time to object in order to show that the critic who sees fit to turn himself into another of the numerous publicity agencies which are busily engaged in selling the film in that way is promoting a complacent and culpable blindness to the fact that the film represents. An American cinema of which *E.T.* is characteristic prohibits that active, critical engagement with cultural value, for which Hollywood has been, in the past, consistently remarkable, and which is one of the prerequisites of value in art. To ignore this is to abrogate the critic's function of getting recognition for the work in which such value is most notably to be found. It is already sufficiently unseemly in Adair, who knows no more of such a function than is to be derived from a querulous hostility to its exercise by others, to exploit the historical limits of early auteur theory so as to question the integrity and belittle the decisive, creative role of writers exemplary in their commitment to the task of contesting inertly received ideas of value. But rather more is at sake, in the present instance, than the apparatchik's translation of discourses which displease the apparatus. It is rather more than unseemly to pass off an unthinking complicity with the most reactionary tendencies in contemporary cinema and contemporary society as the last result of judicious acumen and percipience. One ought to be able to say more about *E.T.* than it is willing to say about itself, and if one persists obediently to being "charmed," the interests one serves are not those of criticism or of the cinema.

Chris Auty, whose article on "the complete Spielberg" appeared in the issue of *Sight and Sound* preceding the one containing Adair's indolent philippic, is not to be suspected of harboring a similar attitude to Hollywood: he is indeed associated, as the film editor of *City Limits*, with a lamentable indulgence of American culture which incites Adair to a particularly pungent display of podsnappery. It is fitting, nevertheless, that the two articles should share the one occasion. Here is Auty on *E.T.*: "For this 'small film' about life 'after school,' with its play of childhood memory, film fantasy and breathless wish-fulfilment, has restored cinema to its right place—the wellspring of dreams." (279) Adair prefers the phrase "populist escapism" to "the wellspring of dreams," but if solemnity came to him as readily as flippancy, he would have written the same thing. Auty makes a great deal of play with the concept, or the word, *populism* himself, and while he seems to regard it favorably, he is never any clearer about what he means by it than he is here, countering the charge that Spielberg's work is tantamount to "some operation of mass seduction, verging on deception":

> Part of the problem is a gap between American and European conceptions of "the masses." The latter, in which a Marxist notion of intellectual leadership still plays an important part, is the more apparently political. The former, fuelled by a kind of Jeffersonian liberalism, appears both bland and individualistic by comparison, apolitical . . . But isn't it unreasonable to accuse Spielberg in particular of a general tendency within American culture? And would we really prefer the lip-chewing, self-consciously liberal politics of a Martin Ritt, Sydney Pollack or Sidney Lumet? (276–77)

What does this mean? If the "conception of the masses" in Spielberg's work reflects a "general tendency within American culture" which is open to substantial criticisms, then we have grounds for making substantial criticisms of Spielberg's work, and to find fault with Spielberg "in particular" is palpably irrelevant. If the criticisms are sound, they are not affected one way or the other by our being able to point to other works and other tendencies which are open to different kinds of criticism—and the proposition that Lumet is the, or an, alternative to Spielberg is gratuitous and absurd. (Lumet's self-consciously liberal politics are of the kind which every way incline, according to the prevailing current, and *The Verdict* [1982] is merely *Star Wars* for grown-ups.) I am not clear, in any case, as to what the two "conceptions of the masses" are supposed to be. Though I would claim to be a Marxist, it surprises me to learn that there is a "European conception" which "still" owes a debt to Marxism. It surprises me still more that my dislike of Spielberg's work can be attributed to any conviction that the masses require (or ought to give?—the confusion of the syntax betrays the confusion of the alleged thought) "intellectual leadership" which Spielberg is failing to provide or which the masses, because of their "seduction," can no longer offer. "Where does 'true' knowledge reside, after all?" Auty rhetorically asks by way of dealing with those who "damn populism generally." (276) The whereabouts of true knowledge need not concern us, but it is still possible to be a little more precise than Auty is in defining the issues involved in an account of Steven Spielberg.

There is no need whatsoever to assume that Spielberg (or George Lucas) is engaged in "mass deception," and there is correspondingly no need to work out a respectable version of the features of his work which that deceptive formula seeks to grasp by invoking either "populism" or Spielberg's "sincerity." It is not only reasonable but obligatory to relate Spielberg to "a general tendency within American culture," but to call it populist and mention Capra can only promote confusion, which is worse confounded if one goes on to argue, as Auty seems to, that populism and Jeffersonian liberalism are the same thing. There is in fact nothing that is properly to be described as populist in Spielberg's work. While he may well imagine that he admires Capra and that he will make his *It's a Wonderful Life* some day, this is hardly evidence of an affinity. It tells us only that he misreads Capra in ways which are deducible from his own films, and even when he aspires to reproduce what he takes to be the Capra idiom (as he clearly does in his episode of *Twilight Zone: The Movie*), he merely succeeds in demonstrating that however "intensely" he feels about it, he actually understands it as a specialized entertainment formula which conduces to agreeable emotions. For Spielberg, the emotions are an end in themselves: he likes to feel them and so he works them up. They are thus very different from Capra's, in whose greatest work the profoundest kind of commitment to populist feeling is inseparable from the undertaking to explore its conditions and its limits. But for Auty, as for Spielberg, there is "Capra and Spielberg," and it is no doubt to the difficulty of contriving a formula for populism capable of accounting for both directors that we are indebted for "the wellspring of dreams" and the role that it plays in Auty's article.

Spielberg has been accused of being "a mechanic triggering off responses from some automated audience," but criticism can demonstrate that he is deeply and sensitively in touch with the collective (for the purposes of the argument, the populist) unconscious:

> On more recent productions, despite his complete freedom now to work as he wishes, the director has surrounded himself with a close-knit group of collaborators and the writing has virtually become a collective process. It is as though the older, essentially private ground rules of "writing" a film are being replaced by shared dreams, by "visualization," by a creative community which deliberately anticipates the collective dream-work of the eventual audience. But this can hardly be called mechanical. (Auty, 276)

Perhaps not, but then the question is wrongly posed. Auty assumes that Spielberg's films must be either cynically manipulative of their audience or at one with it in the "shared dream," and that, if they can be shown to be the latter, there is nothing more that need be said in defense of them. He does not ask what the "collective dream work" is, or where it comes from, or what is at stake in a film's "anticipating" it. It is simply there—and there, simply, is Steven Spielberg, acting in good faith with respect to it.

Auty is propelled toward this remarkable conclusion by his assumption that because Spielberg's films are "hugely popular," there is something invidious in finding fault with them: to criticize the films is somehow to slight or patronize the "masses" who enjoy them. The assumption is grotesquely false, and Auty is wholly mistaken if he believes that the middle-class intellectual is performing a service for the masses by persuading him/herself that they have an essential collective dream or mind of which a Spielberg is representative. Does it follow from the huge popularity of *The Sun* and the *Daily Express* that their editors, too, have premonitory intimations of the content of the collective psyche, and that left-wing thinkers everywhere must find some means of approving of the tabloid press? The popular taste for Spielberg's films has been historically formed in conditions, and by forces, which include Spielberg's films. If the films "anticipate the collective dream work," they do so in a formative way. It is the business of the critic to define what that way is, and to come to an understanding of its relation to those other conditions and forces which make up the cultural situation of the films. If the critic, having undertaken this business, concludes that the films have the effect of perpetuating and authenticating, as "entertainment," an inert, uncritical, and mystified understanding of that situation, to which the films refer in addressing their audience, then s/he ought to say so. It should not come as a very great surprise that capitalism is able to construct, as the general interest, desires and tastes and attitudes which actually conflict with the general interest, and to recoup a longing for change and transformation in the interests of the status quo. Capitalism has always done this, and it will continue to do so for as long as it exists.

It does not follow, however, that because the critic has developed an account of what Spielberg's films are doing which the majority, perhaps, of those who enjoy the films have not, that s/he is thereby committed to a sense, either complacent or guilty, of personal superiority and to a view of the masses as the drugged and stupid victims of deception and imposture. S/he is not obliged either, in a desperate attempt to think well of popular taste, to propound a view of the films as the products of egalitarian communal creativity, or to institute a search for definitions of the discourses of late capitalism which will allow us to think of them as a mere sympathetic witness to feelings that the masses already have. The desires and aspirations to which the fact of Spielberg's popularity attests have potential forms and tendencies other than those to which the films reduce them. When Auty tells us that Spielberg is the disinterested servant of a military communal vision, he is merely, in his own way, collaborating in the mystification. He does so unconsciously, of course, encouraged by his critical method, which is the simplest kind of auteurism and deprives the films of the most elementary cultural context, cinematic and other. There is Spielberg's work and there is the liking for it, but there is no better explanation of the relation between them than that the films deceive the audience or the audience dreams the films, with the artist, in both cases, as intermediary. The one hypothesis is worth about as much as the other, as we may see very clearly if we return the artist, the films, and the audience to the social present that they have in common. The social present, and the intervention in it of *Raiders of the Lost Ark*, are blatantly what they are, and the concern for the masses is seriously defective that contrives (the word seems appropriate) to believe otherwise.

Auty is mistaken, too, in his conviction that an appeal to Spielberg's "sincerity" constitutes a proper critical argument, and that the sincerity can be established by quoting the director to the effect that "everything I do is for an emotional reason [and] not really for a mechanical reason at all." (276) The opposition between an "emotional" and a "mechanical" reason is itself false: there is no pure calculation which exists independently of feeling, and no emotion which does not embody an attitude. We are concerned, or ought to be, with the quality of the "emotional reason," and therefore with the content of the attitudes expressed in it, and the only evidence for them is the text. The mere assertion that a reason is emotional is not a guarantee of its authenticity: all reasons are. If the emotion is meretricious, the fact that it is deeply felt demonstrates something quite different from sincerity. The question is not "Does he believe it?" but "What, on the evidence of the work, does 'believing in it' entail? In what does this sincerity consist, and what are its conditions?" The answers to these questions will determine the value that we are to ascribe to the sincerity; if the questions are put to Spielberg and his films, the answers we get seem to me to be very unfavorable. There is, perhaps, no real reason to doubt that Spielberg is, in Auty's sense, "sincere," but even then there is something equivocal about the sincerity which can describe the dream it shares with the audience like this:

> [*Raiders of the Lost Ark*] is like popcorn, it doesn't fill you up and it's easy to digest and it melts in your mouth and it's the kind of thing that you can just go back and chow down over and over again. It's a rather superficial story of heroics and deeds and great last-minute saves; but it puts people in the same place that made me want to make movies as a child, which is wanting to enthrall, entertain, take people out of their seats to get them involved—through showmanship—in a kind of dialogue with the picture you've made. I love making movies like that. I mean, I'd really still like to do my *Annie Hall*, but I love making films that are stimulus-response, stimulus-response. Anyway, I haven't met my Annie Hall. (McCarthy, 58)

No one could venture to commit himself to sentiments like this in public who was not protected by a very obdurate sincerity. Pressed to distinguish between Spielberg and Lucas, one might say that Spielberg wishes to eat the popcorn as well as make money out of it and that he still aspires, in his innocent way, to "be an artist," should the occasion present itself. Yet the attitude to the audience is, at the same time, obviously cynical, and it is the essence of Spielberg's case that the cynicism and the sincerity consort quite naturally with each other—that they become, that is, a third thing which is neither simply the one nor simply the other. "You see, George and I have fun with our films. We don't take them as seriously [as Scorsese does his]. And I think that our movies are about things that we think will appeal to other people, not just to ourselves. We think of ourselves first, but in the next breath we're talking about the audience and what works and what doesn't." (Sragow, 116–17)

We may think we can imagine Howard Hawks talking like this, but a moment's reflection is enough to reveal that we can't: Hawks could never have said that he didn't take his work seriously, or made that kind of distinction between films that appeal "just" to oneself and films that appeal to "other people," or compared any of his movies to popcorn. It is a condition of Hawks's representative strength that he worked under conditions (in the largest sense) in which his understanding of himself as an entertainer with an audience to entertain was so completely and reliably given, and so little distinguishable from what he most wanted to do, that the question of this sort of attitude to the spectator did not arise. Spielberg's is the attitude of someone who thinks of the audience not as being simply there, for this as for other films, but as a collection of consumers to whom a specific commodity must be sold and in relation to whom, therefore, it is essential to know "what works and what doesn't." Spielberg may well think of himself (or wish to think of himself) as being on an equal footing with a spectator who enjoys the same fantasies, and some such form of fellow feeling with the consumer is, and always has been, available to anyone involved in commodity production. Sincerely held or not, the feeling is, in Spielberg's case, false, and its falseness is deducible from the films and their habitual emotional opportunism. It is difficult to think of oneself as a popcorn salesman who will one day make his *Annie Hall* (1977) (or—the same kind of thing—his *It's a Wonderful Life*) while continuing to enjoy the popcorn in the same way that the purchaser does, and Spielberg's "sincerity" comes down, on the one hand, to his having cultivated an unawareness of the difficulty, and on the other, to his having felt the need to do so. He isn't out there in the audience being thrilled as he was as a boy, but he wants to be, and he has contrived to become unconscious of why he can't. This sincerity is a defect of intelligence—a refusal of it. Steven Spielberg is actually a grown-up man making large amounts of money out of "rather superficial stories of heroics and deeds and great last-minute saves," but he sincerely believes that he is on the edge of his seat with the rest of us, and his simplemindedness is the sincere expression of a genuine bent: he really wishes that adult life didn't make a difference—though no doubt the money helps.

Spielberg's unconsciousness is, in its way (it has much in common with Auty's), an impressive achievement: there is so much of it, and it extends to so many subjects. "Francis [Coppola] lives in a world of his own, George lives in a galaxy far, far away but close to human audiences, and I'm an independent moviemaker working within the Hollywood establishment." And "Michael [Cimino] has a showman inside that doesn't know where he's at yet . . . And once he gets himself a story that's accessible to the masses, he's gonna be hard to stop." And "I think it's bullshit when people say the success of *Raiders* precludes the success of *Diner* (1982). I think a success like *Raiders* feeds the pocketbook that's gonna finance *Diner*. You can't have a *Diner* without *Raiders*. But you can't have good movies without *Diner*. So, we need each other. Should we all join hands and sing, 'I'd like to buy the world a Coke'? (Laughs)." (Sragow, 117)

The significance of the last sentence is that it shows us the point where sincerity stops: confronted by the economic base, even Steven Spielberg isn't quite convinced by it and is obliged to resort to his disarming lack of front to make up. The transition is barely visible, and Spielberg negotiates it with such facility because sincerity is already for him what Jonathan Swift once called the capacity to be "well deceived" (though Spielberg's ingenuousness is too equivocal for one to rest happy in thinking of him as a fool among knaves). He has managed to work out, at any rate, an account of modern Hollywood, and of his own position within it, which is as culpably foolish as it must be, from his point of view, congenial—which provides, indeed, the order of satisfaction that we associate with the films. It is impossible to believe that he doesn't mean it—no one couldn't who was prepared to say it—and it provides ground for the most depressing speculation about the kind of "experienced parent" (his own phrase) that Spielberg will become when he and his friends have realized their professed ambition of "doing to the film industry what Irving Thalberg did to it fifty years ago." (Sragow, 115) Opinions will differ as to the value of what Irving Thalberg did for Hollywood, but it can hardly be doubted that whatever Spielberg does will turn out, conditions having changed so completely, to be rather different. His belief that the Hollywood of fifty years ago could be, or ought to be, revived is continuous with his belief that the fifty years don't matter: the material social conditions, and effects, of his own practice are a closed book to him. With his lack of front to help him, he has actually succeeded in convincing himself that the existence of *Raiders of the Lost Ark* makes it easier to produce "good movies," and that *Diner* is a good movie, and that the "inaccessibility" of *Heaven's Gate* (no one so sincere could find irony in the word) has nothing to do with the historical circumstances in which large numbers of people, including many calling themselves critics, find "the magical essence of storytelling in the cinema" the work of Steven Spielberg.

The unconsciousness about what the Hollywood of Industrial Light and Magic is goes, inevitably, with a total ignorance of what Hollywood was in its heyday. "I essentially pulled from the air the same sense of popcorn pleasure that Ford, Curtiz, Hawks, King Vidor and even C. B. DeMille had available to them. We drank from the same well. It's always been there for anybody who wants to dip a ladle." It is Spielberg's ability to say and mean this which allows him to feel that he is seriously interested in the Hollywood of the past: his sense of value and his sense of history go together. The "even" in "even Cecil B. DeMille" is unmistakably, in Auty's sense, "sincere," and it has the effect of convincing us that the idea of sincerity ought to be dissociated from the art of Steven Spielberg, who is not just pretending that he can't distinguish *She Wore a Yellow Ribbon* (1949) from *North West Mounted Police* (1940)—or *Raiders of the Lost Ark*. And it is all too appallingly clear that Auty can't distinguish either, though, being a critic and an intellectual, he likes to think of the great tradition as the great tradition and sees that the well contains dreams rather than popcorn. We know already that Spielberg's populism "recalls" Capra's, but it is equally the case that his storyboarding is, like Hitchcock's, an "aesthetic virtue." (Auty, 276) While Auty never tells us what an "aesthetic virtue" is, or could conceivably be, he does go on to say that *Jaws* is a "Hawksian celebration of belated male courage," that *Close Encounters of the Third Kind* reminds him of the spirit of Jean Vigo's *Zero de Conduite* (1933), and that *E.T.* is "a kind of cinematic equivalent of Blake's 'Songs of Innocence.'" (278–89)

These ludicrous judgments, by which one would be merely amused if less were at stake, are the perfect complement to Adair's. Auty, of course, "likes" Hollywood and Adair doesn't, but the difference is, in this form, hardly worth having, and the incapacity for discrimination is the same. It is also, where Spielberg is concerned, fashionable and representative—which is why one has to deal with it. I am indebted for the title of this article to Pauline Kael's announcement in the *New Yorker* that "*E.T.* is a bliss-out" ("Pure," 347), but for someone writing in England there seems to be greater point in drawing attention to the domestic equivalent of the same phenomenon. That there is less excuse for them is part of the point. We have it, after all, on Adair's authority that we are to talk about *E.T.* if we wish, and the discourses which allow us to do so ("impressionistic, genre, sociological . . . ") are present in the culture in a way which they're not in New York. Anyone who is capable of learning what there is to be learned from the development of film studies in the last twenty years, and of putting the lessons to intelligent use, ought to see the significance of Spielberg at once (he's hardly complex)—ought too, one feels, to grasp the importance of doing everything that criticism can do to define and contest what Spielberg represents. The tendencies he embodies, if persisted in, would make a valuable popular cinema in America impossible today. Such a cinema would be necessarily very different, and consciously different, from the popular cinema that did exist, the greatness of which is inseparable from the presence of enabling constraints which no longer survive in that form; the strategies of a Sirk or a Minnelli are historically specific, and their value derives from their historical relevance; their significance *now* consists in this fact. If Hollywood of that period continues to be exemplary, it is not because it provides models which ought to be imitated but because it shows us what relevance in the use of convention looks like. The use I have in mind is that which dramatizes, and in so doing makes present, the real cultural contradictions to which convention refers, and in a cinema of which Spielberg is characteristic this can't take place—the conditions are hostile to it. The critic, obviously, cannot change these conditions, but because s/he aims to distinguish between work which is valuable and work which is not, s/he is committed to emphatic clarity on the subject of what the conditions entail—that is, to resistance to them. S/he is otherwise condemned to help to reproduce them. The writing up of Steven Spielberg as an artist is, under the circumstances, a particularly serious mistake (it would be a mistake at any time), and while Auty is, like Spielberg, patently sincere, his sincerity seems likewise to be conditioned by his failure to perceive what he is actually doing. This may be innocence, but it isn't Blake's, and critical writing which is in any way characterized by it has its small contribution to make to the hegemony and persistence of an idiom whose legacy may prove even more disastrous than one can yet suspect.

E.T., Utopia, and the Gothic

In the course of his article, Auty quotes from one of Spielberg's interviews a passage which is in fact, for all the actual use of it, of great critical interest.

> It all begins on Sunday—you take the car to be washed. You have to drive but it's only a block away. And as the car's being washed you go next door with the kids and buy them ice-cream at the Dairy Queen and then you have lunch at the plastic McDonald's with seven zillion hamburgers sold. And then you go off to the games room and you play the quarter games . . . And by that time your car's all dry and ready to go . . . and you drive to the Magic Mountain amusement park and you spend the day there eating junk food. Afterward you drive home, stopping at all the red lights, and the wife is waiting with the dinner on . . . and you sit down and turn on the TV set, which has become the reality as opposed to the fantasy this man has lived with that entire day. And you watch the primetime, which is pabulum and nothing more than watching a night light. And you see the news at the end of that, which you don't want to listen to because it doesn't conform to the reality you've just been through primetime with. And at the end of all that you go to sleep and dream about making enough money to support weekend America. (Auty, 277)

Here, as Spielberg clearly knows from the inside, we have a representative American petit bourgeois life. The tone suggests a critical intention which is yet neither patronizing nor complacent. If we were to go straight from these remarks to the films, we might be forgiven for anticipating something of the complex poise, at once unrelentingly astringent and compassionate, of Sirk's melodrama. Steven Spielberg, as it turns out, is very unlike Douglas Sirk, but it is obviously crucial that Spielberg recognizes, having lived in it, that there is something appallingly wrong with "weekend America" and that life lived in this way is banal and deforming. It may be assumed that the millions who live the same kind of life have much the same feeling about it: it is both absolutely normal and utterly unsatisfying. Because it *is* normal, there is not much that can be done with the dissatisfaction. There it is, a part of experience—sufficiently present to make experience, for the most part, empty, but not present in such a way as to generate the impersonal perspective in which experience could be seen as anything other than natural or inevitable. The cultural resonance of Spielberg's work is a matter of its expressing so acutely the kind of distance from the conditions of everyday middle-class life which that life can be imagined in general to promote in those who have to get through it. It does so at a moment when "living" in this way is again being proclaimed as ideal and exemplary.

The "transcendence" Spielberg offers is exactly what one would expect of a sensibility so conditioned and so formed: it is about as much really transcendent as the "distance" or alienation it aims to satisfy is effectively critical. Its nature can be indicated by a comparison with Gustave Flaubert (though I will add that, much as I dislike Flaubert's work, it would not occur to me to value the two artists at the same rate). Both Spielberg and Flaubert are the products of a specific petit bourgeois culture which they feel to be stupid, anodyne, and oppressive, and both of them are motivated, in their different ways, by the impulse to transcend it. Flaubert's asserts itself in his cultivation of his "art"—art which defines his Olympian externality to the society he despises, and the internal tension of his most interesting work arises from his intense involvement, nonetheless, with protagonists whose attempts to escape the banality of their culture assume forms which are themselves banal. The tension is, ultimately, unproductive and Flaubert's final novel, *Bouvard et Pécuchet*, on which he labored for years and which he never finished, dwells with inert obsessiveness on the absurdity of two *bêtes bourgeois* who labor for years on a massive and unprofitable treatise which they never finish. If bourgeois reality is stultifying and fatuous, it is also final and authoritative and pervades even the projects which aspire to resist it. The art itself, and the heroically indefatigable industry involved in producing it, are not exempt, and the industry of Bouvard and Pécuchet comes at last to exemplify, in that perversely easy way, the absurdity and uselessness of the creative impulse, both as Flaubert invested in it and as such.

Spielberg, by contrast, cultivates the apprehension that there is some Power lurking in the essence of things—a Power of Evil (*Duel* [1971], *Jaws*, *Poltergeist*) or a Power of Good (*E.T.*, *Twilight Zone*)—the intervention of which will demonstrate that the banality and oppressiveness of weekend America are really something else, and that the world in which one feels trapped and from which one wishes to escape is worth having and fighting for after all. The source of the potency of such a vision in the 1980s hardly needs to be demonstrated. Spielberg does not actually believe for a moment that what he calls "the anaesthetic of suburbia" (Sragow, 111) is anything but what he thinks it is, but, for all his desire to "transcend" it, he is quite unable to conceive of any real alternative to it and quite unprepared to countenance the implications of the feeling that alternatives are necessary. A way must be found of convincing oneself that suburbia has an ultimate sanction and a real value: that is, a value that will be *made* real in the act of defending home and family from the excursions of the powers of darkness or which will be re-created and renewed by one's experience of a redeemer. The spuriousness of Spielberg's films derives from their desperate attempt to create the conditions for feelings which, the films are at some level aware, can't legitimately be felt, and intensities of conviction and commitment which can't legitimately be realized.

As a result, it is beyond Spielberg's powers to give any convincing, coherent dramatic substance either to the norms his work reaffirms or to the catalyst, malignant or benign, which enables him to reaffirm them. Because it is never possible to entirely forget that weekend America is monstrous, its salvation is invariably gestural, rhetorical, and more or less blatantly inconsequent: *Jaws*, as I have tried to show elsewhere, remains exemplary in this respect. At the same time, however, because weekend America must be saved, the catalyst must be conceived in terms of saving it; that is, the catalyst must have the effect of demonstrating that America can be cleansed or transfigured while catering at the same time to a sentimental fantasy of escape from or rebellion against the very same culture. Representations of Otherness in Spielberg's work are always visibly afflicted by this contradiction: the Other can never be an alternative to the dominant norms in that they're sacrosanct, but nor can it subserve a convinced endorsement of them, in that the films are aware of what, in practice, the norms are like. The problem is very much less embarrassing, naturally, in those cases where the Other is Evil. Nothing is easier, in the conventions of the horror-thriller, than to take the transcendent value of home and family completely for granted. While it is part of the function of the shark in *Jaws* and the evil spirits in *Poltergeist* to enact an impulse to violate the very things to which the films are supposed to be committed, the image of suburban domesticity under threat is so potent and the narrative donnée so strong that the contradiction need not assert itself in any very damaging form. When the Other is Good, however, the incoherence and pusillanimousness of the Spielberg thematic is blatantly exposed as the films attempt to reconcile the felt need to flee or disrupt America with the desire to believe that nothing is wrong with it.

E.T and *Poltergeist* go together. Even if we didn't have the internal evidence, there is the fact that Spielberg's name appears in the credits of *Poltergeist* as writer and producer, and he describes himself as "the David O. Selznick of this movie"—adding, as any experienced parent might have done, "I'll just say that I functioned in a very strong way." (McCarthy, 56) *Poltergeist* was nominally directed by Tobe Hooper, whom one would feel no compelling need to exonerate from the charge of being its author were it not for the first half of his previous film, *The Funhouse* (1981), which is more distinguished than virtually anything in the genre since *Halloween* and *Friday the 13th*. Its theme, embodied in the image of the funhouse itself, is the way in which the language and imagery of the Gothic and its characteristic thematic concerns (the determinants, functions, and consequences of sexual repression) have been recuperated by American culture, as "entertainment," in the interests of conservative reassurance. The theme is explored with great economy and poignancy, and the prolonged climactic scene of the film's first "movement," culminating in the murder of the fortune-teller, enacts one of the horror film's most disturbing and painful accounts of patriarchal sexuality. The second half of *The Funhouse* is entirely and tediously devoted to the obligatory massacre of teenagers—obligatory, in part, because of the precedent of Hooper. The fact that Hooper seems incapable of sustaining a work (the first forty minutes of *The Texas Chainsaw Massacre* [1974] are, though schematic, not without interest), combined with the mediocrity of his other films, makes it difficult to feel confident that the promise of what is good in *The Funhouse* will be fulfilled. We may give him the credit, perhaps, for the intensity and concentration of the climactic scenes in *Poltergeist*, which might well have been part of something better. They are certainly very unlike anything in Spielberg, who actually remarks that the last fifteen minutes is his "least favorite" part of the film. (Sragow, 114) In fact, the links between *E.T.* and *Poltergeist* are implicit in the films themselves: each, as the toy imagery (for example) attests, is an "extreme" which is produced by the repression of its counterpart.

The content of the extreme is determined by the unity, or otherwise, of the patriarchal family. In *E.T.*, the family has been disrupted by the absence of the father and is cobbled together again through the good offices of a representative of "Otherness," which is conceived of as redemptive and benign. In *Poltergeist*, the family is internally unified and homogeneous and is exposed, in the manner of the post-*Halloween* horror film, to the bad offices of "powers of Evil" which have no significant relation to it—which are defined by the film, in other words, as absolutely external to the order they disturb. At this level—the level of explicit articulation—*Poltergeist* has nothing whatever to say about Evil except that it threatens the family and is therefore deplorable, but we are certainly in a position to make a number of plausible deductions about the nature of the film's unspoken anxieties.

I suggested earlier that it is the tacit thesis of *Raiders of the Lost Ark*, apropos the nuclear holocaust, that "if you are American you cannot die," and I might have made the same point of the *Star Wars* trilogy. For Obi-Wan Kenobe, Yoda, and Darth Vader, death has no real bearing on the fact of life. While the Emperor, for all his omnipotence and omniscience, can be killed decisively merely by being thrown over the banisters, the good father, having died, proceeds to come back again. The recuperation of mortality is a theme which turns out to be characteristic of a number of important contemporary American documents.

The commercial debacle of Tony Bill's magnificent melodrama *Six Weeks*—a debacle in which reviewers of the most diverse persuasions collaborated, in the usual manner—followed inevitably from its reckless interrogation of this theme, and it might be proposed as an interesting exercise to students of contemporary American culture to juxtapose the film with *Terms of Endearment* (or *Testament*) and ask under what circumstances sophisticated modern spectators are prepared to contemplate the idea of their decease. The answer, of course, is when death brings the family together again and provides an occasion for the kind of emotional opportunism and self-display which often passes for great acting and which James L. Brooks uses rather as the space films use special effects: death loses something of its sting when conceived as an opportunity to win an Academy Award. The formula for *Terms of Endearment* is, in effect, *E.T.* plus breast cancer, and the Deborah Winger set piece in which we learn what a far, far better thing it is to have an inoperable malignancy than to have had an abortion ought to be recognized as a locus classicus of Reaganite cinema. If *Six Weeks* hadn't appeared first, one would have assumed that it had been conceived as a direct reply to the Best Picture of the Year. One can understand, at any rate, that a film in which the death of a little girl, unredeemed and irreversible, becomes the focus of a complex dramatic analysis of representative structures of wish fulfillment and fantasy investments in the family is the very last thing which admirers of Brooks's cunning bestseller wish to see.

The significance of, say, the "Jane Fonda Workout" in terms of postfeminist bourgeois discourses about women is obvious, but it also has a more general significance. If we submit ourselves to the stringent regime of the born-again body (and the revivalist atmosphere of the Fonda videotape has its suggestiveness), we can forget about age and coronaries and the carcinogenic properties of the late capitalist environment and the existence of nuclear energy, for we are acquiring a personal solution to the problem of death in all its forms. The physical perfection which Ms. Fonda promotes and sells so successfully testifies to the conquest of what one might call the "social body"—the body in its specific materiality. "Conquest" is clearly the word. There is an element of truth in the slogan "Discipline is Liberation," but it is not that element which gets the stress when Ms. Fonda talks about "the burn" and serves up an exemplary Puritan individualism in the guise of ludic dance and the discovery of solidarity. The "Workout" promises immortality through self-punishment, and expresses the Puritan revulsion from physicality in exactly the way one would expect it to do at a cultural moment when we are all very acutely aware both that the value of the commodified bourgeois body is at a premium and that its health, and the very possibility of its existence, are seriously threatened by forces over which we have, as yet, no control.

Of course, it turns out that Americans cannot die in *Poltergeist* either, but the film's Gothic is centrally a matter of the suspicion that they might. The "horror" which invades the immaculate, petit bourgeois suburban home is the body perceived as—indeed, identified with—a memento mori, and the film's imagery is entirely dedicated to the association of physicality with the charnel and the latrine.

Yet while horror in *Poltergeist* derives from an excremental vision of the body's materiality (the suburban home is built over a graveyard, and the mouth of Hell is an anus), Evil insinuates itself into American domesticity by way, not of the body, but of the most important item of domestic technology, the television set. This duality is the key to *Poltergeist*, and its significance emerges clearly enough when we compare the climactic scenes with those of *Raiders of the Lost Ark*. Suburbia is, in effect, nuked, and if Evil reminds middle America that the body is an organism which can die, it does so in a context of anxiety about American technique which it is the function of the television both to bear and to assuage. Thus, on the one hand, the Americanness of the television is very strikingly emphasized, and in the opening scene the arrival of the poltergeist is associated with the close-down playing of "The Star-Spangled Banner." Conversely, the conventions of the contemporary horror film divorce Evil completely from the culture in which it manifests itself, and in the final shot the fears to which the television has referred can be at once acknowledged and suppressed in the form of a joke. The fears are inspired by that acute and unwilling consciousness of what it is that the television does, for which, in his account of weekend America's treadmill of consumption, Spielberg becomes the spokesman. Given the excremental vision of the return of the body, his description of prime time as "pabulum" and his emphasis, in general, on the ingestion of junk seem significant. The television is the family's sustaining staple diet, and it is from this, the film implies, that the horror derives: one is consuming America, and America visits apocalypse on the consumer.

Such a thought can hardly be countenanced, and it is the strategy of *Poltergeist* to invoke the social fears it presupposes in its audience in such a way as to deflect them onto something else. Consider, for example, the extraordinary moment, stressed by the use of close-up and camera movement, in which the film's patriarch is shown reading a book on Reagan. The shot is unfathomably cryptic, and that is the point about it. It is there in the film but there is nothing that can be done with it. By at once adverting explicitly to the politics of an American present and refusing to define a discourse in terms of which the reference could make concrete sense, *Poltergeist* is able to draw on and to disarticulate its audience's uncertainties at one and the same time.

The ambivalence can be sustained because, whatever the symbolic content of the family's antagonist may be, the family itself is, according to *Poltergeist*, all right. The premise of *E.T.*, by contrast, is that the family is, or has become, all wrong; the advent of the extraterrestrial has for context an experience of the duplicity of the father, who has committed adultery and gone off with his lover. The experience in question is, for the film's purposes, the younger son's: the father's betrayal of the family which he ought to be holding together is dramatically significant because of what it means for Elliott. In this, *E.T.* stands in a complementary relation to *Cujo* as well as to *Poltergeist*: Lewis Teague's film, in which the identical sexual transgression is committed by the mother (played, as in *E.T.*, by Dee Wallace), can comfortably demonstrate the necessity of the father to the son's well-being by staging a grueling account of the effects of his departure, while chastening the mother at the same time. *E.T.* must, of necessity, undertake a more difficult task: its project is to reconcile Elliott to the paternal function from which his real father has alienated him, while accommodating a fantasy of rebelling against his father and dispensing with him altogether.

The project is embodied in the conception of E.T. himself, who is both the Father and the Son: in one of the more vulgar moments of Spielbergian religiosity, he appears in the back of a truck in the archetypal posture of the risen Christ, and he ascends to Heaven a few sequences later. The point is all the more worth making because it has become a standard feature of eulogies of the film that they maintain that E.T. has, in Auty's phrase, "no sex"—though Auty does not go on to explain how we are to read Elliott's outraged injunction to his sister, on discovering that she has dressed E.T. in women's clothes, to "give him back his dignity." That E.T. is male is the essence of the film, and there is nothing in the film which suggests that he isn't. If his maleness sometimes seems rather odd, it is because he is called upon to represent, promiscuously, the supreme patriarch and a fellow child. In his capacity as manifest deity, E.T. serves to invest the formation of Elliott's superego ("I'll . . . be . . . right . . . here.") with that atmosphere of Brucknerian elevation and grandeur: even if the differences from the end of *Return of the Jedi* aren't worth noting, it must be conceded that George Lucas could hardly sustain so exalted a tone. As buddy and disarming klutz, on the other hand, E.T. can be used to rid the father's Oedipal role of its threatening, oppressive, castrating aspects and to license the fantasy that it is possible both to internalize the father as superego, thus acquiring the advantages of maleness, and to remain a pre-Oedipal infant.

Consider, for example, the telepathy sequence, in which E.T.'s drunken odyssey through the deserted family house is juxtaposed, through parallel montage, with Elliott's anarchic rebellion against the authoritarian proprieties of his school biology class. The crux of the sequence is the quotation from *The Quiet Man* (1952): E.T., fumbling with the television, finds himself watching the famous scene in which Wayne seizes Maureen O'Hara and kisses her for the first time. E.T., bemused but aroused, identifies with Wayne, and the identification is relayed telepathically to Elliott, who proceeds to grab one of the little girls in his class and impose on her, charmingly, the masterful embrace for which Wayne has set the precedent. In its Fordian context, the meaning of the scene is rather different from what it means for Spielberg: its function in *E.T.* is to dramatize the process of the exemplary male Oedipus complex in terms of the rejection of the law of the Father. The sequence is a locus classicus of opportunistic Spielbergian "unrealism": in Spielberg movies it is perfectly possible for little boys to transform their schoolrooms into a bedlam with impunity, and to become John Wayne while conducting a successful revolution against the real constraints and material institutions of male authority. One can have the culture, and one's privilege within it, and overthrow it too—all without the least sense of contradiction: the extent to which Spielberg seeks to have it both ways has never been more clearly demonstrated.

Elliott's teacher, like all the adult men in the film, is presented as a figure of sinister impersonal power, and Spielberg chooses to convey the threat the men represent by refusing to show us their faces. We see them instead as E.T., or a male child, might see them: the eye line which the film constructs for us directs our attention to the abdomen. The bunch of keys which hangs so alarmingly at the groin of the man who seems, until the end of the film, to be the prime mover in the campaign to do violence to the extraterrestrial is the film's representative image of male power, and it is crucial to the significance of *E.T.* that the keys are both a threat and an object of desire. Obviously, they signify patriarchal violence: they are a reminder of the sexual crime (the father's adultery) which has destroyed the family, and inasmuch as they are, by definition, what the father has got and the son hasn't, they confront the son with the threat of his castration. Later in the film, Keys and his cohorts invade, violate, and depersonalize the home, which is primarily associated, as is usual in American culture, with femininity, and in which E.T. has found a natural refuge. Yet, while the film regards adult male sexuality with revulsion, and connects it single-mindedly with oppressiveness and aggression, it is absolutely essential to reinstate the paternal function. The thing is accordingly done through the recuperation of Keys, who replaces E.T. as the father who is also a child. At the very moment Keys tells Elliott that he too has always longed for the appearance of an extraterrestrial and takes Elliott's hand in his own, the metabolic systems of Elliott and E.T. begin to diverge. At the same moment, Spielberg shows us Keys's face for the first time, and throughout the rest of the film Keys's groin is correspondingly forgotten. The function of *E.T.*, at this level, is to renovate the patriarchal family by reconciling a boy who has been estranged from the sexual identity exemplified by his father to a new, benign father who has and does not have the phallus.

Yet, while the reconstitution of the patriarchal family is in one sense the point of the exercise, *E.T.* is nothing if not a Spielberg film, and the theological intensities of the final scene are inspired, not by the family or by the relationship between Elliott and Keys, but by the parting of Elliott and E.T. For *E.T.* is primarily a love story, a fact to which Spielberg himself alerts us (if that were necessary) when he remarks, with characteristic ingenuousness, that the narrative first came to him in terms of "boy meets creature, boy loses creature, boy finds creature." (Sragow, 110) As the childlike father, E.T. permits, for Elliott, the expression of a kind of feeling between father and son which is very rigorously censored in patriarchal culture. *E.T.* is hardly readable if we forget that one of the crucial functions of the Oedipus complex is the regulation of bisexuality: when the male child identifies with the place of the father, he is enjoined to renounce a "feminine" relation to him. In this perspective, the *E.T.* fantasy reconciles the internalization of the father (which is prerequisite for the achievement of male heterosexuality) with the kind of rebellion against patriarchy that expresses itself in a refusal to renounce the father as an object of desire. The superego, in fact, becomes the lost object, and E.T.'s "I'll . . . be . . . right . . . here" is both an injunction and a declaration of eternal love. We have the clue here to the characteristically gestural offhandedness with which Spielberg's ending affirms the new family and the new father. Keys may solve the problem of the father's disruption of the family and the couple, and he may secure, in so doing, the normative destiny of the male child, but precisely because he does so, he cannot be used to address the bisexuality of the male Oedipus complex. In the climactic love scene between Elliott and E.T., the creation of the superego is also the formation of a nonsocial Imaginary in which father and son will always be together, united in infantile play.

This kind of sentiment, in which homoerotic feeling is both indulged and censored, is not new in Spielberg's work. In *Jaws*, the male bond between the Roy Scheider and Richard Dreyfuss characters is sanctioned because it is formed in the name of the defense of social values (home and family) which define the bond as "nonsocial," and under circumstances (the pursuit of the shark) which define it as temporary. The films often suggest a certain vague nostalgia for the world of polymorphous infantile desire, but they haven't the moral or emotional energy to do anything more than posit fairytale situations in which such impulses can be unconsciously reenacted in disguise—that is, sentimentalized. No Spielberg film could ever admit to the fact that infantile desire has its bearing for the possibilities of conscious adult life, nor could Spielberg ever commit himself to the Blakean protest of "Infant Sorrow" or "A Little Girl Lost." Childhood in his work is a support to a fainthearted male daydream, which accommodates itself to life in this world through fantasies of regression.

The dream, of course, is very much male. As we have seen, while Spielberg's films are ostensibly committed to the renewal of patriarchal domesticity, they are surreptitiously motivated by a desire to escape it. Since "settlement" and "femininity" go together in American texts, the contradiction expresses itself, where women are concerned, in a covert, diluted, and inexplicit misogyny. At one level of meaning, the role of wife and mother is the ideal role; at the other level, it defines the "female world" which threatens the male American protagonist with emasculation. The consequences of realizing both meanings at the same time are very clearly enacted in *Jaws*, where the shark is both the enemy of the home and the *vagina dentata;* the terrorization of the perfect mother in her perfect house in *Poltergeist* can be related to the same pattern. The most striking case, however, remains *Close Encounters of the Third Kind*, in which Roy Neary (Richard Dreyfuss), like the poltergeist, demolishes the family home in order to build a monolithic, excremental totem-phallus in the middle of the living room before retiring, at the end of the film, to the interior of a spaceship whose inhabitants, like E.T., are both phallic and fetal.

It is fitting, in the light of this account, that E.T.'s last words to Elliott's sister should take the form of a command to "be good," which sums up the content of Reaganite entertainment's address to women in a phrase. Those who continue to be charmed by *E.T.* should ponder it and go on to ask how it is that, in spite of all the mileage that is got from the comedy of E.T.'s culture shock, the protesting cry of "Give him back his dignity!" is reserved for the moment when he is dressed in female clothes. That E.T. should be the feminized father is germane to the fantasy, but for this very reason femininity must be rigorously distinguished from anything that smacks of the female. For all its softheartedness and sunny benevolence, Spielberg's work has its residual asperity, and it is invariably the female that brings it out.

In *Indiana Jones and the Temple of Doom*, the latent neuroticism and unpleasantness of Spielberg's work is offered to us fully realized. The catalyst is Spielberg's fear, manifest in his film's unremitting stridency, compulsiveness, and hysteria, that he will be unable to "hold" an audience which has by now supped full of wonders, and his accompanying conviction that he must, therefore, top every last effect with another even grosser and more lurid. For a man in Spielberg's position, this anxiety about the potency of his magic can hardly be distinguishable from resentment, and *Indiana Jones and the Temple of Doom* is in effect an exercise in savage self-assertion: a brutal assault on spectators whose very acclaim and expectations have now become intimidating; Spielberg clearly feels, understandably, that he cannot afford (in any sense) to do anything that might be construed as "dull." Since Spielberg is, as far as the significance of his work is concerned, as entirely unconscious as it is possible for an artist to be, the frantic effort to load every rift with ore has the inevitable effect of exposing, grotesquely, the system of values and assumptions whose harsh outline is softened, in less desperate works, by an appearance of charm and geniality. Now that *Indiana Jones and the Temple of Doom* is there, we can also see the tendency toward it: Spielberg's investment in overwhelming an audience which he also despises ("*Raiders* is like popcorn") has an element of cynical and sadistic calculation which his dread of losing the audience, even for a second, has brought to the surface. The film's all-pervasive racism is of interest inasmuch as it makes explicit, to those for whom explicitness is necessary, the sublimated racism of the space cycle: the wogs of *Indiana Jones and the Temple of Doom*, good and bad, are Other in exactly the same way, and to exactly the same end, as the aliens of *Return of the Jedi*, as the obvious comparison between the court of Jabba the Hutt and the Maharajah's banquet, or between Spielberg's Indian peasants and Lucas/ Marquand's cuddly jungle bunnies, demonstrates. In *Indiana Jones*, moreover, the monstrous cult of Kali is called upon to bear the responsibility for the film's own violence through a process of disavowal and projection which, in the conditions of Reagan's America, must be seen to have its representative significance. The nervous uncertain treatment of "the-British-in-India," who are briefly taken to task for attitudes and practices affirmed through Jones himself and who collaborate with the American hero in suppressing the natives at the end, is sufficient evidence of the content of the film's subtext. Imperialist violence is seen to be necessary in *Indiana Jones and the Temple of Doom* because the victims of the vile renaissance of the colonized peoples are children. The prospective audience, of course, consists largely of children too, and Spielberg has even seen fit to excise a minute or so from his masterpiece so that British children can be subjected to it unaccompanied by adults.

We may leave it, perhaps, to apologists of the director's Blakean vision or, more safely, to students of the economic and ideological motivation of the campaign against video nasties to ponder the implicit contradiction in this incomparably brutal film's concern for children. It will be enough here to note, in conclusion, that *Indiana Jones* is also exemplary in its revelation of the logic of Spielberg's sexism. The film's subject, at this level, is the formation of a misogynistic homoerotic bond between father and son, consummated through imitative violence and the systematic degradation of the heroine. These are familiar themes in Reaganite cinema, of course, but it is fair to say that *Indiana Jones* gives us something like the ultimate exposition of them: in no other film of the period is one woman called on to be both the "love interest" (by virtue of the conventions of heterosexist narrative) and the focus of intense antifeminist animus. The scene in which Short Round beats up the Maharajah while Jones beats up the thuggish overseer, and the final scene in which Short Round averts his eyes in horror from the heterosexual embrace to which the film is inertly committed by the presence of the woman whom, at the same time, it passionately loathes, provide us with exemplary images of the North American 1980s.

Spielberg's work is undoubtedly distinctive, but it should not be inferred from the fact that I end with him, and that I discuss him at such length, that I think his distinctiveness is of the important kind. It consists, rather, in his exemplary representativeness, and to say that, under the conditions of Reaganite entertainment, *this* is what an individuated sensibility looks like is to make a point against the conditions—and a very important one. The films I have considered are ideological deposits, like yesterday's *Sun* and the *Daily Telegraph* of the day before, and their inertia and their anonymity go together. When the ideological history of Hollywood comes to be written, their significance will be found to consist in this fact.

Prospects

Obviously, the current period cannot last and may, indeed, be drawing to a close already. I hope I have been able to demonstrate what it is about the films which makes their projects, for all the appearance of robust self-possession and triumphalist assertiveness, inherently unstable. The question of what will replace them is more difficult, since it remains to be seen whether the Hollywood cinema has any vitality of convention left. It is not enough to hope that directors will emerge who have more radical sympathies and a greater readiness to contemplate the real conditions of the social present than do Lucas, Spielberg, and Stallone. Artists, however great, do not invent the language that they use or the conditions in which they use it, and the greatness of the popular American cinema has always been inseparable from the quite extraordinary ideological productivity of its conventions, the contradictory diversity of the cultural traditions which fed into them, and the existence of material conditions of production which were hugely congenial to the realization of their significance. The nineteenth-century realist novel, the popular theatrical melodrama, American Gothic, psychoanalysis, montage theory, German modernism—the classical Hollywood cinema had its enabling resources. The immediate background of any conceivable modern Hollywood will be formed by the total exhaustion and reduction to banality of the conventional language and the dominance of practices of production which are in themselves inimical to significant work: a system of commodity production in which the average cost of a feature film (*Variety* informs us) is now between 12 and 15 million dollars and in which each film must make back three times the cost of its production before it goes into profit is not intrinsically favorable to the progressive exploration of cultural contradiction.

It is that last phrase, in fact, which helps to make the fundamental point: any modern popular American cinema of value will have to be in some sense explicitly controversial and oppositional. It is no longer possible to work with radical incisiveness on the structural conflicts and tensions of American bourgeois culture under cover of the prevailing sense of confidence and security which accompanied the emergence and consolidation of American hegemony. Hollywood cinema in the period of its greatness is the most distinguished cinema for the same reason that the English novel is the most distinguished nineteenth-century literature: the very resistless expansion of the supreme imperial power created a space and an opportunity for the critical *bourgeois* text to examine the social conditions (or, some of them—they are critical bourgeois texts) of supremacy. The lesson of Reaganite entertainment is that it is no longer possible to coherently affirm the culture either—for the principle of ironic disavowal which governs "affirmation" in the contemporary entertainment film points, in effect, to "impossibility."

We are left, then, when it comes to prognosis, with a definition of what a valuable modern "Hollywood" *cannot* be—and with a sense of the difficulty of there being one at all. American capitalism and the world system in which its dominance is becoming increasingly precarious are disintegrating, and the social circumstances which make open ideological criticism the prerequisite of value in the American cinema are the same circumstances which militate against it. How, under such conditions, is it possible to sustain a significant conventional language which addresses itself, analytically and productively, to the definition of the real?

It would be foolish to indulge in confident speculation, the American situation being so unstable, and I will end by merely recalling that for all its monolithic appearance, the period has its contradictions. *Cutter's Way, True Confessions, Reds, Heaven's Gate, Blade Runner, Victor/Victoria, Raging Bull, Six Weeks, Scarface* (1983), *Under Fire* (1983), *King of Comedy, Silkwood* (1983), *The Dead Zone*—there is no masterpiece here (though *Raging Bull* comes close), but then one is not primarily concerned for masterpieces at this stage. These films remain facts out of which something could come, and while it is perhaps more difficult now to imagine the future lines of Hollywood's development than at any previous time, we cannot assume in advance that the opportunities which these works represent will not be put to use.

Part Two
Hollywood Movies

Meet Me in St. Louis: Smith, or The Ambiguities (1994)

I n *Capitalism, The Family, and Personal Life*, Eli Zaretsky writes:

> The family, to the Victorian bourgeoisie, was a "tent pitch'd in a world not right." "This is the true nature of home," wrote John Ruskin; "it is the place of peace; the shelter, not only from all injury, but from all terror, doubt, and division . . . So far as the anxieties of the outer life penetrate into it . . . it ceases to he a home; it is then only a part of the outer world which you have roofed over and lighted fire in." It stood in opposition to the terrible anonymous world of commerce and industry: "a world alien, not your world. . . without father, without child, without brother." The Victorian family was distinguished by its spiritual aspect: it is remote, ethereal and unreal—"a sacred place, a vestal temple." As in the Middle Ages, so now with the bourgeoisie, the domain of the spirit had once again separated off from the realm of production. (51)

Meet Me in St. Louis (1944) is set in a precise geographical location at a precise historical moment—1903/4, the turn of the twentieth century—yet the temporal specificity is, instantly, mythic: simply to plot a course within those historical/topographical coordinates is already to proceed across a landscape which has been colonized by mythology, and from which history has been expelled. St. Louis is as much "south" as one can be while remaining "north," and in a film in which the supreme disruption is figured as a move to New York, one set of the ambiguous connotations relating to south is powerfully evoked: the connotations of elegance, refinement, culture, "organic community," which Mark Twain, in his denunciation of the myth, associates with the European tradition of aristocratic, chivalric romance of which Sir Walter Scott is the supreme and most pernicious exponent. (The myth is, then, dualistic, contradictory: alongside the ethos which produces *Gone with the Wind* [1939], the stress on the contaminating rottenness of southern Europeanism—Edgar Allan Poe, *Uncle Tom's Cabin*, *Pudd'nhead Wilson*, William Faulkner. One notes in this context the extraordinary ambiguity of the attitude to the south in, say, John Ford.) Simultaneously, 1903/4 calls up the myth of "Edwardianism"—the last halcyon days of the nineteenth century before the twentieth begins in 1914, to which Sir Edward Elgar, writing in 1917, pays significant tribute: "Everything good and nice and clean and fresh and sweet is far away never to return."

Meet Me in St. Louis is roughly contemporary with *The Magnificent Ambersons* (1942) and *Shadow of a Doubt* (1943), and while the myth is placed in all three films, its invocation in the context of the family (the romance of the family, as opposed to what Sigmund Freud means by "the family romance"—the Oedipal relation with which the films also concern themselves) testifies, in various ways, to its potency. Orson Welles's response to the "magnificence of the Ambersons" is as systematically ambivalent as Vincente Minnelli's to the Smiths, and in Alfred Hitchcock's film (on the script of which the Thornton Wilder of *Our Town* collaborated), Uncle Charlie, the "monster" whose psychosis is directly attributed to the American family, tells his niece, as three generations gather round the family dinner table (children, parents, grandparents in the photo), "Everyone was sweet and pretty then—not like now." Anne Newton, in the same film, not only reads *Ivanhoe* but also aspires, like southern ladies "in books," to gather orchids with white gloves.

The difficulty inside the sense of nostalgia (less apparent in the Hitchcock, which lacks that sensuous response to the object of criticism so characteristic of the Welles and the Minnelli) can be defined by offering, as a third term, Henry James. *Washington Square*, set in the 1830s, written in 1880, is as trenchant an analysis of bourgeois patriarchy and its associated oppression of women as any the realist novel has produced. Yet the book's marvelous tension depends not only on the ambivalent response to Dr. Sloper (both monster and angelic intelligence, both the figure of repressive social law and the supremely refined [self-] consciousness) but also on a topographical ambivalence. The revulsion from the urbanization of New York ("the long shrill city"; "the murmur of trade had become a mighty uproar") is only half concealed by irony at Dr. Sloper's expense and has, as its corollary, the sensuous, inward evocation of the very culture the novel condemns ("This portion of New York appears to many persons the most delectable") and for which, at one point, the narrator actually apologizes ("My excuse for this topographical parenthesis…"). What is "tension" in *Washington Square* becomes, increasingly, vacillation. The culture, after all, determined James's repression of his homosexuality, and that repression (inseparably, the refusal to follow through the logic of the social analysis) produces, finally, the impotent male protagonists who have never "had their lives" so characteristic of the late period (*The Beast in the Jungle*, *The Ambassadors*). The subtext of the latter novel is, indeed, the novel about gayness that James is incapable of writing. The ambiguities of nostalgia emerge very strikingly in *Meet Me in St. Louis* in the singing of "Have Yourself a Merry Little Christmas," in which Esther attempts to console Tootie (and herself) by escaping from the present through creating the future (New York) as the past ("Happy golden days of yore"). The project is doubly, and disturbingly, inflected by giving the song, as context, Tootie's desire to dig up her "dead" dolls from her graveyard and take them with her to her new home.

The New York/St. Louis antinomy is an opposition between oppressive, dehumanized urbanization ("cooped up in a tenement") and the "organic community"; between "the city" and a city which, nevertheless, isn't a city. "It just doesn't seem very big out here where we live."

The New York of *Meet Me in St. Louis* is not the "wonderful town" of *On The Town* (and is the use of "town" there, rather than "city," significant?), but the metropolis of the antiurban tradition discussed by Morton and Lucia White. (1–5) The Whites suggest that the crux of hatred of the city is the hatred of "commerce, industry and massive immigration" (consider the importance of Mr. Smith's being a businessman, and the film's repression, from its ethos of "southness," of the blacks) and that therefore antiurbanism did not emerge, as far as the American city was concerned, until the nineteenth century. They quote Hector St. John de Crèvecoeur, who distinguishes between the "simple and cordial friend-liness they [visitors] are to expect in [the] cities of this continent" and the "accumulated and crowded cities" of Europe. "'They are but the confined theatre of cupidity; they exhibit nothing but the action and reaction of a variety of passions which, being confined within narrower channels, impel one another with the greatest vigor.'" (White and White, 12) The "bad" city, while it suggests compactedness, anti-freedom, the negative of American space, and commerce ("cupidity"), also evokes, in this description, a sense of violent, seething, untrammeled, and implicitly erotic energies—the city as repository of libido, so central to the film noir. Typically, Crèvecoeur admires in contemporary New York both the "enlighten-ment" social values (hospitality, a contained cosmopolitanism) and that sense—crucial, also, in Benjamin Franklin—that America is the place where universal engagement in commerce does not entail destructive competitiveness and is consonant with perfect social stability. Noncompetitive free enterprise not only "binds the whole together for general purposes" but also contains sexuality—"Industry and constant employment are great preservatives of the morals and virtue of a nation." (Williams, *American Grain*, 152–53) To the extent that it draws on Crèvecoeur's preindustrial American city and makes use of conventions for the presentation of sexuality arrived at by a process of sublimation, *Meet Me in St. Louis* and the genre to which it belongs (small-town domestic musical/comedy) suggest a sort of modi-fied pastoral convention.

The years 1903 to 1904 become in fact, the point at which city can still mean "community," and one can compare the film in this respect to *It's a Wonderful Life* (1946). In Frank Capra's film, the myth of community depends for its efficacy on the freezing of the development of capitalism at a certain point: the point before which capitalism's defining characteristic, the desire to produce an economic surplus, has become evident. Hence, the film's central struc-tural opposition between George Bailey (James Stewart) and Mr. Potter (Lionel Barrymore), between the accumulation of capital and the constant diffusion of capital back into the com-munity ("Your money's in Joe's house"), translated into useful, socially beneficial objects; between, that is, "the capitalist" (bad) and the circulation of capital without capitalists, no one at any point making a profit at anyone else's expense. On this level, the film's repeated crises, which finally reduce Bailey to attempt suicide, are essential to its project in that, without them, Bailey would be seen to be becoming Mr. Potter. One can relate this to Zaretsky's remarks to the effect that at the moment of the supreme development of bourgeois capitalism, the family, its basic unit, is imaged as a refuge from it by saying that Capra's film moves toward locating the family within an essentially decapitalized capitalism, and that *Meet Me in St. Louis*, while on one level roundly denying the family's immunity, operates on another as if the denial were not taking place (it can be read, that is, as if it weren't).

One can approach an analysis of the ambiguity through decor, an iconography at which point *It's a Wonderful Life* again provides a point of reference. The imagery of the last five min-utes of the film, after George's "salvation"—snow-laden streets, trees festooned with fairy lights, decorations, presents, warmth, hospitality, "hearth and home"—relates directly to the iconogra-phy of a certain kind of Christmas card, still extant, frequently with a Regency/Victorian/

Edwardian setting: the image, for example, of a coach traveling across a snowy landscape toward the lighted windows of a house just visible in the distance, or of passengers disembarking in the snow before a glowing doorway. Whatever has been done thematically—and *It's a Wonderful Life* has been profoundly subversive—the iconography has its own potency based on a prospective sense of "being at home inside": the anticipation of warmth, security, sociality, apartness from "outside." Consider the way in which, in the first scene of *I Walked with a Zombie* (1943), Betsy's self-confidence, her (illusory) sense of self-coherence, is associated with the spatial confidence of the inside/outside opposition by the device of framing her and her interlocutor against windows beyond which snow is falling—the film being concerned thereafter simultaneously with the breakdown of self-coherence and the dissolution/transgression of boundaries.

The credits of *Meet Me in St. Louis* are set within rococo gilt frames, with cameo insets of flowers in vases, and the film's temporal advances (associated with transitions in nature—the passage of the seasons) are marked by dissolves from a sampler-like image to its "reality." The picture, literally, "comes to life." The first instance of this (the movement from the credits to the narrative), as well as subsequent ones, reinforces the sense of entering the picture through camera movement, through the smooth, elaborate crane-cum-tracking shot which carries us forward into the fiction by accompanying the movements suddenly revealed within it: the horse-drawn wagon heading up the street and then the figure of a boy riding a bicycle toward a large house. The concept of "the frame" will be crucial in the film, and here the entry to the picture which comes to life is the entry to a defined, mythological space, a space of confidence, a conventionalized world bounded, ordered, delimited by a frame, appropriate expectations for which have already been sufficiently defined by the credits sequence. Frame and convention (generic and representational) make the spectacle world cohere, the coherence completed by that self-projection into the frame which the film encourages. Like the Christmas cards, the opening shots set up the anticipation of "at homeness," which becomes, immediately, inseparable from the notion of the family, in that the film invites very strongly an identificatory regression, not to childhood as it was, but to a cultural myth of "childhood-in-the-family-as-it-ought-to-have-been-and-might-possibly-be." The film is the product of a society in which the myth, the need for the idea of the family, is so intensely powerful that it can depend on functioning as a *petite madeleine* for individuals whose particular experience may not correspond at any point to the image of the family that is being offered.

This is the point, perhaps, to suggest certain qualifying elements which feed into the film from other sources. Obviously, if Hollywood affirms the family massively, one must give equal emphasis to the complementary impulse to reject it, both being rooted in the sense of home as "vestal temple," the sacred domain of woman as the embodiment of civilized social values. The most obvious form of the rejection produces that ongoing tradition of flight from home/community/woman from Henry David Thoreau to Jack Kerouac's *On the Road* to Sam Peckinpah's *Cross of Iron* (1977), frequently accompanied by a paradoxical, despairing nostalgia for what has been lost ("You can't go home again"). Equally important is what one might call the "alternative small-town tradition," the first major instance of which is Herman Melville's *Pierre* and which proceeds through Twain (*Pudd'nhead Wilson*, "The Man That Corrupted Hadleyburg") to Sinclair Lewis (*Babbit, Main Street*), and Sherwood Anderson (*Winesburg, Ohio*). It is also significantly developed by James (consider the concept of "Woollet, Massachusetts" in *The Ambassadors*).

In the context of *Meet Me in St. Louis*, certain characteristic elements of the genre need to be stressed.

1. On the first page of *Pierre,* Melville makes the connection between the myth of the small town, a debased pastoral convention reinforced by the antiurbanism of Wordsworthian romanticism, and the sublimation of sexuality. The innocence of this Arcadia ("brindled kine") consists in the ignorance of the energies which will later disrupt it.

2. Those energies are embodied, in the pastoral, by Comus, and the links among sexuality, the devil, and the darker nature of the forest emphasized in John Milton's poem is reiterated, in the New World, in the Paradigm libido/wilderness/Devil/Indian, forces which surround and threaten the community. In *Pierre*, as in *The Scarlet Letter*, they emerge inside the community as female sexuality. Both novels, indeed, suggest versions of "Comus," with the sexes reversed: Pierre and Dimmesdale in the role of "the lady" (who now succumbs to temptation), and the sexuality of both Isabel and Hester associated with "the blackness of darkness" and vast, savage, natural forces (thunder and lightning, the forest). But the attitude to sexuality and to "the fall" is correspondingly more ambiguous, and the tendency to affirm the energies embodied in the women and their liberation of the men as human consciousness is offset by the chaos they unleash and the emasculation they threaten to induce. There is a direct line of descent from Isabel and Hester and her daughter Pearl ("a demon offspring") to the small-town "vamp" (Gloria Grahame, say, in *It's a Wonderful Life*, or Bette Davis, supremely, in *Beyond the Forest* [1949]) to Tootie in *Meet Me in St. Louis* and to the devil-children of the diabolist cycle, Regan and Carrie. It is a line which, as *Pierre* makes clear, has to be associated with the hubris of Melville's heroes: Ahab's vow "in nomine diaboli" has been inherited, in the modern horror movie, by the female child.

3. The characteristic form of the possessed child's rebellion is a repetition of the crime of Satan—the overthrow of the father (or, as in *Carrie* [1976], the phallic mother), the figure of the Law. Pierre's last gesture on leaving his ancestral home is to destroy his father's portrait ("Henceforth, cast-out Pierre hath no paternity and no past"); Tootie kills Mr. Brockhoff; Regan becomes the Devil, kills her potential stepfather and, finally, both representatives of Holy Church. In all three cases the Law of the Father continues to reassert itself, and the child is vanquished.

4. *Pierre* is built on the theme of the Oedipal romance and its enforcement within the idealized nuclear family. Pierre, impelled by love of Isabel, breaks out of his incestuous involvement with his mother only to discover that Isabel is his sister, and in the final chapter, he beholds in the portrait of Beatrice Cenci, the icon of "the two most horrible crimes . . . possible to civilized humanity—incest and parricide." Once more the apparent innocence of the female child ("so sweetly and seraphically blonde a being")

assumes the burden of guilt, but now as the emphasis on "blonde" conveys, the stigma passes from the dark lady to the likeness of Lucy, the archetypal "sweetheart" of the opening chapters, and from her to Pierre, who is guilty in her image. The indissoluble themes of parent-murder and Oedipal confusion which continue to inform the Gothic (*Psycho* (1960), the devil-child films) are also paired in *Meet Me in St. Louis* in which the Halloween sequence has its significance in the rejection of Father and Oedipus complex, the two determinants of the all-American romance.

5. The sense that the domesticated small-town male is castrated is an obsessive cultural preoccupation and surfaces in numerous movies—*Shadow Of a Doubt, Meet Me in St. Louis, It's a Wonderful Life, The Searchers* (1956), *Kings Row* (1942), etc. The castration may be the punishment for rebellion against the Father: for example, Ahab's lost leg; Pierre's vision of Enceladus, and his final cry of "Pierre is neuter now!"; Regan's appropriation of the phallus and her recastration by the two priests in *The Exorcist* [1973]. Alternatively, and far more frequently, the man is castrated by women; the small town is a matriarchy and the phallus is stolen by a monstrous wife/mother: for example, Mrs. Glendinning in *Pierre;* the narrator's wife in Melville's outrageous short story, "I and My Chimney"; Mrs. Newsome in *The Ambassadors;* the inhabitants of the boarding school in *The Beguiled* (1971). The man is unmanned by the contagion of domesticity and is left either absurdly embattled ("I and my chimney will never surrender") or hopelessly lost and ineffectual (Strether) or pernicious (Babbit). If Tootie relates to the first type of Satanic hubris, then John and Mr. Smith relate clearly to the second.

The richness of this material is clearly inseparable from its profound contradictions. To take only the question of female sexuality: while the energies embodied in Hester, Isabel, Regan, and the film noir vamp—Davis in *Beyond the Forest* and Jennifer Jones in *Duel in the Sun* (1946)—are supremely fascinating (and thus, at some unconscious level, espoused) precisely because they are subversive of patriarchal order, as soon as that order has been subverted and the satisfactions of anarchy indulged, order must be instantly reasserted, if only by the punishment of the agent. The rationale of the contradiction emerges most clearly in the extremist cases. Thus, while Isabel frees Pierre from castration by his mother and releases the impulse which rejects the patriarchal law, it is only, as his sister, to trap him in incest and castration once more. Tootie and Regan kill the Father, but the very act entails the dissolution of the Oedipus complex, and must be canceled out. The breakdown precipitated by female sexuality is to be desired, in that the institution it undermines is felt as repressive, but the cost is always too high, in that it is always seen, quite correctly, to involve a threat to possession of the phallus. Time and again woman plunges order into anarchy, but the terms of the new order are always so horrific that the old is reinstated. *The Exorcist* is an almost diagrammatic illustration of the process, and it represents, as such, a partial return to sources: a new inflection of the meeting of the small town and the Gothic, Satan and female sexuality in *Pierre* and *The Scarlet Letter.* It transpires that the small town, the outpost of a civilization created and consecrated in the name of woman, has actually taken the serpent to its bosom. Satan has not been expelled to the wilderness at all. The guardian of the "vestal temple" herself contains the forces which

The small town as matriarchy: Mr. Alonzo Smith (Leon Ames) and the Smith women in *Meet Me in St. Louis*. Personal collection of the editor.

continually threaten to destroy it. Hence the crucial significance of those films in which the link is made between the Lady and the Indian.

The link between the family film and the horror film (touched on by Robin Wood) emerges very concisely in that extraordinary moment in *Meet Me in St. Louis* when, on Halloween night, the Smith house turns into the Bates house from *Psycho*. (Wood, *Hollywood*, 84–85, 193–94) The space of confidence opened up in the first shot of the narrative is strangely lost as a forward tracking shot takes us this time toward a Gothic mansion at night, scarred by the shadow of a dead tree, the orange light of the windows no longer connoting a safe "inside" but assimilated by a dissolve to a shot of lurid skull masks and candles burning inside scooped-out pumpkins. The continuity between the two aspects of the house is carried out in the decor—in the heavy clutter of Victoriana, objets d'art, drapery, and its tone of slightly suffocating luxuri-ousness. Pairs of white candles transform mantlepieces into altars (the "vestal temple"), while the bad connotations of "southness" return in busts and figurines of Moors. *Psycho* makes the undertones explicit with its pastoral/allegorical icon of female nudity, its stuffed birds, its cast of clasped hands, its beckoning baroque statue presiding at the foot of the staircase.

The sublimation of female sexuality (the attempt to "block the hole" in Stephen Heath's phrase) can never rid itself of the perpetual danger that the hole will reassert its presence.

Regression to home and mother—to home as mother—contains the possibility of refinding mother's body, of ending up "inside" with a vengeance (the Bates predicament). Indeed, consider that cycle of films, contemporaneous with the 1940s domestic musical/comedy and the film noir about dead or missing women who remain as portraits, as potent forces immanent in the decor. The cycle is initiated by *Rebecca* (1940), which sets up also the recurrent Hitchcock image-complex of appalling mansion, impotent male, and castrating mother (Rebecca reborn in Mrs. Danvers) which proceeds through *Notorious* and *Under Capricorn* to *Psycho*. The structure is, of course, not simply Hitchcock's but an element of the American Gothic on which Poe worked countless variations.

Meet Me in St. Louis is one site of intersection of various complex strands. Its conventions permit the containment of conflict, but the particular process of containment exposes conflicts with unusual clarity.

If "St. Louis" suggests a myth of the organic community in a lost Golden Age, then the idea of "the fair" is the furthest reach of the myth—"It must look like a fairy land." The last moments of the film—the camera tracking in to a huge close-up of Esther's face on her rapt, repeated murmur of "Right here where we live"—convey an achieved union of the "normal"/everyday and the miraculous. They put forward, implicitly, for the spectator's consent, the proposition that "your home town too is miraculous if you only stop to look at it." (*It's a Wonderful Life* offers a similar conclusion while extending it through the allegorical mode to induce a sense of cosmic confidence in an anthropomorphized universe.) The proposition draws on a strangely secularized variant informed by the "entertainment-as-utopia" syndrome of a familiar assertion of the Puritan ethic—the divine is immanent in the mundane—which lends itself to a multitude of possible inflections: from Herbert's "the daily round, the common task" to Hopkins's "inscape." (Dyer, "Entertainment")

With the exception of the choruses and Judy Garland solos, the songs in *Meet Me in St. Louis* are characterized by a process of naturalization; it is stressed that various characters can't sing "well" (professionally) or aren't used to singing (Agnes, Grandpa, Tootie). The device finds its most beautiful expression in the singing of "You and I," where Mrs. Smith's lowering of the key to accommodate her husband's voice and her quiet, unobtrusive anticipation of the key line ("Through the years . . . ") magnificently convey that reaffirmation of monogamy and family unity through the guidance of woman which culminates in the transformation of solo into duet while, around the singers, the family returns, silent and unobserved. The naturalization both foregrounds the aspect of "performance" and partially covers it: the characters are singing because they want to, not because they are singers.

One can relate this to the way in which the songs are not marked off and isolated as numbers, but erupt out of the narrative, unless the sense of "tableau" or "performance" is justified diegetically, as, for instance, in "Skip to My Lou" or, most conspicuously, the cakewalk, which is explicitly a performance for an audience in the narrative and which places the proscenium arch within the frame. Thus, the first statement of *Meet Me in St. Louis* develops through Lon's humming it sporadically in the course of conversation, Agnes taking it up "naturally" as she goes upstairs, her passing it on to Grandpa, and, finally, its transference to Esther as she arrives in a buggy with her friends: each shift of voice, as it introduces an individual, binding him/her into the family, an emphasis reinforced by the movement of each individual into or toward the house. Thus, Esther's appearance recapitulates the arrival of Lon in the first shot and reinforces the notion of "binding in" by formal symmetry. Subsequently, both elements (naturalization, community through song) are amplified in Mr. Smith's remark that everyone is singing "that song," St. Louis becoming a grand extension of the family. The fluid continuity between musical and nonmusical elements is carried also in the mise-en-scène, in that characteristic flow of movement which both asserts spatial continuity and, as in the work of Max Ophüls, a self-conscious delight in physical grace, in the "musicalization" of the camera: consider, for example, the scene in which John and Esther extinguish the lights, with its complex counterpoint among (a) Esther's deliberate fabrication of "romantic" atmosphere; (b) the acknowledgment of, respect for, and embodiment of the romantic sensibility implicit in the elaborate crane shot in which the scene is realized; and (c) the deflation of both artifice and romanticism which proceeds from John's insuperable stolidity. The "binding in" is extended to the audience by way of that forward craning movement toward the inside initiated by the first shot and repeated as a structural principle thereafter in, for instance, the two dance scenes.

But the first song sequence already introduces conflicting elements, which cluster around the pointed opposition between work and leisure. As Agnes enters the kitchen, she remarks to her mother, "You should have taken a swim with us," to which Mrs. Smith replies, "With all I have to do?" All the singers in the first number—Lon, Agnes, Grandpa, Esther—are nonworkers, and their "freedom" is set against the domestic labor of Katie and Mrs. Smith and the business of making ketchup, which everyone wants to taste different. At once, a tension is set up (and stated, here, in a light key) between the celebration of the leisure and release from responsibility, which is shown to be expressive of, and to produce, unity (Lon, Agnes, Grandpa, Esther, St. Louis all united across space and time in the singing of the song), and work within and for the family which precipitates conflict (the ketchup). Two parallel and mutually opposed lines of suggestion have been established: the wonderful is everyday versus the wonderful is opposed to the everyday, in the second case the singing becoming instantly anarchic in its implications. One might compare the use of "the fair" here with that of the myth of Vienna in *Shadow of a Doubt*. It is at the moment that she is released from work by her daughter at the beginning of the second dinner sequence that Mrs. Newton, primping her hair in front of the mirror, begins to hum the "Merry Widow Waltz," immersing herself in the ethos of "romantic dream," the sexual connotations of which have already been sufficiently established.

The first song is also remarkable for that assimilation of Grandpa to the female children which reasserts itself in the scene in which Mr. Smith announces the family's departure for New York, and which, while it underlines the work theme (the young and old can be "irresponsible" because they are dependents), also feminizes him and places him on a more fundamental level with the women against the man of the house. (One should add that this, too, is ambiguous in that Mrs. Smith's "What about Katie, Grandpa, and the chickens?" gives him and the female servant the status of nonhuman property.) Indeed, *Meet Me in St. Louis* systematically links all the children and Grandpa, with the emphasis on the female children (Lon's contribution is minimal): Agnes and Esther in the first statement; Esther and Rose in the second, with—via the dissolve to the duet from Tootie's "Wasn't I lucky to be born in my favorite city?"—the implicit collaboration of the youngest daughter. It is the father who, in disrupting the song, violates the unity ("For heaven's sake stop that screeching!"), and through him the theme of the oppressiveness of the work undertaken in the name of the family at once becomes explicit.

There are nine song sequences in the film. Of these, all but one ("Skip to My Lou") are initiated by women, and with the same exception, individual male characters feature significantly in only two—Grandpa in the first statement of "Meet Me in St. Louis," Mr. Smith in "You and I." Apart from one line in "Skip to My Lou" ("Lost my partner"), the "hero" does not sing at all. The preeminence of women musically—which coincides of course with the narrative premise—is complex in its implications, and it becomes necessary at this point to consider Judy Garland's solos and their relation to the film as a whole. The first Garland number, "The Boy Next Door," establishes a set of related motifs and images:

1. Woman as predator. The number is preceded by Rose's provocative walk up the porch steps in an attempt to attract John's attention, and then by Rose and Esther strolling out and posing themselves nonchalantly on the balcony for the same purpose. Both strategies are conspicuously unsuccessful.

2. The reversal of the convention which dictates that sexual aggression is the prerogative of the male is contained within and defined by the convention which prescribes marriage as the destiny of the female. Esther and Katie have just been discussing Rose's "problem" ("The brutal fact is she isn't getting any younger"), and throughout the film the concept of "marriage at all costs" is repeatedly foregrounded.

3. Inseparably from 1 and 2, woman as image: both Rose and Esther attempt to draw the attention of the male by creating themselves in, and as conventionalized images of, "femininity." Songs and nonmusical narrative alike emphasize Esther in a frame: the frame of the proscenium arch in the cakewalk, and in "The Boy Next Door," "Merry Little Christmas," and the "Bannister Song," the frame of the portrait, the icon. Indeed, the "Bannister Song" makes the imagery explicit by uniting the connotations of theater and of picture. The number is preceded by the extinguishing of the lamps, the prelude during which Esther's "performance," however unappreciated, is in preparation (the perfume which she "saves for special occasions") and which subtly suggests the lowering of the house lights around the "stage" which the staircase will finally provide. Esther leaves John gazing up at her from the foot of the staircase and, at his prompting ("How does it go?"), takes up the poem into song and herself into poetic image ("He watches the picture smiling"). Elsewhere, the concept of the picture frame is echoed by the frames of window and mirror and reinforced in, for instance, the scenes in which Esther prepares for the two dances, where the adoption of an artificial and oppressive femininity is associated with the donning of costume ("I feel elegant but I can't breathe").

Once again, the image of the frame works in terms both of the narrative and of the relation of spectator to film. "The Boy Next Door" is a courtship display for the absent male spectator in the diegesis (John) and also a performance on set for the absent spectator who will be provided by the screening of the film in a cinema. Just as Esther stages herself in the window frame, longing for John's attention, so Judy Garland the star performs a musical number for the contemplation of the spectator. And, like a spectator, John is passive. He does not sing—he watches.

The terms in which the Esther/John relationship is initiated are structurally crucial. It is emphasized that Esther does not know John and that her imagination has transformed him into an ideal figure: "My only regret is that we've never met/Though I dream of him all the while." John is introduced, from the girls' perspective, standing on the lawn in front of his house dressed in white, the whiteness suggesting not simply an immaculate ideal but also a tabula rasa, an emptiness onto which emotions can be projected. Thus, if Esther's desire at this point is expressed in self-re-creation and self-projection as an image, then the object of desire is perceived in similar terms. Posed in profile with his pipe, John is instantly an icon of "normal," clean-cut manhood, the guardian of heart and home; the complex tone of the scene—and of a great deal of the film—consists in the fact that while the conventions of desire are made ironically explicit (desire is shown to be determined by convention), we are nevertheless invited to feel a degree of sympathetic involvement with characters who are uncritically governed by them.

In his account of the female Oedipus complex which, satisfactorily resolved, initiates normal womanhood and locates the female child "correctly" within the institutions which precede her, Freud suggests that the girl's desire is transferred from the father to the man who, as husband, will replace the father. Glossing this in *Psychoanalysis and Feminism*, Juliet Mitchell remarks that "there is an obvious link between the security of Oedipal father love and the happy hearth and home of later years." (118) By marrying the boy next door, who appears at once in the image of the father, the girl reproduces the family structure and, in the same action, reproduces society. Similarly, the girl relinquishes her hostility to her mother (consider Esther's concern to echo Mrs. Smith's judgment in the ketchup controversy) and identifies with her in relation to the father. This structure remains beneath the open hostility to Mr. Smith in the second half of the film in that the proposed move to New York directly threatens the smooth reproduction of the same social/familial order through the marriage of the two eldest daughters. The female rebellion against the real father (Mr. Smith) operates in the interests of the law of Father (the institutions of patriarchy) and is explicitly concerned to perpetuate the status quo. Similarly, of course, acquiescence in the move north would operate in the same interests. By concentrating on the social construction of desire within the family, the film succeeds in setting up a dramatic context in which the constraints on the female characters to reproduce the patriarchal order become apparent, all the more strikingly because of the apparent impotence of the given father figure.

Mitchell continues, quoting Freud, that it is through her identification with her mother that the girl "acquires her attractiveness to a man, whose Oedipus attachment to his mother it kindles into passion." (118) At the beginning of *Meet Me in St. Louis*, John is living alone with his mother (his father, presumably, dead), and during the extinguishing of the lights sequence, his only response to Esther's perfume is the remark that it reminds him of his grandmother. At the end of the second dance sequence, the Esther/John relationship is ratified in an image which condenses, with perfect simplicity, the logic of the "family romance." Esther, having been duly punished for her conspiracy against Lucille by dancing with each of the "perfect horrors" she has originally selected as Lucille's partners, is finally rescued from the last of them by her grandfather who cuts in in the name of an "oriental" custom which fixes the status of woman as that of an item of property ("When a stranger admires one of your possessions, it's common courtesy to offer it to him"). Esther responds with relief and gratitude ("You're the first human being I've danced with all evening"), and grandfather tells her how proud he is of her acceptance of the penalty he has imposed. The camera cranes up and we see grandfather guiding Esther as they dance toward and behind a huge decorated Christmas tree at the far end of the room. When Esther emerges on the other side, she is dancing with John, and the waltz which the orchestra is playing becomes "Auld Lang Syne." The moment is beautifully exact: as the old year becomes the New Year, John takes the place of the father/grandfather and loves Esther in the image of the mother/grandmother, the connotations of ritual reenactment and repetition underlined by music, imagery (Christmas—the annual festival of the "holy family"), and movement (the unbroken circle).

But the film is significantly more complex than this in ways which have, perhaps, already been implied and which are bound up with John's status as "the ideal." One needs to account for the fact that while, on one level, the Esther/John relationship is offered as a paradigm of the "American romance" (girl meets and marries boy next door), John scarcely exists in the film as anything more than a token and is played and presented with an innocuousness which markedly sets off, by contrast, the intense vitality projected by Judy Garland. One needs to account, that is, for the discrepancy between a dominant ideological project—which is clearly there in the film, which will be read as being there, and which is given in the narrative data—and the contradictory implications set up by the realization of the project.

The point here is the extraordinary way in which John becomes effectively superfluous to the four of Esther's songs supposedly inspired by him, the songs being transmuted into a form of communion between Esther and her own desire. In only one of the four (the "Bannister Song") is John directly physically present, and not only is it sung by Esther, the "smiling picture" of the lyric, in praise of her own beauty ("the loveliest face in town") but also, during the singing, she scarcely looks at John at all, her gaze remaining fixed on some distant space off-camera while John continues to gaze entranced at her. (The device is repeated in "Merry Little Christmas," in which Esther is clearly addressing herself rather than John, whose absence—as Esther's pretext—is signaled before the song begins by the lowering of a window blind, or Tootie, for whom the advice delivered in the song is conspicuously ineffective). Similarly, "The Boy Next Door" culminates in Esther's poses before the mirror in the hallway and her rapt solitary dance, and the first meeting with John is preceded by further intense self-scrutiny in a mirror framed by blue material similar in shade to that of her dress. Downstairs we discover that John is also dressed in blue, and Esther is continually associated with the color throughout the first half of the film.

Esther's creation of herself as a picture comes to appear less as a method of attracting John than as a way of allowing an image of herself to emerge for herself. John functions as an alibi which allows her to dramatize her own desire on a private stage for her own eyes.

Hence, the immediate appearance in "The Boy Next Door" of the image of the mirror, and Esther's performance before it; the "ideal," the "overestimated object" of romantic love which, according to Freud, is always informed by the primary narcissism in which the child "was its own ideal," recedes or becomes the catalyst of those moments in which desire erupts for itself. Consider "The Trolley Song." Esther begins singing it the moment at which she sees John racing after the trolley and catching it at the last minute. This is also the moment at which she turns her back on him to look inside the tram, and the entire song is delivered in the midst of a circle of admiring women who form her background and chorus, gazing in at her as their center. On the line "His hand holding mine," Esther clasps her own hands together, and both her singing and the impulse which informed it are cut short abruptly when Esther becomes aware of John's presence next to her. They seat themselves immediately on opposite sides of the trolley platform and Minnelli dissolves directly to the Halloween sequence. Thus, while "The Trolley Song" is ostensibly precipitated by John's arrival and is dedicated to him as the ideal ("He was quite the handsomest of men"), the actual staging of the number physically excludes the male, and the one moment in which a man intrudes into the performance, by raising his hat to Esther, provokes her withdrawal, shaking her head emphatically.

It is useful at this point to recall Jacques Lacan's definition of desire: "Desire is irreducible to need because it is not in principle a relation to a real object which is independent of the subject, but a relation to the phantasy. It is irreducible to demand in so far as it seeks to impose itself without taking language or the unconscious of the other into account, and requires to be recognized absolutely by him." Thus, one can point to two aspects of "The Boy Next Door." Esther's desire relates to the fantasy of John ("We've never met"), an emphasis underlined by the dialogue before the song ("I want it to be something strange and wonderful"). Simultaneously, the dance before the window captures exactly "the desire to have one's desire recognized," which the scene has already established as a ruling motive.

The songs in *Meet Me in St. Louis* mark repeatedly a point of tension between containment and overflow. They continually override their authority while only being conceivable within its terms. They suggest moments of license and bear as such all the hallmarks of the defining restrictions. Thus, the celebration of female desire in "The Trolley Song" is dramatically contingent on John but does not survive his physical presence. Similarly, while "Skip to My Lou," the communal youth dance, takes place within (is contained by) the Smith household, it clearly functions in part as a rebellion against ideological constrictions: a rejection of hearth and home ("I've run away to a neighboring state") and of prohibitive morality ("I don't care what my folks think"). Indeed, the end of the song is marked by one of the girls falling over onto the floor, the incident suggesting very simply the shock of "reentry," the abrupt transition between two worlds.

More significantly, the very concept of "St. Louis" itself is redefined in this context. From the first scene of the film, the dream of "the fair" is the alibi for the release of those energies which are defined in opposition to "work." Yet, the extraordinary bleakness and flatness of tone of the final scene (to which Robin Wood has drawn attention) is a sufficient testimony to the failure of correspondence between the energies and the ideal in the name of which they have been allowed to emerge. (Wood, "Introduction," 11) It becomes clear, indeed, that in taking the fair as ideal, the energies have been devoted to their own entrapment. The fair is the repressive, quotidian reality etherealized, and the final scene is dominated by imagery of sublimation. The exhibition itself is merely glimpsed, across a stretch of water, as a display of brightly shimmering lights and has been built, we are told, on a drained bog. John, briefly alone with Esther, tells her "I liked it better when it was a swamp and there was just the two of us" before they are summoned to rejoin the family, two nuns shrouded in black appearing spectrally in the background. The connotations could scarcely be more explicit: sexual energies, the life of the body, associated directly in John's remark with the swamp, are to be purified by assimilation to the small-town-as-Celestial-City, and the summoning of the couple to join the family group is presided over by figures suggestive equally of Holy Church and death. Real relations and conditions of existence are sublimated in imaginary ones: the fair, twinkling beyond the mirror line marked by the river (and the final track in on Esther's face suggests strongly that the fair is the outward projection of an internal image), becomes exactly, in Lacan's phrase, "the presence of an absence of reality." It is crucial here that Tootie, though subjected anew—like Esther and John—to the prohibitions of the renewed, reaffirmed, idealized family (she is asked not to eat too much, "you'll spoil your dinner"), proceeds at once to undo the sublimation in her account of her dream (which is to be set against Esther's "I never dreamed anything could be so beautiful")—"I dreamt a big wave came up and flooded the whole city, and when the water went back it was all muddy and horrible and full of dead bodies!" The apocalyptic vision so central to the American Gothic, from Poe to Roger Corman and *The Exorcist*, suggests not simply a wish (it emerges in a dream) or a portent (The Fall of the House of Smith) but also the perception of a reality, of that face of St. Louis concealed by the fair. Just one scene previously, Mr. Smith has declared, "We'll stay here till we rot!" Tootie knows that they are rotten already. It is, perhaps, significant that she shows scarcely any interest in the fair throughout the film.

This sublimation theme has already been firmly established in the treatment of money: Mr. Smith's attempt to repress the energies which find expression in music is balanced by the attempt of the female members of the family to repress the economic reality in which the family is bound up and which dictates Mr. Smith's decision to move to New York. To Rose's "I hate, loathe, despise, and abominate money!" Mr. Smith replies at once, "You also spend it"; the exchange neatly inflects the film's central opposition in economic terms—St. Louis in apotheosis as the fair versus St. Louis as economic unit. Thus, the final scene, as it sublimates sexuality into marriage and family, represses money elsewhere (into "New York," into the swamp), and forgets the problems of the continuing economic viability of the family which Mr. Smith has brought forward ("I've got to worry about where the money's coming from"). The three occasions on which the family is reassembled after the divisive split attendant on Mr. Smith's announcement all depend consciously on the repression of those problems. "You and I," while it reconvenes the family group, affirms not the family but the couple (the family does not join in and is not mentioned in the lyric) and affirms it, too, in isolation from society in "metaphysical" terms of the triumph over time and adversity ("You and I together, forever"). The immediate problem which is, precisely, the family as a locus of conflicting interests—at a moment of economic crisis—is completely avoided. Subsequently, Mr. Smith's change of heart after Tootie's destruction of the snow people is presented unequivocally as a piece of stoical window dressing, the violence of which comes over equally as bitter resentment of the family which has forced it on him, the suppression of his own desires and aspirations, and an attempt to make himself believe that it is, after all, his own decision. Indeed, the "happy ending" is achieved by two displays of "male dominance" which are shown to be victories in campaigns of attrition mounted by the women; the forthright proposal of Rose's suitor ("I don't want to hear any arguments") is at once qualified by Esther's remark—"He's just putty in your hands." The women have won, and the palm of victory is their own entrapment, with their castrated men, inside patriarchal institutions.

This brings us to Tootie, the crux of the film, the register of its defining tensions. If Mr. and Mrs. Smith suggest the couple achieved as basic unit of the family, each with their "sphere" (home and business), and Rose and Esther are characterized by the desperate struggle to insert themselves in the same structure and perpetuate it ("We can't be too particular"), then Agnes and Tootie, the youngest sisters, embody and express a potential anarchy, a possible subversion of the structure. The film is quite clear-sighted about the kind of possibility; there is not a hint of sentimentality, nor any pretence that the return of repressed energies in Tootie are uncontaminated by repression. Consider, for example, her obsession with death (Twain's Emmeline Grangerford in *Huckleberry Finn* affords a useful parallel in contrast), which is used as an overtly neurotic inflection of capitalist possessiveness; she hoards dead matter ("I'm taking all my dolls—the dead ones too. I'm taking everything!"), and part of the impulse behind the destruction of the snow people is the determination that no one else should have them if she can't. Similarly, the dolls suggest a morbid surrogate family in regard to which her inferior status in the Smith house is replaced by the power of life and death ("I expect she won't live through the night").

This last represents, perhaps, the correct emphasis. The power of life and death is the power of the Father, and Tootie's usurpation of the Father's function is the extreme instance of that pattern of reversal of which she is the focus, whereby the ostensible values of the Smith household are inverted and their underlying logic revealed. Thus, for example, in the present case, the obsession with death and physical cruelty comes across both as a distorted recognition of the body (the physical nature which the family ethos represses) and as a magnification of sadism latent in the family group in any case, surfacing in such jocular exchanges as that between Agnes and Katie about the fate of Agnes's cat ("I'll stab you to death in your sleep and then I'll tie you to two wild horses till you're pulled apart!"). It is a measure of the film's intelligence that Agnes and Tootie can be seen both as profoundly subversive of an order based on repression and as themselves already caught up in the network of repressiveness. Both elements frequently emerge simultaneously; Agnes and Tootie's undisguised giggling amusement at Esther's romantic daydream after her reconciliation with John serves equally as an implicit comment on the boy-meets-girl romantic love which the family so easily recuperates and as a type of the oppressive, prying inquisitiveness on which Rose immediately comments ("It's very difficult for a person to have any private life in this family").

Three scenes repay particular attention.

1. The first dance sequence might itself be compared with that extraordinary, because emblematic, moment in *The Exorcist* in which Regan, having been packed off to bed, intrudes on her mother's party while the adults are gathered round the piano singing "Home, Sweet Home" to the accompaniment of a priest, and pisses on the carpet. Agnes and Tootie, likewise sent off the bed, likewise intrude and are compared by John, who sees them first, to vermin ("There are mice in the house"). The grown-ups adopt at once the familiar tone of maudlin patronage ("She's such a sweet little thing"), and Esther attempts to appease Tootie's desire to join in by suggesting that she sing an "appropriate" nursery song—that is, to perform as a child. Tootie refuses vehemently ("You know I hate those songs!") and proceeds, in the face of some opposition, to sing a forbidden ballad ("I was drunk last night, dear mother"), with the word *drunk* censored. The moment is remarkable and of considerable complexity. Tootie's appearance immediately follows the singing of "Skip to My Lou," in which the group's resentments and rebelliousness have been contained in the allowable license of "party high spirits." Tootie violates the license both of the party and of her own role as female child (she should be in bed, should be a sweet little thing), and she does so by mimicking not simply intoxication but also sexual reversal—the presumed singer of the ballad is male. Again, the outrageousness is contained: the song promises future sobriety in return for mother's forgiveness, the forbidden word is not pronounced, and the entire incident is promptly "covered" by the performance of the cakewalk, in which marriage and settlement are reaffirmed ("Two live as one, One live as two, Under the bamboo tree"), as is woman's place within it ("I want to change your name"). It is important here that Tootie's ballad is the only unaccompanied musical number in the film, and that the cakewalk, by emphasizing the conventions of "performance" to a marked extent, restores—formally as well as ideologically—a sense of the proprieties. But there is a residual tension, analogous to that underlying "The Trolley Song." The voice presumed by the lyric, as by the drunkard song, is male, but the lyric is performed by two sisters. As in the other case, while the song affirms the centrality of the male, the performance excludes him, the cakewalk finding a further nuance in giving a song in praise of exogamy ("I want to change your name") to two female members of one family. The ironic play of connotations and contradictions is central to the film's concerns.

2. The Halloween sequence. As I have tried to suggest, *Meet Me in St. Louis* implies a tension between the supremacy of patriarchal institutions and the impotence of particular men. The tension is beautifully expressed by the moment when, while the women of the household are gathered round the dining table waiting for Mr. Smith to come downstairs, a crash is heard from above as he trips over one of Tootie's roller skates. Raising her eyes, Katie mutters dryly: "The Lord and Master!" The phrase is not simply ironic since, in the ensuing sequence, Mr. Smith's decision to vet all incoming telephone calls is a sufficient demonstration of his real power, and the incident also prepares the idea, to be developed later, that he is as much encumbered by his family as the family by him. All these connotations meet in the prevailing suggestion that the power structure

of the patriarchal family is totally insufficient to the exigencies of the reality; while to the extent that they are devoted to circumventing Mr. Smith, the women's actions proclaim that the power structure need not be taken seriously but merely lived with, they serve to reinforce the structure to the extent that they are supremely preoccupied with the necessity of marriage. It is appropriate, then, that Mr. Smith should fall on Tootie's skates, since in the Halloween sequence it is not an individual but the very function of the Father which, through Tootie, comes under attack.

The sequence takes the principle of reversal to its extreme and logical conclusion. The conventions of the domestic musical comedy become the conventions of the horror movie. With the exception of the film's opening sequence shot and the trolley sequence (the latter largely involving, in any case, the use of back projection), the Halloween sequence is the first to take place out of doors, and it is structured by the motif of boundary transgression so fundamental to the horror genre: Tootie moves outward from the space of confidence, the known and established world (for spectator as much as character), through a transitional zone, to that "other space" where her self-imposed task must be executed. The visit to the voodoo ceremony in *I Walked with a Zombie* and Lila's exploration of the Bates house in *Psycho* offer suggestive parallels in that in all three cases the other space exists explicitly in an inverted mirror relation to the known space, and that each sequence moves toward the discovery, by the female protagonist, of a monstrously potent parent figure beyond the last forbidden door. The pattern, and its psychoanalytical implications, are generic givens, and the relation to the descent myth (and thus to structures which overflow the genre—see for instance, Vladimir Propp's analysis of Russian fairy tales) is equally clear: in this case, Tootie has undertaken a mission which, if fulfilled, will entail a reward (acceptance by the other children).

The mission here is parricide, and the spirit of Halloween, as the film depicts it, is a massive, concerted rebellion against the Symbolic Father—the Father as Law, as totem figure, as the embodiment of power and prohibition. Thus, Mr. Smith, the castrated small-town father, becomes Mr. Brockhoff and is endowed, in Tootie's imagination, with all the ideas of absolute power and dark, forbidden energy which the "real" father so conspicuously lacks: sexual potency and control of women ("He was beating his wife with a red hot poker"); indulgence in alcohol (remember Tootie's identification with a drunkard in her ballad); abominable rites ("He burns cats at midnight in his furnace"). It is of the essence, then, that Tootie's crime is not literal murder but a handful of flour in the face: she is not killing an individual but desecrating a totem.

Most significantly, given the film's concerns, the rebellion consists in the rejection of the Oedipus complex: all the boys are in drag, as are most of the girls, including Agnes and Tootie. Momentarily, and fantastically, the basic principle of socialization in patriarchal culture is triumphantly overthrown, gender roles disintegrate, and as household furniture is heaped joyously onto a blazing bonfire around which the children dance like demons or "savages," Tootie, the female child, is unanimously declared, in place of Mr. Brockhoff, "the most horrible of all." It is this triumph of the child which distinguishes the Halloween sequence from, say, *I Walked with a Zombie*, *Psycho*, *The Exorcist*, and *Carrie*; indeed, from the end of *Meet Me in St. Louis*, in which the repressive energies embodied in the parent figure are indomitable and enforce either "tragedy" or the bluff of the happy ending, either "things could not have been different" or "things do not need to be different." If the small-town myth is, as I have suggested, the heir of the pastoral convention, each of them serving to provide extremely formalized models of ideal communities in which sexuality is rigidly contained, then the appropriate analogy for Tootie and the children is Comus and his "rout."

The contagion of anarchy spreads immediately into the world of order. Agnes and Tootie nearly succeed in derailing a tram by placing a dress stuffed to resemble a body across the tracks, and Rose's outraged protest that everyone might have been killed produces from Agnes the sublimely amoral reply, "Oh Rose! You're so stuck up!" Disaster is averted by the intervention, appropriately, of John in the interests of the paternal order, but Tootie's lie (she pretends that John has not rescued her, but beaten her up) immediately precipitates the repetition by Esther in the "normal" world of the crime committed by Tootie in the underworld: Esther avenges her sister by beating up John on his own front porch. The misunderstanding is subsequently cleared up and "natural" relations reinstated, but the raison d'être of the entire sequence is the reenactment of breakdown in the Esther/John relationship with the accompanying inversion of purely conventional gender characteristics (the repeated phrase "you've got a mighty strong grip for a boy"/"for a girl"), and the willing assumption by John of a posture of masochistically passive submission ("If you're not busy tomorrow night, could you beat me up again?"). Indeed, the token of reconciliation becomes John's deliberate adoption in his request to Esther to help him turn out the lights, of the role of timid "femininity" that she has previously exploited ("I'm afraid of mice"). The release of chaos reveals nothing if not that the proprieties are quite arbitrary, perilously fragile, and contradictory: the roles which John and Esther are culturally required to adopt effectively invert the actual characteristics of the relationship.

3. The "killing" of the snow people. While the sequence, which again takes place at night and out of doors, repeats the murder of Mr. Brockhoff, this time in the context of the Smith family itself, the particular inflection is significantly different and profoundly ambiguous. On one level Tootie's impulse is conservative: she dreads the prospective disruption of the status quo and, in particular, the absence of the Father (Esther discovers her sitting up so as not to miss Father Christmas: "I've been waiting such a long time! . . . How will he find us next year?"). On a second level, the attack on the snow people is an attack on the Father, the intensity of which is exacerbated rather than assuaged by Esther's assurances that "some day soon we all will be together," since it is the united family that ensures Tootie's repression. The sequence ends with Tootie and Esther in tears, at the very moment that Esther's stoical insistence that "we can be happy anywhere as long as we're together" breaks down. The suggestion that it is "being together" which perpetuates the misery is very strong, and it is maintained as an undercurrent to the end.

Alfred Hitchcock's *Spellbound:* Text and Countertext (1986)

One can discern in *Spellbound* (1945) the elements of three of Hitchcock's favorite narrative structures: (1) the double-chase, in which the hero, in pursuit of the real villain, is himself pursued mistakenly by the police (for example, *The 39 Steps* [1935], *Saboteur* [1942]); (2) the romantic love story, usually characterized by some form of tension or struggle for mastery between the partners (for example, *Notorious* [1946], *Marnie* [1964]); and (3) the psychopath story, in which the male protagonist is gradually revealed to be insane and criminal (for example, *Shadow of a Doubt* [1943], *Psycho* [1960]). These three simple, schematized structures, or delicate variations and modifications of them, usually coexist in any one film, and in the case of *Spellbound*, one can relate them quite distinctly to explicit ideological projects.

The first of these is the validation of psychoanalysis as, simultaneously, the science of "the truth" and the science of "normality"—a project spelled out for us in the caption which follows the credits. An incomplete quotation from Shakespeare ("The fault is not in our stars, but in ourselves"), which in context has nothing to do with psychological disorder—it is part of Cassius's plea to Brutus for revolution—introduces a preamble which tells us that psychoanalysis is a method of treating "the emotional problems of the sane." Once these have been "uncovered and interpreted," the "illness and confusion disappear, and the devils of unreason are driven from the human soul."

The vocabulary suggests that the attainment of "normality" (reason) is like the entry to a state of grace and that psychoanalysis is analogous to exorcism. This association of science and the casting out of demons, which on the one hand unites an appeal to a belief in the rigorous, objective finality of empirical evidence and on the other an appeal to the mystic notion of ritual purification, establishes psychoanalysis as a kind of secular religion, the embodiment of the union of two forms of ultimate authority.

This emphasis is obviously well served by the use of the detection/manhunt story. Through a variation of the double-chase format, the villain whom the hero and heroine are pursuing becomes the hero's neurosis, and his cure becomes the removal of the stigma of guilt and of abnormality—the assurance of his "innocence." This is intensified by the fact that there is also a "real" human villain involved, Dr. Murchison (Leo G. Carroll), who has to be unmasked by Constance (Ingrid Bergman), just as she has been the driving impulse behind the cure of Ballantyne (Gregory Peck), before total harmony can be restored. The conclusion of the narrative elides the discovery of (a) the hero's neurosis, (b) the real villain, and (c) the "truth"—so that the achievement of psychological certainty is colored by the unmasking of a murderer. The implication is that just as one can assign a crime to a criminal, and solve it, so one can assign a neurosis to a trauma, and cure it. Indeed, the traumatic event in Ballantyne's life is itself a crime, and his triumphant cry as his memory returns—"I didn't kill my brother! It was an accident!"—conveys his liberation from both guilt and disease. The aberrations are cleared away, and a conclusive state of ideological confidence is established, both on the social level (the crime has been solved and the hero is innocent) and on the psychological level (the hero has been purified and is now normal).

The second ideological project is familiar from numerous Hollywood movies: the "managing," independent, professional and/or intellectual woman becomes a "real" woman by falling in love with the hero. In *Spellbound*, this process unfolds in parallel to the hero's cure and is presented, through the imagery and dialogue, as analogous to it. Constance's "manlessness" is characterized by frustration, repression, and the usurpation of the male role, and the film ends with the "cure" of her frigidity and her accession to her proper place as Ballantyne's wife. Her role as an analyst has been played out in the course of the action in that (a) she has cured Ballantyne, (b) she has discovered the real criminal, through psychoanalysis, and (c) she has found "herself." Because the only other patients with whom we see her involved (Miss Carmichael and Mr. Garmes) function as symbolic projections of herself and Ballantyne, there is no need either in narrative or in symbolic terms for Constance to be an analyst anymore. The film begins with both characters "misplaced" inside Green Manors, their "true" identities suppressed (Ballantyne in the role of Edwardes, Constance in that of prim, "sexless" physician). The achievement of essential identity at the end is again reinforced by its juxtaposition with a similar process (the clearing of the wrong man, the revelation of the right man) in the detective story.

The two projects are brought together through the door imagery which informs the whole film. In the opening caption, and repeatedly in the dialogue, the discovery of the causes of neurosis is expressed in terms of the unlocking of doors, and the caption is superimposed over a shot of the stately door of Green Manors, set between pillars in a grandiose, mock-classic portico. At once, the detection of trauma and the detection of the crime are linked. Green Manors is the house of Dr. Murchison, and the film moves toward Constance's final penetration of its "sanctum sanctorum," Dr. Murchison's study, and her unveiling of the mystery, a scene to which I shall return later. The scene culminating in the couple's first embrace is also based on the door motif, most obviously in the shot of a vista of opening doors superimposed on Constance's face to suggest her "release" at the moment of the kiss, but also insisted on in the preliminary detail of the scene: the subjective tracking shot toward Ballantyne's door and Constance's hesitation outside it; her choice of the library door before she dares to enter Ballantyne's room; and finally, the threshold of the bedroom which separates the couple, until Ballantyne crosses it and they are united in the kiss.

I wish to suggest that the scene-by-scene realization in *Spellbound* consistently works against the conclusions of the narrative, and that although every detail of Constance's and Ballantyne's "case" is systematically explained and accounted for, it is implied, equally systematically, that this explicit solution is no solution at all. I will begin by considering the opening of the film.

Spellbound begins by establishing a very intricate pattern of contrasts, similarities, and parallels among the characters, presented through a series of meetings and conversations, as in the following chart:

    I. Miss Carmichael playing cards. Interruption (summons from Constance). Miss Carmichael leaves with Harry, the guard.

    II. Harry and Miss Carmichael on their way to Constance's office.

    III. a. Entry of Harry and Miss Carmichael into Constance's office. Departure of Harry.

          b. Constance and Miss Carmichael. Latter's outburst leads to

          c. Entry of Harry and Dr. Fleurot. Harry leaves with Miss Carmichael.

          d. Constance and Dr. Fleurot, interrupted by

          e. Entry of Dr. Murchison. Departure of Dr. Fleurot.

          f. Constance and Dr. Murchison, interrupted by

          g. Entry of Harry and Mr. Garmes. Constance sees "Dr. Edwardes" through the window as he arrives for the first time. Cut to

    IV. a. Doctors speculating about Dr. Edwardes. Enter "Dr. Edwardes"/Ballantyne.

          b. "Edwardes"/Ballantyne and his new colleagues. Enter Dr. Murchison.

          c. Meeting of "Edwardes"/Ballantyne and Murchison. Exit Dr. Murchison. Fade out.

    V. a. Dining room. Fleurot, Murchison, Constance, and other doctors discussing Dr. Edwardes. Enter "Edwardes"/Ballantyne.

          b. First meeting of "Edwardes"/Ballantyne and Constance. "Love at first sight": crisis.

It will be seen that the conversations are built around the entrances and exits of various characters; this is particularly evident in the third scene, where each conversation is marked by the arrival of the next character and the departure of the previous one. The scene is given a further symmetry by the use of Harry, the guard, who brings in Miss Carmichael in III (a) and introduces Mr. Garmes in III (g) and by the arrangement of the meetings—two with patients, two with doctors, the latter inserted between the former. Let us consider these four encounters in turn, in the light of the ideological projects that have been described.

The film begins with a brief scene (I) in which we see Miss Carmichael (Rhonda Fleming), the "nymphomaniac" patient, playing cards with a group of other patients, the game being interrupted by a summons from Dr. Constance Peterson. Miss Carmichael leaves, saying that she had had "a perfect hand" and "would've beaten the pants off you," and when she enters Constance's office, tells her that she has "ruined a very interesting card game." The sexual symbolism of the game of cards, and the motif of a doctor trumping or spoiling the patient's hand, is resumed in Ballantyne's dream (to be considered more fully later), where the analyst figure miraculously beats Ballantyne with blank cards. The suggestion in both cases is that the cards are loaded inevitably in favor of the doctor, and in both cases the patient's defeat—the repression of sexual drives, the suggestion of impotence or inferiority (Miss Carmichael accuses Constance of wanting to "feel superior" to her)—is followed by an assault on the analyst: Miss Carmichael's outburst, physical and verbal, against Constance, and Dr. Edwardes's fall from the roof. The notion that the patient's symptoms are a response to persecution by a figure of authority is central to the film.

An explicit iconographic antithesis is at once established between Constance and Miss Carmichael. Constance's hair is gathered up on her head in a tight bun; Miss Carmichael's is loose around her shoulders. Constance wears glasses (for a woman, an instant signifier of "intellectuality" in Hollywood movies) and a white, "sexless" doctor's overall, and when we first see her at the desk, she has a cigarette in a holder in one hand and a pen in the other, the phallic symbolism underlining her masculine appearance and her status as an "authority." Miss Carmichael wears a skirt and a loose, plunging blouse, and she is offered very obviously as a type of seductive femininity: she moves with nonchalant, sensuous grace and drapes herself on a chair, in contrast with the erectness of Constance's posture and the precision of her movements. The opposition "doctor/patient" is thus redefined as the opposition "repression or denial of femininity/magnification of femininity"—both being, in the terms of Hollywood convention, abnormal states. The nymphomaniac and the intellectual woman are both seen as threats in that they both possess characteristics regarded as the prerogatives of men: in the former case, sexual aggression, and in the latter, mental penetration (knowledge, and the ability to pursue and acquire it independently), sometimes combined, as in this case, with an institutional position. Constance and Miss Carmichael are both "phallic" women, and it is significant that the scenes II––III (g) begin with the latter's "attack" on Harry with her nails, when she takes his hand in an apparent attempt to seduce him, and end with Constance causing acute distress to Mr. Garmes by cutting open her mail with a paper knife. Again, the ostensible antithesis (abnormal patient attacks her guard/doctor about to resume the attempted cure of her patient) is subverted by the symbolic parallel. Both incidents suggest the transference of potency to the woman and an experience of emasculation by the man—a reading stressed particularly in the second incident by the fact that (1) Constance refuses Mr. Garmes's offer to cut the envelopes for her with "I can do this myself very well" and (2) at that moment she is watching, through the window, the arrival of the man who is going to displace Dr. Murchison.

Thus, Miss Carmichael is related, in the film's symbolic scheme, both to Ballantyne—in that both are Constance's patients and both succumb to breakdown or violence at moments of extreme erotic tension in response to what is interpreted as Constance's aggression—and to Constance herself—in that she is simultaneously sensual and repressed, sexual desire coexisting with a strenuous denial of it.

At the beginning of the scene, Miss Carmichael occupies more or less the position of the skeptical spectator: "Psychoanalysis bores the pants off me." The phrase, which echoes the one she has just used with her opponents in the card game when she speaks of "beating the pants off" them, marks her transition from potency and power as the prospective winner to the subjected role of patient. This strategy, ostensibly the film's raison d'être, is elaborated in the encounter between Ballantyne and Dr. Brulov (Michael Chekhov): a character and, by extension, the spectator, is initiated into the mysteries and made aware of the perspective in which experience/the narrative is intelligible. There is, in fact, a fundamental tension at this point between the film's two projects: the woman who is "presenting" psychoanalysis to the patient who embodies sexual "excess" is herself seen as sexually repressed.

Miss Carmichael, to Constance, is a typical case—she has told "the usual proportion" of lies under analysis. The former, lying on the couch, admits this, and with sudden, uncontrollable vehemence, she launches into an account of how she bit off the mustache of a man who tried to make a pass at her. This castration fantasy, which anticipates Constance's role in the ensuing narrative, is introduced by the phrase "I hate men," on which Hitchcock cuts to a close-up of Constance, clearly alarmed and personally touched by the violence of the confession.

Reacting against this intense self-revelation, Miss Carmichael turns on Constance, denouncing both her as an individual ("Miss Frozen-Puss!") and the notion of "scientific detachment" as such ("You and your drooling science!"). We think back to the transition between scenes one and two, which is marked by a dissolve to Harry and Miss Carmichael in the corridor from the sharp, angular face of a nurse who whispers to Harry as he is leaving, "Don't take your eyes off her!": the dissolve, in preference to the simple cut (there is no time-lapse), suggesting the lingering, prying gaze of the nurse. The notion of persecution through a look is central to the film.

The outburst prompts the arrival of Harry and Dr. Fleurot (John Emery). Miss Carmichael allows herself to be led away, after an attempt to make a pass at Fleurot, which he, in his role of doctor and authority, circumvents. The moment he is alone with Constance, however, he takes up Miss Carmichael's accusations, telling her that her work is "brilliant but lifeless," and that she lacks the "human emotional experience" necessary to "treat a love veteran like Carmichael." His remarks lead into a declaration of his fondness for Constance, which she rejects—"You sense your own desires and pulsations. I assure you that mine in no way resemble them"—and the conversation moves toward a confirmation of the parallel between Fleurot and Miss Carmichael, first established explicitly in the dialogue (Fleurot declares that he feels "exactly like Miss Carmichael") and elaborated in the use of the book which Miss Carmichael has thrown at Constance at the end of the previous dialogue. Fleurot, when his kiss produces no effect, murmurs resignedly that "it's rather like embracing a textbook," and then, as he is about to leave, asks if he can borrow the book, which he has picked up from the floor. He is just telling her that "I think you'd better stick to books" when Dr. Murchison enters the room.

The notion of reading as a sublimation of sexual desire, of the book as a surrogate for a human object, reemerges a few scenes later when Constance, repressing her longing to go into Ballantyne's room, goes into the library instead and gets down Edwardes's book—one of a limited edition which has been personally autographed by the author. Here, it is Fleurot who is forced to seek alternative satisfaction, and it is significant that Dr. Murchison should appear for the first time at the moment of Constance's denial of her sexuality and the arousal/frustration of Fleurot—the two elements which will characterize her relationship with Ballantyne. With the single exception of this third encounter, all the conversations in the scene end with Constance inciting some form of neurotic disquiet in her partner.

Leo G. Carroll's Dr. Murchison is clearly in the main tradition of Hitchcock's villains— charming, refined, immaculately "civilized"—and although the character is not developed, he is an essential part of the film's organization. The Ballantyne/Constance/Murchison relationship anticipates the triangular adulterous affairs of the later films with Ingrid Bergman. In both *Notorious* and *Under Capricorn* (1949), Bergman is caught between an older man, her husband (Claude Rains, Joseph Cotten), who is clearly deeply attached to her, and a younger, attractive lover (Cary Grant, Michael Wilding), the nature of whose love is ambiguous, who is involved in the causes of the heroine's predicament, and who disrupts the marital relationship by intruding into the husband's house. (I am, obviously, schematizing here, but this basic pattern is present and important.) *Spellbound* relates significantly to this structure, though in the nature of the subject, the particular inflection is different.

Murchison, Green Manors, and Constance's position as analyst/intellectual/repressed, "denatured" woman, are inextricably bound together. We can distinguish various elements in their conversation.

1. Murchison seems to materialize out of Constance's rejection of Fleurot, and his arrival drives Fleurot out of the room; the denial of sexuality is underlined by the affirmation of loyalty to Murchison. As Fleurot leaves, Constance tells him that she won't come with him, as she is "in no mad hurry to welcome Dr. Edwardes," and one of her first remarks to Murchison is "You are Green Manors." The hostility to eroticism and to the idea of Murchison's replacement are thus linked together, with, in addition, the hint that just as Fleurot's obsession with sex unites him with Miss Carmichael, so he is "mad" in his concern about Edwardes's arrival.

2. Resignation, maturity, freedom from illusion. Constance tells Murchison that his behavior is "a lesson in how to accept reality," to which he replies, "Don't be too taken in by my happy air, Constance"—an exchange which is charged with irony by the subsequent narrative. Murchison's crime is, precisely, an evasion of the reality of his dismissal, and his very disclaimer augments the effect of his stoicism and Constance's admiration of it.

3. Youth and age. This theme is strongly emphasized in the opening scenes, and both the group of doctors who first meet Ballantyne and then Murchison himself (it is his first remark, as he comes through another door) comment on the fact that Ballantyne is "younger than expected." Murchison tells Constance that it is "the basic secret of science" that "the old must make way for the new"; Hitchcock maintains a subtle balance here between a sense of Murchison as a figure of reaction and repression, resisting the new, and as a victim of the ideological obsession with youth. He is "as able and brilliant as ever," but "having crumpled once, I might crumple again": it is made clear that his breakdown is a response to the threat to his position at Green Manors. He has been "like a new man since his vacation" because the murder of Edwardes has removed that threat.

The main importance of the age/youth antithesis in *Spellbound* lies in its Oedipal connotations, which are variously emphasized in the four main characters: Constance's resentment of Murchison's replacement; Ballantyne's desire for/revulsion from Constance; Murchison's plot against Edwardes, and then Ballantyne; and Brulov's resentment of Ballantyne.

Constance's progress is marked by the gradual movement away from the two possessive father figures, Murchison and Brulov, and the movement toward Ballantyne: a movement which is simultaneously a rejection and a violation of the psychoanalytical practice which they endorse and which, for them, puts her on a level of irrationality practically comparable to her patient's. Hence, the constant identification of love and madness throughout the film: Ballantyne tells

Constance "I think you're quite mad—you're much crazier than I am"; and when he asks her if she will "love him just as much when he's normal," she replies, "I'll be crazy about you." The theme receives its most extensive treatment in a long conversation between Constance and Brulov, when he tells her that a woman in love "is functioning on the lowest level of the intellect." Indeed, his decision to help her rather than turn Ballantyne over to the police is expressed in terms of humoring, and he himself partly assuming, her madness—"I'll pretend to myself that I'm acting sensible for a few days." There is the constant tension in the film between the presentation of a "rational" science and the fact that the only creative use of it we see is based on feelings which are totally irrational (trust, faith, love, intuition) and methods which go against every precept for its successful operation.

As we have seen, Constance's affirmation of loyalty to Murchison (III [f]) is balanced on one side by her rejection of Fleurot and on the other by the scene with Mr. Garmes, the paper knife, and the arrival of "Edwardes"/Ballantyne—the knife suggesting an assumption of potency and an attack on both newcomer and patient (between whom, as we shall see, an important symbolic parallel exists). Her rejection of Murchison in the film's penultimate scene is characterized by the turning against him of the aggression originally excited on his behalf, and it reverses the pattern of scene III: the series of incursions into Constance's room, the repeated agitation and undermining of her position, are balanced by the visit to the study in which she becomes the intruder.

This final confrontation again turns on a transference of sexual potency and is riddled with sexual imagery. Murchison gives himself away to Constance at what is, apparently, his moment of triumph (the "recapture" of Constance, the murder of Edwardes and the conviction of Ballantyne; that is, the elimination of the rivals for Green Manors and for Constance) as they are standing in the doorway of Constance's room, when he says that he knew Edwardes slightly (he has earlier professed never to have met him). Left alone, Constance, disturbed by the remark, walks slowly toward her bedroom, Murchison's words echoing distortedly on the soundtrack; she grasps their significance as she is standing in the far doorway, her arms spread out grasping the uprights of the frame. She goes upstairs, and Hitchcock repeats the forward subjective tracking shot toward the door used earlier for Constance's wary, fascinated approach to the room then occupied by Ballantyne.

The explicit acknowledgment of Freud invites a psychoanalytical reading of the film's imagery, and the use of doors here is especially interesting. For Freud, doors are a female symbol in dreams. Thus, Constance, unshakably committed to Ballantyne, refuses Murchison entry to her room, and the track toward Murchison's door, which places us in Constance's position and which associates the female symbol with the man, exactly expresses the scene's symbolic force. Constance's potency is reestablished by her knowledge of the crime, her penetration of the secret, and her visit is an act of sexual aggression. The shot also creates a link to the earlier scene with Ballantyne and suggests that the breakdown of the men toward which both encounters move is a response to that aggression.

Murchison agrees, unwillingly, to discuss Ballantyne's dream ("Nocturnal conferences are bad for the nerves"), and he comments with paternal condescension on Constance's loyalty, "one of your most attractive characteristics." As he says this, he reaches for his cigarette case, and throughout the rest of the scene, until he throws it away into the grate at the moment of his confession, he is fingering and stroking a cigarette which he never lights. The phallic symbolism of the cigarette, here suggesting Murchison's impotence (because unlit and then discarded), recalls both Constance's first appearance and a moment in a conversation between her and Ballantyne after his breakdown in the operating theater, when he tells her that the only clue he has of his real identity is a cigarette case which he found in his pocket, with the initials "J. B." engraved on it.

After the confession, the cigarette is replaced by the gun, which Murchison also strokes coolly as he points it at Constance. As with Garmes and Ballantyne, the response to the woman's assertion of her potency is violence: her possession of the phallus is barred by his possession of the gun. In all three cases, the men are also responding to Constance's knowledge, her use of her intellect. Garmes and Ballantyne are her patients, the latter constantly attacking her for her insistent probing of his memory (he calls her "a phony King Solomon" and "a smug-nosed old schoolmistress"), and Murchison is now exposed by her detection of his guilt. It is notable also that Murchison remarks on Constance's "agile young mind." Through her association with Ballantyne, she is no longer the object of desire but an embodiment of the threat of youth to age associated with his professional rivals. At the same time, he begins to abuse and ridicule her devotion to her lover ("A love-smitten analyst playing a dream-detective").

Constance triumphs over Murchison in a manner which exactly reverses the procedures of her science. Psychoanalysis as the film defines it is the means whereby the analyst guides the patient toward the recognition of the truth about himself. Constance escapes from Murchison by an exertion of controlling will which is close to hypnosis, staring at him with an unwavering, oppressive gaze and imposing a lie on him—if he lets her go, the police will treat him leniently ("They'll find extenuating circumstances in the state of your health"), and he will be able to continue to work and research in prison. Constance's stare is the final, and supreme, expression of her superior power (earlier in the scene, Murchison has wearily hidden his own eyes behind his hand for a moment), and the man responds by turning his weapon on himself.

The father figure is split into two in the film: Murchison's analogue is Dr. Brulov, Constance's former teacher. Brulov is first mentioned at the moment of Ballantyne's first breakdown at the dinner table, when Constance says that Ballantyne's irrational behavior reminds her of him—a remark which both underlines the emphasis on the neurosis of the analysts and recalls the Freudian formulation that the choice of love object is affected by recollections of a parent (Constance has just fallen in love with Ballantyne at first sight).

The parallels with the other male characters are striking. During his conversation with the policemen, Brulov agitatedly manipulates a knife in his hands, and his response to being questioned again is the remark, "What is this kind of persecution?" From what he says, we learn that his disagreement with Dr. Edwardes at a conference they both attended resulted in an outburst of violence (kicking over chairs) and his furious departure from the lecture hall, and his exasperation at Constance's irrational commitment to Ballantyne induces him to start smoking compulsively—spilling all his matches in the process. The overtones of impotence, sterility, sexual isolation, loneliness are very strong. Brulov asserts that his housekeeper "hates" him (we have seen the housekeeper briefly when the couple arrive at the house—a perfectly innocuous woman, worrying about the professor missing his evening meal), and he describes himself as "living on my own with a can opener." When he is fetching the milk for Ballantyne, he remarks that he is "glad to have company" and that although he longed when he was young "to get alone by myself instead of wasting my time with people," now, in old age, "everything becomes just the opposite." As he is handing Ballantyne the drugged liquid, he is saying that old people cause all the trouble in the world, and the last words we hear before Ballantyne loses consciousness (the camera puts us in his place as he drinks, so that the upturned glass and milk gradually fill the screen) is Brulov's toast to youth —"to when we are young and know nothing." He will later, of course, while Ballantyne is unconscious and "knows nothing," try to persuade Constance to let him have Ballantyne arrested.

Brulov's attitude to the couple ranges from an initial sentimentalism to the resentment of Ballantyne, which has more explicit sexual connotations than in Murchison's case. His first reaction is to canonize them (they pretend to be newlyweds) as the embodiment of an unfallen innocence and purity—the ideal, young, normal American couple—in which the equivalent of the worm in the bud is mental "disease." He tells them that "there is nothing so nice as a new marriage—no psychosis yet, no aggressions, no guilt-complex," and he wishes them "babies and not phobias." We are reminded of a remark by Ballantyne earlier, just after the departure of Mr. Garmes and the mysterious phone call from Edwardes's secretary, when he tells Constance that some fresh air would do them both good, and they can go and see some "sane trees, normal grass, and clouds without complexes." In both cases, the explicit suggestion that there are at least some things which are uncontaminated ("normal" marriage, and the country walk and picnic during which Constance begins to thaw) is quietly undermined by the implication that both speakers are neurotics.

Brulov's second reaction is a belittling, sarcastic revulsion from Constance's foolhardiness and irrationality ("a schoolgirl in love with an actor"). Brulov is, obviously, not identical to Murchison, and their characteristics ("Europeanness," irascibility, excitability, gnome-like old age, as opposed to "Englishness," suavity, self-control, finesse, sinister middle age) are readily distinguished by the film. But in both cases, the presence of Ballantyne emerges as a personal threat. Brulov clearly takes over Constance at once as daughter/pupil/servant ("This morning I get some real coffee!"), and his repeated insistence that personal, emotional involvement and science are incompatible (the remark, for instance, that women make the best psychoanalysts until they fall in love, when they make the best patients—which equates, derogatorily, love and irrationality, and which is one of numerous remarks which suggest that Constance is only saved from "the usual female contradictions" by the discipline of her work) ties in significantly with his advice to her at the end of the film, when both he and Murchison recommend repression and sublimation as a cure for her attachment to Ballantyne.

American ideology is founded quite explicitly on the notion of work as the sublimation of sexual drives: in Benjamin Franklin's words, "Industry and constant employment are great preservatives of the morals of a nation." ("Information," 264). Hitchcock explores the concept extensively in *Shadow of a Doubt*. At the end of *Spellbound*, after the apparent irrefutable revelation of Ballantyne's guilt, Constance has returned to Green Manors. She has returned also to Brulov and Murchison and the authority they represent: that is, to an environment characterized by age, paternal possessiveness, and impotence, Murchison's gun and unlit ciga-rette being balanced and reinforced by the cane which Brulov grasps throughout his conversa-tion with Constance. He insists to her that she can't keep on "bumping her head against reality and pretending it isn't there"; the remark echoes Constance's praise of Murchison's "realism" in III (f), creating a disturbing network of ironies. Brulov's demand that she "accept reality" which, in his role as psychoanalyst, is the nature of his demand on a patient, becomes, in effect, a demand for acquiescence: Constance must accept the law, both psychoanalytic law (he and Murchison have diagnosed Ballantyne as a schizophrenic) and legal process (Ballantyne has been found guilty of murder). Work within that law thus becomes the means of repressing the sense of loss and constructing a "fresh or substitute satisfaction which has become neces-sary owing to the fact of frustration" (Freud's words in a discussion of symptom formation). "There's lots of happiness in working hard—perhaps the most," Brulov tells her, and after he has left, Murchison repeats the injunction to "try to forget things better forgotten."

We thus arrive at the point at which the two representatives of psychological health attempt to direct the heroine on the path toward neurosis: it is at this point that the iden-tity of that science with patriarchal law and its prescribed "normality" is clinched. Indeed, the dialogue indicates that Constance is in a state similar to Murchison's before his "vaca-tion": "I know that feeling of exhaustion only too well. One must humor it before it explodes." Murchison's outlet has been the murder of Edwardes; the outlet for Constance, Ballantyne, and the narrative (their resolution) is the death of Murchison.

Before passing on to the Constance-Ballantyne relationship, it is useful to remark at this point, while the subversion of psychoanalysis is in question, on an incident in which the par-allel between analysis and detection so central to the film's attempt to confirm ideological confidence (Constance becomes, in Ballantyne's words, "a great analyst and a great detective") is subtly undercut. I am thinking of Constance's encounter with the hotel detective who helps her in her search for Ballantyne after he has absconded from Green Manors—an encounter which is elaborated beyond its strict narrative function and which at first sight seems a mere jeu d'esprit.

The detective first rescues Constance from the advances of an obese drunk who tries to pick her up in the lobby, and who sports a phallic cigar—the symbolism, in association with the theme of loneliness and isolation and the desire for Constance to alleviate it ("A fella could live and die in this town and never meet nobody"), uniting him to the film's central father figures. The kindly detective interprets Constance's plight as that of a distraught wife seeking her fugitive husband to beg his forgiveness, and the conversation is built on this confident error, in which, gradually, Constance begins to collaborate to win his sympathy and gain his help. The detective describes himself as "a kind of psychologist," and his reading of Constance's situation is based on what, from experience, he has found to be "the usual psychology," so that the meeting is suddenly recast as that between analyst and patient, with the latter carefully exploiting the complacent self-assurance of the former, who misreads the symptoms com-pletely, treating his subject as a typical "case" (as Constance has done previously—"He fits perfectly into your chapter on the guilt complex"). Her situation has been reversed. This is the first scene in the film (apart from the country walk, in which the collapse of the analyst persona begins) which takes place outside Green Manors, and as the prospective accomplice of a wanted man, she is the victim rather than the representative of institutional authority. There are hints again, here, of the equation of analyst and policeman, mental patient and criminal, in which "abnormality" becomes an ideological offense. It is implied that Constance herself must "break the law"—both police law (by running away with the suspect) and analytical law (by acting "madly")—and join Ballantyne on the wrong side of it before she can help either him or herself. Her "science" must partake of its share of "insanity."

Green Manors itself can be read both as a social microcosm and as a monstrous, perverted family, characterized at once by sexual repression, a claustrophobic lack of privacy, and a pervasive immaturity and childishness. Fleurot's style and manner (slicked hair, thin mustache, smart suit, leering innuendo) suggest the superficially sophisticated, big-city charmer, a familiar inhabitant of film noir, and his encounters with Constance recall those between Joan Fontaine and George Sanders in *Rebecca*. Constance twice remarks on the childishness of the doctors: first reacting against Fleurot's insinuations about her attraction to Ballantyne ("I detest that sort of high-school talk"), and then the concerted sarcasm, led once more by Fleurot ("You look as if you've been having an instructive time"), which greets her on her late return from the country walk and which prompts her to compare the staff dinner table to a kindergarten. Again, in the scene in the library after Ballantyne disappears from Green Manors, the doctors talk casually and unconcernedly about his probable fate, to Constance's acute distress (her feelings communicated to us by a slow track-in to a close-up of her face), and Fleurot turns the conversation into an attack on Constance herself—"A woman like you could never become emotionally involved with any man, sane or insane." Thus, the three male doctors in the film are used to suggest various responses to the fact of sexual repression. If, in Brulov, it gives rise to an idealization of the "normal," a commitment to the supreme value of work as sublimation, and a tendency to see love as a silly female illusion (Constance's love transforms a "schizophrenic" into a "Valentine"); if, in Murchison, it produces psychosis; then, in Fleurot, it leads to malicious callousness: when Constance does not respond to his advances, she becomes the "human glacier"—an accusation which exactly mirrors Miss Carmichael's "Miss Frozen-Puss!" The treatment of Fleurot here (together, of course, with the warmth and intelligence conveyed in Bergman's performance) plays its part in qualifying the ideological project about the making of a "real" woman which I outlined above: although, because Fleurot is so eminently "unsympathetic" in comparison with Ballantyne, the project remains substantially unaffected. One might remark also, in the library scene, on the complex effect achieved by Murchison's coming to Constance's defense, and in terms which echo her comments on the doctors' immaturity: he apologizes that "our staff still retains the manners of medical students" with that consideration and courtesy so typical of Hitchcock's villains (consider, especially, Claude Rains in *Notorious*).

This brings us to the film's central relationship. Constance's devotion to Ballantyne is obviously intended to reconcile the psychoanalytic theme with the emphasis on romantic love and sexual awakening: her role as analyst/detective is effectual because her commitment to his cure derives its force from a love which is repeatedly shown to be "crazy"—precisely *l'amour fou*. On another level, the film almost becomes, through the heroine's name, a fable about the constancy of woman (see, for example, Chaucer's Constance in "The Man of Law's Tale") and the redeeming power of woman's love, which coincides with the religious dimension imparted to psychoanalysis by the introductory caption. Guided by Constance, Ballantyne descends into the inferno of the unconscious and returns whole and sound—a traditional enough romantic theme, which receives its baldest statement in the scene on the station platform about halfway through the film. Surrounded by embracing couples, Ballantyne tells Constance, "There's nothing wrong with me that a good long kiss wouldn't cure," to which she replies, "I've never treated a guilt complex that way before." However, the film constantly implies, on the contrary, that Constance aggravates Ballantyne's symptoms and that his neurosis, whatever account may be given of it in the narrative, is sexual in nature.

One might begin by noting that the incidents associated with the neurosis have erotic connotations. Ballantyne has burnt his hand in a flying accident, and the two crucial traumatic experiences (the death of his brother, the death of Edwardes) both involve hurtling uncontrollably down a slope. They also involve, respectively, a boy and a man, and two of Ballantyne's breakdowns occur when Constance forces him to relive with her what he did previously with Dr. Edwardes (buying the railway ticket, going down the ski run). We think of Freud's suggestion that flying dreams "have to be interpreted as dreams of general sexual excitement," and that "gliding or sliding" are "symbolic representations par excellence of masturbation." (*Introductory Lectures,* 156)   Similarly, the razor scene strikingly anticipates the atmosphere of the shower murder in *Psycho*, in which Norman Bates resorts to a sharp instrument and violence as a substitute for the rape he cannot commit. Robin Wood has suggested that the attempt to explain away Uncle Charlie in *Shadow of a Doubt* as an aberrant monster by means of his childhood accident (ideologically necessary in a 1940s Hollywood film) may also be interpreted as a euphemism for sexual trauma: we are told that Charlie, "such a quiet boy" before the crash on his bicycle ("You didn't know how to handle it"), is perpetually in trouble afterward, as if "he had to get up to mischief to blow off steam." (*Hitchcock's Films Revisited,* 297, 301)   In both films, the "safe" explanation becomes more, rather than less, troublingly suggestive. In *Spellbound*, too, the fact that Ballantyne is a returned serviceman relates the film to a contemporary group of movies (including *The Blue Dahlia* [1946] and *Crossfire* [1947]) dealing with demobilized and/or wounded ex-soldiers and sexual pathology: Buzz Wanchek (William Bendix) in *The Blue Dahlia*, for example, has a steel plate in his head; suffers, like Ballantyne, from amnesia and war shock; and is suspected of the murder of the hero's promiscuous wife.

Ballantyne's dream is as good a starting point as any. In the narrative, the dream is treated as a decoratively esoteric version of "reality," a sort of allegoric distortion of the circumstances of the crime. Dr. Brulov, in response to Ballantyne's skepticism, compares dreams to jigsaw puzzles with the pieces mixed up; it is the interpretation of the dream which reveals the location of the crime, precipitates Ballantyne's therapeutic reenactment of the skiing trip, and finally reveals Dr. Murchison as the murderer. This use of the dream emphasizes once more the suggested parallel of unsolved crime/forgotten trauma. Dream analysis becomes the means by which the mystery of reality is made intelligible: fitting together the pieces of the dream solves the patient and the crime.

The most striking thing about the dream as we are encouraged to read it is the remarkable absence of the personality of the dreamer. Apart from the sequence in which a voluptuous, scantily dressed young woman appears, kissing the players in the casino in turn, and is identified by Ballantyne as Constance (a sequence which Brulov dismisses briefly and wearily as "plain, ordinary wishful dreaming"), the dream images are made to coincide point-for-point to "real" events, as if they were empirical clues. The film purports to be an explication and justification of psychoanalysis, and yet the fundamental Freudian thesis that a dream represents the fulfillment of a wish is mentioned only to be dismissed as comparatively trivial, and it is replaced by an inverted version of the pre-Freudian thesis that dreams "could be used for practical purposes" (Freud's words) (*Introductory Lectures,* 104)—here, not to foretell the mystery of the future but to unravel the mystery of the past. Thus, if the proprietor of the casino is simply Dr. Murchison, there is no reason whatsoever, apart from considerations of narrative suspense, why he should be masked in the dream, since Ballantyne has scarcely come in contact with him and there is no necessity for his identity to be repressed.

I wish to suggest that the dream is an Oedipal dream, and that such a reading is supported by the whole presentation of the Constance-Ballantyne relationship. Ballantyne is playing cards with the bearded authority/father figure, identified for us as the "real" Edwardes but who bears a striking physical resemblance to Brulov, and might be a younger version of him. We should remember that the dream occurs in a drugged sleep which Brulov has induced (the drug concealed in the innocent whiteness of the milk—the color which terrified Ballantyne—and the deceit concealed by Brulov's paternal benignity) and which follows Ballantyne's suspended attempt on his life. The bearded figure defeats Ballantyne with blank cards, that is, defeats him "against reason": his authority and victory are preordained, "givens" of the game, and do not depend on the value of the cards he holds. The proprietor appears and threatens the "father," telling him "This is my place" and "You can't play here." He is masked because he is Ballantyne's surrogate in the dream; the son can express his hatred and jealousy through him and deny them as his own emotions. We then see the father falling from the roof of the house—the wish for his death is fulfilled, the threat enacted. The masked figure appears from behind the chimney carrying a wheel, which he drops onto the roof. The wheel suggests the vagina: with the death of the father, the mother is now sexually available to the dreamer. The camera tracks in on the hole in the hub of the wheel (a deeply suggestive image, given the doors and forward tracks in the film). Suddenly, the screen fills with billowing smoke, and we then see Ballantyne fleeing down a slope pursued by the shadow of enormous wings: seized by guilt and panic, the dreamer is unable to consummate the desired union with the mother and flees from the achievement of his crime. The dream has begun with the image of an eye, and of a man cutting through eyes painted on drapery with a pair of shears, both suggesting the sexual wish on which the dream is based (recall the opening of *Un Chien Andalou* [1929], in which, of course, Salvadore Dali, who designed the dream sequence, was also involved).

The link between the dream and Constance (which, once stated, is "forgotten" in the narrative from thereon) is implied by Brulov himself. Constance is attempting to interpret the winged figure, and Brulov cuts in with, "The figure was you: If you grew wings you would be an angel." The implication of this seems to me fundamental to Hitchcock's presentation of the central relationship. Constance, the maternal, loyal, devoted woman, is also the potent woman, the woman with the phallus, the forbidden woman (the mother): like Miss Carmichael, Ballantyne simultaneously feels desire and denies it, and the series of hysterical breakdowns which he suffers throughout the film are all associated with moments of extreme sexual tension. This, and the fact that Ballantyne is appalled by a particular color, relates *Spellbound* emphatically to *Marnie*, and, more generally, to the recurrent characteristics of the developed erotic relationships in Hitchcock's films. T. R. Devlin, the Cary Grant character in *Notorious*, for example, is based on a similar tension between desire and revulsion, and he tries to transform Alicia (Bergman) into a prostitute so that he can despise her for being one. The ambivalence is further explored in *Under Capricorn*, in Flusky's (Joseph Cotten) complex and vacillating response to his wife's degradation (Bergman once more).

I shall consider the crisis points in *Spellbound* in their chronological narrative order.

1. The first meeting. Constance and the other doctors are at dinner in the refectory, an empty chair (for Edwardes) separating Constance and Murchison and suggesting the rupture which the newcomer will create, displacing Murchison professionally and sexually. They are discussing Edwardes. Constance says that she has read his work and that "I intend to learn a great deal from Dr. Edwardes—I think we all can." Ballantyne comes in and is introduced to Constance, Hitchcock cutting between close-ups of the two while the film's theme tune wells up on the soundtrack—instant signifiers, as Truffaut remarks, of "love at first sight." (119) The conversation turns to the value of sports as therapy for the patients, and Constance takes this up excitedly ("Dr. Murchison always said we never did enough in that direction"). Here, as in the interpretation of the dream (the descent into "Angel Valley"), sport is given unmistakable sexual overtones. Fleurot describes Constance as "frustrated gymnast," and Constance agrees that she misses sports, "particularly winter sports." She begins to tell Ballantyne about plans for building a swimming pool ("an irregular one") and outlines the proposed shape on the tablecloth with the prongs of her fork. Ballantyne is immediately alarmed and overreacts hysterically—"I presume that the supply of linen in this institution is inexhaustible!" Constance tries to gloss over the incident, and she begins talking rapidly about how Ballantyne's behavior reminds her of Dr. Brulov, who couldn't endure the presence of a sauce bottle on the table. Ballantyne sits smiling at her, at the same time trying to smooth out the fork marks with his knife.

   All the important elements are present in this first encounter: Ballantyne's initial attraction, the hint of Constance's repression, the sexual proposition (Constance tries to interest Ballantyne in sports), the association of Constance with the phallus (the fork, and, in addition, the knowledge—about the pool—which she has and he lacks), Ballantyne's perception of her as threat and aggressor, and his hysterical withdrawal, followed by the attempt to erase the mark of her presence. We see also the link between Ballantyne and Brulov and the common element of fastidiousness in their reactions, reinforced later by the similar dialogue given to both in praise of the cleanness of normality. This is important both in undermining the status of the analyst (his reaction is neurotic) and in respect of Constance—all the men perceive her as a threat.

2. The first embrace. After fetching the book from the library, Constance at last summons up the courage to go into Ballantyne's room. He is asleep in a chair in the bedroom with a book in his lap but wakes when she comes in, and Hitchcock cuts between them, separated by the frame of the door. Constance at first pretends awkwardly that she wants to discuss the book, but then abandons this—"I'm amazed at the subterfuge—I don't want to discuss it at all." Again, the blurring of the boundary between "sane" and "insane" is important here. Later, in the scene in which Edwardes's secretary appears and the masquerade is uncovered, Murchison describes the imposter's deceit as "typical of the shortsighted cunning that goes with paranoid behavior." The immediate irony stems from the fact that the speaker himself is the murderer and from his eminent clarity and clearheadedness (the note of scorn for "mental illness" is also important and ties in interestingly with Brulov's idealization of "normality"). One can also relate it to Constance's actions here, the fragile imposture breaking down under pressure. Significantly, she has removed her glasses, and throughout, the spectacles are associated with the scenes in which she is an "analyst," as opposed to the "romantic" scenes. (She puts them on as a disguise in a moment of nervous tension when they are confronted with the two policemen in Brulov's parlor, removing them when the agents leave—an act which, ironically, gives her away to them later.) The whole scene, indeed, is treated, for Constance, as the "unlocking of a door," the discovery of her true self, the driving out of the demon of repression: "What a remarkable discovery that one isn't what one thought one was!"

She still attempts to resist the idea that they are in love—"It doesn't happen like that—in a day." Ballantyne, walking toward her, crosses the dividing threshold of the door. He is gazing at her with hypnotic fixity, while she stands motionless (spellbound), and the image of the staring, controlling eye is central, most notably in the penultimate scene, where it becomes Constance's own: at the moment of her surrender, in the kiss, her eyes close, and we are given the superimposed vista of doors swinging slowly open.

Ballantyne's last line before the kiss is an insistence that they are in love: "It was like lightning striking. It strikes rarely." Afterward, as he sees the black lines on her dressing gown, he pushes her away, reassuring her that "it's not you" and muttering that "something struck me." Immediately, the phone rings, and Ballantyne is told that Mr. Garmes, Constance's patient of III (g), has "run amok," attempted to kill a guard, and then cut his own throat with a razor.

The narrative insists, clearly, that the breakdown is not a sexual crisis ("it's not you"), but the connotations are unmistakable. There is, first of all, the repetition of "strike," linking the embrace and the revulsion from it and establishing the idea of assault. Most important is the extended symbolic parallel between Ballantyne and Garmes. As we have seen, they are introduced into the action almost simultaneously (III [g]) and linked by means of the paper knife, the cutting open of the mail/male becoming an attack on the unwanted newcomer and the patient (it releases his symptoms).

Dr. Constance Peterson (Ingrid Bergman) enters the bedroom of "Dr. Edwardes" (Gregory Peck) in *Spellbound*. Personal collection of the editor.

Ballantyne believes he has killed his brother; Garmes believes he has killed his father—the Oedipal crime which underlies Ballantyne's dream. The second meeting between Ballantyne and Constance takes place in Garmes's presence and is precipitated by him, when Ballantyne rings her and asks for her help and advice with him, interrupting a conversation between her and Fleurot in which the latter is lying on the couch like a patient, revealing his ill-concealed jealousy of Constance's interest in Ballantyne. As Constance tries to explain to Garmes that his guilt is illusory ("a child's bad dream"), Hitchcock cuts away to a shot of Ballantyne watching with fascinated intensity (compare the cutaway to Constance when Miss Carmichael confesses that she "hates men"). When Constance returns late from her walk with Ballantyne, she is told that while they were away "Mr. Garmes became agitated again": the walk has been characterized by the interplay of desire and repression, Constance insisting that love is a "delusion" invented by poets, and oblivious to Ballantyne's interest. The walk scene ends with Constance looking out over the landscape, seeing it for the first time, and declaring "Isn't this beautiful?" while Ballantyne replies "Perfect," looking not at the country but at her, before distracting himself hastily with the picnic.

The Garmes/Ballantyne parallel reaches its crux in the scene of the embrace and in the ensuing scene in the operating theater, in which Ballantyne's breakdown becomes complete as he explicitly identifies himself with Garmes—"You can't keep people in cells! You fools babbling about guilt complexes! What do you know about them?" The imagery of release which is so conspicuously insisted on (the doors; the books which both characters discard before the kiss) is radically subverted by the film's symbolic relationships.

3. During the analytic session at the Empire State Hotel, Constance notices the burn on Ballantyne's hand. She grasps him by the wrist, demanding that he remember the accident. He tries to pull away from her, telling her she's hurting his arm. He becomes hysterical, and finally collapses when her grip is removed. Again, the scene up to that point has been marked by the alternate expression and denial of desire; Constance embraces him and is obviously alarmed when she thinks that he may be married, yet she insists that "it has nothing to do with love." Similarly, Ballantyne's panic is juxtaposed with his assuring Constance, "Thank heaven I can't remember a wife."

4. The first train journey. Ballantyne remembers his accident in the plane over Rome and responds to Constance's pressure with abuse, described metaphorically as blows in the dialogue.

5. The first night together. Just as the couple first met in the house of Dr. Murchison, they spend their first night in the house of Dr. Brulov—under the aegis of the father. The desire/repression pattern here is crucial. Symbolically, it is the couple's wedding night ("I take it this is your first honeymoon"). Alone, they can abandon their pretense (adopted for Brulov's benefit, and which, ironically, never deceives him): through Ballantyne's amnesia ("I can't remember ever having kissed any other woman before") and Constance's inexperience ("I have nothing to remember of that nature either") they seem for a moment the innocent, "unfallen" couple. An ambiguity is introduced by Ballantyne's suggestion that they are "bundles of inhibitions" beneath which "dynamite" is buried. They embrace, but Constance pushes him off, insisting again that she is only his doctor, and that "the doctor occupies the couch—fully dressed," while the patient takes the bed. Immediately afterward, Ballantyne notices the counterpane (white with embroidered white lines) and collapses. There follows the superb suspense set piece in which Ballantyne's anxiety is triggered by the whiteness of the bathroom, and he enters the somnambulistic trance in which he first tries obsessively to shave himself, breaks off and approaches the sleeping Constance with the razor, and then goes downstairs where Brulov is waiting for him.

The phallic significance of the razor is confirmed by the shot in which Ballantyne descends the staircase, an unbroken take which begins with the figure in medium long shot at the top of the stairs and ends in an enormous close-up of his hand, held rigidly at his side, the razor jutting out in front of him. The incident exactly mirrors the end of the first kissing scene, without, in this case, the mediation of Mr. Garmes: the same catalyst (sexual tension with Constance), the same weapon. Mr. Garmes turns on his guard; Ballantyne on Constance and then Brulov, both figures of potent, oppressive authority; and the actual procedure of shaving, which completes Ballantyne's discomfiture (shaving brush stirring the lather in a cup), has clear erotic overtones. As in *Psycho*, sexuality is channeled into violence by the overwhelming force of repression—here, both partners' censorship of desire, and the presence of Brulov.

6. The train journey to Gabriel Valley. They are in the dining car, and Constance is having a meal. She says that in the future she intends to change her style of dress—"I've always loved very feminine clothes, but never quite dared to wear them." Ballantyne stares obsessively at her hands as the fork and knife cut the meat; as Constance goes on, aware of his alarm, Hitchcock cuts to a close-up of his face, glazed with horror, grotesquely illuminated by the flashing lights of a passing train, the clatter of which thunders deafeningly on the soundtrack. The image blacks out.

The fork-and-knife imagery relates back both to the couple's first meeting and to the paper knife scene, and it relates the threat of Constance as the castrating woman to her desire to increase her "femininity." Ironically, her "liberation" as a "real" woman only augments the man's neurosis, defines its nature more clearly. In the previous train scene, the noise of a passing locomotive and the reflection of its lights on Ballantyne's face became, simultaneously, the roar and the glare of his flying accident. Now, the repetition of that imagery links economically the connotations of the various events involved—the "accident," Constance with a knife, femininity, the journey toward "winter sports" in Gabriel Valley.

7. The ski run. The connotations of winter sports have already been described, and the descent of the slope on skis is clearly a sexual culmination for both Constance, "the frustrated gymnast," and for Ballantyne. The scene begins with Constance looming over him, ordering him sternly to put his skis on, and throughout the run, he is staring at her with the utmost repugnance and loathing. It is at this point that the ideologically compulsory resolution of the conflict (Ballantyne finds salvation through his relationship with Constance and remembers that he is "not guilty," the Oedipal trauma canceled out) intrudes at the expense of the logic of the symbolism, as if Norman Bates were to be redeemed by Marion Crane as he tore aside the shower curtain. Hereafter, Constance's potency is not a problem for the hero or the narrative (Ballantyne, now "cured," can declare that his love is "beyond cure"), and it can be directed against the villain: as we have seen, Constance's gaze deprives Murchison of the use of his gun, and her use of her knowledge, which unmans Ballantyne, can become beneficial.

Such an interpretation helps to make sense of the connection between Murchison and Ballantyne created by the mise-en-scène: the repetition of the subjective tracking shots toward the door before the love scene and the suicide scene, and the two ostentatious subjective trick effects—Ballantyne drinking the drugged milk, and Murchison shooting himself. The threat to the hero of the woman and of her teacher/father, Brulov, can be resolved when it is directed toward "the monster"—the darker and more dangerous father figure.

The film ends with the achievement of "normality" and reconciliation, the exorcism of the "demons." Constance now accepts and invites the public kiss from which she shrank before ("We don't want to attract attention"), and the union is blessed by Brulov, who repeats an earlier remark that "Any husband of Constance is a husband of mine." Given the nature and role of fathers in the film, this is a deeply ambiguous suggestion: one might compare the end of *To Catch a Thief* (1955), in which, in the last shot (also an embrace), Frances Stevens (Grace Kelly) informs John Robie (Cary Grant) that mother will be coming to live with them. It should be noted, also, that Constance is still wearing a suit!

I have tried to indicate the ways in which a work designed, ostensibly, in praise of the science of "normality" continually subverts its surface project. The way in which that subversion is achieved (the blurring of the "normal" and the "abnormal" so that any definition of either becomes uncertain; the indication of insoluble conflicts in the main sexual relationship) suggests that Hitchcock's presence is a crucial factor in it. One can make no claim for *Spellbound* as an achieved work of art: the discrepancy between surface and implication, the grotesque uncertainty of tone (especially noticeable in the wildly clashing conventions of the acting), and the frequent banality of the script testifying only too clearly to Hitchcock's profound unease. The film's interest lies in the nature of its "badness": in the tension between the affirmation and justification of fundamental ideological assumptions and a repressed meaning which is everywhere at odds with them.

Detour (1993)

Edgar G. Ulmer's *Detour* (1945) was filmed in six days on a minimal budget. No one noticed its existence when it was released, and although it has since acquired what Leonard Maltin calls a "deserved cult following," its true stature has never really been appreciated, and such critical writing on it as there is tends to misrepresent it. It is also quite scandalously difficult to see if one lives outside North America: at the time of writing, no commercial print exists anywhere in Europe (although it has just become available on tape in Britain). A work can hardly be recognized as a classic if no one has access to it, and yet there seems to me no doubt that *Detour* deserves classical status. It is not only one of the greatest film noirs but also one of the most demanding and audacious narratives ever produced in Hollywood.

The Unreliable Narrator

> This is the excellent foppery of the world, that, when we are sick in fortune, often the surfeits of our own behavior, we make guilty of our disasters the sun, the moon, and stars: as if we were villains on necessity, fools by heavenly compulsion, knaves, thieves, and treachers by spherical predominance, drunkards, liars, and adulterers by an enforc'd obedience of planetary influence: and all that we are evil in, by a divine thrusting on. An admirable evasion of whoremaster man, to lay his goatish disposition to the charge of a star!
> —William Shakespeare, *King Lear*

It is hardly possible to watch *Detour* without becoming aware that the film seems to attach great importance to the idea of fate, and it has sometimes been argued that the whole work is pervaded by a depressed and nihilistic determinism. For example: "Ulmer's films reveal that the director does believe in intangible forces . . . [like] externally imposed fate . . . which circumscribe the free will of his characters. They exercise little or no control over their destinies." (Belton, 153) Certainly the film's hero, Al Roberts (Tom Neal), seizes every opportunity to insist that a malicious destiny is responsible for all his troubles. "From then on," he tells us, apropos of the death of Haskell (Edmund MacDonald), "something else stepped in and shunted me off to a different destination than the one I'd picked for myself." A few scenes later, fate intervenes once more by introducing Al to Vera (Ann Savage), the only person in the world who is in a position to know that Al must have stolen Haskell's car and disposed of its original owner. "Just my luck picking her up on the road," he says, and proceeds to complain that this gratuitous calamity is typical of "life," which delights in giving fate the opportunity to "stick out a foot to trip you." His experiences as Vera's traveling companion and putative spouse reinforce Al's conviction that he is the helpless plaything of the gods, and as the police car draws up beside him in the final shot, he leaves us with the warning that "fate, or some mysterious force, can put the finger on you or me for no good reason at all." As far as Al is concerned, everything that happens to him is completely arbitrary. He has come to a bad end because providence assigned him one, and as he surrenders to the inevitable, he has at least the comfort of knowing that things would have turned out much better if he had been left to his own devices.

Vera is neither an impartial nor a sympathetic observer of Al's predicament, but when she tells him, with the lack of feeling which comes to her so naturally, that "you got yourself into this thing," she has the film's unqualified support. The whole meaning of *Detour* depends on the fact that Al is incapable of providing the impartial account of the action which convention leads us to expect in first-person narratives, and when we examine the film's detail, we discover that his commentary has a dramatic status quite different from that of O'Hara (Orson Welles) in *The Lady from Shanghai* (1948) or Philip Marlowe (Dick Powell) in *Farewell, My Lovely* (1944). O'Hara and Marlowe are to be thought of simply as speaking the truth, both about themselves and about the narrative world in general. They may be mistaken, but they never equivocate, and their impersonality is never questioned for a moment. Al's commentary, however, though it is not hypocritical—he plainly believes every word of it—is profoundly self-deceived and systematically unreliable. "Did you ever want to cut away a piece of your memory and blot it out?" he asks us as the film goes into flashback, implying that the truth of what he is about to say is guaranteed by the pain involved in remembering it. In fact, Al's memory of the past is in itself a means of blotting it out, and his commentary, far from serving as the clue which leads us infallibly to the meaning of the narrative action, is like a palimpsest beneath which we may glimpse the traces of the history he has felt compelled to rewrite.

Our suspicions are (or ought to be) aroused by the betraying discrepancy between Al's description of his relationship with Sue (Claudia Drake) and what we are shown of their last evening together. According to Al, he himself is "an ordinary, healthy guy" and Sue is "an ordinary, healthy girl," and when you "add those two things together, you get an ordinary healthy romance" which is "somehow the most wonderful thing in the world." It may be thought that Al protests too much, and it is certainly difficult to reconcile this rhetoric with the couple's actual behavior, the most striking feature of which is the suppressed mutual frustration of partners who want completely different things, both for themselves and for each other. Sue insists that they have "all the time in the world to settle down" and wishes to postpone their marriage until each of them has established a successful career. Al wishes to "make with the ring and license" at once—not because he is in love, as he wishes retrospectively to believe, but because he has in practice abandoned his expressed ambition to become a concert pianist and decided instead to assume the character of the embittered failure who might have made something of himself if fate had not strewn his path with rocks and briars. He has no obvious reason to suppose that he will be incapacitated by arthritis by the time his great chance comes, or that he will be obliged to make his Carnegie Hall debut in the basement, "as a janitor." He has simply concluded that this is the way life must be, and the willed (if unconscious) defeatism implicit in his attitude to his blighted career is the first sign of his habitual tendency to attribute his own choices, and their disastrous consequences, to forces external to himself.

Since Al's desire to marry Sue is in fact inseparable from his jaded acquiescence in the necessity of his own failure, it is hardly surprising that his treatment of her is consistently peremptory, and there is no real evidence that he is even fond of her. Indeed, he refuses so much as to listen to, let alone discuss, her plans for their future, even though she makes it clear that she is doing what she thinks is best for both of them, and as soon as he realizes that she is not prepared to bow to his wishes, he virtually breaks off the relationship, with calculated churlishness, and walks off on his own in a sulk. However, Al is more than willing to take advantage of Sue's initiative once it has occurred to him that advantage can be taken, and his dramatic change of heart, experienced as the revival of love, is actually inspired by the dawning of a suspicion that a future with Sue might, after all, be a better bet than a future without her. A customer in the nightclub has just rewarded his efforts at the piano with a "ten-spot" of which he remarks, significantly, that "it couldn't buy anything *I* want," and if he now discovers that he is devoted to Sue after all and is even ready to "crawl" to California to join her, that is because the fantasy of her success, however irrational, at least contrasts favorably with his current prospects. "It was nice to think of Sue shooting for the top," he tells us. The ten-dollar bill is a painful reminder of the limits of what he is likely to gain through his own industry (the waiter who hands it to him rubs salt in the wound by remarking that he has "hit the jackpot"), and he therefore sets out to gain what he can from Sue's.

Ulmer uses these brief, and extraordinarily elliptical, expository sequences to define his hero as a man who lacks all sense of aim and purpose, who is essentially indifferent to everything but what he takes, at a given moment, to be his own interests, and who, above all, instinctively rationalizes his convenience on all occasions, either by absolving himself of responsibility for his actions completely or by providing himself with a spurious but flattering account of his motives. We have thus been carefully prepared to understand why Al behaves as he does when Haskell dies. It is, of course, crucial that Haskell's death is the result either of a genuine accident or of natural causes: we have seen him taking pills regularly, and since his body is already completely inert when it falls from the car, it seems likely that he has simply died in his sleep. The question is never resolved and is, in fact, immaterial—though it is certainly important that Al, who has noticed the pills, should choose not to become aware at this point that Haskell may have been mortally ill. He opts instead to convince himself that if he tried to tell the truth, no one would believe him: that even Haskell, in the unlikely event of his recovery, "would swear [Al had] knocked him on the head for his dough," and that he therefore has no choice but to get rid of Haskell's corpse and appropriate his effects, which is "just what the police would say [he] did even if [he] didn't." The necessity of this remarkable course of action is so obviously dubious that Al feels constrained for once to anticipate our incredulity, and refers testily to "that 'Don't-make-me-laugh!' expression on [our] faces." At some level, he seems to recognize that his actual motive was pure greed, but, unlike Vera, he cannot bring himself frankly to admit that he is primarily interested in money and will go to any lengths to get it. The very fact that he should be driven to prevaricate with us only serves to emphasize the intensity of his need to think well of himself, and he fairly bombards us with far-fetched and superfluous alibis, including the culpable negligence of Emily Post in failing "to write a book of rules for guys thumbing rides" so that they have some means of knowing "what's right and what's wrong." Al is a parasite and an opportunist of the most cynical kind, but he can grasp his opportunities only if he has first disavowed his reasons for doing so.

Given that he has just concealed a dead body in a ditch and is now driving a stolen car, Al has the most compelling of motives not to pick up a hitchhiker, and Ulmer's treatment of his fatal rendezvous with Vera is the single most astonishing example of the film's oblique and cryptic narrative method. We are not explicitly alerted to the fact that Al's decision to give Vera a lift stands in particular need of an explanation, and Al himself has nothing to say on the subject beyond the simple observation that "there was a woman . . ." as he draws into the gas station. Ulmer merely shows us what happens, just as he showed us the events which precipitated Al's earlier decision to join Sue in California, and we are perfectly at liberty to take both incidents at face value, as if no more were at stake than the hero's realization that he needs his beloved after all or his honest sympathy for a stranded wanderer. We can perceive that these crucial choices are in any way problematical only by relating them to what Al has said, done, or inadvertently revealed in previous scenes, and while Ulmer makes it possible for us to ask the appropriate questions, he also declines to tell us that we need to ask questions at all.

The only clue we are offered on the present occasion is easily overlooked, for it consists of an apparently innocuous passage of narration in the sequence at the motel where Al spends the night between Haskell's death and the advent of Vera. He tells us that he will have to go on pretending to be Haskell until he gets to "some city in which he can be swallowed up," and then adds, "In a city I should be safe enough." "Some city" is a vague destination, and the phrasing is significant because it suggests that Al is no longer thinking of joining Sue, of whom we hear no more, indeed, until after Al has realized that picking up Vera was a disastrous mistake which tragically has put "a greater distance between Sue and [himself] than when [he] started out." It has already been intimated to us that Sue swims in and out of Al's consciousness with the ebb and flow of his financial prospects, and Ulmer now implies that he comes to Vera's rescue because his newfound wealth has given him the sense that he is a free agent, economically and sexually. He no longer feels a need to bank on the hypothesis that Sue will "click" in California, and since Vera seems to be available, he offers her a ride for much the same reasons that Haskell did. Even when Vera has revealed her true colors and Sue has accordingly been restored to favor, Al is still prepared to hedge his bets. He telephones Sue furtively from the apartment which Vera has rented, she herself having at last retired for the night, but decides at the last minute not to speak and hangs up, telling himself, "Not yet, darling! Tomorrow, maybe . . ." The operative word is "maybe." Al is not yet sure whether or not he will be able to dump Vera and get away with some, at least, of the profits from the sale of Haskell's car, and he refrains from rashly building a bridge which he may not have to cross.

In the brief interlude before Al finds out who Vera is, he recalls his first impressions of her, and they are fascinatingly incongruous. He begins by telling us that "she looked as if she'd just been thrown off the crummiest freight train in the world," but a few moments later he is reflecting on her beauty: "not the beauty of a movie actress, or the beauty you dream about when you're with your wife," but a "natural beauty [which is] almost homely because it's so real." These contradictions are the residue of the process of rationalization and revision to which all Al's memories have been subjected: he denies any sexual interest in Vera by portraying her, in opposition to the accredited archetypes of male erotic fantasy, as a generic farmer's daughter, and he insists at the same time that he could not possibly have guessed what she was really like from her disarmingly folksy appearance. "She seemed harmless enough," he says, and in the sense that Vera's demeanor does not actually proclaim her identity, this is true, if hardly remarkable. The fact remains, however, that Al's commentary is tellingly silent about the overwhelming impression of Vera's sexual knowingness which Ulmer and Ann Savage communicate to us in the extraordinary reverse tracking shot that accompanies her steady and deliberate progress toward Al's car. Al misreads the evidence of her sexuality as evidence of an invitation to him, and his opening gambit is the standard observation that Vera reminds him of a girl he once knew in Phoenix. Her response is less than encouraging ("Are the girls in Phoenix that bad?") but, before he can proceed further, she has discouraged him permanently by raising the subject of Haskell.

Given both the radical influence of psychoanalysis on film noir and Ulmer's background in the culture of Weimar Germany, it seems as likely as such things ever can be in the absence of external evidence that the idea of Al's narration in *Detour* was arrived at by way of the concept of secondary revision. Sigmund Freud argues that our recollection of the past is governed by a mechanism of unconscious censorship, such that memories of events which we find too distressing to acknowledge are either repressed completely or reworked by fantasy so as to eliminate their potentially traumatic elements. Between them, repression and secondary revision allow us to remember the past inaccurately but without excessive pain, and the task of the analyst is to restore the memory's true contents to full consciousness by working back from the contradictions, anomalies, and silences which invariably characterize the censored materials that the patient currently recalls. While there is not, and cannot be, an exact analogy between reading a film and the procedures of the psychoanalyst, Ulmer certainly obliges the spectator of *Detour* to deduce the film's meaning from the discrepancies between two incompatible discourses: the dramatized action, and the hero's interpretation of it, the second of which has been distorted in ways, and for reasons, that Freud describes in the theory of censorship.

We should also bear in mind that the undermining of the authority of the narrative voice is a recurrent feature of literary modernism. Many of the late tales and novels of Henry James, for example, present us with a first-person narrator ("The Turn of the Screw," "The Sacred Fount") or a central consciousness (*The Ambassadors*, *The Beast in the Jungle*), who fails, or refuses, to understand the significance of the action and who gives an account of it that turns out to be false. James never explicitly warns us that we cannot trust the governess's every word in "The Turn of the Screw," any more than Ulmer explicitly announces that Al's version of the past is inaccurate and self-serving, although, on the other hand, neither artist misleads us by suppressing or withholding the signs of the narrator's tendentiousness. The information we need in order to distance ourselves from the point of view of the protagonist is always potentially available, and if we fail to notice and make use of it, we cannot blame the author for deceiving us. The whole point of the strategy of unreliable narration is that we cannot gain access to the work until we have discarded the lazy assumptions and preconceptions about narrative which we have derived from other works and on which we tend inertly to rely in making sense of new ones. The assumption that we can always believe what "I" says is especially hard to renounce, not only because the sole obvious alternative to it seems to be that the narrative is simply nonsense but also because our instinctive identification with "I" makes it necessary for us to doubt the reliability of our own perceptions and judgments before we can doubt the narrator's. Unreliable narration undermines the reader's *suffisance* along with the narrator's authority, and the sense of disorientation it induces is so extreme that one is hardly surprised that *Detour* is one of the few movies which have dared to make use of it. (The most extraordinary examples are *The Devil Is a Woman* [1935], *Letter from an Unknown Woman* [1945], and *Le Plaisir* [1951].)[1]

Gender

The four protagonists of *Detour* are the products of a single culture, but Ulmer never allows us to forget that this culture (whatever else may be said about it) is permeated by inequalities of sexual power, and that Sue and Vera are oppressed as women. Sue is the only character in the film whose ambitions for herself do not in any way entail the exploitation of others and who is prepared to plan her own future on the assumption that she has interests in common with someone else. The ambitions may be banal and unattainable, and the understanding of common interests entirely conventional—she wishes, in the end, to marry Al and settle down—but she nonetheless retains a capacity for disinterestedness to which her lover is a stranger and which allows him to use her for his own purposes. Ulmer emphasizes, of course, that Sue does not wait on Al's approval or support before leaving for California and that her decision is as much an attempt to escape from the degradation and harassment to which she is routinely exposed by her work in the nightclub as it is an initiative on behalf of the couple. Al fails to comprehend either motive, and, indeed, when Sue tells him that a drunk has made advances to her during the evening, his reaction ("What drunk?") is so peculiar that she takes him up on it: "What does it matter what drunk?" Sue knows that her present situation is intolerable, and she has the independence required to go ahead with her project in the face of Al's opposition, but she does not see that the ideal of heterosexual domesticity to which she remains committed makes her vulnerable to forms of masculine predatoriness more insidious than the unwanted attentions of the customers in the club. Both the roles that are available to her—nightclub hostess and girlfriend/wife—are equally oppressive and demeaning, and the material success of which she dreams, even if she were to achieve it, would not spare her the consequences of the structural inequalities between the sexes which Al and Haskell take for granted. We cannot hope to understand Vera's role in the film, or the hysterical stridency and excessiveness of Ann Savage's glorious performance, until we have grasped this fact.

Ulmer prepares us carefully for the appearance of a heroine who may be found rebarbative by prefacing it with Haskell's sadistic and lubricious account of his unsuccessful attempt to rape her. As far as Haskell is concerned, Vera was, in a quite literal sense, fair game. "I was fighting with the most dangerous animal in the world: a woman!" he declares, with the hunter's hyperbole, when Al inquires about the scratches on his hand. If women are wild animals, then it follows virtually by definition that they are also quarry. In any case, Haskell had the right to expect a gratuity for picking her up in the first place: "Give a lift to a tomato, you expect her to be nice, don't you? What kinds of dames thumb rides? Sunday school teachers?" Ulmer insists on both the egregious nastiness of the language and the nagging sense of impotence which Haskell's vainglorious bravado conceals, for he at once goes on to add that Vera "must have thought she was riding with some fall guy" and then to display the still more impressive scar ("Infection set in later") incurred in the knife fight which obliged him to leave home fifteen years earlier. Haskell recalls this scrap as a "duel," and makes much of the fact that the wound was inflicted by a sabre. Later, in the diner, he goes to great lengths to cut a dashing figure in front of the waitress and hints broadly that he is a man of means ("Keep the change!"). Haskell plainly feels that he has an image to keep up, and since Vera (who bears no scars) seems to have been more than a match for him, it may be inferred that his lurid rhetoric is primarily intended to impress himself and other men. (Al, who knows that "lots of rides have been cut short by a big mouth," is the perfect audience: "She must have been Tarzan's mate!") However, Haskell is the more, not the less, dangerous for his suspicion that he is "some fall guy" who has a right to use women to compensate him for his failure, and Ulmer offers him, in all his unpleasantness, as a fitting representative of a society in which success is both elusive and a prerequisite for the achievement of a sense of manhood.

Vera takes it as given that all men, with half a chance, will treat her as Haskell treated her. She clearly sets out to "rook" Al in exactly the same way that he rooked Haskell, who was in turn preparing to rook his own father, but her spontaneous rapaciousness is actually quite different in kind from that of her male antagonists. The most obvious indication of this difference is the hectoring aggressiveness of her manner. Vera is not a trickster like Al and Haskell, and she does not try to deceive, disarm, or win the confidence of her chosen victim. On the contrary, she goes straight for the jugular in order to dispel any illusion that her womanhood makes her susceptible either to physical violence or to seduction. It is not enough for her to present herself as Al's (or any man's) equal, for in the world of *Detour*, where nothing matters but the power to impose one's will on others, the concept of equality has no positive meaning. Vera needs to establish that the inequality of the sexes has been *reversed*, not eliminated, and her every word and action is designed to convince Al that she can do exactly what she likes with him ("I'm not through with you by a long shot!") and to rub his nose in the humiliating fact of his complete subordination to her ("In case there's any doubt in your mind, *I'll* take the bedroom!"). Vera points out, justly, that Al is the author of his own downfall ("Not only don't you have any scruples, you don't have any brains!"), and Ulmer unmistakably invites us to take pleasure in the comeuppance of this obtuse and pusillanimous egotist at the hands of a woman of such formidable wit, energy, and intelligence. Indeed, the dialogue of some of their exchanges and the theme of the discomfiture of male presumption and complacency by a female anarchist suggest the direct influence of screwball comedy, and for all that *Detour* is an unusually bleak film noir with a tragic ending, it is very easy to detect within it the makings of a Howard Hawks farce.

Al Roberts (Tom Neal), the hapless protagonist of *Detour*, with Vera (Ann Savage). Personal collection of the editor.

Vera, too, believes in fate, but if Al conceives himself to be its passive and blameless victim, she succumbs to necessity in a spirit of self-assertion, on the principle that adversity can and must be turned to advantage. "That's the trouble with you, Roberts! All you do is belly-ache," she tells him, adding (for reasons of which we are not yet aware) that there are "plenty of people dying this minute who'd give anything" to be where he is. Al replies, characteristically, that "at least they know they're done for: they don't have to sweat blood *wondering* if they are." Vera's contemptuous response—"Your philosophy stinks, pal"—may he charged with irony by the fact that her own philosophy is no better, but it is a tribute to the complexity and maturity of Ulmer's moral sense that he should wish to give Vera's judgment substantial positive value while enforcing the irony at the same time. Like Al and Haskell, Vera acknowledges no higher imperative than personal gain, but while their acquisitiveness signifies no more than their uncomplaining acceptance of the priorities of their culture, Vera's is also determined by an impulse to resist her oppression by men. She acquiesces in the quotidian brutality of capitalism with exemplary ruthlessness, but even as she does so, she is struggling against masculine dominance, and Ulmer attributes the appropriate importance to this struggle, and to the pungent critical insights which it has generated, without exonerating or indulging the lack of "scruples" that Vera shares with Al. Vera has the greater right to her scorn for the Al Roberts worldview because she knows that she is dying of consumption, and she could easily lay claim, if she wished, to all the alibis for immorality that Al is so anxious to establish in his own pathetic case. She refuses to do so, and Ulmer contrasts Al's habitual self-deception unfavorably with Vera's remorseless honesty. Her values may be despicable, but she never pretends, to herself or anyone else, that they are anything but what they are.

The profound poignancy of Vera's character has less to do with her awareness of the imminence of death than with her desire to cling to the possibility of a relationship with Al which is not based on power, despite the fact that such a relationship is no longer feasible, partly as a result of her own actions. As soon as she has rented an apartment for them in the name of "Mrs. Charles Haskell," her behavior toward Al becomes startlingly ambivalent. She continues to flaunt her mastery over him while also making it increasingly obvious that she wants to have sex: her invitation to share her whiskey, which Al refuses, is intended to encourage not merely intimacy but camaraderie ("If I didn't want to give you a drink, I wouldn't have offered it!"). The clue to the significance of this unexpected development is Vera's insistence, for no apparent reason, that the windows of the apartment must always remain closed. She has no more renounced the ideal of "the home" than Sue, her more conventional counterpart, has, and Vera wishes to think of the apartment as a place of privacy and seclusion which has no connection whatever with the world outside it and which operates according to completely different principles. Beyond the apartment's walls, the eternal struggle for supremacy continues, and Al, like all men, is a potentially deadly enemy who must be blackmailed and humiliated into total submission, but Vera has only to close the windows to create a new order of things in which power no longer matters and in which, as "Mrs. Charles Haskell," she can enjoy Al's affection and comradeship.

By the time she reads the news about the approaching demise of Haskell's father, she is prepared to surrender her monopoly of all present and future spoils and to offer Al an ongoing working partnership based on complete economic equality. Even as she plans to cheat Haskell's family out of a fortune, Vera continues to press the claims of reciprocity and mutual responsibility on her reluctant companion, and she seems to envisage a future of collaborative swindling and chicanery in which she and Al exploit everyone but each other ("We're both alike, born in the same gutter!"). Vera is certainly capable of perceiving the ironies of their situation as a couple, but when she suddenly exclaims, "You don't like me, do you, Roberts?" her consternation and disappointment are perfectly genuine, and she remains utterly unaware that the fantasy of a shared domestic refuge from the laws of the jungle by which she herself abides is unrealizable. Al's offended amour propre is a major obstacle in her path, but he has (to do him justice) a certain right to object to being imprisoned, and the harder Vera tries to force him to accept her own distinction between the apartment and the outside world, the more absurdly unreal this distinction becomes. She finds herself in the paradoxical position of seeking to perpetuate her utopia by the coercive methods she wishes to reserve for the road ("I've got the key to that door!"), and the battle for supremacy which began before they reached their haven is inevitably reproduced within it, first as an intensified form of conventional marital bickering, and finally as a lethal game of one-upmanship in which each threatens to betray the other to the police.

They at last come to blows in a struggle for possession of the telephone which will shortly become the instrument of Vera's death, and she tearfully rebukes Al for the violence which her own bluff has helped to provoke by telling him that he is not "a gentleman." Vera does not actually believe (when she is sober) that gentlemen exist, and she herself has done nothing to merit consideration as a lady, but it seems sadly appropriate that she has in the end no better model for the kind of heterosexual partnership she wants than an archaic and idealized version of the inequalities with which she is already familiar.

America

No arts; no letters; no society; and which is worst of all, continual fear and danger of violent death; and the life of man, solitary, poor, nasty, brutish, and short.
—Thomas Hobbes, *Leviathan*

None of the central characters in *Detour* has a fixed abode, and even the marginal figures with a settled existence and a role to play in the maintenance and reproduction of what remains of social life are engaged in occupations—running motels and diners, policing highways, buying and selling cars—which relate in some way to the wanderings of others. Ulmer emphasizes the protagonists' social rootlessness through their propensity to change their identities. Al becomes Haskell, Vera becomes the new Haskell's wife, and Haskell himself has written a letter to his father in which he pretends to be a salesman of hymnals. We never even know if Vera is the Ann Savage character's real name: she tells Al only that "You can call me Vera if you like." The denouement leaves Al without any viable identity at all: "Al Roberts" is listed as dead, and "Haskell" is wanted for murder.

The protagonists have more in common than their mobility. They are all running from places to which they do not wish to, or cannot, return; they all want to settle down again happily and permanently; and they all believe that this aim can be realized only through the acquisition of wealth. Since none of them has any clear idea about where the wealth is to come from, their journeys have the logic, or illogic, of gambling—literally in Haskell's case, metaphorically in that of the others. They have nothing concrete to lose and no certain prospect of gain, and so they stake their lives on a throw of the dice in the hope that the risks they incur will be rewarded by a fortune. Haskell has set himself the goal of making a killing on the races and dreams of returning in triumph to Florida, where he has just been swindled, "with all kinds of jack." Sue longs for a brilliant career in Hollywood, and Al decides, off the cuff, to go along for the proceeds, while reserving the right to play the market until they materialize. Vera, who is coming from "back there" and going nowhere ("L.A.'s good enough for me, Mister"), seizes the unlooked-for opportunity presented by Al's folly in the same buccaneering spirit that prompted Al to rob Haskell, and she is later willing to improvise her own and Al's future around a newspaper story which she discovers entirely by chance. All four gamblers lose. At the end of the film, Vera and Haskell are dead, Sue is working as a hash-slinger in a cafeteria, and Al, who can neither stay where he is nor go back to where he came from, is vaguely heading East in a desultory attempt to postpone the evil day when he will he arrested for Vera's murder. The film's title is profoundly ironic: none of the protagonists is in a position to make a detour, for they have no itinerary to depart from.

Al, Vera, Sue, and Haskell cannot be seen merely as individuals: the fact that they are traveling toward the west, in the footsteps of the pioneers, suggests plainly enough that we are to think of them in terms of a classical American mythology which represents individual enterprise as heroic and as the means of realizing an ideal social project. The ideological connection between individualism and democracy was always willed and tenuous, but in practice it makes no sense to connect them at all, and Ulmer argues in *Detour* that the two terms contradict rather than complement each other. The world he shows us is technically a modern bourgeois-democratic civil society, but it is actually governed by the principles which obtain in Thomas Hobbes's "state of nature," before the implementation of the social contract, where human beings "are in that condition which is called war: and such a war as is of every man against every man." (*Leviathan*, 100)

Ulmer embodies the contradictory concept of the savage, or nonsocial, society in his use of the metaphor of the road. This metaphor recurs frequently in American narratives, and it is almost invariably used to celebrate individual resistance to the constraints of an intolerably oppressive, conservative, and regimented culture. Actually existing American society is seen as an insuperable impediment to the full self-realization of the individual, and the road becomes the last sanctuary of the true American spirit, which can survive only by taking flight from the social world constructed in its name. This use of the road metaphor turns the mythic American ideals on their head. It employs exactly the same terms of reference—heroic individualism and democratic society—but takes the irreversible debasement of the latter for granted and goes on to affirm the former through characters whose refusal to participate in social life comes to signify a rebellious vindication of America in spite of itself.

By contrast, Ulmer preserves the connection between individualism and American social institutions established by the original myth, and he uses the metaphor of the road to argue that this connection manifests itself in practice, not as a democracy of heroes but as an exceptionally inhumane and brutal capitalism. Ulmer's road is not a refuge for exiles from a culture in which America's ideals have been degraded; it is a place where the real logic of advanced capitalist civil society is acted out by characters who have completely internalized its values, and whose interaction exemplifies the grotesque deformation of all human relationships by the principles of the market. Al, Vera, and Haskell are isolated vagabonds whose lives are dedicated to the pursuit of private goals which they set themselves ad hoc, in the light of their own immediate interests, and who collide with one another in a moral vacuum where human contacts are purely contingent, practical social ties have ceased to exist, and other people appear as mere use values to be exploited at will. The ambiguous connotations of the image of the road—which can suggest both social and extra-social space, both a planned system of communication between society's parts and a void that separates them—correspond perfectly to Ulmer's view of America as a society which negates society, and it is significant that the only character in *Detour* who is traveling because he has a social task to perform is the long-distance truck driver who approaches Al in the diner in the opening sequence. The driver is lonely and "needs to talk to someone," but Al rebuffs him ("My mother taught me never to speak to strangers"), and he is forced to withdraw, explaining that he was only "trying to be sociable." It is a key moment: in *Detour* the desire to be sociable is doomed to remain unsatisfied.

The corollary of the reduction of society to a loose aggregate of competing individuals is the reduction of culture to the language of sport: when the characters of *Detour* wish to relate their own actions and projects to a larger public world of common values and shared assumptions, they resort at once to a metaphor drawn from baseball. Sue refers to Al and herself as a "team," says that they have been "struck out," and describes her move to California as an attempt to get out of "the Bush League." Vera tells Al that "life's like a ball game," and you have to "take a swing at whatever comes along" or else you'll "wake up and find it's the ninth inning." Later, Al tries to dissuade Vera from going ahead with her plan to acquire Haskell's inheritance by informing her "that's how people end up behind the eight ball." Even the rhetoric of American democracy has evaporated, and the only surviving impersonal warrant for the conduct of private life is a discourse of winning and losing derived from the national team game.

The impression of radical cultural impoverishment which *Detour* communicates so powerfully is fundamental to the film's meaning. Given Al's refusal to admit responsibility for his actions, it is at one level extremely important that the characters should be seen as the makers of their own history, but the fact that Ulmer overrules his hero's appeals to fate does not mean that he fails to take account of the objective determinants of the characters' behavior. They are free agents in a world which privileges the material well-being of the atomized individual above all else and which unofficially encourages the most vicious, unprincipled, and irresponsible forms of personal rapacity; they exercise their freedom in exactly the way that these circumstances would lead one to expect. Vera and Haskell know that they are dying, but this knowledge, far from qualifying, actually exacerbates their voraciousness. As Vera says, she is "on [her] way anyhow," and the approach of death only strengthens her conviction that she is accountable to no one but herself. She is also intensely aware of the limitations of this kind of detachment from the world, and Ulmer's recognition of the incorrigible survival, in however compromised a form, of the human need for society gives the film's pessimism its tragic character.

Notes on *Pursued* (1996)

The main concern and emphasis in Raoul Walsh's *Pursued* (1947) might be described as the social determination of neurosis. The film belongs to a key area of Hollywood cinema that embraces films in many genres, from the musical (*The Pirate* [1948]) to the western (*The Searchers* [1956]) to the thriller (*Shadow of a Doubt* [1943]), and deals in the form of symbolic drama with sexual repression in the bourgeois American family.

The film establishes that, with the exception of Jake Dingle (Alan Hale), all the characters—Jeb Rand (Robert Mitchum), Thorley Callum (Teresa Wright), Adam Callum (John Rodney), Ma Callum (Judith Anderson), Grant Callum (Dean Jagger), and Prentice McComber (Harry Carey Jr.)—are clearly being "pursued," literally or metaphorically or both, and they are "in pursuit." Hence, the pervasive use, as a background, of the vast, precipitous walls of rock, dwarfing the riders below, which become associated symbolically with the repression of which Grant is the source and, finally, the victim. The flashback that makes up the bulk of the film begins and ends with the mountains: Ma, and then Grant, emerge from their shadow in its opening scene, and the chase in which it culminates is dominated by them. They recur, too, with the death of Adam, Jeb's departure for the war (he rides away toward them), and the colt incident, in which the young Jeb, standing over and accusing Adam, is framed from a low angle against them. The mountains suggest, strikingly and simply, the inescapable repressiveness of which the characters are simultaneously embodiments and victims.

Jeb might be described as the "subject" of the flashback to the extent that we are invited to believe that he is giving an account of his experience. In fact, the strict subjective authenticity of the flashback is violated constantly throughout the film, and once it has been established that the action is occurring "in the past," there is no attempt whatever to restrict us to Jeb's consciousness, on the (correct) assumption that the audience won't notice what is, in "realist" terms, a fundamental discrepancy. Thus, the flashback does not constitute, in any consistent sense, a "first-person narration"—a claim one might make for, say, Edward Dmytryk's *Murder, My Sweet* (1944). *Pursued* works in a way more closely comparable to an Alfred Hitchcock film, encouraging us to identify with the emotional predicament of the central character. There are eight key scenes in the film in which Jeb does not appear and which he could not know about:

1. the conversation between Ma and Grant in the hotel
2. Grant's temptation of Adam at the homecoming celebrations

3. Adam's conversation with Thorley after his fight with Jeb
4. the consultation of the jury at the inquest
5. Grant's temptation of Prentice
6. Ma's conversation with Thorley after Jeb's proposal
7. the gathering of the Callums after the wedding
8. Thorley's rejection of Ma in the denouement

Even in the scenes in which Jeb does appear, we are constantly allowed to become aware of things of which he is not—the song sequence is the clearest example of this. Thus, Jeb can be described as the "subject" of the flashback only in the dramatic sense: he is the protagonist of a narrative which is centrally concerned with the nature of his experience. He is not in any sense the narrator of the film; he is merely the figure with whom the audience identifies.

In the sequence which precedes the opening of the flashback, as Jeb struggles to remember, the phantom figure of Grant appears to him, framed in the barren landscape by the ruined uprights of the doorway, with splintered wooden spars jutting into the image from above. The image establishes, first, the diffuseness of the threat that Grant embodies. It is a threat which crosses time (a generation) and is here associated with the arid desolation of the surrounding country, thus confirming a symbolism already implicit in the first shot of the film: the great block of mountains looming over Thorley as she rides to meet Jeb at the burnt-out ranch at Bear Paw Butte, where the killing of his family took place. Subsequently, Grant acts through Adam, Prentice, Ma, Thorley, and the war. He is both an individual and an all-pervading force. Second, the phantom is (a) an intruder from outside who (b) suddenly appears. These elements, in juxtaposition, suggest an ambivalence that will be central to the film: Grant acts consistently in the name of the family and its purity—that is, in the name of the basic institution of bourgeois democracy—and he is here associated with the disruption of families, death, sterility, and the past.

Nothing in the film encourages us to believe that the child Jeb is not remembering the killing of his family as it "really" happened. The superimpositions of the ghostly images of spurs vividly suggest that already, a few moments after it has occurred, the event has become nightmare and, in the way in which the spurred boots appear to be trampling on the child, redefine the motif of subjection, vulnerability, persecution that is stated in the first shot of the distant rider—here, Jeb "crushed" by his neurosis.

The cry of "Daddy! Daddy!" by the child in the flashback is followed by the narrated remark "But my father wasn't there," which is perfectly true: his father has been killed and the body dragged out, as we see at the end. The narration merely attempts to explain why the child's cry was unanswered. The significant point here is that on the cry "Daddy! Daddy!" Walsh cuts to a shot of Ma Callum, prostrate, and dragging herself toward the trapdoor. What is being stressed is "Ma-as-father," a status which the film quickly confirms: Ma is fearless, aggressive, independent; Ma is owner of the ranch, head of the family; Ma is associated, both here and at the end, with a phallic rifle. She is associated not with the word *mother* but with the phrase "*your* mother" (Jeb is speaking to Thorley). Part of the significance of the very striking birth imagery in the opening scene and its echoes (Jeb lifted out of the dark hole into the light;

Ma's wagon emerging out of the black shadows of the mountain into the moonlight; Ma letting light into the dark cabin, first by opening the door, and then by lighting a lamp) is its irony: the birth is preceded by massacre, and the stages of the emergence into light and safety (hole, clearing, cabin, flight) are steps toward collapse and disintegration.

Ma's first action on bringing the young Jeb into her house is to light the lantern on the table. During her conversation with him after she has seen Grant at the hotel, they are framed with a lamp between them—one on a low table, the other in a bracket on the wall. The same configuration is used for their farewell as Jeb leaves for the war (a lamp on a table between them, and beyond it a fire in the grate; another lamp on the wall as they part at the door), and in the scene following Jeb's visit to Bear Paw Butte, which ends with a very "posed" low-angle medium shot of Jeb, the globe of a lamp filling the right of the frame, and another "balancing" it in the background. In the following scene—Jeb's break with Adam, and Thorley's failure to reconcile them—all three characters are framed with lamps beside and/or behind them, and during the song sequence, lamps separate Jeb and Thorley, and Thorley and Adam. Toward the end of the film, this motif comes nearest to explicit presentation: consider, for example, the extraordinary moment in which Thorley carries a lamp into Ma's bedroom after her drive with Jeb, the scene lit in such a way that Thorley's face is in complete darkness, all the light concentrated on her white blouse, which glows with luminous brilliance. Later in the same scene, when she is telling Ma that she intends to kill Jeb, Thorley is framed behind the bars at the foot of the bedstead, an unlit lamp on a table beside her. The wedding-night sequence exploits similar compositions.

The film begins with the "flashes" of the massacre (the destruction of a home) and proceeds through a narrative in which exterior scenes involving gunfire (or lightning in the visit to Bear Paw Butte) are interspersed with interior scenes in which all the characters are separated, dominated, surrounded by lamps and fires. The Bear Paw Butte scene, for example, is preceded by one in which Thorley rejects Jeb's plan of elopement and is followed, via a wipe of Jeb fleeing home in long shot while the storm rages around him, by a shot of Thorley throwing wood on the fire. Thorley's name is habitually abbreviated to Thor, the name of the Norse god of thunder and lightning—and of the home. The lamp motif reaches its climax in the attempted murder of Jeb on the honeymoon night, when Thorley shoots at him and hits a lamp instead. The imagery has suggested throughout that the household is a circuit of repressed tensions which are released in the gunfire, and the images of lamp and gun are linked in the figures of the women: Ma, whose "crime" is responsible for the interior shooting of the traumatic scene and who lights the first lamp; and Thorley, who becomes the radiance of the lamp she carries and then, in her white bridal negligee, becomes the bearer of the gun. The home and its representatives, the women—the keepers of the flame—become the "keepers" of the hero's neurosis.

In this respect, *Pursued* strikingly resembles Hitchcock's *Spellbound* (1945), in which the sexual pathology of the hero (Gregory Peck) is also associated with the threat of a dominating woman. In both cases, too, the woman is associated in her turn with a malevolent, dangerous, possessive male figure: here, Grant Callum, in *Spellbound,* Dr. Murchison (Leo G. Carroll) who is, implicitly, impotent. While *Spellbound* seems to me to invite an Oedipal reading, the emphasis in *Pursued* is somewhat different.

Let us now consider the nature of the original traumatic event. Ma Callum, married to Grant's brother, commits adultery with Jeb Rand's father. In revenge, Grant wipes out the Rands; Jeb's parents, sister, and brothers are killed, as is Grant's brother (the deceived husband), and Grant himself loses his arm. There are two basic issues here: (1) Ma has broken a social/sexual taboo. She has had an erotic relationship outside marriage and has thus violated the concept of the family; and (2) Grant sets himself up as a figure of (ideological) retribution in the name of family honor—that is, in the name of the family as an inviolable social/moral absolute. The relationships of the original event are repeated and elaborated in the main narrative, with Jeb in the role of his father, Thorley in Ma's, and Adam in Grant's. Grant and Ma survive from the previous generation—Grant attempting to complete his revenge on the Rands and on Ma (thus explicitly, as before, on the side of retribution), and Ma attempting to cancel the guilt she feels for Jeb's losing his family by adopting him into her own (thus, ostensibly, on the side of conciliation).

The main narrative thread of *Pursued* is therefore the feud between two tight, nuclear families, which is associated quite explicitly with the perversion, morbidity, and repression of sexual impulses and the disruption of a love affair. It may be compared with the feud in Mark Twain's *Adventures of Huckleberry Finn*, a novel that represents the classic statement in American art of disgust with and rejection of the family: everything in the book proceeds from complex variations on this dominant theme. For Grant, Ma's crime is that "she forgot she was married to a Callum"; at the end of the film, his coercion of the remnants of the clan to finish the feud after Jeb's marriage to Thorley is rooted in the idea of family solidarity: "Seeing as we're all Callums, I don't have to tell you what we're going to do about it." His obsession with family purity is directly linked to his symbolic impotence through the wounded shooting arm, which he loses in the act of vengeance, and the final eruption of the Callums evokes strong parallels with the vicious, perverse all-male families which recur so significantly in John Ford's films—*My Darling Clementine* was made in 1946, the year before *Pursued*. The incest theme, which is fundamental to the film, develops around the Callums, in Grant's revulsion at Ma's adultery, and Adam's attachment to Thorley. It is inseparable, that is, from the associations of "family purity" and "impotence" which accrue to Grant and the surrogates whom the lost arm compels him to use (Adam, Prentice, his relatives).

Grant is continually linked with the defense of the basic institutions of American ideology: the family; "correct" sexual morality ("thou shalt not commit adultery"); patriotism (he appears as the recruitment officer for the Union army, leading the volunteers in the oath of allegiance, and a portrait of Lincoln presides over his office); hard work and application (he incites Adam's resentment of Jeb by pointing out that dedicated labor goes unrewarded while praise is heaped on the glamorous war hero—"Too bad they don't have a brass band for a good cattle-tally!"); and the law (he appears as the county prosecutor at the inquest). These associations permit a series of disturbing and subversive ironies. Thus, the war (first mentioned by a figure identical to the poster Uncle Sam as "a real shooting war") becomes perverse, the defense of the great, clean American family, a magnification of the destructive sexual pathology embodied in Grant, with guns replacing the lost phallus. (An interesting cross-reference here is Dmytryk's *Crossfire*—made, like *Pursued*, in 1947—in which a similar link is implied between war and unresolved erotic tensions, and in which the psychosis of Montgomery [Robert Ryan] is connected with an obsession with the inviolability of country and family—"He don't respect the service, he don't respect his mother.")

Such implications are a key strategy in film noir, in which, again and again, the villain is there to suggest that American ideology gives birth to monsters. Other elements in the film, of course, are there to place such implications safely. Thus, while Grant's association with American law and order is inherently subversive, his villainy can be used to suggest also that he is a corrupted individual and that the institution itself is basically sound. Hence, the importance of the coroner at the inquest, whose sound common sense can intuit Jeb's innocence and Grant's malicious hypocrisy and triumph over the indifference of the jury ("Don't stand to reason that a man that shot down a dozen fellas in battle [would] shoot down his own brother without givin' him a chance"). The reaffirmation of the benign, homely, incorruptible rightness of American justice does not cancel the more disquieting inference, although it is clearly meant to do so.

Ma attempts to resolve her crime and her responsibility to Jeb by adopting him into her family, and the film's central irony derives from the fact that Grant's impulse to vengeance and Ma's to reconciliation both involve the repression of Jeb's true identity. Killing him and adopting him both become efforts to destroy him as a Rand (as his father's son). The key scenes here are those which follow the colt incident. Ma infers at once that Grant is responsible, and she seeks him out to tell him that she "won't let [him] start it up all over again" and that "that night ended it for [Jeb]." The dialogue continues:

> **Grant:** A night like that don't have an end! What happened then'll make him do things just like spirits were whispering in his ears, saying "Kill! Kill! Kill!"
> **Ma:** The spirits may speak to you, but not to him. I don't believe in your spirits.

When Ma insists that she loves Jeb "like my own son," Grant replies, "What makes you think that boy loves you?" and he threatens that he will "leave that Rand alone—let him grow up— just to see what happens to you when he's big enough to start asking questions," assuring her that "someday you'll wish I hadn't missed my shot." Ma emphatically denies this ("That's one day that'll never come! He's a good boy"), but on her return to the ranch, she takes Jeb aside at once, and when she is certain that he remembers nothing, insists that "What you don't remember don't matter. You belong here with us now . . . Don't ask questions of the past—it has no answers for you. Grow up strong in the love that's here for you. As long as you love in return nothing can happen." When she adds "You do love us, don't you, Jeb?" he makes no reply.

In the next scene, Ma, in the presence of her children Adam and Thorley, adopts Jeb into the family officially—that is, in terms of property. Everything we have or ever will belongs to you three from this day on," she says and, embracing them all within her arms, tells them: "You three yourselves are the finest thing there is—a family." The adoption is ratified by Ma's once more taking Jeb aside and asking him if he would "like to use our name today." Jeb declines this: "If you don't mind, I'd like to use my own name—Jeb Rand." Ma hesitates, then smiles and embraces him; at once Jeb backs away from her in horror as the memory intrudes into consciousness.

Ma's action turns on her need to deny Jeb the knowledge of his past because of her role in the death of his family; the tensions result from the imposition of a family relationship where none exists. The law which has been offended is the ideological proscription of adultery, so that Jeb becomes a "signifier" of guilt. Thus, the first real threat to her relationship with Jeb follows his discovery of Bear Paw Butte, and the renewal of his demands about his identity and his past ("I want to understand"), which she bitterly rejects. The relationship is one, not of repressed love, but of repressed fear and resentment.

The American psychiatrist Morton Schatzman offers a critique of Freud's analysis of the Schreber case, in which Freud arrived at his theory of the nature of paranoia. Schatzman suggests that Freud disregarded the particularities (social, familial, ideological) of the context in which Schreber's "paranoid" symptoms were produced. Schatzman suggests that the social/ideological context which Freud discounts in his analysis of Schreber is that of "the authoritarian, patriarchal, nineteenth-century family," a structure which "(like many today), was a factory for authoritarian ideologies." He concludes that psychoanalysis has, to some extent, "protected and acquiesced in" those ideologies, with their assumptions about "the position of women and children" and their "cosmological" connotations—"a male God atop a hierarchy of accomplices, deputies and servants" (consider Grant Callum in *Pursued*). Considering this repressive, totalitarian ideological context, of which "threatened and actual castration" was a part (both as a punishment for masturbation and as a "cure" for "mental illness"), he suggests that Freud's proposed explanation of "castration fears" in terms of phylogenetic memory, hallucinated (unreal) persecution by the father, and "the discovery of the female genitals," are "gratuitous," and that Freud's choice of data (Schatzman renames them "capta"—the taken) and the actual methods of his analysis embody unquestioned ideological assumptions. (Schatzman, 104–10)

Schatzman distinguishes between repression as defined by psychoanalysis ("an intrapersonal defense built to ward off real, imagined, or phantasied harm") and what he calls "transpersonal" repression: "A person (often a parent) orders another person (often a child) to forget thoughts, feelings, or acts that the first person cannot or will not allow in the other . . . If the first person's aim is to protect himself from experience of which he fears the other may remind him, if the other experiences too much, the order serves as a transpersonal *defense*." (121) This is exactly analogous to Ma's attitude toward Jeb, and her defense becomes "an attack on the other person's experience." (121) Schatzman suggests that both the symptoms of the person who is called "paranoid" and the behavior of the "paranoidogenic person" (his term for one who generates paranoid states in others) can be explained in terms of an identical "sequence of operations" on repressed or forbidden desire—"denial, reversal and projection"; these operations can be described as reversals in syntax and are socially determined. (122–24) It is interesting to bear in mind, too, Schatzman's contention that "paranoidogenicity . . . may be 'inherited' . . . by each generation teaching the next one to fear certain possibilities of mind" (129)—a contention suggested in the whole procedure of Jeb's adoption and in the development of the Ma/Thorley relationship in the second half of the film.

By killing Grant, Ma is symbolically ratifying a relationship analogous to the one for which she was punished. Just as the birth imagery of the traumatic scene was undermined by the prevailing intimations of death, as Ma brought Jeb simultaneously into light and safety, and into the family and repression, so Grant's death becomes Jeb's birth: Jeb tells Ma, "You've given me back my life." The final image of the film—the couple, on horseback, riding away from the camera, the ruined house, and Ma—clearly celebrates a (romantic) release from the constrictions of the family, which is seen as essentially death oriented. Ma is thus rejecting the perversion of the law of the Father (in retributive, sexual morality) embodied in her brother-in-law, and by which she, too, has been contaminated. The two generations are reconciled when the older generation destroys its own, exteriorized perversity. The suggestion is that the forces which Grant represents, and which are shown insistently throughout the film to be interior to all the characters, can be absolutely exorcized (*Spellbound* again provides an interesting parallel) through the death of the "villain."

Thorley's role here is to emphasize the essential difference between herself and Ma: "You lost the man you loved. He died here. My man won't—unless they kill me too!" Thorley's rejection of Ma here is crucial. In their conversation just before the marriage, Thorley has agreed to a temporary separation from Ma until Jeb has been killed—"We'll be together again soon." The intention at this stage is to regress to the sterility of the family relationship once the outsider has been killed. At the climax of the film, this intention is reversed. Thorley accuses her mother of having "failed" Jeb's father and herself, and of having withheld the truth from Jeb through shame, the charges representing, in effect, an indictment of the ideology of the family which dictates that Ma's love is a "crime," imposes guilt for it, and demands that consciousness of it be repressed. The film's inability to contain its own subversion of the family is very clear. The ending can work only because there is no equivalent of the taboo of Ma's marriage vows to be broken: bourgeois ideology can easily accommodate the "nonsocial" romantic couple. Thus, despite the ostensible reconciliation, Jeb and Thorley ride away from family and civilization at the end, like Huck Finn lighting out for the Territory.

The incest theme in *Pursued* comes nearest to explicitness in Adam's attachment to Thorley. Adam is clearly presented in parallel to Grant. He occupies Grant's "place" in the younger generation (brother, instead of brother-in-law, to the offending woman, so that his "perversity" becomes correspondingly more pronounced), and there are again suggestions of impotence: (a) the obsession with his sister (as a part of the ranch that he inherits by right); (b) his general ineffectuality; (c) the abbreviation of his name to "Ad" (this relates, too, to his constant association with the account books—"Add"—such that his potency is not in his sexuality, but in his control of the ledgers, and Jeb threatens not only his possession of Thorley but his sole right to the accumulating capital of the ranch); and (d) the implication that he is not properly virile (Thorley calls him a "back-fence gossip"). In the scenes preceding the ambush, he and Grant are deliberately blurred together, so that both become embodiments of one force: we see, first, Adam resolving to ride into town in pursuit of Jeb ("Looks as if we're gonna have to set things right"); then, at the end of the sequence at Dingle's place, as Jeb is beginning his ride back to the ranch, Grant appears, suddenly and inexplicably, out of the darkness and vanishes again. Finally, Adam ambushes Jeb in the ravine. The blurring is appropriate, since

Jeb Rand (Robert Mitchum) feels the deathly constraints of the family in *Pursued*. Personal collection of the editor.

Grant has, symbolically, "possessed" Adam, their conversation in the saloon on the day of Jeb's homecoming being treated both as temptation by the devil and temptation by repressed desire. Grant emerges out of Adam's disquiet at Jeb's safe and glorious return.

In Adam's confrontation with Thorley after his fight with Jeb, we are presented very economically with two facets of sexual repression. Thorley "solves" the problem of her desire for Jeb by admitting him into the family—that is, by desexualizing her desire and trying to perpetuate the relationship which makes the desire a problem in the first place. Thus, when Adam asks her in horror if she hates him, she replies that she loves him, and that "I always thought the three of us would never be apart." Adam's response is practically a declaration of love: "Three! Three! You're always saying that! Why does *he* count? It's you and me!" Thorley's "solution" is an aggravation for Adam: her need to desexualize her desire for Jeb and adopt him as brother actually inflames the erotic tension for Adam. Thorley accuses him of thinking of her as his property: "The ranch has been a wife to you . . . because you don't *have* a wife! Well, I don't belong to it! You can take me off that dog-eared tally-book you carry around!" Capitalist possessiveness and incestuous possessiveness are linked, the enclosed family unit being seen as the breeding ground for both.

The Adam/Jeb relationship is complex and important. Consider the scene at the beginning of the film, when the three children meet for the first time. Lying in bed, his head toward the door, is a boy (Adam) clad in a white nightshirt, his hands behind his head compulsively gripping the ironwork of the bedstead, as though in pain or distress. As his figure is too distant to be distinguished clearly, our first impression might be of a woman in childbirth—or, at least, in intense pain and anguish. The camera pans left, and Jeb climbs on to the other end of the bed. We become aware of a girl (Thorley), her head at the other end of the bed from Adam's. When Jeb and Thorley look at each other for the first time, this is shown in the one image, without cutting. By contrast, Walsh cuts between close-ups of Adam and Jeb staring at one another, conveying at once an opposition, on which the subsequent narrative will enlarge, and a symbolic likeness—Jeb's face left of frame, Adam's right of frame, suddenly become, across the cut, reflections of each other. Adam's initial strange movements increase this suggestiveness, as if he, like Jeb, were possessed by a nightmare.

The symbolic significance of the parallel is clinched in the song sequence, part of the "thanksgiving," as Ma calls it, for Jeb's safe return from war. The scene is based almost entirely on an exchange of surreptitious glances between the characters (it is analogous to the dance scene): the celebration of family togetherness is characterized by silent, private communications from which at least one person is always excluded. The scene begins with a medium shot of a table in the sitting room with the three "children" gathered round it: Jeb in uniform, standing, left of frame; Thorley standing next to him; and Adam sitting, resigned and despondent, his body hunched up, his eyes fixed on the floor. Ma comes in from the background, carrying a bottle of wine and glasses on a tray. She proposes a toast—"Welcome to my son Jeb"—and Thorley, unseen by the others, prods Adam and gives him an admonishing look to make him join in. She says to Jeb, "To you, Jeb—and you must drink to me," putting her arm around him. As the camera pans around the table from left to right (Jeb-Thorley-Adam-Ma), we see Adam noticing Thorley's gesture, and looking away again bitterly.

The climax of the scene is the singing of the "Londonderry Air" by Adam and Jeb to the tune of the music box, as they used to do as children. The camera pans up from a close-up of the box to frame Jeb and Thorley in a low-angle medium shot, and Jeb begins to sing on his own: ". . . once more I waken/ The sweetness of thy slumb'ring strain;/ In tears, alas, farewell was taken." Thorley moves out of frame right at the end of the second line, leaving Jeb alone. At the beginning of the next line ("And now in tears we meet again"), Walsh cuts to a medium shot of all four characters from roughly behind Jeb, and we see Ma, noticing that Adam is looking down sadly, put her hand on his shoulder and smile at him. On the next line, Adam joins in: "Yet even then our peace was singing/Her halcyon song o'er land and sea." Beyond the table, Ma and Thorley exchange smiles, and then Thorley glances between Adam and Jeb, neither of whom are looking at the women, both being totally absorbed in the song. For the last two lines, Walsh cuts to a medium close shot of Adam and Jeb, Jeb left of frame looking down, his head above Adam's, Adam right of frame, looking off left—a composition that seems to "contain" the opposing close-ups of the two boys on the bed: "Though joy and hope to others bringing/She only brought you tears to weep." As the song ends, Jeb nods slightly in Adam's direction, and they exchange a brief glance. There is a sudden, sharp cry of pain from beyond the frame, which turns out to come from the dog, but is clearly intended to evoke, at first, a human voice. Everybody laughs merrily, their unity apparently confirmed. The next scene is the communal meal which breaks up with the beginning of Adam's jibing, resentful provocation of Jeb, the insistence that Jeb is an intruder ("I call it the Rand share").

The scene is remarkable for the polarization of the male and female characters on each side of the table, both pairs united, the men oblivious of the women, and for the fact that Adam and Jeb are brought together, for the only time in the film, by a song which implies betrayal by a woman. This is emphasized by the final cut, which leaves only their faces in frame for the last two lines of the song. At the same time, they actually look at each other only for an instant—Walsh enforces their separateness even within the bond established by the song's theme. In both song and narrative, peace, reconciliation, reunion across time are allegorized as a woman (Ma brings Jeb into the family; Thorley acts as mediator between Jeb and Adam; Ma brings in the communion wine; both women coerce Adam into the celebration by touching him); in the treatment of the last lines, the men are seen as victims of the woman as peacemaker, who is transformed into the woman as destroyer. One thinks immediately of Ma's rejection of Jeb after the inquest into Adam's death: "For me, you're walking up the gallows steps! I built that gallows. I tied the noose. All the love I had for you is dead." She has been building the gallows all the way through the film, from the moment when she rescues Jeb from his hiding place. The birth imagery, then, is significant here, the inference being that both as an agent of disruption (Ma's adultery) and as an agent of reconciliation (Ma's, then Thorley's, adoption of Jeb), the woman is lethal. Two families disintegrate because of Ma's crime; a third disintegrates through her attempt to absolve it. In both cases, the destructiveness is seen as ideologically determined—Ma cannot love Jeb's father because adultery is forbidden; Thorley cannot love Jeb because Ma has made him her brother.

Let us compare the song sequence with the dance sequence. The dance is the scene of the first meeting between Jeb and Thorley after Adam's death: like the song, it shows us a reunion after a long passage of time. Jeb arrives with Dingle, who, in the second half of the film, becomes Jeb's business partner. The dance begins with Jeb's "appropriation" of Thorley, who acquiesces against her will and her expressed intentions ("I'd rather have people look at me than dance with someone I hate!"). Walsh cuts from the couple to (1) Ma in close-up. She sees what Jeb is doing and is obviously furious and desperate. She turns right. Cut to (2) Grant in close-up. He also looks right. Cut to (3) Jeb and Thorley dancing. Cut to (4) Grant continuing to look right. Cut to (5) Thorley's suitor, Prentice, coming into the room in medium long shot, carrying some glasses of punch for Thorley and himself.

The cutting in the sequence suggests a telepathic transference of intent. Ma silently evokes Grant's intervention: he, in turn, and in a repetition of her movements, silently evokes Prentice as his instrument. The whole movement is initiated by Thorley's repressed rage at Jeb's approach, which is an expression of [his] desire for her and which, of course, takes advantage of the fact that etiquette requires her compliance. The exchanged looks in the song sequence convey the two women's desire to achieve unity. Here, the family tensions have already exploded, and the looks convey the desire, once more silent, private, and inexplicit, to force a dissolution. It is now Prentice who brings the communion drinks, and he is made to relinquish them for a gun.

Walsh cuts back a wide shot of the room full of dancers (6) and then to Jeb and Thorley (7). Cut to (8) Ma in close-up, looking as though searching for someone. Cut to (9) Dingle in medium shot, looking off right, then left. Cut to (10) Grant going over to the orchestra in medium long shot, to get them to finish the dance. In this sequence (a) Grant initiates his move against Jeb; and (b) the shot of Dingle "intervenes" between those of Ma and Grant, prefiguring his decisive intervention in the duel between Jeb and Prentice.

Jeb has now adopted Dingle's style of dress— an immaculate black suit—which is also the costume worn by Grant Callum throughout the film (except in the traumatic scene). Dingle is benevolent, Grant is malign; both are "tricky." Grant operates through deceit and hypocrisy, under the cover of law, and is distinguished by a certain diabolism in his ability to possess and manipulate other characters, in his "dispersed presence." Dingle owns a gambling den called the Honest Wheel and refers to himself as "Honest Jake Dingle." He also runs a crooked game, and we see him instructing one of his croupiers, through a loaded glance, to see that Jeb wins at roulette, deliberately in order to counteract Jeb's previous "bad luck" with Adam—"Maybe you played into a cold deck." He also provides and deals the cards with which Jeb wins at poker. An explicit antithesis with Callum is established in the dialogue, Dingle telling Jeb before the card game that "Luck's sure riding on your shoulder tonight," and Jeb telling Thorley at the end of the film, before the shootout, that "There was a black dog riding my back, and yours, too." Dingle's last act in the film, before his abrupt disappearance from the action, is to disarm Grant: the camera tracks back from a close-up of the gun in Grant's hand as he hides in a dark alley to ambush Jeb and reveals Dingle behind him, covering him with another gun.

Thus, while Grant suggests malignant trickery (ambushes, facades, hiding up the back way), Dingle's trickery is attentively, kindly providential, operating the wheel of fortune on Jeb's behalf. Most important, Dingle is presented in opposition to any idea of family, so that the offer of a partnership at the Honest Wheel ("We'd make a great combination, you and myself") counterbalances the threat of enforced adoption at the ranch. Both Adam and Thorley explicitly disapprove of gambling, the former, when he throws Jeb out, associating it with laziness as opposed to work and earning your money, which are part and parcel of the family ethos ("You've been drawin' that money for lyin' in the shade. Lucky if I didn't have six of my riders stretched out beside you playin' pitch.") The opposition of male companionship/"irresponsibility"/rejection of family on one hand, and marriage/"responsibility"/family life on the other, is central to American culture, and Jeb is a victim of this tension, his black suit emphasizing a link with both Grant and Dingle. This also helps to explain the love-duet aspect of the song with Adam, both men finding a momentary unity as the victims of a woman.

Similarly, we note an important sexual opposition. Jeb's persecutors are either aggressive, potent women (the woman with the phallus) or men who are shown as impotent and "unmanned." Prentice succumbs to Grant's temptation precisely because Grant works on his doubts about his "virility." Grant insinuates that unless he avenges Jeb's "insult" to Thorley at the dance, "You're not the man I took you for," to which Prentice replies, lowering his head in shame so that it is obscured by shadows, "I'll do what's right." He adds a moment later that he is "not much good with a gun." We have seen him earlier, during the recruiting sequence, behind the counter in his father's store, resentful that "Dad won't let me" join up, this father/son pair forming a contrast to Grant and Jeb through the former's evident determination, as one of the soldiers remarks, "to get [Jeb] into this war." It is one of the film's main strategies to imply that the parent, whether protective or aggressive, generates anxiety in the children, the anxiety being traced back to its roots in ideology—here the relation between war and "manhood": impotent father-figure tries to send youth off to war; protective father keeps son away from war, thus creating fear of impotence.

Dingle, as opposed to all these, is individually potent (the wheel, the disarming of Grant) and/because he lacks a family. The problem of the film is to reconcile Jeb's "potency" with an ideologically approved relationship (marriage) that will not be sexually repressive. This is achieved through the symbolism of the wedding-night sequence. Jeb surrenders his gun to Thorley so that she can kill him with it, and at the very moment at which she possesses the weapon, Thorley discovers that she is unable to use it ("Your hand shook—but not because you hate me"). The battle of opposing wills—imaged as opposing stares—is resolved by her surrender. Thus, the defeat of the forces of sexual repression is simultaneous with the woman's perception and admission that she has loved the potent male all the time. It is by means of this procedure that *Pursued* can present the family as "a factory for authoritarian ideologies," in Schatzman's phrase, and yet move toward the affirmation of the basic unit of the bourgeois family—the couple, rendered as reborn (fully virile) male, and reborn (fully devoted) female. The conclusiveness of the denouement is an insistence that "it will be different from now on."

We are now in a position to describe the series of breakdowns which Jeb suffers during the action, and which represents a complex network of tensions:

1. The traumatic event, which establishes Grant Callum as the agent of persecution (in Schatzman's terms, "the paranoidogenic person") and identifies him with socially determined sexual repression, in the name of the family.

2. Jeb embraced by Ma, which associates Jeb's neurosis with an attempt to absorb him into the Callum family, and thus with a threat to the identity to which he clings. The correlation between Ma and Grant at this point has already been discussed.

3. The war. The breakdown here is associated both with Grant's persecution (he is the recruiting agent) and with the impediment of Jeb's union with Thorley. In their final conversation before Jeb leaves for the war, each confesses to the overwhelming repression of desire which has been forced on them by the imposition of the family relationship ("I had to go on every day pretending. Watching you all day, letting you touch me, at night going in my room, lying there thinking about it."), and which is now perpetuated by the intervention of the war.

4. The discovery of the ranch at Bear Paw Butte, which follows Thorley's rejection of Jeb's proposal to elope and her insistence on the decorum and propriety of courtship, the desire here to "pretend we didn't grow up together" ironically balancing her previous protest against having to "pretend" to think of him as a brother. Thus, the emergence of the trauma (accompanied by a sense of suffocation—"Suddenly I couldn't breathe") is prompted, not by a kiss, but by the repression of it: Jeb's anxiety is a response to Thorley's ridiculing of his premonitions and her barring of his desire to escape from the family, a denial which takes the form of subjecting him to the etiquette through which alone sex can be naturalized in bourgeois society. Thorley's proposition has a double function from her point of view. It secures Jeb as a potential

husband while at the same time distancing indefinitely the physical consummation of marriage—even the most innocuous physical contact is forbidden "'til you've bought the ring." By the same token, it keeps Jeb "in the family," it keeps "the three of us together," it preserves the nonsexual communion of childhood. After the death of Adam, Thorley uses the courtship proprieties as a weapon: they become her means of humiliating Jeb and of masking her plan to destroy him on the wedding night ("That moment he thinks he has me, he'll lose everything.") The courtship scene exactly reproduces the images of it conjured up earlier by Thorley, and the references—through the wine ("just for Christmas and holidays") and the music box ("An old-fashioned tune. Some people don't care for it") to the song sequence—underline the fragility and illusoriness of that apparent reunion. Here, bourgeois good manners become, literally, masks for murder, and Jeb, in his humiliation, denounces them: "It's worse than fighting and yelling in the streets!"

5. Prentice's burial. Prentice, as we have seen, is Grant's surrogate, and the attack by the two "paranoidogenic" agents releases the memory of the original persecution— "He was one more part of the mystery of people hating me. I had that feeling of some lost and awful thing come over me again"—and Jeb's narration at this point is juxtaposed with the spurred, trampling feet of the pallbearers in an echo of the traumatic scene.

The Family in *The Reckless Moment* (1976)

Much recent work on the western—and the reading of *Young Mr. Lincoln* (1939) by the editors of *Cahiers du cinéma* has been crucial here—has explored the genre's Garden/Wilderness antinomy in terms of the attempted exclusion and negation of Desire (sexuality, violence, the "lawless"—classically embodied by the Indian) and its subjection to a prohibitive Law. It is legitimate to develop the thesis, not only for the Hollywood cinema as a whole but also for the culture itself: it is implicit from its origins that the cost of the democratic American community is repression. Discussing Benjamin Franklin in *In the American Grain*, William Carlos Williams remarks: "It is necessary in appraising our history to realize that the nation was the offspring of the desire to huddle, to protect—of terror" (155); the virtues embodied in *Poor Richard's Almanac*—the ideal of "sobriety, industry and frugality," through which Americans can "soon become masters, establish themselves in business, marry, raise families, and become respectable citizens" (152, 156); the ideal of an economy based on the harmonious interdependence of "useful members of society" who are individually independent and self-reliant; the work ethic, which is inseparable from the idea of social morality ("Industry and constant employment are great preservatives of the morals and virtue of a nation")—all these are characterized by Williams as products of the need to build "strong walls and thick shutters," to "keep out the wilderness with the wits," to repress everything which threatens the security (the economy) of that whole which the Constitution "binds . . . together for general purposes." (Franklin quoted in Williams, 148) Indeed, Williams makes the connection between the suppression of the Indian and the denial of the body emphasized by the *Cahiers'* text, and his remarks coincide with Freud's suggestion, in "Inhibitions, Symptoms and Anxiety," that human "sociability" is dominated by the death instinct. (Vol. XX, 168)

The fundamental dialectic of the need for and the flight from community, variously inflected, but almost invariably expressive of violent sexual tensions, can be traced throughout American art. Its literature, for example, develops out of the vision of a misanthropic hermit (Henry David Thoreau) and out of Edgar Allan Poe's themes: of the morbid, incestuous family; the protagonist's unending battle against burial, suffocation, appropriation of the body (beautifully applied to the predicament of the American male in two of the most appalling of the tales, "Loss of Breath" and "The Man That Was Used Up"); and the association of culture and an encroaching, increasing heritage of guilt (Freud's theme in *Civilization and Its Discontents*). Similarly, *Moby Dick* begins with Ishmael's evocation of the entire respectable, working population of the New World "athirst in the great American desert," gazing out toward an ocean which is associated, symbolically, with the prairie, dreaming of "forbidden seas" and "barbarous coasts." The structural pattern of *Billy Budd*—an ambiguous innocence/ignorance (Billy) placed between the demands of the Law (Vere and his "set forms") and the "monster" whose monstrousness stems from sexual repression (Claggart)—is echoed in that of one of the most subversive Hollywood "family" films, *Shadow of a Doubt* (1943). It is appropriate that the "charming community" in which Lucia Harper (Joan Bennett) is imprisoned in *The Reckless Moment* (1949) should be named Balboa, after the Spanish conquistador who helped to bring European civilization to the New World and who was the first European to look out over the Pacific in the direction of that "passage to more than India" which Walt Whitman describes as the aim and impulse of the American Dream.

One can associate *The Reckless Moment* with a (trans-generic) cycle of films which emerge in Hollywood during the 1940s alongside the themes and iconography of film noir and which express that increasingly disturbed preoccupation with the tensions and ambiguities of "settlement" and the family which reaches full, conscious, elaborated expression in the work of, say, Nicholas Ray and Douglas Sirk in the 1950s. I want to indicate here some points of connection and resemblance before passing to Max Ophüls's film itself.

1. One might reasonably begin with the western. Jacques Tourneur's *Canyon Passage* (1946) is built entirely on a series of variations on the theme of "settling and wandering," significant here because of an insistent thematic emphasis on money and economics: what we see is the emergence of American capitalism. The film begins in Portland, the meeting (trading) point of the East (capitalist civilization and refinement) and the frontier, and the town is created in terms of mud, commerce, and gold worship ("A man can choose his own gods"). That equation recalls Norman O. Brown's thesis in *Life Against Death* that the phrase "filthy lucre" is a symbolic truth and that capitalism, with its acquisitiveness, its rates of interest, and the "sacred" significance it gives to gold, is the heir of "the magic-dirt complex" of "archaic" cultures and, as such, represents—from a psychoanalytical viewpoint—the definitive triumph of sublimation (the denial of the body) and the death instinct, whereby "dead matter" is cathected with libido, the "worthless" becomes the "priceless," and gold "the visible god." (248, 300, 302–3)

   At the other end of the trail is Jacksonville, the pioneer town, with its insecurely repressed violence (the brawls, the lynch mob—"Why didn't you kill him?"/"Would that have been more fun?") and sexuality. Indeed, Bragg (Ward Bond), whose rape of two squaws provokes the Indian war, is associated not only with Lestrade (Onslow Stevens), the gambler who is the leading representative in the town of parasitic, exploitative capitalism, and whose sexual impotence/sterility is strongly inferred symbolically, but also, crucially, with the "hero" (Dana Andrews)—"I guess we're both restless men." The burgeoning little town "contains" both Portland (gold worship; gambling as a way of life emerging logically from the ideal of self-reliant individualism) and the wilderness. The moral ambiguities are all-pervasive and finally contaminate the hero (himself a trader—a commercial go-between), whose cheerful self-confidence ("This is Jacksonville, U.S.A.—we sail with the tide!") and sense of immunity are progressively undermined. Similarly, the kind of settlement implied in the isolated little cabin of the Dancer family ("This is my fort"—see, for example, Williams on Franklin) is shown both to be perpetually vulnerable to the eruptions of Savagery (with the traditional generic connotation of id energies) and to depend for its survival on their denial and repression (settling down—"Caroline don't like movin' around and changin'"), bringing with it notions of inheritance and repetition across the generations. Caroline's (Patricia Roc) ambition for her children is that they will do exactly what she and her husband have done.

2. The crux of *Shadow of a Doubt* is the confrontation of Young Charlie (Teresa Wright) and her Uncle Charlie (Joseph Cotten) in the 'Til-Two nightclub, the archetypal film noir underworld dive which Alfred Hitchcock locates at the heart of the ideal American small town, Santa Rosa, California. The film is built on the systematic subversion of apparent extremes, which are rendered iconographically through the imagery of ostensibly antithetical genres. Thus, on the one hand, Uncle Charlie's pathology is presented as American ideology gone mad—he is the purifier, the killer of "useless," unproductive women with undemocratically excessive accumulations of wealth. He embodies a hopeless nostalgia for an illusory Golden Age of togetherness and rural community ("Everybody was sweet and pretty then"), and he shares with his sister Emmy (Patricia Collinge) the fastidious cleanliness (he is "neat and fussy") which, as a touchstone of bourgeois manners, is also invoked, as Robin Wood has noted, in the opening shots of the Lewton/Tourneur *Cat People* (1942). ("Shadow Worlds," 66) Uncle Charlie yearns for both the family and the home, and he is possessed by the compulsion to destroy them: the imagery of his dialogue in the nightclub (ripping off the fronts of houses to reveal the "animals" inside; the universe as "a foul sty"; the sense that the unrelenting clarity of vision which pierces the repressive hypocrisy of social forms and dares to look into "the blackness of darkness" is, inevitably, a plunge into madness) recalls irresistibly the imagery with which Ahab is created in *Moby Dick*—"Strike through the mask!"; the breaking of the quadrant; the image of "the wretched infidels . . . who refuse to wear colored or coloring glasses upon their eyes," and who "gaze themselves blind" at the prospect of a universe revealed as a "charnel." (Melville, 354) The film can be seen as a major instance of a theme which has characterized American art from Thoreau to Norman Mailer's "white negro"—the problem of the perversion of fundamental energies which cannot be accommodated by bourgeois-capitalist American democracy. The answer to the problem has been found, to date, in various forms and degrees of monomania, ranging from misanthropic hermetism (Thoreau) to psychosis (Ahab, Claggart, Hitchcock's "villains") to a kind of self-induced psychosis (the anarchy of Mailer's hipster). It is fascinating to note (the structural similarity being so close) that in both *Shadow of a Doubt* and *Billy Budd*, the reaffirmation of a Law which has been shown to depend on sexual repression involves a betrayal of the "psychopath" figure.

The family life of the Newtons in *Shadow of a Doubt* is characterized by constant and habitual repression: the use of overlapping dialogue, the sense of individual self-absorption and co-presence without contact, conversations in which the members of the family do not look at or listen to one another create an overwhelming impression of isolation. The image of the youngest son being nagged and/or petted by his mother and portrayed, always, as strangely alienated, recurs in numberless family films (it is still there in, say, Robert Altman's *Thieves Like Us* [1974]). A marvelous inflection of the generic type of the smart, precocious, tomboyish younger sister produces, in Anne Newton, a little girl characterized by a sustained autistic withdrawal from reality into movies (her ambition to look like Veronica Lake) and, predominantly, books—she wants to become a librarian, and is introduced refusing, literally, to take her head out of *Ivanhoe*, the classic novel of sublimated romantic dream by an author who epitomized, for Mark Twain, the rottenness of the European inheritance. She also has a dread of "movin' around and changin'" ("I don't want to get carried away"), a profound conservatism ("It's wrong to talk against the government"), and in her love of horror stories and her repressed resentment of the family ("I broke my mother's back three times"), anticipates by thirty years a crucial contemporary development in the horror film.

One might compare the mother/daughter relationships in Hitchcock's film and *The Reckless Moment*. At the party at the end of *Shadow of a Doubt*, where Young Charlie silently forces her uncle to leave Santa Rosa by wearing the ring which, earlier, suggested their symbolic marriage, Emmy, to the hushed embarrassment of the company, violates the bourgeois taboo on the public expression of distress and breaks down at the prospect of the disintegration of the family. Hitchcock clinches here the parallel between Emmy's entrapment as wife and mother ("You sort of forget you're you . . . your husband's wife") and the future facing her daughter. The idea of the reenactment of the repressive family structure through the children is crucial in both films. *The Reckless Moment* moves toward the moment at which Bea inherits her mother's fur coat, the immersion in the role of bourgeois womanhood being accompanied in both cases by the rejection of a (very ambiguous) male intruder (Darby, Uncle Charlie) who has been attractive in the first place because of the romanticization of desire encouraged by the family's restrictions. Similarly, both films end with a renewal of self-repression by the mothers and the return to an impotent (Joe, who "might as well be dead") or an absent husband. One might note here that Emmy, on being relieved of her preparations for the meal by her daughter just before the second dinner scene (Young Charlie has just discovered that her uncle is a murderer), immediately begins to hum the "Merry Widow" waltz—the tune which symbolizes the sublimated romantic dream of which all the characters are, variously, victims.

As Ronnie Scheib points out, money is central to the film. (56) Indeed, it begins with the landlady's horror at Uncle Charlie's carelessness with his banknotes. Part of what Young Charlie discovers in the "descent" which culminates in a bar straight out of the nightmare capitalist city is an economic reality. In the bank sequence, her real involvement in bourgeois values is indicated in her shocked dismay that her uncle makes jokes about money, embezzlement, and the acquisitiveness of banks, and we remember the conversation with her father in which, when he tries to dispel her depression by telling her that he has been given a raise, she replies, "How can you talk about money when I'm talking about souls?" The bourgeois obsession with money-values is counterbalanced by a fantasy which excludes the consciousness of money; the unmasking of Uncle Charlie entails the recognition that the money he has invested in her father's bank and the ring he has given her are "filthy lucre," made even filthier by theft and murder. Hence, a further connotation to the film noir bar, where Young Charlie meets another alter ego—the waitress who was in the same class at school with her, who has worked her way through "half the restaurants in town" and reached bottom, and who would "just about die for a ring like that." The notion of repetition and circularity (bourgeois routine and inheritance; the recurring pattern of the waitress's descent; the neurotic repetition of Uncle Charlie's existence) permeates the film and is rooted in the circulation of capital.

3. The main narrative of *It's a Wonderful Life* (1947) is built on the repeated frustration of George Bailey's (James Stewart) desire to leave his hometown because of his commitment to other people, on the conflict between individual creative impulse (his ambition to become an architect) and the restrictions and responsibilities imposed by family and community (the need to maintain the bank he inherits from his father, the last bastion of benevolent private enterprise in a town otherwise absorbed by malign corporate capitalism). The central flashback culminates in a financial crisis, precipitated by someone else's carelessness (Bailey is constantly greeted by the antagonism, indifference, or inefficiency of the townspeople), which releases all the repressed resentment and frustration built up during a lifetime of self-abnegation: in one of the most painful scenes in the history of the cinema, he turns on town, home, wife, and children before going out to commit suicide. His salvation by his guardian angel (Henry Travers, the father in *Shadow of a Doubt*) is clearly intended to recuperate the subversion of the ideals of fulfillment through family and devotion to others (one might compare the film with F. Scott Fitzgerald's *Tender Is the Night*, in that both concern men who are totally drained in the process of nourishing those around them). In fact, the extraordinary sequence in which Bailey is shown what the town would have been like if he had never been born serves to confirm the vulnerability of the bourgeois order, the repression on which it depends. The angel conjures up a vision of the film noir city, in which Bailey encounters family and friends now totally brutalized amid the raucous darkness of Raymond Chandler's "mean streets," and the penultimate scene is a visit to an enormous graveyard (in an inverted version of Scrooge's vision in *A Christmas Carol*).

One might single out two points. In the absence of Bailey (the potent male who defines the town's significance), his wife is revealed as the local librarian, dowdy, bespectacled, totally inhibited. In the absence of the family, the role of the Negro is reversed: the black maid, who is central to the Bailey household, is treated with "liberality" and deep affection and, at the end of the film, is given the most prominent place (the last) among the townsfolk who donate money to restore Bailey's fortunes (that is, she accepts cheerfully her servitude to the white bourgeoisie), and she is replaced, in our first glimpse of Pottersville—the inside of a murky, crowded bar—by a Negro playing a piano, placed in the very middle of the image.

Very obviously, money is once more crucial in the film's scheme: the unfeeling syndicalist-capitalist (Lionel Barrymore), symbolically impotent (his crippled legs), is opposed to Bailey's sympathetic, paternalist benevolence. (Both here—in the assumption that social problems can be alleviated significantly by a benign individual controlling money—and in its narrative strategies and the amazing intensity and vitality of the realization, Capra's film invites a comparison with Dickens.) Potter's money is filthy, insidiously acquired ("magic-dirt"—see Brown's analysis of the Devil as the heir, under capitalism, of the trickster god; *It's a Wonderful Life* has a succession of temptation scenes), and associated with death and sterility (Potter comes into his own at times of death and disaster). Bailey's money is creative (the housing estate) and fertile; indeed, the creativity is given religious connotations when the bank's last two notes, from which future prosperity must grow, are named "Momma and Poppa Dollar." The final scene—love, gratitude, community, respect, expressed through gifts of money to save Bailey from bankruptcy—is a triumphant assertion of the latter emphasis, just as Potter's diabolic currency reaches its ultimate expression in the "negative vitality" of the infernal city. The conviction that the bourgeois order depends on repression and sublimation is underlined by the dualistic treatment of money, if one follows Brown's suggestion that capitalism depends on the final denial of the "anal-erotic" sources of the money complex. Thus, Bailey's money, and Bailey's town, are carefully purged of any connection with capitalism and its distinguishing feature (Potter's motive)—accumulation (in the psychoanalytical terms employed by Brown, hoarding excrement/dead matter): Bailey's money is (a) entrusted to him on a personal basis by his friends; and (b) constantly going out again for the good and enjoyment of the community. It defines an "archaic economy of gift giving [on] the principle of reciprocity" rather than a capitalist economy (possession, hoarding, interest, debt). In the capitalist city, not only desire but also the bodily origin of the money complex becomes evident, and must be denied. The community celebrated at the end of the film represents the sublimation of both.

4. *The Woman in the Window* (1944) begins with Professor Wanley (Edward G. Robinson) seeing off his wife and children as they leave New York for a holiday in the country. The rest of the film consists of what we eventually discover is a dream, in which Wanley is picked up by a beautiful, mysterious woman (played by Joan Bennett), returns to her apartment—where he kills her enraged lover in self-defense—and, after a disastrously clumsy attempt to get rid of the body, becomes increasingly, insidiously incriminated. The imagery of Bennett's first appearance (Wanley gazing at her portrait through a window, and the reflection of the "real" woman suddenly materializing beside the painting) suggests a fulfillment of repressed desire: Wanley, temporarily released from responsibility to his family, invokes the sexuality which is habitually denied and which the doppelgänger symbolism locates within himself. As in *The Reckless Moment*, the act of transgression leads to death and, in turn, the effort

to dispose of the body—"the body" signifying here both sexuality (the original surrender to desire) and the corpse (in both films, an inhabitant of the underworld by which the "murderer" has been contaminated and symbolically linked to him/ her). During the investigation, Wanley increasingly excites the suspicions of his friend, the police commissioner (Raymond Massey), subtly exposing himself through "mistakes" which suggest a need to be punished: the narrative moves toward his literal exhaustion and the surrender of Eros to the death instinct, in which the only final means of repressing the body and the guilt imposed for desire becomes suicide. In both films the desperate ineptitude of the "cover-up" is emphasized, and in both, a blackmailer appears (Dan Duryea in Fritz Lang's film). In both films, too, a tender, hopeless love, which is never physically consummated, develops tentatively between the "family" figure and the intruder from the underworld. (I am suggesting only a generalized similarity here: obviously, the pattern of relationships is not exactly congruent.) *The Woman in the Window* ends, like the other films, with a deliberate reinstatement of repression. Appalled by the surrender to and punishment of desire enacted in his dream, the professor rejects in horror the advances of a second woman who approaches him as he is taking another look at the portrait.

In Ophüls's film, iconography and emphases similar to those I have tried to describe recur. I want to indicate a few significant points.

1. After a series of static shots of boats moored in the harbor, and one of the house, we are introduced to camera movement and movement within frame simultaneously in the pan which shows us Mrs. Harper's car crossing a bridge. Already, the Balboa/Los Angeles opposition elaborated in the opening scenes has been implicitly undermined, and one might compare, again, the opening of *Shadow of a Doubt*, in which the striking antithesis of Lehar's Vienna and industrial wasteland is subverted by, among other things, a shot of a bridge.

2. As Mrs. Harper enters Darby's hotel, the money theme is introduced, associated with (a) exploitation and trickery. We overhear a man remarking, "I don't think that game was on the level," and learn later that Nagel is in charge of illegal gambling. This connotation, through Darby, blurs into (b) the sexual connotation, introduced through the blonde in her fur coat, and another overheard remark about the new singer. (c) Both adhere to Mrs. Harper herself in the course of the action, through her attempted "bribery" of Bea over Darby, and, of course, the fur coat. (d) Money and sexuality are immediately associated with descent—initially into the city itself, subsequently into the underground bar (with its neon cocktails sign) for the conversation with Darby.

3. When she first finds Darby's body, Mrs. Harper looks desperately up and down the vast, empty beach, and two cut-in shots show a white bridge on one side and a black on the other. Like Herman Melville's "Bartleby," the action of *The Reckless Moment* unfolds between white and black walls, in a "zone" of grayness—the blurring of extremes.

Joan Bennett, as Lucia Harper, in *The Reckless Moment*. Personal collection of the editor.

4. As in the other films, the descent into the underworld is a descent into the capitalist metropolis. It has been pointed out in the analysis of the opening of *The Reckless
Moment* that financial transactions are crucial throughout, and the thematic emphasis
on the ideological repression of women involves Mrs. Harper's discovery that she has
no individual, socially recognized economic status. Within the home, as bourgeois
wife, she has charge of the household accounts and some limited control of money
(the loans to her son). Outside it, she is constantly dependent for money on other
people (Donnelly during the telephone sequence in the store and, subsequently, bank,
loan company, and pawnbroker). The money-raising trip to Los Angeles must be considered in detail here.

a. We see Mrs. Harper working at the accounts, trying to discover ways of saving
money and concluding that she can at least "cancel that suit I ordered" (as in *It's
a Wonderful Life*, the theme of self-denial). Sybil hands her the cigarette holder
that Donnelly has bought her, and she remarks casually that she will take it back.
(She never realizes about the gift, which remains unique as a money transaction
in that it is a present, involving neither debt nor profit; it is concealed, and it is
generous rather than self-interested. The saving of cigarettes is significant, given
the film's themes, in that it involves making money out of inducing illness, a
point which is insisted on every time smoking is mentioned ["Wouldn't it be

226

simpler if you didn't sell the cigarettes?"]. This is inseparable from the association of Mrs. Harper's chain-smoking with the repression or frustration of emotional energy, to which it is a neurotic [death-oriented] response.) The camera cranes down from behind Mrs. Harper's head onto the open ledger.

b. In the next shot, we see her going downstairs into the vaults of the bank, the top of the image dominated by a metal grill which seems to weigh down on her head. The manager is explaining to her that "we have to have your husband's signature" for any withdrawal from their account. She is wearing, for the first time in the film, the fur coat which symbolizes her status as bourgeois wife—the allowable "luxury" which is her reward for her entrapment, and in the pocket of which the lost shopping list will finally be discovered.

c. The loan-office sequence. The imagery here is deeply ironic. A Christmas tree stands just inside the office door, and the interviewer's parting words to Mrs. Harper are "Merry Christmas." A picture of the signing of the Declaration of Independence is prominent in the decor. A single flower in a slim glass vase stands on the interviewer's desk ("I grow them in my garden"). The iconography suggests the finest aspirations of American idealism and, more generally, of bourgeois-capitalist democracy: the celebration, through the Holy Family and the birth of the redeemer, of the concept of togetherness in the nuclear family—this irony permeates the film, as it does *It's a Wonderful Life* (Consider also Sirk's use of Christmas and present giving in *All That Heaven Allows* [1955]); "life, liberty and the pursuit of happiness"; the transformation of the wilderness into a garden. These implications are counterbalanced by others of isolation and imprisonment (the glass partitions) and of oppressive power (Mrs. Harper dominated by the interviewer, whose head fills the foreground of the image, or is reflected in the glass behind Mrs. Harper, or is photographed face-on from a slightly low angle, with the reflection of the name of the company cast in a semicircle on the wall above her).

It is crucial that the interviewer is female. She is the only woman in the film who has any status in the patriarchal culture outside the home, and that status is economic. Her treatment of Mrs. Harper is belittling and patronizing, and she confirms and amplifies the notion that Mrs. Harper has no place apart from her husband's ("How much do you think you could pay back every month?"), coldly dismissing the only possessions of financial value which she does have—her jewels ("We don't have a pawnbroker's license"). Ironically, the jewels, with the coat, are not only all that she is permitted to own, as bourgeois wife, but also the mark that she herself is owned: they testify to her husband's wealth. The woman who has an acknowledged position in the patriarchal order as the voice of the law ("It's state law, you know") confronts the woman who, in the absence of her husband, but defined absolutely by tokens of him, has none at all—the vital point being that neither can exist outside a place allotted by respective men.

The tragic irony of the film lies in the fact that this is, essentially, Donnelly's point of view, and he devotes himself single-mindedly to protecting Mrs. Harper's family and her entrapment within it. Donnelly is characterized by a sort of nostalgia for and idealization of the bourgeoisie from which he feels he has fallen (consider Nagel's "I remind you of what you are," and Donnelly's own conviction of his "damnation," the inevitability of his predicament, the impossibility of change), and in the name of which he is even prepared to let an innocent man be executed for Darby's murder ("If he gets it for this, it'll be the only good thing he's done in his life . . . Don't be thinking of the right and the wrong of it"). Significantly, he twice associates Mrs. Harper with his mother, in both instances in connection with the woman as redeemer, as a figure who has faith in him and inspires him to "start over," but whom he must betray through his own incapacity: a psychoanalytical reading of the character is in order, in terms of a desire for the mother which must be repressed and denied and can only find expression through the attempt to restore her to the father (her role as wife and mother).

Similarly, the tremendous personal energy conveyed through Joan Bennett's performance and Ophüls's direction of it (the constant, restless movement of character and camera) is devoted entirely to self-entrapment, self-repression. One might, again, compare Capra's film, though Capra is more optimistic about the social values and (partial) individual fulfillment which the repression is supposed to promote. (Not only the very different visions of the American and the European artist but also the difference between a male and a female protagonist are important here.) One might define a crucial tension in the films under discussion as that between two alternative forms of the expression of energy: (1) diffusion outward into community or family, with the (perhaps intolerable) repression of individual desire which this may entail; (2) fulfillment of desire/transgression of law, which is shown in every case to lead to the release of chaos. The attempt to find a non-repressive social group (that is, non-repressive law) which can accommodate active individual energy (though, obviously, a perennial human concern) may be described, perhaps, as a defining characteristic of American art.

d. The final stage of the descent is the visit to the pawnshop, which is framed by long tracking shots following Mrs. Harper down a dark, crowded street, the music blaring with violent, monotonous insistence on the soundtrack. The scene reinforces the imagery of separation and imprisonment (counters, metal grills) and, crucially, the sense of cultural dislocation—the pawnbroker, at the heart of the film noir city, keeps humming "Home, home on the Range" throughout. (See, for example, the use of western conventions in *It's a Wonderful Life* to suggest the discrepancy between romantic, individualistic aspiration—"George lassoes the moon"—and social entrapment—"George Bailey lassoes stork.") He describes the jewelry as "a little old-fashioned," restating the motif of personal humiliation through the aspersion of possessions; we think of Bea's remark earlier, "Mother, you really are terribly old-fashioned." The pawnbroker proceeds to exploit Mrs. Harper's evident need by giving her less than the jewels are worth. The scene ends with another striking echo of *Shadow of a Doubt*—in her desperate hurry, Mrs. Harper, like Young Charlie, nearly steps under a car, both women plunged into recklessness, the neglect of habitual caution, by the encroachment of the underworld.

5. During the ferry sequence, Donnelly tells Mrs. Harper, "You have your family, I have my Nagel." She angrily rejects the comparison (interestingly, in financial terms—Nagel and Donnelly, as "a couple of blackmailers held together by a mutual interest in cheating people," are opposed to her son, who "earned" his money working in a factory). She also denies that she is a prisoner ("I don't feel like one"), though she has assented earlier, after a long pause, to Donnelly's observation about her never getting away from her family. In fact, the Nagel/family parallel is of the essence of the film. We feel in both cases that a relationship from which neither character has been able, or even willing, to escape has imposed the systematic repression of individual potential.

6. The character of Sybil is beautifully used in the film, the relationship with Mrs. Harper gradually built up until, by the end, the outsider by race and status is the only member of the household with whom Mrs. Harper can make open contact. One might compare the process by which, in Richard Fleischer's *Mandingo* (1975), the ideological limitation of the possibilities open to the "white lady" (Susan George), both social and psychological, is associated with the predicament of the Negro slaves. The other members of the family ignore Sybil, take her for granted, or treat her as an inferior: consider old Mr. Harper's irritable "Sybil, you know I drink tea," or Bea's petulant anger when, trying to escape from the row with her mother, she finds that Sybil hasn't ironed her dress yet, to which Mrs. Harper responds, "You're not to talk like that to Sybil." (One should note here the deeper complexity established by our awareness that Bea's "repression" of Sybil—treating her as a slave—is a direct response to her mother's attempt to repress her—treating her as a child.)

Ophüls makes use of two devices to indicate Sybil's deep concern for and attachment to the family—specifically, to Mrs. Harper. (1) The exploitation of long-take, deep-focus shots with a family group in the foreground, and Sybil watching and/or listening anxiously in the middle distance, as in the first telephone conversation with Mr. Harper, and the conference between Mrs. Harper and Bea in the kitchen during Donnelly's visit. (2) Sybil's demand if she can be of any help runs like a leitmotif through the film. Mrs. Harper constantly refuses it until the final sequence, which is introduced and interspersed by renewed offers of aid ("Would you like me to go with you? . . . You call me if you need me . . . You'd better take your coat"), the total unselfishness and generosity thrown into relief by their polar opposite in Nagel's total self-interest ("I don't care about your daughter, your son, your husband, or anybody else"). The acceptance of Sybil's help follows on directly from the decision to help Donnelly and take responsibility for Nagel's death, from the admission that "My way of doing something made everything wrong." The symbolic complex here—the decision to reveal Bea's involvement with Darby and her own with Donnelly (and thus the acknowledgment of what she has been trying to repress, essentially desire and the body); the sudden association with two people from outside the family, both her inferiors in social status, both non-WASP—is the crux of the film. Momentarily, the nuclear family and its preservation ceases to become an absolute for Mrs. Harper, and it is at this moment that she allows herself to break down for the first time, her emotional turmoil beautifully conveyed in the brief lowering of head onto hand as she kneels to take out the first-aid equipment to dress Donnelly's wound.

In this context, Sybil's judgment of Nagel ("He's not a nice man, Mrs. Harper") and Donnelly ("I like Mr. Donnelly") assume great—but completely unostentatious—force and significance. One can compare the character with John, Stefan's valet in *Letter from an Unknown Woman* (1948), and in both cases Ophüls associates their quiet, unassertive constancy with an intuitive discernment and understanding which the other characters are denied (consider John's long, intense, gentle look at Lisa as she hands him the books he has dropped; or, supremely, his silent acknowledgment, at the end of the film, that he has remembered the woman his master has forgotten).

7. The underworld depends for its existence and its potency on the repressiveness of the "civilized order": what the latter defines as "sin" is the former's investment. Thus, Nagel is in charge of illegal gambling, and indeed, Donnelly calls Darby's letters "collateral," adding, "We want to liquidate our stock while the market is high," Ophüls stressing here that Donnelly is using Nagel's words. Brown's psychoanalysis of money is again suggestive here in its thesis that the psychology of economics is the psychology of guilt; he quotes Freud's reading of Dostoyevsky, to the effect that "a burden of guilt had taken tangible shape as a burden of debt." (*Life*, 266) In *The Reckless Moment*, the underworld holds a negating culture to ransom by demanding payment for transgression: underworld, entrapment in cultural patterns and assumptions (the past), the perversion of repressed sexuality, and money thus form a symbolic nexus. The film's psychoanalytical insight is very concise indeed, the imagery and the structure of characterization creating an analogue for the structure of neurosis. Inherited cultural law demands repression (defines the limits of desire) and imposes guilt for what is interpreted as crime/sin/violation. The neurosis consists in the dynamically increasing necessity to devote conscious energies to rejecting and "undoing" transgression, the undoing imaged here as "paying off": "the dead past employs labor, the living vitality and power of the present." (Fromm, 94–95)

8. Male sexuality in the film is either degraded and vicious (Nagel) or variously impotent or ineffectual—Mr. Harper (by his absence), Darby (his smooth, shallow, insidious gigolo manner), Donnelly (his entrapment by and submission to Nagel), the grandfather. Eroticism is either poisoned or emasculated, and it is part of the pervasive tragic irony that the only creative, liberating act—Donnelly's rejection of Nagel—is directed to perpetuating sterility.

9. Of the films mentioned, *The Reckless Moment* is the one whose subversiveness is least recuperated by the narrative/thematic concessions which are, obviously, obligatory in a popular commercial film. One can see the potential for such an operation in, for example, Mrs. Harper's remark to her father that "There's nothing wrong that Tom's coming home won't cure." It is "placed" definitively, however, by the last shots of the film—by the final shot at the scene of the car accident, with the headlights of the Harpers' car vanishing in long shot into an engulfing darkness, and the dissolve to the darkness of Mrs. Harper's bedroom, in which she is prostrate on her bed in tears; by the deliberate perfunctoriness of Bea's sudden arrival with the news that Donnelly has confessed; by the final image, which frames Mrs. Harper through the banisters of the staircase, sinking down behind them with her back to the camera. The impression of a woman on the verge of breakdown, desperately denying, in the light and in the presence of her family ("With the whole team 'round the phone I could not say . . . "), the emotion she can only express in darkness and solitude, inverts the significance of the closing line ("Everything's fine—except we miss you terribly"). The stability of the united family is restored at the cost of permanent denial.

The Exorcist (1978)

n an attempt, here necessarily selective, to account for the current diabolism cycle in American movies and its dominant form—the devil as a child whose "innocence" is stressed—the following phenomena seem significant.

1. William Peter Blatty's novel *The Exorcist* is preceded by a page of epigraphs: a passage from the story of the man called Legion in St. Luke's Gospel; a transcript of an FBI wiretrap of a conversation between two Mafiosi about torture; a Jesuit priest's eyewitness account of Communist atrocities; and three words which Blatty deems able to speak for themselves—Dachau, Auschwitz, Buchenwald. These heterogeneous texts are all reduced to one essence—the Devil is lord of this world ("There's no other explanation," the priest remarks). Political threats to Christian/capitalist democracy (Communism) and products of it (the Cosa Nostra) become, indistinguishably, with Nazism, the powers of darkness, a cosmic force of evil which is by definition archetypal (that is, outside historical determination) and, implicitly, beyond control. Everything in the film of *The Exorcist* (1973), from the use of sound in the Iraq sequence to the very movement of the narrative (Chris's skepticism—"You're telling me I should take my daughter to a witch doctor?"—broken down to "I want a priest, not a psychiatrist"), is designed to overwhelm the audience with superstition and a conviction of its helplessness. The new power of the Devil suggests a society convinced of its own corruption but unable or unwilling to conceive of an alternative; the recent tendency to produce mass rituals of self-condemnation, punishment, and catharsis has resulted in two structures in which the crisis point is variously objectified as natural disaster and supernatural invasion (the horror of the latter recurs constantly in American culture). The horror movie increasingly forgoes the disaster movie's insistence on the final restoration of ideological confidence, but *The Exorcist*, in its allegiance to the purifying/sublimating rites of Catholicism, retains it. One notes, for example, the dedication to "The Story Behind *The Exorcist*": "To William Peter Blatty, for instilling in his novel, his film and in us, the feeling that everything would finally be alright." The price of confidence, here, is its perfunctoriness and, psychoanalytically, its meaninglessness (Regan "forgets"). Indeed, one might hazard that part of the pleasure of *The Exorcist* (and of its importance as a symptom) lies in the undermining of social confidence by inducing a state of anxiety which cannot be satisfactorily allayed.

2. The emergence of Women's Lib and Gay Lib as threats to patriarchal family and its associated sexual "norms." The fear of homosexuality in the context of clerical celibacy is strong in Blatty's novel, and Karras's final cry to the Devil of "Take me!" is actually inspired by Regan's first explicit accusation that he is gay—a detail which the film suppresses. Connections among social disintegration, sexual liberation, and "retribution for sin" emerge here (consider the emphasis on the shark-as-Satan in the novel *Jaws* [1975]), with connotations, again, of inevitability (Christian prophecy in *The Omen* [1976]; the "age of Saturn"—of familial cannibalism—written in the stars in *The Texas Chainsaw Massacre* [1974]).

3. The Women's Lib movement has fostered in America a Children's Lib movement. (See Firestone) Implicit in the image of the devil-child is the problem of what happens to the concept of innocence if the Freudian theory of infantile sexuality is true, and Regan suggests a delayed cultural acknowledgment of, and revulsion from, that obscene suggestion. The accession of sexuality and self-definition where purity and dependence have been endows the child's transformation from angel into demon with an impeccable logic (which Brian De Palma's *Carrie* [1976] submits to analysis). One can trace, notably in the work of Alfred Hitchcock, the association of the Devil with the return, through a child, of the sexuality repressed in the American home, right back into classical Hollywood: Uncle Charlie in *Shadow of a Doubt* (1943) and Norman Bates in *Psycho* (1960) are both ancestors of Regan and Carrie.

4. The recurrent suggestion in white American culture that America's destiny, simultaneously fulfillment and annihilation, is inevitably apocalyptic. One might note the obsessive (and insistently sexual) image of the "vortex" in Edgar Allan Poe ("The inevitable catastrophe is at hand") and the extraordinary moment in Herman Melville's *Clarel* (crucially, post–Civil War) when America, having been compared to a whorehouse and an arsenal ("the slumberous combustibles, bound to explode"), is shown its future in the image of the beast emerging from the sea in the Book of Revelations. Damien in *The Omen* is traced to the same text.

The Devil in *The Exorcist* is given a very specific form—that of the Pazuzu, a minor Mesopotamian deity with none of the connotations of the Christian Satan.[1] Such a choice instantly imposes the Christian dualism on a non-dualistic culture, universalizes a particular sense of evil; the determining factor here, however, is the Pazuzu's physical appearance. The horror in the film is that a little girl should be possessed by a devil whose penis is a serpent. Regan-as-devil becomes the phallic, castrating woman (she seizes the psychiatrist, who invokes her, by the testicles), and she is endowed with a parody-perversion of "masculine" characteristics—bass voice, violence, sexual aggressiveness, unladylike language. Immediately, an Oedipal theme emerges. The early scenes establish Regan's suppressed resentment of her mother ("You'll be sorry!") and of the presence of Burke Dennings, whom she is convinced her mother is going to marry ("I heard differently"). She subsequently turns into a boy, commits the Oedipal crime, and becomes the man of the house, the contest being reenacted, during the exorcism, as the battle with God the Father.

The main body of the film rests on the opposition between Regan's (Linda Blair) potency and Karras's (Jason Miller) impotence, the opposition being rooted in our sense of the similarity of their predicament. Crucial here are the two mother-child relationships, and the series of narrative/thematic parallels between Regan and Karras in the middle stretch of the film, juxtaposing the first tokens of Regan's possession with the conflict in Karras between resentment of his mother (the punching bag scene, which immediately precedes the party where Regan pisses on the carpet) and the guilt to which it gives rise (the nightmare, which immediately follows the violent trembling of Regan's bed and which locates the devil imagery of the Iraq scenes—black dog, Pazuzu medallion—in Karras's unconscious). The oppression of child by mother, suppressed in the Chris/Regan scenes, becomes explicit in the scenes with Karras; yet, conversely, it is Regan who makes explicit what Karras wants to do, simultaneously asserting her sexuality, revenging herself on home and family, and, as devil, refusing guilt for both. Karras's "passion" ("Take me!") allows him both to affirm his loyalty to the Father (God, Father Lankester Merrin) and to avenge himself on his mother (whom he has previously "seen" for a moment on Regan's bed) by beating up Regan as she sits triumphant above Merrin's corpse.

If the film allows the repressed to find expression, and gratification, in an absolutely objectified form (possession by the devil), it moves inexorably toward the punishment (renewed repression) of that gratification. The movement is inseparable from the presentation of the female characters and from the formulation of the central conflict in terms of castration. The opening scenes in Iraq juxtapose watchful, mysterious, threatening women in black (the last of them, hideously disfigured, almost knocks Merrin [Max von Sydow] down in her carriage) with blinded men, the reading of blindness as castration being reinforced by the stress on Merrin's extreme physical debility. The impulse to degrade women is already there in the spectacle of Regan's mother Chris (Ellen Burstyn) collapsing in desperation, but its full force is reserved for the treatment of Regan.

The symbolic premise of the action, established on Regan's first appearance, is that rejection of ideological construction as "a woman" is diabolical. The story of the man riding a beautiful gray horse ("I think it was a gelding"), and the ensuing request for a horse of her own, already poses castration as the necessary consequence of Regan's liberation. The Ouija board sequence, with its amazing verbal innuendo ("I think you need *two* people, honey"; "No, you don't—I do it all the time") fixes the association of pleasure-in-sexual-awakening with the devilish. It is vital that the film can only conceive Regan's sexuality as masculine (culturally defined) and unnatural (because masculine in the wrong place). Having acquired the phallus, Regan must be castrated again; yet whereas the scene of her possession is heavily loaded sexually (the terrified cries of "It's burning! He's trying to kill me!" replaced, at the climax, by "Fuck me! Fuck me!"), sexuality is withdrawn from the various assaults on Regan by men, all of which become attempts to cure her. The crux of the exorcism becomes Regan's levitation/erection and its subversion by the two male priests ("The power of Christ compels you!" endlessly reiterated), the moment of castration figured in the strip of flesh torn from Regan's leg as she descends. The representatives of patriarchal religion restore Regan to the family as female child "in the Name of the Father." Male dominance is reasserted, but with a necessary ambiguity: both priests (Father and Son) are killed, the reconstituted family is conspicuously without a father, and the emphasis on male emasculation (by women) cannot be fully recuperated. Thus, it is not a real but a symbolic authority which is reconfirmed: the Name of the Father as the Law (God) and the family as patriarchal unit survive the absence of their representatives. Indeed, the repressiveness of the film consists of allowing a taboo to be broken in order to reimpose it. We are allowed Regan's subversion of ideology, but in a form so inherently monstrous as to pre-conclude that the restoration of that ideology (read as "normality") is necessary.

Throughout the film, Regan fulfils the function which Norman O. Brown suggests that Luther ascribes to himself—the revelation of the sexuality beneath the sublimations of a Catholic culture ("The Pope is the Devil Incarnate"). (*Life*, 228) On this level, both (a) the dualism maintained in the conscious discourse of the film is inverted and (b) the attack on sublimation is itself seen as filthy. As Brown remarks, "As long as basic repression is maintained, a return of the repressed can take place only under the general condition of denial and negation"—that is, the death drive. "The unconscious self is perceived, but in an alienated form, as the not-self." (*Life*, 231) One might compare here the opposition in *The Exorcist* between well-appointed, bourgeois, WASP domesticity and immigrant, working-class slum with Hitchcock's use, in *Shadow of a Doubt*, of the iconography of small town and infernal city.

The repressed returns in various forms.

a. Anality. The McNeil home is characterized in terms of lightness and brightness. In the first shot inside it, Chris turns on a lamp, and the next sequence juxtaposes the first noises in the attic with Chris's white negligee, white flowers, and white candles on either side of a table, as if on an altar. Chris is "a very nice lady," and Lieutenant Kinderman has seen her in a film called *Angel* six times. Regan's first action as devil is to piss on this niceness, as all the adults, gathered round the piano, sing "Home, Sweet Home" to Father Dyer's accompaniment (he has just imagined heaven as "a solid white nightclub with me as the headliner")—a moment which, in our sense of what, through Regan, is demanding recognition, becomes a crux of modern American cinema. The anal imagery is subsequently transferred to Regan's vomiting, once over Merrin's vestments and once in reply to Karras's question about his mother's maiden name.

b. The de-sublimation of Catholic mythology, most emphatically of the concept of the immaculate conception—the Devil enters Regan through her vagina. The theme recurs later in the masturbation with the crucifix ("Let Jesus fuck you!"), in both cases inseparably from Regan's discovery of her body ("D'you know what she did, your cunting daughter?"): blasphemy, refusal of sexual guilt, and the theme of the "thankless child" (Regan as the namesake of one of King Lear's bad daughters) are fused symbolically. (Compare here De Palma's treatment of Carrie's enforced ignorance of menstruation.) The de-sublimation of the Virgin Birth is linked to the castration imagery through the desecration of the statue of the Madonna, which takes the form of endowing her with three monstrous, red-tipped phalluses. The defacing of the archetype of woman as Good Mother, uncontaminated by sexuality (by a body), again connects Regan's awakening with appropriation of the phallus and castration of the male (significantly, it precedes the disruption of the party).

c. Sexual practices officially regarded as abnormal and disgusting—fellatio and sodomy. One can distinguish two points of attack: the concept of motherhood as the place of female sexuality ("Your mother sucks cocks in hell!"), and clerical celibacy. The relationship of Karras and Father Dyer, treated very much in terms of "just good friends," has as its complement the torrent of homosexual abuse with which Regan greets the two priests during the exorcism. Here, as elsewhere, the Devil survives on the notion that there are certain things which are naturally unnatural, and it is scarcely startling that gayness and assertive female sexuality should emerge simultaneously as the Other.

Jaws (1979)

The keynote of Peter Benchley's novel *Jaws* is an immitigable contempt for everyone and everything. It is the post-Watergate best seller, a novel of complete disillusionment, cynicism, and despair, which arouses and exploits, with dazzling efficiency, every phobia of the middle-aged, middle-class, menopausal American male. The mayor has sold his soul to the Mafia; the country is racked by threats of economic recession, unemployment, racial violence; law and order is disintegrating; the environment is being polluted; everyone is motivated by greed and self-interest. The hero, Police Chief Brody, is worried about his spreading middle and his ability to attract his wife, who yearns for the upper middle classness from which she descended to marry him and who seduces the young, rich, predatory intellectual who loves sharks. The novel is intensely mysoginistic and, most striking of all, intensely anti-youth: young people are either "Aquarians" or complacent zombies, both types being regarded with equal scorn and both inseparable, in Benchley's mind, from drugs and promiscuity. The shark is progressively identified with everyone including, finally, Brody himself. There are hints throughout that it is some sort of retribution for sin, a vengeful materialization of the ills of America, which include everything from rampant black rapists and ax-murderers to avaricious storekeepers who don't object to Amity becoming a garbage dump if there's profit in it. What is genuinely disturbing and subversive in the novel is constantly trivialized by the shrill, simplifying generalizations of its symbolism and by its perverse refusal of any alternative to a culture it shows to be corrupt. We are invited, instead, to immerse ourselves in Brody's mounting sense of inadequacy and outrage, his dread of youth, women, effete culture, anarchy, permissiveness, and personal impotence. The novel—and its success—are symptoms of the failure of psychological and cultural confidence.

The tone and purpose of Steven Spielberg's film are as far from this as it is possible to be. The new *Jaws* (1975) might best be described, perhaps, as a rite: a communal exorcism, a ceremony for the restoration of ideological confidence. The film is inconceivable without an enormous audience, without that exhilarating, jubilant explosion of cheers and hosannas which greet the annihilation of the shark and which transform the cinema, momentarily, into a temple. Annihilation is the operative word. It is not enough for the shark to be killed, as it is in the book, only two feet from a helpless, hopeless hero whose two companions have already been devoured, and who has, himself, been implicated too disturbingly in the tensions which the shark has released. The film monster has to be, literally, obliterated. Evil must vanish from the face of the earth.

Crucial in this change of strategy is the removal of the adultery subplot and with it all trace of conflict within Brody's (Roy Scheider) family. Stephen Heath has discussed the film in terms of an unresolved displacement of sexuality onto the shark. ("*Jaws*," 513) It seems to me, rather, that the extraordinary concentration of erotic imagery in the opening sequence (the double row of wooden fencing; the boy's repeated remark, "I'm coming! I'm coming!"; the phallic marker-buoy) suggests the shark's temporary usurpation of sexuality, this tying in with the central theme of male territorial rivalry and with the fact that, once the shark has been established as "masculine energy" in the first attack, sexual connotations are conspicuous by their suppression (in comparison both with the novel and the horror genre). "Possession of the phallus" is the essence of the territoriality theme, and the ending perfectly resolves it, potency being transferred, by right of conquest, from the supreme representative of destructive lawlessness to the policeman's rifle. Similarly, Heath's comment that after the girl, "all the victims are male and the focus is on losing legs," while not actually untrue (although only one leg is lost), significantly distorts the film's emphasis, which is that the shark attacks a woman and children—that is, the home, the family, the basic unit of American democracy. ("*Jaws*," 513) Thus, although a man is killed in the pond sequence, the thematic point here is to stress, by abstention, the near-death of the hero's son in a secluded pool where he has been sent for safety. This is clearly a deliberate structural choice, in terms both of the sequence of the attacks (a girl offshore; a little boy inshore; Brody's little boy in the pool) and of the material employed; there is no equivalent to the pond sequence in the novel, and the film also introduces the potential threat to the Boy Scout swimming contest.

The weight given to the vulnerability of children and the need to protect and guard them is there from the first scene in the Brody house, Brody warning the kids away from the swings and Ellen washing a cut on her son's arm. It is reinforced throughout the first half of the film (the death of the Kintner boy; Brody's son in his new boat; the baby sitting lost and in tears amid the panic on the beach), and all the home scenes create a pervasive sense of the supreme value of family life: a value clearly related to stability and cultural continuity so that the shark becomes a threat to the inheritance of ideology (consider, for example, the beautiful little sequence in which Brody's son sits watching him at the table, imitating his gestures and expressions). Mayor Vaughan is revealed to be totally corrupt at the moment at which he hisses to Brody that he is perfectly willing to let his own children go swimming. Indeed, the emphasis on children is linked explicitly to the regeneration theme. Ellen tells Brody that their boys may grow up afraid of water, like he is, to which he replies at once, "I don't want that to happen, you know that." The shark's death not only cures his own neurosis—it preserves his children from it.

Along with the adultery plot, the film also abandons the theme of the social class divisions within Amity, based on the distinction between all-year residents and summer visitors, and centered on Ellen. The Brodys are re-created as the nice, average, bourgeois couple, their sexuality and aspirations perfectly accommodated by their marriage. What does remain, crucially, is the fact that they are New Yorkers, a note sounded on their first appearance (the business of Brody's accent). This is important for the confidence theme in two respects. (1) It places Brody outside the insularity and predatory acquisitiveness of the community ("You're not born here, you're not an islander"). Thus, although he succumbs temporarily to the persuasions of the authorities, he is not, like the natives, intrinsically corrupt, and the film can move toward an expiation of the failure of responsibility defined in safely nonsocial, symbolic terms. (2) On the journey out to Ben Gardner's boat, Brody tells Hooper (Richard Dreyfuss) that in Amity, as opposed to New York, "one man can make a difference." The contradiction to this implied by the shark's presence and Brody's moral weakness is canceled when Brody kills the shark single-handedly, the implication being that individual action by the one just man is still a viable force for social change.

In fact, the concentration on the hunt seems designed to distract us from the real problem, which is not the shark at all, but the city council. The personal catharsis for the hero (and, by identification, for the audience), by which he is simultaneously purged of his guilt and cured of his lifelong dread of the sea, conveniently ignores the fact that nothing has been done about Mayor Vaughan. *Jaws* is a monster movie in which the hero kills the wrong monster, and this would seem to confirm Robin Wood's thesis that the disaster is meant to stand in for—and thus to discount—revolution. (*Hollywood*, 180) Brody's ability to enter his house justified is also felt to justify the house ("The tide's with us. Keep kicking!").

The hunt is built on a simple pattern of dramatic reversal: the two self-confidently potent figures are defeated, and the man whose confidence has been challenged, and potency undermined, is victorious. We are given a version of *Moby Dick* in which Ishmael kills the whale. The supermasculine, proletarian Hemingway hero with his harpoon fails; the upper-class, adolescent, technologized intellectual with his "power-head" fails. Triumph is reserved for the fallible middle-class cop, Everyman with a rifle, a bourgeois Leatherstocking with *la longue carbine* who has previously been excluded from the phallic communion of the others and is left toying with a coil of rope while they compare scars (the red badge of courage) and toast each other's legs. More exactly, Hooper is implicated in the victory, but only by proxy—through the gritty, tenacious improvisation which transforms a piece of apparently useless scientific equipment into a weapon.

The relationship between the three men is significant here. In the novel, both Quint and Brody detest Hooper, their dislike forming common ground between them (though Benchley carefully refrains from following through the logic of Brody's development, and exonerates him from wishing Hooper dead), and Hooper is killed before the final confrontation with the shark. In the film, the camaraderie of Brody and Hooper is constant from the beginning, culminating in the classical American image of the "marriage" of two men, or at least a conservative variation of it—they are returning to society, not in flight from it. Here, as elsewhere, the film gets it both ways, the defense of home and family consummated in an emotional union which excludes them.

It is as important for the film to get rid of Quint (Robert Shaw) as to get rid of the shark. Alone of the three men, he is identified both with the destructive potency of the monster and the voracious callousness of the community ("Pay me or suffer all winter"). As a native of Amity and an embodiment of its evils (self-interest, commercialism, complacency), he can be used as a scapegoat for them. Even more interestingly, the film's treatment of him suggests not only a bourgeois aversion to and dread of a bourgeois caricature of the proletariat ("Don't give me that working-class hero crap'") but also—returning to *Jaws* as a rite—the symbolic sacrifice of a particular concept of the hero. Thus, although the film preserves the "prove your virility by slaying the sacred animal" syndrome (*The Bear*, *The Old Man and the Sea*), it transfers its allegiance—ostensibly—from the ideal of asocial masculinity to the ideal of the law-and-order man, the defender of bourgeois ideology. It is clearly significant that a working-class character should appear centrally for the first time in the disaster cycle in such a form.

This may help to explain the extraordinary clash of conventions in the film's acting. While Roy Scheider appears to be playing in a realistic drama, the curiously sexless schoolboy embodied by Richard Dreyfuss and Robert Shaw's Quint—all yo-ho-ho, rolling eyeballs, and dirty limericks—are straight out of "Boy's Own." The changes here are related to the softening of the novel's sexual theme, and they have the effect of making the only given alternatives to the hero (ideologically, morally, sexually) slightly unreal. Monogamous, heterosexual normality is reinstated between Peter Pan on the one hand and dangerous potency on the other. The one crucial addition to the novel is Quint's account of the sinking of the *Indianapolis*, the ship which transported the Hiroshima bomb, which was torpedoed on the return journey, and two-thirds of whose crew were devoured by sharks before they could be picked up. The three men find a brief solidarity through an expression of mutual alienation: Brody, who is excluded from the exchange of phallic boasting (Quint and Hooper together in two-shot, seated; Brody apart in medium shot, on his feet), is brought in for the singing of "Show me the way to go home." Implicit here—as in the entire first half of the film—is a sense of the shark as Moloch; the scene comes close to identifying the men as victims of American ideology, suggesting the link between sacrificing bathers on July Fourth ("Amity means friendship") and sacrificing servicemen in the war to end war ("world peace for democracy"). In this light, the hint of subjection and helplessness in Quint's theme song ("For we've received orders") becomes as important as the rejection of women ("farewell and adieu to you, fair Spanish ladies"). Logically, the scene implies complete despair, since both "home" (America as Amity/America as warship) and "outside home" (sharks) are murderous, with the three men suspended between them in a sort of limbo. Hence, the imagery: a motionless boat on a dead sea at night; the renewal of the shark's attack on the word *home*; the scene's conclusion on the failing of the boat's lights. The film, committed to the reassertion of the bourgeois order which its premise undermines, works toward the dissolution of the group which can only become a group through its members' recognition that, really, they have nowhere to go.

Mandingo (1976)

> **Beatrice:** Alsemero, I am a stranger to your bed. Your bed was cozen'd on the nuptial night,/For which your false bride died.
> **Alsemero:** Diaphanta!
> **De Flores:** Yes; and the while I coupled with your mate/At barley-brake; now we are left in hell.
> **Vermandero:** We are all there, it circumscribes here.
> —Thomas Middleton and William Rowley, *The Changeling*

The arbiters of taste have spoken. The critics have indicated their almost unqualified rapture over Robert Altman's *Nashville* (the modern, adult American movie) and their unanimous antipathy to Richard Fleischer's *Mandingo* (both 1975). If I begin by picking on Geoff Brown's pocket review in the *Monthly Film Bulletin*, it is both because that magazine is an official publication of the British Film Institute (thus, one would suppose, representative of informed and responsible critical judgment in this country) and because Brown purports to give an objective synopsis of the plot, which he succeeds in perverting in several interesting and important respects. (178)

1. We are told that Blanche is "flighty," a word which suggests coquetry, capriciousness, and infidelity. I can only suggest that Brown is thinking of the genre stereotype of the Southern belle portrayed in Kyle Onstott's original novel, since Fleischer's character evinces none of these traits. In the courtship scene, she does indeed pretend to be a coquette, for reasons which are well-defined in the narrative, but it is the whole point of the film that she attempts continually and vainly to elicit some affectionate response from her husband, and she is never shown as being in the least interested in any other man. She induces Mede to have intercourse with her not out of flightiness, but from long-continued sexual frustration and a desire to avenge herself on her husband for his infidelity. The description of Blanche effectively reverses the emphasis of theme and action.

2. "Other slaves on the plantation" do not "soon resent Mede's preferential treatment and servile manner." They do in the book, but not in the film. It is one of the most disturbing aspects of the reviews that their authors are apparently unable to distinguish between feebly organized, overwritten pulp fiction and the delicate precision of

a complex dramatic narrative. Fleischer shows us hardly anything of Mede's contact with the Negroes, apart from the moment in which a group of female slaves see him off to the fight at New Orleans and clap and cheer him heartily, which would seem to suggest his popularity. One particular slave, Mem, does resent Mede, again for clearly defined reasons, and the fact that he is a conspicuous exception is another rather significant point which seems to have passed Brown by. It is, rather, Blanche who resents Mede, not the blacks. Nor does Mede ever act in a manner which could remotely be described as servile. He behaves constantly with enormous personal dignity, and his commitment to Ham is based on feelings of love, loyalty, and gratitude.

3. "When [Warren] Maxwell learns of the baby's color, he easily persuades the doctor to let it bleed to death, thus preserving the family honor." That an error of this magnitude, which undermines the whole meaning of the end of the film, should have been allowed to pass prompts one to ask whether Brown bothered to see it at all. Once more, the point is that Hammond Maxwell does not order the murder of the baby or learn about it until it has been done. Dr. Redfield is solely responsible for the decision, which he executes himself, moved by the ideological assumption that the child of a white woman by a black man is a monster. He then tells Maxwell and Ham that the child was stillborn in order to spare them and shelter Blanche from their recriminations. The act thus represents a complex interweaving of social determinations, human compassion, and a desire to keep the peace. Immediately afterward, Redfield provides Ham, without demur, with the poison he uses "to kill old niggers who can't work no more," which he knows Ham will use to kill Blanche. Redfield is a doctor within a given society in which the children of miscegenation, worked-out slaves, and white women who consent to intercourse with Negroes can be dispensed with. The fact that he is characterized as a physician who kills people is not unimportant.

4. "Agamemnon . . . aims at Hammond, but suddenly shoots his master instead." Mem shoots Maxwell, as will be seen, for precise reasons which are of the essence of the film's theme and of Mem's own characterization. Brown's phrasing implies an arbitrary bloodbath.

Brown and his fellows all try to portray the film as at once irredeemably disgusting and too ridiculous to warrant anything but flippancy: *Sight and Sound* magazine's *Film Guide* announces, for example, that although *Mandingo* is morally reprehensible, its "atrocities" are "palatably ludicrous." Kenneth Robinson in *The Spectator* thinks it "nice" that the audience with which he saw the film was "quite convulsed" by the scenes of violence and infidelity; he takes this as evidence for his comforting conclusion that he need not take it seriously either. He "is sure" that "when somebody is accused of exploiting a social problem," as Fleischer undoubtedly is, then "the problem is not as great as it was," so that we can all sigh with relief and settle down to a little effortless slumming. (387) Nigel Andrews, in the *Financial Times*, takes a similar line. He describes the Deep South as "America's cultural id, a world of lurid passions thinly camouflaged by gentility," but instead of elaborating this fundamental point, he takes refuge in the belief that the release of these suppressed energies in *Mandingo* produces some sort of camp pastiche, and he proceeds to indulge in a good giggle along with Robinson. Yet, it is remarkable how many critics apologize for taking so much time over such a "farrago." They profess to be nauseated but are still unwilling to leave the film alone until they have expressed their superiority to it.

Robin Wood has suggested that British film criticism has two main characterizing values: (1) the fallacy of 'Realism', and (2) the concept of 'Good Taste'. The reception of *Mandingo* confirms the judgment. Thus, on the one hand, one finds the moans about James Mason's Southern accent and the quibbles about authenticity, the latter taken to an extreme by Derek Malcolm, who while willing to accept black concubines and Negroes who rape their white mistresses as historical truth, draws the line at the use of young Negroes to cure rheumatism. On the other, there are the universal accusations of the film's excess, accompanied by comprehensive lists of enormities and tut-tutting about the effect this will undoubtedly have on race relations. "The truth is hardly the point," proclaims Malcolm, "it is what use is made of it that matters," before revealing his inability to gauge such a quality. It must obviously be said that it is completely irrelevant whether any of the incidents depicted in the film took place—once or a million times, in the Deep South or anywhere else—just as it is completely irrelevant whether the kings of ancient Britain were wont to divide their kingdoms among their daughters, or whether Scottish lairds had conversations with witches on foggy moors. It is extremely easy to ridicule *King Lear* by recounting its plot with occasional choice misstatements—there is a long and honorable tradition of such work, culminating in Tolstoy—but the result can only be satisfying if one is willing to believe that because a play involves blindings, hangings, thunderstorms, parricide, and madness it is a bad play. I neither know nor care whether James Mason sounds exactly like a real plantation owner in 1840, just as it does not trouble me that Garbo plays Anna Karenina with a Swedish accent, or that in *Under Capricorn* (1949), Ingrid Bergman is supposed to be Irish. Any work of art presents one with a set of conventions which one can either accept or refuse. However, if one refuses them on the grounds that one doesn't like them, or because they fail to coincide with what one imagines reality to be, one should not expect one's judgment to be taken seriously. As for Malcolm's straining credulity, one can only recommend him to Dr. Samuel Johnson's reply to those critics who objected to the violation of the unities, to the effect that "he who can imagine so much can imagine more." Once I have accepted that Macbeth talks to witches, I am not moved to leave the theater when he starts seeing ghosts as well.

Antecedents

Like any great work of art, *Mandingo* can stand on its own, and one might sufficiently place derision such as this by detailed analysis—which I intend to do. But it is important, first of all, to situate the film in a cultural tradition which was, until very recently, considered to be beneath the contempt of adult sensibilities, and which clearly still is when it manifests itself in a new film by a director who is not fashionable rather than in literary texts which have become respectable, and thus harmless, classics.

American literature provides numerous examples of the image of an appalling mansion inhabited by a monstrous and perverted family. It is already there, just beneath the leisurely good-humored surface of James Fenimore Cooper's *The Pioneers*. There is the fundamental tension between the beginnings of civilization in a New World and the survival of the "civilized" culture of the old, epitomized in the Temple house, which is built, grotesquely, in "the composite order"; between the young democracy and the importation of an inherited feudalism with the trappings of aristocracy. (viii) The tension is repeated in the house's owner. His name is Temple—he is his house; the town is named after him, suggesting at once the aristocratic ambiance—that it is his child, a creation of his blood, and that it is a monument to himself, an assertion and celebration of ego.

Temple's wife is dead. His only heir is his daughter, Elizabeth, and the book begins with her return from school "to preside over a household that had too long wanted a mistress." (Cooper, 34) The opening also introduces a comic Negro slave called Agamemnon, who "owing to the religious scruples of the Judge" is the servant of his friend (and alter ego) Richard Jones. Jones "commanded a legal claim" to the slave's respect, and early on we see "Aggy" caught in "a dispute between his lawful and his real master," for both of whom he "felt too much deference . . . to express any opinion" in the matter. He is eventually induced to side with Jones, of whom he "stood in great terror" because he "did all the flogging . . . in the main." (52) Jones habitually calls him "you black rascal" and "you black devil," but Cooper goes out of his way to stress at the same time Aggy's devotion, and that after the incident, "the most prefect cordiality was again existing between them." (53)

We also meet the town's physician, Dr. Elnathan Todd, whose supreme reputation and dubious knowledge are expressed in imagery which resumes the motifs of grotesque architecture (the reputation is built on a "foundation of sand" with "somewhat brittle materials") and of superficial, "civilized" propriety (the "blind desperation" of his remedies is concealed by "all the externals of decent gravity and great skill"). (70–71)

Elizabeth's arrival and her first glimpse of the house (it is stressed that the end of the journey is a descent into a valley from a great height) take on, in the description, a nightmarish quality, which Cooper characterizes, nevertheless, as an awakening, a dreadful refinement of perception. The main characters are a heterogeneous group of European refugees who are contrasted with Leatherstocking and Chingachgook, both ambiguously a mixture of the civilized and savage, both at home in the wilderness, both brothers rather than master and slave. Cooper struggles to suggest, largely through the novel's *jeune premier*, Oliver Edwards, a possible reconciliation of the extremes.

Edgar Allan Poe takes up and elaborates these themes. In "The Fall of the House of Usher," we once more find the descent by a stranger to the appalling mansion, the imminent extinction of the family (which hangs on in the diseased and cadaverous Roderick Usher), the decadent and perverse remnants of European culture, the sibling incest, the association of degenerate sexuality with money-power and death, the ultimate apocalyptic catastrophe with one survivor. In *The Narrative of Arthur Gordon Pym*, Poe's most complete work, the monstrous house becomes the monstrous ship, the "large, hermaphrodite brig," which the starving, shipwrecked heroes encounter as it drifts—reeking—across the ocean, peopled by corpses "in the last and most loathsome state of putrefaction." (667) Its grinning figurehead is revealed as the remains of one of the sailors, on which a huge carnivorous seagull is gorging itself, a sight which, even as it nauseates him, brings to Pym's mind "for the first time" the thought of cannibalism, to which they later succumb. (668) The ship is thus explicitly an image of Pym's unconscious impulses; it emerges out of the desires which are already fully formed within. This delightful novel also contains an account of the bird life of Desolation Island which is, in fact, a hilarious and ghastly parody of American pioneering and family life, based on the territorial imperative, cannibalism, and an innate propensity for mutual theft. In addition, there is a mysterious half-breed (the "dusky, fiendish and filmy figure" into whose arms Pym plunges ecstatically from a cliff at the climax of the story); a symbolic representation of black slavery as divine law; and Pym's final union with the Absolute, a figure whose skin "was of the perfect whiteness of the snow." (735)

From Poe onward, these images and themes are endemic to American literature. We think of Nathaniel Hawthorne: the Pyncheon household in *The House of the Seven Gables,* and Donatello's castle in *The Marble Faun*, associated through the Roman ruins with an inescapable heritage of European guilt and corruption. This theme resurfaces in Henry James: consider Osmond's houses in *The Portrait of a Lady*, in which the images of Isabel's entrapment turn her into a companion of the prisoner of the Inquisition in "The Pit and the Pendulum." We think of Melville: Poe's bird colony reappears in "The Encantadas," his "hermaphrodite brig" in "Benito Cereno," with its skeleton figurehead adorned with the inscription "Follow your leader," its Negro revolt, and its complacently oblivious white "hero." Bannadonna's "Bell-tower," built by armies of slaves, is an assertion of self-destructive hubris and individual potency, and the symbolism of *Pierre* is based on the succession of houses and monuments which Melville presents. We think of Mark Twain: the account of the Shepardson-Grangerford feud in *Huckleberry Finn*, which associates the Southern slave ethos with the perversion of sexuality in the separation of the lovers and the figure of the sweet, idealized little girl who composed graveyard poetry. We think of William Faulkner: decaying mansions, incest, miscegenation, generations of family interbreeding culminating, in *The Sound and the Fury*, with an idiot screaming obscenities in a ruin.

Falconhurst in *Mandingo* is part of a central tradition of American art which uses the image of a building to express the conflicts in the American psyche. It is surely deeply significant that the genre described by Leslie Fiedler as the American Gothic, the genre precisely devoted to laying bare the chaotic undertow of the New World consciousness, should reemerge on such a scale with the failure of confidence in an increasingly powerful presidential administration. (126–61) *Mandingo* clearly relates to the disaster cycle, with Falconhurst as a microcosm of America, and to recent developments in the horror movie involved with the disintegration of the family. Like *Rosemary's Baby* (1968), *The Exorcist* (1973), and *It's Alive!* (1974),the film shows the birth of a child which is seen as an epitome of conflicts in society, and which constitutes a threat to the ideology depicted.

If the American Gothic provides us with one perspective on *Mandingo*, then Jacobean tragedy—particularly, I think, Thomas Middleton—provides another. We find in *Women Beware Women* and *The Changeling* the same concern with the ideological oppression of women, the same association of socially determined sexual repression with the eruption of violence, the theme of masters and slaves, personal relationships perverted by financial greed and the will to power, and the contamination of the young by received values in which they are immersed and which they cannot consciously question. The connotations of Italy for a Jacobean audience (treachery, sexual license, assassination, luxury, atheism, Machiavelli) might reasonably be compared with those of the Deep South for us. Neither country "exists": both provide symbolic landscapes and sets of conventions through which the "cultural id" can be expressed in narrative. It is worth pointing out, however, that *Mandingo* differs from, say, *Women Beware Women*, in that there is no use of violence or catastrophe to avoid the issues raised in the action, and nothing of that tendency to associate vitality with villainy at the expense of the "positive" characters, in whom the artist does not believe and who are accorded an incredible and meaningless final triumph. It has long been a popular critical pastime to squabble over the status of Jacobean drama, but since there is no agreed definition of either tragedy or melodrama, it is sufficient for my purpose here to say that Fleischer, like Poe and the Jacobeans, set out to create a setting in which the "excessive and unpleasant" can be naturalized, and rendered as art. This provides a convenient get-out for members of the audience who wish to ascribe what they are given to the inherent vulgarity of the material. The journalist-critics, who all use melodrama, quite unquestioningly, not as a technical term but as a word of abuse, are habitually and proudly types of that select band.

There is a crucial and relevant passage in Louis Althusser's essay on "Ideology and the Ideological State Apparatus":

> In the ordinary use of the term, subject in fact means: (1) a free subjectivity, a center of initiatives, author of and responsible for its actions, (2) a subjected being who submits to a higher authority and is therefore stripped of all freedom except that of freely accepting his submission. This last note gives us the meaning of his ambiguity . . . the individual is interpellated as a (free) subject in order that he shall submit freely to the commandments of the Subject, i.e., in order that he shall make the gestures and actions of his subjection "all by himself." There are no subjects except by and for their subjection. That is why they work "all by themselves." (169)

The Subject, for Althusser, is the Absolute, the law which is unquestionable, and he compares the structure of ideology to, firstly, a system of mirrors in which, while each individual subject is subordinated to the central, absolute Subject, that individual can also contemplate, in the Absolute, "its own image (present and future)." Secondly, he compares it to a family, "the Holy Family: the Family is in essence Holy," through which we are "absolutely" guaranteed "that everything really is so, and that on condition that the subjects recognize what they are and behave accordingly, everything will be all right: Amen—'So be it.'" ("Ideology," 169) Thus, it is important that *Mandingo* is a family film, based on the irresolvable tension between ingrained ideological assumption and the promptings of a human nature which is not ideologically determined, but ideologically perverted. We should remember also that the questioning of, disgust with, and flight from the family are recurring obsessions in American art.

These remarks point to the extraordinary complexity of the image of slavery in *Mandingo*. It is the premise of the film that all the characters, white and black, are slaves. Its portrayal of ideological imprisonment is expressed through the imagery of a genre in which the repression of the black man has always carried more or less explicit sexual overtones; they are there in the title itself, which refers to a superior strain of Negro for whose breeding, to produce studs and gladiators, Falconhurst is famous.

I have said enough, I hope, to indicate the sheer triviality of spirit in which *Mandingo* has been discussed. To dismiss it as debased erotic sensationalism is just as absurd as the dismissal of Poe on the same pretext; to describe it as antiblack as wrongheaded as a similar description applied to, say, "Benito Cereno." Poe and Melville can now be incorporated without excessive dismay in university syllabuses, but one wonders how much understanding is involved in the acceptance, and the doubts increase every time a work such as Fleischer's film provokes a chorus of offended yelps from the guardians of culture. D. H. Lawrence's words in the first chapter of *Studies in Classic American Literature* are still very much to the point. We have "declined to hear" the "new voice in the old American classics . . . out of fear." (7) *Mandingo* is one of the richest and most mature expressions of that voice in recent years.

The Film

What debt, if any, Norman Wexler's screenplay owes to the stage adaptation of *Mandingo* I cannot say, having neither seen nor read it, but a few words about Kyle Onstott's novel are in order. It sets out to be a "terrible indictment" but ends up as a covert endorsement of the status quo. This is particularly evident in the treatment of Blanche. Onstott pays lip service to the theme of the oppression of women, but Blanche is presented throughout with such contempt and disgust that the ostensible purpose counts for nothing. The same holds true for all the white women in the novel, notably Blanche's mother (who appears only briefly in the film), who is portrayed as a hysterical, hypocritical grotesque. Similarly, although Onstott occasionally criticizes the Maxwells, they are nevertheless the standard by which all the other white characters except Wilson are judged and found wanting (Blanche's home and family, for example). Maxwell Senior frequently appears benign, the treatment of the slaves is shown as exemplary, and there is scarcely a sign of discontent, let alone the rebellion of a figure like Cicero. Big Pearl is shown as being rapturously eager to sleep with Ham (Maxwell Junior), and Mem, a central figure in the film, is peripheral in the novel, with no characteristic but laziness (significantly, Fleischer and Wexler make him much older than Onstott does). The novel is verbose, flabby, and repetitious, with nothing of the expressive narrative organization of the screenplay, which both omits several wandering subplots and condenses and reorganizes the events which it retains, most notably in transposing Ham's meeting with Ellen so that it precedes his proposal to Blanche (Onstott repeatedly tries to exonerate Ham by implying that he would never have gone through with the marriage if he had seen Ellen before). The entire honeymoon sequence is new, as are the scenes in the brothel and the two fights which take place there (there is a brothel in the book, but it is nothing like Madame Caroline's and has no thematic significance). Charles and Mede are new characters in the film, and Fleischer's main theme of Ham's inner conflict is worked up from what remains, with Onstott, a series of unsystematic asides. There is, finally, the vital change in the ending: in the novel, Maxwell Senior survives, and Mem plays no part whatever.

We are introduced in the first shots of the film to Falconhurst as a dilapidated semi-ruin surrounded by drooping, overgrown vegetation. Its owner, Warren Maxwell (James Mason), hobbles out of the house leaning on a stick to supervise the sale of a line of Negro slaves. Maxwell himself is crippled with rheumatism. His son, Hammond/Ham (Perry King), who appears at the end of the scene, has a crippled leg and walks with an awkwardly pronounced limp, the result, we learn later, of a riding accident when he was a child. During the sale, Brownlee (Paul Benedict), the trader, picks out one of the slaves, Cicero (Ji-Tu Cumbuka), who will later be the leader of the slave revolt, and who is being sold precisely because he is an agitator who "stops others from doin'." Brownlee throws a stick and orders Cicero to retrieve it. He is impressed by the slave's nimbleness and guesses that "he might last seven, eight years" in the sugar plantation. He asks Maxwell if any of the slaves have been castrated, and Maxwell replies with some pride and irritation that "on this plantation there's no altered nigger."

There is nothing insistent in the symbolism, but the contrast between the rebellious slave who can run—who, ironically, is valuable because he can run—and the master and his heir who can only hobble, quietly makes its effect. The naturalistic explanation of Ham's limp is unimportant. The fact that both father and son walk badly suggests hereditary impotence and extends the physical decay of the house to its owners. Falconhurst is, explicitly, a slave-*breeding* plantation. Straightaway a link is established between the brutality of slavery and the social and physical degeneration of the Maxwells: in nourishing the order on which their power is based, they have, paradoxically, brought themselves to the point of extinction. The metaphor works simultaneously on a political and psychological level. The agony of the slaves has reached a point at which Cicero can emerge as a rebel, and repressed energies and impulses, ignored or unacknowledged, have acquired a force which must assert itself in catastrophe.

The sexual theme is intensified in the ensuing dinner scene. It is preceded by the visit to the Mandingo "wench," Big Pearl (Reda Wyatt), who is ill and can only be cured, the doctor pronounces, by having intercourse with Ham. Falconhurst has preserved the concept of droit du seigneur, but feudal privilege has been transformed into superstitious lore (it is something the master must do, on known medical grounds), and as Ham leaves the dinner to go to Big Pearl, Brownlee remarks to Maxwell that Ham looks like "a right vigorous stud." Ham is himself a slave. As much as the Mandingos, he is kept for breeding purposes: his destiny is to provide an heir to perpetuate the line, and in this context, his name (Hammond is almost invariably abbreviated to Ham) becomes subtly suggestive. He is Hamitic, a white Negro, a brother of the slaves, preordained to servitude. From this fundamental identity the theme of ideological imprisonment is developed, in conjunction with the theme of sexual roles.

The significance of the names is implicitly there in the novel, but it is fully realized in the newly structured narrative of the film. The dinner scene introduces Mem (Richard Ward) and Lucrezia Borgia (Lillian Hayman), the senior slaves of the household. Mem/Agamemnon is the king in chains. At the beginning of the film, he comes out of the house behind Maxwell. By cutting between them, framed against the facade, and the slaves lined up below for sale, Fleischer separates Mem from the blacks and unites him with the house and his master. At the same time, the low angle, with the house towering above them, suggests that they too are dominated and oppressed; the house and the ideology it embodies are the real masters in the film. In the prison scene, in which Mem, at Cicero's request, reads haltingly a few lines from the Bible scrawled crudely on a piece of paper ("But by Thee only will we make mention of Thy name"), Cicero says that they were all free and princes in their own land. Throughout the film, Mem is used to show the appalling indignity in which the slave must acquiesce for sheer self-preservation. Maxwell asks him if he has a soul, and he replies, on cue, "A lazy, no-account, God-forsaken nigger can't have no soul, master." There is also the extraordinary, and presumably coincidental, identity of his name with that of the slave in *The Pioneers*. There was already uneasy humor in Cooper's comic nigger, who submitted to one master's "truth" to avoid a whipping and then begged him "to protect him from the displeasure" of the other. (53) Fleischer's character (not Onstott's) shoots his master when named with the same epithets which his ancestor accepts. The transition over two hundred years epitomizes the entire development of American culture.

Lucrezia Borgia is the cook, and where Mem's first appearance introduces the concept of innate dignity degraded, hers associates it with the subjection of women. Maxwell remarks that she has produced twenty-six children, and adds, "She bred out now—too old." Quite without resentment, Lucrezia replies, "Yes, sir." She is named after the legendary (European) murderess, an archetype of the idea of woman as treacherous temptress. Yet in the film, it is Dr. Redfield (Roy Poole), the guardian of life, who is the poisoner, and it is Lucrezia who vainly attempts to prevent Blanche from killing Ellen's unborn child by whipping her stomach, and who finally cradles Blanche protectively in her arms when Ham discovers the color of his supposed son. Lucrezia's cheerful acceptance of Maxwell's remark typifies the attitude of the slaves to their slavery. With the exception of Cicero and Mem, the slaves accept their lot as part of the order of things. When Blanche (Susan George) arrives at Falconhurst, Lucrezia joyfully embraces her (to Blanche's obvious distaste), saying to Ham, "Ever since your Ma died I been wanting another pretty white mistress."

The dinner scene also quietly initiates the characterization of Ham. Redfield mentions the abolitionists, and Maxwell, instantly enraged, declares that "slavery was ordained by God." Ham reminds his father quickly that losing his temper irritates his rheumatism. Later, when Maxwell has learnt about the "cure" (he has only to plant his feet on a Negro boy for the "misery" to drain away) and turns toward the boy murmuring, "That's mighty interestin'," Ham gets up abruptly and leaves to go to Big Pearl. At a second viewing, Ham's two attempts to "block" his father—first by asking him to calm down (a request which, simultaneously, conveys a genuine concern), and then by leaving—make their full impression, as does the irony of his departure to sleep with a female slave to "cure" her at the moment at which his father is considering "sleeping with the boy" to cure himself. All that we learn about Ham is implicit in this moment. The pathos and beauty of the character, perfectly realized in Perry King's performance, lies in the contradiction, of which Ham cannot become consciously aware, between an instinctive compassion and tenderness (the impulses of his individual humanity) and the order which he habitually accepts—he is torn apart in the efforts to be loyal to both. A capacity for complete emotional commitment coexists with an inability, socially determined, to understand what it implies. The film centers on his sexual relationships, where the war between the naturalized constraints and personal response is most intense.

The scene with Big Pearl follows that in which she is bathed by her mother in a tub of evil-smelling liquid in preparation for the meeting ("Smells good to white noses") and is given instructions on how to behave. The theme of parental domination and the acquiescence of the child is thus restated in terms of the Negroes: in both cases, after merely token and unco-ordinated resistance, the child submits, with the equivalent of Althusser's "Amen—So be it," the acknowledgment of necessity. It is important that two of the elements of this scene—the immersion of the slave before use by the master (a sort of grotesque parody of baptism) and Ham's dipping his finger in the water, withdrawing it at once in distaste—are repeated in the bathing of Mede (Ken Norton) in the cauldron, thus linking the sexual prostitution of Big Pearl and the prostitution of Mede as a gladiator, and suggesting Ham's unconscious revulsion from both.

The scene's bleakness derives from the reduction of sexuality to a duty. A custom, which has developed in order to justify the exploitation of the female slaves, has calcified into a degrading ritual, which neither the servant nor the supposed master desire; the whole presentation of the encounter suggests the bull led to the cow. Ham's hesitant tenderness and unease and his intuitive awareness that Big Pearl is far from finding her duty "right joyful," as her mother has told her it is, are crystallized in his physical helplessness. His disability reduces him suddenly from masterful white overlord to a human being who has to ask for help with his boots. At the same time, to fulfill the request, Big Pearl must kneel to him, and thus confirm her servitude, and the potential human oneness is canceled out. She doesn't answer Ham's question about whether she is happy but merely lies back on the bed in silence.

Fleischer cuts away, first to a shot of an old negress dragging off a little boy who is lying down outside the hut, trying to squint under the door—the same little boy who has followed Ham at the beginning of the scene and whom Ham has driven off; then Fleischer cuts to the chained slaves in the prison hut, awaiting transportation to their new masters. The editing unites in slavery the prisoners and the "lovers," a connection stressed by the lighting—both rooms are suffused with an oppressive reddish glare. The inhabitants are all lost souls, trapped in hell—the two sets of characters intermesh, as they do in *The Changeling*. The curiosity of the little boy, a recurrent motif of the film, suggests once more the acceptance of the world which characterizes everyone we see. As Mem is hung upside down to be whipped, the boy crouches down in front of him and says, "Boy, you sure look a-funny hangin' up!" One might compare Fleischer's emphasis here with Sam Peckinpah's in *The Wild Bunch* (1969). Peckinpah is essentially sentimental: he transforms children into animal-baiting monsters in the anguished recognition that innocence does not exist in a corrupt world; if children are not sweet little angels, they must be diabolic instead. Fleischer simply shows the inquisitiveness of a young mind calmly learning how things are. He is in the process of becoming a slave.

Ham's meeting with Ellen (Brenda Sykes) is the focal point of the film. Ham is returning with his cousin, Charles (Ben Masters), to the latter's house to meet Charles's sister, Blanche, whom he is virtually bound to marry. On the way, they stop at a neighbor of the Maxwells, Major Wilson, so that Ham can borrow Wilson's Mandingo slave, Xerxes, whom his father wishes to breed with Big Pearl. The dual purpose of the journey again enforces a parallel between Ham and Blanche and the Mandingos. Maxwell wants an heir for Falconhurst and

James Mason, as Warren Maxwell, in *Mandingo*. Personal collection of the editor.

sends Ham to propose to Blanche; he wants to mate his prize slave and sends Ham to get the father. The parallel is stressed by the fact that Ham has had intercourse with Big Pearl himself. At the same time, Ham also wants a Mandingo slave, which links him with his father: "They makes the best fightin' bucks . . . I craves one my own self, one that can whop anyone." Ham's need for a "fighting buck" is inseparable from the sense of impotence induced in him by his crippled leg. He can't "whop anyone," so the slave can do it for him, can assert and confirm his potency. After one of Mede's training sessions, Ham flings his arm round joyfully, saying, "You lucky buck, able to fight like that!" Hence, the supreme and dreadful irony of the ending, when Mede literally asserts his master's potency by making love to his wife, and is killed for it.

251

Charles is presented as an inverted mirror image of Ham—they were close as children, they are the product of the same environment—through the incident of the whipping of Mem. Ham has caught Mem reading from the Bible. He realizes that Mem must be punished but inwardly recoils from the thought, and the dilemma is made explicit when he goes to his father's bedroom to discuss the matter. Maxwell insists that Mem be blinded—"One eye—work as hard, don't give no more trouble." Ham, arranging mosquito netting around the bed, squashing an insect caught in it, seeing to his father's comfort, insists equally doggedly that "a larrupin'll do." The inner conflict (and its unconsciousness) is conveyed in the contrast between the words and the action. As Ham is himself preparing for bed, Mem, waiting on him, taking his clothes (that is, in the position occupied by Ham in the previous scene), asks him if he will pray for him, and Ham replies coldly that, since he can read, he should be able to pray for himself, but adding at once, "Mayhap tomorrow, after you've been larruped."

It is at the moment when the tensions reach an extreme in the whipping scene that Charles appears. Ham, after instructing a slave not to hit Mem too violently, watches the first blow, and then leaves. (Not looking is his habitual safety valve, frequently accompanied by a muttered "Damn!"—the only way in which he can prevent his instinctive sympathy with a slave from rising into consciousness. He turns away in the same manner from Charles's assault on the black girl, from Mede's "hot bath," from the execution of Cicero.) Charles arrives, criticizes the slave's halfheartedness, and begins to lash Mem violently. Ham bursts in yelling, "Who the hell are you to touch my niggers?" and almost attacks Charles before learning who he is. The slave-owning ideology ("my niggers") and the unacknowledged disgust with it are inextricably confused.

In the encounter with the two slave girls, these themes become infinitely more complex in their involvement with the film's sexual concerns. Wilson presents his two visitors with Ellen and Katie as part of the hospitality of the house. Charles walks round them, looking them over, and starts mauling them. As his hand goes between her legs, Ellen swings away in terror toward Ham. Charles asks her incredulously if she is a virgin, and then he pushes Katie toward the bed, telling Ham, "You can take the virgin. I don't care for hard work." Charles tears off Katie's dress and throws her face down over the side of the bed, lashing her with his belt as he begins to undress. Ham flees into the next room, followed by Ellen, and sits down sweating and trembling. There follows what must surely be one of the most beautiful and moving love scenes in the cinema—moving in the complexity, depth, and honesty of its emotion, superbly realized by Fleischer and his actors.

What we see is the momentary dissolution of ideological barriers through mutual human tenderness. "Momentary" is the word to stress; Fleischer's treatment is totally clear-sighted and unsentimental. He dissolves, for example, from the final embrace to the Price and Birch public market for "slaves and mules" in New Orleans (again, note the aptness of the names—capitalism and the lash), where we see Ham being offered "a capital woman and her three children by one of the dealers and turning away, cheerful and unconcerned, with the remark, "They ain't worth it." The beauty of the union lies essentially in its fragility. The love scene becomes the first, halting contact of two outsiders—the slave and the cripple—united in their horror at a sight which epitomizes the concept of slavery in the film: namely, the use of another human being for a personal satisfaction, specifically sexual, which denies and degrades their humanity. The injured leg, which Maxwell and Brownlee lament, which mars Ham's perfection as a specimen of white mastery, and which is symbolic of an inheritance of corruption, also makes possible the link with Ellen, who—uniquely in Ham's experience—actually comments on it, then dismisses it as irrelevant. Similarly, at that same time, her color and status become irrelevant for Ham; he twice renounces mastery over her, first by transforming his order to her to look him in the eyes into a request, and then by telling her, "If you don't like me, you don't have to stay." In this context of the abrogation of authority, Ellen expresses her desire to "please" him, which suggests not the submission of a servant, but the emotional commitment of a lover. Ham's final surrender of controlling power is expressed through the kiss toward which the whole scene moves. In the other room, he has seen Charles kiss Katie on the mouth, and is appalled. Here, at first tentatively and finally with a complete abandonment of all remaining self-consciousness and shame, he brings himself to do the same to Ellen. Whereas Charles's kiss was an expression of debased lust, Ham's represents the release of his humanity, desire transformed by tenderness and insight. The scene is built on a wonderfully simple use of camera movement. As Ham makes and repeats his plea to Ellen to look at him, Fleischer cuts between close shots of the two, the camera slowly, almost imperceptibly, tracking in on each. At the end of the scene, as they lean back on the bed, the camera again tracks in, this time on both of them, united in the one image.

The auction scene is placed between the meetings with Ellen and Blanche; the structural choice (again, a departure from Onstott) reinforces the ambiguities in Ham's impulsive purchase of Mede. Mede, firstly, is "the Mandingo my Poppa craved all this time." There is also Ham's need to compensate for his sense of impotence and inferiority. Most important, he is spurred into bidding for Mede by his disgust with a German widow who wants to buy Mede as a lover, and who, with business-like thoroughness, puts her hand beneath his loin-cloth to feel his genitals ("I don't buy the pig in the poke"). The incident obviously parallels Charles's groping at Ellen. Here, Fleischer introduces another of the themes seen by Fiedler as central to the American Gothic—the "homoerotic" love of the white man and the "savage."(13) Mede's name is thus significant. It is an abbreviation of Ganymede, the beautiful youth who arouses the passionate desire of Jupiter and is stolen from the earth to be the cupbearer of the gods on Olympus. The qualifying irony is very strong, given the un-Olympian characteristics of Falconhurst and its inhabitants. Fleischer suggests it at once in the shot in which we are shown Ham in the left of the frame, triumphantly counting out his money and muttering to himself, with Mede to his right, towering above him, silent, dignified, and serene in his humiliation, looking at him calmly with his hands on his hips.

Throughout the rest of the film, we see Ham's love for Mede developing to the point at which it transcends the desire to use him as a means of indirect self-assertion—the point at which he wants to throw in the towel during the fight with Topaz. Afterward, he goes against his father in insisting that Mede will not fight again. When Ham returns to Falconhurst, he brings with him his three lovers, two of whom (Mede and Blanche) were intended to restore the reputation and power of the dynasty, and all of whom precipitate its destruction. The catalyst of the final catastrophe is Blanche, the "white lady" whom he was sent to get and to whom he is not personally committed, rather than the black slaves whom he loves, has met accidentally, and has bought on a spontaneous impulse.

To say this, however, is at once to realize its inadequacy to the complex relationships of the actual film. Blanche's first appearance immediately follows the purchase of Mede. Like Mede, she is for sale. When Blanche is asked if she thinks Ham is handsome, Charles blurts out that "What matters is Cousin Ham thinkin' Blanche is pretty," implying that the completion of the financial deal between the two families depends on the satisfaction of the male purchaser. The outburst takes place in an ornate drawing room, the "mounting" in which Blanche has been placed to set her off. The camera advances toward the group through a doorway which frames them on sofas and chairs as in a painting, while on the soundtrack (a brilliantly suggestive touch) a harpsichord plays a variation of the theme previously associated with the slaves at Falconhurst. In the following scene between Blanche and Charles, we see that she is prepared to go to any lengths—and to collaborate in her own degradation as an object of display—to "get out of this house and this family." Ham is the opportunity of escape: "He's a fine catch—good-lookin', rich, romantic, bin to New Orleans, comes from far away." The romantic dream, in which fairy-tale illusion and acquisitive opportunism are balanced, is one face of the attitudes fostered by the polite, genteel seclusion of Blanche's home. The other is the incestuous relationship with Charles, which he fights desperately to preserve. He threatens to reveal it to Ham, to which Blanche replies instantly that "He wouldn't believe you, and Poppa would throw you out." The moment is poignantly ironic. Charles has brought Ham to his house (and with Ham the disruption of his affair with Blanche) at his father's insistence and in his father's financial interests. Equally, Ham returns to Falconhurst with the elements of his destruction, again moved by his father's concern for the future. Later in the film, Blanche, enraged by Ham's neglect, by jealousy of Mede and Ellen, and by sexual frustration, summons Mede to her room and forces him to have intercourse with her, threatening that if he doesn't, she will tell Ham that he has raped her. When Mede says that Ham won't believe her, she replies, "He'll believe me. He won't believe a nigger!" In the event, Ham does not believe the rape story. This irony overlays the other, whereby Blanche comes to occupy the place of sexual blackmailer previously occupied by her brother. In her blind and desperate attempt to escape from the unnatural constraints of her family, Blanches rushes headlong into another prison.

Blanche is the white lady (another obviously significant name); like her namesake in *A Streetcar Named Desire*, she is used to explore the assumed incompatibility of sexuality and "being a lady." The theme has already been broached in an earlier scene between Ham and his father, in which the slave-owning ideology is identified with a notion of the fundamental bestiality of sex. Ham says that he "wouldn't know what to do with a white lady" and that in any case, he doesn't want to give up having black mistresses. Maxwell replies that a wife "wants you to have 'em. Saves them from havin' to submit"; he tells Ham that when making love with a white lady they must always keep their clothes on, as white ladies dislike the sight of naked flesh (we learn later that Maxwell was a "hell-raiser" in his youth, and frequented Madame Caroline's white brothel). The restriction of unfettered erotic love to the humanly irresponsible, exploitative relationship of a master sating his desire on a slave suggests the alienation of the human body from the idea of "civilization," which is equated with a sterile etiquette of "refinement." Sexual relations with a woman of his own race are effectively impossible for Ham. The female slave as whore and the white lady as untouchable goddess complement one another. Susan George's beautiful performance expresses superbly the tension in Blanche between what she knows a white lady must be and do and the desire which she must consequently repress. The tension manifests itself in the co-presence of apparent rejection and underlying invitation ("You come to buy me—take a good look at me! . . . You crave I undress?"), culminating in their first embrace. Blanche tells Ham not to kiss her yet "less'n it's just a cousin kiss," and at once leans up and kisses him passionately on the mouth.

The terrible doublethink involved in "civilized" sexuality is vividly brought home in the honeymoon sequence. We see Blanche posing with two dresses in her arms in the bedroom of the New Orleans hotel, framed in a doorway as she was at her house, asking Ham which color suits her best, and admiring her wedding ring with childish excitement. The subliminal link supplied through the doorway shot is taken up again in the use of mirrors. As Ham storms out of the room at the end of the scene, the camera frames Blanche's reflection in a huge mirror, and she is constantly caught in the mirrors over the fireplace and in the wardrobe in her room at Falconhurst. One might single out the scene in which Maxwell turns on her furiously after he has learned about her attack on Ellen, dragging her to the mirror so that she can see her disheveled hair and clothes—"Ain't you got no pride?" He orders her to comb her hair and make herself attractive to Ham, and when she tries to protest that "it's Hammond's fault" and that he wants her to do "dirty things in bed" as his wenches do, tells her, "Then you are goin' to do dirty things so's you can get him in your bed and keep him there!" He proceeds to lock her in the bedroom with Ham to "get down to business": "I ain't lettin' you out till you done pleasurin'." The sexuality which Blanche yearns for but has to think of, through a lifetime's indoctrination, as "dirty," has been movingly conveyed in the moment when she confesses to Ham that she has been drinking to get up the courage simply to ask him to touch her. Again, the mirror dominates the image as she desperately caresses Ham, who is sitting impassively in a chair before her. He pushes her away and leaves, remarking, "You sure are a strange kind of white lady." This continuous association of Blanche with frames (her entrapment as an icon) is emphasized by the fact that once she arrives at Falconhurst, we never see her outside the house again, and only three times outside the bedroom, which becomes, with its sickly, yellow light, an image of, at once, a prison cell and of Blanche's own disintegrating psyche, the obsessional, morbid world of frustrated erotic drives.

Ham is both a fellow prisoner (Maxwell locks both of them in) and one of the jailers, in that he believes in and imposes the repressive, denatured stereotype of the white lady. It is part of the nature of things that a white man should have sex with slaves and whores before and after marriage, but for a white lady not to be a virgin on her wedding night is monstrous; the husband's rights of possession have been violated ("Who pleasured you before me?"). The transition from the hotel to Madame Caroline's brothel is typically concise. From the mirror shot of Blanche, beating the bed with her fists and screaming repeatedly in despair that she was "pure," Fleischer cuts to a door opening inside the brothel, a well-dressed man coming out into camera and blowing a kiss back to the naked white prostitute, who is being attended like a queen by her servants. The two frames link the women: Blanche is, in the use to which

Maxwell and Ham want to put her, no more than a prostitute—a body to produce the desired heir. At the same time, the cut establishes a contrast. Ham's flight from bedroom to brothel expresses the tragic, absurd incoherence of his notions of sex. He flees, in effect, from a bride who disgusts him because she is not white lady to white whores who are professionally not ladies. Instinctively but illogically, he chooses the uncomplicated world of the brothel to wipe out his shattered illusion (though on being faced with it, he awkwardly withdraws).

The establishment of Madame Caroline, described before the wrestling match as "New Orleans's main patroness of manly and recreational sports," reveals the complete degradation of both whites and blacks. We see Negroes in white-powdered wigs and elaborate silk livery waiting on the pleasure of their masters as the white prostitutes do, in a world governed by the power relations of masters over servants and the exchange of sex for cash (Brownlee, the slave trader, appears there as Ham's sponsor and guide). The brothel's walls and drapes are red, evoking both erotic desire and blood. It is essential that the film includes—under the heading of manly recreation—both whoring and the slaughterous contest between Mede and Topaz, announced by the master of ceremonies as an "epic battle" and presided over, from a box, by Maxwell and Madame Caroline, the slave breeder and the courtesan, sitting together like king and queen—the masters of the revels.

Maxwell's first inquiry about Mede is: "He pure? I don't want no half." Mede is then sent straight away to Big Pearl, who, Ham discovers, is Mede's sister. Maxwell waves aside the objection ("Works sovereign with animals—works fine with niggers"), and when Ham asks what they do if the product of the union is a "monster," replies calmly, "Snuff it out!" The moment obtains its full significance in the context of the ending. Fleischer dissolves from the scene of Mede's intercourse with Blanche to Ham's discovery that Big Pearl has just given birth to Mede's son. Ham, overjoyed, cradles the child in his arms, while Mede stands by, head lowered, in guilty silence (compare the proud, lofty gaze of the auction scene). The child is, symbolically, Ham's own—he first had intercourse with Big Pearl, and Mede "compensates" for his doubt of his own full virility. Yet the juxtaposition with a scene in which the roles are reversed (Mede makes love to Ham's wife) charges it with irony. Big Pearl's son, the incestuous child which represents the triumph of Maxwell's breeding plans, seems to foretell Blanche's son, the child of miscegenation and adultery. It is the latter which is considered to be the "monster" which Ham himself "snuffs out." Maxwell, too, is pleased with Mede's baby and Ham whispers to him, so that Mede can't hear, "Weren't no harm, Big Pearl and Mede," at which precise moment Blanche enters the room, beautifully dressed, charming, elegant—the perfect white lady. Maxwell offers Mede some money, which Mede silently ignores; Ham remarks, "I reckon Mede's just too proud to take that money, aren't you, Mede?" As Mede leaves, he exchanges glances with Blanche for a second. This series of painful ironies is capped by the closing exchange between Ham and Blanche. Ham tells her she is "behavin' most ladylike," and after a pause, she blurts out, "Well, I'm with child." Ham stares at her. Then, smiling, "Is that the reason you're actin' so nice?" He embraces her, with subdued affection, for the first time since the honeymoon. The camera tracks in on Blanche's face, in which the joy at being accepted and touched by her husband is mingled with incipient horror.

Mede's role is defined, in addition, by its juxtaposition with that of Mem. After the train-ing fight, Ham orders Mem to see that Mede is bathed and fed, and Mem smilingly replies, "Yes sir, Master Hammond," turning and grimacing at him with furious resentment as soon as his back is turned. The self-disgust is then vented on Mede: "When you gonna learn the color of your skin, Mede?" Mede returns, "Just as soon as you stop puttin' on your smilin'-nigger face to Master Hammond." Fleischer shows us here two faces of self-oppression and makes it impossible for us to feel any complacent superiority toward either. Mede collaborates in his own degradation out of a selfless loyalty which drives him even to kill Topaz so that Ham will not lose face. In the final scene, as Ham is forcing him to climb into the cauldron of boiling water at gunpoint, Mede appeals in the name of that loyalty, relying on the belief that Ham acknowledges and reciprocates it: "You know I never do anythin' against you, Master! I always respects you!" Ham's face contorts, and he discharges his gun into Mede's shoulder.

Mem has no such commitment to his oppressors, and he acts the self-deprecating "smil-ing nigger" to keep his skin and what comfort he can; his criticism of Mede wells up out of his helpless loathing of his own submission. The desolating force of the catastrophe stems from the complex interplay of loyalties between the four characters involved. Ham first shoots Mede as Mede is declaring his respect for him; he shoots him again as Mede's uncomprehending hor-ror (he seems more amazed than hurt) expresses itself in a denunciation: "I thought you was somehow better than a white man. But you is just white!" From the moment at which he sees the dead baby, Ham's actions have the relentless, obsessive drive of a machine ("Ain't no other way")—his senses and his mind have been shut off. Blanche has twice been "pleasured" for him by men who do not have his absolute rights, the second time by a black slave he has loved: he has been ousted from his place in the order as white overlord of his woman and his servant. Mede was to have counterbalanced the consciousness of the crippled leg, but his "possession" of Blanche only confirms it; the gun and pitchfork, the power of life and death, are Ham's final means of asserting his potency. Similarly, the use of the cauldron becomes significant. Before, when Mede was being "toughened up" for the fight, Ham could not bear to watch him get into it. Now he uses it to kill the "fighting buck" it was one of the means of creating. The shooting of Mede on the word *respects* is Ham's frantic denial of his human involvement with him; the violence is another blocking action, an attempt to resolve the intolerable opposing pulls of ideological revulsion and personal emotion. And he shoots Mede in the shoulder, where Mede gave Topaz his fatal wound. Symbolically, Ham is murdering a fellow slave and alter ego.

Mede's denunciation provokes the second attack, a consequence of and reaction against the first, this time to block Ham's sense that he has betrayed a trust, and with it his true emo-tional loyalty. It is this attack which finally moves Mem to the rebellion he has been unable to make throughout the film: as Ham turns against Mede, Mem commits himself to him. Once more, the action is shown as painfully divisive. Mem backs away with the gun, begging Ham not to come any nearer, the need to avenge Mede's and his own degradation counterbalanced by the ingrained habit which still compels him to call Ham "Master" even as he points the rifle at him. Maxwell has been standing in the background throughout, offscreen most of the time: an observer, as at the fight; the figure of the retributive authority which Ham is enacting before him. He calls Mem "You crazy nigger! You loony black bastard!"—and Mem turns the gun on him and kills him. Maxwell falls in the doorway from which he and Mem emerged at the beginning of the film, and Mem runs away. Ham is left, literally, with nothing. The violence has resolved his divided loyalties by annihilating both of them.

The full, complex impact of the denouement can best be felt by juxtaposing it with the slave revolt. It is preceded by the scene in which Ham, having just rejected Blanche's desperate plea to him to touch her, leaves her to sleep with Ellen, and he grants Ellen's request that if the child she is expecting is a boy it can go free. Ham's initial fury (he assumes at once that Ellen herself "craves to be free" and becomes suspicious of the genuineness of her attachment to him) dissolves in the face of her assurances (she takes slavery for granted for a woman) and, above all, of her tears—he cannot bear the sight of her crying. Fleischer cuts at once to the announcement of the uprising. It is as if, by acceding to Ellen's demand, Ham has released the forces that threaten the order of which he is a part.

The emotional center of the rebellion sequence is the confrontation of Cicero and Mede. Mede pursues him through the woods after Cicero has been shot in the leg and catches him. Just as Mem has done, Cicero accuses Mede of being "a white man's animal": "What you think you is—a hound dog?" If Mede hands him over, "you gonna know you kill a black brother." Mede lets him go but hesitates just long enough to allow Cicero to be caught by two of the white pursuers, a superb example of the recurrent use of narrative action to express psychological tensions—Mede partly wills the capture of a slave who has been disloyal to his master. Cicero repeats his denunciation at the hanging, as Mede will finally denounce Ham. In the face of the uneasy, silent crowd, he declares that Mede's action proves and perpetuates the total slavery of the Negro and that a race which was already in bondage ("You peckerwoods was slaves in your own land!") has enslaved a free people. Ham, obviously deeply disturbed, pulls Mede away, and we cut to their departure for the match with Topaz. A group of female slaves, including Ellen, clap and dance with delight as Mede tells Ham, "I whops anyone you wants, Master."

It is typical of the complex and subtle power of the film's method that Cicero and the rebellion, though thematically central, are presented without conspicuous emphasis. Cicero himself is not used as a mouthpiece for liberal humanitarianism nor made strikingly sympathetic as an individual, although in his proud, unwavering, and finally self-sacrificing assertion of the human dignity and the social and political rights of the Negroes, he embodies values which the action implicitly endorses. The film needs Cicero, but as part of the defining context in which its central concern with the characters who are not ideologically aware can be honestly developed. Thus, the importance of the parallel between Cicero and Mem: Mem, before the rebellion, voices Cicero's accusation that Mede is becoming a "white man's animal," and after it, inherits the denunciation made at the hanging ("Not every black man gets a chance to kill another black man!") in connection with the killing of Topaz. But the point of the parallel is precisely to underline the human complexity of the ideological issues. Addressed to this particular character (Mede) by that (Mem), the remarks introduce a whole range of ambiguous personal issues which make approbation or condemnation trivial and irrelevant. We are not, that is, dealing with a tract on racial discrimination.

One can also read Mem's whispered criticisms as the germs of a questioning and doubt, consciously rejected, in Mede himself: both incidents occur when he has been beaten to the ground in combat. Consider the aftermath of the fight with Topaz. Mede fights on for his master, abandoning the restraints of hand-to-hand combat to destroy his opponent, literally, by tooth-and-nail. Fleischer juxtaposes this with the close-up of his anguished face as, feted and applauded, he watches the mutilated body being dragged away. Similarly, we have the contrast between Ham's euphoric vicarious triumph ("Poppa! We won! We killed him!") and his horror and compassion—a conflict which culminates, on the drive home, in a partial rejection of his father. While Maxwell is full of the supreme importance of the victory in terms of social prestige and "fancy money," Mede, sitting on the back of the cart, mutters dully, "Ain't nothin' worth all this fightin', killin'." Ham spontaneously half-turns in the driver's seat for a moment and touches Mede's arm. Maxwell is appalled and demands of Ham if he is "goin' to let him say that." Without looking at his father, Ham replies, "Reckon I am." The movement away from Maxwell is confirmed in the following scene, in which Ham gives Ellen the earrings his father intended for Blanche, and by the final break with Blanche, precipitated by her hurt and furious departure from the dinner table when she sees Ellen wearing them. Yet it is symptomatic of Fleischer's unwavering "inwardness" with his theme that the extreme of Ham's commitment to the slaves should coexist with an affirmation of his loyalty to his father, and I want to end by examining the sequence in question.

Blanche returns to her room and starts smashing ornaments in a fit of hysteria, the violence, as always, providing the only outlet for frustration which never becomes consciously defined. It is significant, the frustration being primarily sexual, that the nucleus of the violence should be a bedroom: we remember the prelude to the whipping of Ellen, when Blanche reeled drunkenly about the room lashing the walls and furniture, concentrating her rage on the rocking chair in which Ham was sitting when he rejected her plea to him to touch her ("I need you!"). Now, again, Ellen prompts the second outburst, and Blanche screams at Ham, "You might as well brand your name on her face—and on mine—so everyone knows us is the women of Hammond Maxwell!" It is ironic both that the original idea of the jewelry was not Ham's but his father's and that in her jealousy of Ellen, Blanche should state exactly what it is that unites them in their oppression. Ham's tenderness in giving the earrings to Ellen, who tells him that they are "pretty enough for a white lady," can exist beside the unthinking insensitivity with which he gives Blanche the necklace. Her disgust with him is countered and barred by the emergence of his disgust with her, and he demands that she tell him who her first lover was. Blanche replies, "You know who it was! You just afraid to ask!" Ham instantly names Charles and storms out when she assents. She calls after him, "We was fifteen! We only did it once!"—a heartbreaking moment in which the whole agony of sexual repression and ideological guilt is concentrated. Blanche is leaning on the bed as she speaks. (The cycle in which she is subsequently involved—copulation, birth, death—all in the one bed, expresses the desecration of the processes of love and regeneration in the society depicted. The poison is given to her as a restorative.)

We cut to Maxwell and Mem herding together the slaves who are to be sold to get money for the building of Ham and Blanche's new house. The camera tracks past the crowd, and we see a husband saying good-bye to his wife and assuring her that "Master wouldn't sell me to no mean man." She, oblivious, in tears, replies that "We ain't never gonna see each other again"

—a touch, deliberately stressed (the voices continue on the soundtrack as the camera moves on, thus associating the lines with the whole crowd), which gains much of its force from its proximity to the previous scene. Maxwell comes to a female slave, Didie, whose child is to be sold. Earlier, when Ellen begs Ham not to sell their child, she has added, not yet reassured, "You're gonna sell Didie's sucker," to which Ham has replied, "That's different." His personal concerns exist apart from the general order which he takes as a matter of course. Now Ham tells Didie to take her child back, emphatically lifting it out of the cart when his father protests and sending Didie off with it. Maxwell tells him he's a fool, and Ham replies, walking away, his back to him, "Mayhap. Just how I feel." He asks Ellen to come with him, and she climbs on, kneeling behind him with her arms on the back of the driver's seat. Maxwell is again enraged and shouts after Ham, "I don't understand you!" Ham goes over and kisses him on the cheek.

The scene is a crux of the film. For the first and only time, Ham makes a gesture of compassion and humanity to a slave with whom he is not personally involved, and it is shown as being precipitated by his revulsion from Blanche, in which his indoctrination by the ideology is most evident. He can allow Didie to keep her child, whom he had previously been quite unconcerned about, because his wife's reaction to her repression (which is, equally, his own repression) disgusts him. The same disgust prompts in part the desire to take Ellen with him—he is aware that Blanche is watching them from the balcony—and Ellen's posture, kneeling behind and below him, yet at the head of the procession, exactly expresses her dual status as slave and consort. The double rejection of his father is balanced by the kiss, the token of the love for and involvement with him which Ham can never renounce. The tragedy of his unawareness is compressed in that one phrase, "Just how I feel." The moment at the end of the film when he pushes Ellen aside as he marches on inexorably to exact his revenge, saying, "Don't think that 'cause you get in my bed you're anythin' but a nigger!" is terrifyingly credible.

The scene ends in a coda which encapsulates its meaning. Fleischer cuts from a shot of a huge Negro woman falling face down in the dirt as the wagon to which she has been clinging in despair gathers speed to a long shot from the balcony of the procession getting under way. The camera pans round and tracks rapidly across the balcony toward Blanche, who is watching, wearing a disheveled white dress. The camera moves into a close-up of her face, then pans down and cranes forward in the direction of her gaze. We see the procession turning away from us down the drive. Ham looks back over his shoulder for an instant, and then away again. We cut to Blanche sitting in her room at the beginning of the scene in which she sends for Mede, and the overlap of the music from one scene to the next points up the continuity of Blanche's state of mind: the use of Mede is a direct response to what she saw. The elaborate shot recapitulates the thematic development to that point in preparation for the denouement. Ham, below Blanche, turns his back on the house. He is at the extreme of his revulsion from the whites (father and wife) and his involvement with the slaves; yet, he is taking them to an auction to get money for a house for himself and a bride he hates. Blanche, above him, is at once associated with the house and a prisoner of it, at once a figure of oppressive power (her physical elevation) and a victim (her exercise of power can only be self-destructive). The camera movement, the simple cut, and the precise use of sound evoke again that sense of interrelatedness within and between scenes and actions which is so typical of the film as a whole.

My purpose has been to show that *Mandingo* is a great and achieved work of art. If it is deeply involved with a tradition in American culture discernible from its origins, the film is also representative of a second tradition—that of the classical narrative Hollywood cinema—in a way which, say, Altman's films evidently aren't. One feels it continuously, in its assurance, fluidity, economy, and formal conservatism, as a supreme example of a conventional art form.

In *My Darling Clementine* (1946), Henry Fonda's Wyatt Earp sat on the porch of the sheriff's office in Tombstone, dexterously balancing himself on the rear legs of his chair, the town becoming an image of the burgeoning community of America and Earp of the benevolent patriarchal authority which made it possible. In 1975, America is not the youthful desert town, but the corrupt, rotting mansion, and the chair on the porch is occupied by a cripple with his feet on a Negro boy. All the racial and sexual conflicts which John Ford's film was just about able to contain are explicit and diagnosed in *Mandingo*. Think of Indian Joe—"Indian—get out of town and stay out!"—and Chihuahua—"Get back to the reservation where you belong!" Chihuahua is a paradigm case of the whore/wench, the natural inferior through both her sex and her race (part-Mexican, part-Apache) who is associated with the degeneration of the white man (Doc Holliday). It is impossible to conceive of a more perfect example of the "white lady" whose clothes cannot be removed than Miss Clementine Carter, saint and schoolmistress. *Mandingo* is an exploration of the nature of these assumptions, which it follows through unsparingly to a conclusion of desolating bleakness. Ham is left, like Ishmael, "another orphan" amid the wreckage of America, and with no Rachel in sight in search of her "missing children." Yet the ending avoids, as well as sentimental evasion, sentimental despair. If the action progresses toward total collapse, it conveys at the same time, largely through Ham and Ellen, an overwhelming sense of human potential. In its rigorous vitality and energy, it embodies qualities which are the opposite of defeatist. *Mandingo* is a masterpiece of Hollywood cinema.

10 (1981)

oward the end of *10* (1979), Jennifer (Bo Derek), with whom George Webber (Dudley Moore) has been romantically obsessed throughout the film, seduces him, and they repair to bed to make love to the accompaniment, at Jennifer's suggestion, of a record of Maurice Ravel's "Bolero." They are interrupted by a telephone call from Jennifer's husband, David (Sam J. Jones [David Hanley]), whose life George has earlier saved and who is now recuperating in the hospital. The effect of the call on George, who at once becomes unable to perform, significantly redefines our understanding of his sexual fantasy, which appears to have been close to realization. It has always been clear that, in the manner of such obsessions, George's desire is fueled by private needs and intensities which are wholly indifferent to the real nature of the object onto whom they are projected, but it might have been thought—on the evidence of his daydreams and periodic investigations, through a telescope, of the sexual exploits of a neighbor in the house opposite his own—that his interest in Jennifer lay essentially in the prospect of a sexual fling. It transpires, on the contrary, that it is precisely Jennifer's relaxed, hedonistic attitude to their encounter which George finds distressing. What he wants is exclusive romantic proprietorship—a relationship, in other words, identical in form to the one which dissatisfies him—and his discovery that, for Jennifer, the pleasures of the evening imply neither the betrayal of her husband nor renunciation of him in favor of permanent devotion to George, releases a torrent of self-righteous prudery: "There's more to life than turning on and screwing to Ravel's 'Bolero.'"

We are not concerned, that is, with the revamping of the theme of "male menopause" to which the film, insofar as it has been discussed at all, has been reduced, if by male menopause we mean the last-ditch indulgence in irresponsible promiscuity which the phrase customarily denotes. George's desires are more complex and contradictory than that. He wants monogamy all right, in the sense of being found "special," and Jennifer's response—"As far as I'm concerned, I'm very special"—helps to define George's case as the familiar one of needing "love" for self-definition and ego-reinforcement, the ideal corollary of the acquired sense of "specialness" being the self-abnegation of the partner who bestows it. The untiring sexual prowess of his neighbor supplies merely an irritant, or catalyst, for a character whose Oedipal attachments are not to be invested, in Don Juan's manner, in an eternally unsatisfied magpie acquisitiveness; yet, the scenario which has as its upshot George's finding himself at last in bed with his ideal does bear all the hallmarks of the family romance.

George first sees Jennifer, in bridal white, en route to her wedding, and desire at once collides with the law in the wonderfully literal form of a police car. The frisson generated by the fantasy from the start derives from the fact that the image of Jennifer appears to reconcile virginal purity (no one has "had" her) and Oedipal prohibition (she is subject to another man). The Mexican events seem to promise the opportunity of breaking the prohibition without the inconveniences of the accompanying guilt, which will be allayed by the saving of David's life. The "adult" fantasy of glamorous voluptuousness is mediated by the infantile fantasy of displacing the father in the affections of the mother and opens up the possibility of an unrecognized gratification of older impulses. As soon as the insistent third party intrudes again, and it transpires that there is no prohibition after all—and thus no "specialness" to be won—the entire emotional structure crumbles, the beneficent mother is suddenly perceived, correspondingly, as "easy," and George retires in piqued disarray.

George's desire that monogamy should reenact the lost plenitude of selfless maternal devotion has as corollary the cynical contempt for women which finds expression, near the beginning of the film, in the discussion of the meaning of the word *broad* with his lover, Samantha (beautifully played by Julie Andrews). The scene is preceded by George's first glimpse of Jennifer, and then a tense evening with Sam, near the end of which George, sidling up to the telescope, has seen his neighbor desultorily buggering a girlfriend in the course of a game of pool. The juxtaposition of the two modes of objectification—idealizing and lubricious—suggests with marvelous economy the complementary nature of apparently contradictory drives: whether as unique vehicle of a grand passion or nameless prop in a display of achieved and effortless mastery, the woman's function is to obliterate the sense of being at once "invalided" and "invalid" to which George confesses at his birthday party.

It is perfectly logical, then, that during the first half of the film, the onset of romantic intoxication can coexist with the disastrous attempt to pick up the young woman in the café and the excursion to his neighbor's orgy, and that George should find himself in pursuit of Jennifer only after Sam has discovered him in flagrante. He is still capable, even then, of moaning desperately, alone in his bedroom on the first night in Mexico, "Oh Sam, come and save me!" and of investing in grand passion while also asserting, on the phone to Sam, that his absence is temporary and therapeutic ("I love you too much to put you through all that rubbish"). Thus, while at one level George does not know what he wants, everything he does is nevertheless contingent on the need for an indulgent mother figure. As long as Sam is somewhere in the background, the house on the other side of the hill is a consuming attraction, and monogamy is felt as constraint. Conversely, it is the apparent foreclosure of his options with Sam which finally propels George at full tilt toward Mexico, where monogamy is felt as romantic. It is quite characteristic of him that he can begin to suspect, after his arrival, that the woman he has just left is a source of protection, solicitude, and salvation after all.

The function of the "broad" sequence is to define the real nature of Sam's unsatisfactoriness from George's point of view: that so explicit and astringent a critique of male sexism should figure here as a dramatic crux ought, one feels, to have provided sufficient evidence of the nature of the film's intentions. If the relationship is inadequate to George's requirements, it is less because it is sexually exclusive than because Sam strenuously insists on her own sexual equality within it, and subsequent developments amply confirm the point that George's voyeurism is premised on a desire to subordinate female sexuality to his own rather than on aspirations to promiscuity. Indeed, the argument is broken off when George reveals the essential nature of his position by bursting out with "I wouldn't mind losing like a man if you weren't so damned determined to win like one." Neither monogamy nor polygamy in themselves can satisfy the kind of desire implied by the designation of "sexually emancipated ladies . . . as broads," since both—unless certain conditions are fulfilled—may equally exacerbate the feeling of being "invalided." Polygamy on Jennifer's terms is as undesirable as monogamy on Sam's, the serene assurance of possessing the phallus being irremediably compromised in either case by the woman's intransigent autonomy. The real object of George's quest is the benign maternal figure who will simply bestow the phallus and refrain from jeopardizing the gift by giving evidence of a desire of her own.

10's substantial achievement is attended by obvious limitations and ambiguities. If the film is keenly aware of its protagonist's representative unpleasantness, and its wit is continuously a matter of his discomfiture and embarrassment—of the gap between self-serving romantic fantasy and the real conditions (subjective and objective) which impede its successful realization—there is, nevertheless, a disturbing tendency to reinstate him which manifests itself most clearly in the treatment of Hugh (Robert Webber), George's collaborator, and Mary Lewis (Dee Wallace-Stone), the woman he meets in Mexico. While both characters are offered as variations on the theme defined by George, they are figures not of comedy but of pathos. To say as much is already to indicate a radical uncertainty in the kind of comedy of which George is the subject. The "broad" sequence demonstrates clearly enough that George is an exemplary figure; the dialogue emphasizes repeatedly ("As far as you're concerned, or any man for that matter, virtue has everything to do with it") that certain characteristic features of heterosexual maleness are in question. At the same time, it is possible to read his behavior as a temporary aberration induced by crisis. Again, while much of the humor depends on the discrepancy between George's actual physical characteristics and the conventional iconography of the romantic lover, he is also represented as being attractive and desirable. It is clearly significant, in the light of these hesitations, that we are encouraged to feel that the unsatisfactoriness of Hugh's and Mary's relationships is germane to their "condition"—the condition, respectively, of a gay man and a middle-aged woman—and that both are explicitly used at various points to recuperate George. Thus, in conversation with Sam, Hugh becomes the medium for an enumeration of George's merits which culminates in the claim that he is "a genuine genius"—a proposition which is presented here, quite without irony, as a reason for Sam's continuing to tolerate him but which nothing in the realized character remotely substantiates. Similarly, while George's inability to make love to Mary Lewis is obviously to be explained in terms of George, we also seem to be invited to endorse her own attribution of it, on the basis of a similar experience in the past, to herself ("Some of us just don't bring out the man in men"); later, her remarks to the bartender about the "unfairness" involved in middle-aged men looking "distinguished" and middle-aged women "looking old" reaffirm George's physical attractiveness rather as Hugh has reaffirmed his remarkable abilities.

These uncertainties are particularly striking in Hugh's case in that the film, in its early stages, far from privileging the heterosexual protagonist, has used Hugh emphatically to place him: George's petulant baiting of Hugh in the second scene in the beach house is associated with envy, and Hugh's robust response (he calls George "the Anglo-Saxon heterosexual bore of all time") is given complete support. But one need only compare Jennifer to Hugh's beautiful young lover, who is presented, in the usual way, as venal and exploitative, to become aware of the limits within which Hugh can appear as a positive figure. The failure of the gay relationship is objectively given for the film, and Hugh—consigned at the end to poignant and inevitable loneliness—becomes the mouthpiece for the recommendation of any permanent relationship at any cost ("Kill if you have to, George, but don't lose that lady"). This has obvious repercussions for the presentment of Sam, whose decision to take George back is quite unmotivated (indeed, inexplicable) and whose character itself is the site of unresolved tensions and ambiguities. The direct cut from Jennifer to Sam on stage, in an eighteenth-century setting, singing the number with which she has been constantly associated ("I give my heart just to one man"), seems to suggest a negative judgment on the artifice and archaism of exclusive relationships; the association of Sam both with this concept of monogamy and with the positions she defends in the "broad" sequence has an arbitrariness which can be related to the film's failure to define a couple relationship which is neither exclusive nor "promiscuous" in the pejorative sense. Jennifer's marriage to David, which offers the possibility of doing so, is wholly unexplored, and the gay relationship is automatically assimilated to an inert stereotype of the loveless, the predatory, the transient. Given these blockages, the film can only resort to the mechanism of the "change of heart" and reinstate a relationship whose conflicts have not been resolved and a hero who has been irreversibly undermined.

The Great Waldo Pepper (1981)

One wouldn't have gathered from the way in which the film was discussed when it appeared that *The Great Waldo Pepper* (1975) amounted to much more than "the same kind of thing" that had been offered already by *Butch Cassidy and the Sundance Kid* (1969) and *The Sting* (1973). Both its predecessors achieved an enormous popular success, which was sustained on their re-release, as well as satisfied the unexacting demands of critics who really despise commercial movies but are ready, in moods of relaxation, to jovially succumb to the kind of opportunistic fluency which makes no bones about its calculation. *The Great Waldo Pepper*, however, failed dismally at the box office and failed to come up with the invitations to have knowing fun which excite journalistic approval. Both facts bear eloquent testimony to the significant differences between George Roy Hill's third film with Robert Redford and its forbears—differences which primarily have to do with the attitude we are to adopt toward the hero.

In *Hermes the Thief*, Norman O. Brown gives an account of the mythological archetype of the tricksters: Hermes and Mercury in Greek and Roman legend, Coyote in North American Indian tales, Loki and Puck in Norse and English folklore, respectively, are all avatars of this type, and Herman Melville's *The Confidence-Man* represents its most complex and sophisticated literary deployment.

> Depending on the historical circumstances, the trickster may evolve into any one of such contrasting figures as a benevolent culture-hero nearly indistinguishable from the Supreme God, a demiurge in strong opposition to the heavenly powers, a kind of devil counteracting the creator in every possible way, a messenger and mediator between gods and men, or merely a Puckish figure, the hero of comical stories. (Brown, 46)

The "theft" with which Hermes is associated is distinguished from "robbery" and from the physical prowess of the robber-hero Herakles by connotations of fraud, stealth, and deceit, which give evidence of magical powers and which manifest themselves in many ways besides stealing. Thus, Hermes is variously the patron of sexual seduction, the master of runes and talismanic formulas, and the sorcerer. While the trickster becomes purely evil when incorporated, as the devil, in Christian myth (while retaining, of course, his alluring and charismatic quality), his pre-Christian forms combine positive and negative characteristics: destructive guile coexists with the properties of culture-hero and "giver of good things."

Melville's novel is set on April first aboard a ship of fools called, ironically, the *Fidele*, which functions as a microcosm of American society, and the myth provides the basis for a critique of the structures of ideological confidence which sustain white American democracy: the successive avatars of the trickster appeal for confidence and, in betraying it, demonstrate the mystified nature of the values they have pretended to uphold. This use of the myth is a recurrent motif in the American Gothic; it is central to the work of Mark Twain, appears again in Jack Kerouac and Thomas Pynchon, and defines the hero function in Clint Eastwood's western *High Plains Drifter* (1973), whose protagonist, like Melville's confidence man, is at once Devil and Nemesis.

The assimilation of the trickster to the asocial homoerotic couple is not without precedent (Huck Finn serves very radically as a critical trickster figure), but in *Butch Cassidy* and *The Sting*, the conjunction is simply at the service of an appeal to romantic identification with the male outlaw. In *Waldo Pepper*, the male romance, while thematically crucial, is both radically redefined and displaced from the center of the narrative. The concern here is with a hero whose appearance as the hero itself is an act of trickery; the film is single-mindedly preoccupied with the ideological determinants of his masquerade and, inseparably, the emotional needs it fulfills. Waldo Pepper (Robert Redford) is the trickster-god who comes "down from the heavens—all for you," and whose plane, the "Mercury," bears the winged helmet as insignia; his potency, however, derives not from his own magical properties but from social readings of him (including his own) which come to seem increasingly problematic as the film goes on.

It is crucial for the film's purposes that the effect of Waldo's charisma should be dramatized, in the opening scene, through Scooter (Patrick Henderson), the little boy who fetches gasoline for Waldo's plane in return for "a free ride at the end of the day." It becomes clear in retrospect that Scooter's attitude to Waldo is very much Waldo's to Kessler (Bo Brundin): by incorporating the boy into the mechanics of the spectacle which creates the hero, Waldo regenerates in Scooter his own need for the charismatic father, and in so doing, Waldo achieves the Oedipal displacement characteristically associated with the wanderer's disruption of domesticity (compare, say, the effect on Young Charlie of that exemplary trickster figure Uncle Charlie in *Shadow of a Doubt* [1943]). While for Scooter's father (James N. Harrell) "an honest day's work is what I call special," Waldo is invested with the glamour of a moment in which the mastery of technology can appear not as work, but as magic. That the moment is as good as over is intimated in the dialogue: the show by which Scooter has been dazzled was "the best in over a year," and Waldo himself attributes the decline of barnstorming to the fact that "people have just got used to airplanes." At this stage, we're not yet aware of the full extent of the artifice involved in Waldo's performance—we know no more than Scooter that the Kessler story is false—and the withholding of information encourages us, if not to endorse Scooter's adulation, to expect at least a nostalgic lament, in the manner of the aging gunfighter cycle, for a form of heroism outstripped by history. We are invited to become involved in Waldo's own assessment of himself as a romantic icon, all the more substantial for the approaching triumph of the mundane.

The complicity is immediately disturbed by the introduction of Mary Beth (Susan Sarandon) in a manner which, at once, creates a parallel between her and Scooter and brings to full explicitness the theme of the trickster as a seducer in whose seductiveness guile is irreducibly an element. The image of flying itself, and the language through which Waldo appeals to romantic dissatisfaction with domesticity ("It was OK the day I got married, and I didn't much mind the day I first fell in love, but seeing the sky with the Great Waldo Pepper—that beats 'em all!"), are already implicitly erotic; furthermore, the scene in the cinema, in which Waldo, who has seen the film (*The Son of the Sheik* [1926]) before, captivates Mary Beth with his miraculous ability to anticipate Valentino's exploits correctly ("Know what I'd do if I was him?"), brings into focus the link among seduction, trickery, and self-dramatization as "the hero." It follows that the terms in which Axel (Bo Svenson) deflates the illusion ("He's been telling you stories and getting you drunk so's he can work his way with you") acquire a significance which extends far beyond the particular case. Waldo can only realize himself as the image he needs to be by exciting in others an intoxicated commitment to him as the real embodiment of the social myth of the hero; his self-confidence is directly contingent on the confidence trick. Scooter is the prototype of a succession of figures for whose own romantic intensities Waldo becomes the catalyst and who are appropriated as accessory figures in the elaborate mise-en-scène required for the enactment of Waldo's imagination.

The death of Mary Beth exactly halfway through the film effects as abrupt, unexpected, and audacious a shift of tone as the drowning of the child in *The Marrying Kind* (1952): nothing that has gone before prepares us for it, and its function, in radically preempting any further indulgence of Waldo, is to enforce a critical reassessment not only of the previous action but also of the nature of our investment in what Waldo represents. The sequence corresponds to that, near the beginning, in which Waldo has sabotaged the landing gear of Axel's plane, causing it to crash in the middle of a shallow lake. The tone there was comic and invited an amused complicity with the successful trickster, undisturbed by any sense of the pain or injury incurred by his victim. Waldo doesn't set out to kill Mary Beth or Ezra (Edward Herrmann)—on the contrary, he risks his own life to save them—but it is vital nonetheless that even if he is not the immediate agent of their destruction, it is a logical corollary of the same self-aggrandizing project which expresses itself, apropos of rivalry with Axel, in the claim that "this is my territory." Mary Beth's dream of becoming the "It Girl of the Skies" refers us directly to the cinema scene and to the commitment to the realization of romance which—if, obviously, given in the culture—Waldo has, in his own interests, encouraged. Ezra is testing out the plane in which Waldo aspires to perform, before Kessler does, "the last great stunt"—the outside loop. It is no part of the film's case against Waldo that he is knowingly vicious; indeed, to make him monstrous in the simple sense would be to confine an argument about an objective ideological function to an account of an aberrant individual. As Dillhoefer (Philip Bruns) puts it, "You're not a bad sort, Waldo, but you're dangerous. People die around you." The danger is a fact, not of particular wickedness, but of the acting out of a concept of "maleness" which is both romantically charismatic and, immediately, murderous. Waldo himself remains enclosed within the myth to the last: in the sequence following Mary Beth's death, he can still present himself to Newt (Geoffrey Lewis) as the guardian of romantic liberty ("You gonna license the clouds, the rain?"), and Ezra's fatal crash inspires him to project his own responsibility for it onto the watching crowd ("Goddamn vultures!"), which he vengefully proceeds to dive-bomb in another plane.

Waldo's relationship to Kessler is the crux of the film: if he seeks to appear as the hero to others, it is primarily because he needs the hero himself. For the mythical tale of the dog-fight doesn't involve beating Kessler—Waldo describes himself to Scooter as "the second-best flier in the world"—but being acknowledged by him as an equal. It is the need for the gesture of recognition ("Over Hürtgen Wood Ernst Kessler saluted me") which has been accorded, by some freak of fate, to another ("It should have been me!") which gives the myth its emotional intensity. It also implies, of course, the source of the intensity. Aviation, for Kessler as for Waldo, is at the service of a desire to simplify and idealize; flying facilitates the recovery of a sense of order and coherence which is felt to have existed in the past and which is very intimately bound up with confidence in the self and its potency. "Everything was in order: the world made total sense." The experience of "total sense," in Kessler's remark, is at one with the conviction that he and his adversaries are governed by a code of "courage, honor, and chivalry," the impersonality of which purges of egotism the struggle for prowess and victory. At the same time, the very brevity, purity, and intensity of the moment in which the self is distilled ("It seemed too little—like a cheat") gives to the act of combat the significance of a sexual consummation: indeed, the recovered sense of disinterested social and ethical allegiances (skill and honor) is conjoined, for both men, with an achieved erotic communion with a lost object.

In Kessler's case, the object is his first wife, Lola, after whom his plane is named: "They all left me, but Lola is the only one that I still seek out in clouds." For Waldo, the object is Kessler himself, and through Waldo's feeling for him, the film dramatizes with great subtlety and tact that essentially dialectical nature of the male Oedipus complex (analyzed by Freud in "The Ego and the Id") whereby the father becomes both identification figure and love object. The salute for which Waldo yearns is the sign that he has achieved union with Kessler in the sense both of becoming him and of coming with him: the astonishing final shots of Waldo's ecstasy suggest unmistakably an orgasmic release and fulfillment. If the film ends before his plane lands, and dissolves from his face to a monochrome photograph with the date of his death inscribed beneath it, it is because the consummation of his relationship with Kessler leaves him in an imaginary state in which nothing further is possible.

The concluding scene takes place on a Hollywood set where Kessler's life story is being filmed, and where the ironies of Waldo's position are brought into perfect focus. While his own emotional needs define him as the quintessential product of a society in which the heroic role is massively reproduced, Waldo appears to himself, in his disagreements with the director, Werfel (Roderick Cook), as a spokesman for authenticity against Hollywood's romantic falsification of history. At the same time, Hollywood provides the only condition in which his fantasy can be realized, and the contradiction is beautifully embodied in the moment when Waldo, watching rushes in a viewing room and reacting with incredulous contempt to the suggestion that a plane crash should be faked, suddenly realizes that the footage is a representation of his own fantasy scene. Leaving the room, he discovers Kessler's plane on the set before him. If Robert Altman's desperate attempts in *The Long Goodbye* (1973) to distance himself from the hero are so many symptoms of his helpless involvement with him, *The Great Waldo Pepper* is sufficiently in possession of its critique of the hero, and of Hollywood's part in his social viability, to avoid the slightest suggestion either of self-exonerating cynicism or of sentimental collusion.

The Other Side of Midnight (1981)

From the very outset, *The Other Side of Midnight* (1977) proposes the investigation of a woman's guilt ("Innocent or guilty, Noelle?") as the organizing principle of its dramatic world. The question is germane to melodrama, and not least to one of its most characteristic and durable narrative patterns: the tale of the innocent young woman lured into sexual transgression by an irresponsible seducer and subsequently visited with consequences—whether loss of social status, ostracism, loss of a child, or secrecy purchased at the cost of embitterment and rancorous obsession—from which the seducer is spared, temporarily or permanently, by virtue of his being a man with unimpeachable social credentials. Noelle Page (Marie-France Pisier) obviously relates to this type, which has its forbears in such heroines of Victorian low and high culture as those of *Way Down East* (1920) and *Tess of the d'Urbervilles*, *The Scarlet Letter*, and *Felix Holt*. The 1930s "confession" cycle in Hollywood offers innumerable variations, one of which—Robert Z. Leonard's *Susan Lenox* (1931)—strikingly anticipates *The Other Side of Midnight*'s theme of a woman who, abandoned (if for different reasons) by her lover, prostitutes herself in order to achieve a position of social power from which she can control his destiny and humiliate him.

In the literal sense, of course, Noelle is innocent, but this "answer," while crucially important—in that Constantin Demeris (Raf Vallone) is in a position to have her punished for a crime she did not commit—is subordinate to a rigorous critique of the terms in which the question is posed. The function of bourgeois law is to protect bourgeois property and the social relations which sustain it. The function of the language of bourgeois law is at once to universalize the social interests inscribed within it, which then appear as "the public interest" rather than the interests of particular groups and classes, and to extrapolate the action defined as criminal from its determinants: that is, to individualize it, so that it appears as a matter of personal moral responsibility. This double movement—the universalization of interests, the hypostasization of actions—transforms a real question as to the determinants of an action and the interests which constitute its illegality into a mystified one—"innocent or guilty?" A preference for the first question over the second implies neither sentimental charity nor moral quietism, and *The Other Side of Midnight*, eschewing facile "exoneration," is precisely concerned with the objective social forces acting on Noelle which lead her to behave in the way she does: social forces which both provide the conditions for her history and insist on reparation for it.

Noelle, as we first see her, has been subjected to two contradictory sets of injunctions, both originating in her family and, specifically, her father. On the one hand, "You are a princess—you are above the rest"; on the other, "You have beauty—it's your only weapon of survival." Each of these opposing principles fulfills needs of the father: respectively, the idealistic and the practical. His insistence that Noelle's "natural" rank is out of true with her social one allows him vicariously to transcend his own social position through her; she has been molded, as a result, as that type of frailty, vulnerability, and "innocence" which is (quite without her own volition) most inviting to exploitative advances and least able to cope with them. At the same time, he is quite willing to prostitute her to secure himself in a more material sense ("A few things to comfort me and your mother against whatever comes"), and he adjures her to pursue the same course ("End up in a yacht—in a villa!"). Both injunctions define Noelle in relation to men—romantically ("You are a princess" has its echo in Larry Douglas's [John Beck] "You're magnificent") and cynically (you get on by using sex)—and it is crucial for our understanding of her subsequent trajectory that these apparently distinct imperatives, whose continuity she acts out, are articulated at this early stage in sexual and class terms: in terms of women "succeeding" through men, and of the upward mobility of the petit bourgeoisie.

It is the class theme which establishes a parallel between Noelle and Demeris, just as the imbrication of class with patriarchal relations defines their fundamental asymmetry. The likeness and the dissimilarity are demonstrated with great precision in the extraordinary scene in which Noelle, having been invited by Demeris to a banquet, ostentatiously walks out in the middle of the self-aggrandizing monologue about his rise from humble origins with which Demeris has been regaling his guests. The incident generates a complex irony. Noelle is defying the proprieties of an occasion engineered to gratify Demeris's desire to dramatize his own authority before an audience rendered quiescent by having accepted his hospitality; she refuses, with insolent publicity, the role of mirror for the male ego, and we refer her gesture to the scene in which she has waited, in vain, at Victor's for the meal with Larry that will never take place. At the same time, the process of unscrupulous self-advancement that Demeris is describing ("I learned quickly to estimate the odds against me—and I beat them") is analogous to hers. Demeris, though, holds his power at his own discretion; Noelle's is achieved by proxy—as a "mistress"—and the motif of the three invitations, only two of which Noelle can refuse with impunity, indicates clearly enough that the efficacy of sex as a weapon is strictly curtailed by conventions imposed by the male. Noelle can only withhold her labor and her deference up to a certain point—the point at which the patriarchal nature of capitalist social relations determines different points of access to one social hierarchy.

If Noelle has been prepared to experience her affair with Larry as the discovery of her own authenticity, Larry feels it as another conquest: "He's already shot down more girls than he'll ever shoot down German pilots." For Noelle, the relationship is definitive; what it means for Larry is embodied in the glib, disarming seducer's routine ("This is the boy, that's the girl—where will it all end?") which is later recycled for Catherine Douglas (Susan Sarandon). Noelle's revenge takes the form of accommodating herself to power structures of patriarchal sexual relations with one man in order to invert them with another. Significantly, her first move is to "ground" Larry; given the link which the film has already set up between potency in the air and Don Juanism, the metaphorical implications of Larry's unemployment make themselves felt. Noelle appropriates the phallus: from now on, Larry can only get up in the air as her employee—"Be always on your best behavior, know your place, be available when I want you."

But the mere fact that only a reversal of roles has taken place is sufficient to remind us that the new relationship is a determinate product of the institutions which it seems to displace. Noelle continues to define herself in terms of her consuming desire for Larry ("If I could do without you, I would"): romantic self-surrender has been transformed into an obsessional need to overpower and master, but Noelle's existence remains absolutely contingent on him. Analogously, the condition of this (in any case, partial and compromised) disturbance of sexual roles is a curiously double-edged relation to Demeris, in which Noelle appears, as regards Larry, in Demeris's position of class and sexual oppressor, while becoming an accomplice in her own oppression as regards Demeris himself. For the only way in which she can acquire exclusive rights in Larry is by being owned in her turn by a patriarchal figure who defines himself as the Old Testament God to the power of "n" ("a head for an eye, and a heart for a tooth"). This complex network of correspondences is neatly summed up in the remark "You have bought the air," addressed to Noelle by the private detective she has hired to track Larry down: her power is real, but it is Demeris's both in the sense that she has used his money and that in using it, she has become like him.

The Noelle-Larry-Demeris triangle, then, is eminently a capitalist structure, and Noelle's romantic love is at once a transgression and an embodiment of principles of ownership and possession. For Noelle herself, it is, very self-consciously, romantic and grand: the line from her film script ("In the name of love I lived, and in the name of love I died") clearly expresses her own sentiment and suggests to the spectator the extent to which the objectively oppressive function, for women, of "love" of this kind has become a lived experience of self-realization at a heroic pitch. Noelle goes to her death with the rhetorical self-absorption of the Senecan hero, feeling defeat as victory through the medium of a romanticism so intense that it has transcended its need for an object; she does not notice, waiting in her cell, the gunfire that signals Larry's execution, which cannot now disturb her preparations to assume in imagination the role of wife (she is dressed in bridal white) that she's earlier told Larry she has earned. The common trope which associates the perfect consummation of romantic love with annihilation points to the fact that it is supremely in death that the simultaneously narcissistic and acquisitive nature of passion—the desire at once to have completely and to be completely the object of desire—can be satisfied.

It is of fundamental significance that Noelle's desire for Larry enlists her in the destruction of another woman, Catherine, who is oppressed by the very same structures of patriarchal power as she is. Similarly, of course, at the end of the film, Catherine's revenge on Larry lures her into complicity with the destruction of Noelle—depicted in the extraordinary courtroom scene in which all the men in the film gather together as Noelle's accusers to bring down upon her the retribution of patriarchal law—the point of the final scene (set, ironically, in a convent) being to suggest that Catherine has collaborated with Demeris in the pretense that she has been drowned. It is in this context that the pertinence of the film's complex narrative structure becomes clear: the intercutting of the two narratives dramatizes the process whereby two women who are potentially united in terms of their common experience of oppression are, in fact, mobilized against each other and for, though in different ways, the patriarchal-capitalist status quo. Noelle's pivotal position in the dramatic world can be gauged by pointing out that she partakes of both Demeris and Catherine and acts out the contradictory logic of a social position so defined.

But if the narrative parallels Noelle and Catherine, it also contrasts them, and given the nature of the contrast, the film's handling of Catherine's development becomes distinctly problematic. For the Catherine of the early scenes is a very different character from Noelle: her handling of the taxi driver on her arrival in Washington; her active pursuit of Bill Fraser (Clu Gulager) and the bluntly expressed disappointment ("Shit!") with which she greets his failure to respond; her negotiation of the filmmaking sessions and of Larry's attempts, first to embarrass her and then to pick her up—all display a resilience, self-sufficiency, and self-confidence which have no equivalent in her counterpart. It is significant, then, that the film has to resort to an abrupt ellipsis in order to shift her into alcoholic degeneration, and the brilliance with which Susan Sarandon handles the transition (hers is perhaps the finest in a series of exemplary performances) doesn't conceal the fact that it is not dramatized but imposed, under cover of an aside in the dialogue about the number of women who developed a "drinking problem" during their husbands' absence in the war. Catherine's own remark to Larry that "I knew you were lying, but I didn't care because I loved you" doesn't help matters: we haven't been shown (as we have with Noelle) how or why she came to love him, and the very insistence with which the film seeks to justify the process only reinforces our sense of its tenuous and contrived connection to the character initially created. The arbitrariness here, and the connotations of "fate" or "predestination" which accrue to Demeris through his isolated appearances at an early stage in both narratives before he has actually become involved with either woman, invite the damaging criticism that the film's inevitability is constructed by sleight of hand and that Catherine's subordination to Larry, and Demeris's final triumph, have been pre-given in a way which involves the suppression of the potential resistance that Catherine embodies. The dramatization of the oppression of women, as is so often the case in even the most distinguished melodramas, builds in the impossibility of the struggle against it, so that patriarchal relations seem at once intolerable and mysteriously impermeable and women are compelled to assume the role of "victim." This clearly limits the film's achievement, but it doesn't outweigh or invalidate its substantial insights, or diminish one's gratitude for it at a moment when *Urban Cowboy* (1980), *Honeysuckle Rose* (1980), and the rest are setting the tone for a systematic anti-feminist reaction.

Part Three
European Cinema

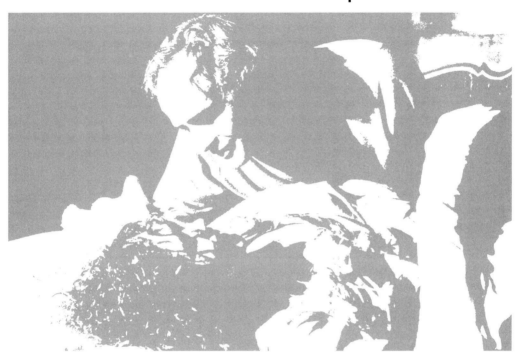

Sexuality and Power, or the Two Others (1977–1978)

In the context of the coding of "masculinity" prevalent in Western culture—the association of biological maleness with particular codes of behavior and response and particular conventions governing the thinking and presentation of self—male homosexuality can be variously conceived ideologically. It can become the repository of "bad" maleness, whereby unacceptable extremes of attributes felt to be characteristically masculine (sexual aggressiveness, the power drive) or of behavior culturally condoned for men (promiscuity—that is, nonmonogamous relationships) can be projected outward onto a figure and denounced. This image produces, ultimately, the popular belief that every member of the Nazi Party was gay, and that fascism and gayness are virtually synonymous. The image is, clearly, intimately involved with repression. Hence, the insistence in popular culture with which gay figures appear in connection with supremely valued male friendships, so that the charge can be definitively placed: the threat of the gay character consists in the sense either that he retains, toward men, predatory emotions taken as given in attitudes of men toward women (he's after *you*), or that he shares with women "natural" weaknesses and shortcomings which render gay men unfit for the high demands of comradeship (they are inclined to be treacherous or unreliable *in extremis*, unable to take hardship, longing for comfort, swayed by self-interest).

Thus, the gay man as a figure of menace (for example, fascist) retains the phallus, his possession of which threatens the castration of the straight man (he wants to take me as his object, use me like a woman). Alternatively, the homosexual may be conceived as castrated (no better than a woman) and can become, with the removal of the threat to possession of the phallus, a figure of comedy: attitudes here range between tolerant amusement (gay men are charming, entertaining, epigrammatic) to that derision which, in continuing to imply a sense of menace, testifies to that obstinacy with which the gay figure oscillates between being simply phallic and castrating or simply castrated and insists on dwelling in some unsignposted no-man's-land between the two. The connections between this schematic typology and a typology of women is crucial—the castrating figure who endangers ideological boundaries opposed to the castrated figure who can be accommodated within them—and the recuperable gay man tends to be placed within contexts regarded as the province of women (fashion, hairdressing, forms of "excessive" civilization)—outside the home, but ideologically safe.

The recent appearance of *Drum* (1976), the disreputable sequel to *Mandingo* (1975), provides a useful point of reference. Steve Carver's film is primarily interesting in that the impulse to propitiate the black man is balanced by the necessity of reconfirming the ideological confidence of the white man, both projects converging in the loading onto homosexuals of the sense of threat which can no longer be attached safely to Negroes. Thus, the guilt of white oppression is carefully shifted from Hammond Maxwell (Warren Oates), who is portrayed as endearingly bewildered and well-meaning, to the vicious, European, aristocratic gay man.

The axis of that shift is the question of castration. Maxwell does not punish his slaves with castration; the homosexual does, and when his advances to Drum (Ken Norton) are refused in disgust, he responds by attempting to have him castrated. At the climax of the film, Drum castrates the homosexual, in a moment of supreme catharsis for whites and blacks alike, the status quo affirmed through an action which provides vicarious revenge for one-half of the audience and self-absolution for the other. Similarly, while Maxwell is associated simultaneously with a lack of culture (his treatment of his slaves is assimilated to a sort of "natural innocence") and domination by conniving women (the prudish "lady" who aspires to his hand and his purse and who is intent on "sivilizing" him; the lascivious daughter whose unquenchable desire for black men is the root of the final apocalypse), the homosexual is associated with effete salon culture (un-Americanness) and with power relationships (his attempt to seduce Drum, his brutality toward his white lover). It becomes evident here that the presentation of gayness cannot be considered as an isolated phenomenon; it is inseparable from the whole of the film as ideological construct. Thus, for example, the film's self-image as pro-black statement coexists with its use of Ken Norton as sex object and its exploitation of the archetypal Western fascination with/fear of the black man as an embodiment of libido. The narrative premise (Drum as slave and object of desire) places Drum in that situation of enforced passivity as object for "the active controllers of the look," which Laura Mulvey has analyzed in images of women, and permits the identification of white oppression with the expression of desire by women and homosexuals. Drum-as-slave means, essentially, Drum feminized, deprived of the phallus (his place as man), reduced to the status of "a sign which is being exchanged in patriarchal culture," threatened with castration. (Johnston, "Film Practice," 321) The "natural" sexual paradigm is subverted, the man is unmanned, and the phallus appears in the place where it cannot be except as horror (see, for example, *The Exorcist* [1973], where the threat of the castrating woman and the threat of gayness again coincide, more explicitly in the novel than in the film); the dreadfulness of the male homosexual resides in the fact that he both possesses a penis and yet remains "that which is not male." (322) Accordingly, the moment of Drum's self-liberation, the moment at which he becomes the hero, is the moment at which he castrates the homosexual.

The film is concerned not with the horror of slavery, but with the horror of patriarchy disintegrating, and it consistently reaffirms a classical image of maleness, in terms both of what is desired (Drum/Norton's "beautiful body") and of what is done. It is significant here that Drum's male gayness is balanced by the brothel madame: also refined/European; also associated with castration (the amazing moment in the dinner party sequence in which in reply to the homosexual's recommendation of castration for recalcitrant slaves, she proposes a toast to castration "for all men"); also associated with gayness (her relationship with her black maid). Here, however, crucially, the gayness is presented positively, the apparent liberalism serving only to set woman more firmly in her place. The film can only present female gayness without disgust because (a) both women—Drum's real and his surrogate mother, respectively—are devoted to the best interests of the film's supreme embodiment of "maleness"; (b) the relationship does not endanger the patriarchal order—the madame, after all, serves it by prostituting other women; (c) the madame is pointedly dissociated from and hostile to the male homosexual, so that any sense of shared ideological oppression is voided; (d) women being creatures of the flesh anyway, emotional attachments can be allowed physical expression, although true male companionship exists on a higher, spiritual plane; and (e) the madame's "Europeanness" relates her to a type of exotic pansexualism (Greta Garbo, Marlene Dietrich) whose sexual charge is defined by an aura of "masculinity." It is the moment at which the madame becomes a threat to men, through the alarming subversiveness of her toast, which calls down the wrath of God upon her in the final holocaust.

The ideology of male friendship suggests an attempt to rewrite "homosexual" as "homospiritual." It represses, or places, women and sexuality in the same movement and is typically dualistic (women, if at all, for the body; men for the free spirit), permitting physical contact between men only in variously sublimated forms (shared labor, spectator sports, communal drinking, the "manly" professions). Indeed, the attitude to women defined by the macho code of masculinity is inseparable from the need to disavow bisexuality: it is originally self-repressive. Clearly, the ideology is capable of various complex permutations. Consider, for example, the work of Joseph Conrad. It is possible in *Victory* to trace a direct relationship among the values embodied in male comradeship, the presentation of the "feminine creature" in white whom Heyst first glimpses amid the "cruel, sensual, and repulsive" spectacle of the ladies' orchestra, Heyst's "infernal mistrust of all life," and the appearance—as the novel's supreme representative of evil—of "plain Mr. Jones," whose gayness is coded as violent misogyny (that is, he does not idealize Woman) and the power drive. A similar complex of associations can be discerned in, say, *Heart of Darkness*, in which gayness does not figure at the level of narrative except, momentarily and ambiguously, through the harlequin ("It isn't what you thinks"). Mr. Jones and Mr. Kurtz share identical imagery and connotations (extreme potency, extreme physical "length" and emaciation, deathliness, ghostliness, control of the savage, a capacity to elicit unquestioning loyalty, whiteness), and both are closely linked to the male protagonist. The explicit emergence of homosexuality, however, brings with it the emphasis on Mr. Jones's willful, self-conscious delight in evil; the attempt to allegorize him ("I am a sort of fate"); and the full elaboration—in one of the most disastrous portrayals of a woman in prose fiction—of the Feminine as Redeemer, Conrad's obsessively repeated characterization of Mr. Jones as a "cadaverous specter" emerging as a desperate attempt to prevent the reader from noticing that all the vitality in the novel has been concentrated in the repressed. The development is latent in *Heart of Darkness*: Marlow's assertion that "women are always out of it"; the distinction between the Intended, that "soul as translucently pure as a cliff of crystal" whose "mature capacity for fidelity" must be based on ignorance, and Marlow, whose "loyalty to the specter of my choice" is based on self-knowledge and becomes totally debilitating; Mr. Kurtz's "unspeakable rites" and the association of energy with the powers of darkness—all become significant as reaction-formations of relationships between men in which sexuality is repressed. One might compare here the opposition between Nina and the vampire in *Nosferatu* (1922).

It is primarily through American culture, however, that the concept of "a world without women" has become operative ideologically in contemporary Western society. Sam Peckinpah's *Cross of Iron* (1977) suggests, initially, an attempt to foreground the homosexuality implicit in it (consider the intercutting of the birthday party with Stransky's discovery of the two gay soldiers), and it is possible to isolate the exact moment at which the film reneges on the analysis potential for it: the moment in the hospital sequence where Steiner (James Coburn) refuses to answer Eva's (Senta Berger) accusation that he is returning to the front because he is afraid of what he will be without war. His silence raises two related problems for the film: the search for alternatives has been, implicitly, refused (it is stressed that Steiner loathes the institution of which he is a part), and the form of that refusal is the flight from woman (significantly named) for a type of male comradeship ("I've missed you!") whose erotic component must be vigorously suppressed. Narratively, the disavowal of sexuality and the rejection of change are inseparable and produce, together, that "inevitable" movement toward closure in the film's second half: the embracing of a despair which is offered as "existential predicament" but which is, in fact, structured by the possibilities the film will not admit.

The notorious violence of Peckinpah's films can be thought of in these terms, the violence again offered in terms of a "human condition" (Peckinpah's allegiance to Robert Ardrey) or cosmic persecution ("God is a sadist, and he doesn't even know it"—the God Herman Melville uses to "place" Claggart in *Billy Budd*) but coming over repeatedly as the other term of a repressed sexuality for which "the Nature of Things" functions as an alibi. The sexual charge binding Steiner's platoon returns as "community through violence," as the loyalty, efficiency, and skill of institutionalized thuggery ("Good kill"), the platoon being possible, by definition, only within the detested institution yet uncontaminated by it—somehow hermetic, the last "good place." In Steiner's choice of the men, and in the necessity of desexualizing that choice, the violence is guaranteed to be sexualized in the slow motion which celebrates it, in the sensual massacres of writhing limbs and tormented bodies, coming in blood. The progressive stultification of Peckinpah's work—the ideological closedness which gives, logically, the end of *Cross of Iron:* maniacal laughter subsiding into the weary apathy of "Oh, shit!"—relates interestingly to the impossibility of development within the films of Howard Hawks, development being contingent in both cases on taking male relationships beyond a certain point.

The denial of gayness in *Cross of Iron* is interesting and important.

a. While all the characters in the film are German, those who are presented in any degree positively or sympathetically are played by American or English actors, and the three bad Germans—a Nazi, a Junker aristocrat, a homosexual—are played by German or Austrian actors. The Nazi has his cock bitten off by a woman and is used as a sort of scapegoat to appease a sense of war guilt and guilt toward women ("Now we're even!"), the whole scene being offered with an air of "paying one's dues." The homosexual is triumphantly mown down with a machine gun in slow motion (identically, Steiner's self-consummation/self-repression) in a moment which rhymes exactly with Norton's revenge in *Drum*. The aristocrat, who has been thoroughly unmanly throughout, is ritualistically humiliated in the final scene where he proves to be unable to handle his gun. Thus, the three "other" figures, all of whom are linked thematically—consider the extraordinary shot in which the homosexual and his boyfriend are introduced, framed by a doorway (that is, immediately and, necessarily, *outside*) and by a mirror, as Stransky's reflection—are castrated, literally or symbolically, leaving Steiner holding the gun which, although it can do him little good, he must nevertheless retain, given Peckinpah's allegiance to the American tradition of individualist anarchism which refuses both existing societies and the imagination of others. Similarly, all three characters are treacherous, hypocritical, and unreliable; two, including the homosexual, belong to the hated officer class; the homosexual is flawed, additionally, by a longing for luxury, his Achilles heel being his desire to return to the decadent softness of life in Biarritz.

b. It is implied that the gay relationship is emotionally trivial and nonreciprocal ("I do what I am ordered"), both elements being inextricably bound up with the conceptualization of gayness, in its "dangerous" manifestations, as almost emblematic of the will-to-power.

While it is obvious that the bourgeois American "revolution" and the Marxist-Leninist Russian revolution are phenomena of a completely different order, it is significant, precisely because of the difference, that a limited but illuminating analogy appears between Sergei Eisenstein on the one hand and Melville and Walt Whitman on the other (quite apart from the influence of the American writers on Eisenstein's later theoretical work, notably the essay on "Color and Meaning," which takes as epigraph a line from a poem in *Leaves of Grass*). All three, in their early work (Melville up to *Moby Dick*; Eisenstein up to *Alexander Nevsky* [1938]), establish themselves very self-consciously as the mythologists of a new order envisaged primarily in terms of spiritual and physical communion between men. Whitman proclaimed and celebrated his gayness: in Melville and Eisenstein, its expression is suppressed or sublimated for various reasons (in Eisenstein's case, one should note that homosexuality was "forbidden" by the Soviet government in 1935). Thus, for example, while the opening chapters of *Moby Dick* present one of the most charming and intimate images of gay love yet achieved (within obvious ideological limitations—sex roles are largely retained, Ishmael becoming the girl from the East), and while the gay imagery, here and throughout the novel, is staggeringly explicit, Melville invariably insists on denying the presence of sexuality ("the unbecomingness of his hugging a fellow male in that matrimonial sort of style" [*Moby Dick*, 33–34]), and whenever gayness surfaces explicitly, it is made monstrous, unnameable except through euphemism ("what some sailors become after years at sea"). For all three artists, women are marginal, excluded, or present only in the most perfunctory and unsatisfactory of stereotypes: consider, for example, the business of the rival lovers in *Alexander Nevsky*, and notably the extraordinary scene in the aftermath of the Battle on the Ice, where the erotic/emotional commitment is transferred to the relationship between the two men.

With the failure of the myth, both Eisenstein and Melville create last works in which a simpleminded innocent (Vladimir, Billy Budd) is destroyed by a homosexual monster (Ivan, Claggart). *Billy Budd*, written some five or six years before the appearance of Freud's early work (and first published thirty years later, roughly contemporaneously with the first English translations of Freud), already makes, implicitly, the psychoanalytic reading of Desire and the Law, of the process of repression, and the novel's supreme interest lies largely in its status as one of those boundary works in which opposed structures of argument and explanation (in this case, Freudian and pre-Freudian psychologies) are simultaneously present in a state of mutual tension. Throughout the first half of *Billy Budd*, Melville worries away repeatedly at the problem of explaining Claggart and arrives, finally, at a simple and, in ideological terms, momentous alternative: Claggart "would have loved Billy but for Fate or ban." (88) Melville opts for Fate, the concept of socially determined sexual repression (which still remains a presence in the text) being held in abeyance to that of a universe governed by a principle of evil (or at least, the arbitrary) in which Claggart becomes, like the scorpion, a "natural monster," "for whom the Creator alone is responsible." (78) In Eisenstein's *Ivan the Terrible* (1944), as I shall attempt to argue later, the exploration which Melville cannot yet make is made through procedures which enact, in the same movement, a deconstruction of the mythology of *October* (1928).*

The revolution of *October* is a phallic revolution, a tremendous upsurge of male energy. Consider, for example, the opening sequence of the film (the demolition of the statue of the tsar) in the light of the recurrent statue motif which reaches full expression in the gods sequence and which depends on interweaving connotations of religion, militarism, capitalism, and sexuality. Crucial here is the Marxist theory of surplus use value and the suggestion that, under capitalism, commodities tend to become fetishized, the ultimate fetishes being gold and silver, which become "independent incarnations . . . of the social character of wealth." (Marx, *Capital*, 573) Thus, the golden Baroque Christ of the gods sequence, whose radiating beams "rhyme" with the radiating arms of the Indian idol, becomes the supreme capitalist fetish—a commodity occulted with mystical power (Marx's "gold-chrysalis") and constituting, as such, an emblem of state oppression (the union of monarchy and church). The force of the whole sequence, indeed, depends on its two-way reference: religion is secular, and secular power is religious/superstitious. Simultaneously, the imagery invokes the Freudian concept of fetishism: the fetish as substitute for the sexual object (and retaining, in Freud, its totemic significance). The last of the idols is linked to its predecessors not only by rhymes of shape, texture, volume (that is, affectively) but also by its complete elaboration of the intellectual dominant of the sequence, its jerkily swinging arms suggesting at once artifice, toy (childishness), and impotent phallus. The connotations here play back to the Kerensky/Napoleon and Kerensky/peacock sequences (plaster statues, crystal goblets, decanters, toy soldiers, chess pieces—again, multiply coded in terms of the religion/militarism/capitalism/sexuality complex which is fully reconstituted in the image of Kerensky crowning the chess piece) and forward to the images of "Country" (medals, epaulettes, regalia). The sequence culminates in the triumphant reinstatement of the original fetish object—the tsar's statue becomes erect again.

The statue motif is grounded in the antinomy between dead, stony capitalist monuments and the vital potency of the Bolsheviks, already implied in the opening shots of the film. The statue of the tsar, segmented by the montage into a set of fetishes (crown, scepter, orb), is

---

* *October* (aka *Ten Days That Shook the World*) was codirected by Grigori Aleksandrov.

juxtaposed, as it is torn down/castrated by the masses, with a set of phallic images which establish very precisely the connotations of the revolution: (a) Ropes being pulled taut—the destruction of the old order. (b) A host of Bolshevik men raising their rifles in the air. The rifle, as both mechanism (metal) and potent fetish (the fire in the tube), becomes a crucial Bolshevik emblem, and the narrative is repeatedly punctuated by these enthusiastic communal erections. (c) Scythes being raised into the air—ambiguously (1) the capacity to make the land fertile, to bring forth plenty from Mother Russia, and (2) a death/time image—both echoing rifle and ropes and suggesting the harvest of time, the fulfillment of natural/material process.

The extraordinary ideological ambiguity of Eisenstein's position as mythologist can be gauged, in this context, by the depiction of the arrival of Lenin at the climax of the "Waiting" sequence, in which "the whole repertoire of the bourgeois myths" (Barthes, *Mythologies,* 147), particularly the religious myths crucial to the anticapitalist/imperialist imagery, is reactivated to image Lenin as the creating Logos—the potent male deity whose word (the banner) and breath (his appearance is accompanied by tumultuous winds) animate the silent, motionless, male crowd. The gradations of Lenin's emergence (we see his effect on the crowd and the wind-tossed, screen-filling banner before we see his figure) evoke Eisenstein's description of the introduction of Peter the Great in Pushkin's *Poltava* ("Word and Image," 49–55), and the device recurs in the coronation scene which opens *Ivan the Terrible.* The exclusion of women from the unleashing of Lenin's energy is emphasized contextually—we have just seen the women, also silent and motionless, waiting in bread queues in falling snow—and *October,* like Eisenstein's *Potemkin* (1925), celebrates the revolution as an emanation of male vitality which makes possible the joyful expression of male unity and comradeship.

This preoccupation emerges early—in the scene in the trenches with the exchange of hats—and is expressed most beautifully in the reconciliation of the Bolsheviks and the Savage Division, in which an initial antagonism is dissolved through personal contact and the gift of the word which releases a unity already implicit ("the Bolshevik leaflet spoke their language"). The gift is returned by the Cossacks in the form of a dance which is transformed by the montage into a hymn to Whitman's "merging" (men and languages "one under their diversities"), Eisenstein intercutting a Bolshevik and a Cossack dancer with increasing rapidity until it is almost impossible to distinguish between them. The dance, that is, becomes a form of asexual intercourse. One must note here that it is predominantly, though not exclusively, a particular image of male beauty which Eisenstein celebrates—the beauty of heterosexual "virility" variously embodied in the swarthy, menacing darkness of the Cossacks (consider the extraordinary sensuousness of the sword partly unsheathed from its scabbard) and the muscular, blond ruggedness of the agitprop posters, and in the mutineers in *Potemkin* and the Kronstadt sailor in *October* whose imposing massiveness (in low-angle close-up) bars the way to the twittering, bourgeois old men and women (shot from above).

In *October,* this goes with an extreme hatred for and revulsion from women, who insofar as they are allowed any active part in the narrative, are associated exclusively with the forces of reaction. (The obvious exceptions—the women of the bread queues; the girl of the bridges sequence—relate directly to traditional stereotypes of bourgeois ideology and are conspicuous by their passivity: wives and mothers waiting at home, the dead blonde girl and her white

Lenin appears before the crowd in *October*. Personal collection of the editor.

horse as emblems of violated purity. They are coded for ahistorical, symbolic meanings and excluded from the process of the revolution.) The libido repressed from the male relationships is imposed on the other (the feminine) and returns as threat, with consequences which extend far beyond "images of women" and make themselves felt at every level of meaning.[1]

Consider, for example, the murder of the male Bolshevik demonstrator by the bourgeois women which immediately precedes the Raising of the Bridges. The first two shots of the sequence are (a) Medium shot of the demonstrator, clutching a banner. Behind him, in

284

extreme long shot, is the statue of an Egyptian sphinx. (b) The left of the frame is entirely filled by an open parasol, its owner concealed behind it. The man with the banner enters the frame from behind it in medium long shot.

The sphinx introduces the Egyptian variant of the statue motif, dominant in the bridges sequence and intermittently recurrent thereafter, Egypt clearly suggesting repressive, totalitarian, royalist power at its extreme (the Pharoah as god). The sphinx did not become exclusively female until its absorption into Mediterranean mythology, but its presence here, towering behind the doomed Bolshevik, evokes not only the complex of connotations already suggested (and already heavily loaded sexually) but also that blurring of the human into the bestial which is immediately transferred to the women. The play of forms in the second shot (open parasol—material stretched taut on a round frame—against banner—material limp on a staff) establishes a sexual symbolism which is, in the development, partially confirmed and partially reversed: the parasol eliminates space and dwarfs the man, overwhelming him spatially in anticipation of the subsequent onslaught and suggesting an engulfing vagina. At the same time, the women become phallic monsters, jabbing at the man's naked torso with *furled* parasols and castrating him (one of them stamps on the shaft of the banner, breaking it) in a scene which, with its dominant water imagery (horse, man, banner, pamphlets, all lost, in turn, to the current of the river), directly evokes the murder of Pentheus by the Bacchae. Significantly, Eisenstein links the scene, inversely, to the male camaraderie of the trenches through the use of hats, the murder being characterized by the flashing white plumes of the women's bonnets (juxtaposed, in the montage, with the whiteness of the horse and the long, uncovered blonde tresses of the girl). Similarly, the woman in the boat with the tsarist officer joins in the attack when her lover's cap is knocked off by the Bolshevik. The editing here is crucial: (a) Woman stamping on the banner in triumph, breaking it. (b) Grimacing tsarist soldier crouched over a machine gun, firing out of frame left. (c) Long shot of the approaching carriage as the horse collapses and skids forward onto the bridge. The symbolic nexus here (castrating woman with bared teeth; firing soldier with bared teeth; massacre of the innocents; violent tsarist oppression) is contained within, and defined by, imagery of erection and collapse, the rising bridges, rampant women, and impassive, monumental faces intercut with the dying fall of the revolution. The bridges sequence is followed by the procession of manacled, enervated Bolshevik prisoners, mocked in their passage through the streets by an old man and a woman.

The imagery here can be connected with other statements of the statue motif: that, for example, involving the figures and connotations of nymphs and angels, where the tsarist-Christian faction again becomes inseparable from a dangerous blurring of gender roles. The danger is Janus-faced: reactionary men are turned into women (impotent/castrated), reactionary women into men. Hence, in the first instance, the cut-in shots of female harpists are used to characterize the Mensheviks and to identify them with the provisional government and the tsarists (the three are more or less inseparable in the film): the image rhymes with the shot of the old cabinet minister, framed beyond a pane of glass on which a lyre has been engraved, who is pretending to strum it with his fingers. The effeminacy/castration theme is fully elaborated through Kerensky in his collection of phallus substitutes and his limousine with its nymph-like figurehead. He is first seen, after the peacock sequence (Eisenstein cutting from a shot of the peacock's backside to the palace doors opening for Kerensky to go in), lounging in the empress's bedroom where later, after his favorite fetish, the Napoleon statue, has been broken, he throws himself onto the cushions of a sofa, ass in the air. Eisenstein cannot resist repeating the backside joke, and Kerensky is juxtaposed with a row of horses' asses in the imperial stables.

Conversely, the bourgeois harpies of the bridges sequence are transmuted, in the second half of the film, into the members of the Women's Death Battalion; it is at this point, crucially, that a fascinating incoherence emerges within the film's imagery. Once more, the statue motif provides a starting point, this time in its "classical Greek" variant. During the surrounding of the Winter Palace, there is a sequence of four shots in which a huge, mock-classical statue of a seated woman is, increasingly, festooned with the figures of male Bolsheviks, motionless in heroic postures, their rifles erect, the sequence taking its tone from the first shot of one man sitting on the statue's shoulder, the bayonet of his rifle jutting out across the woman's throat. This passage can be juxtaposed with the intercutting of the Women's Death Battalion guarding the barricades around the palace and the statue of a standing Grecian female looking out over the river, silhouetted against the skyline. In the second shot sequence, the statue is being used positively: woman-as-soldier is grotesque by virtue of her deviation from the image of classical femininity which the statue embodies, and to which the rhetoric of the composition gives an imposing majesty and grandeur. Similar dislocations emerge at each appearance of the Women's Death Battalion, but one can single out, for the present purpose, two instances.

a. The arrival of the women in the winter palace. We are shown classical statues hung with army greatcoats, bottles, muskets, and canteens. The women proceed to occupy the tsar's billiards room, and the imagery suddenly acquires an almost hysterical intensity. A bra is draped over a rack of phallic cues; a thin woman stretches scrawny shoulder blades; a fat woman leans back on a table revealing a hairy armpit; shiny faces are dabbed with powder puffs; two women in uniform dance together, while two others look on exchanging remarks which need no title to elucidate them. The sequence ends in a direct cut to the nymph-figurehead of Kerensky's Rolls Royce. What is most interesting here is the extraordinary incoherence precipitated by Eisenstein's undisguised revulsion: the women are, after all, the last people on earth one would ever expect to see using a powder puff. The imagery depends on the sense that they are desecrating the palace; that they are monstrous because they are like women, biologically (the vagina-armpit) and ideologically (the powder puffs); that they are monstrous because they are *not* like women (their physique, their clothing, the hint of lesbianism); and that they are primarily monstrous because their nakedness (the uncovering of the body for the only time in the film) unleashes the return of the sexuality repressed in the male relationships. The sense of sexual confusion is crystallized in the moment at which the two male Bolsheviks, unable to decide whether the woman above them on the barricades is male or female, settle for the safe neutrality of "friend," any latent hint of *human* community firmly placed by the woman's reaction (scorn) and the playing of the scene as comedy at her expense.

b. The use of Auguste Rodin's "Spring" and "The First Steps." While gayness only becomes explicit in *October* through physical contact between the women, in order to be degraded (compare the token gay male so vital for the male-duo/road movie), the two statues are used to reinforce the conviction of "woman's place" endangered by the Women's Death Battalion. As before, the ideological coherence of the statue motif is fractured. Each Rodin statue is both a supreme bourgeois work of art and a supreme expression of the ideology of exclusive, heterosexual passion which long precedes the bourgeoisie and which is (has been), like the ideology of motherhood embodied in "The First Steps," essentially inseparable from the "givens" of Nature. The solitary communion of the female soldier with the Rodin, in which her yearning (for man) increasingly enforces a sense of her own "unnaturalness," is immediately followed by the surrender of one of the women's detachments and immediately preceded by, and intercut with, shots of the old man pretending to strum the lyre—a juxtaposition which, in the unfathomable vagueness of its meaning, testifies sufficiently to the radical disruptiveness of the women's presence in the film. Two attitudes toward "culture"—as a standard from which the woman has deviated; as a token of the old man's insulation and irresponsibility (shooting has just broken out outside)—exist, intractably, side by side.

The themes and images I have been considering culminate in the sequence, at the end of the film, in which a group of male Bolsheviks, led by one of the Kronstadt sailors, ransack the tsarina's bedroom, presented here as the sanctum sanctorum of bourgeois/royalist privilege and the supreme emblem of its oppressiveness. The scene functions on several levels. (a) It is an extended metaphor-cum-euphemism for the massacre of the Romanovs which, obviously, cannot be shown. (b) It suggests the symbolic murder of repressive parent-figures, a reading which becomes important in light of the use of the child in the last shots of the film. (c) The room is a vast clutter of fetish objects—Christian (altar, icons of saints, Christ, and the Madonna), bourgeois/royalist (ornaments, knickknacks), personal (the photograph of Nicholas, with the imperial eagle emblazoned across his jacket)—and represents the final, most complete statement of the royalism/capitalism/religion/fetish complex, simultaneously trivial (the oppressive institutions in microcosm) and supremely pernicious (emblems of the oppressive institutions as the "culture" and luxury of privileged individuals). (d) The triumph of the phallic revolution is imaged as the symbolic violation/dismemberment of the female body. Two shot sequences are crucial here, and must be examined in detail.

The first relates directly to the Women's Death Battalion, several members of which have fled to the bedroom at the beginning of the scene and hide in an alcove when they hear the Bolsheviks approaching. The men burst in and start smashing up the room, leaping on the bed and jabbing underneath it with bayonets. Then comes (a) a slow-motion shot of a bayonet ripping open the mattress; (b) two of the women cling together in terror, wincing as if in pain; and (c) the mattress is impaled on the end of the bayonet, hanging down in two folds like a woman's breasts. Just as in the winter palace scenes the film attempts to associate the Women's Death Battalion with both effete, bourgeois womanhood (powder puffs) and a betrayal of womanhood, so here, through shot (b)—the fulcrum of the series—the women-soldiers and the tsarina are subjected simultaneously to the revenge of the phallus-as-bayonet, to which the use of slow motion in shots (a) and (c) gives an appalling sensuousness. Significantly, the women, who up to this point have been shown to be fearless, are reduced here to helpless terror, the élan of the sequence, as in many horror movies, consisting in the presence of prostrated women threatened by the unleashing of male libido. The women's courage is either grotesque or insubstantial, and its total abeyance here to "natural" timidity adds luster to the potency of the Bolsheviks.

The second sequence is longer and more complex; it is built on the identification of what we are shown with what the Kronstadt sailor sees as he gazes around the room.

a. Close-up of the head of Christ in the icon on the wall, one hand raised, palm out, left of frame. There is a close physical resemblance to the photograph of Nicholas wearing a fur cap, and it is crucial here that the imperial chamber is associated not only with women but also with "effeminate" men, the third image being Kerensky. In the context of the next three shots, the hole in Christ's palm is connoted as a vagina symbol.

b. Close-up of the torso of a statue of a shrouded, but exposed, woman wearing a classical robe, the camera panning down to her vagina. Given the extreme infrequency of camera movement in *October*, its employment here is particularly striking.

c. A small, round white bowl with a short handle, partially concealed by two bars in the foreground.

d. A white washbasin. Shots (c) and (d) both continue the vagina symbolism and rhyme with an earlier shot of the tsarina's commode, which one of the Bolsheviks has touched gingerly with horrified bewilderment. The elegance, the cleanness, the smooth whiteness conceal filth; vagina becomes anus. The association of bedroom/femininity/anality again links the tsarina to Kerensky.

e. Medium shot of the icon in (a), Christ now revealed as blessing the standing figures of Nicholas and Alexandra.

f. Longer shot of (d), the tsarevitch now revealed standing in front of his parents. In *October*, as in *S/Z*, "the symbolic field is not that of the biological sexes; it is that of castration" (Barthes, *S/Z*, 36), of which the icon is slowly revealed to be the emblem: "feminized" Christ blesses the union of woman and "feminized" man and its progeny, opening up the prospect of an infinite posterity of femininity. Christianity, imperial power, and castration are allied.

g. The sailor turns aside and spits in disgust.

h. Long shot of the bedroom, which is suddenly inundated by a violent explosion of feathers from the torn mattress as the concentrated force of the sequence's disgust bursts out of containment. The revenge on/repression of femininity is carried over to the following sequence in the wine cellar, where, through the montage, the Bolshevik sailor who stops an old woman looting appears to be smashing the bottle he seizes from her across her face.

The whole sequence, in fact, foregrounds very pointedly the sadomasochistic impulses in Eisenstein's work, the scope of which Peter Wollen has suggested to be (and which can be read as the complement of) the partial and distorted return of the sexuality repressed from the images of male brotherhood. (*Signs and Meaning,* 36) Thus, male activity repeatedly finds expression as the perpetration of violence, and male passivity as an ecstatic, voluptuous surrender to it. One notes, in the first instance, not only innumerable passages in the silent films but also the Battle on the Ice, which in its extraordinary repression of any sense of pain, is transformed into a series of "turns" for the exhibition of irrepressible, invulnerable vigor. One notes, in the second instance, the rhetoric of restraint and prostration fully elaborated in the surviving footage of *Que Viva Mexico!* (1932) and *Bezhin Meadow* (1937), implicit in *Potemkin,* and inseparable from Eisenstein's obsession with the image of the crucifixion (see Christ-as-woman in *October*). The Mexican sketchbooks, with their endless variations on that image, become "required looking" here, and they suggest that the Passion is inseparable in its turn from the corrida, drawings of crucified bulls juxtaposed with others of Christ buggering the thieves on the cross. The related connotations of martyrdom, passivity, and impalement produce, variously, the ripping of the mattress in *October* (to which the unauthorized presence of frightened women is so necessary) and the shooting of the hostages in the Kazan sequence in *Ivan,* which evokes St. Sebastian as much as the crucifixion. It was in Mexico, too, that Eisenstein became interested in *Macbeth,* and specifically in the murder of Duncan as the ritual sacrifice of the innocent, which, with specific homosexual inflections, becomes one of the major themes of the second part of *Ivan.* Given this associative complex, it is clearly significant that the rhetoric of "the agony" invariably coincides with those moments in which the male body appears naked, the celebration of nudity and the infliction of punishment (within, and to some extent by, the film) fusing inseparably together.

It is useful at this point, in connection with the appearance of male gayness as the imposition of and submission to power, to juxtapose Eisenstein and Pasolini. (See Dyer, "Pasolini.") The massive eruption of homosexual guilt to which *Salo* (1975) is the testimony can be related in detail to Pasolini's previous work: there can be no doubt, for example, as to what Julian's (Jean-Pierre Leaud) desire to fuck pigs in *Porcile* (*Pigpen* [1969]) is supposed to represent—but I shall limit myself here to *Arabian Nights* (1974), a work in which, beneath the ostensibly extreme dissimilarities, everything in *Salo* is implicit.

a. Compare the picking-up of the three young Arabs in *Arabian Nights* with the rounding-up of the prisoners in *Salo*. The scene in the earlier film should be compared in its turn with the opening sequence in the marketplace, in which the central heterosexual couple is established. While the Zumurrud/Nuredin relationship is created in terms of choice (Zumurrud chooses her buyer), reciprocity (Nuredin desires her), and mutual tenderness, the Arab boys are chosen and enticed by the old man with the promise of food, drink, and luxury for which the price will be his sexual satisfaction. There is no suggestion that the old man's desire is reciprocated, and whereas the heterosexual union culminates in a love scene of great delicacy and charm, the young men are last seen lined up in a row, with simulated grins, for the old man's inspection. Zumurrud

and Nuredin are the same age, are presented as physically beautiful, and have intercourse. The man is older than his victims, is presented as a predator lusting after the
youth and beauty he no longer possesses, obtains sexual satisfaction by talking about
it and looking at his object, and is a prototype of the image (common to *Arabian
Nights* and *Salo*) of repressive, aged, ambiguously potent/impotent parent-figures
spying on and desecrating the beauty of youngsters. Gayness becomes both indistinguishable from the exercise of power and "sadistic looking," and the apparent attempt
to distance the atrocities of the Circle of Blood (which are shown through glass, bars,
and binoculars) is more than somewhat undermined by the fact that we are placed
consistently in the position of the voyeur. The theme of sexual excitation through the
recounting of a text, stated for the old man, and interesting in light of the trilogy as a
whole, becomes, of course, the basis for *Salo*.

b. Compare the incarceration of young people underground in *Arabian Nights* with
the whole of *Salo*. The demon sequence (Franco Citti with a ginger rinse) relates
directly to the Circle of Blood, and, like the analogous sequence later in the film,
culminates in an image of homosexual intercourse figured as monstrous, destructive,
and perverse: the demon's embrace which, after a flight through the air, leads to his
partner's metamorphosis into an ape; the murder of the little prince, in bed, the man
sitting astride him and plunging a knife into the small of his back. In the final scene of
the film, as Richard Dyer has noted, homosexual sodomy becomes the threat of degradation and pain ("Don't hurt me too much"), and while, in *Salo*, the prisoners are
allowed to form unrepressive heterosexual and, in one instance, lesbian relationships,
male gayness is reserved entirely for the tormentors. ("Pasolini")

c. With the exception of one sequence (the succession of mutual betrayals), *Salo*
establishes a polar opposition between the active monstrosity of the fascists and the
passive purity of their victims, and although the film is set, initially, in a particular
historical period, it is as essentially removed from history as the films of the trilogy.
The repression of context, and the apparent impossibility of rebellion, create fascism as absolute, irresistible, and undefinable (except as "perversion"); the loading
of an extremely suspect "positive value" onto predominantly heterosexual relationships between beautiful people entails that projection outward of "bad" libido which
materializes in the threatening, infernal, anal landscapes of *Salo* and the last scene
of *The Canterbury Tales* (1972) and the arid deserts of *Teorema* (1968) and *Porcile*.
The fact that Pasolini insists both on asserting the value of liberated sexual energy
and on regarding his own sexual energies as monstrous produces that extraordinarily repetitive movement toward Hell so characteristic of many of the late films,
and it becomes questionable whether Pasolini's conception of sexuality is liberating
at all. In *Teorema*, where the awakening of the repressed bourgeois-capitalist family
is in question, sexuality is entirely destructive, with the ambiguous exception of a
member of Pasolini's mythologized peasantry who, nevertheless, renounces sexuality entirely. In *Porcile* and *Medea* (1969), libidinal energy is inseparable from "abominable rites" (cannibalism, pig-fucking, human sacrifice), the repression of which is

preordained. Indeed, the dominant impulse is toward the reinstatement of repression: *either* sexual release is totally incapacitating *or* the only alternative is between primitivism/sexuality on the one hand and culture/repression on the other (that is, there is no conceivable post-tribal culture which would not be repressive). The temporal regression of the trilogy saves Pasolini from having to face the problems raised by the temporary environment of *Teorema* and *Porcile*, whose parable-forms accentuate the obvious fact that without radical social change, the liberation of an individual who is thereby left to his own resources in a repressive environment can produce only breakdown (*Teorema*) or asocial, self-destructive, individualist anarchism (*Porcile*). It does *not* solve the problem of what is to happen to gayness if liberation remains at a premium, and *Arabian Nights* can only work by vigorously suppressing it (explicitly and deliberately in the final scene) and, in consequence, affirming a set of values scarcely distinguishable from prevailing ideological norms. Thus, it comes as no great surprise to discover: that the infidelity which the film asserts is as "splendid" as fidelity is exclusively male, Zumurrud and Aziza remaining miserably celibate throughout; that the film is single-mindedly phallocentric, all the stories being built around men and the worship of men being a constant motif; that the vagina is the natural place for the phallus (the bathing scene with Nuredin and the three girls); and that the final scene, as it rejects gayness, simultaneously confirms male-dominated heterosexuality, Zumurrud shedding the vestments of power, assuring Nuredin that she does not have the phallus, and announcing herself to him his "slave."

I have suggested that, in *October*, the cohesiveness of the revolution is achieved through the sublimation of homosexual libido (brotherhood) and, crucially, the presence of the charismatic male (Lenin) as creating Logos. Similarly, the film establishes two congruent sets of oppositions: male (Bolsheviks) versus non-male (castrating women, effeminate men), and natural potency versus unnatural or artificial potency. That is, *October* assimilates the revolution to a mythology of phallic power, and if the "hero" of the film is the mass, it is a male mass whose sexual connotations have been largely repressed from the film's consciousness, to return as the "perverse" among the reactionaries. In *Alexander Nevsky* and *Ivan the Terrible*, in response to the cult of personality, the hero as patriarch, as the figure of the Law, as phallus, is reinstated. This movement, although it represents on one level an inversion of the silent films (one has only to compare, for instance, the opening shots of *October*—the dismemberment of the statue of the tsar—with those of *Ivan*—the creation of the tsar as living statue, rigid and erect—the two sequences related in inverse rhyming order as the destruction/emergence of the Father through the subtraction/addition of fetishes), is also, on another level, entirely consonant with them, the gradual revelation of Ivan at his coronation corresponding to that of Lenin in *October*. It is that concentration of phallic potency in "the man," however, which precipitates the emergence of the sexual dimensions of power and permits that deconstruction of the mythology of patriarchy undertaken in *The Boyars' Plot* (*Ivan the Terrible, Part II* [1958]), the appalling cost of which, to Eisenstein himself, is well-known.[2]

Eisenstein's position in the Soviet Union in the 1930s was, for various reasons (his theoretical preoccupations, his gayness, his long sojourn in Europe, America, and Mexico), constantly precarious, and the period is a history of aborted or unrealized projects and campaigns of vilification. *Alexander Nevsky* was not initiated by him but made at official request, to which Eisenstein appears to have submitted with a mixture of irony and resignation ("there are situations when you have no choice"). (Barna, 206) The first part of *Ivan the Terrible*, however, was Eisenstein's own project, prepared and realized in the context of the Nazi advance on Russia and the demand for the mass production of propaganda films. Read in isolation (*The Boyars' Plot* cracks it open at once), Part I elaborates a clear, simple ideological project. "This film is about the man" who seized autocratic power to unify Russia, to reclaim lands lost to alien powers, to crush self-interested internal factions in the name of "the Great Cause," and to lift the nation out of feudalism into the modern world. On this level the film becomes a hymn to the triumph of the will over the loneliness and misery of power, human loss, and the betrayal of friends, culminating in the identification of Ivan/Stalin with a Christ (Eisenstein's "Passion" theme) who renounces his agony and assumes the stoic grandeur of the Jacobean hero ("The Tsar of Muscovy is still undefeated"). (See T. S. Eliot.) The Kazan sequence reiterates the pseudo-heroic compositional rhetoric of *Alexander Nevsky* (the great man against the clouds) and dissociates Ivan from the arbitrary cruelty of Kurbsky in the hostages incident. Most crucially, Ivan's trust in the people is shown to be unshakable ("The call of the people will express God's will"), and the film rests on the distinction between duplicitous, self-seeking Boyars and aristocratic minions, and the faithful brotherhood of the Iron Ring.

Similarly, Part I affirms the symbolic oppositions of *October*, again in terms of a sexual typology. The paradigm is established at the coronation. Anastasia is associated visually with the smiling, fresh, innocent faces of peasant women and verbally with the land of Russia, specifically its rivers. Eli Zaretsky has noted that "the ideal of motherhood was associated with the re-emergence of Great Russian nationalism and the idea of the 'Motherland' during the 1930s," and he links this to that resurgence of the "psycho-social heritage of male supremacy" which dissipated the "deep commitment to the emancipation of women" with which the Bolshevik revolution began. (*Capitalism*, 100–101) Thus, Anastasia becomes the focus of the symbolic complex—Motherland/fertility/purity/wife and mother/"loyal slave to the Tsar of Muscovy," in which the two "good" images of women in *October* (the domestics of the bread queue, the blonde martyr/muse of the bridges) are fused. Opposite Anastasia is that one-woman Death Battalion Euphrosyne, the castrating mother par excellence, who, like her forbears, is associated with the forces for reaction and the preservation of the past, and who, throughout Part I, is presented consistently as a sexual threat. During the wedding sequence, Eisenstein intercuts the embrace of Ivan and Anastasia with shots of Euphrosyne watching malevolently, and the conflict culminates in the deathbed sequence in which the two women—in black and white, respectively—move in simultaneously from opposite sides of the frame to flank Kurbsky and vie for his support for their respective sons. Subsequently, Euphrosyne insists on murdering Anastasia herself, her blanched face engulfed in darkness as she murmurs, "That I shall undertake." As in *October*, the dichotomy of women coexists, on the "axis of castration," with a dichotomy of men: Anastasia finding her complement in the Iron Ring (the phallus in place), and Euphrosyne hers as the phallic, castrating mother in Vladimir, her son (idiot-cum-pansy) and Kurbsky, whose jealousy of Anastasia she incites. These symbolic oppositions exist as conflicts within Ivan himself, and the willed refusal of despair and prostration at Anastasia's bier affords the moment for the transference of loyalty from the dead woman to the Iron Ring, the sublimation of libido into brotherhood which simultaneously becomes a means of fulfilling her injunctions to and aspirations for him and is ratified by an oath over her body and a kiss on her brow. One might invoke here Eisenstein's admiration for John Ford's *Young Mr. Lincoln* (1939) ("Mr. Lincoln") and juxtapose the bier scene with the scene at Anne Rutledge's grave in the film. In both cases, the protagonist's loss of the woman "must be read as the real origin both of his castration and of his identification with the Law": from this moment, Lincoln/Ivan does "not have the phallus; he is the phallus." (Editors of *Cahiers*, 517)

The bier scene—indeed, the moment at which libido is redirected into the power drive— is the turning point of the film, the moment at which, in retrospect from *The Boyars' Plot*, the subversion of Ivan-as-hero begins. In the context of Part I alone, the triumph of tsar over man can be, and was, read affirmatively; the film was a massive success and won the Stalin Prize. In the context of the whole, the same triumph initiates the deliberate and systematic inversion of the symbolic scheme previously established which produces Ivan as the castrated and castrating monster in Part II. Given the explicit homosexual connotations of the scene, this seems the point at which to note some adverse criticisms of the film advanced by Noel Purdon in an otherwise trenchant article on gay cinema.[3] Purdon's strictures relate entirely to what Eisenstein is recorded as having said about the film, which he takes on trust, rather as he takes on trust that the ecstatic male nudity of *Que Viva Mexico!* is evidence of "relaxation and expansion." Eisenstein's remarks completely fail to explain—and are indeed contradicted by—the extraordinary transformation of Vladimir in *The Boyars' Plot*, where he suddenly ceases to be the buffoon of Part I, and the discrepancy foregrounds the nature of *Ivan the Terrible*'s supreme importance for gay cinema. If Pasolini's work is characterized by conscious gestures toward self-liberation which are consistently undermined by the very images in which they are expressed, *Ivan the Terrible* is marked by a radical questioning of the mythologies within which Eisenstein's images have been structured—the mythology, primarily, of phallocentrism. One need only consider, here, the development in the use of Nikolai Cherkasov as the film progresses, which corresponds exactly to the development of Vladimir. While Pasolini's regression to the past serves primarily as a means of evading the question of how liberation can take place without radical social change, the past of *The Boyars' Plot* is there to suggest the structural continuity of patriarchal organization, within which any essential change is impossible and repression inevitable; all conflicts which are expressed inside its terms finally cancel out and reproduce the structure. *Salo* implies that "fascism" can be explained ahistorically, as a sort of spiritual state, in terms of some people who are perverts wanting to have power over other people who are not. Eisenstein relates the perversion of sexuality to particular structures and ideologies of power; he is concerned, that is, not with homosexuality as perversion but with the perversion of homosexuality (and other forms of sexuality). *The Boyars' Plot* is a liberating work not because it fabricates images of "liberated" sexuality (which it nowhere attempts to do) but because it analyzes the mechanisms of repression with a rigor which few films have approached.

The film's projects can be gauged partly by its use of Shakespeare. I am thinking here not only of the Vladimir/Euphrosyne scene in *The Boyars' Plot* (with it pervasive, ironic references to *Macbeth* through which the positions of Macbeth and Duncan are reversed) but also of two quotations which encapsulate the development of the whole.[4] Thus, at the beginning of Part I, the visit of the Tartar envoy from Kazan and the insulting gift of the knife transpose the tennis-ball scene in *Henry V*, the siege of Kazan which follows being analogous to the siege of Harfleur. At the end of the Nebuchadnezzar sequence in *The Boyars' Plot*, the warrior-king gives place to Richard III, Ivan's "Then terrible I will be" (and his masquerade as a monk) recalling Richard's "I am determined to prove a villain."

The abandonment of the "hero of the people" proceeds in accordance with the systematic repudiation of the black/white antinomy on which Part I is based, the opening sequence of *The Boyars' Plot* making the antinomy explicit in order to subvert it. Sigismund's court is a chessboard (knights, bishops, king/"queen," pawn [Kurbsky] becoming queen by reaching the opposite edge of the board), in which, however, the reality of the color distinction is already tenuous: the three bishops are on the same side, but two are white and one black. When the chess metaphor recurs, in the Nebuchadnezzar sequence—black and white pieces taking their places from opposite ends of the cathedral—the distinctions between the sides (Heavenly Tsar/Earthly Tsar) have become meaningless, while their structural congruence as patriarchal factions has become crucial, the film moving dialectically toward the identification of white and black. The movement is continuous (consider, for example, the scene in which Philip, in black, sitting between the coffins of the Boyars, is juxtaposed with Pimen, in white, standing beyond him beneath the icon of a skeleton, both men holding a staff), but one sequence in particular, for the present purpose, should be noted.

The sequence begins with the conversation between Pimen and Euphrosyne which concludes with Pimen's assertion that "Philip is more useful to our cause as a martyr." As he speaks, Pimen, who is, as always, wearing white, moves forward into camera and makes the sign of the cross, the movement of his hand casting deep shadows over the brilliant whiteness of his face. In the following shot, Euphrosyne, in a rhymingly inverted movement, is drawing back from the camera in horror. As Pimen leaves, she whispers, "White cowl, black soul," and as she speaks lets fall her own black cowl to reveal a white one beneath it. Euphrosyne's immediate attempt to enlist Vladimir in the conspiracy against Ivan rhymes in its turn with the enlistment of Peter by Pimen which has preceded it, Eisenstein establishing two corresponding symbolic pairs, Peter/Vladimir and Pimen/Euphrosyne. As Pimen declares that "only the pure in heart" is fit to murder Ivan, Eisenstein cuts to a medium shot of Vladimir, cowering on the floor in terror. At once, Peter's face moves into frame in close-up, hiding Vladimir, who then cranes round behind him so that both heads are framed together. The links then multiply, Pimen's blessing/curse of Peter ("With the dead be sealed") echoed in the Euphrosyne/Vladimir dialogue, where Euphrosyne's love for Vladimir becomes indistinguishable from exploitation of him ("Why must I be sacrificed?"). The film's central preoccupation, the perpetuation of a single structure through the insistence of the past in the present (psychoanalytically, the dominion of the death drive), is inflected repeatedly as the possession of children by parents, the transformation of the young into pawns/sacrificial victims (Vladimir, Peter) or, in the Ivan/Basmanov variant, their absorption into the Law of the Father (consider Basmanov's gift of his son to Ivan at Anastasia's bier, and the juxtaposition, within the frame, of Fyodor Basmanov and the choirboys in the Nebuchadnezzar sequence). In either case, whether enlisted for or against the Father (Ivan), the male children are interpellated within patriarchal structures as a means of reproducing them.

The symbolism is clinched in the concluding shots of the sequence in question.

a. Vladimir and Euphrosyne, brightly lit, wearing gold and white, clinging together as they retreat from the camera. Malyuta moves in from the bottom of the frame until the blackness of his back hides them from sight and fills the center of the frame.

a. Close-up of Malyuta's face, brightly lit. He raises the goblet which Euphrosyne has used to poison Anastasia, and which he is returning to her as a token that her guilt has been discovered. The goblet is shrouded in a black cloth, and Malyuta's face is slowly concealed behind it. He moves the goblet to the side, so that his face becomes visible again, but still engulfed in shadow. He moves the goblet further away, the shadow vanishes, and a brilliant white light falls onto his face as he leans forward into camera.

The shots link Malyuta and Pimen, the shadow of the poisoned chalice and that of the sign of the cross. The return of the emblem of Euphrosyne's conspiracy against Anastasia initiates Ivan's conspiracy against Vladimir, in which, through her exploitation of him, Euphrosyne becomes, symbolically, a partner. The return of the guilt of the past introduces that sequence of ritualized, ceremonial repetitions of the past which constitute the color sequence (black and white meeting in red) and in which the triumph of past over present becomes absolute.

The threat of the phallic woman to the "natural" possession of the phallus by the man which dominates *October* and Part I of *Ivan the Terrible* ceases to be significant in *The Boyars' Plot* along with the project of affirming phallocentrism. One can point to four central male/female relationships in the film—Ivan and Anastasia, Ivan and his mother, Ivan and Euphrosyne, Vladimir and Euphrosyne—and the emerging pattern of symbolic displacement within and between them is crucial.

a. Anastasia and Ivan's mother are clearly linked in terms of dress and physical appearance, and both are poisoned by the Boyars. Ivan's first and last assertions of power, as boy and man, are provoked by the desire to avenge the deaths of mother and wife respectively, the third term being the scene at Anastasia's bier after the repetition of the original loss—"I will be Tsar"/"The Tsar of Muscovy is still undefeated"/"My hands are free!" Ivan recuperates loss by becoming the phallus, and the movement toward apparently ever-greater freedom is a movement toward ever-greater repressiveness and self-repression. It is stressed in the flashback that the first move is both (a) directly a displacement of the father (Ivan is aroused when the prince of the Boyars lies on his mother's bed), and (b) Ivan's self-insertion into the battle for possession of the phallus which has preceded him and to which the deaths of his parents are attributable in the first place. He is simultaneously victim and oppressor, and his conviction of self-determination is illusory from the first.

b. In the color sequence, a series of reversals takes place. Ivan subjects Vladimir as he himself, in the flashback, has been subjected by the Boyars, to mock ceremonials which culminate in a coronation; to this extent, Vladimir is the young Ivan, while Ivan becomes the Boyars and repeats the crime against himself. The murder of Vladimir is thus self-murder, the final act of self-repression necessary to becoming the phallus. At the same time, Vladimir is Anastasia, and the orgy becomes an obscene parody of the wedding banquet, the servants bearing the figures of black ornamental swans instead of white. Thus, Ivan-as-the-Boyars is also repeating the crime against Anastasia. To this extent, Ivan's possession of the phallus involves the perversion of libido into the power drive and, identically, the total repression of "femininity" (his own, Anastasia, the gentleness of Vladimir—"Who'd want to be Tsar?"—which has by now become the emotional center of the film). Finally, the dragging away of Vladimir's corpse from Euphrosyne echoes the dragging away of his mother from Ivan. The film's symbolism has moved full circle. Taking the place of his first oppressor, Ivan confronts in his vanquished enemy an image of himself. The force of the ending depends on the sense that Euphrosyne and Vladimir both occupy places previously occupied by Ivan, and that the struggle for power under patriarchy can be defined in terms of that set of positions in relation to the phallus.

The dominant elements of Part I of Ivan the Terrible are relevant to the exploration of the sexuality of power undertaken in *The Boyars' Plot*. The first centers on Anastasia and relates directly to the sexual paradigm of *October*. Anastasia is never a sexual presence in the film, her function being simply to define the "place of woman" in relation to the "Great Cause" embodied in the man. Opposite this, there is Ivan's sublimated homosexuality, the presence of which emerges, appropriately, in the wedding sequence, where Kurbsky's explicit sexual desire for Anastasia is juxtaposed with the transfiguration of Ivan's desire for Kurbsky and Kolychev by his self-identification with the cause ("If I need you, answer my call"). The only moment of tender physical/emotional contact between Ivan and Anastasia, immediately before her murder, arises out of her consoling him for the absence of his male friends. The (initially) positive connotations of Ivan's sublimation (dedication, selflessness, fortitude, fidelity, heroic/ tragic self-isolation) are juxtaposed in turn with the negative ones of Kurbsky's (obsequiousness, treachery, self-interest, effeminacy)—a variation, in fact, on the opposition between Kerensky and the Bolsheviks. Kurbsky is as jealous of Anastasia as of Ivan, the jealousy of the former implying the frustration of the power drive ("Marriage is the end of friendship"), and he continuously exploits Ivan's asexual devotion in order to gain power over him (consider the embrace of the deathbed sequence).

This narrative/thematic thread of Part I, within which Ivan's sublimation can be read as being affirmed, is counterbalanced by the prevailing eye imagery and its derivatives. From the coronation scene onward, Ivan's power is concentrated in his eyes. Eisenstein withholds the appearance of Ivan's face until after he has been constituted as the phallus through the bestowal of the imperial regalia (his creation as the totem figure), whereupon he turns to the camera, and the motif of the castrating stare is immediately inaugurated. Ivan's emergence as the castrated is, simultaneously, his emergence as the castrator. Again, the wedding sequence is crucial. As Ivan puts his hand on Kolychev's shoulder and says, "If I need you, answer my call" (the moment linking the sublimation of homosexuality, the wedding, and Ivan's identification with the cause), Eisenstein cuts from the banquet chamber to the courtyard and the eruption of the anti-Boyar riot, the male crowd bursting into the palace and disrupting the feast. The quelling of the mob—Ivan both espouses its cause ("weed out the treason of the Boyars") and harnesses its energy ("A state without reins is as uncontrollable as a horse without a bridle")—proceeds through the castration of Malyuta (Kurbsky dashing the candlestick from his hands, Kolychev pinning his arms behind his back, both forcing him onto his knees before Ivan), the castration of the mass by Ivan's eye ("He sees right through you"), and threats of decapitation for traitors. That is, the mob both functions as the return of the libido repressed by Ivan's espousal of Anastasia and the Motherland and, in that Ivan simultaneously adopts it and emasculates it ("The Father of us all!"), precipitates the renewed repression of libido into the power drive. The rioters become Ivan's sons, and the film proceeds directly to the crushing of the rebellious sons, the Tartars of Kazan.

The Kazan sequence elaborates the symbolic implications of the eye motif. Consider the following series: (a) a long shot of Ivan on the hilltop, alone, silhouetted against the skyline, gazing off toward Kazan; (b) three quick shots of the mine beneath the walls of Kazan—a candle burning down at the center of a radius of fuses leading to barrels of gunpowder; (c) a long shot of Kazan, as the mine detonates, the debris and smoke from the explosion radiating outward from the central point.

The rays of fuses and explosion are linked visually to Ivan through the image of the sun on his breastplate (a circle surrounded by radiating beams), and the detonation is initiated by a shot whose rhetoric associates the gaze of the conqueror with his isolation as the figure of the Law ("Look, my son! The Tsar of all the Russias!"). Subsequently, the assimilation of Ivan-as-the-sun to Ivan-as-castrato/castrating eye produces the extraordinary icons of the scene with Philip at the beginning of *The Boyars' Plot*: the council chamber dominated at one end by the inverted head of a ceiling-long icon of God, hair and beard radiating like the rays of the sun, and at the other, behind the throne, by the face of a sun tormented, shorn of its beams, partially obscured by the feet of the God-icon. The two icons make present the two related aspects of Ivan's elevation to being the phallus—his potency (God/tsar) and his impotence (the face obscured by feet recalls the shots of Ivan enthroned as a boy, his feet dangling awkwardly above his footstool), the two faces confronting each other, from either end of the room, like inverted reflections in a mirror. The imagery here has been prepared throughout Part I. Thus, after his castration, Malyuta becomes "the Tsar's eye," and the icon of an enormous staring eye, surrounded by candles (a religious/imperial fetish), spies on Anastasia and Kurbsky as Kurbsky, imagining that Ivan is dying, attempts to take his place. Most crucially, the eye motif is contained within the performance of Cherkasov, the film's development being one with the shifting of the meanings expressed through his body. Thus, the unbending erectness and the ecstatic gaze offscreen of the inspired redeemer (the codes of *Alexander Nevsky*), when they are reinstated at the end of *The Boyars' Plot*, have been filtered through, and become the products of, the rigid, angular distortions and obsessive, paranoid stare which Eisenstein drove Cherkasov to breakdown to create.

In this context, it becomes possible to examine more clearly the place of sexuality in *The Boyars' Plot* and its implications for gay cinema.

a. One should note first the residue, in the opening sequence in Sigismund's court, of the concept of the effeminacy of the reactionaries, inherited from *October* and certain aspects of Part I. Sigismund, like Kerensky, is associated with effete luxury, mechanical fetish objects (the movements of the knights), imperial statues (real and dehumanized human), and imperial women (the ladies of the court); his audience with Kurbsky is rendered, with extraordinary explicitness, as decadent homosexual flirtation, Kurbsky presenting his sword and Sigismund stroking it languidly with jeweled gloves. Subsequently, this aspect of Eisenstein's self-oppression is definitively abandoned, and Vladimir, in whom its development is clearly potential, escapes it completely in Part II, where he becomes, essentially, a new character.

b. Also potential in Part I is another self-oppressive archetype: all gay relationships are exploitative. Thus, Ivan could emerge as the tragic victim of his need for men who only want to obtain power through him, and who invariably betray him. In the context of the whole, this reading becomes insignificant, and the film develops instead a theme which effectively inverts it: the universal contamination of all the central relationships by ego drives.

It becomes necessary here to return to the scene at Anastasia's bier. Basmanov offers his son to Ivan in order to consolidate a position of power for his family; the Iron Ring is defined, through a parody of Christ's injunction to the disciples to renounce everything and "follow me," in terms of those who can only gain by servitude to the tsar and "the dictates of his will." Basmanov forces Fyodor onto his knees before Ivan (compare the identical ritual imposed on Malyuta), and Ivan, after fondling his hair obsessively, asserts his power over both ("You presume to instruct us!"). The presence of the corpse of Anastasia, who has also declared herself "a loyal slave to the Tsar," defines the moment's significance.

a. Close shot, from above, of Anastasia's face in the coffin.

b. Close shot of Ivan, who turns away from the bier and looks off left at Fyodor (offscreen).

c. Low-angle close shot of Fyodor, looking up at Ivan (offscreen), his face radiant and adoring. The shot is back lit, and in soft focus.

d. Close shot of Fyodor in profile, left of frame. Ivan's face moves in right of the frame and leans forward until it is almost touching Fyodor's. Fyodor murmurs, "You are right!"

Montage, lighting, and composition transform Fyodor into Anastasia's equivalent and her successor; Ivan saves himself from despair by turning from a relationship whose power component is implicit (tsar/"loyal slave") to relationships explicitly based on control to which the men submit in the interest of their own power drives. Sexuality reappears in the form of an "urge to mastery" (Freud, *On Narcissism*) and Ivan's assertion of sexual power over Vladimir can be read in terms of undoing his own earlier passivity to the Boyars.

The Boyars' Plot proceeds logically from this renunciation of sexuality. Consider the Ivan/Malyuta scene, which immediately follows Ivan's self-prostration to Philip and immediately precedes the hallucinated cry and the discovery that Anastasia was poisoned. The scene works in two ways, both consonant psychoanalytically. (a) Malyuta functions here as an ego projection of Ivan's paranoia, inciting fear of betrayal by Philip, to whom he has just given his trust. Malyuta has already been established symbolically as Ivan's "eye," the bearer of his castration, and the scene begins with a medium shot of Ivan alone, the conversation with Malyuta continuing for the length of two shots before the latter is actually seen. On this level, the scene becomes a narcissistic-megalomanic inner colloquy. (b) With Malyuta as a narrative figure, the scene suggests both a pact with the devil ("My soul I yield for the Tsar") and a sexual seduction, the dialogue culminating in the elision of the two ("Damnation for the Tsar's caress"), marked by Ivan's possessive kiss. Again, what is crucial here is the perversion of sexuality by the exigencies of power. Thus, having failed to coerce Philip into submission, Ivan abases himself to him and then, immediately, in the scene with Malyuta, he reacts violently against his vulnerability to reconfirm his supremacy. Similarly, in the name of maintaining power (his first remark, offscreen, is "Why give the bishop such power over you?"), Malyuta abases himself to Ivan, calling himself Ivan's "faithful cur" and stroking the fur of Ivan's mantle as if the tsar himself were a dog.

From the bier sequence onward, Ivan and his two male rivals, Philip and Pimen, constantly carry staffs, the clashing diagonals of which form the dominant compositional motif of the Ivan/Philip scene. The jutting staff also dominates the scene with Malyuta. As he leaves, he brushes against it, and it remains vibrating slightly in its socket, while Ivan, stiffening and staring obsessively ahead, rises slowly to his feet and becomes erect. The juxtaposition of the instances of Ivan's erections (the bier sequence; the submission of the masses in the final scene of Part I; the Malyuta scene; the final appearance in the cathedral) and those of his impotence (the deathbed sequence; the initial reaction to Anastasia's death; the end of the confrontation with Philip; the mock-bow to the enthroned Vladimir which suddenly produces a real sense of powerlessness), can virtually define the theme of the phallus, possession of which necessarily depends on the abasement/humiliation/ degradation of the other.

The Boyars' Plot ends with the orgy in Hell in which all the dominant structural oppositions are finally subverted. It counterbalances the Nebuchadnezzar sequence. Both are "mystery plays" set in a cathedral designed to abase an opponent: the first staged by the Boyars and culminating in Ivan's self-dramatization as "the Terrible"; the second staged by Ivan in revenge on the Boyars, who are under the illusion that they are controlling the masquerade, and culminating in Ivan's triumph. Both are dominated by fire imagery (the Burning Fiery Furnace, the flames of Hell in the banquet chamber, the Doom painting in the cathedral) and by the exploitation of the powerless (the choirboys [and the characters they represent], Peter, Vladimir).[5] Eisenstein makes the connection explicit in the ironic reference to Belshazzar's Feast which immediately precedes the orgy, Euphrosyne crying ecstatically "God's finger!" as she seizes the goblet, whose significance she does not, at that point, understand. Ivan, as both the master of the revels and the hand that writes, becomes equally God and Nebuchadnezzar's son, and the distinction between "Heavenly Tsar" and "Earthly Tsar" maintained by the Boyars disintegrates along with Ivan's conviction of his messianic vocation.

With extraordinary precision, Eisenstein reveals that all the avatars of the Father (hence, the significance of the masquerade) are one, and the orgy becomes the marriage of Heaven, Hell, and Earth, with Ivan as Satan, Jehovah, and finally Tsar of all the Russias. Thus, the black dervishes of the orgy become the black monks of the cathedral; Vladimir's transition from banquet to cathedral/sacrifice is accompanied by the choir's anthem, "Awake my soul!"; and the murders are introduced by the affectation of piety ("Let us address ourselves to the Almighty") and followed by Ivan's self-justification/self-deification before the altar. The color sequence is, at every level, a resolution of dualisms.

Inseparably, the orgy reveals the final dominion of the death drive over sexuality, repressed libido returning explosively and destructively in the vortex imagery of the dancing. The crucial element here is the antimony between Vladimir and Fyodor Basmanov. As I have suggested, the orgy explicitly recalls the wedding sequence, with Vladimir in Anastasia's place and Fyodor—the exercise of power over whom has replaced, for Ivan, the passionate submission of his wife—now transferred to the place occupied by Euphrosyne in the wedding festivities. Thus, Fyodor inherits Euphrosyne's threatening gaze at the intimacy of the imperial couple, but he is also in league with Ivan; the double connotation both confirms Ivan's movement toward identity with the Boyars and makes explicit the implication that the original festivities have been broken off by an eruption of the repressed (the mob). At this level, that suppression and denigration of the non-male which structures the symbolic field in *October* is foregrounded by *The Boyars' Plot*, the orgy being designed entirely to degrade and overpower the only character in the film who has no interest whatever in the possession of the phallus. Vladimir's very gentleness renders him vulnerable and ineffectual, and his transformation by this point into a repository of values—the absence, that is, of a creative alternative—is a sufficient token of the film's despair—its status as a negative statement, though one of uncompromising extremeness.

The repression of femininity is supremely imaged in Fyodor's appearance in drag as the soloist in a song threatening the Boyars with decapitation. The masquerade as the non-male becomes the ultimate assertion of the supremacy of the phallus and the castration of the other (see Mulvey; Johnston, "Femininity and the Masquerade"), and Fyodor exists as both a mockery of Anastasia and Vladimir and as an organ of the tsar. Thus, his headdress takes up for the last time the ray motif established—in the Kazan sequence—in the context of Ivan's emasculation of the rebellious, and Fyodor, like Malyuta before him, is transmuted, after his submission (forced onto his knees), into the bearer and perpetuator of Ivan's castration (note the pronounced phallic connotations of his dress). It is Ivan-as-phallus that determines the form of the orgy, in which images of gayness and of women are debased simultaneously. Repressed libido can only return as the anti-life, as the seduction/exploitation of Vladimir ("Ah, Brother Vladimir, you don't love me!") which represents, at the same time, Ivan's exploitation—in the interests of power—of the personal predicament which the possession of power has induced ("I'm just a poor, abandoned orphan whom no one pities"). Similarly, Eisenstein stresses, throughout, Ivan's contempt for and oppression of the individuals he has appropriated, drama-tized as the contempt of God for his creation ("You are my slaves! I raised you from the dust! . . . I express my will through you!"). The color sequence, as the scene in the tsarina's bedroom revisited, realizes "that horrible mixture of sensuality and cruelty" which, in *October*, is only there as a symptom.[6]

October ends with the beginning of time and the emergence of a new generation, figured as the liberation of a child: the son of the proletariat is seen first in ecstatic triumph and then sleeping peacefully in the throne of the deposed father while Lenin announces that "We must now set about building a proletarian state in Russia." *Ivan the Terrible*, like the aborted *Bezhin Meadow*, ends with the murder of a child as a blood sacrifice to the father, who rules on. In *October*, the mass raising of guns expresses and affirms the phallic brotherhood of the revolu-tion. In the last shot of *Ivan the Terrible*, the members of the Iron Ring raise their swords in tri-umph behind Ivan as he sits in state and proclaims that the era of "the sword of righteousness" is at hand, the image suffused in a garish, bloodred glow. Eisenstein's last film is not simply, and comfortably, an indictment of Stalinism. Rather, it works through an analysis of the ideological structures that have dominated Western culture, and its extreme importance can be estimated in terms of its subversion of them.

Their Finest Hour: Humphrey Jennings and the British Imperial Myth of World War II (1989)

Humphrey Jennings's reputation stands as high as that of any director in the history of the documentary, and he is widely regarded, in England at any rate, as one of the two or three greatest artists the British cinema has produced, if not the greatest *tout court*. Jim Hillier's judgment of Jennings's most famous film, *Fires Were Started* (1943), is perfectly representative:

> Although particularized in time and place, the film's formal and symbolic qualities, together with its humanity, give it a universal significance outside of time. It is the masterpiece not only of Jennings but also of the British documentary school and the whole British cinema. (98)

My own disagreement with this evaluation of Jennings is extreme, and the reader is forewarned, therefore, that what follows definitely represents a minority viewpoint: Hillier's account (and there is little else to point to) is all the more worth reading as a counterbalance. I should add, too, that while (naturally) I do not think I am biased, it is certainly true that my difficulty with Jennings's films is bound up with the fact that they seem to me to exemplify some extremely depressing things about official British culture in general, and the relationship to it of British social democracy in particular. Obviously, North American readers will not be capable of being depressed in the same way, and this may well affect their reaction to the films.

Jennings is in many ways an exceptionally attractive figure. He was a socialist and, unlike most British film directors of his period, he was also highly cultivated. His interest in culture, moreover, was both intelligent and advanced. It came under the heading of what would now be called "cultural studies," and throughout a large part of his life he was working on a book called *Pandemonium* (left unfinished at the time of his premature death) about the relationship among industry, science, literature, and society in England since the Industrial Revolution. This political, or sociological, interest in the culture of the past was accompanied by an allegiance to modernism: Jennings helped to organize—and indeed, exhibited his own paintings in—the first surrealist exhibition in London in 1936. At the same time, as we might expect from the subject of his book, Jennings was not in the least a cultural elitist: if William Shakespeare, John Milton, and William Blake were, for him, "a permanent frame of reference," he also knew and loved contemporary popular culture and drew on it extensively in his work. (Hillier, 63)

Finally—as if all this were not enough—in an age in which John Grierson was proclaiming that any preoccupation with aesthetics was trivial and that the virtue of the documentary was that it "allowed an adventure in the arts to assume the respectability of a public service" (70), Jennings had the temerity to suggest that English Renaissance theater provided a model of an artistic practice in which poetry and social analysis ("*connaissance*—we have no word for it—naturally") were continuous with each other, and that "it still seems just a possibility" that British artists in the present might aspire to produce a similar synthesis. (71) Nothing could sound more promising, and there would be every reason to expect that an artist with expressed interests and convictions of this kind would end up, in practice, creating major work. And yet—or so it seems to me—the promise was not fulfilled, and in the work itself the interests and convictions, though in a sense present, are present in a notably debilitated, impoverished, and conventional form. Jennings has been visibly defeated by the cultural situation in which he worked, and I want to suggest how and why this is so.

The War as Golden Age

We may begin with an incident, cited in Hillier's essay, in which one of the director's friends recalls Jennings having told him, "firmly and passionately, that good films could only be made in times of disaster." (110) This remark tells us a great deal, not only about Jennings's films but also about the dominant British myth of World War II—a myth which was already there, as the films demonstrate, while the war was still being fought and which is incorrigibly there to this day. The myth has its basis in what was, objectively, Britain's unique situation in World War II: it was the only European country which, while being persistently blitzed, bombarded, and threatened with invasion, was never actually occupied by German troops. Britain's experience of German imperialism was significantly different, therefore, from Poland's or France's or the Soviet Union's experience of it. There was carpet bombing and there was a Battle of Britain, in which many people fought heroically and many people were killed, but no Nazi atrocities were committed on British soil, there were no concentration camps, there was no occupying army, there was no resistance movement, and—above all, perhaps—there was no experience of collaboration, either by the British ruling class, within which there was many a willing candidate, or by members of the general community. The ideology corresponding to Britain's peculiar and, comparatively speaking, privileged position in the Europe of the Third Reich has two principle components: it emphasizes on the one hand the homogeneity, the unambiguous political unity, of British wartime society, and on the other the triumphant success of British resistance to invasion. The British fought as one man, and although there may have been times when we were down, we were most certainly never out. The central symbol of this ideology is the Blitz of London, and its exemplary charismatic image is the dome of St. Paul's rising with imperturbable majesty above the ruined landscape in the early morning as the all-clear sounds—the very emblem of the invincibility and the wholeness of British culture. In one version of it, these feelings about the war are very intimately connected to feelings about the empire, and the war becomes the last moment at which it was possible to experience Britain (wrongly) as a great imperial power, but the imperialist content of the war myth (a myth which we may call "Churchillian") need not be this explicit and is, perhaps, more commonly sublimated into a sense of embattled, intransigent British isolation and exceptionalism. At the time of the Battle of Britain, Europe had fallen, the United States had not yet entered the war, Britain stood alone, and, unlike "other countries," it won.

In one sense, of course, the social unity of wartime Britain was very real, and it is all the more necessary to distinguish carefully between the nature and conditions of the social solidarity on which the British war effort actually depended and the ideology of the war which was developing at the same time. For this solidarity had, in practice, a specific class character: it was directly contingent on the presence, within the wartime governing coalition, of representatives of the Labour Party and on the fact that the prosecution of the war was linked, more or less from the outset, to the planning of a number of fundamental domestic social reforms which were later implemented by the Labour government after 1945. In other words, British war unity was characterized not by the suspension of class politics or class struggle but, on the contrary, by the British ruling class's recognition that it could not pursue its own war aim—to wit, the crushing of Germany's resistance to the hegemony of British imperialism—without making major political concessions to its own domestic class antagonist, large sections of which were intensely hostile to prewar Toryism in general and to Churchill in particular. There could be no more striking evidence of the material content of the popular aspirations which secured the united British nation than Churchill's overwhelming defeat by Labour in the 1945 general election; indeed, the welfare state was the victory which the British working class won by fighting the war. The ideology of war unity, by contrast, is continuous with the idea that "Britain at war" was a society in which class interests—identified, needless to say, with the pursuit of selfish and self-serving political goals by groups who ignore the interests of the social organism as a whole—were dissolved or transcended, and this ideology has generated an emotion which can only be described as "war nostalgia." The war is recalled, with a lump in the throat—or, in the Thatcherite rhetoric of the Falklands period, with crazed revivalist enthusiasm—as that magic moment when all the class and social contradictions of British culture evaporated and the British people, bloody but unbowed, enjoyed for a while a sense of common purpose and disinterested mutual dedication to a common cause which has since been tragically lost. While no one would claim that the United States, the USSR, and France did not also develop their official myths of World War II, this nostalgic longing—this conviction that the war represents "the good old days"—is surely peculiar to the British case. It is impossible, I think, to imagine a Soviet representation of the siege of Stalingrad which fondly recalls the hours when the characters were trapped in the only building in the city which had not been captured by Nazi troops, or a Polish representation of the Warsaw ghetto which construes the German occupation as a lost utopia, but from a very early stage there was a British myth of the war as a golden age.

Fires Were Started

Fires Were Started shows us this ideology in the process of being manufactured; the film itself is already a nostalgia movie (as Hillier virtually concedes, though he does not pursue the logic of this description). (90) The film was made in 1943, three years after the Blitz and British victory in the Battle of Britain and some months after the Red Army's triumph at Stalingrad, the turning point of the whole war. At this time, German air attacks on London had significantly diminished, and the invasion of Britain, given Germany's disaster on the Eastern front, was no longer a real possibility: Jennings's actors were firemen who had been seconded from duty to take part in the filming. It is not strictly true, then, that the film was produced in "a time of disaster" (a perfectly appropriate phrase for the first three years of the war). On the contrary, it was produced at a moment when the Western allies and the Soviet Union had visibly conquered the initiative and when it had become apparent that Japan and the Third Reich could no longer win the war: the tide had also turned in North Africa—following the Allied landing in November 1942 and Montgomery's victory at El Alamein—and in the Pacific—at the Battle of Midway. The time of disaster, in which alone good films can be made, must be conjured up for the purposes of making them, and Jennings accordingly returns to the moment of potential defeat: emotionally, potential defeat is an indispensable prerequisite of the successful enactment of war nostalgia because hardship and suffering, in their turn, are indispensable prerequisites of the ideal social unity which the war is supposed to represent.

Like so many war films, *Fires Were Started* is about the creation and consolidation, through combat and death, of an all-male group which is offered as a microcosm of the social order for which the men are fighting, and in this case the creation of the group embodies a fantasy about the reconciliation of classes: the central theme is the initiation of the middle-class fireman, Barrett (who is familiar with poetry), into a unit which otherwise consists of working men. The larger social hierarchy of civilian and military authority within which the group is inserted—and which is plainly, on the film's own showing, a class hierarchy—is noted in passing and then taken completely for granted: the class-free male bonding of the firefighting unit may well correspond to some kind of social ideal, but it has no more extensive social implications, and it certainly does not inspire any reckless challenging or even tentative questioning, of class structures external to the group. Jennings's emotional investment in the Blitz—or rather, in the idea of it—is an investment in highly specialized social conditions which allow him to envision the magical disappearance of British class society without ever having to confront the question of what, in practice, the struggle to achieve a classless society would involve. This society simply comes into being, courtesy of the *Luftwaffe*, and since the Luftwaffe is so urgently required to bring the vision of *Fires Were Started* into contact with the real world (to the satisfaction, at least, of Humphrey Jennings as a maker of documentaries), it is summoned up again to drop a few more incendiaries and create in general the state of universal misery on which the realization of the film's utopia depends.

Consider, for example, the famous song sequence. Its subject, explicitly, is the invocation of the classless male group by the new middle-class recruit through the performance of "popular" (that is, in the film's terms, "class-free") music. Barrett, sitting at the piano, strikes up "One Man Went to Mow"; one by one, in obedience to the strains of each successive verse, the jolly workers enter; with the appearance of the last man, the air-raid siren promptly sounds. The sequence is a locus classicus of the sentimental self-deception for which *Fires Were Started* is consistently remarkable. Jennings clearly thinks that he is saying—and requires us to think that we are feeling—"Oh, my God! Here they come again! How terrible!" The sentiment which the film actually expresses, however, is "Thank God they're back!" Without those bombs raining down, a British film director committed to socialist ideals would be obliged to turn his

The creation and consolidation of the all-male group in *Fires Were Started*. Personal collection of the editor.

attention to the British rather than to the German state, but as things are, the external enemy can be allowed to distract us from the impediments to those ideals which exist in Great Britain itself. The allegedly classless group is constituted within British class society—and, moreover, in its defense—but because of the Germans, the protection of this society and the fantasy of transcending it can be experienced as one and the same thing.

In fact, of course, the male group is not classless at all, as we may readily deduce from the fact that Barrett figures in the song sequence as its Orpheus. *Fires Were Started* is primarily engaged by the idea of the acceptance of a middle-class intellectual by the workers as "one of us": having undergone a rite of passage (literally, a baptism of fire), Barrett is enrolled as an honorary member of the working class in the context of a social world which continues to be organized by structures of class power. In that this fantasy of a more equitable and comradely life is unhappily contingent on other people being blown to smithereens, we are perhaps entitled to claim that the fantasy is a rather insensitive, or at the very least a thoughtless, one, and it is obviously significant in this connection that Jennings almost completely ignores the suffering caused by the Blitz. No civilians are killed, not a soul is made homeless, the fire which the characters are fighting takes place in a deserted warehouse, and the narrative's suspense (such as it is) derives from the danger that the fire will spread, not to anybody's home, but to a munitions ship (also deserted) at anchor down the road. Bombs fall, but the plucky telephone operator picks herself up, dusts herself off, and starts all over again. The Blitz, in this supposed documentary, is utterly and grotesquely unreal: it is reduced to little more than a portentous symbolic thing, the virtue of which is that it allows the business of cross-class male bonding to proceed. The role of women in the film consists of answering the telephone, providing the chaps (or blokes) with pints of beer to speed them on their way, and wheeling round the tea trolley to welcome them home again. Naturally, in the documentary context, the film's system of gender roles is camouflaged by the usual documentary alibi: the firemen actually were firemen in real life, and women actually did answer the phone and make cups of tea. This alibi is, as always, completely spurious, and once we have taken note that the realistic effect of *Fires Were Started* is continuous with the naturalization of a dramatic world which is strikingly stilted and factitious—which is hardly distinguishable, indeed, from the dramatic worlds of contemporary British fictional war films—then the alibi collapses in ruins. Jennings's vision of the end, or erasure, of class does not extend to a vision of the end of patriarchy, and as we shall see when we come to *A Diary for Timothy* (1945), the sexism of his work is a critical symptom of a more pervasive imaginative and political debility.

If no civilians are killed in *Fires Were Started*, one of the firemen is, and the death of Jacko, the emotional crux of the film, provides a useful point of transition to the analysis of *Diary*. Jacko raises in a particularly acute form the problematic nature of the role played in Jennings's movies by his intellectual and cultural interests. Hillier makes the point that the war was associated in Jennings's mind with the symbolism of Tarot cards: he identified the Blitz with "*la Maison Dieu*," a card which represents a house struck by fire from heaven and which functions in the Tarot pack as an image of cosmic fatality. (91) Tarot symbolism entered modern bourgeois high culture by way of "The Waste Land," and one's suspicion that Jennings (who greatly admired T. S. Eliot) derived his interest in the Tarot from this source is confirmed by the remarkable similarity between his treatment of Jacko and Eliot's use of another key Tarot card, "*le Pendu*." In "The Waste Land," the Hanged Man is one component of an elaborate symbolic structure derived from various fertility myths, and he appears in the poem as an avatar of the fertility god whose death redeems, and restores the fecundity of, the earth. Hillier himself does not suggest that there is a connection between Jacko and the Hanged Man, but in the light of Jennings's interest both in the Tarot and in Eliot, the relationship seems fairly obvious, and two rather different issues arise from it.

In the first place, I think we may claim with something like certainty that no one who had not been expressly told that Humphrey Jennings was interested in Tarot cards could possibly deduce this interest from the mere reading of *Fires Were Started*, and to this extent the symbolism of la Maison Dieu remains purely private, an esoteric personal preoccupation of the artist's. The symbolism is not realized in the film and plays no part whatever in its communicated significance, and this extraordinary discrepancy between private intention and enacted public meaning is suggestive of the extent of Jennings's imaginative disengagement, both from the material reality of what purports to be his subject matter (Britain at war) and from the audience whose long-suffering heroism he believes himself to be valorizing. Perhaps the point can best be made by saying that while Alfred Hitchcock did not suppose that the audience of *Psycho* (1960) would be familiar with psychoanalytic theory, nor Douglas Sirk that the spectator of *Imitation of Life* (1959) would have an expert's knowledge of the theory and practice of epic theater, we do not feel in watching these films that they have been written in an arcane metalanguage which is accessible to their authors but not to the people in the seats. On the contrary, Sirk's and Hitchcock's intellectual interests, which derive from bourgeois "high culture," manifest themselves in their work as the profound exploration, and reinvention, of the expressive possibilities of the popular artistic forms of the thriller and the melodrama, and it is taken for granted that the "intellectual interests" (if that's the right phrase) can be, as dramatized, communicated to the audience for which the films have been made. In *Fires Were Started*, we cannot escape the impression that the audience is being patronized. "Here," the film seems to say, "is the experience of the British at war. To me it means la Maison Dieu. The British at war, noble as they are, won't get it, and it doesn't matter whether they do or not." This assumption that the sensibilities of the director and the anticipated spectator are radically different—and the accompanying attitude of class patronage—are endemic to sponsored documentary filmmaking in Britain in the 1930s and '40s, and they help to explain why Jennings's commitment to both "high" and "popular" culture, which looks so promising in theory, fails to achieve an adequate correlative in his artistic practice.

In the second place, when we return to *Fires Were Started* armed with the knowledge that it is indeed informed by the symbolism of the Tarot pack, we are primarily struck (it seems to me) by how little the difference is that this knowledge makes. The symbolism adds nothing to the complexity or richness or resonance of the film's imagery; it only confirms its impoverishment by introducing a rather more pretentious, mystified, and alienated gloss of the simple literal meanings we would have picked up in any case. It was already apparent that the film construes the Blitz as an abstract symbolic event which allows men of different classes to bond. To be told that, as far as the director was concerned, this symbolic event was the fire from heaven which strikes the imprudent unawares but which may also prefigure some form of ultimate enlightenment or unification is merely to have confirmed one's initial impression that the attitude to the Blitz in *Fires Were Started* is grossly unacceptable. The construction of Jacko as le Pendu, the sacrificial fertility god, makes it clearer still that Jennings is, in effect, looking to the Nazi blitzkrieg for redemption: the British have been, or will be, bombed into transcendent national unity, and the deaths (suitably distanced and mythologized) which unfortunately result are thus redemptive in that it is through them that the unity is achieved. *Night Mail*, in 1935, had represented this unity as the existing reality of prewar British society, at once embodied by and achieved through the wage labor of a representative group of workers. By the time we get to 1943, the same unity is understood to be contingent on a perpetual rain of high explosives. *Fires Were Started*, it might be said—to adapt a famous phrase—is the continuation of *Night Mail* by other means.

A Diary for Timothy

A Diary for Timothy was made a little over a year after *Fires Were Started*, between the summer of 1944 and the spring of 1945, just before the war ended. It is Jennings's last major work, and it shows us, with painful clarity, where war nostalgia led him; even if the film had not been made, it might have been guessed, I think, that this is where a man who relied on World War II to reconstitute, through hardship and self-abnegation, a lost organic culture would inevitably end up. The war is nearly over, though one would never know it. The Red Army has crossed the Vistula, the American and British armies are sweeping over the Rhine, Warsaw is being liberated, the defense system along the British coastline is being dismantled, six years of the most excruciating warfare in human history are finally drawing to a close—and Humphrey Jennings is languishing in a quagmire of bitterness, disappointment, and depression. He seems altogether happier with the Battle of Arnhem, which, in that it was a total disaster, allowed the British to go on suffering as one nation for a few months longer. "Death came to many of us by telegram on Christmas Eve," intones Michael Redgrave on the soundtrack apropos the human costs of Hitler's last offensive on the Western front. On the other hand, it is death which binds us together, and what on earth are we going to do without it? Confronted with the imminent defeat of European fascism, Jennings can do no more than comfort himself with the thought that peace is "just as dangerous" as war, that mining accidents will continue even if air raids do not, and that the future may well be even more appalling than the past.

At one level, of course, the whole point of the film is that it is the business of Timothy, the beaming bourgeois baby to whom the diary is addressed, to make sure that peace was worth fighting for. Nevertheless, on another level, the investment in imagining the future as a sort of prolongation of the war is unmistakable: by 1944, war has become for Jennings the glue which holds Britain together. This spiritual need for the war explains the absence, here and throughout Jennings's work, of any sense of the tragic and the mood of enervation—the shocking lack of moral and emotional energy—with which he contemplates the prospect of the end of hostilities. Jacko dies in *Fires Were Started* and death comes to many of us in *A Diary for Timothy*, but these deaths are poetical abstractions, and the idea of death involved is essentially that voiced in the poem which Jennings obliges one of his firemen to read aloud in *Fires Were Started*: "O eloquent, just and mighty Death"—a curious sentiment, it might have been thought, in the context of World War II. The war is experienced, and re-created, as a solemn national pageant in which, war being war, death naturally figures. While there is no doubt a vague atmosphere of melancholy, it is no part of Jennings's purpose, and it is perhaps beyond his powers to dramatize any feeling of pain or loss or waste or suffering. The deaths are as purely emblematic as the lives which preceded them, moments of pathos in a national spectacle whose concrete reality is already distanced and attenuated, even as it takes place, by a thick crust of nationalist metaphor. One of Jennings's major themes is that "Britain Can Take It" (to quote the title of one of his first wartime films), but he never really conveys what "taking it" involves. Again, it is the idea, in the abstract, of "British resistance" which inspires him—if "inspires" is the word for these rather frigid texts. There is no equivalent anywhere in Jennings's work for Frank Capra's presentment of the siege of Leningrad in *The Battle of Russia* (1943) or—even more strikingly—for his presentment of the Blitz in *The Battle of Britain* (1943). Capra understands the Blitz, not as la Maison Dieu, but as a practical struggle, and it is the sense of a practical struggle which he communicates, whatever the ideologies are in terms of which that struggle is perceived. Jennings's Londoners, by contrast, are not historical persons but archetypes who live and die as signifiers of a mythic national *Geist*.

Since it is disaster which constitutes the nation and which permits Humphrey Jennings to make good movies, the end of disaster arouses nothing but gloom: there is going to be a national crisis and a crisis of narrative material. The really pressing question, therefore, is whether or not the white, male middle-class baby will be able to "cope with freedom," and Jennings can only resolve this agonizing doubt by offering Timothy to us as a potential national Messiah. In the Christmas sequence, which culminates in a close shot of his chubby cheeks with "O Come All Ye Faithful" blazing on the soundtrack, Timothy is explicitly identified with Christ, to whose unusual domestic situation his own exactly corresponds. The Father is absent (though under modern conditions, and through the good offices of the General Post Office, it is possible for God to communicate with his only-begotten son by mail), and the mother, it would seem, since she can hardly be thought of as the type to go sleeping around, is a virgin. Those requiring confirmation of the ignominious nature of the role assigned to women in *Fires Were Started* need look no further than *A Diary for Timothy*, in which that role has been reduced to the thankless task of giving birth to the Savior.

If the embarrassing excessiveness and insistence of this imagery of miraculous redemption convey anything, however, it is the willed, hopeless, and desperate lack of conviction with which Jennings resorts to that redemption: one's sense of creative possibility in the future must be pretty well exhausted if one is obliged, in defining it, to speculate on the imminence of the Second Coming, and for all Jennings's rhetorical inflation of his innocuous protagonist, it is the spirit of exhaustion, of course, which prevails. Jennings's real attitude to the shape of things to come is very much more adequately conveyed by his injured airman's ambition to go to the South Seas, become a beachcomber, and do nothing at all. Now that he is no longer fighting, Jennings has lost interest in him. He cannot be imagined as being anything but a "British airman" or as aspiring to anything, once he is out of uniform, but a life of feckless indolence—in a foreign country! Indeed, the most disturbing and unpleasant feature of *A Diary for Timothy* is the way in which, the war over, the archetypal British—so admirable when they were suffering and dying as one nation—become the focus of a quite different set of feelings, and the emphasis now falls on their susceptibility to the lure of venal moral relaxation on coral islands and the fear that they will be unable to sustain, under conditions of peacetime comfort (or worse), the bracing sense of common purpose which came so readily when they were being bombed. This attitude of Jennings toward the audience is implicit in the film's commentary, the more tellingly so for Jennings's abandonment of voice-over narration in his earlier wartime films. On the face of it, the commentary is addressed to Timothy, but it is also plainly addressed to the film's spectators, whom Jennings now views as a collection of moral infants who stand in urgent need of exhortation and admonishment. The tone is that of a kindly but earnest headmaster who feels he has reason to believe that every one of his pupils is about to go to the bad.

The nature of the position which Jennings has reached is painfully betrayed in the extraordinary sequence built around a performance of the graveyard scene from *Hamlet*: the production, starring John Gielgud, is represented as taking place in contemporary London so as to naturalize the sequence in terms of the documentary convention. We begin with the grave digger's famous joke about the English: asked by Hamlet (who is, of course, in disguise) why the Prince of Denmark has been sent to England, the grave digger replies that it is because Hamlet is mad: "'twill not be seen in him there; there the men are as mad as he." Uproarious laughter in the theater. Jennings then cuts to a group of rescue workers at a bomb site, one of whom, thinking he has found a survivor under the rubble, calls sharply for quiet, thus initiating a standard British comic routine whereby a request for silence, passed from mouth to mouth, generates more and more noise. It transpires, however, that the warning is a false alarm, and the rescue worker turns to his companions and tells them, offhandedly, to "carry on." We then cut back to the theater for Hamlet's great speech to the skull of Yorick, the king's jester: "Where be your jibes now, your flashes of merriment that were wont to set the table on a roar? Not one now to mock your own grinning?"

What Jennings thought that he was doing in this sequence it is impossible to tell: the enacted meaning is distressingly clear, but one cannot imagine it to have been fully conscious. The "British at war" have become a stale joke: the rescue workers are extras in a Will Hay comedy; there is no body buried under the ruins. As we have seen, the war was never fully real for Jennings in the first place, but now that its end is in sight, heroic firemen and sacrificial hanged men are replaced by generic Cockneys, and the British character becomes the object of a querulous and cynical irony which culminates in the juxtaposition, through parallel montage, of Yorick's skull, unearthed by the grave digger, and the absent bomb-site victim. Shakespeare uses Hamlet's speech to dramatize his protagonist's neurotic revulsion from death. Hamlet once loved Yorick ("Here hung those lips that I have kissed I know not how oft"), but in death he becomes nothing more than a symbol of the futility and transience of life in the body, and the speech ends with Hamlet throwing the skull aside in disgust. In the new context created for the speech by Jennings, Hamlet's reaction to the skull, critically placed by Shakespeare, is surreptitiously endorsed, and the speech comes to represent Jennings's feeling about the inhabitant of the bombed-out house, about the British he has mythologized, about the myth of the war he has dedicated himself to perpetuating. "Dost thou think Alexander looked o' this fashion i' the earth?"/"E'en so."/"And smelt so? pah!" In the midst of all the spurious uplift about Timothy, salvation, and the fragile promise of fresh young life, Hamlet's "pah!" tells us where *A Diary for Timothy* actually stands. At a moment when one might have thought that an artist with socialist sympathies would be pondering what might be made of the massive defeat of the European right, Jennings recalls the past, and anticipates the coming period, from a position of total nihilism.

Jennings and the British Documentary Tradition

It goes without saying that more is at stake here than the personal sensibility of Humphrey Jennings: his sensibility is representative. Hillier ends his essay with the words: "Perhaps, consciously or unconsciously, [Jennings] lacked a new vision, confidence in the future. And perhaps the world he looked at lacked it too." (120) The world he looked at? All of it? Jennings is very different from Grierson (typically, Grierson thought him a dilettante), but they have in common the fact that their enthusiasm for "the people" and "the common Man" and their conviction of "the dignity of the worker" absolutely depend on the common Man's being safely contained by the social order of the capitalist nation state. He is, of course, a marvel, but he is marvelous only in his capacity as a working part of the organic social body. Jennings takes up this attitude toward "the British people," quite uncritically, from the British documentary tradition which his own work continues, and although the attitude is obviously deeply conservative, the tradition encouraged Jennings to mistake it for a form of socialism. Grierson, after all, was capable of advancing the astonishing claim that *"Night Mail* and *Housing Problems* were the films of a Tory regime gradually going socialist"* (though he does not tell us whether or not this remarkable tendency on the part of the Stanley Baldwin administration was successfully consummated under Neville Chamberlain and Winston Churchill); and Harry Watt could say in all sincerity that "we were trying to give an image of the working man, away from the Edwardian, Victorian, capitalist attitudes." (Barnouw, 100, 90) The intellectual and political confusion, or disingenuousness, implied by that list of adjectives and that description of *Night Mail* forewarn us of what we have to expect when we watch the films, and while Jennings was very much more sophisticated than either Watt or Grierson, his sophistication, given his failure to question the assumptions embedded in the tradition and conventions he inherited, was not of much help to him. "He was attracted by the imaginative materialism of Marxism but felt, for example, that Blake's 'Song of Los' said all there was to be said about owners and men in the context of the Industrial Revolution and says it much better than Marx did." (Hillier, 65)

It may be agreed that Blake developed a profound critique of the Industrial Revolution which retains its importance to this day, but to argue that this critique is "better" than Marx's is nonsensical and absurd, and the principle effect of Jennings's remark is to call into question the nature of the allegiance to Blake. We may feel that an artist who finds himself praising Blake on these grounds would also be ill-equipped to criticize the conventions of the British documentary from a socialist position, and might even end up using them in such a way that no one could deduce he was familiar with Blake's critique of industrialism at all. It seems reasonable to suppose that Jennings's conviction of Blake's superiority to Marx as a critic of capitalist society has to do with Blake's being British and with the fact that Blake tried to convince himself, in his later work, that Jerusalem could be built again "in England's green and pleasant land." F. R. Leavis has argued that the belief in the possibility of restoring Jerusalem represents the weakness (inevitable in the given historical circumstances) of Blake's position (*Nor Shall My Sword*, 11), but whether or not one agrees, as I do, it is quite indisputable that there is something very wrong with a love of Blake which leads, in practice, to the assertion that Jerusalem will be created by Timothy, and nothing could be more remote from the intensity and moral passion of Blakean "imagination" than the inertia and inanition characteristic of late Jennings. The idea of Jerusalem has degenerated in *A Diary for Timothy* into mawkish bourgeois escapism which can be correlated, on the one hand, with Jennings's refusal, or inability, to conceptualize the transformation of the social world in concrete terms and, on the other, with the flaccid and indulgent despair in which he emerges from World War II. "It will all have to go, it has been a terrible mistake!" he apparently remarked near the end of his life, "surveying the industrial landscape of Battersea." (Hillier, 120) This sentiment is the exact counterpart of the hope that England will be redeemed by Timothy, and it is just about as helpful.

In the context of the British documentary tradition, which was the only cinematic tradition which Jennings had behind him, all his potential strengths go for nothing: they are turned, in fact, into positive weaknesses. His ardent and informed preoccupation with English cultural history is assimilated into an idealistic, and almost mystical, English nationalism; his attraction to "the imaginative materialism of Marxism" and the Blake of "The Song of Los" is reduced to sentimental populism; and his complex and wide-ranging aesthetic allegiances manifest themselves as the kind of pretentious bombast which passes for "art" in 1930s British (and American) documentary filmmaking. The beautiful images of *A Diary for Timothy*, and E. M. Forster's unctuous commentary, embody the same notion of cultural seriousness which produces the pastiche of Walt Whitman on the soundtrack of *The River* (1938), W. H. Auden's ode to the post office in *Night Mail*, and Virgil Thomson's submodernist musical scores, and while we cannot doubt that Jennings genuinely loved Shakespeare and Milton and Beethoven, they appear in his work only as museum pieces—as "High Culture" in the most conventional, academic, and deadening sense.

The weaknesses of the British documentary tradition are, in effect, the weaknesses of British social democracy: an account of why *Industrial Britain* (1933) and *Night Mail* and *A Diary for Timothy* are bad films turns inexorably into an account of the drastic ideological limitations of Labourism, and in particular of its historical failure to disengage itself from, or provide a coherent and intelligible alternative to, the assumptions and discourses of the dominant class culture. "Jennings's political views were certainly left-wing," (Hillier, 65) but these views do not get into his work, and if one were asked to give one's reasons for saying that his films could not have been made by a high Tory, it would be difficult to do so on the basis of their politics. He hopes vaguely for a better world: that is about it. This world, however, though better, will not be in any essential way different, and if Jennings is completely incapable of formulating any progressive social aim or project, that is because he is imaginatively complicit in the very ideologies which such a project would be obliged to contest.

Metaphor and Mimesis:
Madame de . . . (1982)

T he booklet on Max Ophüls, which was published to coincide with major retrospectives in Edinburgh and London, is an inept and embarrassing document. Even its editor is not quite convinced by its pretensions and feels compelled to construct elaborate alibis which will allow him to disclaim responsibility for the mysterious process whereby a publication appearing under his name inexorably consolidates critical positions to which he is explicitly opposed. In a series of prefatory remarks to an introduction entitled, with coy tendentiousness, "Familmographic Romance," Paul Willemen inveighs against "certain idealist ideological discourses" which might seek to posit Ophüls as a source of coherence in "the work that is generally ascribed" to him. (*Ophüls*, 1)

Over half the booklet is taken up by interviews with or writing by Ophüls, and in his own contribution Willemen finds occasion to "substantiate" two critical hypotheses by referring to the director's remarks. An emergency exit is nevertheless available: Willemen is the unfortunate victim of "industrial and ideological, institutional pressures" which have "prefabricated" his task for him—so completely, it would seem, that it is impossible to discuss his own work as editor as part of the structure of prefabrication which is supposed to determine that work. (1) It is moreover impossible, according to Willemen, either to conceive of another method or to provide an account of the "pressures" and their mysterious ways, since there is "no 'subject position' available within the institution" from which to do so. The proclamation of this all-purpose *salve mecum*,* and the accompanying gestures toward the categorical imperative, are followed at once by a surrender to the most conventional auteurism and to a banal form/content dualism which, despite the impressiveness of its credentials, is practically indistinguishable from that which dogged Ophüls criticism in the days of Roy Armes, Richard Roud, and Lindsay Anderson.

It is curious—and ought, one feels, to trouble the writer rather than provide his excuse—that a serious analytical discourse should proceed from the assumption that it is objectively incapable of extricating itself from discourses which it claims are incompatible with it. The oddity, however, has at least the merit of drawing our attention to the substance of the claim. The fault, perhaps, lies not in Willemen's stars, nor in the Kafkaesque impediments of "the

---

* *Salve* in Latin is a greeting that means "be well" or, essentially, "hello." *Mecum* means "with me." So *salve mecum* is "be well with me" or "hello along with me," both of which are nonsensical. What Britton seems to be suggesting here in wordplay is that Willemen is offering a sense of ideological determinism as an excuse for his self-imposed critical limitations. Thanks to Professor Carol Merriam, Department of Classics, Brock University, for this explanation.

institution," but in his method and its presuppositions. I do not wish at this point to embark on a developed account of the complex epistemological, political, and aesthetic issues raised by the realism debate. Since the only interest which the Ophüls booklet can be said to have lies in its neat demonstration both that a concept of realism is necessary in order to discuss Ophüls and that the epigones of materialist film theory can do no more than announce the necessity of succumbing to idealism, a few preliminary remarks are therefore in order.

A recent book by Rosalind Coward and John Ellis, *Language and Materialism*, provides a useful starting point. "The business of realist writing," the authors argue in a eulogy to Roland Barthes's *S/Z* in chapter four,

> is, according to its philosophy, to be the equivalent of reality, to imitate it. This "imitation" is the basis of realist literature, and its technical name is mimesis, "mimicry." The whole basis of mimesis is that writing is a mere transcription of the real, carrying it over into a medium that exists only as a parasitic practice because the word is identical to, the equivalent of, the real world. (47)

Despite the fact that the concept of mimesis was formulated some years before the appearance of the genre, mimetic/realist writing is identified with the bourgeois novel which, for the purposes of the theory, is viewed as a homogeneous entity: all bourgeois novels operate within the same mode, which determines a particular relation—alike, invariable—between reader and text. Mimesis, identified through a pun with "mimicry," offers itself as a transparent representation of a reality existing "out there"—an offer it is able to make, we are told, because mimetic writing adopts the strategy of repressing its status as writing and insinuates an illusory identity between signifier and signified. There is thus a correlation between the fact that mimesis attempts to conceal the process of articulation in language and the fact that it naturalizes what it describes. "The realist narrative," Coward and Ellis continue, "functions to uncover a world of truth, a world without contradictions, a homogeneous world of appearances supported by essences." (49) In other words, realism/mimesis functions so as to naturalize bourgeois social relations, and the authors propose an analogy between the way in which "realism stresses the product and not the production" and that in which capitalist exchange relations conceal the oppressive relations of production within which commodities are produced, the commodities appearing "naturally" on the market as pure exchange values "naturally" equivalent to particular sums of money.

The most immediately striking thing about this argument is that it disposes of the question of writing a priori: if realist writing can be defined in terms of the conflation of signifier and signified, then it won't be necessary, clearly, to consider realist writing. The premise of Saussurean linguistics is that the relation between signifier and signified is arbitrary: language, we know, consists of negative differences, and all that is required of the signifier is that it be distinct from every other signifier in the system. If we accept this proposition, we are potentially committed to a form of linguistic naturalism: either the signifier/signified relationship is arbitrary or it is motivated, and if it is motivated, it is also, by definition, an ideological imposture—a form of false consciousness. A nonarbitrary relation between signifier and signified must be conceived of not as a fact of the social existence of language, but as a social mystification of its essential nature. It is therefore perfectly logical that Coward and Ellis should reduce Marx's theory of commodities and their exchange to a matter of false appearances and transform an account of the material social form of the process of reproduction into an idealist dualism of reality and its illusion.

The slide into what is, in effect, an opposition between the nature of language and its misleading cultural accretions can be attributed to the working through of a tendency implicit in the second basic distinction of Saussureanism—that between *langue* and *parole*. For Ferdinand de Saussure, the language system (langue) is "social," "essential," and "homogeneous," and therefore theorizable. Speech (parole) is "individual," "accessory," and "heterogeneous," and therefore inaccessible to theory. But when Saussure calls langue social, it is only in the banal sense of "non- or trans-individual": he leaves out of the word *social* the very concept which alone gives it substance—the concept of a specific historical situation. By defining langue and parole as an opposition between the social and the individual, by excluding the individual discursive act from the social, only to reintroduce it as an effect-of-system, Saussure effectively ensures that the social existence of meaning (its stability and its transformation) is inconceivable. The Coward/Ellis model of realist writing embodies an identical fallacy: they propose a supposed "social" form which simply deposits its variants.

In order to proceed further, we must reject both the hypothesis that the signifier/signified relationship is arbitrary and Saussure's conceptualization of langue and parole. The relation between signifier and signified is not arbitrary but historical, and it is produced within the specific social conditions which include the activity of speech. Not only are languages inseparable from other social practices, they are also the medium within which other social practices are articulated. This is precisely the specificity of languages—they are the social practices by means of which reference takes place. Semiotics is important inasmuch as it draws our attention to the inevitable tendency for the act of reference to "naturalize" the relationship between the sign and its signification. Clearly, language depends for its usefulness on stability of meaning, but I may well be unaware of the fact that the signifier carries an evaluation of, and defines an orientation toward, the signified. In other words, the basic condition of language—the need for semantic stability in the conduct of social life—is thereby the material basis of ideology. But at the same time, because languages are always embedded in social practice, the possibilities of meaning—or of "practical consciousness," in Marx's phrase—are not fixed, but continuously inflected and redefined. Semantic stability and semantic change are facts, not of language per se, but of the relations which define its use and the values it realizes, and it is only through the concept of historical process that we can begin to think of languages as systems of evaluative signification which always precede individual speakers but which are present as discourse only within the exigencies of a complex social present.

Let us return at this point to the Coward/Ellis account of mimesis, which will doubtless have surprised attentive readers of Aristotle. The poem, according to the *Poetics*, imitates human actions "either as they were or are, or as they are said or thought to be or to have been, or as they ought to be." In other words, as Paul Ricoeur points out in an admirable passage in *The Rule of Metaphor*, Aristotle abandons the Platonic usage of mimesis, whereby even nature is an imitation of its idea, and he proposes instead the dialectic of a generative and a referential function. "As for mimesis, it stops causing trouble and embarrassment when it is understood no longer in terms of 'copy' but of redescription": it is not a literary form, but "the 'denotative' dimension" of what Aristotle calls *muthos*, or fable. Mimesis, in fact, becomes inseparable from *poiesis* (poetry)—the heuristic discursive activity of the poem: "there is mimesis only where there is a making." (35–43, 244–45)

The dialectic of reference and production embodied in mimesis and the location of that dialectic in the activity of writing which constitutes the text are crucial for an alternative account of realism. The Coward/Ellis model is formalist and essentialist. It hypostasizes a particular discursive mode—the mimetic/realist—as the necessary product of particular formal strategies (also hypostasized) such that all "realist" texts enact identical discursive procedures and identical positions of reading. While a concept of the determinate historical characteristics of, say, the novel is invaluable, inasmuch as, in Marx's phrase, "production in general is an abstraction, but a useful abstraction if it actually emphasizes and defines the common aspects and thus avoids repetition," the value is contingent on the recognition that "the general concept is itself a multifarious compound comprising divergent categories" and that the specific object is not production in general or the novel in general, but precisely the specific object. By presupposing the irrelevance of "writing," Coward and Ellis produce, in place of Marx's useful abstraction, a Platonic form which renders any possible concrete instance and any rigorous abstraction from it alike inconceivable.

Let us consider, by way of illustration, a passage from George Eliot's novel *Middlemarch*, cited by Colin MacCabe in the course of an argument more or less identical to Coward and Ellis's, as supremely exemplary of the way in which realist prose "denies its own status as writing." (MacCabe, "Realism," 9)

> He [Mr. Brooke] had never been insulted on his own land before, and had been inclined to regard himself as a general favorite (we are all apt to do so, when we think of our own amiability more than what other people are likely to want of us). When he had quarelled with Caleb Garth twelve years before he had thought that the tenants would be pleased at the landlord's taking everything into his own hands.
>
> Some who follow the narrative of this experience may wonder at the midnight darkness of Mr. Dagley; but nothing was easier in those times than for an hereditary farmer of his grade to be ignorant, in spite somehow of having a rector in the twin parish who was a gentleman to the backbone, a curate nearer at hand who preached more learnedly than the rector, a landlord who had gone into everything, especially fine art and social improvement, and all the lights of Middlemarch only three miles off. (Eliot, 274)

What conclusions does MacCabe draw from this remarkable passage? "A classic realist text," he tells us, "may be defined as one in which there is a hierarchy amongst the discourses which compose the text and this hierarchy is defined in terms of an empirical notion of truth." The narrative prose or metalanguage, "which being unspoken is also unwritten," abstracts "the meaningful content from the useless form" of other discourses in the text ("discourses" being used here in a vulgar sense to signify the dialogue of the characters) and reveals their relationship to the truth, "the final reality," which it embodies in itself. Thus, in the present case, "the discourses of Dagley and Mr. Brooke are revealed as springing from two types of ignorance which the metalanguage can expose and reveal." (8–10)

If we turn our attention to the first sentence of the second paragraph quoted—and, we must believe, pondered—by MacCabe, we find the phrase: "Some who follow the narrative of this experience may wonder at the midnight darkness of Mr. Dagley . . . ." We have followed, not an experience, but the narrative of an experience; the foregrounding of the speaking voice carries here an emphasis on both the characteristic substance of the genre (the experience of the characters) and its conventional medium (narration). Experience is a property of "real" human beings; narration is the making of heuristic fictions. George Eliot emphatically alerts us, that is, to the dialectic proper to mimesis, and in so doing—another way of saying the same thing—proposes the four terms of the "dramatic poem": experience, the dramatic world, the narrative voice, and the reader.

Why does she do so? A clue is to be found in the phrase "midnight darkness." Attuned as we are to the speaking voice, we pick up at once on the declamatory, melodramatic note which the image strikes. Midnight darkness is indeed very dark, and the hint both of hyperbole and of Gothic gloom establishes a register quite distinct from that of the prose which precedes it. The discord consolidates our sense of the significance of tone and of the reader/writer relationship and refers us back to the opening phrase: "Some who follow the narrative of this experience may wonder at. . . ." Those who do so wonder, it is implied, may not have grasped the dramatic function of "the narrative of this experience." The foregrounding of narration has the effect of compelling us to reconsider our reading, and perhaps to criticize it. Moving on to the end of the paragraph, we discover that midnight darkness is implicitly juxtaposed with "all the lights of Middlemarch." This is the standard of illumination in relation to which the profound obscurity which envelops Mr. Dagley is to be measured.

We are given, then, an apparent antithesis between enlightenment and the darkness of ignorance, and the function of the prose which, across the sentence, links the two phrases is to encourage the reader to question both the terms of the antithesis and the appropriateness of the antithetical structure as such. This function is carried, once more, by the tone of the narrative voice: the irony undertakes to demonstrate both the unreality of the antithesis and the fact that the structure of class relationships in *Middlemarch* is such that the antithesis is available, as a means of interpreting reality, to individuals occupying particular social positions in the community. The passage, in other words, is not about the "ignorance" of Brooke and Dagley (the ascription of ignorance to Dagley is, in any case, the judgment of the rector, the curate, and the landlord) but about the way in which the criterion of enlightenment involved can be located in particular class positions and serve to rationalize the necessity of the social status quo: if Mr. Dagley wanders in midnight darkness, it is because his ignorance is as hereditary as his grade, and he is constitutionally incapable of reaping any benefits from the superb advantages of his environment or of attaining the standard of his social betters. Nor is the passage about this in the sense that this is its content, its extractable paraphrase. The negative judgment of Mr. Dagley's intelligence and the critique of that judgment are enacted in the writing—in that extraordinary tonal counterpoint which gives us at once the voice of the gentleman to the backbone, bemused by the necessity of enumerating the obvious representatives of the cultural vanguard, and the ironic undertow generated—for example—in the association of fine art, social improvement, and the class credentials of the rector's spine.

It is crucial for Eliot's purpose that the first clause in the complicated verbal structure of the second paragraph should draw the reader up before a possible complicity with Mr. Brooke and insist that the question which has been raised—the question of the position from which reality is interpreted and meaning attributed to it—is one which immediately concerns him or her. It is of the essence of what follows that the meaning of the sentence is not a matter of its informational content: were we to read it with that presumption, we would reach some such conclusion as MacCabe arrives at (and Eliot can be excused, perhaps, for her failure to anticipate an attribution of "transparency" to a passage which is systematically concerned to pose narration as a substantive issue). The meaning *is* the process of articulation, and it is dramatized in a verbal movement which conducts an analysis of the very perception which it seems to validate. The irony—the tone of voice—makes of the reader and the writer the pivots of this dramatic process. It is precisely because the narrative prose is "unspoken" that it is written: "the narrative of this experience" is constructed, and the foregrounding of the terms of narration becomes inseparably, for the reader, the dramatization of conflicting ideological allegiances.

The analysis of this passage from *Middlemarch* allows us to take the discussion of mimesis a stage further. If mimesis embodies a dialectic of imitation and "making"—if, that is, mimesis is denotative—we can conclude, with Ricoeur, that "mimesis serves as an index of the discourse situation, that every act of discourse issues from a position and postulates the reality to which it refers." (*Rule,* 43) The forms of creative mimesis construct a dramatic world from within a set of conventions—more or less complex, and possibly contradictory—which define the nature of their set toward a reality external to themselves. The mimetic function, in other words, does not presuppose any belief in the literal possibility of the represented world or the actions which constitute it. One can think of any number of works which undoubtedly put forward "imitations of human actions" and which directly oppose any such belief. The conventions of many, though by no means all, of the forms of bourgeois realism do construct a very direct relationship between the dramatic world and a contemporary social reality: the class relationships defined in the passage of *Middlemarch* are a particularized fictional denotation of general patterns of relationships that have an objective existence independent of their representation. To say no more than this is to say less than nothing and to lay oneself open to the inane formalism which allows one to imagine that one has said anything at all significant about *The Grapes of Wrath, The Sound of Music* (1965), *L'Assommoir,* and *Toad of Toad Hall* by describing them all as "classic realist texts." (MacCabe, "Realism," 12)

Even MacCabe, however, feels the need "to make distinctions" within the area he has so liberally marked out, and busily sets about to find a criterion by which to do so. After an elaborate preamble, to which Karl Marx, Friedrich Engels, Vladimir Lenin, and Bertolt Brecht are summoned to lend their authority, he comes up with his trump card—content analysis. "Thus a classic realist text in which a strike is represented as a just struggle in which oppressed workers attempt to gain some of their rightful wealth would be in contradiction with certain contemporary ideological discourses and as such might be classified as progressive." (16) Really? Even the bourgeois press is prepared, in some circumstances, to acknowledge that a particular strike is a "just struggle" and that the workers are hard done by, but then the phrase "certain contemporary ideological discourses" is so portentously vague that it is hard to know what MacCabe means by it. Similarly, a strike might be represented as a just struggle by a Trotskyist, a Stalinist, a Maoist, an anarchist, a social democrat, or even, perhaps, a member of the British Communist Party *couleur de Hirst*; it would be so far from being useful as to be actively misleading to describe all these representations as "progressive." A thesis which concludes that *Cathy Come Home* (1966), *Z* (1969), and *War and Peace* are all progressive texts wouldn't seem to have got us very far, but since MacCabe's conviction that the narrative discourse in classical realism "is not present . . . as articulation" (MacCabe 12) necessarily excludes the consideration of writing, he finds himself attaching importance to, on the one hand, a wholly untheorized notion of the author's conscious political "sympathies" and, on the other, a banal concept of the mode of presence of ideologies in discourse. He is thus able to argue, at one and the same time, that: (a) "subject matter is a secondary consideration for realism [since] what typifies the classic realist text is the way the subject matter is . . . articulated" (MacCabe, 20); and (b) since articulation is homogeneous and, moreover, a kind of negative, in that it is never present as such, the criterion of progressive realism is subject matter.

Once we have committed ourselves to the transparency theory of realism, we find that we have two major strategies to hand for the recuperation of those realist texts which we wish to redeem, or which seem to escape from the confines of the theory. One, as we have seen, leads toward a fixation on content—a kind of halfhearted Zhdanovism, festooned with provisos and disclaimers. The other might be defined as the "aesthetics of subversion," and it leads toward a fixation on "style." This tendency is certainly present in MacCabe's essay, if in a relatively primitive form; in the Ophüls booklet, it manifests itself in its full glory, and by one of those remarkable coincidences which Monsieur de . . . finds so natural, finds itself trapped in a predicament identical to that of the less-sophisticated formalism against which it fulminates. Indeed, this new formalism is so sophisticated that it no longer recognizes itself and imagines itself to be an entirely new animal. Style and content are not "wholly independent," *pace* Armes, nor do they correspond, as we had once imagined. On the contrary, we can now perceive that content is a "pretext" for style, and that Ophüls's films "are not 'about' their subjects in any direct manner, [but] spectacles in their own right." (Willemen, *Ophüls*, 74)

It does not become clear what a spectacle in its own right is, or in what way it differs from the "triumph of form over content" celebrated by Roud in *Max Ophüls—An Index* (6), but Willemen is nearby, lest we despair, with still more radical insights. For Willemen, style—now passing incognito as "the registers of text construction"—inscribes both "a breakthrough of excess" repressed by "the Law" and the process of repression itself. In those instances in which it is deemed that "the registers of text construction" have some kind of dramatic motivation, however vague and unspecified, "the Law" appears to be synonymous with the "rigorous social order" created within the narrative world. Thus, we are told, for example, that the camera's movement in the crane shot of the Maison Tellier in *Le Plaisir* (1952) is generated by that which

is repressed within the walls of the brothel. Elsewhere (and predominantly), Willemen identifies the Law with "a coherent scenario." (*Ophüls*, 73) In other words, narrative equals repression
and style the return of the repressed, or to give the whole thing a dialectical flavor, a mixture of,
simultaneously, the return of the repressed and the reinscription of repression.

While it should by now be something of a truism that artistic forms are historically determinate and that the languages they employ and the models of coherence they construct negotiate reality in ways which are also historically determinate, it would never occur to me to give
an ahistorical definition of "coherence" per se as repression in the Freudian sense. Lacanian
discourse theory and its derivatives encourage Willemen and his collaborators to reiterate the
familiar self-fertilizing, self-perpetuating trilogy of order, subversion, and the reimposition of
order, at the service here of a binary distinction between style and narrative and an unusually
elaborate but simpleminded auteurism: having abandoned Ophüls as origin and only beget-
ter, we conclude that the films themselves posit none other than "Ophüls." The Cartesian ego
which we have so noisily and contemptuously abandoned turns out to be the goal of the journey. The result is a perfectly conventional list of formal devices, deprived of any context either
dramatic or cultural, and assigned a hypostasized, independent signifying value. It becomes
impossible at the same time to distinguish between particular films, all of which, because they
are "Ophüls" texts, do the same things in the same ways. We have certainly rid ourselves of the
naive assumption that the film can be attributed to the auteur and only to him/her, but at the
price of recreating the auteur as effect-of-structure and of abandoning any concept of style as
a formative process.

Madame de . . . (The Earrings of Madame de . . . [1953]) begins, as it ends, with a close shot of
the objects which, by their circulation, define at every point the relations between the film's
protagonists—the heroine's earrings. Louise (Danielle Darrieu) needs money and is deciding
what to sell; after a brief inventory of her possessions, she concludes that the earrings have the
least value for her. The decision precipitates at once the appearance of a series of contradictions
which the earrings both embody and conceal—contradictions already adumbrated in the title
and the introductory caption. Madame de . . . , we are informed, seemed destined to lead "*une
jolie vie sans histoire*"; were it not for "*ces bijoux*," it is probable that nothing would have happened. Yet it is precisely the earrings which, as a token of marriage—they were a wedding gift
from her husband—seemed to guarantee Louise's exclusion from history in the first place. A
similar paradox is embodied in the title: even as Louise is defined absolutely as "wife," the
omission of her husband's surname implies the insecurity of the definition—its tenuousness.
In both cases, the signs of Louise's containment within patriarchal order raise in the same
moment the possibility of her transgression.

The first two transactions around the earrings precede the start of the film: the jeweler
sells them to Monsieur de . . . (Charles Boyer), who in turn gives them to Louise. These transactions establish the social norm of exchange, which is coextensive with "histoire" as a process
in which men are active and women passive: "We sell to men because of women," as the jeweler
puts it. The original sale is, explicitly, a matter of property and capital: the earrings figure as a

Danielle Darrieux in the man's world of *The Earrings of Madame de. . . .* Personal collection of the editor.

commodity, and the exchange of money defines the social relationship between the individuals involved as that of buyer and seller. In the second case, however, the real social relationship established by the earrings emerges in a sublimated form: there is no explicit question either of an exchange or of Monsieur de . . . acquiring property rights in his wife. In becoming a wedding gift, the earrings appear not as an exchange value but as a token of disinterested affection. This exchange, which does not appear as such, has for function the termination of exchange—it removes both the earrings and Louise from the market. The conditions of the gift should, ideally, transform the earrings from an economic quantity into an abstract moral quantity: they should surrender their exchange value and acquire a personal value which makes them "priceless." At the same time, in becoming Louise's property, they signify that she has become the property of her husband; Louise owns them only because she is owned in her turn. It is the failure of coincidence between these two facts which have previously been reconciled—the fact that the earrings are her property and therefore at her disposal, the fact that they are her property only because she is her husband's wife—which initiates the movement of the narrative.

Thus, the circuit of exchange precipitated by Louise's decision to sell the earrings is automatically transgression, which is registered here by the fact that their sublimated exchange value has reemerged. It is crucial, moreover, that the transgression is located not in a self-conscious desire to transgress—not in a manifestation of rebellious or rebarbative will—but in an objective contradiction in the relations of women and property, which emerges, as it were, by chance. Louise does not sue for divorce but sells her husband's wedding gift in order to maintain herself, without embarrassment to herself or her husband, in the marriage which has ceased to have significance for her. In other words, Louise displays at this point the characteristic unconsciousness of the melodramatic protagonist; she lacks any means of conceptualizing her actions or the forces which determine them. Much of the film's extraordinary poignance derives from the fact that the degree of impersonal judgment she attains at the end ("The woman I was made the woman I am") is a measure both of the extent and the limits of her progress. The woman she is is still far from being wholly available to her.

To raise the question of consciousness is to proceed at once to a discussion of camera movement: the opening shot introduces the recurrent motif—consider also the two ball sequences and Louise's desolate walk on the beach—of the tracking shot which at once accompanies and observes the circular movement of the characters. "Accompanies and observes" is the appropriate emphasis: camera movement simultaneously enacts the characters' entrapment and defines for the spectator the critical position from which the analysis of that entrapment becomes possible. This dialectic of insideness with/outsideness from the dramatic world is not "Ophülsian" *tout court*: it is the characteristic mode of significant mimetic art, and its formal means are infinite, but it is—it must be insisted—a fact of the writing of the work. It testifies to that possibility which is open to mimesis of constructing critical metaphorical models of reality, and its tendency is not to solicit but to resist and disturb identification. The style/content dualism is only resolved in this—that content is never present except as style, and that style is a positive articulation which has the potential to transform its own modes and thus to redescribe that which is "imitated." Ricoeur concludes: "Poetic discourse faces reality by putting into play heuristic fictions whose constitutive value is proportional to their power of denial." (*Rule,* 239) The medium of those fictions is not some eternal form—"representation"—which, like God or the Idea, is and ever shall be—but the activity of discourse, which is alone the criterion of the status of the dramatic reality and of our relation to it.

The first shot moves from and returns to the earrings, but while the intervening camera movement is determined by Louise's movement, she is only there in the shot as a hand and a series of reflections; both her movement and her physical presence are mediated by the objects which surround her—objects which acquire a more substantial existence than her own. Our first glimpse of her face is as a reflection in an ornate oval mirror as she holds the earrings to her ears: she appears, both to herself and to us, in an absolutely objectified form, the crucial distinction being that our sight of her foregrounds the objectification. There is a gap between our perception and Louise's, dramatized, in the process of the shot as a whole, in the forty-five-degree angle which separates the line of the shot from Louise's gaze. Holding up the earrings, Louise imagines that "After all, I can do as I like with them." The illusion of autonomy is nourished by the very image which demonstrates its insubstantiality.

The first three sequences—in house, church, and jeweler's shop—are bound together by three motifs: the act of exchange, the conspicuous presence of white candles in the decor, and the scrutinizing male gaze (the general's portrait in the reception room; the soldier praying in the church; the jeweler and his young assistant). At once, the "private" realm and the realms of commerce and the spirit are associated with one another, and in terms which establish succinctly the central preoccupations of the film.

1. "By the currency of the circulating medium, the connection between buyers and sellers is not merely expressed. This connection is originated by, and exists in, the circulation alone." The relationships between the characters in *Madame de . . .* exist alone in the circulation of the earrings. Marx argues that it is characteristic of the commodity economy that things are "personified" and relations between people converted into "entities." (Marx, *Capital,* 137) Isaac Il'lich Rubin comments:

> By the "materialization of production relations" among people, Marx understood the process through which determined production relations among people . . . assign a determined social form, or social characteristics, to the things by means of which people relate to one another. . . . By "personification of things," Marx understood the process through which the existence of things with a determined social form, for example, capital, enables its owner to appear in the form of a capitalist and to enter concrete production relations with other people. (22)

The apparent contradiction "can be resolved only in the dialectical process of social production, which Marx considered as a continuous and ever-recurring process of reproduction in which each link is the result of the previous link and the cause of the following one." (22)

Marx's theory of fetishism has been indignantly traduced of late by those who have embraced Barry Hindess and Paul Q. Hirst's "reformulation" of historical materialism, on precisely the ground that recommends it (temporarily—Coward, in her polemic against the Birmingham Institute, endorses Hirst's recidivism) to Coward and Ellis—that it postulates a dualism of reality and its illusion and thus a concept of ideology based on perceptual misrecognition. Ironically, the most strenuous advocates of these grave charges are frequently unabashed Lacanians, whose conceptualization of ideology in terms of discursive "subject-positions" precisely devolve upon metaphors of vision: Coward, for example, finds herself able to approve Jacques Lacan's reworking of the early Marx/Engels metaphor (explicitly discarded in Marx's mature work) of the camera obscura. But alas, the Hirstian critique of fetishism depends upon an initial idealist reduction of it, underwritten by the belief (so irresistible for psychoanalysis *à la rive gauche*) that there is no specifiable reality external to discourse. Marx does not argue that given social positions entail, for the individuals who occupy them, the misrecognition of a reality which is itself unproblematic, still less that reality is a construction of discourse—an assertion which is simply incompatible with materialism. On the contrary, he argues that there are a number of mechanisms specific to capitalist society whereby it "necessarily appears to its agents as something other than it really is." (Bhaskar, 88) If Louise imagines that "I can do as I like with them," it is not because she is deceiving herself, or failing to grasp the self-evident, but because the social relations which include her and the earrings, and within which the categories she employs to articulate her experience have been produced, present the earrings to her in a systematically mystified, or fetishized, form.

Bhaskar continues:

> The very forms in which social life presents itself to experience embody funda-mental category mistakes (such as the presentation of the social as natural in fetishism or the "interpellation" of individuals as free agents in their constitution as subjects) . . . [and] through the theorem of the necessity of phenomenal forms for social life, they are themselves internally related to (that is, constitute neces-sary conditions for) the essential structures that generate them. (21)

The failure of Louise's desire to be contained by her marriage opens up, "accidentally" and unwittingly, the objective, socially necessary contradictions between what the earrings are and what they appear to be—between their (tacit) value assigned by real relations of property and exchange and their phenomenal form as Louise's own pos-session, which she, as a free agent, can dispose of as she chooses.

Crucially, there is no question here, or at any later stage, of "radical consciousness": the ideologies precipitated by the phenomenal forms of real relations continue to gov-ern Louise's decision to sell the earrings even as her action issues in a contradiction, the development of which, with its gradual ramifications in consciousness, is consid-erably postponed. And while it is perfectly true that in *Madame de . . .* we are not deal-ing with a continuous process of reproduction, but with a process of transgression—a disturbance of social relations—this truth needs to be specified. On the other hand, "probably nothing would have happened."

The effect of this is to vacate any concept of the "radicalism" of desire: there is no equivalent in the world of *Madame de . . .* for the confused and mystificatory business of the "revolutionary of the heart" which informs *Lola Montès* (1955). The value which the earrings acquire as Donati's (Vittorio De Sica) gift—a value illumined by the dis-covery of the "true" self, by the "authenticity" of desire—remains fetishized: the status of the earrings as a fetish in the Freudian sense (as a stand-in for the absent phallus) is a particular manifestation of a structure of necessarily fetishized value forms in the Marxist sense. What Louise experiences as lost authenticity is a form of reification which complements that which she rejects, and which is distinguished from it by the fact that she has invested her desire in it. The grandeur of "all for love and the world well lost" cannot survive the implication of the forms of love in the practices of the world it violates.

On the other hand, while the decision to sell the earrings is already in principle a transgression, it does not yet disrupt the social relations which have assigned to the earrings their social form as a signifier of marriage. Monsieur de . . . is quite prepared to tolerate Louise's deception, for while the earrings have been sold, the role of donor has not been challenged. Indeed, the earrings immediately come into his possession again, and he uses them to terminate his relationship with Lola. Engels remarks in *The Origins of the Family, Private Property and the State* that the logic of patriarchal monogamy finds its supreme expression in the Code Napoleon, which institutionalizes male adultery on the condition that the husband's mistress does not enter the conjugal home. (125) The earrings can be given by Monsieur de . . . to another woman, but not to Louise by another man, and the crucial fact is less whether or not Louise has the earrings than the power of gift. Thus, the film's crisis is precipitated when, for the first time, Louise takes control of the circuit of exchange by buying the earrings herself. Even after they have become Donati's gift, it has been possible for Monsieur de . . . to compel Donati to sell them to the jeweler and, later, to force Louise to give them to his niece. In becoming Louise's property in her own right, the earrings pass beyond male control; no further exchange is possible, and on terms which the woman has decided. We can thus distinguish, as regards the nature and extent of the transgression involved, among the original sale, the lover's gift, and the wife's purchase, the third being the only transaction which is absolutely outside recuperation. At the same time, of course, the third transaction represents, on another level, the most extreme form of Louise's subjugation: while she has transgressed the form of the social relations of exchange, she has by no means questioned all the values assigned to the object of exchange—and, therefore, to herself—by those relations. The earrings are now in her power, but her evaluation of them represents her complete enslavement by Donati—by a socially proscribed romantic passion which is the negative analogue of her subordination to her husband.

2. In the second ball sequence, Louise declares, as she dances with Donati, "I detest the world! I only want to be looked at by you." The incident functions partially to reinforce the continuity between the attitudes to Louise of husband and lover: Louise's remark comes in response to Donati's expression of his jealousy of another man who has spoken to her, which echoes Monsieur de . . . 's "Your suitors irritate me" on the steps of the opera. At the same time, as Louise, assigning the world to oblivion, dramatizes herself through the classical rhetoric of romantic love ("Kingdoms are clay"), she posits herself once more as an object for the male. The series of male glances—bemused, indulgent, fascinated, dominating—which follow her in the three opening sequences, and which bind together the three "realms" of bourgeois society, imply not simply an external agency, for it is in relation to them that Louise, contained or transgressing, defines herself, her activity, and her aspirations. Self-realization at once takes the form of self-objectification and reaches its apotheosis in the fetishization of the earrings, in which the reification of human relations and the personification of the thing finds their extreme expression.

3. From the very beginning, the Church—and with it the concept of a transcendent, suprahistorical power external to social life—is firmly located in society: Louise's prayer is the first act of exchange we are shown (a candle in return for a blessing), just as her final prostration before the same altar, in which she makes an unconditional renunciation of her desire, is the last. If Louise, with the encouragement of Donati and

her Nanny, sublimates the purely social logic of her relationship with her lover in terms of Fate, then at the end of the film she conceives of socially determined self-abnegation as a voluntary sacrifice to eternal Providence. The series of "fortuitous" encounters with Donati, perceived by Louise as the work of destiny, are offered by the film as the working through of a determinate process which the sale of the earrings makes possible, and the Fate which operates in the first meeting at the customs post is decidedly material—Donati is trying to pick Louise up (one might compare Lisa's experience of her encounter with Stefan in *Letter from an Unknown Woman* [1948]).

It is of the essence, indeed, that the logic of the relations "not merely expressed" but realized by the earrings cannot be defined in metaphysical terms. On the one hand, the circulation of the earrings, arising out of an objective contradiction in the marriage relation, assigns to Louise, Monsieur De . . . , and Donati the roles of, respectively, wife/mistress, husband, and lover. On the other hand, the process of these relationships assigns complex and contradictory significations to the earrings. But while the earrings realize the connections between these specific individuals, the positions assigned by them and the values which accumulate in them are determinate. "Wife," "mistress," "husband," and "lover" do not come into being, as social forms, with the characters, and the emphasis on inexorability in the film proceeds not from an abstract fatalism but from the rigor with which the metaphor of the earrings enacts the reified forms of the relations available to the characters.

These impersonal relations, realized by and invested in an object, are repeatedly juxtaposed with interpersonal exchanges characterized by a discrepancy between formal surface (what is said) and significance (what the speaker means or, for some reason, does not articulate), by interruptions and impediments, by the unspoken, the misleading, or the superficial. As they dance in the first ball sequence, in an endless series of circles, Donati and Louise discuss the other guests and the situation in Montenegro; when Donati visits the house, they discuss the battle of Waterloo. Donati and Monsieur de . . . transpose their mutual awareness of being rivals for Louise into an exchange about fencing and billiards. In the first bedroom sequence, Louise lies to her husband, who in his turn lies, in effect, to her, as well as taking a silent pleasure in his awareness of her lie and his ability to exact, surreptitiously, an apology for it. In the second bedroom sequence, Monsieur de . . . , having drawn from Louise's remarks a meaning she does not intend, but which, given their ambiguity, they make available, proceeds to a course of action which will have an effect directly contrary to the one he wants. Ophüls, in both cases, dramatizes the complete lack of contact between the characters in the mise-en-scène as well as in the dialogue. The first meeting between Monsieur de . . . and the jeweler is constantly interrupted by the sound of a cannon and by the speakers' attempts to find a language which will negotiate the encounter to their mutual satisfaction while eliminating, as far as possible, any hint of impropriety. Language conceals, distracts, dissimulates, formalizes; what the characters say is determined by what they cannot or will not say, and this in its turn is determined by the relations constructed by the earrings.

✳   ✳   ✳

Any fully adequate account of *Madame de . . .* would need to define the film's relation to, on the one hand, the structures and iconography of the cinematic melodrama, and on the other, the nineteenth-century novel of adultery: that most insistent genre of bourgeois realism which embraces, for example, *Madame Bovary*, *Le Rouge et le Noir*, and *The Scarlet Letter*, and which reaches its apotheosis in *Anna Karenina*. Such an analysis would reveal interrelationships at a number of levels. The attempt to analyze a network of oppressive social/sexual relationships through the image of the circulation of a commodity with phallic associations links *Madame de . . .* with, for example, Alfred Hitchcock's *Notorious* (1946), John Brahm's *The Locket* (1946), and indeed, George Eliot's *Daniel Deronda*, which uses the exchange of the two necklaces in ways strikingly analogous to Ophüls's rewriting of Louise Levéque de Vilmorin. Similarly, the horse-riding incident (an Ophülsian invention), in which the heroine's first public demonstration of her concern for her lover is precipitated by a riding accident, makes explicit reference to Tolstoy's novel.

I will limit myself here to the significance of a particular concept of the heroine, brilliantly analyzed by James Walton. In a discussion of the "enforced passivity" of the persecuted heroine in bourgeois literature, Walton writes:

> The heroines of all these novels are the victims of a world which sees them simply as opportunities for lust and avarice, which depersonalizes them . . . But the love which destroys them is really a way for these heroines to assert personality, a desperate alternative to the depersonalization which the masculine world imposes on them. . . . The elaborate insistence on the absolutely compulsive nature of passion . . . is a way of avoiding active subversion of the male world . . . Any female aggression to alter this unjust . . . world would contradict in its assertiveness and independence the utter helplessness required for heroic status and for the erotic and pathetic pleasures such heroism delivers to the audience.

Walton concludes:

> Barred from effective entry into the world of power and action, [these heroines] cause that world to enter them. They exhaust it. Each represents the novelist himself, who contrives to show us that no external world is exhibited in his pages, only private vision. Their mirror-image within the fiction is a demonic persecutor who assumes their guilt, provides them with tragic stature, and vanishes, pleading, like Lovelace, "Let this expiate!" Such narcissistic structures derive their broad appeal from the close affinities between the heroine-as-artist and each member of the middle-class reading audience. His disadvantages and compensations are a specialized form of theirs. In debt for their very identity to the institutions which, like Chinese boxes, enclose them, they know that the strength of these institutions makes submission and passivity, however unheroic, the cardinal virtues. For them, inwardness alone provides transcendence, and their world within has heroic dimensions. "*Madame Bovary*,

c'est moi" is the signature of a bourgeois imagination . . . that dreams of power through self-immolation but reaches, in Conrad's phrase, for "a direct grasp upon humanity," the aim of "artists, politicians, thinkers, reformers or saints." (33–35)

We don't need to look further than to *Lola Montès* to discover the dangerous temptations which this pattern represents: the possibility of its realization is inherent in the structures of Ophüls's work, and there could be no clearer indictment of the superficiality of the formalist preoccupations of the Willemen reading than its failure to make necessary discriminations within the oeuvre and its mistaking of a tendency to elicit a narcissistic identification with the heroine for a tendency to elaborate the objectification of her. The critique of the subjugation of women within patriarchal social relations, and of their objectification for the gaze, pleasure, and profit of men, is systematized within the films at a very early stage (by the time, at least, of *La Signora di tutti* [1934]), and there is never any question of a direct complicity with it. Indeed, it is the prerequisite for the particular pattern of identification involved: *Lola Montès* can conduct so rigorous an analysis of the construction of woman as spectacle precisely because of its ulterior commitment to a metaphysic of "woman" as the location of an authenticity perpetually betrayed—the source of a possible transcendence endlessly lost within relations of oppression which the film at once deplores and universalizes.

The Heath/Willemen problematic of representation as per se the representation of woman—the concept of "relations sustained in cinema, as cinema," which necessarily produce, "according to the rules of patriarchy," a structure within which woman is deposited as "the signifier of desire . . . for that other signifier, the look"—is unable to analyze this process because it collaborates with it. (Willemen, *Ophüls*, 71–72) The structural necessity of the objectification of women is the term of *Lola Montès* itself, and a critique which endorses that term can only achieve, ironically, a new variant of the banal reflection theory of realism—a theory no longer concerned with the transparency of a reality external to the text, but with the transparency of a hypostasized model of the construction and perception of the text. Trapped inside the Chinese boxes of "the institution," Lola and Willemen are always already articulated by the structures which include them. They can never find a position from which to speak, and we are forever denied the transcendence we can be sure that they embody. The pseudo-feminism of *Screen*, which arises as a possibility from Lacanian discourse theory, makes of *Lola Montès* a peculiarly attractive proposition: Representation must construct Woman as the subject of desire and is always, at the same time, the "effecting and the effect" of Me. Nothing is left but the perpetual return of a male Cartesian ego in the wake of its expulsion, perpetually lamenting its collusion with and predication by the unalterable institutions which its theory necessitates.

Ophüls is not Josef von Sternberg, and nowhere achieves that radical reformulation of *Bovaryisme* whereby the identification of the male artist with the female protagonist takes the form of an identification with female activity—with a positive critique and redefinition of patriarchal forms, values, and institutions including the terms of the representation of women. "I am Marlene" is, to that extent, the progressive reformulation of "*Madame Bovary, c'est moi*," though it involves Sternberg increasingly in peculiar problems of his own. The greatness of *Madame de. . .* consists not in the fact that it resolves or moves beyond the ascription of "submission and passivity" to the heroine, but in that it enacts at once an incomparable elucidation of its social determinants and a systematic displacement of the form of relation to the heroine which Walton describes.

The denial of "heroic status" for Louise goes with the demonstration that the socially determined limitations of her sensibility are such that "assertiveness and independence" can't be conceived of by her—or rather, that they assume determinate forms which return her to passivity. The corollary of this is the refusal of identification: the Ophülsian "writing" locates the protagonists in a rigorously specified commodity capitalism. Through the dramatic parallel-in-contrast between Louise and the earrings whereby Louise is both peculiarly the object of exchange and (with the general and Donati) the subject of an objective social process governed by exchange, the "writing" breaks out of that deadlock within which the heroine's passivity can be associated with transcendence unredeemed.

It ceases, indeed, to be a question of passivity at all, and by transferring our attention to determinate activity, the film is able both to honor the specific character of women's oppression and to refer it to social relations which determine the conscious activity of women and of men. The moment of "transcendence" in which the heroine finds, through self-abnegation, at once her temporal defeat and the vindication of "the world within" (her *Dark Victory*) becomes, in *Madame de . . .* , the final act in the circuit of exchange. The gift of the earrings in marriage by a man cannot remove but only temporarily contain and conceal the contradictions of the contract: it can never guarantee that the heroine's personal valuation of the object (her desire) will remain in harmony with its signification. The heroine's exclusion from history can only be assured by her unconditional renunciation in a contract with a party who guarantees nothing—by her "Though he slay me, yet will I trust in him." Louise cannot be secured by giving *to* her, on the hypothesis that she will always desire the gift and its conditions, but only by exacting *from* her what she always will desire. In the first case, a gap remains between Louise and the earrings—a gap in which problems can arise. In the second, the gap is closed: Louise, as it were, becomes the earrings, surrenders herself, and "consents to" a complete and successful objectification. Thus, the "*don de Monsieur de . . .* " which precedes the action is displaced by the "*don de Madame de . . .* " which terminates it—by that "voluntary" offering in which Louise and her desire can at last be fixed and embodied in the earrings. The fact that the movement of the earrings has been reversed but that they remain the earrings is the mainspring of the film's irony—its means of demonstrating that Louise's desire always remains a determinate product of the reality which fails to contain it. That the film does not leave room for a positive transgression is the limitation that attends its achievement, and while it is a limitation of which one should be aware, it does not affect one's tribute to the way in which *Madame de . . .* , in articulating and redefining the terms of a major historical genre, constructs the most lucid and suggestive analysis of the dominant form of sexual relations under capitalism which the cinema has given us.

It is appropriate to conclude by considering two dramatic moments which, in their juxtaposition, help to specify some of the points I have tried to make about the film: (1) the long tracking shot past the windows of Louise's bedroom which concludes the sequence in which Monsieur de . . . , convinced that Louise's desire to leave Paris signifies her desire to end the relationship with Donati, insists that she stay. From a position outside the house, the camera tracks from window to window, accompanying Monsieur de . . . as he closes and fastens them and draws the curtains; (2) the scene in which Monsieur de . . . visits Louise in her prostration after the second ball sequence, which has ended with Donati's breaking off the relationship ("I am no longer with you, Louise"). Monsieur de . . . orders Louise's maid to open the curtains, which, after consulting Louise's wishes, she refuses to do. As soon as she has gone, Monsieur de . . . opens them himself, causing a flood of sunlight to pour over Louise's couch, to her intense discomfiture and distress.

The two scenes make use of one of the most familiar iconographic motifs of film melodrama (Vincente Minnelli's *Madame Bovary* [1949] and *The Cobweb* [1955], Douglas Sirk's *All I Desire* [1953] and *All That Heaven Allows* [1959], Charles Vidor's *Gilda* [1946] provide immediately striking examples)—the window as an image of entrapment, particularly the entrapment of women. It might appear at first that the scenes have the effect of producing Monsieur de . . . simply as his wife's oppressor: in both cases she is prostrate and compelled to submit to the exercise of his will. The simple pathos engendered by such a reading might seem to be confirmed by referring the first scene to the conclusion of the first ball sequence, to which it is clearly linked by the image of the extinguishing and obscuring of lights, as well as by the elaborate camera movement accompanying the figure who shrouds Louise in darkness. Louise mentions to Donati, as they dance alone, that her husband is coming home the following day; thus, the closing of the curtains at a later stage reiterates the motif, and explicitly makes Monsieur de . . . the agent of a process which the mere prospect of his presence has already, through a surrogate, initiated.

The matter becomes more complex as soon as we note that the tracking shot in the window-closing sequence makes it clear that Monsieur de . . . is trapping himself as much as Louise: we are concerned once more with an ironic counterpoint between a conviction of self-determination experienced by a character and the scrutiny of its determinants. Monsieur de . . . has just announced that Napoleon was wrong only twice: at Waterloo, and when he said that one should always run away from romantic entanglements. We will later discover that Monsieur de . . . has an enormous painting of the Battle of Waterloo on the wall of his drawing room, but it is already implicit in the mise-en-scène that his correction of Napoleon's strategical errors, and the crisp, decisive precision of the maneuver with which he "takes control" of the affair, define a kind of self-confidence which is radically misplaced.

It is the confidence, in fact, of the metteur-en-scène himself, which Monsieur de . . . 's knowledge of Louise's prevarication has allowed him to indulge in the earlier bedroom sequence. Monsieur de . . . has felt himself to have privileged access to the "reality" of the fiction which Louise wishes him to believe and makes his own use of the discrepancy between the true story and the lie, both to ease Lola's departure by giving her the earrings and to corroborate his characteristic sense of an ironic outsideness from the reality of which he is part. The initial sale of the earrings does not disturb but actively reinforces this sense: Louise may have initiated the action, but he is confident that he has knowledge of its secret, and can thus silently reassume a position of superiority to her ("*Pardon? Je vous demande pardon*"). The confidence expresses itself in his readiness to let Louise imagine she has deceived him—that is, ironically, to indulge her sense of autonomy—and the first bedroom sequence ends with the opening statement of the motif of extinguishing lights, enacted here by Louise herself.

Monsieur de . . . knows the plot and has taken control, as far as he is aware, of its trajectory: let Louise believe, if she will, that she is the author of this drama and its successful resolution. Hence, the deep dramatic resonance of the window-closing sequence, which makes fully present the latent irony of the first bedroom scene. Even as Monsieur de . . . defines the parameter of the dramatic space, the camera suggests that he is not the maker of the mise-en-scène but an actor within it. To that extent, the perspective of the tracking camera on Monsieur de . . . is analogous to the perspective he had previously taken on Louise, with the difference that the dramatic irony isn't of that kind which allows any hint of superiority. It is, on the contrary, the medium through which the film effects our critical recognition of our involvement, and it is crucial that the prevention of identification doesn't encourage some illusion of objectivity. Indeed, it is no small part of the film's irony that it displaces Monsieur de . . . 's, which cannot survive his implication in a world he can no longer simply observe.

It is of equal importance that the irony doesn't spare Louise; the position defined for us in the scene in which Monsieur de . . . abruptly opens the curtains he has previously closed can be taken as a characteristic product of the film's general principles. Monsieur de . . . 's gesture prohibits, on the one hand, any concessions we might wish to make to Louise's morbid withdrawal into romantic despair. In the early stages of the film, we are quite deliberately lured into reading Louise's heart complaint as a manifestation of "coquetry," as a strategy which goes with her internalization of a particular female role of "charming irrationality" ("*Moi et la raison!*"). It is only later that it becomes apparent that Louise is really ill and that "*cette faiblesse que vous avez au coeur*" implies not simply an organic complaint; it becomes a metaphor for the systematic impoverishment and curtailment of emotional resources and allegiances produced by Louise's oppression. We are forced to revise our judgment and to recognize both the determinants and the consequences of behavior which we might have been tempted to find "delightful." But if Monsieur de . . . can be used here to separate us from Louise, and from her beloved Nanny's indulgence of her despondency, the echo of the earlier scene in which Monsieur de . . . has closed the curtains reminds us of his complicity in the process, the conclusion of which he deprecates. His solicitude for Louise is movingly genuine, but he is demanding of her a resilience and robustness which everything in their relationship has served to destroy, and which his ironic attitude toward her has neither encouraged nor required. He has indulged Louise's role of "charming light-mindedness" and raised himself ironically above it; to that extent, the opening of the curtains suggests an attempt—pathetic in its insufficiency—to counteract the history in which he has been an actor. The gap between the peremptory assertion of control and the failure to recognize the nature of the process the character wishes to change has never been greater.

Thus, the two moments I have singled out can be assimilated to a number of interrelated motifs which have the function—among other things—of dramatizing a network of mutually oppressive relationships, in which the characters entrap both themselves and others. If Louise's extinction of the candles above her bed at the end of the film's first movement is associated with the paradox of the sale of the earrings and the lies contingent on it—Louise settles back in the happy belief that she has not damaged the marriage which defines her oppression and which has no real value for her—then the reappearance of the same motif registers an awareness of the same relationship as an impediment to her desire. The entrapment which she has, with some relief, consolidated, is suddenly experienced as entrapment—with an irony all the deeper, for the spectator, for the fact that romantic love is experienced simultaneously as the promise of liberation. At the same time, in taking over the function previously acted out by Louise "on her own," of containing her within the marriage, Moniseur de . . . perceives the reinforcement of his own and his wife's oppression both as a solution to the problem, rather than an exacerbation of it, and as an expression of love for her ("*Je t'admire, et je t'aime*"). The oppression has always been mutual, and Monsieur de . . . 's "I have tried to be the man you wanted me to be" carries great force, but it never generates an adequate recognition of its corollary. Here, as throughout the film, consciousness continually lags behind, and fails to sufficiently grasp, its determinants.

Thinking about Father:
Bernardo Bertolucci (1977)

"History is a nightmare from which I am trying to awaken."
—James Joyce, *Ulysses*

Bernardo Bertolucci's films seem to me to take as their theme a matter which has preoccupied a great deal of recent film criticism: the ways in which the individual is, in Louis Althusser's phrase, "interpellated as a subject" in ideology, in which the Symbolic Order of the culture is inherited, internalized, perpetuated. In offering various proposals for a psychoanalytical reading, the model of psychoanalysis to which I will refer is that developed by Norman O. Brown in *Life Against Death*, a work which adheres, as its title implies, to the concept of the death instinct outlined by Sigmund Freud in *Beyond the Pleasure Principle* and subsequently abandoned by much post-Freudian psychoanalysis (with the crucial exception of Melanie Klein and her followers). Rather than proceeding to an abstract array of concepts, I shall introduce them as they apply at points of crucial significance in the films.

At the beginning of *The Conformist* (1970), Marcello is picked up at his hotel by Manganiello, and they set off in pursuit of Professor Quadri, Marcello's former teacher, whom he has been hired to assassinate. In the car, Marcello is clearly oblivious of what Manganiello is saying to him. The camera tracks in slowly on his face, which is smiling mysteriously, and a dance tune fades in on the soundtrack. Bertolucci cuts to a recording studio, and the track in continues, this time toward a huge wall of glass which separates us from the recording area and through which we see a dazzling white decor, a small orchestra, and three girls in green and white dresses clustered round a microphone in the middle, jigging and swaying to the music of the song they are singing. Marcello is pacing back and forth in front of the glass partition, on our side of it, talking to Italo about his need to conform: "I want stability, security . . . an impression of normalcy. . . . When I look in the mirror, I seem to look different from everybody else."

The imagery gives us an extraordinarily complex visual and aural metaphor for the structure of ideology. The radio broadcast conveys an impression of normalcy to its listeners, and the essence of their experience of it is their blindness—they cannot see what they hear. A link is at once established both with Italo's literal blindness and with the film's central image of Plato's cave, proposed during Marcello's first conversation with Quadri. One might describe Marcello's conformity in terms of the progress from the proposed thesis on the cave under Quadri's tuition to the fulfillment of the need to sit down in front of the wall with the prisoners.

The glass partition here becomes an analogue both of the wall and of the cinema screen, on which we "see only the shadows projected on the back of the cave . . . the reflections of things." The image allows us to experience more than the radio listeners, and it simultaneously gives us a figure of that extra experience through Marcello, who wishes to be absorbed into the normalcy on which the scene beyond the glass gives us a (critical) perspective.

The broadcast attempts to naturalize ideology and to sublimate physical reality. The song the girls sing is called "Who is happier than I?" and the title of the program—"the Archangeli program of light music"—assimilates the happiness to a state of celestial bliss and contentment. The colors of the girls' dresses suggest nature, fertility, innocence, purity, amid the antiseptic cleanness of the decor, and the song is followed by a man doing imitations of birdcalls. This onslaught of joy and Natural Process provides the context in which Italo's propaganda broadcast will take effect. He speaks, not of a political but of a spiritual alliance, a mystical union authorized by Nature ("their deep kinship") between two images—"the Prussian image of Mussolini, the Latin image of Hitler." The progress of the broadcast might be summarized thus: unsurpassable happiness (the song) and Nature (the bird imitations) can reach their mutual zenith in a preordained spiritual union (the Axis). The emphasis on history is crucial: the sequence of unparticularized rhetorical abstractions culminates in the notion of historical inevitability—assimilated to the "natural" order of reality—and of history making.

The conceptual network—the re-creation of the present as the past (Italo tells us that previous alliances have "left a mark on history"), the ever-expanding family structure (the individual listener made to feel contentedly at one with Nature, the movement of time, the etherialized marriage of nations)—coincides with the theory of history as neurosis which is the crux of Brown's reading of Freud. Brown associates the fear of separation and expulsion, which is the impulse behind social formations, with the sequence of traumas of separation (from birth to the castration anxiety) which constitute infantile sexuality. Ideology is what returns the subject to the family, what deprives him of his individuality ("You want to be the same as everybody else"), and thus of the anxiety created by separation. The terms of Italo's broadcast extend the project of reunion to the historical level, so that the illusion of being taken up in history making becomes the ultimate assurance of security.

The notion of conformity as regression recurs constantly. *Before the Revolution* (1964) begins with the words of the conforming Fabrizio, safely married to Clelia, safely absorbed into bourgeois society—"Now I am tranquil, clinging to my roots. I feel as if I no longer exist": the return to the womb imaged as death. Then, in the sequence of Fabrizio's run through the streets of Parma to meet Clelia in the church, Bertolucci establishes a set of correspondences fundamental to all the films.

1. The identification of Christianity—specifically, Catholicism—with the bourgeoisie: "sin is the rejection of bourgeois values."
2. The indication of an ideological split in Fabrizio, suggested in terms of books. Fabrizio describes himself as carrying a volume of Pascal in one hand and "Songs of the Greek People" in the other, and he goes on to speak of "vague desires of freedom stifled by Catholicism," Pascal representing here the morbid sacrifice of individuality to the

prohibitions of a repressive God. The notion of imprisonment by books (the inherited culture) is a leading theme, here and in *Partner* (1968): consider, for example, the moment of Jacob's breakdown, his increasingly desperate verbal revolt (the humming of "The Marseillaise," the repeated cry of "Throw down the mask!") finally succumbing to an admission that "it is necessary to build walls" as he adds book after book to the pile in front of him, finally disappearing behind them. In both films, too, the book imagery is inseparable from the pervasive references to *Moby Dick*. The reference is made explicit at the end of *Before the Revolution* in the intercutting of Fabrizio's wedding (the pledge of his conformity) with a scene in which Cesare, Fabrizio's former teacher, reads from Herman Melville's novel to his young pupils. But the reference is also implicit in an analogous scene in *Partner* in which the revolutionary Jacob shows his class how to make the bomb which will "strike through the mask" that conceals reality. In *Moby Dick*, the *Pequod*, like Fabrizio, is balanced, "though sorely strained, you may well believe," by conflicting books (the heads of John Locke and Immanuel Kant), inspiring Ishmael's comment—"Oh, ye foolish! throw all these thunderheads overboard, and then you will float light and right." (*Moby Dick*, 277) Melville's themes of cultural entrapment, of the dialectics of consciousness, and of the classic variant of the Oedipal project suggested by Ahab's quest, are obviously important for Bertolucci. Fabrizio is, finally, unable to escape from books. His words are always somebody else's ("I have to speak like a book to sound convincing").

3. A parallel between marriage to Clelia ("the sweetness of life I don't want to accept") and ideological submission. Fabrizio's appointment with Clelia is in a church, the church is in the center of Parma, and "the church is the pitiless heart of the state." Clelia is introduced after a series of close-ups of the heads of statues of saints, so that she seems to become a religious icon (during the opera scene, Gina likens her to a portrait by Parmigianino), and the scene ends with a close shot of Fabrizio, his head inclined against a pillar, his eyes vacant—already, implicitly, belonging to the body of Mother Church.

4. The association of the river—a symbol, traditionally, of life, fertility, creativity—with the class divisions of bourgeois capitalist society; it separates the rich and the poor. At the turning point of the film, Fabrizio accepts his own conformity as historically inevitable ("There is no way out for us children of the bourgeoisie") by identifying himself with Puck, the bankrupt aristocratic landowner, in his lament for the fact that "the river is finished. We must forget it."

We can extend the discussion by returning to the recording studio scene of *The Conformist*. The singers beyond the partition anticipate Julie, whose role is structurally equivalent to that of Clelia in the earlier film. We first see her jigging aimlessly to the music of a record player, and she is presented as utterly devoid of ideological awareness: a perfect product of the cultural image of femininity presented by the singers, the ideal of charming, dependent vapidity. Marcello both marries and despises her for this ("She's an ordinary girl full of petty thoughts and petty ambitions"). His contempt suggests Marcello's projected self-disgust as well as the Freudian concept of the conflict of ambivalence toward the mother, a crucial motif in the film; in the scenes in which Julie and Marcello's mother first appear, he is seen covering their nakedness. The scorn also serves, crucially, to distance us from Marcello. Although Julie is portrayed with ruthless honesty, we are not invited to feel superior to her, and her childishness, in any case, is thematically complex, allowing her access to the bisexual experience from which Marcello is in flight but making her politically indifferent and ideologically innocent.

Psychoanalytically, the scene connects (a) the longing gaze at the impression of normalcy embodied by the singers; (b) the expressed desire to be the same; (c) the attraction to Julie; (d) Marcello's placing of his hands on his own body where Julie's breasts would be as he tells Italo that "maybe it's her body, her sensuality" that he likes about her. Thus, the normal life which Marcello tells the priest he is going to build slowly and carefully suggests what Brown describes as the "pure pleasure-ego project"—"the dream of union with the world (the mother) in love and pleasure" achieved by "repudiating the external world" and projecting anything unpleasurable outward into it. (*Life*, 40–52) What he, in fact, achieves is brilliantly and economically conveyed in the scene with his daughter at the end of the film. Bertolucci implies the continuation of the pattern through the new generation: father and daughter, in identical positions of prayer, facing each other like reflections against a wall painted to represent a brilliant blue sky with fluffy white clouds, the child repeating the words of penitence and subjection to the Holy Family.

Thus, on one side of the glass, we see the unreal, purified hermetic world from which the external world is banished. Marcello is on the other side, in the darkness, with Italo, and when Italo goes round into the studio to take the place of the singers, presenting to Marcello's gaze the reality of the normalcy of which they were a sublimated image, Marcello hides his face. Bertolucci makes brilliant use here of the reflections in the glass, superimposing over and beside Marcello the image of Italo reading his speech with the aid of a Braille manuscript. In all the car scenes, we constantly see Marcello through the glass of window or windshield, sometimes additionally obscured by torrential rain. The normal life can be built only at the cost of permanent, violent repression of the nature of the self. Italo is blind, committed to fascism, and, clearly, homosexual—Marcello's alter ego who, at the end of the film, becomes, with the change of regime, Marcello's scapegoat. Indeed, the entire film turns on the attempt to repress bisexuality, a rejection which Freud suggests is the essence of "the neurotic conflict between the libido and reality," and the murder of Lino, the chauffeur, is carefully organized in these terms. We see groups of adults watching with complete indifference as Marcello, wearing a conspicuous sailor suit, is beaten up for his effeminacy by a mob of his schoolfellows. He deliberately stops Lino's car, and when they arrive at the house, again leads the chauffeur on, telling him he has a present for him, "a revolver—a real one." Lino replies, "I have a gun, too," and also "a beautiful oriental kimono." The child's attitude vacillates constantly between response/incitement and retreat.

The bisexual theme is taken up by Anna, Quadri's wife, and by the two brief appearances of Dominique Sanda which precede this final incarnation, both associated with the scenes in which Marcello commits himself more and more inexorably to the murder of Quadri (the visits to the ministry and the brothel). Marcello shoots Lino in the left side of the head; the prostitute

(Sanda 2) has a scar in the same place; Anna is shot there at the end of the film. There are further links in terms of arousal/repression of desire, as in the Lino scene. Marcello spies on Sanda 1 with her lover, receives a disdainful, imperious look, and recoils. Anna asks him, when she has found him watching her with Julie, "Do you always spy on people like this?" His embrace of the prostitute is interrupted by Raoul ("We're wasting time!"), who gives him the murder weapon while opening, with an ornamental cracker, the walnuts he conceals in the lap of a naked statue of a recumbent woman. The sequence of violent denials, which culminate with the reappearance of Lino on the night of the fall of the fascist government to which Marcello has conformed, may be compared with Marcello's dream. He is blind (one of the prisoners in the cave). Manganiello, the alter ego whom he has earlier used to beat up his mother's lover (thus a "father"), is driving him to Switzerland (neutrality, Never-Never-Land) to be operated on by Quadri. Quadri saves his sight (release from the cave). Anna is in love with Marcello and deserts Quadri for him (winning of the mother from the father). The dream comfortably resolves all the contradictions, and Bertolucci immediately juxtaposes it with the reality. The car in which Anna is escaping with Quadri comes into sight, and as Manganiello comments on this ("Sometimes love can work miracles"), Marcello picks up and loads his gun.

The conformity theme in *Before the Revolution* is differently inflected. Fabrizio's socialism itself is immediately established as a form of regression, a flight from pain ("I used to be in constant anguish"), the grasping for a comprehensive meaning which can accommodate even one's mistakes, and which repeats the essential structures of religious belief. This willed commitment, which is accompanied by an incapacity for and continual retreat from deep emotional contact, is juxtaposed with the confusion and alienation of Agostino, Gina, and Puck, who are intensely alive emotionally but who, in very different ways, either despair of or are directly opposed to political liberation. The film is built on complex variations on the themes of time and of the nexus isolation/independence and unity/conformity.

1. Agostino is a runaway who has to keep coming back. Fabrizio callously accuses him of escapism and tells him that "people who run away from home make me laugh." The condemnation is already deeply ironic, given that the film flashes back from the words of a Fabrizio who has conformed. After Agostino's suicide, Fabrizio, wearing a dinner jacket and seated at his father's table, launches into a coolly posed valedictory for him, ignoring the presence of Gina, whose need for his help and attention is clearly as great as Agostino's was.

2. Gina takes over Agostino's role—the boy's performance on his bicycle is echoed in the sequence in which she poses for Fabrizio in different types of spectacles, the link stressed by the music—and Fabrizio's desertion of each to visit Cesare is followed in both cases by breakdown. Gina's despair, like Paul's in *Last Tango in Paris* (1972), stems from the experience of separation/ independence/death. She speaks in anguish of her father's death, associating it with her own ("I dreamed I died, too"), and the consciousness of survival is one both of vulnerability and of an increased, meaningless vitality which has to be wildly dissipated to deny death ("One feels like moving about, talking, gesticulating"). Consider her encounter with the little peasant girl,

Evelina, who has been left alone, locked up in an enormous house, and whose endless chanting song and refusal to speak to her reduce Gina to hysteria, the child clearly presented as Gina's "image." One notes, also, Gina's desperate telephone call to her psychiatrist which follows the loss of Fabrizio to Cesare, in which she pours out her dread of separateness, displacement, exposure.

3. There is a constant sense of entrapment in time. Fabrizio's first remark to Agostino is "What time is it?" before sending him off (a) to "join the Party"; (b) see *Red River* (1948), a beautifully concise irony. After her arrival in Parma, Gina sits on her bed and spreads photographs of her childhood around her in a circle, first looking at them and then turning them over one by one. The themes of time and isolation come together in the scene in the camera obscura, with which—on the question "Where will we be in autumn?"—the first half of the film ends. In the love scene, Fabrizio's confession that he is glad they made love in the room where he played as a child is balanced by his fear of discovery and by the bleakness and lack of fulfillment implied in the treatment of their physical contact (on the one occasion when they are shown in one shot, they are in long shot and surrounded by darkness).

4. The film moves from a resurrection which never takes place (the connotations of rebirth in "Just before Easter, 1962" set against the idea of the Church as sterilized bourgeois institution) toward three "festivals of unity" which become tokens of disintegration. Fabrizio's final acquiescence in the status quo takes place at the opening of the Milan opera house, during a performance of *Macbeth*. The use of Giuseppe Verdi here suggests the emasculation of culture by the bourgeoisie, with the name which embodied the cry of *il Risorgimento* (Vittorio Emmanuele, Re d'Italia) reduced to the label for a great occasion. As Gina remarks: "Our beloved Verdi! All that we are not! Enough Verdi! I'd prefer Mozart." Fabrizio's failure is the failure of Italian culture, and one's impression here is reinforced by Bertolucci's remarks about Verdi in a recent interview, which stress "this sense, which was constantly being confirmed, of a relationship between Verdi's creativity and the reality of that countryside." (Bertolucci, "Interview")

Fabrizio's remark to Cesare during the parade scene that "People accept everything" finds its echo when his mother, showing Gina the box where he is sitting with Clelia and her parents, tells her "He accepts everything now." If the film emphasizes the failure of a popular revolution, it is because the bankruptcy of its middle-class intellectuals is felt to be inseparable from a general complacency and unawareness: the parade is merely a display of flag-waving, as barren, culturally, as the night out in the name of art. All the inadequacies interlock in a complex web. Thus, Fabrizio's assertion that the workers want to mingle with the bourgeoisie and improve their living standards is balanced by Cesare's "Why not?" The attempt to renounce responsibility for Agostino and pass it on to the party leads, when Cesare again intervenes ("Why expect the Party to do what you didn't?"), to the articulation of the need for the party to replace God, to transcend the weakness (the ideological subjection) of human individuals. Agostino is subliminally present throughout the scene in the figures of the bicyclists (a recurrent motif, often sounded in connection with Gina—her photographs, her breakdown outside the florist's shop) and in the glimpse of the proletarian boy who told Fabrizio about Agostino's suicide and is now employed in putting up banners for the parade. In the earlier scene, the boy's crossing of and emergence from the river (with its associations of cultural/economic dislocation), and his triumphant cry of "I've got a job," are juxtaposed with the sense of entrapment and irresolvable despair which have led Agostino to kill himself. Now he still has his job, but the political radicalism of the parade is an illusion—the dominant order continues. The film's political pessimism ("Men make their history in a milieu which conditions them") is reflected in the treatment of education. Fabrizio wants "a new sort of man—one wise enough to educate his own parents." Yet the irony of the Cesare/Fabrizio relationship is that, in rejecting the father, Fabrizio reinvents him. Our last sight of Cesare, telling his pupils the story of an attempt to kill God the Father, is counterbalanced by the defeat of the pupil whose intellectual rebellion is determined, and thus negated, by the need for a cultural and psychological security which orthodox belief cannot satisfy but which inherits its forms.

The spiritual conflict here is elaborated in an early scene in *Partner*, in which we see Jacob, seated in the room which his subversive alter ego is later to describe as phony, amid piles of books, his stentorian, melodramatic quotations from Antonin Artaud (artistic indulgence over form presented as the infernal alternative to the gestures of despair made by victims of ideology) interspersed with petulant shrieks for "Petrushka!"; the landlord who likes to act as a servant is mending Jacob's trousers in the kitchen. Petrushka suggests the cultural Father who pretends to be at your service, the master who appears to be the puppet (Althusser points out that the subject always has the illusion of independence). He was once a prompter ("the world is collapsing for lack of prompting"), and his first line is "Mother, give me the sun!"—Oswald's last line in Henrik Ibsen's *Ghosts*, which reveals his final contamination by his father's syphilis. When Petrushka gives Jacob his clothes, he also gives him a dead herring (a rotten penis). The image recurs in *The Conformist* through the anonymous letter which accuses Marcello of having inherited VD from his father (symbolically true, the father's "patrols" echoed in Marcello's mission). Central to *Partner* is the conflict between an attempt to find self-expression (the destruction of the superego through the improvised revolutionary spectacle) and self-dramatization (the self dramatized as the discourse of the father). Hence, for example, the suicide scene in which, following Artaud's supreme prescription for self-determination ("By suicide, I . . . shall for the first time give things the shape of my will"), Jacob 1 casts himself as Socrates and is derided for it by Jacob 2 ("Don't play the fool!"). Hence, also, the scene with the ham actor, who teaches his pupils to overact so that "you won't do it on the stage because you'll be ashamed."

One can relate such a concept to *The Conformist*. Consider Marcello's poses with his gun after the assignment to kill Quadri is confirmed, and the self-important, dapper arrogance of his strutting gait, so beautifully undercut by his smallness. This, and a deliberate emphasis in style and imagery on the overblown rhetoric of fascism, create fascism as a form of theater: the subject (Marcello) is placed, and dramatizes himself, within a rhetorical discourse which is not recognized as such. On his way to Julie's house (marriage, a normal life), Marcello walks past a vast wall engraved with Latin inscriptions—a monument to the Caesarian dictatorship in the image of which Italian Fascism inscribed itself, and to which, in his turn, Marcello seeks to

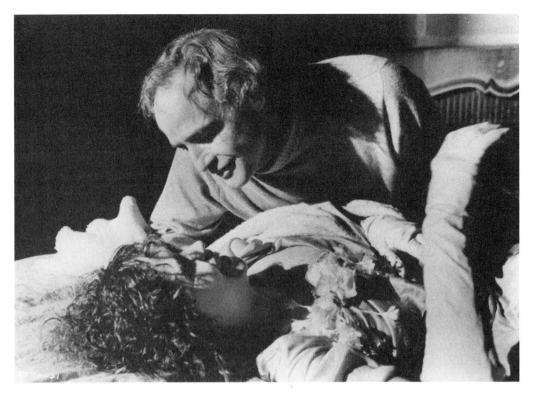

Paul (Marlon Brando) and Jeanne (Maria Schneider) in *Last Tango in Paris*. Personal collection of the editor.

conform. The imagery of pictures in the brothel scene works in a similar way. The scene begins with a shot of a painting of a landscape and dissolves from that to the landscape itself, now with Marcello standing in it. Marcello's conformity is a projection of self into the "imaginary relations" which constitute the ideology of fascism. *Last Tango in Paris* extends the theme to include the nature of "normal, civilized" sexuality itself: in Paul's words, "the tango is a rite." The dancers in the ballroom go through their predetermined motions with the inexorable precision of machines, their eyes dead in their heads.

I wish to proceed to *Last Tango* by way of the treatment of sexuality in *Partner*. Consider the terms in which Jacob's spectacle is described. It must "free the passions, prohibit prohibitions" and is transformed into a sort of communal orgasm: the actors must break into the power station, plunge the city into darkness, and regenerate the light, which "must come rhythmically, obsessively." The spectacle is individual (it "must begin at home") as well as social, sexual, and political. The camera moves over the arena in two continuous, circular panning shots, and an ironic counterpoint is established between the verbal demand for total revolution and a movement which suggests continuity, the impossibility of breaking the circle.

The figure of the detergent seller is important here. She has been introduced earlier, immediately after the construction of the bomb which is to be used to rediscover reality. Her eyes are closed, and false eyes have been painted on her eyelids (compare the blindness motif and its connotations in *The Conformist*). She is selling Splash, the purifying liquid, which does not kill dirt indiscriminately like all ordinary detergents, but "frees things from a state of temporary imperfection without traumatizing them." The girl does not know who her employers are, but she is sure they're clean people. She declares love to be dirty, but sex is her great selling technique, and she seduces Jacob. We later see her painting swastikas on a wall, and just as her first appearance follows, and undermines, the bomb scene, so the announcement of the spectacle in the arena is followed by Jacob's surrender to her, both of them rolling around in the foam and water from an overflowing washing machine to the accompaniment of a pop song which proclaims that "It's biological!" The conceptual network here—imprisonment in the discourse of the unknown employer, alienation from the body, philosophical dualism (spirit/matter, cleanness/dirt)—is fully developed in *Last Tango*, in which the ideological construction of sexuality becomes the dominant theme.

One might begin with the film's pervasive excremental imagery. Consider the sequence in which Jeanne returns to the apartment in her wedding dress, having been unable to go through with the marriage to Tom. She finds a dead rat in the bed and becomes hysterical, refusing to let Paul touch her and declaring, "I can't make love in this bed anymore. It's disgusting!" Paul is sardonically indifferent, offers her the rat as food, and goes to get some mayonnaise for garnish ("I'll save the asshole for you!"). This is followed by the scene of Paul bathing Jeanne which culminates in the discussion of the possibility of human contact, when he tells her, "You won't be able to be free of that feeling of being alone . . . until you go right up into the ass of death . . . till you find the womb of fear."

The film can be read, I think, as a version of the descent myth in which what has to be discovered is the physical reality which the sublimations of the Symbolic Order attempt to deny. The published screenplay contains a scene omitted from the released film, where Paul, after Jeanne has accused him of confusing the sacred and the profane, tells the story of a man who, while waiting to make love to his girlfriend, is seized with horror that his feet are dirty, and he gets one of them stuck while trying to wash it in the bowl of a toilet. (Bertolucci, *Last Tango*, 64–74) Bertolucci is concerned here with the archetypal dualism of Western society, which through Catholicism has been endemic in Italian culture (*The Divine Comedy* is, of course, the supreme example: Virgil and Dante leave the inferno and begin their ascent toward the stars by crawling past the devil's anus—"by such stairs we must depart from so much evil"). In terms of Brown's reading of Freud, one can see the film as a dramatic exploration of the processes of a society organized by the death instinct (the flight from death and sexuality, from life in the body).

1. Rosa's mother attempts to deny the fact of her daughter's death through religion ("I'll prepare a lovely funeral chamber with lots of flowers") and thus to repossess her as a part of herself ("She's my baby girl, Rosa"). Guilt and death must be washed away ("Absolution and a nice mass"), even though Rosa wasn't a believer. We later see the body laid out ("You're your mother's masterpiece"), white, purified, redeemed from decay and damnation by makeup and ritual. Paul's last act as he leaves is to wipe off the undertaker's lipstick (she never wore makeup), describing it as shit. One thinks of Jacob in *Partner*: "People believe themselves immortal. One must give them back a sense of death."

2. Paul's abuse is invariably scatological: he returns the culture to the anality which it denies (as Brown shows, this is characteristic of a long tradition of anti-Catholic polemic). Jeanne and Tom's exploration of the past culminates in an idyllic walk through the garden while Jeanne describes "my cousin Paul, my first love," whom she remembers playing the piano. As they reach the trees ("For me, those trees were a jungle"), they find a group of immigrant boys shitting there, and chase them off. Bertolucci cuts to the apartment, Jeanne trying to tell Paul about her father, whom she describes in terms of his uniform and his "shiny, shiny boots." Paul's reaction is "What a steaming pile of horseshit! . . . Everything outside this place is bullshit!" The essential contrasts between Tom and Paul are all implicit here: Tom pushes Jeanne backward (literally) into her past; Paul attempts to obliterate or degrade it; and the entire sublimation theme is expressed in the opposition between Tom's camera and Paul's penis. Both men imagine themselves in terms of their respective instruments, and one can compare Paul's remark that "If you look real close you'll find me hiding behind my zipper" with the moment in which Tom transforms himself into a camera craning down onto Jeanne.

3. There is a striking class/racist theme: the children who defile Jeanne's jungle, and who are driven off by a maid named, significantly, Olympia, are defiling bourgeois culture/privilege/sublimation, just as Paul is. In a later scene, Jeanne's mother is edgily evasive about a photograph of her husband's Berber mistress, and she clings to his boots ("They give me strange shivers when I touch them") and his gun. She adds that she "tried to keep several [Berbers] in the house, but they make terrible domestics." The white bourgeoisie is thus linked, symbolically, with imperialism, possessions/ownership (people and things), sexual and political exploitation (the native mistress), fetishism, and hoarding the dead (a motif which recurs with Rosa—"all these little knickknacks left behind"—and her mother—the embalmed body). Once again, the connotations of sterilized sexuality, accumulation, possession, fixation on the past are concentrated in Tom's camera, which seeks to trap everything it records.

4. Paul's opening cry of "Fucking God!" suggests a grotesque inversion of the concept of the male creator, such that fucking (the transmission of the sperm) becomes not an image of creativity but of subjection—the train which thunders above his head implies the sterility of the male thrust. Thereafter, blasphemy is crucially important in the film, both in asides such as Paul's confession that he has studied whale-fucking at the University of Congo and in the sodomy sequence. As he is buggering her, Paul forces Jeanne to repeat a sort of ritual chant against the family: "Holy Family, church of good citizens. The children are tortured till they tell their first lie. Where the will is broken by repression. Where freedom is assassinated by egotism." Buggery derives etymologically from the Bulgari, a sect of the Albigensian heresy which was viciously suppressed by the Catholic Church for its denial of the value of the sacraments and the reality of Christ's incarnation, and for espousing a dualistic doctrine that the world was the creation of the Devil, procreation being seen as the greatest of sins since it perpetuated the bondage of humanity to the spirit of evil.

This poses very concisely the essential ambiguity of the film. Paul's "heresy"/buggery—the blasphemy against God the Father, against the Church, against the patriarchal bourgeois family, against the ideological assumption that sex without procreation is sin—reproduces, for Jeanne, the pattern of coercion and repression which Paul denounces in the "Holy Family." In rejecting the Father, Paul comes to embody him, and it is explicit in the film that the very structure of genital sexuality is "loaded" ideologically. In the scene with Tom in her father's house, Jeanne reads a passage from *La Grande Larousse* ("Here are my cultural sources") in which masculinity is defined in terms of penis and femininity in terms of menstruation. Paul's object in taking the apartment and in banishing both the past and external reality is to become himself "fucking God"; it is this impulse which Brown, following the later Freud, sees as the essence of the Oedipal project, in which "the fantasy of becoming father of oneself is attached to the penis, thus establishing a concentration of narcissistic libido in the genital. There it remains, even after the destruction of the Oedipus complex, burdening with fantasies of possession not only the sexual relations of men to women, but also the relations of fathers to sons; sons, as the father's heirs, perpetuate the father." (*Life*, 118)

As in Brown's account of the Oedipus complex, Paul's movement toward the apartment is a response to an experience of separation (the flight from death)—Rosa's suicide. It is crucial that there is not even a tentative explanation of the suicide. It is simply a fact, inescapable and inexplicable: the violence of Paul's outburst against Rosa's mother when she asks him why is an index of his own despair. An apparently arbitrary decision to die becomes an expression of freedom; like the presence of Marcel, Rosa's lover, "the husband's double whose room was the double of ours," it presents Paul with the fact that he has been dispensed with.

If Tom rapes Jeanne's mind (her own accusation), then Paul rapes mind and body—the aim of both is possession. Hence, the irony of, say, Paul's explanation of what women have done to him: "Either they always pretend to know who I am, or they pretend that I don't know who they are, and that's very boring." Paul tries constantly to remain inscrutable or ambiguous ("Think I was telling you the truth?") while claiming complete knowledge of Jeanne and accusing her incessantly of hypocrisy, lying, sublimation. Like God, he knows all, yet is unknowable. Similarly, his attack on sexual escapism in the bathroom scene—Tom will transform Jeanne's body into a fortress where he "can feel comfortable enough and secure enough so that he can worship in front of the altar of his own prick"—is a partial self-portrait. The moment in which Paul allows her the active sexual role by letting her bugger him with her fingers is characterized by (a) his commandment of her, and (b) a torrent of excremental abuse in which she herself becomes the reality which must be degraded. By the time that he is ready to offer her something like a reciprocal relationship, after his descent into and rebirth from the "arse of death" in his final confrontation with Rosa, Jeanne's choice is no longer that between full sexuality and the barren, desexualized ritual of *"le marriage pop"* but between two forms of appropriation. At the end of the film, when he finally corners her in her mother's flat, he puts on her father's military cap with a sort of insolent swagger and asks her, "How do you like your hero?" The shooting is presented quite clearly as yet another act of repression, the desperate withdrawal from Paul turning into flight from sexuality itself.

I wish to end by returning to the Bertolucci interview already mentioned, bearing in mind the thematic preoccupations I have tried to describe. He is talking specifically about *1900* (1976), but the remarks have a more general reference, not only within his own work but also to a predicament with which any artist with Bertolucci's professed aims and ambitions is bound to be faced. One is struck by his allegiance: to particular cultural traditions—that epitomized in the interview by Verdi, which is felt to be vitally related to Italian life; to the cinematic tradition represented by Josef von Sternberg, Max Ophüls, Orson Welles, and so obviously present in the extraordinary stylistic exuberance of Bertolucci's work—the delight in sensuous movement and the play of light and shade, the meticulous attention to and dramatization of details of decor—all reaching full expression, significantly, since *Partner*; and, finally, to the realist tradition and, with it, the acceptance, "quite shamelessly," of "narrative codes taken from the nineteenth-century novel" which give the illusion of "the Force of Destiny," of the necessary order of experience. Bertolucci also speaks of his desire to reestablish for himself and his audience a sense of continuity with the past, and adds that he both does and does not think that such a continuity exists.

It is clear throughout that Bertolucci sees both the thematic of his work and his own artistic impulses in dialectical terms—in terms, that is, of the acceptance, presentation, development, and attempted reconciliation of fundamental contradictions. The need for a large popular audience and for creative dialogue with it—a need which involves, of course, the use of artistic codes which are more or less generally accessible, and therefore heavily loaded ideologically—is balanced by a need to reject that audience and challenge conventional codes. Conflicting attitudes to art within Marxism itself come into play here: compare Antonio Gramsci's suggestion that Hollywood is the great potential medium for socialist art precisely because of its huge public (123) with the artistic theory and practice represented by the work of Jean-Luc Godard and Jean-Pierre Gorin—the search for "an image which has not been used before" and the identification of all bourgeois narrative/visual codes as institutions of capitalist ideology. Bertolucci's dilemma is everywhere apparent. To be popular means to compromise, to acquiesce in "the grossest Hollywood-imperialist speculation," to be defiled—but also to adopt sets of conventions which can be critically inflected with a purpose which "is fairly and squarely ideological." "Pure monologue" (Bertolucci's description of *Partner*, a film which is deeply influenced by Godard in its radical violation of the single diegesis and its conclusion that the Symbolic Law of which Jacob is a product and to which he succumbs is a manifestation of "American imperialism") is diseased, sectarian, narcissistic, cinephiliac—but also the form of posing and challenging the assumptions embedded in received language, "a film against the market and a certain way of making movies." Godard explicitly repudiated Bertolucci after *The Conformist* because it was financed by American capital. All the films (except *Partner*) fundamentally adhere to homogeneous narrative, and their various complex formal structures and devices are firmly rooted in it: the dislocating, elliptical time schemes of *The Conformist* and *The Spider's Stratagem* (1970); the use, in the former work, of Dominique Sanda; the funeral sequence in *Before the Revolution*.

I do not want to suggest that I am subscribing to any crude notion of what Bertolucci himself calls autobiographism by relating the excremental imagery in *Last Tango* to a very striking use of metaphor in the interview, by which the "sublime purity" of Jean-Marie Straub is opposed to the anality of Hollywood ("Good films can be born . . . in shit-heaps"): but it seems to me of crucial importance that both instances should involve the concept of descent into and rebirth from the past. An analogy with Marcel Proust, for example, is conceived in excremental terms—memories as "little spasms of vomit." The films attempt to pose, for the spectator, the cultural/ psychological processes of subjection in ideology by dramatizing the conflict of rebellion and conformity in the characters and by presenting the codes of that dramatization as codes even while maintaining them. The debt to Freud lies in the repeated emphasis that the need to retain the Father determines even the form of the rejection of him. One is justified, I think, in making use of Freudian concepts in reading Bertolucci's work because the undermining of the proposition that "*la vie est a nous*" (the message of the flashing neon sign with which *The Conformist* begins) is structured psychoanalytically. That life is not ours because we have parents—whether we try to escape from ideology (Paul) or immerse ourselves in it (Marcello)—is implicit at every point.

In keeping with this, the local realization of the films is founded in a sense of contradiction and tension which the narrative makes no attempt to place or to solve, and I will conclude by pointing to a scene from *Last Tango* which can be taken as typical of it; the scene with Paul and the maid, Catherine, in the bathroom where Rosa committed suicide. While she is mopping up the blood, Catherine is telling Paul about her interrogation by the police, and in doing so, she describes the account of his own history which she has been compelled to give—a matter of endless, aimless wandering from country to country and job to job (the classic itinerary of the deracinated American) which has led to Paris, marriage for money, limbo: "What does he do, your boss?" "Nothing." The concept of exile recurs throughout the films. We think of Jacob's sublimating version of it, in *Partner*, in his story of the white cosmonauts trying to return to their native planet, which accords so beautifully with his self-dramatization as Socrates (suicide as a return to the world of ideal presences) and which is balanced by his alter ego's autobiography, a sort of mingling of the careers of Alexandre Dumas's Edmond Dantès, Jean Genet, Arthur Rimbaud, and Napoleon in a reiterated pattern of imprisonment/ escape/freedom/imprisonment, culminating, like Paul's, in the unanswered question—"First meeting with . . . ?" Here, Bertolucci evokes through Paul not only the predicament, so familiar in the twentieth century, of American exile in Europe (the *Tropic of Cancer* syndrome: think of Jeanne's "Do you think that an American on the floor in an empty house eating cheese and drinking water—is interesting?" Paul nods and proceeds at once to "possess" her) but also the experience of separation on, simultaneously, cultural, psychological, and metaphysical levels. If the opening of the film recalls Dante (Paul in "the middle way," middle-aged in the middle of a bridge in the middle of the bourgeois metropolis), it is to introduce a comedy set in a universe which is not absolutely meaningful but absolutely arbitrary, and in which a God who has been rejected intellectually lives on in human needs and impulses.

Paul and Catherine are separated by partitions of mottled glass—additionally obscured by smears of blood—and both characters are captured at times in the mirror of the bathroom cabinet. The compositional elements here are vital for the film. Consider (a) the first scene in the apartment, with its imagery of dividing walls, communication by telephone, Paul moving away from the light as Jeanne throws open the shutters; (b) the scene between Paul and Rosa's mother, built on spatial, emotional, and philosophical apartness, which ends with Paul's attempts to maintain himself in the dark by menacing the people who watch him from lighted doorways; (c) the scene, again with Rosa's mother, where Paul turns off the lights in the lodging house and "the whole joint goes bananas," the isolated, derelict inhabitants in their separate rooms suddenly at one in their "fear of the dark"; and (d) Jeanne's last act on leaving the apartment is to close the shutters—the ideas of spiritual progress (return to the world from the room which smells) and repression of the body (marriage to Tom, acceptance of the bourgeois order, and a suspect maturity ["We can't joke like this—like children. We're adults."])—are inextricably confused.

As Catherine talks, Paul looks out through the window (another pane of glass) at a Negro couple in a building opposite, the man holding a saxophone, the woman crouching in front of him, sewing a button on his trousers, biting off the thread near his crotch. The oppositions here—life (the sexuality of the couple) against death (Rosa's suicide); union (the couple entire) against separation (Paul apart from Rosa, Catherine and the blacks); the present (the couple caught spontaneously in a moment of continuing time) against the survival of the past (Paul's history, and the remains of his wife); saxophone against razor; reciprocal sexuality against the voyeur—are all based in the ambiguous image of masculine potency with which the film is largely concerned. The image of sexuality which Paul sees through the window is dominated by the potent male, the woman crouching before him and serving him. The scene in the bathroom presents us with the spiritual and physical bankruptcy of the potent male. Both rooms are characterized by redness—ambivalently, eroticism and death. Paul looks down from his height like God, and it is the flight from the spectacle of Rosa's bathroom which generates the project to become God in the hermetic world of the apartment, to reaffirm the controlling power he now glimpses through the glass. Simultaneously, the fact that he is removed, separate, only looking, suggests his impotence. The tensions in the imagery are underlined through the counterpoint of Catherine's monologue: Paul and Rosa "didn't have children"; the policemen treat Catherine "like dirt," make her reenact Rosa's suicide, and one of them "pushes me in a corner and tries to paw me"; and the scene ends with the unresolved question of whether the razor is or is not Paul's—Catherine gives it to him ("Here's your razor") and he denies it. A moment later, we see him washing his hands (self-absolution?) at the sink. It is significant here that though Catherine continues cleaning up through most of the scene, she has made no obvious progress by the end of it; the blood appears to be irremovable.

The sense of conflict, contradiction, disorientation is profoundly characteristic of Bertolucci's work as a whole; his films have moved progressively toward the suggestion that the conflicts are inherent in the very construction of the human individual.

Living Historically: Two Films by Jean-Luc Godard (1976)

I do not think that the critical problems raised by Godard's recent films have been faced with sufficient rigor. The purpose of this article is both to suggest their nature and to offer certain qualifications of and disagreements with interpretations which I think misleading. It is obviously of supreme importance in attempting to arrive at an understanding of the nature of political cinema to grasp the differences between *Vent d'Est* (*Wind from the East* [1970]) and *Tout Va Bien* (*All's Well* [1972]), films which propose two distinct directions in which such a cinema might develop. I think that a fruitful starting point is the discussion of what "living historically" means in *Tout Va Bien*. Let us consider the context of the film's central scene.

It is preceded by the two interview-monologues of the two leading characters. The end of the strike to which the first part of the film has been devoted is announced, over a shot of the factory's facade, in a news bulletin which juxtaposes it with a report on the latest incidents in Vietnam. The newsreader's voice is flat, impersonal, indifferent: both events are merely items of news, without any context except the bulletin in which they are mentioned, which in its turn has its given time slot in a schedule of other programs. It is a stopgap, like the advertisements; it is the national television network announcing its objective scrutiny of reality, its own commitment to make us aware, without bias, of what is going on in the world. Television has already been identified, in the film's prologue, with the bourgeoisie; the commentary declares that part of the context of the action will be the work of the classes, and we see "workers working, farmers farming, and the middle class middle classing." The balancing image for the work of the middle class is a current affairs broadcast, from which we catch one line of dialogue: ". . . a program on which radicals and socialists can agree."

"Middle classing" is the middle class perpetuating itself in its own image. On the television screen, it views objectively the objective reality of the world and exercises its liberal concern for humanity; it looks at its politicians trying to reconcile all political differences so that the country may go on to greater material prosperity, united in self-interest. The aim of the middle class is to achieve that rationalization and equilibrium which Guidotti, the manager of the Salumi factory, expounds with such delight; to unite all opposing elements in a bland and confident materialism which is, in fact, as gray and barren as the screen which celebrates it. The flat, flickering image purports to show a truth in appearances which it does not for a moment attempt to make us understand, and it reduces that truth to a succession of photographs. It is a false objectivity, the invention of a cast of mind which thinks it pays sufficient tribute to a mutual humanity by being aware of "what is happening." The report is the official truth, which tells us as little as the facade of the factory which the image shows us, or the colored picture of it which one of the strikers paints out. It ignores all the complications which the film so far has established (the phrase "it's more complicated" runs like a leitmotif through the strike scenes as "be more precise" does through the prologue).

Godard cuts to the recording studio and shows us the other face of Janus: from the pious grays of reality caught in the act to the garish brilliance of advertising. In the middle distance, beneath a flood of lights, surrounded by a darkness from which a clutter of cameras and equipment loom out, a couple of girls in brightly colored stockings are rehearsing for a take on a raised podium. They are wearing clumpy shoes; their movements are heavy, ungainly, and crude. Jacques (Yves Montand) sits at the foot of the pedestal directing the proceedings, the faithful servant of his product. The news report continues over the new image, and the juxtapositions achieved—factory front, television screen, bulletin studio—constitute a little poem on capitalist society. Just as the news honors and perpetuates a lack of knowledge under the guise of providing it, advertising exists, in Norman O. Brown's words, "to create irrational demands and keep the consumer confused: without the consumer confusion perpetuated by advertising, the economy would collapse." (*Life Against Death*, 258) In his book, Brown, quoting John Ruskin, sees advertising as representative of the whole science of political economy, which insofar as it

> relates to the advantage of one of the exchanging persons only, it is founded on the ignorance or incapacity of the opposite person. . . . It is therefore a science founded on nescience. . . . This science, alone of sciences, must, by all available means, promulgate and prolong its opposite nescience. . . . It is therefore peculiarly and alone the science of darkness. (258)

Advertising and the news both come down to the same common denominator. Both depend on maintaining "the ignorance or incapacity of the opposite person"—on subjugating him to the consumption of the goods as delivered. The one operates by creating a consciousness of lack and, thus, of need; the other by creating a consciousness of what "is" which is in fact ideologically loaded, and which induces an attitude to reality devoid of any sense of personal involvement or personal responsibility. Thus, the television encourages both a complacent comfort with regard to the order of the world and a fearful, insecure demand for more of what capitalism is devoted to producing. Its revelations are blinkers. Such, for Godard, is the politics of the middle class.

There follows the long take of Montand's interview with a silent, unseen questioner— Godard, conscience, us. He describes himself as "a filmmaker who occasionally makes commercials—it's a nuance I insist upon." Montand conveys brilliantly a sort of testy, defensive wariness—the uncomfortable knowledge that he occupies a position he can no longer defend under rigorous, inexorable scrutiny. He describes his involvement with the uprising of May 1968 ("I was ripe for May") and his previously incomplete political commitment, characterized as a pose in the fashionable position, an unthought association without any real personal validity: voting Communist was "a knee-jerk conviction"; he was with the right "radical" people in the right places at the right times. May, his abandonment of filmmaking, and his affair with Susannne (Jane Fonda) are all connected. Of Susan he remarks, "We went through May together," and it is vital for Godard's purposes at this point that Montand's revaluation of his position as an artist should be inseparable from a poIitical revaluation, involvement with communal action, and a deepening relationship with another human being—social, personal, and artistic life can have meaning only in their interdependence.

Yet at the same time, we feel the incompleteness of the change. Montand was "active and not active," his concern was "serious, and it wasn't." He has rejected the plan of filming the David Goodis novel as "an obscene undertaking" in the circumstances, has considered it "more honest" to make commercials, has been figuring out what he can, or will be allowed, to do "within the political system." He has a plan for a film on contemporary France. But he has actually done nothing—as Fonda tells him in the film's central scene, they have been "living on that honesty for four years"—and it is clear that although his personal commitments have changed, he still lacks a full realization of the necessary continuity of individual life and its context. The affair with Susan exists in a vacuum, and the stasis it has reached at the start of the film is a direct result of this isolation.

When we first see him, Montand is offering a girl (over the phone: throughout the film, "mechanized communication"—radio, telephone, television—is associated both with a lack of contact with reality and with a failure of human contact) the leading part in a commercial for razors, in which, through the customary leering innuendo, sexuality is degraded into a sales gimmick and women into erotic objects. The relationship with Fonda, instead of serving as a point of mutual growth and enrichment, has dried up and shriveled in on itself. Affair and work have become equally a matter of unquestioned, sterile habit. It is significant that he speaks slightingly in the interview of the movement to "reeducate intellectuals—that discouraged a lot of friends of mine, especially C. P. members." Later, after the break with Fonda, he recognizes that although he has dropped "the old style of doing things," he has unconsciously retained the former methods of thought, and that what is needed is "new form for new content," a radical reformulation of the processes of analysis themselves, and not a mere reshuffling of patterns of behavior.

Of his involvement in the strike, Montand says that he felt "out of place," like an actor who has forgotten his lines, and we see here the beginnings of an honesty not apparent during the events themselves. In the scene in Guidotti's office, Montand rounds on Guidotti with aggressive abusiveness, from a position, apparently, of complete self-satisfaction: his hands are clean; he is not implicated in the meaning of the strike. When Guidotti attempts to reassert himself, Montand replies that he feels perfectly at ease and that "Tout va bien." We do not see either of them: the camera remains all the time on Fonda, sitting on the desk and gazing thoughtfully, critically, at him. At one point, the soundtrack gives us what she is thinking—"You're wasting your breath." She never indulges in a similar outburst, and when she speaks to Guidotti, it is only to get information for her article. Later, when they are released, one of the strikers asks them, "You're reporters, aren't you?" Fonda replies, "Yes"—she is at the back of the image among the strikers. Montand is in the foreground. The two moments indicate very exactly the ambiguity of Montand's position—where, precisely, is he—and the confident assertiveness exhibited in the first is a sufficient indication of the hardening of sensibility which his involvement with advertising has produced.

The matter is not neatly tidied away at the end of the film. The scene in which he breaks with Fonda is an echo of that in which he made the offer of the job at the beginning. In both scenes, he is in his place of work—studio and office, respectively. In both he is speaking over the phone. His manner and tone are slightly callous, superficially unconcerned. He tells her that he "feels like working. It's not dramatic. . . . We must draw on our own energies—that's how you grow." After he has rung off, his secretary asks him if anything is wrong. Looking down, preoccupied, shutting out the thought of it, he replies that "Tout va bien." We are left with the sense of the fragility of the new position to which he has moved. It may be the beginning of a new responsive awareness and insight, or a move back to square one. He may be immersing himself in work to suppress the consciousness of what the break means to him. We are not even told whether or not the work is the documentary project he has mentioned. None of our questions is answered.

Significant in this respect is the overlap of the Montand interview with Fonda's. Montand breaks away and tells us that he must get back to his work—work defined for us in the shot which follows. We see, in the back of the frame, the blurred legs of the dancers on the distant podium and, in the foreground, an image of them reproduced on the screen of a television monitor—the harsh, blaring music on the soundtrack underlining in its endless, strident monotony and predictability the repetitive and graceless movements of the dancers. The double image, itself "doubled" by the music, summarizes perfectly the nature of television advertising—the devotion of vast quantities of money, time, energy to one image and one theme, endlessly reiterated, endlessly self-reproducing, devoid of emotion, and eventually, through the length of time over which the image is held, devoid of meaning. The mind switches off and simply allows the relentless insistence of the sales talk to flood over it. The legs of the real girls are mere fuzzy blurs of color in the background, but the monitor screen is in sharp focus. Reality disintegrates, and only its image remains. Montand is nowhere visible—his world has absorbed him.

From this the film cuts to the rejection of Fonda's article on the strike, and then, at once, to her sitting down—tense, overwrought, desperate—in front of the camera and blurting out "I've had it." Thus, whereas the Montand sequence, which begins and ends with Montand immersed in his habitual chore, places his very self-interrogation in the context of a reacceptance of the world of advertising, that mental criticism not consolidated by any action (nor is there any indication in the interview that Montand has any positive or defined intention of making a break—the film project is mentioned in passing, a thing he has thought of doing), the Fonda sequence, on the other hand, begins with an outburst of furious exasperation, depicting her inability to get beyond the first sentence of her broadcast—and her dismissal of it as "crap"—and it ends with the scene toward which the whole film moves, in which she forces Montand to come to terms with their relationship and their work. Throughout the action, she is presented as the more open of the two, the more tentative, questioning and responsive to experience, less hidebound and secure in her accustomed attitudes. We have already noted Godard's emphasis on her silent criticism of Montand's diatribe against Guidotti; when Montand remarks contemptuously, "Management is always out of it," she replies, "What did you expect?"

The decisive moment in the strike sequence, which establishes the first contact between the strikers and their hostages, is precipitated by Fonda's impulsive action. The camera tracks slowly along the upper floor of the factory. Everyone is still and motionless, the opposing parties shut off from one another by walls and partitions. Even the workers' frustrated chanting has ceased, and all that either side can think to do is to kick each other up the arse: Guidotti's remark that "A kick up the arse is the way to handle them" immediately precedes Fonda's action and counterbalances the workers' chant, which has mounted in fury and vehemence and is accompanied by total physical immobility: the workers remain sitting and standing where they are. The tracking shots over the factory, opened up for us like a doll's house, follow a progression which reveals an ever greater silence and isolation and less and less activity, culminating in the deadlock against which Fonda reacts.

The strike, like the Montand-Fonda relationship, has petered out into sterility, as the film implies it had to do. It is a spontaneous, undirected protest against intolerable constraints and indignities, but it is stressed that the strikers have no real awareness of what they are doing or aiming for. The strike never gets beyond "how good you feel thumping someone who's down on you"—the sheer desperation of "Getting mad must mean something." Without conscious aim and strategy, it can only develop into a war of attrition which management must eventually win. Part of the poignance of the film is everybody's sense of confusion. Under analysis, everything gets more and more complicated, there is more to be taken into account, always the necessity for greater specification and precision: a necessary prelude to such an analysis is shown to be direct, honest, face-to-face confrontation, the willingness to admit to confusion and dissatisfaction, and to plunge in and follow it through unsparingly—not with the guarantee of discovering lucid answers, but with the hope at least of clarification, of pushing further back the obscurities and boundaries.

Hence, the importance of Fonda's sudden decision to leave Guidotti's office and go speak to the women strikers. The stalemate is broken. The act paves the way for the later full-scale discussion of the meaning of the strike; for the seminar (think of the student's "Fiat is my university" in *Vent d 'Est*) in which Fonda and Montand participate with the workers; thus for Fonda's article; and thus, finally, for the confrontation with Montand—it is the rejection of the article which focuses the unrest which erupts in their conversation. At the same time, the talk compels the workers to articulate what they have been doing and why, to conceptualize their action. The strike is broken because it exists in a social and intellectual vacuum, is random and isolated. The discussion, the article, the film *Tout Va Bien* itself, are steps toward the opening out of a context in which the meaning of social and personal responsibility can be formulated and discussed. There can be no creative discussion without full consciousness, and there can be neither, the film suggests, without a sensitive awareness of and concern for human beings. This is the import of Fonda's action. The desire to question them, learn about them, move nearer the truth of the situation in which they and she find themselves is a desire of her humanity. The women are specific individuals degraded by appalling, dehumanizing conditions of work, and it is Fonda's response to this, and her willingness to deepen it so that it can take on the substance which she needs in order to write her article, which the film is about.

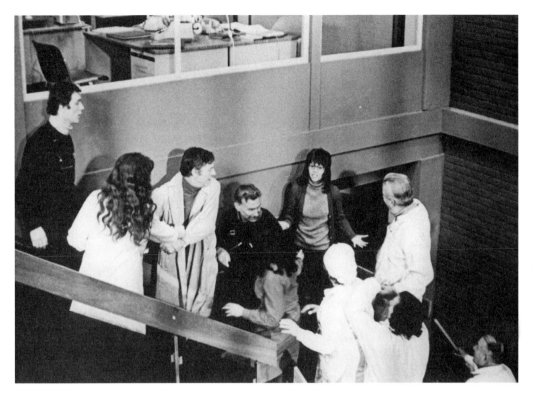

Jacques (Yves Montand) and Susan (Jane Fonda) are caught in the strike in *Tout Va Bien*. Personal collection of the editor.

In the interview, we learn that Fonda, as much as Montand, has been living off the events of 1968. Just as he is comfortably ensconced in the advertising business, she has become known as a specialist in left-wing radicalism, and has been promoted because of it. Unlike Montand, who only becomes aware of it after their discussion, she already knows as a consequence of the strike that "the facts demanded a new style. They make you talk about them in a different way." It is the sense of this need, and the inability to fulfill it—the feeling that she is using the style, words, and concepts of the radio network which employs her rather than realizing her own perceptions in forms she has evolved for herself—which precipitates her "breakdown." Her employers don't want her copy, and she is "incapable of writing it." She has tried to be radical in an outmoded language and has been, instead, adopted by it—her words have written her. "The further I go, the less I understand." Alienated in her confusion from the system and the strike, she is "a correspondent who no longer corresponds to anything."

Godard suggests this lack of correspondence with brilliant simplicity and economy: Fonda's broadcasts in English are overlaid on the soundtrack by a French translation in another voice. She is an American in France, and an intellectual suddenly directly involved in class conflict: an incomplete and partial overlay of different worlds, without a home, a country, a language, a firm commitment. When we first see her at work in the film's prologue, she is in full swing—poised, fluent, self-assured, and uncritical of her position. We watch her in the studio with a complacent smile on her face. When the recording is over, she is told that "that was fine"; the smile broadens, and she murmurs, "Yeah." Godard cuts immediately to the factory. What Fonda is saying is obliterated by the welling-up of the French translation. The assured position is an illusion. Beneath it lies a chaos of contradictions: the questions about herself and her work she has never asked, and the absence of real relations which she has never noticed. We do, in fact, hear the first line of her remarks—she is quoting, to the effect that "the written press is dying." Her manner, her face, the way she sits in her chair and holds her script—all declare loudly that the radio press, and herself above all, are alive and well. She, if nothing else, is justified.

The fact that her preconceptions prove rapidly more vulnerable than Montand's suggests that, based as she is in a medium which propagates "bourgeois ideology," and using its language, she is still a reporter, an observer. She has at least some contact with a world beyond the lurid fabrications of an advertising studio; she has the initial readiness to look. What we see in the narrative is the increasing willingness to question her way of looking. The scene in which she abandons her broadcast after two abortive attempts to begin it is the counterpart to that which ends the prologue. The camera places us behind the recording engineer in his booth. Fonda is in the far background, separated from us by a transparent partition; like the engineer, we hear her voice over the sound system. The distance, the obstructed vision, the disembodied impersonality of the voices, and the harsh artificial light and stark decor evoke once more that sense of co-presence without contact, of alienation from all reality, that characterizes the world presented in the film.

There follows the scene with Montand in their flat. It begins and ends with conspicuous errors of continuity—Godard wishes both to make it stand out in sharp relief, to play up its centrality, and to make sure that, at this vital point, our attention is sufficiently distanced from automatic identification to make us feel the reason for that centrality. Fonda is irritable and depressed. Montand attempts to shrug it off ("Don't panic. You're just jammed.") and resents having to be bothered with it. They quarrel, and he finally remarks that he'll "end up wondering why they're together." From the next room Fonda replies that he should start wondering why they're together, and she takes up what he has said casually about the things they habitually do—eat, make love, go to the cinema, and so on. Montand, speaking generally, abstractly, can name three things. She makes him repeat them; then, specifying the incidents of the previous day, she names ten. Again and again, like the female voice in the prologue, she insists that he be precise ("You've got to say more!"); that he "think his dissatisfaction through around the headings" he has suggested; that he admit that "sex alone satisfies him less than it did three years ago." The "more" that is needed is "a picture of us at work," and the film juxtaposes shots of Montand in the film studio and Fonda at her office learning about the rejection of her article with a monochrome photograph of a woman's hand holding a man's penis.

What *Tout Va Bien* rejects is the concept of the mutual exclusiveness of "public" and "private" life presupposed in modern society. And more than this. The stark, clinical monochrome of the photograph confines sexuality to what Freud describes as "genital organization." We can quote again from Brown's *Life Against Death*: "The ultimate essence of our desires and our being is nothing more or less than delight in the active life of all the human body." (30)

Thus, human sexual love is reduced to the one term, and this reduction parallels the process by which the body itself is seen as apart and "private"—removed from the domain of the world, the domain of work, business, the mind. Fonda insists that Montand recognize (and she tells him that originally he taught it to her) that, as lovers, they are not reducible to their genitals; that they are two human individuals existing in a complex social context in which they are, essentially, what their actions and commitments over that entire range make them; that the quality of their personal relationship and the quality of their whole social existence are inextricably involved, reflect and engage each other; that full, mature sexuality cannot grow from experience that is not constantly, questioningly, and openly concerned with contemporary reality. What the film offers is a definition of human responsibility. In a capitalist society, in the subtle network of preconceptions and assumptions that that implies, we cannot responsibly avoid political commitment.

One of the most striking things about the film is its attitude to sexual relationships—its abandonment of the ideal of the stable, monogamous, romantic couple which is expressed in our first sight of Montand and Fonda together on the riverbank, alone amid the fertility of nature. At the end of the film, their affair may have reached the point at which it is no longer necessary to either of them: they may have given each other all that, at that time, they can give. This in no sense invalidates the relationship. It was bound up with the total revaluation induced by the events of May, but the developing maturity of the couple may require that their union should not be permanent. This is part of the flexibility of attitude and the unceasing interrogation of what is that *Tout Va Bien* demands.

The double ending expresses a complete refusal to summarize and impose intractable conclusions on the filmmaker, the characters, or us. Fonda and Montand may return to each other or they may not. The separation, their individual fulfillment of what they feel is incumbent on them as artist and journalist at that time and in those conditions, may consolidate what has been valid and creative in their union or it may not. We are only told that they have begun to "live historically," and the final shot of the film imposes a similar obligation on us.

In a long tracking shot which echoes those of the factory and supermarket scenes, the camera travels over a road and onto a desolate, barren wasteland in the midst of Paris despoiled, brown, littered, stretching out beneath an oppressive, dreary sky. It tracks in its journey over the surface of a brick wall and onto the wasteland again. On the soundtrack, we hear a banal pop song which declares that "the sun is shining over France"—that "tout va bien." As the camera passes over the wall, we hear the noisy shouting of a mob and the voices of the factory scene—in turn, Guidotti, the Communist Party union representative, and the young radical. As the wasteland opens up once more, the song floods back. What the shot suggests is that France, 1972 (or England, 1976—our lived present) is our factory, our supermarket, our treadmill, complete with bright and bouncy music-while-you-work, the eternal sunny reassurances from those whose interest it is to make us believe that we've never had it so good, and to which the image itself—the bleak, inhuman, devastated ugliness of factory, shopping center, and urban development—gives the lie. In this context of reality and imposed illusion, the film places the voices of the strike, which pierce through the concealing wall: manager, workers, and the so-called workers' representative, who in fact collaborates with the ideals and aims of the employer (greater material prosperity for all) and demands higher wages for the same degradation, repressing the knowledge that, "admittedly," the workers cannot gain any fulfillment in the system as it is. (His speech, we remember, is delivered against a background consisting of a red wall, in the center of which is an enormous photograph of the factory's product on display on a butcher's slab. He is a half-and-half man attempting to balance the irreconcilable.)

The film implies, I think, that these voices are part of our lives, that we are involved and implicated in the struggle they express, and that we can no longer live without analyzing what they are saying and coming to terms with it; without learning to question, to be undogmatic and receptive, to let our beliefs and convictions lie open always to the possibility of constructive change.

The concept of living historically which Godard explores in *Tout Va Bien* is essentially an attempt to define a valid artistic discipline—to construct a style which can lead beyond the impasse which is reached in *Vent d'Est*. The "positive," as opposed to the simply abusive, criticism which the earlier film has received is of little help in coming to terms with it, in that it tends largely to ignore the contradictions with which it is riddled. Here is James Roy Macbean, for example, in his introduction to the published script: "Godard's recent films are politically pointed, to be sure; but although the verbal commentary is prominent—if not pre-eminent— the films are not exhortatory. There is nothing demagogic in Godard's approach either to cinema or to politics." (104)

Comments of this sort get us nowhere and blind us to the nature of what is achieved in *Tout Va Bien*. *Vent d'Est* is, quite simply, one of the most repressive films ever made. For most of its length, the soundtrack is devoted to the commentary, delivered by a female voice at a speed which makes it at times incomprehensible and in an almost unvaried monotone. The effect of watching the film, as distinguished from reading the script, is a state bordering on hypnosis. This commentary is designed to give us "the right answers." We are told who is right and who is wrong; the goodies and the baddies are as clearly labeled as if they rode white and black horses. (This is a failing which, to some extent, also contaminates *Tout Va Bien*. The film's main weakness is the treatment of Guidotti as the comic strip capitalist magnate, which introduces a tone of facile caricature totally at odds with the prevailing complexity and which further undermines the figure of the young radical who, needless to say, wears black and sports a droopy mustache—everyone's idea of the handsome proletarian hero.) Everything is systematically explained and placed; oppositions are lucid and incontrovertible.

"The theory of Marx-Engels-Lenin has universal value. It should not be considered as dogma, but as a guide to action." The film is torn apart by the tension between the idea of Marxism as providing a method of analysis and of Marxism as the receptacle of eternal truths which only have to be stated, so that instead of analysis, we get shrill emphatic generalizations. To state that a theory has universal value is the very antithesis of the analytic spirit, and the two sentences are basically contradictory. Having dismissed "representation" as Stalinist, all that is left to the film (and it follows its logic as far as it can without stopping altogether) is to present us with a blank red screen while the voice of the prophet intones on the soundtrack. As in *Tout Va Bien*, great stress is laid on specification and precision—"the concrete situation"—but this is matched by nothing in the film's thought, method, or realization. Both images and soundtrack tend to complete generality: a wall of unvaried color and the Necessary Truth—that is, the Truth is red—all we have to do is think Marxism. The film precisely forbids analysis or, rather, the analysis has been made, and the only positions left are those of unbeliever or proselytizer. I myself find a reading of the script a far more satisfactory and rewarding experience than watching the film: one has, at least, an opportunity to grasp the ideas, which the film repeatedly denies.

It is only because of the unquestioned acceptance of Marxism as The Word that Godard can dismiss "the Western" as a monstrous weapon in the hands of bourgeois ideology and, at the same time, make a film which violently denounces every political position but its own and elevates a rigid orthodoxy (with its own historical determinations) to the status of a transhistorical heal-all. It is the same acceptance which allows him to deal so complacently with the guerrilla violence that the film ends by proposing, and the treatment here is very revealing. We see shots of the manufacture of homemade bombs: the plans for their construction, hands putting them together, and so on. For the first time, the commentary slows down from its breathless, relentless gabble to an extremely slow, emphatic, rhythmical precision—almost a chant—which repeats over and over again the same instructions: "Think. Manufacture. Simplify. Reflect. Learn. Learn." We are not shown any explosions. We are not shown a devastated supermarket with the dead and wounded being carried away after one of the apocalyptic visitations which the commentary advocates. Instead, Godard gives us a metaphor in the form of several books of matches, each with a cigarette tucked behind the match heads so that they will all ignite at once when the cigarette burns down. As the matches ignite, Godard cuts to a shot of a ruined factory, with the noise of an explosion on the soundtrack. We are shown a square full of people, some of them playing boule while the commentary tells us that the denunciation of guerrilla violence is the squeamish hypocrisy of "bourgeois humanitarianism" which tries to cover up "the daily reality of bourgeois terror."

Godard's treatment of this sequence is a piece of the most appalling dishonesty, in that it exactly reproduces the practice of the aesthetic he is rejecting. Instead of attempting to make us aware of a reality—in this case, a terrorist attack—the film substitutes a metaphorical equivalent which purports to express it, but which effectively excludes any comprehension of it. The image of the books of matches, plus the sound of the explosion, is supposed to show us revolutionary action: in fact, the impoverishment of the image, its trite obviousness and banality, are a sufficient measure of the sloppiness of thought and paucity of feeling which can even suggest it as being adequate.

I am reminded by a great deal in *Vent d'Est* of some remarks made by George Orwell in his essay "Inside the Whale." Orwell quotes two stanzas from W. H. Auden's poem "Spain," about the Spanish Civil War, and picks out the phrase "the conscious acceptance of guilt in the necessary murder." Here is part of Orwell's comment:

> Notice the phrase "necessary murder." It could only be written by a person to whom murder is at most a word. Personally I would not speak so lightly of murder. . . . Mr. Auden's brand of amoralism is only possible if you are the kind of person who is

always somewhere else when the trigger is pulled. So much of left-wing thought is a kind of playing with fire by people who don't even know that fire is hot. (516)

One would scarcely describe Godard as an "eager-minded schoolboy," Orwell's phrase for "the typical literary man" of the 1930s, and he is certainly not a worshipper of Moscow. He is also, I should imagine, aware that fire is hot; at least he's more aware than Auden was. Nevertheless, as one watches the scene in *Vent d'Est* in which a girl reading Proust's "Les Beaux Quartiers" is menaced with a hammer and sickle while the commentary announces "Death to bourgeois culture" and builds up to a cry of "Death, fire, death," Orwell's judgment, and indeed the whole spirit of the socialism he himself advocates, come repeatedly to mind. The sort of action which *Vent d'Est* recommends, and the manner of the recommendation, depend precisely on that simplification which the commentary stresses—the elimination from the mind of everything except the one dehumanized perspective in which alone existence has meaning.

No image, no art, is repressive in itself. It is context which determines significance, and context, in part, consists not of some reified abstraction called "representation," but of a method of representation, the series of formal choices by which an experience is made available to the spectator. These choices can give a greater or lesser degree of opportunity for the play of human intelligence and creative involvement, the degree of freedom being intimately involved in its turn with the nature and range of what is offered: the "content" in art is inseparable from the "forms" in which it is realized. In *Vent d'Est* there is only one unarguably right way of looking, so that all that is left to the film is an endless announcement of its presuppositions, among which Godard, by nature the most inquisitive and skeptical of artists, is left wandering in search of a coherent style. All that the spectator can do is take it or leave it. He has only, exactly, the role of consumer which Peter Wollen considers that "modernism" (and *Vent d'Est* as an example of it) dispels. I know of no work of art in which I am given so little to do.

＊　＊　＊

I want now to consider in detail some matters raised by various critics in their discussions of recent Godard. I begin with an article by Wollen on *Vent d'Est*. Some of Wollen's suggestions (for example, that "the constructive principle of the film is rhetorical, rather than narrative" ["Godard," 502]) are helpful and enlightening. Others will be familiar to anyone who has seen three or four of Godard's films: the attack on the assumed irreconcilability of "fiction" and "reality," on a single, homogeneous narrative and linear plot, on audience identification, and so on. There are other points, however, which I cannot accept, and it is these, and the "counter-cinema" which Wollen uses them to imply, which concern me here.

The essay is arranged as a discussion of the "seven cardinal virtues" of "revolutionary cinema," which *Vent d'Est* is supposed, approximately, to embody, and which exist in opposition to the "seven deadly sins" of "Hollywood Mosfilm." On what one might call the side of the sheep, we find the process described as "foregrounding," or "making the mechanics of the film text visible and explicit," as opposed, on the side of the goats, to "transparency," or language which "wants to be overlooked" (503) Wollen's main exhibit is the workers'-control sequence, in which the surface of the film stock is scratched.

> What [Godard] seems to be doing is looking for a way of expressing negation. It is well-known that negation is the founding-principle of verbal language, which marks it off both from animal signal-systems and from other kinds of human discourse, such as images. However, once the decision is made to consider making a film as a process of writing in images, rather than representing the world, then it becomes possible to conceive of scratching the film as an erasure, i.e., a virtual negation. (504)

The passage depends, obviously, on the assumption that "verbal language" is inherently superior to "other kinds of human discourse," an assumption which depends in its turn on a supreme valuation of what one might describe crudely as "cognitive content"—verbal language is able to convey generalities and abstractions. Indeed, Wollen describes the Stalin sequence in the same film as being "about the problem of finding an image to signify 'repression.'" (504) Apparently, the ideal is to give the image "a semantic function within a genuine iconic code," and "the Baroque code of emblems" is suggested as a satisfying analogy. Both the drift of the argument and the particular example are significant. As Rosemary Freeman shows in her excellent *English Emblem Books*, the emblem technique—"a detailed pictorial and allegorical presentation of ideas," which can be correlated point by point "with the moral doctrines taught in the accompanying poem"—was a product of the disintegration of the "one unified allegorical conception of the meaning of life" prevalent throughout the Middle Ages, in which all things "derived their meaning from, and were always referred back to an established and integrated scheme." (19–20) That is, the technique depended on the partial preservation of habits of thought which outlasted the collapse of the religious system which gave them significance, in which they were expressive of "the collective experience of everyone." The emblematic image establishes "fixities and definites" which no longer exist in the terms of a reliable cosmic order; "allegory has become an interest for its own sake, instead of a means of interpreting the universe." (31) Freeman locates here "the forced and arbitrary nature" of emblematic imagery, and she suggests that the popularity of the emblem books is partly attributable to the fact that in them, that imagery was "required only to exist, not to function; . . . those elements in the medieval scheme which still had meaning locally could be preserved in them without reference to, or need for, a coherent framework." (21)

It should be obvious from this that the "code of emblems" has a particular historical significance, is the product of particular cultural determinants and concepts of imagery which no longer obtain. Without the context of the systematic, symbolic worldview, the emblem becomes stiff and impoverished; "the details are laboriously enumerated and attached to a figure that is, and remains, lifeless." (21) Infinitely further removed as we are than the emblem writers were from any assured and generally accepted symbolic cosmos, it is rather difficult to imagine any analogous technique of "image-building" which would not be intolerably and ridiculously laborious.

But perhaps Wollen believes that a Marxist universe should now stand in for a Christian one, and this ties in significantly with what he has to say about "collective fantasy." In the passage in question (section six), he is, apparently, talking about "the masses" and suggests that a revolutionary cinema must set about creating fantasies through which the spectators can be made to desire the revolution, as previously they were made to desire the indefinite perpetuation of capitalism on the principle, presumably, that one can use the Devil's tools for the Lord's work. Wollen does not specify how one should go about reconciling the pleasure principle with Marxism, or what form the proposed collective fantasies should take, but limits himself to saying that it is "a complicated matter to articulate" the "different modes of discourse" appropriate to fantasy and "scientific analysis," and that Godard's solution is not the right one. ("Godard," 507) One can only agree. I think that Wollen is entirely right in his description of the "blow up the bourgeoisie" elements in the film (they remind me irresistibly of the last reel of *Air Force* [1943], in which the Japanese fleet is blasted to oblivion in a similar spirit of sadistic wish fulfillment), although I do not see how they can be separated from the rest of it, or how one can speak of "the ideology and the political theory" as if they were distinct entities. All three seem to me to be completely consistent, in Godard's film as in Howard Hawks's.

There is no earthly reason why, since "negation is the founding principle of verbal language" (Wollen, "Godard," 504), one should conclude that film "language" is exactly analogous and should produce an equivalent. How, in any case, do scratches on an image "negate" it? Nor is it clear from Wollen's remarks what it is that Godard is trying to negate. The image (that of the film company in a meadow) has no immediately apparent positive force—to me, at least—and the attitude which we are meant to take toward the discussion we half-see is very clearly spelled out for us by the commentary. I find the sequence in question evidence of a creative stalemate rather than creative vitality; by this point in the film, any image, any "bourgeois representation," must be furiously suppressed. The trite, perfunctory obviousness of the images that we are allowed to see can, I suppose, be taken as types of the "genuine" iconography which Wollen envisages. The cavalryman and his fellow are unmistakably "emblems" and tell us one fact at every possible opportunity.

Wollen's essay repeatedly expresses a desire to bypass three or four centuries of European culture—the period, roughly, since the Renaissance (and, implicitly, the emergence of the bourgeoisie), since "the rise of the novel, the representational painting"—and to return to the good old days when a painting was a "text which could be 'read '" ("Godard," 506); one thinks of the passage in Wollen's *Signs and Meaning* in which he advocates a criticism "maximizing lucidity and minimizing ambiguity," in which the connotations of imagery are described as strictly indeterminable and, as such, of no concern to "the scientist" which the critic should be. (153)

Wollen' s denigration of post-Renaissance art depends entirely for its substance on the claim that we no longer "read" it: it does not "create" meaning but "conveys" it; and "meaning . . . was regarded as representation of the world." ("Godard," 506) It is difficult to find anything in this that actually corresponds to any art one could mention. Landscapes by J. M. W. Turner, Caspar Friedrich, Vincent Van Gogh, and Paul Cézanne, obviously, are representations of the world, but considering that there are marked differences of representation, it doesn't seem that one has said anything very illuminating about them by describing them as such. Each one will have an "iconographic" significance which only a "reading" of the particular painting can suggest. (Friedrich, incidentally, is a perfect example of an artist whose "pure representation of the world" has a very precisely formulated and very schematic iconographic force.) It appears that perspective equals representation equals instant meaning—an equation I find it impossible to understand except in terms of Wollen's aesthetic bias. He tells us, similarly, that "from the seventeenth century onwards," language (that is, the monstrous bourgeois novel) characteristically "effaces itself" as it conveys meaning by representing the world. ("Godard," 503) Does Charles Dickens's or George Eliot's or Henry James's language "efface itself"? If Wollen really believes that these writers intend their language "to be overlooked," one can only recommend him to a novel of his choice. The notion becomes even more fantastic if one applies it to poetry: Keats no more wants us to ignore his language than does George Herbert or the writer of *Beowulf,* nor could we if they did.

Colin MacCabe is another critic who thinks that Godard shows the bourgeois novel in a rather unfavorable light. He arraigns "the classic realist text," and *Middlemarch* as an example of it, on two counts: it "cannot deal with the real as contradictory," and it ensures "the position of the subject," through the medium of the authorial voice "in a relation of dominant specularity." ("Realism," 12) This is precisely what *Vent d 'Est* does and what *Middlemarch* does not. In Godard 's film, we are given, through the pronouncements of the commentary, the position from which all reality suddenly becomes intelligible, the position of absolute truth from which all the contradictions of existence miraculously dissolve like dew in the sunshine. In what sense can this be said of George Eliot's novels? We are to believe that the nineteenth-century novel extracts "the meaningful content from the useless form" of the characters' recorded remarks and places them in a narrative context which is that of the truth. "The narrative discourse cannot be mistaken in its identifications because the narrative discourse is not present as discourse—as articulation. The unquestioned nature of the narrative discourse entails that the only problem which reality poses is to go and look and see what Things there are." (MacCabe, "Realism," 12)

The first point is trivial, and easily countered. The novel as practiced by George Eliot is a choir of individual voices, of which the author's is one; there are few novelists who realize their people in greater detail, with more particularized attention, or who are so intensely aware of the minutiae of individual speech. Even to suggest that the language of a character in an Eliot novel is so much "useless form," a sort of husk from which the author winnows a grain of meaning which is then given some clinically authoritative form in the framing commentary, is to suggest at the same time that one is incapable of experiencing the novel at the most direct and immediate level. The "commentary" does not make the voice superfluous; the two work together, formally inseparable, mutually consolidating. The characters' language is an essential part of themselves. It is the way they organize their conscious experience, the movement of their thought. That language's tone, vocabulary, rhythm—what these express, imply, leave unsaid—are manifestations of a human individuality. What the commentary tells us about them makes us more responsive to those manifestations, makes possible a complex counterpoint between what we hear from their lips in a particular context and what we know of the context itself and what has produced it; between what they say and acknowledge and what they do not or cannot say and acknowledge. MacCabe's distinction between meaningful content and useless form in a character's language, or any language, is plainly meaningless. No novelist, unless s/he is a very bad one, invents characters who embody attitudes of varying degrees of rightness which the narrative can then place in the name of a Truth to which it has access. Novels are not about "truth" in that sense.

According to MacCabe, the "metalanguage," or authorial voice, "being unspoken, is also unwritten." ("Realism," 24) But we have only to read the first paragraph of *Middlemarch*, or any other great bourgeois novel, to be intensely and immediately aware of a speaking voice with its own unique emphases and modulations. Our experience of the novel is the experience of that language also, of somebody telling a story *in his/her way*. This is what style means. And part of the pleasure of reading is this sense of being engaged with a conscious-ness expressing personally its personal perceptions—what Jane Fonda is trying to do in *Tout Va Bien*. A George Eliot novel does not proclaim "This is the Truth"; it says something more like "This is what I see"—the novel is essentially the realization of that. As I read it, I am aware both of the "I" which is the author, and of the structure which it builds up: a network of relationships which becomes ever more complex as the reading proceeds; a network of con-nections, resonances, discords, references back and forth, the sense of which it is the purpose of a reading to discover.

The terms of the meaning are the terms of the particular work of art: every work exists "like itself" and in no other way. To say, as MacCabe does of *Tout Va Bien*, that "the narrative serves simply as the method by which various situations can be articulated together" by the spectator is mere critical sleight of hand and linguistic imprecision. ("Realism," 24) The "situ-ations" are articulated together; the linear progression from the first shot to the last is one order of the film, just as that from the first to the last word of *Middlemarch* is one order of the novel. Within it, there are others, which readers must find for themselves. This is their "work," which makes their reading exactly that and no one else's, but their exploration takes place within the made order of the art. The difference between *Middlemarch* and *Vent d'Est* is that in Godard's film there exists a supposed objective Truth which it can simply present as such and which automatically validates it: in the words of the central character of Bertolucci's *Before the Revolution* (1964), "Even if you make a mistake, it has a meaning." This is what must make the film so supremely comforting to those who can agree with it.

In Eliot's novel, there are also values which the artist holds supreme, which are thought to give human life significance, mature purpose, responsibility. But these values are not imposed on or given to the reader, do not take the form of absolute moral polarities which give all approbations and denunciations a legal force, and cannot be held in any sense to make reality finally soluble. Mr. Casaubon does not embody values which Eliot endorses, but the values by which his are felt to be inadequate are realized, are expressed and formulated, within the terms of the novel; they are not imported to it, but made to emerge from it. Nor can we feel that Mr. Casaubon is an item of human rubbish which we can discard or to whom we can feel superior because he does not measure up. The character is a human being, created as such by another, and felt as such by us.

Finally, the values Eliot prizes do not entail some sort of neat resolution of human problems. Take the ending of *Daniel Deronda*. The whole meaning of the counterpoint between the two strands of the plot is that this cannot be so. The Deronda plot ends with Deronda's marriage and his involvement in the Zionist movement established, his break with the constrictions of the past and his faith to what is vital in it complete. The Gwendolen plot ends completely openly, balancing, on the one hand, the movement toward maturity, self-awareness, commitment to something beyond the self—which has been initiated and nurtured under Deronda's influence—against, on the other, Gwendolen's vulnerability beneath the burden of the past, the incompleteness of her development, and her isolation. She is left with nothing but the fragile beginnings of the full independent humanity which Deronda has already achieved. George Eliot 's novel can admit precisely that refusal of resolution, that incompleteness, which *Vent d 'Est* cannot.

The pre-Renaissance art to which Wollen suggests that *Vent d'Est* returns also appears to be largely imaginary. Another of his "sheep versus goats" distinctions is that between the "closed" and "open" text-"openness" being largely a matter of "quotations, allusions, parodies, citation of authorities," in which the artist's "own voice is drowned out and obliterated behind that of the authors quoted." ("Godard," 506) He cites pre-Renaissance literature and "the battle of the books" as exemplary of this. One might say, first of all, that the citation of authorities in medieval texts had various functions: a method of displaying the erudition of the author; a method of gaining acceptance by appeal to recognized and universally respected sources; a method of embodying a particular dramatic conflict or moral dilemma; a method of reconciling and synthesizing contradictory (say, Christian and classical) sources. There is also the typical delight in abundance and variety, in the retelling, reworking, and collecting of familiar stories. And to describe the battle of the books as a "meeting-place in which different discourses encounter each other and struggle for supremacy" (506), as if no authorial intention were involved, is totally inaccurate, since the whole point of the form is that it is organized according to a strict polemical purpose. None of this corresponds to the spirit of Godard's films.

The fact that *Une femme est une femme* (1961) is "obviously derivative from the Hollywood musical" makes it no more or less of a work "harmonized within its own bounds," creating its own terms of reference and its own relations, than a Vincente Minnelli musical. (Wollen, "Godard," 505) Nor does Godard's own remark that *Le Mépris* (*Contempt* [1963]) is "Hawks and Hitchcock shot in the manner of Antonioni," although it may have tangential interest, like any authorial comment, help us very much with the nature of *Le Mépris*. (Godard quoted in Wollen, "Godard," 505)

Wollen goes on:

> Godard is like Ezra Pound or James Joyce, who, in the same kind of way, no longer insist on speaking to us in their own words, but can be seen more as ventriloquists' dummies, through whom are speaking—or rather, being written palimpsests, multiple *iederschriften* (Freud's word) in which meaning can no longer be said to express an intention of the author or to be a representation of the world, but must, like the discourse of the unconscious, be understood by a different kind of decipherment. (506)

What it comes down to is that the author him- or herself (if one may speak so personally) is a sort of passive receptacle from which discourses emerge, rather as a medium vomits ectoplasm. The fact that Ezra Pound, James Joyce, and Godard refer to the work of other writers and filmmakers, and parody or imitate various other styles, is extended to suggest that their works are the determined pronouncements of something or other, some mystic scribal power, which seems on the whole to be a hybrid of cultural history and the murmurings of the unconscious. The books have "an independent life of their own," and the writers are dead—or at least inanimate. If one is logical about this, one ends up with a very strange definition of the phrase "in their own words," by which it could only be applied to a virgin tongue which no one has ever used before. Because Pound refers, implicitly and explicitly, to Homer, Dante, and Confucius, is he any the less Ezra Pound, who makes the reference at a particular point, in a particular context, with a particular purpose? It is extremely likely, given Pound's extraordinary familiarity with these and other writers, and their relevance to the themes of his work, that not all the references are deliberately, consciously formulated. This means neither that they aren't there nor that they aren't vitally expressive of the "intention of the author." "Intention" as Wollen defines it (that is, conscious plan) is obviously not the whole of art, nor does anyone pretend that it is. But this indicates the superficiality of the definition rather than the absurdity of using the term, intention in a work of art being a far more subtle and complex matter than Wollen seems to believe.

No work of art is simply a "representation of the world." The most perfunctory snapshot entails a choice of some kind in that one snaps one thing rather than another, from one angle rather than another. On the other hand, no definition of "the world" can be confined to physical reality, and the works of art to which another work refers are part of the world. Think of poems such as "The Waste Land" and "The Ancient Mariner," two very different examples of works in which practically every image (in the first case, every extractable "idea" as well) can be traced to a known source outside the poem. It would be as absurd to suggest that, in the former, Dante, Charles Baudelaire, and so on "drown out" T. S. Eliot's voice as to say that, in the latter, reports of various sea voyages drown out Samuel Taylor Coleridge's. The suggestion in the last case is patently absurd—it seems to me equally so in the first. If one knew Dante only from Eliot, or Pound, or Geoffrey Chaucer, one would know a very different writer in each case. Godard belongs to a long line of modern authors (the first great example is Herman Melville) for whom civilized culture has become a sort of playground in which the artist can disport him- or herself, and one can gauge an essential movement of Western civilization by observing the way in which the spirit of the play turns from an exhilarated, but already deeply ironic, delight to conspicuous desperation. Wollen's intentness on the virtues of "counter-cinema" leads him to ignore, even to discount, the tone of the work.

In *Tout Va Bien*, Godard returns to the depiction of "an action," the presentation of a narrative with "characters": the meaning of the film, as we have seen, is that politics and individual life are inseparable. In the light of the later film, it seems evident that the dehumanization and the political repressiveness of *Vent d'Est* are similarly connected: the essential denial of the creative involvement of the spectator goes with the political dogmatism and the absence of any human consciousness within the film, the reduction of the actors to so many emblems. Yet it seems possible to find this admirable. Here is Stephen Heath, discussing distantiation:

In the French film *Septembre chilien* [1973], the voice of the woman militant in the final interview is spoken over by Simone Signoret; where the woman's voice is flat, anonymous almost, *political* (that of a specific struggle), Signoret's brings with it emphatic emotion and individual pain, a heroization, a certain non-political "human message," the feeling of those Signoret roles of today, the resolutely determined yet deeply—and frailly—affected woman. . . . It is these effects that Brecht's theory seeks to locate and to refuse.

In his essay on *Touch of Evil* (1958), Heath brings up what he calls the "problem" of the "use of the face" in film, "the tendency—of which the close-up is the ultimate mode—to an 'inevitable' individuation round the expression of the character (character constructed from this expression)," and cites, as if an appalling contradiction were involved, *State of Siege* (1972) as "a film that runs its political action into the predicament of consciousness." ("Film and System Pt. 2," 104) I have not seen *Septembre chilien*, and I would agree with the denunciation of the sort of calculated, sentimental effect intended to lure us into an ecstasy of self-indulgent emotion, which may well be the case here. What is alarming, however, is the apparent assumption of a necessary contradiction between "political" and "individual," and the implications of a phrase such as "non-political 'human message'" considered as an adequate paraphrase of the latter. How can we make sense of a "specific struggle" unless in terms of the specific aspirations, aims, pains—feelings—of the specific individuals specifically involved in it? How can we reconcile that "specific" and that "anonymous"? How can an individual be anonymous at all? Do people involved in political struggle miraculously discard their individuality to become merely representative or embodiments of "The Struggle," which exists apart from them? How, unless they were conscious of action to be taken, of ends to be achieved, of values and motives which drive them and which they wish to establish or defend, could they be involved in action at all? How are we, unless we too are conscious, to experience anything beyond a certain impersonal, uncommitted curiosity about them—unless we can feel the human cost and relevance of their struggle to themselves and us? And how can a close-up, or any other kind of shot, make the expression of a human face individual? Human beings, and revolutionaries above all, would appear to be, for Heath, a type of zombie.

Commitment is a specific act of the whole being. One might say of *Vent d'Est* that it attempts to impose a generalized intellectual commitment, and that its artistic failure can be defined in terms of the contradiction which that implies. One cannot commit oneself to anything—one cannot even be aware of the issues involved—without a complete (emotional and intellectual) grasp of them. *Tout Va Bien* takes that as its theme, and the film's method is not an imposition of "knowledge"—a set of truths and solutions—but an attempt to create that feeling awareness of our context which makes us fully individual, and which makes responsible commitment possible.

"Foxed": *Fox and His Friends* (1977)

I t was very illuminating—if disconcerting—to see Bob Cant's review of *Fox and His Friends* (1975) appearing in the same issue of *Gay Left* as Richard Dyer's admirable analysis of "Gays in Film." In discussing, among other works, *The Bitter Tears of Petra von Kant* (1972)—also by Rainer Werner Fassbinder—Dyer seems to me to have said very pointedly what also needs to be said about *Fox*: the film tries to suggest that gay relationships can be taken as a valid metaphor for the exploitiveness of bourgeois-capitalist society as a whole. ("Gays," 16) I found the film offensive in the extreme. And since it is possible, apparently, for a popular audience—let alone a gay socialist—to read it as a damning indictment of the bourgeoisie, I feel it is important to raise one or two points in reply.

1. There is no mention in the article of the reception of the film in the bourgeois press. David Robinson remarked in the *Times* to the effect that the chronicle of exploitation is all the more convincing for being set in a homosexual milieu, and that it represents an honest and realistic picture of gay relationships. ("Matter") Such comments are typical of what has been the general emphasis. This would seem to suggest both that a concern with The Problem of Homosexuality, as Cant puts it, is rather more central to the film—and to its reception by the audience—than he tries to imply and that its supposed subversion of bourgeois assumptions is rather less so.

2. The film's German title, *Faustrecht der Freiheit* (literally, *Fist-Right of Freedom*), carries connotations of the survival of the fittest, which, indeed, is the English title provided by Peter Cowie in his *International Film Guide 1976*. Clearly, social Darwinism has been crucial for capitalist ideology, and a film concerned with its ramifications within institutions and personal relationships might be interesting and valuable. What is objectionable in *Fox* is that the notion is introduced not as an ideological category but as the inevitable order of the reality depicted. In other words, the ideology is reinforced. A Fate motif is introduced in the opening scenes in the fairground (consider the obtrusive emphasis on the deserted Big Wheel, revolving inexorably like the Wheel of Fortune), in the dialogue ("That's Fate!"), and in the device of the lottery, on which the plot turns. One can, perhaps, attribute part of the film's critical success to this carefully contrived impression of "tragic" necessity. Insofar as *Fox* portrays "the homosexual predicament" and reinforces deep-rooted preconceptions about it, the film allows the spectator to sit back and think, "God! What awful lives

they lead!" Insofar as it permits identification with the dumb loser, and enforces the generalization "This is how things are in this world," it encourages acquiescence in the movement of the narrative and, ultimately, in the status quo. The spectator can leave the cinema filled with an ennobling compassion for a despised and rather pathetic minority group, and with a complacent conviction of his own, and everybody else's, helplessness. *Fox* is, in fact, the least ideologically subversive of films.

Cant talks about Fox's "lack of choice" in a context which implies that there is a direct analogy between choice in immediate personal relationships and our lack of control "over the economic destiny of the countries" we live in. This is a fatuous equation; it is difficult to see how any individual movement toward self-determination, or any radical political action, could begin or even be conceived if it were true. It is deeply significant that there is not the slightest mention of Gay Liberation in the film, not a glimpse of a character, gay or straight, who either wants or knows how to break out of the repressive environment. The only characters who are permitted any degree of distance from the central action either observe it in a spirit compounded of self-interest and resignation (Uncle Max, Eugen's father) or are provided with sterile, bitter tirades of disgust and self-disgust (Fox's sister). The film concludes that one is "inside the whale," in George Orwell's phrase, and one can't do anything about it. The "lack of choice," the "downhill-all-the-way" structure, in which everything goes wrong with somewhat facile regularity, depends upon the deliberate choice of an ineffectual protagonist, whose defeat is inscribed from the start. *The Merchant of Four Seasons* (1972), another Fassbinder film, works in the same way. In both cases there is an attempt to immerse the spectator in the process of disintegration.

3. Cant suggests that *Fox* is "about the corruptive nature of capitalism," and that the film is seriously concerned with the economic determination of human relationships. This formula seems to me objectionable on several counts. Unless one is willing to accept that "filthy lucre" is a subversive concept, and that people with money tend to be unpleasant is a significant judgment on "the pressures of capitalism," it is difficult to point to any coherent, serious awareness of the "economic structure of a society." Bourgeois audiences find no difficulty in accepting the proposition that "money corrupts all relationships." And the victimization of the loser by rapacious hangers-on has become a staple narrative structure precisely because it so emphatically confirms complacency, allowing us to feel outraged by a collection of vultures who are very definitely not us.

If the film were really concerned with the perversion of human relationships under capitalism as that which is reflected in the lives of a particular group of people (in this case, homosexuals—and if that is not the concern, then the use of gayness is superfluous), one would require the following:

a. An exploration of what it means to be gay in a working-class environment, and how this differs from what it means to be gay in an upper-middle-class environment. As it is, Fox-as-proletarian does not exist in the film beyond such qualities as bad table manners and bourgeois myths, which see the proletarian hero as

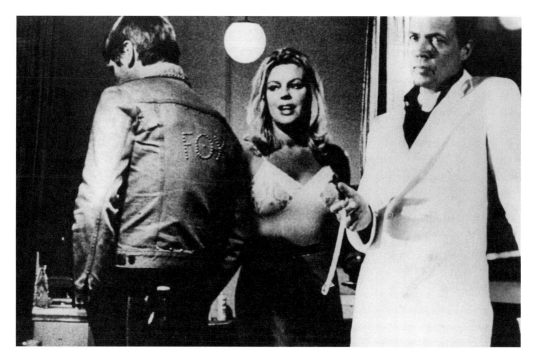

Director Rainer Werner Fassbinder as the ineffectual protagonist in *Fox and His Friends*. Personal collection of the editor.

slightly (or, as here, exceptionally) stupid, gullibly generous, emotionally sincere (as opposed to the affectation and superficiality of the bourgeoisie—consider Eugen's "We're not starry-eyed lovers anymore"), and sexually potent, in a modern variation on the "close-to-the-earth" syndrome. The class theme is, in fact, only trivially present, and the film's central conflict would remain if Fox were an aristocratic gay visitor from Mars. Cant does seem aware of this at some level, since he can talk at one point about relationships being "more than just a matter of good individuals and bad individuals" and at another about the fable of "the innocent abroad in an evil world," without any acknowledgement that there might be some contradiction between the two.

b. An exploration of why and how the bourgeois gays depicted have come to acquiesce in the institutions of the society which oppresses them. As it is, there is no sense whatever in the film that gayness and bourgeois ideology are in any way incompatible. Indeed, as the action progresses, and the bourgeois gays whom Fox has met at the beginning appear one by one in positions of exploitative power, any distinction between victimization by predatory homosexuals and victimization by a predatory bourgeoisie becomes so blurred that we are left with, at least, the impression of an alliance for mutual benefit. It clearly needs to be said that although gay relationships may become exploitative under capitalism, as any relationships may, the attempt to elide the two is pernicious.

c. A sense of gay oppression. There is nothing in *Fox* to show that gayness is sub-ject to ideological, social, or legal constraints. Why no awareness of the eco-nomic and ideological factors which determine the existence of, say, the gay bar? Why no mention of the social stereotyping which associates gayness with interior decorating and sultry boutiques? Why is gayness taken as paradig-matic of "a world which is self-conscious and yet desperate not to face up to its own reality"? I quite agree with Cant about the symbolism of boutique and antique shop, but that symbolism has nothing essentially to do with gayness at all. Instead of exploring gay lifestyles in terms of their various, complex deter-minants, Fassbinder presents them as a kind of existential metaphor, an image (deprived of any ideological context) of "exploitiveness" which perpetuates every received idea about homosexuality—its squalor, its ephemerality ("one affair after another"), its triviality, its decadence (the scene with the singer, an imitation-Dietrich backed by an enormous photograph of a naked muscleman), its inhumanity.

Unlike Cant, I feel that the inhabitants of the bar are consistently portrayed as callous, petty, and malicious, and I found the use of the plump flower seller's attempted seduction of Fox to arouse an automatic response of revulsion from the grotesque quite intolerable. Once all the stereotypes and the finality of "the predicament" have been affirmed, the spectator can be invited to feel pity. One can point to a comparable procedure in *The Tenderness of Wolves* (1973), which Fassbinder produced, where after all the fuss and bother about the activities of the murder reflecting the viciousness of capitalist society (a theme which, again, is not significantly there in the film but which has earned it consider-able praise—including that of *Gay News*), we come back, through the use of Bach's "Have mercy, Lord, on me" for the opening and closing titles, to the real business of "grief for sin," and the pitiable pervert Fassbinder seems to me, in fact, the archetypal watered-down radical, whose extraordinary current popu-larity with bourgeois critics can be associated with the opportunity his films provide for becoming aware of, and condemning, some of the more obvious unpleasantness of the middle class without having too many basic assump-tions disturbed in the process. The recurrent tone of rather frigid irony, shad-ing at times into the misanthropic, is admirably suited to this purpose, as to the enrollment of the spectator in a stable position from which the inevitability of the action can be observed.

4. Many of the film's targets are reassuringly noncontroversial and curiously anach-ronistic. Elegant table manners, a familiarity with French cuisine, cultural philis-tinism, and the "family tradition" of Châteauneuf du Pape are easy, comfortable foes from which we can dissociate ourselves without difficulty. To gauge the thinness of Fassbinder's conception, one has only to place these scenes beside, say, the Christmas scenes in *All That Heaven Allows*, a film made in Hollywood in 1955 by Douglas Sirk, for whom Fassbinder is always declaring his admiration, but who is completely with-

out Fassbinder's rather glib fatalism (consider, as an example of it, the way in which Fox and Eugen come across their Arab pick-up in "The Meeting Place of the Dead"). In Sirk's film the insidiousness of the oppression of bourgeois good manners is felt and conveyed with a subtlety and insight beside which the meal scenes in *Fox* seem dismally obvious and crude.

5. Cant implies that there is no alternative to "gay chauvinism" on the one hand and the "fairly accurate picture of one part of the gay world" which he claims *Fox* to be on the other. One can readily agree that "the gay ghetto is not a pleasant place," that it is inadvisable to pretend that our lives are "heroic" (do we pretend that?) and that we, like everyone else, are subject to social and ideological determination in various ways, some of which are beyond our immediate control. This is not the same thing as saying that we should countenance a film such as *Fox*—whose unawareness of ideology is quite staggering, and which attempts, in a most simplistic and destructive way, to appropriate what it calls "the gay world"—as an all-purpose metaphor for a rotten civilization. There seems to be a widely held belief—attributable, presumably, to fear of a charge of "gay chauvinism"—that we should commend and applaud every "exposure" of the "jungle-like atmosphere" (Cant's fine phrase), which we, more than any other class of people, are thought to breathe. Chauvinism is now, of course, a loaded word and probably, in the present context, an inappropriate one if all that is meant is a degree of enthusiasm for Gay Liberation which various bourgeois/liberal observers feel to be "excessive." I think that "proper pride" is admirable and sorely needed, especially at the present time. On the other hand, a clear, honest, coherent portrayal of the ways in which gay relationships are repressed, perverted, curtailed in bourgeois-capitalist society might be equally admirable. This is not what *Fox* is. Its version of homosexuality degrades us all and should be roundly denounced.

Part Four
Film and Cultural Theory

In Defense of Criticism (1986)

It is nowadays the case, perhaps, that the word *criticism* tends to sound recherché—to suggest nostalgia for the days before film studies became intellectually strenuous. A few years ago it passed as a commonplace in advanced circles that criticism ought to be, and might become, "scientific," and the older word evoked in itself the morass of impressionism and empiricism from which the discussion of art should be promptly rescued. Today, a new set of discourses adjure us not to criticize but to "deconstruct," and deconstruction, whether or not it is properly scientific, certainly suggests an activity at once more bracing and more precise than any in which the student of culture was traditionally engaged. The new vocabularies are awesome—at any rate, they have attracted a good deal of publicity—and it is correspondingly necessary, if one thinks the concept of criticism worth reviving, to undertake to be as clear as possible about the intention with which one employs it.

No film theory is worth anything which does not stay close to the concrete and which does not strive continually to check its own assumptions and procedures in relation to producible texts. Much of what has passed for film theory in the last decade is principally remarkable for its solipsistic and opportunistic character, and it is curious that discourses which arraign "representation" and "realism" on the ground that they serve, in essence, to naturalize a bourgeois worldview should be committed also to methods of analysis which are programmed to produce exactly the conclusions which the reader is presumed to hold in the first place. The interests of film theory are not served by finding in every "realist" text a confirmation of the Lacanian (or Foucauldian or Derridean or whatever) "problematic," or by proselytizing for the mass production of "modernist" texts which flatter the presuppositions embodied in the attack on realism. Characteristically, and deplorably, such theory reduces the objects it purports to theorize to mere pretexts for rationalizing the validity of its own premises, and it makes a virtue of its refusal of all cognitive controls by denouncing any concern for the material integrity of the text as "empiricism."

All intellectual fashions have their slogan, and the proposition that "theory constructs its objects," seductive and comforting as it is, is now part of the thinking literary person's common sense. This proposition, when it is not a truism, is little more than a self-serving scholastic fiction and a license for intellectual irresponsibility, and that conception of theory is illegitimate in which the necessarily creative and formative nature of discourse is understood as a means of freeing the theory in question from the elementary critical obligation of demonstrating its own pertinence. Such theory is anti-theoretical, as well as a betrayal of the function of criticism.

It is also possible to regret the abusive, trivializing misappropriation of political—in particular, of Marxist and feminist—idioms for which structuralist and post-structuralist film theory have been responsible, and of which the banalization of the word *materialist* (as in "materialist film practice") is representative. Whatever the intentions of specific users (often, doubtless, "good"), the effect in general of this usage has been to give a spurious political gloss to discourses which are in fact innocent of all politics; as a result, the language of socialism has been conscripted for service in the realm of manners and polite good form. It has been reduced, in fact, to a sign—a sign that one is familiar with the forms and keepings of a fashionable academic world in which such idioms are common currency but which issues, nevertheless, into that public world where the major struggles of our time are being fought out.

It is in the nature of fashions to change. Ten years ago, before the ripples of 1968 had subsided, it was necessary for advocates of the Lacanian theory of subjectivity to qualify the phrase with the adjective "materialist"—for at that stage, one was committed, if one was committed at all, to the project of articulating psychoanalysis with historical materialism. A few years later, when the irreducible economism and class-reductionism of Marx's thought had become clearer and historical materialism had been superceded by Michel Foucault's theory of power, the adjective was superfluous, even embarrassing. Had it not been discovered that Marx was befuddled by the most vulgar realist epistemology, and had not Foucault asserted that Marxism led to the Gulag archipelago? Clearly, materialism would have to go.

In film studies, politics ought to be more than a matter of esoteric vocabularies that are useful while they happen to be "in" but which can be discarded as soon as they happen to go "out." Marxism is a politics—not just another academic hermeneutic.

It is now, and for some time has been, apparent that the claims once made for the significance and intelligibility of the successive structural-isms as "critical theory" were exorbitant. Among other tests, Sebastiano Timpanaro's *On Materialism*, the volumes from the Harvester Press on *Issues in Marxist Philosophy*, Fredric Jameson's *The Prison-House of Language*, the polemics against Louis Althusser by Simon Clarke and Edward Thompson, and Perry Anderson's essay "In the Tracks of Historical Materialism" have all made memorable contributions to the necessary demolition work, from a wide variety of socialist positions. While Terry Lovell's book *Pictures of Reality* has performed the valuable service of introducing some of these critiques for readers whose main concern can be assumed to be the politics of culture, it can hardly be claimed that film theory has yet begun to take stock of, or even positively to acknowledge, the radical challenge to the assumptions on which, throughout the '70s, the film theory worth engaging with was based. It is clearly significant that Lovell's book (for all its limitations an important one) has had no visible effect or influence—it has been, in fact, disgracefully ignored—and if the petering out of *Screen* as a major force inertly reflects the passing of the structuralist "moment," nothing of value has emerged to replace it. Indeed, film theory seems now to proceed on the assumption that nothing which need concern us has really happened, or that honor is sufficiently served or face saved by hole-and-corner intellectual expediency. The need for a coherent, systematic film theory—a political priority until so recently—has been studiously forgotten.

If, in such a context, one feels the need to stress the word *criticism*, it is because the structuralist record in the performance of the critical function has been, on the whole, a poor one. Given what structuralism is, that fact hardly provokes surprise: "It is in the last resort immaterial" for Lévi-Strauss (who in this respect is perfectly representative) "whether the thought processes of the South American Indians take shape through the medium of my thought, or whether mine takes place through theirs." (*Structural Anthropology*, 13) Whether "closed" or "open," "realist" or "modernist," the text "produced" by this method has always been exhausted in advance and cannot but serve to authenticate the discourse which articulates it. It is quite inconceivable that the text might tell creatively for the assumptions of the critic. During the structuralist heyday it was hardly necessary for the critic to be able to read, or even to make a plausible show of doing so. S/he was required instead to be an expert (at least for the purposes of social solidarity) in structural linguistics, structural psychoanalysis, Marxist theory (selected), the history of philosophy (abridged)—even the higher branches of mathematics. Expertise consisted not in the capacity to grasp the relevance of these disciplines and to put them to firsthand use, but in one's readiness to apply the orthodox formulae to whatever object that offered. It was tantamount to exposing oneself as an empiricist or (worse) a Leavisite to admit to an addiction to close reading or to maintain that a text's relation to the ideologies implicit in its own modes and conventions could be determined only by an analysis of the text.

It has distinct bearings for theory that texts should be read closely, and to the extent that theory impedes or discourages close reading, or surrenders it to contingency, theory disqualifies itself for the use of the theorist of film.

Of course deconstructionism, which—things being what they are—has found a natural home in the university, offers close reading of a kind, though it is possible to doubt that the kind is the right one. However, for the modernized, swashbuckling literary academic, it is the indicated idiom, and those with an eye to the right journals can hardly afford not to cultivate it. The university presses desperately compete in the manufacture of Derridean prose, and only the most indefatigable labor among the groaning library shelves would make it possible to take cognizance of the "state of the art," or to pronounce with a measure of confidence on whether it is or is not legitimate for the deconstructionist to adhere to materialism, Freudianism, feminism—to any, indeed, of the Old Pretenders who continue to voice their tired and importunate claims against the new regime.

The cachet of the sophisticated form of academic agnosticism which deconstruction is is very understandable. Even at its most recondite and abstruse, there was still, perhaps, something unengagingly political about the Lacanianized materialism which flourished in the early '70s—something which intimated, in however gestural and paradoxical a way, of the necessary interconnection between the concerns of aesthetic theory and "life." It may well be that the unfortunate combination of arbitrariness and dogmatism which marked the political rhetoric of the Lacan period has had the effect of confirming the academic's constitutional timidity about getting mixed up with politics in the first place, and the mandarin features of the earlier project unmistakably point forward, in any case, to what has replaced it. But it would not be proper merely to conflate the kind of thing that used to be found in *Screen* with the indiscriminate "deconstructions" of the artifacts, major and marginal, of the Western tradition which now grace the pages of innumerable scholarly journals.

Deconstructionism is the exemplary product of deradicalization, and the historian of literary tastes in the twenty-first century, should we reach it, can be expected to have a word or two to say about the coincidence between the rise of Jacques Derrida as the presiding deity of the literature department and the less-specialized political ethos of the Reagan era. No one will dispute that there is pleasure to be derived from the conviction that all totalizations (that is, all political positions) are false, and for the critic who wishes to nourish such a conviction without inviting the deadly epithet "liberal," the new discourse, with its air of astringent modernity, combines two obvious sources of credit.

But alas, the critic is committed to totalize. S/he will do so in any case in that s/he uses language, and the idea that any discourse can abdicate from politics is an illusion.

The business of theory and the business of criticism cannot, in practice, be hived off from one another, and the cost of an attempt to do so is one of the fundamental lessons of the structuralist/post-structuralist phase. The cost is measured in academicism of the worst kind: narcissistic, pedantic, introverted, self-perpetuating, apolitical. Obviously, there can be no criticism without theory, but it is equally the case that there can be no viable theory without a viable sense of the nature of the critical function. Theory, for the critic, is—or ought to be—the discoveries of relevant criticism expressed as principle, and criticism is at once the practice and the critique of theory, where "practice" consists in the attempt to define the value of objects whose significance cannot be construed in advance. Unless the critic understands what the aims and conditions of this practice are, s/he will not come up with any principles worth having: they will have no intelligible connection with the kinds of activity in which the critic actually engages.

Criticism is the systematic reading (that is, the evaluation) of texts. Like all other activities, it takes place in the present. Like all other critical activities, it presupposes a principled attitude to the politics which constitute the present. The business of the film critic is to arrive at an understanding, on the basis of that attitude—which ought to be as alert and as conscious as possible—of what is of value in the past and present of the cinema and to ensure that this value is recognized for what it is, and has the influence it ought to have, now. The critic's theory should be seen in the light of this business and in no other, for there is no other test for the intellectual relevance of theory.

Criticism today, if it is to have any substance at all, must be explicitly oppositional: the critic's concern with artistic value is a concern to arrive at a sense of the conditions of profitable and progressive intervention in a dominant culture of daunting banality and impoverishment. It by no means follows from this that one is committing oneself to the enforcement of some aesthetic "line" or orthodoxy. The grounds for being opposed, on principle, to the notion of a socialist orthodoxy in aesthetics were classically expounded half a century ago by Leon Trotsky, and only the conservative or (it amounts to the same thing) the critic with a stake in the notion of critical "impartiality" will maintain that political conviction and responsibility are synonymous with monolithic intransigence. (Trotsky, *Literature and Revolution*)

The critic for whom the conditions of profitable and progressive intervention are of interest will be centrally concerned with popular culture. For me, this interest is continuous with the belief that the advanced views on representationalism are, for all purposes of theory, criticism, and practice, false, and that whatever may be retrieved from them and put to other uses, their basic assumptions are dangerously misleading. They act as an impediment to significant theory; to the reading, in their specificity, of particular texts; and to constructive political strategies in contemporary filmmaking. The opposition between realism and modernism, between the closed and the open text, between the film which constructs you as a subject and the film which does not is, as construed, entirely unacceptable, and it has had the most disastrous consequences for film studies.

The valorization of the avant-garde—the backing of a Jean-Marie Straub/Danièle Huillet or a Peter Wollen/Laura Mulvey or a Peter Gidal or a Berwick Street Collective as representatives of the, or a, progressive cinema—is not an intelligible political strategy, and it is legitimate to be disturbed by the value which has often been attributed to such work. The theory which finds value of that kind here takes for granted categories and political conditions which need to be challenged. It is necessary to reject the view according to which the popular cinema (or any cinema which can be vaguely construed as realist) is an object of urbane, ironical, or diagnostic scrutiny and the various "avant-gardes," imputed or actual, acquire a privileged political significance for theory and practice alike.

It is necessary to plan for radical interventions in a culture which extends beyond the academy and its associated institutions, and if it is important to make judgments about, and discriminations within, the various complex traditions of popular narrative filmmaking, that is because they have creative implications for progressive work in filmmaking and film studies in the present. Indeed, the mapping of this enormous field has barely begun, and many of the guides that are most often handled and most widely publicized are seriously defective.

The '80s of *Rambo: First Blood* (1982) and *Je vous salue, Marie* (*Hail Mary* [1985]), to take two obviously representative works, are not a creative period, and the difficulties of a contemporary film criticism follow from this: the contemporary world cinema is remarkable for the absence of significant development and innovation, and it would be difficult to come up with even a handful of films from the current year which are even of minor interest. That criticism in itself cannot affect this situation is obvious, but it is therefore all the more necessary to attempt to maintain the sense of what an oppositional film culture is, or might be. The time, in fact, is now ripe for a reconsideration of the past and a revaluation of methods and strategies on the basis of a cogent radical position.

For Interpretation: Notes Against Camp (1979)

> Genet does not want to change anything at all. Do not count on him to criticize institutions. He needs them, as Prometheus needs his vulture.
> —Jean-Paul Sartre, *Saint Genet*

One. It almost seems at times to have become a matter of common acceptance that camp is radical, and the play *Men* by Noel Greig and Don Milligan provides a convenient example of the process by which I imagine that to have come about. *Men* offers itself as a polemic against "the straight left"—an abstraction which it embodies in one of its two central gay characters, a shop steward in a Midlands factory and, in secret, the lover of Gene, a camp gay male for whom the play attempts to solicit a besotted and uncritical reverence. Their relationship is seen to be continuous with the dominant patterns of heterosexual relationships, and it is presented as a synonym for them, though there is no attempt to consider, or even to acknowledge, the social pressures which have gone into producing the similarity. The play concludes that the political struggle in which Richard, the shop steward, is engaged at work can be assimilated to "phallic" power drives (we are not allowed to forget that he is known to his fellow workers as Dick), and offers, in Gene's plangent cry of "Socialism is about me," what it takes to be the corrective emphasis. How "socialism" is to be defined or in what way, exactly, it can be said to be about Gene are not matters which the play finds it proper to discuss, although it becomes clear enough that Richard's activities (from which women workers are pointedly excluded except, in one instance, as the "victims" of a strike action) lie beyond the pale. Indeed, Gene's intimate relation to socialism is very much taken as a given. His ignorance of, and indifference to, politics is repeatedly stressed, yet he is somehow instinctively in line with the proper ends of political action; in the final scene, Gene becomes the medium not only for a series of vague and tendentious aphorisms about patriarchy ("Men, like Nature, abhor a vacuum"), portentously delivered in a spotlight, but also for the savage, cruel, and self-righteous scapegoating of Richard, who is endowed with the moral responsibility for his oppression. *Men* concludes that Richard should allow himself to become "nervous, sensual, and effeminate"—as dubious a set of Moral Positives as anyone could reasonably demand—and indulges itself in *A Doll's House* ending which we are asked to take as a triumph of radical intelligence. Richard's confusion, desperation, and self-oppression are neither here nor there. It is all "his fault," and we can take due satisfaction in his comeuppance: his guilty secret has been discovered by his workmates, and his just desserts are at hand.

The point I wish to make is that Gene's camp is taken as an automatic validation of the character. He has nothing to recommend him beyond a certain facile charisma and a few slick epigrams, yet his five-minute tour de force telephone monologue at the end of the first act is considered sufficiently impressive to "place" the portrayal, in the preceding thirty minutes, of Richard's political involvement. *Men* arrives at its assessment of camp by a simple process of elision. The Richard/Gene relationship is "like" a man/woman relationship. Therefore, Gene's camp is continuous with woman-identification: that is, it is "like" a feminist discourse against patriarchy. Therefore, camp is the means by which gay men may become woman-identified = radical = socialist, and we can carry on camping and "being ourselves" with perfect equanimity (camp, of course, is always "being oneself") in the serene assurance that we are in the vanguard of the march toward the socialist future. The play does not seek at any point to demonstrate the validity of this spurious set of propositions. They are simply data, and as such, they relate significantly to certain characteristic assumptions of bourgeois feminism. Juliet Mitchell has argued, for example, that the "political" and "ideological" struggles are conceptually and practically distinct, the one to be fought by the working class and the other by the women's movement. She even goes so far as to suggest in *Woman's Estate* that the revolution must now come from within the bourgeoisie. (179–82) Gene, while ostensibly working class, is very much a mouthpiece for bourgeois aspirations, and *Men* compounds Mitchell's fallacy both in its uncritical assimilation of camp to feminism and in its implicit assertion that there is no conceivable form of organized political activity which would not surreptitiously reiterate patriarchal power structures.

Two. Camp always connotes "effeminacy," not "femininity." The camp gay man declares, "'Masculinity' is an oppressive convention to which I refuse to conform," but his nonconformity depends at every point on the preservation of the convention he ostensibly rejects—in this case, a general acceptance of what constitutes "a man." Camp behavior is only recognizable as a deviation from an implied norm, and without that norm it would cease to exist; it would lack definition. It does not, and cannot, propose for a moment a radical critique of the norm itself. Being essentially a mere play with given conventional signs, camp simply replaces the signs of masculinity with a parody of the signs of femininity and reinforces existing social definitions of both categories. The standard of "the male" remains the fixed point in relation to which male gays and women emerge as "that which is not male."

Three. Camp requires the frisson of transgression, the sense of perversity in relation to bourgeois norms which characterizes the degeneration of the Romantic impulse in the second half of the nineteenth century and which culminates in England with aestheticism and in France with the *decadence*. Camp is a house-trained version of the aristocratic, anarchistic ethic of transgression, a breach of decorum which no longer even shocks and which has gone to confirm the existence of a special category of person—the male homosexual. Camp strives to give an objective presence to an imaginary construction of bourgeois psychology. The very term "a homosexual" (of which, finally, the term "a gay person" is only the recuperation, albeit a progressive one) defines not an object choice of which any individual is capable, but a type with characteristic modes of behavior and response. Sartre has analyzed, in relation to Genet, the process by which a determinate social imperative ("I have been placed in such-and-such a role") can be transformed into existential choice ("Therefore I will take the initiative of adopting it"); that process describes the fundamental complicity of what may appear to be an act of self-determination. (Sartre, chapter 2) Camp is collaborative in that sense.

Four. "Subversiveness" needs to be assessed not in terms of a quality which is supposedly proper to a phenomenon but as a relationship between a phenomenon and its context—that is, dynamically. To be Quentin Crisp in the 1930s is a very different matter from being Quentin Crisp in 1978. What was once an affront has now become part of life's rich pageant. The threat has been defused—and defused because it was always superficial. Camp is individualistic and apolitical, and even at its most disturbing, it asks for little more than living room. Susan Sontag's remark that "homosexuals have pinned their integration into society on promoting" the camp sensibility seems to me exact, and in its exactitude quite damning. (290) It is necessary, in making such a judgment, to dissociate oneself from any simple form of moralism.

Clearly, until very recently the ways of being gay have been so extraordinarily limited that the possibility of being radically gay has simply not arisen in the majority of cases. But in a contemporary context, gay camp seems little more than a kind of anaesthetic, allowing one to remain inside oppressive relations while enjoying the illusory confidence that one is flouting them.

Five. The belief in some "essential" homosexuality produces, logically, Jack Babuscio's concept of "the gay sensibility," of which camp is supposed to be the expression. "I define the gay sensibility as a creative energy reflecting a consciousness that is different from the mainstream; a heightened awareness of certain human complications of feeling that spring from the fact of social oppression; in short, a perception of the world which is colored, shaped, directed and defined by the fact of one's gayness."(40) This formulation contains two false propositions: (a) that there exists some undifferentiated "mainstream consciousness" from which gays, by the very fact of being gay, are absolved; and (b) that "a perception of the world which is . . . defined by the fact of one's gayness" necessarily involves a "heightened awareness" of anything (except, of course, one's gayness). I would certainly accept that oppression creates the potential for a critical distance from (and action against) the oppressing society, but one has only to consider the various forms of "negative awareness" to perceive that the realization of that potential depends on other elements of one's specific situation.

It is clearly not the case that the fact of oppression entails a conceptual understanding of the basis of oppression, or that the fact of belonging to an oppressed group entails ideological awareness. "Consciousness" (which is, in itself, an unhelpful term) is not determined by sexual orientation, nor is there a "gay sensibility." The ideological place of any individual at any given time is the site of intersection of any number of determining forces, and one's sense of oneself as "gay" is a determinate product of that intersection—not a determinant of it. It seems strange, in any case, to cite as exemplary of a gay sensibility a phenomenon which is characteristically male and with which many gay men feel little sympathy.

Six. The failure to conceive of a theory of ideology is continuous with an untenable theory of choice. Sontag, adopting a summarizingly crude behavioristic model, remarks that "taste governs every free—as opposed to rote—human response," and associates "taste" with an ethereal individuality which transcends social "programming." (276) Babuscio develops the same line of argument: "Clothes and decor, for example, can be a means of asserting one's identity, as well as a form of justification in a society which denies one's essential validity. . . . By such means as these one aims to become what one wills, to exercise some control over one's environment." (44) Neither writer seems aware that, as used here, "identity" and "freedom" are problematic terms. In order to explain the fact that gay men gravitate toward certain professions, one has to adduce the "discredited social identity" of gays as the determining factor of the choice rather than suggest that the choice alleviates the discredited social identity. (Babuscio, 44) The professions in which male gayness has been traditionally condoned (the theater, fashion, interior decoration, and so on) are also those in which women have been able to command a degree of personal autonomy without threatening male supremacy in the slightest, since "real men," by definition, would despise to be involved in them. It is scarcely permissible to explain the association of gay men with the "luxury" professions in terms of a collection of individuals who discover, by some miraculous coincidence, that the assertion of their identity leads them to a single persona.

Seven. Whatever differences they may have on other points, the three most fully elaborated statements on camp to date (Sontag, Babuscio, Richard Dyer) are all agreed that camp taste is a matter of "style" and "content," ignoring the fact that style describes a process of meaning. The camp attitude is a mode of perception whereby artifacts become the object of an arrested, or fetishistic, scrutiny. It does not so much "see everything in quotation marks" as in parentheses; it is a solvent of context. (Sontag, 289) Far from being a means for the demystification of artifacts, as Dyer asserts, camp is a means by which that analysis is perpetually postponed. ("Being") The passage from "determinate object" to "fetish" preserves the object safely and reassuringly in a vacuum.

Eight. All analysts of camp arrive eventually at the same dilemma. On the one hand, camp "describes those elements in a person, situation or activity which express, or are created by, a gay sensibility" (that is, camp is an attribute of something). On the other hand, "camp resides largely in the eye of the beholder" (that is, camp is attributed to something). (Babuscio, 40–41) The latter seems correct to me in most cases, and the generalizing tendency indicates very clearly camp's essential facility. Camp attempts to assimilate everything as its object and then reduces all objects to one set of terms. It is a language of impoverishment: it is both reductive and nonanalytic, the two going together and determining each other. As a gay phenomenon, camp is a means of bringing the world into one's scope, of accommodating it—not of changing it or conceptualizing its relations. The objects, images, values, relations of oppression can be recuperated by adopting the simple expedient of redescribing them; the language of camp almost suggests, at times, a form of censorship in the Freudian sense. There is, of course, a certain mode of contemporary aestheticism which is aware of the concept of camp and whose objects are constructed from within that purview; as a rule, though, the conception of camp as a property either begs the question or produces those periodic insanities of Sontag's essay, whereby Alexander Pope and Mozart can be claimed for the camp heritage as masters of rococo formalism.

Nine. According to Dyer, John Wayne and Richard Wagner can be camp. To perceive Wayne as camp is, on one level, simply too easy, and doesn't make any point about masculinity which would not instantly earn the concurrence of any self-respecting reader of the *Daily Telegraph*. Of course, Wayne's "way of being a man" is a social construct, as are all "ways of being a man"—including the camp one—and to indicate as much doesn't seem particularly significant. On another level, which "John Wayne"? The Wayne who advocates, on screen and off, Lyndon Johnson's policy in Vietnam and McCarthyism, or the Wayne of John Ford's westerns? Wayne "means" very different things in the two cases, and while those meanings are intimately related, they cannot be reduced to one another. To perceive Wayne merely as an icon of "butchness," which can be debunked from, apparently, a position of ideological neutrality, is either complacent or philistine. Similarly, to regard Wagner as camp is, on one level, only silly, and no more to be tolerated than any other kind of silliness because it masquerades as critical analysis. On another level, it preempts the discussion of the real problems raised by Wagner's music and the cult of Bayreuth (the discussion initiated by Friedrich Nietzsche), and ends by corroborating the vulgar bourgeois critique of Wagner's "overblown romanticism." The "camp insight," in these and many other cases, is little more than a flip variant of the worst kind of right-on liberalism.

Ten. In his essay, Babuscio attempts to construct a relationship between camp and irony which, it transpires, turns on the same unresolved contradiction as that which afflicts the definition of camp itself. "Irony is the subject matter of camp, and refers here to any highly incongruous contrast between an individual or thing and its context or association." By the end of the paragraph, the irony has become a matter of the "perception of incongruity." (41) One should note, first, that irony is badly misdefined: it does not involve incongruity, and it is not, and can never be, "subject matter." Irony is an operation of discourse which sets up a complex of tensions between what is said and various qualifications or contradictions generated by the process of the saying. Furthermore, it is difficult to see in what way any of the "incongruous contrasts" offered as exemplary of camp irony relate either to camp, irony, or "the gay sensibility." Are we to assume that, because "sacred/profane" is an incongruous pair, a great deal of medieval literature is camp? Most importantly, Babuscio ignores the crucial distinction between the kind of scrutiny which dissolves boundaries in order to demonstrate their insubstantiality—or the value systems which enforce them—and the kind of scrutiny which merely seeks to confirm that they are there. As a logic of "transgression," camp belongs to the second class. If the transgression of boundaries ever threatened to produce the redefinition of them, the frisson would be lost, the thrill of "something wrong" would disappear.

Eleven. Babuscio quotes Oscar Wilde—"It is through Art, and through Art only, that we can shield ourselves from the sordid perils of actual existence"—and adds, approvingly, "Wilde's epigram points to a crucial aspect of camp aestheticism: its opposition to puritan morality." (40–41) On the contrary, the epigram is a supreme expression of puritan morality, which can almost be defined by its revulsion from the danger and squalor of the real. Puritanism finds its escape clause in the aspiration of the individual soul toward God, in a relation to which the world is at best irrelevant and at worse inimical, and Wilde simply redefines the emergency exit in aesthetic terms. Sartre remarks of Genet that "The aesthete's Beauty is evil disguised as virtue." (404) I would rephrase him to read: "The isolation of style is the aesthete's dirty trick on the concept of value, and the constant necessity to analyze and reconstruct concepts of value."

Twelve. Camp is chronically averse to value judgments, partly by choice (evaluation is felt to involve discrimination between various contents, and thus to belong to the realm of "High Culture," "Moral Seriousness," etc.), and partly by default: the obsession with "style" entails both an astonishing irresponsiveness to tone and a refusal to acknowledge that styles are necessarily the bearers of attitudes, judgments, values, and assumptions of which it's necessary to be aware, and among which it's necessary to discriminate. "The horror genre, in particular, is susceptible to a camp interpretation. Not all horror films are camp, of course; only those which make the most of stylish conventions for expressing instant feeling, thrills, sharply defined personality, outrageous and 'unacceptable' sentiments, and so on." (Babuscio, 43)

What is "instant feeling"? Or, for that matter, feeling which is not instant? And what are "stylish conventions"? The conventions of the horror movie are complex and significant, and they cannot be discussed in terms of a chic appendage to a content which is somehow separable from them. Certainly, horror films express "unacceptable sentiments"—indeed, they exist in order to do so—but to read them as "outrageous" in the camp sense is to protect oneself from their real outrageousness, to recuperate them as objects of "good-bad taste" (which is what bourgeois critics do anyway). Once one has effected the impossible and meaningless distinction between "aesthetic and moral considerations" (Babuscio, 51), it becomes perfectly feasible to associate the critical intelligence of Josef von Sternberg movies with the coy, vulgar, sexist fantasizing of Busby Berkeley musicals, or to confuse the grotesque complicity of the Mae West persona with the "excess" of Jennifer Jones's performance in *Duel in the Sun* (1946) or Bette Davis's in *Beyond the Forest* (1949), where excess is a function of an active critique of oppressive gender roles. While ostensibly making demand for new criteria of judgment, camp is all the while quietly acquiescing in the old ones. It merely takes over existing standards of "bad taste" and insists on liking them.

Thirteen. Camp has a certain minimal value, in restricted contexts, as a form of *épater le bourgeois,* but the pleasure (in itself genuine and valid enough) of shocking solid citizens should not be confused with radicalism. Still less should "the very tight togetherness that makes it so good to be one of the queens," in Dyer's phrase, be offered as a constructive model of "community in oppression." (Dyer, "Being," 50) The positive connotations—an insistence on one's otherness, a refusal to pass as straight—are so irredeemably compromised by complicity in the traditional, oppressive formulations of that otherness, and "camping around" is so often little more than being "one of the boys" by pink limelight. We should not, *pace* Dyer, feel it incumbent on us to defend camp on charges of "letting the side down" or wanting to be John Wayne. Camp is simply one way in which gay men have recuperated their oppression, and it needs to be criticized as such.

The Ideology of *Screen* (1979)

The work undertaken by *Screen* during the past seven years has established itself, clearly, as the most significant development in contemporary film criticism. Equally clearly, it has provoked considerable opposition of an abject and defensive kind, and the period in question has been characterized not simply by the dominance of *Screen* but also by the scarcity of serious critical response to it. In such a situation, it is only too easy to appear reactionary, and one must insist at the outset that disagreement should not be taken as an endorsement of Barry Norman.

Screen's major achievement is not to be denied: it has forced the question of ideology on our attention, invoking in that context materials developed by structural linguistics, semiology, and psychoanalysis. It has challenged the notion of "film criticism" as a self-defined realm in splendid isolation and insisted that it must seek all the time to define its concerns theoretically. I assume that such definition is a political act, inseparable from any responsible engagement with the arts, and that the investigation of the cinema as an ideological institution should involve a commitment to ideological, and thus political, change. This may represent common ground on which disagreement can profitably take place. I shall begin by considering the major intellectual sources of *Screen*'s intervention and proceed from there to various appropriations of them which have been made either within the magazine or by writers associated with it.

Althusser

The alliance between Louis Althusser and Jacques Lacan (both in Althusser's work itself and in *Screen*) is of interest in terms both of certain theoretical contradictions which the two have in common and of the differences which the union has, remarkably, survived. Each one emphasizes the return to a collection of texts (the work of Karl Marx and Sigmund Freud, respectively) that, whatever qualifications, refinements, or reformulations they may require, provide a number of fundamental certainties, objective truths, which have been distorted or abandoned by subsequent theoreticians. Both men assert that their particular practices constitute a "science"—a word which they, with equal vehemence, seek to dissociate from empiricism (verification by experimental practice) and from idealism (the postulation of a transcendental subject), but which is, nevertheless, necessary *as* a word. (Althusser, *Essays in Self-Criticism,* 116) Both are antihumanist in that they deny the primacy of the self-conscious subject as a theoretical category and suggest that the subject is an ideological construct whose conviction of self-determination is illusory. While Althusser has openly taken Lacanian psychoanalysis to his bosom, Lacan's attitude toward Marxism is studiously ambiguous; he has remarked both that he has developed the only theory of subjectivity consonant with materialism and that Marx can be grouped with Jacques-Bénigne Bossuet, Arnold Toynbee, and Auguste Comte as an ideologist whose "role is somewhat too slender for scientific progress," felicitous though the "ideals" that he provides may be. (Lacan, *Ecrits*)[1] This last would seem to provide sufficient conditions for friction, and one has to ask why there has been, ostensibly, so little. A clue can be found, I think, in the profoundly contradictory relationship between Althusser and Lacan, and the dominant concerns of post-Cartesian Western philosophy.

Abolishing the Cogito

Althusser's conception of René Descartes is characteristic of the illusory anti-Cartesianism which marks the varieties of structuralism and which *Screen* has absorbed: while dutifully renouncing "the central category of imaginary illusion, the Subject" (*Essays in Self-Criticism*, 136), classically embodied in the cogito ("I think, therefore I am"), Althusser adheres unshakably to the theoretical procedures of which the category of the subject is the only guarantee. The aim of Cartesian method is the construction of indubitable knowledge by "the rational deduction of consequences" from the starting point of "what is completely known and incapable of being doubted." (Descartes, 10) The historical significance of Cartesianism consists in the suggestion that the ground of all certainty is the "self's intrinsic evidence of its own existence . . . even whenever it is doubting" (Grene, 71); it is crucial, however, to insist (a) that one can retain both the procedures and the objectives of Cartesian method even if the original certainty is not explicitly the self, and (b) that "the *cogito* is not an argument but an event." (Grene, 72) By suggesting that the cogito is a philosophical argument for self-existence and then saying "I reject it," Althusser is able to cleanse himself of Cartesianism to his own satisfaction, while at the same time conducting an inquiry which consists precisely of that series of acts of a pure and attentive mind which Descartes sought to achieve.

The operation is exemplified by some extraordinary remarks on "the process of knowledge." (Althusser, *Essays in Self-Criticism*, 187) Here, as throughout the book, Althusser quotes a sentence from Benedict de Spinoza's *Ethics*: "It is just because we possess a true idea that we can also say that what is true is the sign both of itself and of what is false." Althusser feels able, in all sincerity, to define this perfect formulation of the Cartesian ideal as "Spinoza's resolute anti-Cartesianism," and goes so far as to reveal the sleight of hand by which he achieves it. The weight in the phrase "we have in fact a true idea," Althusser tells us, lies not on the "we" but on the "in fact." All that we have to do is to displace the emphasis from "we-as-subjects" to the "true idea" that "we" possess, and at once we have discovered not only the road to truth (we can now produce more true ideas "according to the norm" of the first) but also a new subject, defined now in terms of the access to certain knowledge rather than the perception of his/her own existence. Althusser fails to perceive that the quest for objective truth (which he and Lacan have in common with the whole tradition of Western philosophy) necessarily presupposes the centrality of the subject as a theoretical category. The placing of confidence in "what we can clearly and evidently intuit or deduce with certainty" (Descartes, 13) and faith in the subject are indissolubly involved. Each guarantees the other.

Having discovered that Spinoza is an anti-Cartesian, Althusser now perceives that he is also "on close terms [with] the Marx of *Capital*, together with Lenin" (*Essays in Self-Criticism*, 188), and he proceeds more or less to reiterate the realist theory of knowledge while asserting strenuously that he is doing nothing of the kind. Identifying Spinoza's "true idea" with "Marx's concepts" so that all subsequent knowledge becomes "dependent on the *fact* of the knowledge which we already possess" (188, italics in the original), Althusser defines the process of knowledge as the movement toward "the thought-concrete, the thought-totality, which . . . presents itself as knowledge of the real-concrete, of the real object." In the passage from a "true idea" to "knowledge of the concrete" (194), Althusser manages to achieve a method of logical, objective certainty, which for all the gestures in the direction of materialist process, reveals its origins in such concepts as "real history" (185)—the "intimate relations" which exist "in diametrical opposition [to] the appearance of things." (194) This is precisely the contention that "there is knowledge which is knowledge of the real" which a recent editorial in *Screen* declares that "we have consistently opposed" (Nowell-Smith, "Editorial," 5–6), though Althusser's dominant tendencies have never been inexplicit. The same project is fundamental to Lacan and provides, explicitly, the raison d'être for his use of mathematics—that language by means of which "the real" can be made manifest.

Even more significant, in this context, is the relationship between Althusser and Immanuel Kant: in attempting to solve the problem of knowledge, both reach an identical impasse and propose an identical escape clause. Kant wishes to assert, against David Hume, that it is possible to arrive at what he terms synthetic a priori judgments—that is, knowledge which is neither simply tautologous nor derived by induction from experience. He distinguishes, within a priori knowledge, a pure portion, uncontaminated by empirical content, "in which reason determines its object entirely *a priori*," and another portion derived by the addition of empirical concepts. All "sciences properly and objectively so-called," Kant suggests, are characterized by that pure, theoretical reason which has no need to refer to experience to justify its judgments; the only two instances he offers are mathematics and physics, the first of which is quite pure and the second partly so. Needing then to explain how these sciences come into being, Kant produces a theory which Althusser has since refurbished as the "epistemological break." Kant writes:

> I believe that it [mathematics] long remained . . . in the groping stage, and that the transformation must have been due to a revolution brought about by the happy thought of a single man in an experiment—an experiment after which the road that must be taken could never again be missed, and the sure path of a science was entered upon and signposted for all time to come and into the infinite distance. (*Critique of Pure Reason*, B X-XI, quoted in Grene, 128)

The Immunity of "Science"

As soon as ideology becomes theoretically central, the question arises of constructing a critical distance from it, of articulating its operations and thus opening up the possibility of change.

The concept of the epistemological break (apart from the phrase "in an experiment," the passage from Kant is a good enough definition of it) functions as the emergency exit from ideology. It is deeply colored by the quest for a sort of existential confidence which recognizing the construction of "lived relations" in ideology has fatally undermined. Indeed, one might discuss Althusser's project in terms of a desire to reaffirm the concept of "the real" by ceasing to define it as lived experience (phenomenologically) and grounding it instead in that which is "revealed" through the mediation of "a system of new scientific concepts." (*Lenin and Philosophy*, 39) "Marx's discovery [allows us] to get to know what really does exist." (*Essays in Self-Criticism,* 56) We have at our disposal a philosophy which "no longer merely 'interprets' the world" (69), but gives us its formula and which, in doing so, "rejects all or part of its prehistory, calling it erroneous." (113) We are asked to accept that this clever version of idealism is really "materialism" ("the only real history, the history of the material life of men"), but its philosophical credentials are obvious enough. Reality is deceptive and illusory: one must penetrate it, transcend it, tear it aside so as to discover its pure form. "Science is then the real itself, known by the action which reveals it by destroying the ideologies that veil it." (*Lenin and Philosophy*, 38)

More exactly, materialism emerges as a curious hybrid which might be defined as "positivist idealism." The "scientific or theoretical practice" which Althusser sets out to define in *Reading Capital* is measured by "what is commonly called theory, in its 'purest' forms, those that seem to bring into play the powers of thought alone (e.g., the mathematics of philosophy), leaving aside any direct relation to 'concrete practice.'" (59) Even the vocabulary echoes the Kantian formulation, and the suggestion that mathematics is the quintessence of "pure theory" is consistent from Descartes to Lacan. Althusser suggests that "the knowledge-effect is exercised in the pure forms of some strict science" (*Reading,* 62), and that it is to be distinguished from the "ideological knowledge effect," the two existing in a relation similar to that between the a priori and the a posteriori in Kant. In the case of the ideological knowledge effect, the process of knowledge is "impure," marred by a resort to social/empirical data which interrupts the process of proof. On the other hand, on the analogy with mathematics, it is axiomatic that "the truth of a theorem is a hundred per cent provided by criteria purely internal to the practice." (*Reading,* 59) The practice is "its own criterion," and one reaches a point at which "scientificity" is guaranteed by internal coherence. Thus, for example, in a response to criticisms by Julia Lesage, Ben Brewster, Stephen Heath, and Colin MacCabe assert that "a critique of . . . [psychoanalysis] can only be based on an examination of how [its] concepts work within it." (85)

The effect of these formulations can be studied very conveniently, as I have suggested elsewhere in discussing Althusser's essay "Freud and Lacan" in *Lenin and Philosophy*. The characterization of science is idealist to the extent that it gives us access, in Sebastiano Timpanaro's phrase, to "another reality truer than phenomenological appearances." This emphasis produces Althusser's contempt for what he defines as "empiricism"—a contempt which, as Timpanaro again points out, depends on blurring the distinction between "the experimental [and] lived experience in the irrationalist sense." (*Lenin and Philosophy*, 186) In his presentation of psychoanalysis, Althusser proceeds logically to the positivism which is the necessary correlative of his idealism: that is, to the notion of "fixed" scientific concepts and of "bodies of knowledge" which, in its unawareness of the provisional nature of scientific knowledge and its reification of the various "practices" as fixed, exclusive, self-consistent, and, above all, independent of the knower, are effectively antiscientific in nature. And when Althusser insists (supporting himself on a definition of the "natural sciences" which depends on their objectification) that a science is constituted by the appropriation of "an object of its own," he succeeds in reaffirming the most reactionary demarcation of subject boundaries. This is consolidated, ironically, by a torrent of specious and sentimental rhetoric which transforms Lacan into the beleaguered guardian of a science which "violates the existing frontiers." (Althusser, *Lenin and Philosophy*, 203)

A similar point emerges, again, in the *Screen* reply to Lesage: as science, psychoanalysis "cuts across, largely and differently, those [accepted fields of interest], constituting new 'objects,' new points of interrogation." The very phrasing implies a definitive status for the hypotheses of psychoanalysis, which, if it "is not to be applied 'from outside,' so to speak" (Brewster et al., 87), can be used with confidence to redefine everything else. It is significant here that in his evasive and naive remarks on structuralism in *Essays in Self-Criticism*, Althusser should fail to perceive his own profound affinities with structuralist procedures and proceed to take structuralism to task for its "vague and changing themes" (128) which lack the requisite "unity of a systematic conception."

Again and again in Althusser's work, the concepts which are under attack reassert themselves in this way in the very formulations designed to place them—most significantly in the recurrent operation by which "practice" is purged of the notion of "process" to rigidify as "the 'truth' of the knowledges that Marx produced." (*Reading*, 59–60) Indeed, *Essays in Self-Criticism* is remarkable for the attempt to maintain both that Marx's theory is a sort of talismanic charm ("Marx's theory is all-powerful because it is true" [170]) and that "it has to be explained by the conjunction of the material, technical, social, political and ideological conditions which determine it." (148–49) This latter seems to me to be the correct emphasis (how could it not be?), and yet as soon as one acknowledges it, the concept of science which Althusser wishes to maintain disintegrates. Cartesian science cannot survive any theory of ideological determination, and Althusser is reduced to a limited series of moves which have the primary purpose of evading the issue.

Althusser's evasiveness and his need for some token of a radical break between ideology and science follows from his undialectical conception of ideology. It is necessary to be able to make generalizations about the characteristics of "bourgeois ideology." But Althusser attempts to argue that ideology can be conceived in opposition to modes of knowledge that are not ideologically determinate. His analysis thus becomes, by definition, incapable of suggesting how ideology functions historically. *Essays in Self-Criticism* certainly raises such issues but fails to grapple with them precisely to the extent that Marxism refuses to accommodate the concept of "philosophy" in the classical Western sense to which Althusser is, albeit uncomfortably, committed. Althusser is concerned with the search for "specific and indisputable facts" (148), and vociferous lip service to "contradictory tendencies" does not protect him from regression to very simple antinomies whose relations are anything but dialectical.

Antihumanism

Consider, for example, Althusser's much-vaunted "theoretical anti-humanism," by which individuals are to be considered as "simple bearers of functions" within the social formation. (*Essays in Self-Criticism,* 195) Let us be quite clear about this: it seems to me that Marx's anti-humanism states a crucial theoretical principle and that the relevant passages in Althusser's *Essays in Self-Criticism* (206) are acceptable only insofar as they reiterate positions already taken up by Marx in the *Grundrisse* [*Outlines of the Critique of Political Economy*]. "Society does not consist of individuals, but expresses the sum of interrelations, the relations within which these individuals stand." (Lacan, *Ecrits,* 682) At best, Althusser's remarks merely gloss Marx's; at worst, they sentimentalize them by associating antihumanism with that aspiration toward "the real" which informs the science/ideology distinction ("If Marx does not start out from man, which is an empty idea, that is, one weighed down with bourgeois ideology, it is in order finally to reach living men"). (Lacan, *Ecrits,* 817)

But the model of ideology which can be constructed from Althusser and Lacan seems to me incapable of grasping "the sum of inter-relations" mentioned by Marx in any but the most schematic form. Rather, it makes the familiar structuralist reduction, whereby material relationships ("relationships natural to individuals within specific and limited relations of production" [Marx, *Outlines,* 162]) vanish into relationships which are produced ahistorically. Thus, the repeated claim that the Lacanian structures are subject to particular historical inflections (see, for example, Heath, "Anata Mo," 60–62) emerges as little more than a rhetorical device—a gesture toward dialectics which is instantly canceled by the very terms of the system. The system is inherently resistant to the historically specific; it cannot acknowledge its possibility without disintegrating. Lacan deals with givens of the human condition, explicitly unrelated to the social—like the "fall into the Imaginary." One cannot then go on to say, "But of course, there is no subject outside of a social formation," when the exclusion of the subject from the social formation is the major premise of the system.

Marx's antihumanism is the basis of a theory of social being; that of Althusser/Lacan is the necessary forgetfulness of the idealist fallacy. One accepts, of course, the crucial significance of "those more or less long-lasting features of human reality" with which Timpanaro is concerned when he cites the concepts of *la longue durée* and *la très longue durée* developed by the historian Fernand Braudel. But Timpanaro emphasizes at once that these features must be articulated "in materialist rather than objective-idealist terms," and it is at this point that Lacanianism, of all the versions of psychoanalysis, is the least qualified to produce significant results. Lacan's antihumanism is, quite simply, a calculated means of evasion. Similarly, some degree of hypocrisy or misguidedness is evident in Althusser's attempt both to repudiate structuralism and to hold onto his "theoretical anti-humanism," since the latter represents an extreme of idealist structuralist reductionism.

The intellectual flabbiness becomes startlingly apparent in Althusser's language. "In philosophy, you can only think . . . by the use of metaphors" (*Essays in Self-Criticism,* 107), Althusser declares with some solemnity, going on to suggest that it is a matter of some moment whether we think of the "continent of history" as emerging or as irrupting—or, indeed, as both.

It emerges in the ordinary sense: this means that it is not born out of nothing, but out of a process of labor by which it is hatched, a complex and multiple process, sometimes brightened by a flash of lightning, but which normally operates blindly, in the dark, because "it" never knows where it is headed, nor, if ever it arrives, where it is going to surface. (112)

If the quality of philosophical thought is really to be judged by the quality of the metaphors which express it, what are we to make of a process of labor which could also be a baby—or perhaps a mole—whatever its sense of direction, and of subterranean flashes of lightning which can cure blindness? This sort of lumpen poeticizing, which Althusser has presumably caught from Lacan, is the corollary, in its sheer confusion, of an intelligence which has adapted itself to maintaining the most blatant contradictions simultaneously, and the tension here between science-as-process and science-as-thing ("it") indicates a fundamental difficulty. What intelligible concept of process can possibly obtain within a system which defines "the discourse of scientific proof" as "a phenomenon which imposes on thought-categories (or concepts) a regular order of appearance and disappearance," and which functions, independently of the subject, as a "mechanism" for producing knowledge? (Althusser, *Reading*, 67)

Knowledge: Product or Process?

Discussion can be focused by reference to Paul Willemen's "Notes towards the Construction of Readings of Tourneur," wherein he asserts that the ability to

> construct a reading . . . implies a certain degree of familiarity with the theoretical concepts necessary for the work of transforming [the] raw material into the finished product of the reading. Unfortunately, these concepts (i.e., the means of intellectual production) are at present the exclusive property of a small number of the educationally privileged; but there is no reason whatsoever why this should remain the case. (18)

I shall return later to the suggestion that the text has no priority over the reading. What concerns me here is the simplistically literal-minded appropriation of Marxist terminology, and the objectification which follows in its wake.

The concept of a reading as a "finished product" is inadmissible. The act of reading is never finished; it is open to perpetual transformation, precisely to the extent that the reader's social/intellectual context is never fixed, the text as his/hers entering constantly into new relations. Similarly, to describe a concept as a piece of property that can be acquired, so that by owning a set of concept—things one can busily set about constructing a reading—thing of one's own, completely goes against what I take to be meant by the phrase "the means of intellectual production." Concepts are not that means—they are its raw material; the point is not to acquire particular (and supposedly ratified) concepts, but to gain access to the processes of conceptual thought, which might well entail challenging the concepts. The reification of concepts here is constantly on the verge of blurring into eminently un-Marxist positions (that, for instance, of Basil Bernsteinism, with its pious hope of bestowing "universalistic meanings" on the deprived),

390

but the positivistic emphasis which underlies it is explicit in Althusser and points up a continuous, and disabling, uncertainty in *Screen*'s intervention. "We believe that effective knowledge is not a matter of fixed and settled sciences but is itself a process of production within which object and theory are constructed and reconstructed." (Brewster et al., "Reply," 113) This, in response to internecine strife, is very admirable; one readily concurs. But how does it square with the above, with recurrent linguistic usage ("the knowledge it [psychoanalysis] produces . . ."—again, knowledge as product), with the constant reiteration of Lacan's account of the genesis of the subject (see, for example, MacCabe, "Presentation"), with the (very Althusserian) paradox in the above-quoted assertion that psychoanalysis "cuts across" existing boundaries to "constitute new 'objects'" which it founds "as science"? The tension between the assertion, on the one hand, that knowledge is, and is achieved in, process, and the recourse, on the other, to certain dubious "knowledges" which are offered as achieved products; between the renunciation of "fixed and settled sciences" and the instant resort to "discourses of scientific proof" which inscribe the "continents" anew with, now, a guarantee of "scientificity"—these conflicts have been constant and have contributed to that extraordinary theological ethos of deliberation-inside-certainty which is the hallmark of the work that has been produced. There has been plenty of disagreement, but always within the "given," which is emerging increasingly as Lacan.

There, contradictions entail, as corollary, an inability to perceive the intellectual implications of certain choices which is at best, naive, and at the worst, dishonest. Consider this, for example, from Steve Neale's review of Robin Wood's *Personal Views*.

> *Screen* sees theory not as a system for providing values, but as a system for providing knowledge, i.e., a body of concepts whose importance lies in producing a form of understanding that does not entail a necessary dependence on institutionalized authority, be it that of the critic or teacher, but rather provides, through its system of conceptual elaboration and definition and its procedures of application and testing, a potential alternative to that authority. (120)

The passage illustrates what seem to me the disabling limitations of *Screen*'s position with almost diagrammatic simplicity. The scientificity of "knowledge" is produced by a grammatical trick: "a body of concepts . . . [produces] a form of understanding." The human agency—the particular, material (and therefore, necessarily, ideological) process which the concepts of "use" and "knowing" imply—is expelled from the formula, and the "body of concepts" is endowed with some miraculous life which generates "understanding" independently of anyone doing the understanding. As soon as one suggests that understanding is an active, material process, then the ideological immunity of "concepts," and of the persons propounding or working with them, evaporates. To indemnify the "objectivity" of concepts by a piece of syntactical sleight of hand so that the system, and the procedures interior to it, come to appear independent of subjective intervention (using, knowing, acting) is a very cheap trick and, of course, profoundly anti-Marxist. Similarly, the claim that *Screen*, of all institutions, has abandoned "institutionalized authority" seems to be a slightly risible suggestion. Quite apart from the status of Lacan, the conceptual model employed in the quoted passage was institutional-ized some centuries ago by Sir Isaac Newton and Descartes and has since proved of no small assistance to those who would prefer to believe that knowledge exists apart from questions of ideology and social power. The "potential alternative" mentioned in the closing phrase is an imaginary construction.

Thus, the crux of the passage is the opposition between "knowledge" and "values," and the thesis that knowledge is value free. F. R. Leavis being in question, one is used to the usual—the institutionalized—misapprehension that Leavis is concerned with a "system for providing values," although his own repeated disclaimers are explicit enough. "No one, then, who knows what 'standards' are and what is the nature of critical authority could talk of 'fixed standards' or of 'providing them with a legal backing,' and no one who understands the nature of a judgment could talk of 'imposing accepted values.'" (*English Literature,* 47)

What is at issue here is the fact that the attempted divorce of "knowledge" and "values" itself enforces the very institutionalization which Neale claims to oppose. Leavis's refusal to define "life," "significance," and "value" is precisely the acknowledgment that "values" are not fixed—that they cannot be, since they are produced in a continuous "corrective and creative interplay of judgments." It is Neale's position, not Leavis's, that entails fixed standards—the standards produced by the closure of a system which guarantees the tendency of its own oper-ations. If language is ideologically determinate, then the very use of language in the process of knowledge is a work in and on values. It is in that use and that process—which, Leavis stresses, are necessarily continuous and collaborative—that the "object" comes to be "there," can be articulated ("object" meaning here both the world of, say, the text, and, through the "process of creation in response to the poet's words," the world of the reader's activity). Neale reduces "val-ues" and "knowledge" to things—bodies with internal functions which are somehow redeemed from external ones—and maintains that the one thing is different from the other thing.

Leavis's epistemology tends to suggest that "values" and "knowledge" are inseparably in process in language and that that process is work in and on "a public world." The world comes to be present only through the process, and—one might go on to say—it is only through the process that the articulation of change becomes possible. Language is a material process in and by which worlds are made present—with "making present" as the condition for consciousness, analysis, transformation—and in and by which knowledge and values come to be in produc-tion. "Material" connotes an emphasis on particular modes and terms of discourse and their determinations—an emphasis which entails, implicitly in Leavis and explicitly in Paul Ricoeur ("Structure-Word-Event"), an attack on the structuralist ideology of synchrony, the science of states of system proposed by Ferdinand de Saussure as the proper object of "scientific" lin-guistics. I will return to these matters in a later article and only now suggest that they contain, potentially, an alternative to the objective-idealist model of language proposed by the various structuralisms—by, most significantly, Lacan.

The uneasiness of Althusser's position can be indicated by placing beside the banish-ment of history, anthropology, sociology, and biology from the psychoanalytic "continent" in the Lacan essay the tentative query with which it ends: "Is it inconceivable that the historical variation of these latter structures [kinship, ideology] might *materially* affect some or other aspect of the instances isolated by Freud?" (Althusser, *Lenin and Philosophy,* 217, italics mine) An encouraging thought but one for which Althusser, given his premises (what does the query imply, if not an influx of empiricism?), is unable to account. Significantly, there emerges at this point both a distinction between "formal" and "concrete" structures and a certain disquiet about the ideological determinants of psychoanalysis. It says a great deal about the decisions and revisions of *Essays in Self-Criticism* that Althusser does not feel compelled to commit himself to any further reflection on the subject.

Lacan

"The virulence with which psychoanalysis rejects such a primacy [of the subject] has ensured it . . . the living gratitude of those who see it as marking an irreversible break with all idealism and religion." (MacCabe, "Presentation," 8) One might be forgiven, as one studies the pages of Lacan's "*Fonction et Champ de la Parole et du Language en Psychanalyse*" (*Ecrits*), for believing that one was present not at a lecture on the topography of a new scientific continent but at a *rite de passage* for the postulants of some dark and mystical faith, an exposition of the riddles of the universe. Indeed, the first sentence of the introduction informs us that the "form of man's power" is about to be revealed; the second compares Freud to Prometheus; and the third introduces a usage of the concept of "the word" (capitalized in Anthony Wilden's translation) which will be shortly assimilated to that of the creating Logos. Throughout the text, Freud himself is transformed into a felicitous combination of the Father and the Son, and his followers into apostles. Psychoanalysis is at several points identified with Zen, and in the closing passages, the "gift of the Word" is ratified by the passage from the *Upanishads* with which T. S. Eliot concludes "The Waste Land." Previously, a lament for the alienation of man behind "the wall of language which sets itself up against the word" (Lacan, *Ecrits,* 282) has recourse to the opening lines of "The Hollow Men." We learn that Dr. Schreber left behind the key for the "decipherment" of paranoia "in the lava of his spiritual catastrophe" (244); that the death of the Rat Man in World War I, "concluding the case with the rigor of destiny, elevates it to the beauty of tragedy" (303) in a happy reconciliation of the grandeur of Fate, the exigencies of science, and the symmetry of art; and that the "human condition" finds satisfactory expression in the image of a blinded rabbit with myxomatosis gazing sightlessly toward the setting sun—a predicament which is again described as "tragic" (280), although Lacan is silent as to its beauty.

A certain use of language is clearly involved here, as in the metaphor of the two lavatories in "*L'instance de la lettre*" (Lacan, *Ecrits,* 449), and in the elaborate syntactic convolutions and sub-Baudelairean mugging of Lacan's style (what is our rabbit if not *Le Cygne* with long furry ears?). One may doubt, though, whether "the avoidance of a metalanguage" quite covers it. MacCabe's alibi for Lacan ("Presentation")—borrowed from Althusser—whereby conceptual integrity becomes the symptom of a neurosis might seem to provide cover for the most flagrant irresponsibility; indeed, what emerges is a cunning mixture of romantic anthropology, psychoanalytic revisionism, mysticism, self-advertisement, secondhand existentialism, and selected concepts from linguistics so ostentatiously spurious as almost to invite refutation.

The Incarnation of the Word

In "*Fonction et Champ*" and "*La Chose Freudienne*," Lacan elaborates a myth of the origin of language which bases itself on the exchange of symbolic objects in "archaic" cultures—objects which are deliberately "useless" and which function "primarily as signifiers of the pact which they constitute as signified." (*Ecrits*, 272) Lacan continues: "In order for the symbolic object liberated from its usage to become the word liberated from the *hic et nunc*, the differentiation does not depend on its material quality as sound, but on its evanescent being in which the symbol finds the permanence of the concept." We have embarked on a voyage toward sublimity: an object that depends for its efficacy on the suppression of its material existence gives place, not to an acoustic image, but to Word-as-essence-of-spirit. The symbol becomes superfluous, and the concept appears more substantial (the word "takes on flesh") than the object (capable of being absent) of which it is a "trace." Having come thus far, an elementary logical shift takes us still further: "It is the world of words that creates the world of things—the things originally confused in the *hic et nunc* of the all-in-the-process-of-becoming—by giving its concrete being to their essence, and its ubiquity to what has been from everlasting: an eternal possession." (*Ecrits*, 276) Amen.

We are dealing, then, with a Christian myth of the incarnation of the Logos fed back through Platonism: the word was made flesh and "tends to become the thing itself." (Lacan, *Ecrits*, 242–44) The world of things is the realm of becoming, of "matter increate," insubstantial, without form, void, to which the Logos imparts substantial life, giving access to a world of pure forms located no longer in a Platonic heaven but in the order of language—the Symbolic. Hence, for Lacan, the significance of the "fort/da" game. In *Beyond the Pleasure Principle*, Freud offers the child's game of discarding and retrieving a spool of thread as a paradigm case of that "compulsion to repeat" which is described as the essence of the death instinct and which Freud, by dint of an astute examination of the animal and vegetable kingdoms, finds to be implicit in "life itself." (Vol. XVIII, 15) For Lacan the game functions as the repetition in the finite world (the individual) of the original mythic birth of language (simultaneously, Lacan tells us, the "murder of the thing"): the signifier (fort/da) ambiguously creates/takes the place of the signified, and the child enters the symbolic system. Despite his (perfectly correct) diagnosis of the ideological function of the myth of origins in *Reading Capital* (62), Althusser makes no demur at this point in his exposition about one of the most outrageous examples of it in Western thought. One should add, perhaps, by way of distinguishing between Freud and Lacan, that Freud introduces his foray into biological determinism in *Beyond the Pleasure Principle* by remarking, "what follows is speculation, and often far-fetched speculation at that" (Vol. XVIII, 24); he stresses constantly that his own findings are provisional and subject to emendation and qualification and that when he feels his conclusions to be dubious, or his data inadequate or incomplete, he says so. This is not to say that Freud feels these admirable scruples as often as he should, but in the context of the formula for the unconscious, the schema of psychosis, and the cosmology of the "mind of man," it is as well to bear it in mind.

Concepts of Determinism

Bourgeois humanism bridles at the concept of determinism, and it is arguable that the refusal to acknowledge determinism in one sense (individuality and social process are subject to determination by forces other than self-conscious volition) encourages a surrender to determinism in another—that sense of helpless prostration in the face of forces which cannot be conceived as socially determinate without undoing the original premise, and which have to be recuperated as elements of the human predicament. Marx, and to a certain extent Freud, demolish the humanist position between them, and it becomes necessary to construct a theory, not of self-determined/self-determining individual subjectivity, but of the ways in which individuals are incorporated in social practices, in which social norms are internalized and perpetuated.

It is clear, I think, that such a project might take various forms; we are immediately concerned here with the form which has evolved under the aegis of structuralism. As a philosophical orientation, structuralism might be described as "Marxism for queasy stomachs" in that an interest in trans-individual, collective phenomena expresses itself in a constant attempt to transcend the particular and reveal—to use the English title of Foucault's *Les Mots et les Choses*—"the order of things." Structuralism is certainly interested in the culturally specific, but predominantly as an instance of the "laws of the human order," of forms of determination which are immanent in "social being." That is, it aspires to a sort of cosmology of social space, and given such an emphasis, Althusser's need for Lacan suddenly becomes explicable. Structural psychoanalysis offers the possibility of constructing a theory of macrocosm and microcosm (implicit, in any case, in every manifestation of structuralism from Saussure onward) whereby each individual, as a subject, becomes structurally coincident with the whole. Each subject mirrors "ideology"—*is* "ideology" in microcosm. The project is already blatant in Althusser's essay "Ideology and Ideological State Apparatuses." Man—that indispensable philosophical nonentity which Althusser makes a great show of pooh-poohing as a bourgeois myth, but on which his essay depends at every point—is immersed from before his birth in "the" family, "the" law, "the" church, "the" educational system, all of which categories are sublimely unproblematic, producing mutually coherent determinations which lock in "man." At the center of the system is God, now known as the Absolute Subject, of whom, we are to believe, each individual feels himself to be the image. Everything fits, everything is coherent: Althusser's Marxism consists in saying that the great chain of being is a bad thing.

But how is everything coherent? At this point, the psychoanalytic reinforcements arrive. Lacan shows us how man goes through the mirror phase and the Oedipus complex and how man is structured in a system called "language" which imposes subject-positions on him. Man is constructed in the imaginary. So we have our theory of social being, which is more or less good for any conceivable instance of social being, and what is more, we have got rid of man, because man is an imaginary construction. Q.E.D.

Consider the following passage:

> The object of Lacanian psychoanalysis is linguistic: the speech of the patient, the dream as productivity of meanings. The unconscious motivation, that is, the position of the

subject, is looked for in the particular configurations of discourse. In other words, the object of attention is production of representations in discourse through a particular subject position as the place of meanings. . . . The identity of a particular articulation is only produced according to the position of the subject in language. The sexual history of the individual which, at one level, psychoanalysis describes, traces the processes of splitting by which the effect of consciousness is produced in language. In the same moment, psychoanalysis indicates how every utterance could be said to inscribe a material position, a subject position, which is different in each utterance. (Coward, 78)

The argument—which, naturally, takes a pathological model for granted—rests on an analogy between the process of meaning in dreams and the process of meaning in waking discourse, in both of which the position of the subject is produced by the movement of the discourse. The speaker is an effect of the unconscious; he does not speak, "he is spoken." If the analogy is correct, what follows from it? One consequence is that we cease to be able to account for the specificity of dreams, which surely become explicable only on the hypothesis that the process of meaning involved is significantly different from that of waking discourse. Among the other consequences of analogy (none of them helpful) are the following:

a. We cease to be able to account for any form of discourse in which "the unconscious motivation" and "the position of the subject" are not synonymous terms, or, rather, we assume that the latter will always be sufficiently covered by the former.

b. We assume either the existence of a certain power relationship between two speakers, such as exists in the analyst/patient relationship, or a Cartesian knower capable of fixing "the identity of a particular articulation."

c. We assume that a particular articulation has an identity.

d. We cease to be able to account for structured conscious discourse—for example, a poem or our own argument—or we assume that the structure is unconsciously motivated. Covertly, we assume the immunity of our own self-consciousness, guaranteed by our access to science.

e. We assume that "the effect of consciousness" can be discussed entirely in terms of an individual's sexual history.

f. We make the extraordinary, and indeed nonsensical, claim that discourse involves "the production of representations," a position elaborated at the end of the essay, where Rosalind Coward endorses Lacan's analogy between subject-positions in language and the position of a spectator watching an optical illusion. (103) A confused adaptation of the Freudian hypothesis about the transformation of word-presentations into thing-presentations in dreams (so that the dream is, literally, the production of representations) is transferred directly to the concept of speech, with consequences of which the convenience fails to distract from the absurdity. "Representations" of what? Is it possible even to suggest that there may be an analogy between the position of a finite spectator perceiving an optical illusion—which will be identical for any spectator occupying that position—and the "position" of a speaker in an act of articulate speech? Indeed, we are left with the proposition—sufficiently banal—that language represents in an illusory way. The subject-positions which it imposes on us cause us to misperceive what is really there. The formulation is unusually gross, but it does represent the logical conclusion of that pat conjunction of the mirror phase, Althusser's theory of ideological misrecognition, and the relation of spectator to film so familiar from the pages of *Screen*.

The "materiality" of the signifier in the Lacanian myth of language (and one notes, above, that subject-positions are of course "material") is in itself merely a terminological quip—an "evanescent being" endows a "concrete being" with "essence." It is achieved at the cost of the disappearance of the signified ("the murder of the thing"), which then becomes the pretext for that mystical rapture which culminates in the apotheosis of the signifier, the creating Word. To say that in any given discourse the signified is the product of the ordering of the signifiers is, at one level, to state a commonplace: meaning is contextual. It is not the same thing as saying that the signifier is a founded entity within a "law of symbolization," and it does not solve the conceptual problems inseparable from the terminology, which if Derrida's analysis in *L'Ecriture et la Différence* is correct, are insuperable. Derrida suggests that the very concept "sign" presupposes a "transcendental or privileged signified" (a myth of "presence") and is thus determined "utterly and completely and throughout its entire history" by the Platonic dualism of "the sensory and the intelligible." (Derrida quoted in Jameson, *Prison-House*, 185–86, n17) (Timpanaro makes a similar point, while distinguishing Saussure sharply from his appropriators.) The alternative, within the given terms, must be to fetishize the signifier which, as Anthony Wilden points out, actually takes the place of the sign and must be concerned to repress henceforth the concept on which it depends. (Wilden in Lacan, *Language*, 144) The results can be read in, say, "*La Chose Freudienne*" (Lacan, *Ecrits*, 401), in which "signifier," "sign," and "signification" come to be used virtually interchangeably.

Irrigating the Wasteland

The Freudian determinism implicit here is of precisely that kind which follows from the inability to conceive of a theory of social subjectivity. It is characterized by a pervasive sense of the closure of history and the inalienability of "primal man" (Freud, "Thoughts"), which produces those elements in psychoanalysis that function, in Eric Mottram's phrase, as "alibis for disaster." In Lacan, this becomes a sort of existential angst tempered by elegant quietism and no small degree of self-regard, whereby the supreme act of the apostle of the Word becomes the assumption of the being-for-death, the entry into "the life of history . . . the perpetuated tradition of subject to subject" through the medium of annihilation. (*Ecrits*, 320–21)

There is no space here for that analysis of Lacan's intellectual sources which, given his extraordinary reputation, is now an urgent priority, but one should note, alongside the Platonizing tradition, the influence of a species of cosmic malaise (from Blaise Pascal through Søren Kierkegaard and Jean-Paul Sartre) and the tendency to compensate for it by a type of religious self-aggrandizement, by going "High Church" in the various available religions. Lacan's fondness for certain aspects of Eliot is not without its explanation. Lacan is basically a loss-of-faith, desert-of-the-modern-world man who has managed to adapt psychoanalysis to fill all the important existential gaps, and for whom the Symbolic serves as a somewhat calcified version of the concept of "tradition" in Eliot. "*L'aggressivité en psychanalyse*," for instance, offers the following by way of social analysis:

> What we are faced with, to employ the jargon that corresponds to our approaches to man's subjective needs, is the increasing absence of all those saturations of the superego and ego ideal that are realized in all kinds of organic forms in traditional societies, forms that extend from the rituals of everyday intimacy to the periodical festivals in which the community manifests itself. We no longer know them except in their most obviously degraded aspects. (*Ecrits,* 121–24)

"Jargon" apart, this is the exact tone of the literary gentleman recoiling from the horrors of "Technologico-Benthamite Society," down to the very vocabulary ("the organic community") and the aside about bingo halls and football matches; though, one should add, the nearest analogy is not so much Leavis, who has a highly, if inaccurately, developed sense of social dialectic, as Eliot/Sir James George Frazer refurbished with the idealism of Claude Lévi-Strauss. Clearly, psychoanalysis supplies the requisite re-saturation of the superego and, in the predictable form—doctrinal, hierarchical, absolute—the religious paradigm. The persona which Lacan has so assiduously developed is that of *le maître*, the shaman (see Lévi-Strauss's remarks on shamanism and psychoanalysis in *Structural Anthropology*), the Parisian reincarnation of the holy man of those "traditional societies" where persons who have gained access to the mysteries can count on receiving the proper respect.

The golden age pastoral of Lacan's myth of origins obtains much of its force in this context. As anthropology, it is somewhat more than absurd, but as an Edenic fantasy, which Lacan's language openly celebrates, it is indispensable. It describes a state in which "the life of *natural* groups" is governed by a set of perfectly congruent acts of exchange which correspond to "the *laws* of number" (*Ecrits,* 276–77, italics mine), a state in which mathematics mediates the synthesis of Nature and Culture, and which is ratified by "the Word." This sublime "harmony" has now, alas, been lost, and we are left today in a "social hell," cursed by that "isolation of the soul" which is the cost of individuality. "The cosmic polarity of the male and female principles," nicely catered to by the kinship system, has been "abolished," and we can see the "social consequences in failure and crime" (unspecified), which are entirely attributable to subjective dysfunctions in "man." (*Ecrits,* 123–24) The valorization of a set of nonexistent "forms and keepings," the ostentatious refusal of historical specificity, the belief in therapy and in the therapist as priest of the Word, the fear of the collapse of cosmic principles—the conjunction is certainly familiar, though never before under the name of Marxism.

If the Lacanian positive is accounted for by the muttering of "Da da da (Submission, gift, grace)" (*Ecrits,* 322), we should, nevertheless, give some consideration to his despair. Crucial here is the recurrent theme of "man eternally enchained by his symbols," of which the Schreber case becomes the paradigm ("the ego is a paranoid psychosis"), and in which the potential radicalism of Freud's finest work goes to seed. Schreber was a German judge whose autobiography

Freud analyzed and from whose experience Freud developed the concept of paranoia. A comparison of the three major analyses of the Schreber case—Freud's, Lacan's ("Traitement possible de la psychose," *Ecrits*), and Morton Schatzman's—seems to me crucial for anyone concerned with the possible development of psychoanalysis. The exercise indicates very clearly the extent to which both Freud and Lacan are incapable of comprehending the social determinants of mental illness and are unconcerned with any attempt to do so.

The mirror phase serves Lacan both as an alibi for aggressivity ("the ego is founded in radical conflict"—(*Ecrits*, 101) and as a version of the Fall, the central point being, as is stressed in phrases such as "primordial discord" and "an organic insufficiency of [man's] natural reality," that the primary alienation which constitutes the ego precedes "its social determination." (*Ecrits*, 450–52) The merging of this, the myth of linguistic origins, and Lévi-Strauss's account (*Structural Anthropology*) of the symbolic function, with its emphasis on transhistorical, "non-temporal" laws of the unconscious ("the vocabulary is less important than the structure"), produces a theory of predestination in which symbols "envelop the life of man in a network so total . . . that they bring to his birth, along with the gifts of the stars, if not with the gifts of the fairy-spirits, the design of his destiny." (Lacan, *Ecrits*, 279)

Language

While the use of words in that sentence comments on itself, *Screen*'s own language seems to demand some notice here, since it has been one of the main areas of contention. Stephen Croft's defense of *Screen* against the accusations of the essay "Psychoanalysis and Film" (Buscombe et al.) concedes one of its adverse judgments—that difficult concepts have been inadequately explicated and contextualized—but Croft's general position on this issue is, to say the least, naive. (15) He claims that the difficulty of the writing in *Screen*, as in Lacan, "aims to point up the error of assuming language to be transparent . . . and thus to avoid some of the incursions of ideology into the text by forcing the reader to work to grasp the signifieds." (15) There are two fallacious assumptions here.

    a. That while language and, thus, the act of reading are ideologically determinate, the process of "working to grasp the signifieds" is not. Thus, the simple expedient of convoluting one's syntax and employing an esoteric vocabulary guarantee the production of a distance from "ideology." Nonideological concepts are rendered opaque so that they can subsequently be made transparent through "work." The argument rests on a classical rationalist belief in the power of Reason to dispel error and ignores the obvious fact that the work of comprehension will be conducted in language as well. Since Lacan believes he has discovered eternal truths—"the analytic discourse . . . attains a real" (*Séminaire*, 118)—the ideological determination of his own theoretical activity never emerges as a problem. But it is dangerous for a Marxist to assume that he/she has a "signified" which, could one only find the signifiers, would be ideologically inviolate.

    b. That ideology intrudes into a text. Language and texts are either ideologically determinate or they are not; if they are, ideology is not a disreputable visitor whom one can choose or not choose to admit. But Crofts takes it as given that the "new ideas" can be "uncontaminated by the ideology"—that is, they can be themselves ideology free. This is clearly continuous with *Screen*'s definition of "science" and amounts to an idealist definition of writing, the aim of which becomes the maintenance of the purity of ideas amid the unfortunate tribulations of their material inscription.

One accepts, obviously, that Lacan's concepts are difficult and generally unfamiliar, and that "only ideological notions are self-evident," but neither of these propositions involves taking Lacan at his own valuation. If Freud has been comfortably assimilated by bourgeois capitalism, it is not because his writing is not sufficiently "difficult" but because he is eminently assimilable. Those elements of psychoanalysis which, though expounded with perfect clarity, are ideologically repulsive (for example, the sexuality of children) have been repressed. If Lacan is apparently being assimilated even more easily, despite his "difficulty," it is because he is infinitely less dangerous. Indeed, the hermeticism is part of the glamour—Lacan is a "star," and as such he becomes interesting. But it is, predominantly, the sort of interest which attaches to a symptom—which leads one to ask not "Is he a serious thinker?" but "Why is he fashionable?" Lacan is the seer of an antisocialist culture struggling to interpret its own obsolescence in terms of "the human predicament," simultaneously diagnosable and unalterable, and his style is a function of such a role. By turns magisterial and supplicatory, florid and austere, lyrical and "scientizing," comfortable and jaded, tormented and ironic, it is the precision instrument of a system whose closure has become a source of ease, the motley for every gesture of comfort and despair. One can explain all and change nothing, and what remains is a kind of antic solemnity, half-joker, half-mandarin.

Lacan's language is, explicitly, the discourse of initiation (see, for example, "*Fonction et champ*"), and its use carries with it the danger of lapsing into cliquishness. If *Screen*, as an ideological institution, has sometimes suggested a thinking-man's Bloomsbury Group, it is less a question of the books one is expected to have read (though, as Crofts admits, a certain hauteur as regards the presentation of concepts has been a problem) than the implied attitude to the books themselves. It is clearly desirable—indeed, a priority—that as many people as possible should be able to use Marx and Freud, but (crucially in the case of Freud) "use" involves a critical faculty. If all that one had to rely on were the pages of *Screen*, one would be bound to imagine that the premises of Lacanian psychoanalysis were quite unchallengeable, and could be taken as "truth." The manner in which they have been presented has succeeded in producing awe and bewilderment, unquestioning acceptance, or hysterical denunciation—all of which are obstacles to intelligent activity. There has not been the slightest attempt to place Freud, Lacan, Roland Barthes, Althusser, Julia Kristeva, etc., ideologically. Each of them might be taken as an individual working in an ideological vacuum producing "knowledge," whereas one is subjected to endless vulgar and trivial misreadings of, say, Leavis, in relation to his class position (Don McPherson even manages to trace a line "from Leavis into contemporary pop journalism"). One hears nothing about the class position of Lacan or MacCabe, and one can only assume that science is the universal solvent of class positions. The tone of *Screen* implies repeatedly that one either "believes" or one does not, and that if one does not, one must be either very lazy or very stupid. The assumption appears to be "Is it really necessary to explain all this? Isn't it obvious?" The absence of explanation and contextualization is, in fact, continuous with the absence of significant disagreement and has reached the point at which actual misrepresentation has taken place: to describe Lacan as an anti-idealist, for example (MacCabe, "Presentations," 8), is to commit oneself to a palpable untruth.

It seems to me that the dominant tendency of *Screen* has been to encourage an essentially uncritical attitude toward crucial areas of recent thought, and that the magazine itself has assimilated what Neale describes as "the central contradiction of the literary magazine *Scrutiny*: that between its role as vanguard and its role as elite." *Screen*'s "role as vanguard" has been increasingly suspect precisely because it involves the primacy of certain "bodies of knowledge" in a way which Leavis's very different intervention, with its own ideological limitations, did not. The use of language has made itself felt most keenly here. One respects the need to overthrow the "tyranny of common usage," which is very real, but the tyranny of hermeticism is as dangerous.

Lacan's pretensions to science are no less insistent, though somewhat more disreputable, than Althusser's. Lacan also dissociates himself elaborately from "positivism" and the "fictitious, or even simulated, principles of the experimental method," proposing instead "a return to a conception of true science" developed by Plato, in which "exactitude is to be distinguished from truth." (*Ecrits,* 284) This Truth to which Lacan has gained access both purports to be the expression of "that august voice" which issues not simply from the Other but from great creating Nature herself and claims as its "instrument . . . the mathematical symbol." Hence, the fondness for formulas and related appurtenances of precision by which the eternal structures of *l'esprit humain* can be expressed algebraically. The allegiance to mathematics is consistent through to the most recent seminars: "Only mathematicisation attains a real—and it is in this that it is compatible with our discourse, the analytic discourse—a real which has nothing to do with what traditional knowledge has upheld, and which is not what it thinks it is—reality—but, rather, fantasm." (Lacan, *Séminaire,* 118) This revelation of the order of things comes to Lacan as he unwinds the coils of his latest genuinely scientific discovery, the Borromean knot.

Given Lacan's honesty in making the debt to idealism so explicit, to the extent of assimilating the fort/da to the Platonic myth of the dyad (see some interesting remarks on the binary opposition in Jameson, *Prison-House,* 119), it seems more than perverse to appropriate these flights of fancy as "materialist theory of language." One would expect that in such a system the "real" would be a problem, and one is not surprised to find that object *a*, the instance of the real, finds its most sublime expression in the look, "reduced, by its nature, to a punctiform, evanescent function." (Lacan, *Séminaire,* 73) Object *a*, the loss of which constitutes the subject, functions in the Lacanian system to represent "a part, or detached spare part, of the apparatus here imagining the body" (*Ecrits,* 682), and it figures as the object of desire (which is unattainable). It partakes of Freud's theory of the stages of sexual organization (oral, anal, genital), and object *a* can represent the breast, excrement, and the phallus insofar as they are lost objects—"an unthinkable list if one does not add, as I do, phoneme, look, voice—the mere nothing." (817) Thus, for example, object *a* is not the symbol of the phallus, but of the lack of the phallus. If, therefore, object *a* is the "instance of the real," the real disappears at once into "a function which sublimates it even before it exercises it" (682), the function being that of an "index finger" indicating an absence. Lacan solves the problem of the real by making its sublimation a given of the system, and the Platonic model (the distinction between object *a* and the function it only "partially" represents) is particularly striking here.

The increasing impossibility of establishing any significant distinction between the Imaginary and the Symbolic goes along with the closure of the Symbolic which, as a concept, is totally insufficient to account for any creative act of meaning. On this level, the fort/da, in which "the child" acquires/is acquired by the signifier, manages to identify the first subjective act of meaning with the submission to social meaning (hence, its value as an idealist axiom). That is, we are dealing with a language model which fixes absolutely a set of forms for consciousness and which theorizes the entry into language as the surrender to meanings which always exist prior to, and apart from, any particular speaker.

Given this closure, which among psychoanalysts only Norman O. Brown has challenged—and that within a tradition of libertarian anarchism which leads, finally, to *Love's Body*—two attitudes to the "cure" become possible. The first, fed equally by Freud's misanthropy and his experience of the "vortex" of the Great War, concludes (in his "Analysis Terminable and Interminable") that therapy is effectively inconceivable. The second, equally reactionary, declares that "the question of the termination of the analysis is that of the moment when the satisfaction of the subject finds a way to come to realization in the satisfaction of everyone." (Lacan, *Ecrits,* 321) In other words, having been cured of his neurosis, a conforming subject is reinstated in the social structures which produced him/her, a project decorated by Lacan with quantities of rodomontade about gaining access to the Word and acquiescing in natural process. Lacan's insistence on the construction of the individual in language—which is a crucial insistence—becomes, in the very moment of the mystification of the signifier, the premise not of a science but of an existential metaphysic, which cannot be salvaged for socialism by patching it onto an almost equally suspect appropriation of Marx. The impossibility is sufficiently demonstrated in Althusser's own stab at it in "Freud and Lacan."

Claire Johnston's "Towards a Feminist Film Practice: Some Theses," following Kristeva, responds to the problem of the necessary intractability of the Symbolic by covertly reintroducing, under and against it, a concept of "semiotic process" which does service for that of "creative meaning." ("Practice") This unfettered primal language of radical difference is "analogous to the primary process and the drives," all three undergoing repression on the entry into the symbolic. Thereafter, the semiotic process is discernible only in its transgressions, through which "the unifying instance of signifier/signified which forms identity and the coherence of the sign" is fractured to produce the "feminine in a repressed form." (323–25) At this point there is a very romantic identification of madness with "poetic language" as the "primary example" of the crisis of difference, and of both with the "feminine"—a conjunction which makes sense polemically, if not conceptually.

This model of feminism, which also underlies the films of Peter Wollen and Laura Mulvey, seems to me most dangerous in its implications. As right-on, together, liberated political beings, we have abandoned the notion of the unfathomable mystery of Woman, only to see it replaced by "the voice of the Sphinx"—the Feminine as "the unspoken and the unspeakable," the Freudian "dark continent," the voice of the poet and the madman, a mysterious, repressed, volcanic life force. Kristeva's argument, in fact, merely grafts "the eternal feminine" onto a collection of romantic/anarchist stereotypes—the wise fool, the demonic poet, the spontaneous disruption of social forms—and then offers the result as sexual politics. While both are clearly comprehensible as a response to oppression, the "feminine" as here defined seems to me as illusory as the "gay sensibility," and in Kristeva's definition of the "Feminine," which is essentially mythic (it is eternal and ahistorical), psychoanalysis has become little more than a means of reinforcing the most cherished dreams of Romanticism. We have come, in fact, full circle. Kristeva and Johnston have perceived that "the symbolic and patriarchal ideology are not a separate realm" (indeed, in the given terms they are indistinguishable), and now the semiotic process emerges as a reaction-formation to the limitations of the original concept of the sign. Once subjectivity and "social identity itself" have been conceived in terms of insertion into the linguistic circuit—the symbolic exchange—the process of signification which the definition represses is reinvented as the subversion of it.

Suture

Screen's use of psychoanalysis has culminated, to date, in the adoption of the concept of suture, to which a lengthy dossier has been devoted in a recent edition of the magazine. (Winter 1977/78) Extremes frequently possess a certain clinical interest, and if the available returns—which are vapid to a degree—are scarcely commensurate with the labor of illuminating the prose, it is useful here to pause at a set of arguments which recapitulate and amplify, more generously than even parody could desire, the tendencies I have described.

"Suture names the relation of the subject to the chain of its discourse; we shall see that it figures there as the element which is lacking, in the form of a stand-in." (Miller, 25–26) As defined, the need for suture is clear enough: it is offered to bridge the gap opened up by the collapse of Althusser's theory of the interpellation of the subject which, as Stephen Heath—following Paul Hirst—has perceived (Heath, "Notes," 71), presupposes, like the cogito itself, the very category it is meant to establish. With suture, by contrast, the attempt to theorize the subject as the effect—the creature—of the "signifying chain" attains its apotheosis. Whatever one's sense of the effrontery of passing off Jacques-Alain Miller's piece on the "logic of the signifier" (24–34) as serious and significant, the article has the virtue of catching a particular ideology at a pitch of confidence, at a moment when the currency of the outrageous and the specious allows brazen displays which seem to betray themselves.

Leaving aside the question of his language—and the paper, delivered originally to Lacan's seminar, flaunts the predictable vices—Miller manages to be definitive in four crucial respects.

a. In a passage which almost exactly—and, one presumes, accidentally—paraphrases the Cartesian formulation about "the rational deduction of consequences," Miller describes the logic of the signifier as "a minimal logic in that within it are given those pieces only which are necessary to assure it a progression reduced to a linear movement, uniformally generated at each point of its necessary sequence." (25) The Cartesian guarantee has rarely been evoked so succinctly.

b. As "a general logic [whose] functioning is formal in relation to all fields of knowledge" (25), the logic of the signifier completes the structuralist reduction. Taken together, (a) and (b) insure at once the necessary veracity and the generality of that logic.

c. The logic of the signifier "should be conceived of as the logic of the origin of logic—which is to say, that it does not follow its laws but that, prescribing their jurisdiction, itself falls outside that jurisdiction." (25) Thus, the logic of the signifier possesses the immunity which was once felt to be the prerogative of deities. It is the unmoved mover. Like Althusser's science, it exists outside the operations of which it is absolutely the measure, and which, as Miller would have it, it can be said to ordain.

d. These minor sallies and alarums are mere preliminaries to the sustained broadside of mathematicizing that follows, in the course of which the ideological function of mathematics for structuralism is made beautifully explicit. From Pythagoras to the end of the nineteenth century, there was an intimate connection in Western philosophical thought between mathematics and theology. The influence of Pythagoras on Platonism was immense, and Lacanian psychoanalysis, as the supreme refinement of structuralist method, can best be understood as a contemporary instance of a long series of attempts (which include Descartes, Spinoza, and Gottfried Leibnitz) to discover mathematical axioms in metaphysics. The claim that "the signifying chain is *structure of the structures*" (34, italics in the original) is a theological proposition, and if Miller can assert that the logic of the signifier describes the origins of logic while at the same time exempting itself from its laws, it is because mathematics—for structuralism as for Platonism—constitutes the activity of *nous* (mind/spirit). As both the principle of organization and the means by which that principle can be grasped—as, in effect, the tautology of the principle—it dispels, by definition, the curse of being contained within its own terms of reference. Miller's discovery of the formal principle of "all fields of knowledge" simply ratifies Lévi-Strauss's declaration that "the important thing is not man's point-of-view, but that of God" (quoted in Timpanaro), and it is very proper that Miller should begin his demonstration with the perfect sublimation of the real. While we already know from Lacan that the birth of the signifier is "the murder of the thing," Miller can demonstrate that "the emergence of the numerable" transports us, like Gerard Manley Hopkins in Ireland, to a third remove: "a number is assigned to a concept which subsumes objects." (Miller, 27) Pythagoras asserts that "all things are numbers," Plato that God is a mathematician, and Lacan that mathematics "attains the real" (that is, ideas in the Platonic sense): the knowledge of number is God's point of view.

I do not wish to embark at this stage on a refutation of the detail of Miller's argument, as this would involve discussion of some length, both of his ignorance of the history of mathematics (the claim that "the foundation of arithmetic [is] empiricist" states, in fact, the reverse of the case) and of his badness as a mathematician. (27) I will concentrate instead on his basic project and the larger misconceptions on which it is based. The project is quite simple: Miller wishes to establish an analogy between the series of whole numbers and "the signifying chain" of verbal discourse. The argument runs as follows:

a. Following Leibnitz, "identity" may be defined thus: "Those things are identical of which one can be substituted for the other without loss of truth." (28) Truth is predicated on a thing's identity with itself.

b. Following Gottlob Frege, the assignation of number may be defined thus: "The number assigned to the concept F is the extension of the concept 'identical to the concept F.'" (28) The possibility of number is predicated on the concept of a thing's identity with itself.

c. In order to produce the succession of numbers "without any reference to the real" (29), it is necessary to invoke the zero, defined as the concept "not identical with itself." Since truth has been defined in terms of self-identity, the zero therefore "subsumes no object."

d. Although in the order of the real the zero, by definition, is impossible, in the order of number it is the first number, and it is counted as "one." The zero number sutures (stands in for) "pure and simple absence" (nothing) and is counted as a number; it is the first non-real thing in thought." (30) The representation of absence as "zero" and the counting of zero as "one" "determines the appearance of the successor." (31)

e. Miller continues:

Now, if the series of numbers, metonymy of the zero, begins with its metaphor: if the 0 member of the series, as number, is only the standing-in-place suturing the absence (of the absolute zero) which moves beneath the chain according to the alternation of a representation and an exclusion—then what is there to stop us from seeing in the restored relation of the zero to the series of numbers the most elementary articulation of the subject's relation to the signifying chain? (32)

One would have thought that "what stops us" is quite apparent; the attractiveness, at any rate for Lacanianism, of an analogy between the series of numbers and the "chain" of verbal discourse is grossly obvious. The Platonic bias of Miller's argument becomes most explicit in (e), where we are asked to believe that the zero number is a metaphor of some "absolute zero" which the number both excludes and represents, but it emerges, crucially, much earlier in the proposition that self-identity is the support for the assignation of number. The example which Miller provides—the assignation of number to the concept "child of Agamemnon and Cassandra" (28)—reiterates an argument in the "Thaetetus" which suggests (incorrectly, as Bertrand Russell demonstrates in *History of Western Philosophy*), that the concept "one" can be assigned to objects when it is only applicable to "unit-classes." This confusion has lamentable consequences for Miller's initial postulate (a number is assignee to a concept which subsumes objects), since it transpires that the "logical dimension," built on the concepts of self-identity and "redoubling" (of object by concept by number), is simply a matter of bad syntax. The only field of human inquiry in which it is possible to speak of "*the thing insofar as it is one*" (italics in the original) is theology—but I am reliably informed that we have left all that behind us.

In ordinary circumstances, Miller's attempt to play the numbers game might be counted on to revoke itself, but since the intention (at least of *Screen*) is so evidently not facetious, it demands a rejoinder. As Russell remarks, "pure mathematics consists of tautologies" (*History*, 168), and it follows that mathematical truth "is truth of a very peculiar sort," admirably defined by Leibnitz's statement about identity, quoted above. It cannot be emphasized too strongly that this definition of "truth" is specific to mathematical truth, and that in any other context it is either unhelpful or irrelevant. Numbers are neither abstractions from percepts nor metaphors for absent absolutes; they are, in Russell's phrase, "logical fictions" (169), the succession of which is determined by a conventional necessity. Crucially, the series of numbers is totally unambiguous; it precedes and is independent of anyone using the series. "Two" must follow "one" or the numerical fiction will break down. Anyone wishing to add "two" and "one" has a limited series of moves available, and if the answer is not "three," then the mathematician is in error. As a system, the series of numbers is complete (although in principle infinite), and acts of meaning are absolutely determinate according to a few very simple principles, to the extent that "significance" and "correctness" are synonymous. In that the series "one, two, three . . ." is given, by definition the metaphor of a "signifying chain" is not inexact, but it scarcely needs to be said that the relation of a user to a system of this kind is a phenomenon of a completely different order from that of a user to verbal language.

When Heath remarks, of the latter, that "since the system of signifiers is by definition complete, the subject can only be entered there as this structure of lack-in-being" ("Notes," 52), the "lack-in-being" is merely a deduction from a false premise. As soon as one contests the completeness—or indeed, the existence—of any such system for verbal language, the concept of the subject remains interesting only as a kind of sophism, one, moreover, of insufferable crudity. It is a corollary of the necessary priority of the series to any user that its meanings and relationships are both autonomous and static. Indeed, the system is partially defined by its exclusion of the possibility of structural or semantic change, which would deprive it of its usefulness. While certain structural features of verbal language may be, for practical purposes, finite, semantic fluidity is here, on the contrary, a condition of usefulness and a product of use. If the "system of signifiers" were complete, and all subjects "entered there" in a relation of lack, language would be inconceivable beyond the parrot level, and change of any kind, other than that which was induced, would cease to take place, since thought would be impossible. Suture, whereby the subject becomes the effect of a prior system of meaning, is, as a concept, an evasion, since all it postulates is a subject in process within stasis, and the one cancels the other.

As soon as the analogy with the series of whole numbers is made, and language becomes an autonomous "signifying system" existing apart from users or contexts of use, it is no longer possible to formulate the essential questions, and any gesture in their direction, without a major theoretical shift, is doomed to impertinence. Thus, on the one hand, Lacan's attempt to dissolve the *langue/parole* distinction with the concept of *lalangue* succeeds only in producing a vague and tendentious parody of Noam Chomsky which regresses to a pre-theoretical state of mystical portentousness (*lalangue* as "inconsistent multiplicity . . . which affects us first by everything it contains as effects that are affects"). (Heath, "Notes, 51) On the other hand, Michel Pécheux's theory of "discursive formations" (Heath, "Notes," 69–73) simply reiterates the reflection theory of language, whereby "discursive formations . . . represent 'in language' corresponding ideological formations" of which, again, subjects become the effect—"represent" functioning there as the notional (and totally inadequate) exemption from the proposition that discourse is ideology. The static quality of Pécheux's theory—the absence of dialectics—is striking: "Words, expressions, propositions, etc., receive their meaning from the discursive formation in which they are produced," and which determines "what can and must be said." ("Notes," 70) This has a certain limited usefulness, but it is clearly insufficient to suggest that there is some one-way determination of meaning by "the conjuncture," in which those meanings are held unambiguously to the extent that what must not be said cannot be said. Any interesting Hollywood movie can be used to demonstrate in a moment that what can be said and what cannot be said *are* said simultaneously.

What Pécheux omits from his "discursive formations" is the element of which, one presumes, they were designed to take account, and that is the fact of discourse. Leavis's controversy with F. W. Bateson over the reading of Andrew Marvell's "Dialogue" (Bateson; Leavis, "Responsible Critic") is exemplary in this respect. Bateson, by dint of careful references to the discursive formations, attempts to establish what the poem can and must be saying; Leavis, by reading the poem, demonstrates with cogency and rigor what the poem *is* saying. The demonstration comes down, effectively, to this: that the poem is a critique of dominant discursive modes. In other words, semantics is creative, or to put it more exactly, Marvell's poem—and any act of discourse—is a field of tension between the given and the "doing" of the utterance. The given itself will always be enormously complex—far more so, certainly, than Pécheux's "given position in a given conjuncture," which appears to be more or less homogeneous—far more so than what Heath, in the term "preconstruction," describes as the "ready-made positions of meaning that a film may adopt." (Heath, "Notes," 74) If the definition of "preconstruction" is inadequate, how much more so then is that of discourse, in which "the signs and orders of language itself" being part of the given, all that remains is a kind of superficial tinkering, the reconstruction of the same from "different materials." ("Notes," 75) If this is really the case, and if "the signs and orders of language itself" can be packaged as "preconstruction," it is not difficult to conclude that "the movement of the spectator making the film" and the "construction of the subject" must be synonymous terms, or that suture must describe an objective fact, since the premises do not admit of any other hypothesis: to fix the signs and orders of language is to fix the possibilities of discourse and of thought. Language has become a kind of Kantian category. With the achievement of this august transformation, there seems very little left for structuralism to do.

Finally, the dossier on suture demonstrates—if that were still necessary—that the concept of ideology appropriated and elaborated by *Screen* has become theoretically useless, and has to be abandoned. The concepts of the logic of the signifier, and of the construction of the subject in that logic, are radical impediments to any theory of discourse. Lacan can congratulate himself—and it is no mean achievement—on having made the unconscious into conscious mental activity and the historical process of meaning virtually undiscussable; it is to be doubted whether what we gain in bad mathematics sufficiently counterbalances the loss.

Juliet Mitchell

The pernicious effects of Lacanianism are strikingly apparent as regards the development of what is potentially radical both in Freud and in work outside psychoanalysis whose intellectual/political integrity one respects. Thus, in the final section of *Psychoanalysis and Feminism*, Juliet Mitchell resorts to that analogy, constructed by Lévi-Strauss on the transport-service theory of language, between the linguistic circuit and the kinship system; to that insistence on the founding function of the incest taboo which, as has been repeatedly demonstrated, is not a universal and which depends, in Lévi-Strauss, on the confusion of the functions of the incest taboo and exogamy (see, for example, *Fox* [1983]); to, finally, the elaborate superstructure which Lacan has erected on Lévi-Strauss and which, while eagerly exploiting certain congenial elements (such as the concept of mana, interpreted as that supreme entity the pure signifier, "pure form without specific content"), carries to its logical extreme the suppression of historical specificity to which Lévi-Strauss was increasingly drawn.

Beyond all this, however, and determining it, is the attempt to make Freud cohere—a project discernible in the very organization of the book—as an achieved body of theoretical work. While one can understand the ideological position which produces such an impulse—and in her introduction, Mitchell quotes from *Psychanalyse et Politique*: "In the ideological and sexual fight, the only discourse that exists today on sexuality and the unconscious [is] the discourse of psychoanalysis (Freud, Lacan) and semiology" (Mitchell, xxii)—one should add that simply because psychoanalysis is all there is (and Mitchell accords to R. D. Laing none of the indulgences meted out to Freud), an act of wholesale recuperation is neither politically nor intellectually desirable. Psychoanalysis does not cohere. It is riddled at every level with gaps, contradictions, uncertainties, and hesitations.

Thus, an apparently minor point in Mitchell's book turns out, on consideration, to be crucial. She quotes a passage from Freud's famous letter to an American mother about her son's gayness: homosexuality "cannot be classified as an illness; we consider it to be a variation of the sexual function." (Mitchell, 11) At this point, an interesting hiatus occurs in the quotation: the phrase omitted is—"produced by a certain arrest of sexual development." The absence can scarcely be regarded as innocent, since Mitchell proceeds to omit passages from the end of the letter referring to "the blighted germs of heterosexual tendencies," the blossoming of which Freud "cannot promise to achieve." (Freud, "Letter to an American Mother," 787) Thus, we are given that portion of the letter with which persons of liberal sympathies might be expected to concur, and the entire book is characterized by a tension between what Freud is saying and what, from a certain perspective, he can be maneuvered into saying. In the present instance, the tension is that between a theory of sexuality in which normality is "an ideal fiction," and one in which heterosexuality, nevertheless, is regarded as a point from which perversions and inversions can be theorized as "arrests." Both theories are present in Freud, usually in close proximity (see, for example, *Three Essays on the Theory of Sexuality*) and in a state of mutual tension. To this extent, bisexuality is that crux of psychoanalytic theory which Freud is never able unambiguously to conceptualize, and the failure has consequences of a scope which cannot be narrowed simply by choosing the explanation one prefers. Similarly, the "Psychogenesis," offered in *Screen* in reply to Lesage, as exemplary of Freud's "awareness of social relations" serves rather—while it does indicate that to a degree—to demonstrate the point at which that "awareness" breaks down in the extraordinary explanation, guaranteed by the Oedipus complex, of the patient's suicide attempt.

Freud's radicalism is potential, not achieved. The priority now is neither to use his work as a sheet anchor nor to decorate it with shamanistic charms, but to rethink it from the base up, avoiding at all costs the assistance of *l'esprit humain*. In this context, the posture of resigned religiosity of Lacanianism should not offer even a *last* resort.

Roland Barthes

The difficulties of dealing with Barthes appear most strikingly, perhaps, in those texts in which he can be said to be at his best. *S/Z* and *Sade/Fourier/Loyola* are clearly distinguished by passages of great precision and insight, but one is continually brought up short by perception of the ideological positions which the "brilliance" entails.

Barthes can be associated with a certain French romantic attitude to crime which can be traced from the Marquis de Sade through Gustave Flaubert, Charles Baudelaire, Joris-Karl Huysmans, Jean Cocteau, and André Gide, to a sort of apotheosis in Jean Genet, and which has been enormously influential (feeding, for example, Jack Kerouac, into the hipster anarchism of the Beat Generation). Barthes emerges from this as a kind of salon dandy for whom the "erotics of the text" constitute the defining tenet of a metaphysics of transgression. Thus, Sade's textual practice becomes "a language" of crime, or "new code of love," the crime consisting in "transgressing the semantic rule: . . . the act *contra naturam* is exhausted in an utterance of counter-language . . . to transgress is to name outside the lexical division, the basis of society, for the same reason as class division." (Barthes, *Sade,* 27) To propose the ambiguous analogy proposed in that last phrase (is "class division" the basis of society or is it not? Is it identical with, prior to, or a consequence of lexical division?) is to advance, as the quintessence of subversiveness, the subversion of linguistic rules—*"lese-language."* Thus, for example, "it is syntax, and syntax alone, that produces the supreme immorality" (102), or "crime begins only in form, and paradox is the purest of forms." (168) The "elegance" of syntactic crime is assimilated, as we might expect, to mathematics (157), the status of which seems to vary between affording, as here, a paradigm of refinement or, as in Lévi-Strauss, Althusser, Lacan, Foucault et al., a type of that purity of discourse ("the pure language of the combinative" [Barthes, *Sade,* 108]) which guarantees the banishing of the ideological.

This latter is, in its turn, associated with the subversion of representation. Thus, the "textual book, textured of pure writing" which inhabits the Sadean text is pure in that it does "not tell, but tells that it is telling" (Barthes, *Sade,* 35), just as, in Foucault's description of *Las Meninas* (Foucault, *Order,* 16), "representation in its pure form" emerges at that point at which representation is itself represented, in a work which gives us the "manifest essence" of representation. Again, the language tells us that we are dealing with a search for a Platonic essence of "text," beyond the realm of becoming, ideology, signified, etc., in which a pure signifier, "unimpoverished by any constraint of representation (of imitation)" (Barthes, *S/Z,* 5) and "free from any referential illusion" (Barthes, *Sade,* 110), gives us access to a realm of pure textuality. The "classic texts" which one is still permitted to validate—the texts which Barthes finds it in him to "consent to write (to re-write), to desire" (Barthes, *S/Z*, 4)—are those in which it is possible to discern an immanent textuality, a sturdy resistance to the bonds of the *scriptible*. Hence, that admirably "writerly" practice, rife of late, of totting up tables of acceptability whereby movies can be graded according to what is perceived as their violation of the conventions of representation or, as Barthes might say, their unhappiness in the flesh. Hence also, the insistent gravitation toward works in which it can be maintained that the means of representation is made manifest within the work, frequently on the scantiest grounds. Thus, MacCabe, in a reading of *American Graffiti* (1973), actually goes so far as to fabricate two moments in which, we are to believe, radical difference is introduced into the text. The reading of both moments is evidently spurious—even MacCabe is forced to concede that the editing in one of them "has a certain diegetic motivation" ("Principles," 17)—but the flimsiness of the evidence is as nothing beside the desire that it should be there. A similar argument, in praise of Vincente Minnelli, may be found in *Screen* several issues later. (Nowell-Smith, "Minnelli and Melodrama," 117–18)

Exorcising Ideology

The consequences of Barthes's position emerge fully in *Le Plaisir du Texte* and the essay on "Diderot, Brecht, Eisenstein." The modern text is "the impossible text," the impossibility relating directly to that fetishization of the signifier so central to Lacan and producing an ideal of linguistic practice in which, logically, any nonarbitrary method of organization opens the floodgates of "the ideological and the imaginary." (Barthes, *Pleasure*, 14) In his concern to cleanse himself of what Frederic Jameson calls "the guilt of language," Barthes resorts to a set of oppositions between classic and modern texts of which the import emerges in the plangent cry with which "Diderot, Brecht, Eisenstein" begins and ends—"When are we to have music, the Text?" The nature of the concern with mathematics here—aligned, with music, against the geometrical cast of representation—is sufficiently defined by its appearance as a strut to prop up the reinvention of Paterism (all art aspires to the condition of music) and its association with an aesthetic which leaves us, in *Le Plaisir du Texte*, with a reworking of the form/content opposition, newly appointed in a debased version of Saussure (form = the signifier) and a sort of swooning sensualism ("language lined with flesh").

Sade, Charles Fourier, and Saint Ignatius Loyola are exemplary because, supposedly, their texts tend toward that "non-originated, non-determined material" which is the condition of the signifier, and which is consummated in the "atopia" of the ideal text. "From this atopia the text catches and communicates to its reader a strange condition: at once excluded and at peace." (Barthes, *Pleasure*, 29) It seems that, as "aristocratic readers" (13), our only refuge from the Platonic cave of ideology is the blubbery belly of George Orwell's whale, "a sort of islet within the human—the common relation." (16) The social implications are alarming, and Barthes does not hesitate to follow them to their conclusion, clothing himself the while in the vestments of socialistic piety. Thus, while we are treated to sporadic displays of *saeva indignatio* on behalf of the People (38)—sixty years ago, Barthes would have called them the Poor—all he can offer by way of political commitment is "a drift, something both revolutionary and asocial, [which] cannot be taken over by any collectivity, any mentality, any ideolect." (23) When he is not defining revolution as an opium trance, Barthes presents, by way of criticism, both an analysis of a sentence from *Bouvard et Pécuchet* which concludes that its "excess of precision" (excess by what standard is not made clear) marks it as "pure language," and an analogy between reading *War and Peace* and speeding up a striptease act. (11) These gems glitter in the same setting as that description of narrative as an Oedipal process which is offered to us in *Screen* as a serious critical judgment.

It is quite impossible to separate cleanly the sort of thing which Barthes wishes to advocate (a marriage of "pure form" and a limp-wristed individualistic hedonism) from his descriptions of its converse. Against what is of value in *S/Z* (the isolation of certain rhetorical structures) must be set the sheer vagueness of the use to which the Saussurean terminology is put and a conception of reading as "an act of lexical transcendence which can stand as a definition of the idealist fallacy." (Barthes, *S/Z,* 83) We are told that "the object of semantics should be the synthesis of meanings, not the analysis of words." (92) The extraordinary disjunction there of "words" and "meanings" opens the way for the assimilation of reading to a search for "forms," the blurring of the concrete instance into "the generic word it continually attempts to join." This explicit Platonizing is decorated with the predictable mystical tinsel ("A maya activity, as the Buddhists would say") and leans, for its alibi, on the assertion that such an operation is already immanent in the text. If, then, we are concerned to find meanings beyond words, it should scarcely come as a surprise to find that we can separate the signified from the signifier and declare that signification is the path of truth, since our conclusion is given a priori. Barthes is helped in the present case by the choice of *Sarrasine*, which is not only a detective story but also a *roman à thèse* of amazing schematism. But indeed, what awareness of specificity can remain when the detail of realization in language can be dismissed as "the prattle of meaning"? (Barthes, *Pleasure,* 4–5)

The conjunction of ideology, the imaginary, and representation which finally produces, in Barthes, the posturing dilettantism of *Le Plaisir du Texte*, gives us in Althusser's "Letter on Art" (*Lenin and Philosophy,* 221) the positivistic distinction between affect and cognition: art gives us "experience," science gives us "knowledge," science being defined, again, as "the abstraction of structures"—that is, a sort of transcendent certitude. In Lacan's analysis of Hans Holbein's painting "The Ambassadors"—swallowed hook, line, and sinker by MacCabe ("Principles," 14)—we discover that without a jolt, "the spectator" is incapable of comprehending that a painting is "a set of traces left by a paintbrush," a claim based on that analogy with the mirror phase which, while strenuously asserting the "non-reduction of the *relation*" (Brewster et al., 87) between the forms of representation and the mirror phase, depends on the reduction at every point. Along with the sententia, MacCabe inherits the maudlin pathos of the Master's prose ("that endless movement which can find satisfaction only in death"). (MacCabe, "Theory and Film," 16)

The "homological" argument as a basic structuralist tenet deserves closer attention. In "Lessons from Brecht," Heath, like Christian Metz and Barthes, proposes a direct analogy between the structures of fetishism and representation. (106) Freud's paper on fetishism suggests that the fetish is determined by the perception that the mother does not have a penis, and the simultaneous "disavowal" of that perception, the fetish working as a safeguard against the acknowledgment of sexual difference. The crucial word is "disavowal," a process which,

Freud remarks elsewhere, "would, in an adult, mean the beginning of a psychosis." ("A Case of Paranoia," vol. XIX, 253) Heath suggests that the fetishistic structure "operates a split between knowledge and belief." ("Lessons," 107) This is not true, in that "knowledge and belief" are consciously held (or at least preconsciously), and neither arises as a problem for the fetishist (the fetish is there, precisely, so that they should not). The ensuing analogy with representation depends on an opposition between "a knowledge—this exists—and a perspective of reassurance—but I am outside this existence." This proposition is characterized neither by disavowal nor by a tension between knowledge and belief. A little further down the page, the definition of fetishism has broadened out into "the essential denial of work, production, the refusal to grasp the positions of subject and object within that process" (see also the reply to Lesage, where an impenetrable analogy between "work" and "heterogeneity and process" is proposed). "Denial" and "refusal" take us even further from "disavowal," and we perceive that the Marxist and Freudian definitions of fetishism are being elided, at the cost of some distortion, and the resulting makeshift is being referred back to the concept of representation. This concept itself undergoes changes of emphasis, referring initially to the "separation" of spectator and spectacle, when a strict analogy with Freud's account is required, and later to the spectator's "ignorance of the structure of his production"—a phrase which also need have nothing to do with disavowal. This extraordinary botch, which presents itself insistently as a structural analogy, can of course be transferred sexually at will. Thus, for example, in reply to Lesage, "it is the representation itself which is the endowment of the penis." (Brewster et al.) Barthes—need it be said?—takes the argument to its extreme and proceeds to construct a monolith of fetishism/representation so unshakable as to produce the memorable conclusion: "Nothing separates the shot in Eisenstein from the picture by Greuze (except, of course, their respective projects . . .)." ("Diderot, Brecht, Eisenstein," 34)

"Closed" and "Open" Texts

The question this opens out—the notoriously embattled subject of the "open text"—has been explored through arguments which range from the silly to the obvious. Wollen's dissertation on "Ontology and Materialism in Film" proceeds toward the shattering *trouvaille* that "style is a producer of meaning," a proposition with which everyone has been familiar since, at least, Leavis, and which we now discover to be "the fundamental axiom of a materialist aesthetic." The banality (and one passes over the evident confusion between "style" and "form") is accompanied by an equal misconception, to the effect that "style" in pre-modernist art can be adequately discussed in terms of "spontaneous idiosyncrasy or a mere manner of writing . . . fundamentally subordinate to the sovereignty of the signified" (20) (and one passes over the suggestion, in the previous sentence, that it can't). This belief obtains very widely. Thus, for instance, the style of *Touch of Evil* (1958) is "the decorative inscription of Welles as 'artist'" (Heath, "Film and System Pt. 1," 111), or in the Burch/Dana "Propositions," the style of Max Ophüls "takes the form of decorative patterns tirelessly woven around a more or less 'theatricalized' anecdote," according to a theory of the "amplification of codes" that leaves one, intellectually, at the level of Richard Roud. (Burch and Dana, 47) (One should add that in other respects, Heath's article is not to be compared with the sustained fatuousness and hectoring stridency of Burch and Dana.)

Each instance has recourse to Barthes's distinction between "style" and *écriture*, which falls at once on the use of the word *style* at all. Can one discuss, for example, Hamlet's "I have of late, and wherefore I know not, lost all my mirth. . ." in terms of a "spontaneously idiosyncratic" elaboration of the basic signified "I am pissed off"? The opposition of "a structure of signifieds" (classic text) and "a galaxy of signifiers" (modern text) implies, as in Lacan and elsewhere, that the two are conceptually separable, in that the modern text can attain a "pure signifier" and the classic text somehow subordinates the signifier to the signified. (Barthes, *S/Z*, 5)

Indeed, *S/Z* regularly provides instances of woolly terminology as flagrant as Lacan's. We find that "a single signifier" is analogous to "a single statement" (35), and that "signified" has become synonymous with "meaning." (79) "Meaning" has been separated, in effect, from textual process, and by the end of the paragraph, signified is indistinguishable from "signification." To this extent, Barthes's attempts to deal with the "plurality" of classic texts are liable constantly to collapse into doublethink. Thus, in an analysis of *Ivan the Terrible* (1944, 1958) in "The Third Meaning" (*Image-Music-Text*, 64), he tries to maintain that the film's nonnarrative structures are actually counter-narrative, networks of "signifiers" which in some way declare their independence of what is termed—in a damaging giveaway moment—"the story (diegesis)." We have here a perfect illustration of that familiar intellectual trick whereby, once an untenable definition has been established, an inordinate and distorted significance is attached, for good or ill, to instances which show the definition to be incorrect. Thus, once we have decided that the classic text is a "structure of signifieds," we suddenly discover classic texts which are not. They can then be theorized as types of the aspiration to *écriture*.

It has been axiomatic since Leavis's analysis of the realist novel as "dramatic poem" that the classic realist text (to retain, for a moment, that insignificant phrase) is capable of embracing minute, complex, nonlinear symbolic/poetic structures, and it seems more than perverse of Barthes, on making the discovery for himself, to conceptualize it wrongly. It is, indeed, true that the nonnarrative structures of Sergei Eisenstein's film are nonlinear—but does one really need to be told this? Conversely, to suggest that the narrative becomes the mere "fellow traveler" to the flight of the pure signifier is simply to fall victim to the limitations of a false system. This particular passage is quoted approvingly by David Bordwell, Janet Staiger, and Kristin Thompson at the end of some remarks on Yasujiro Ozu (70) which base the claim for his modernity on a series of "quotations," compiled with laborious erudition and effectively deprived of any semantic context, either within individual films or within Japanese culture. Bordwell et al. manage to tell us that Ozu's films have nonnarrative structures and that they look rather different from Hollywood movies, but the attempt to read the use of space and graphic play as essentially unrelated to narrative ends up, like Barthes, in aestheticism: "The object's lack of function creates a second formal level alongside the narrative: its motivation is purely 'artistic.'" (65) So explicit a lapse is rare, but its like is implicit in *Screen*'s presentation of the "modernist" position.

One might go so far as to say that it accounts for Wollen and Mulvey's *Penthesilea* (1974), and for the reputation it enjoys. What is one to conclude when, after a lucid—indeed, brilliant—analysis of "narrative space," Heath invokes *Penthesilea* as an instance of the "radical transformation" of the relation of subject and film? ("Narrative Space," 107–8) What can one actually find to justify such a reading? The film, which is larded with quotations from the fashionable scriptures, displays a crushing literal mindedness. The second section, in which the camera leaves and rejoins Wollen as he wanders, in a mauve lounge suit, through the precincts of a luxuriously appointed suburban villa telling us about *l'amour fou*, does indeed grant a certain autonomy to the movement of the camera and foreground the space of the recital. But why should this be interesting? Why should we be concerned with "rediscovering the space" of this bland dwelling at such laborious length? Unless, indeed, the rediscovery of space is to be valued for its own sake, as Heath implies. And if the procedure really constitutes a foregrounding of "the ordering of signifiers" (Wollen, "Ontology," 20), what substantial work are the signifiers being ordered to produce? None whatsoever—beyond that obsessive "auto-referentiality" discussed by Jameson (*Prison-House*, 119), through which "form" is transliterated into a sort of ultimate "content." Indeed, in the article cited, Wollen refers us to that dissertation by Roman Jakobson in which "the poetic function of language" is defined as "the set (*Einstellung*) towards the MESSAGE as such, focus on the message for its own sake." ("Ontology," 20) Again, all we are left with is an aestheticist axiom.

Elsewhere, *Penthesilea* is remarkable for the suppression of the historical specificity which Heath seems to imagine it emphasizes. It seems to me, rather, almost a locus classicus of an idealist reading of history, which one might associate with the fact that the film does not exist beyond a very conspicuous level of intentionality. Thus, every concrete instance in the film is blurred and assimilated to some transhistorical "predicament of Woman," the fuzziness constantly producing massive misjudgments of effect. During the opening minutes of Section Four, for instance, throughout which a speech by the American feminist Jessie Ashley is delivered directly to the camera with an objectionably fruity Girl Guide heartiness, one imagines that some adverse judgment is intended as to the historically conditioned limitations of Ashley's rhetoric (the sentimentalization of the working class; the phallic imagery—"masses of aroused womanhood," eagles with wounded wings; the general tone of messianic vagueness). As the sequence progresses, it becomes clear that incredible as it may seem, this is not the case, and that both Ashley and the performance are being offered "straight," as it were, the straightness remaining unbent by the do-it-yourself distantiation effects with which the sequence is liberally endowed. One's impression is confirmed by Mulvey in an interview in *Screen* (Johnston and Willemen, 125) in which we are told that the speech seriously "states the case for class politics" in a way which "is just as relevant to the situation here in England." The sentimental idealist liberalism of *Penthesilea*'s feminism is to some extent dealt with in *The Riddles of the Sphinx* (1977), which is far more open, complex, and interesting, though the film's gestures toward the "concrete situation" (setting up a crèche for the children of working women) are somewhat undermined by endless narcissistic speculations on the mysteries of Woman.

The question of order in art crops up, variously, in the closed and open text antinomy, in the concept of the reader's productivity, and in Barthes's influential description of "the very process of story-telling" as an Oedipal structure. (*Pleasure*, 47) By "art" I mean a "made object," an artifact which has a concrete existence in a certain order—an order which produces certain structures of meaning. These structures will be historically determinate and, variously, complex, mutually qualifying, or contradictory, but inasmuch as the text is, in Ricoeur's phrase, "fixed by writing," meaning is not arbitrary. That characteristic phenomenon of twentieth-century art, the work which is, theoretically, interminable (Ezra Pound's *Cantos*, Charles Olson's *Maximus* poems, William Carlos Williams's *Paterson*, and so on), does not imply that meaning is any the less determined by structures of made relations, any the less an "injunction of the text." (Ricoeur, *Hermeneutics*) Thus, to suggest in the name of some hypothetical openness that *Vent d'Est* (1970) refuses to "place the spectator" in the position from which it wants to be read is to say something which is essentially meaningless. (MacCabe, "Theory and Film," 11) In its materiality, the text itself is the placing, in regard to which "reading is concretely accomplished in an act which is . . . what speech is in regard to language; namely, an event and instance of discourse." (Ricoeur, *Hermeneutics*) The reading will also be historically determinate in any particular case. To this extent, Leavis's concepts of "the third realm," though clearly inadequately theorized (without a concept of ideology), and of a reading as a "process of creation in response to the poet's words," are potentially infinitely more sophisticated than MacCabe's auto-critique, which merely succeeds in swapping one untenable position (the text as "immutable structure") for another ("the text has no separate existence"), and which leaves us with the banalities of Vladimir Lenin's analysis of Leo Tolstoy and the historicist reductivism of a "class analysis" dependent on an undialectical notion of "class" which has been untenable for at least 150 years. (MacCabe, "Theory and Film," 22–24, 25)

The nullity of Willemen's account of "productivity" can be gauged on the same scale. On the one hand, raw materials "possess their own particular characteristics, thus facilitating or preventing a number of operations." ("Notes," 17) Two pages later, they actually acquire "structural properties," which would indeed seem to constitute a limitation. On the other hand, we are offered, in the name of "productivity," a model of reading indistinguishable from that "mere subjectivism" which would be sententiously lambasted if it appeared in the guise of Durgnatism ("Wouldn't it be interesting if . . .?") but which acquires instant respectability from the name of Barthes. No one for a moment denies that "writing and reading are two moments of equal value," and clearly, for the reader, the text "comes into existence" in the reading, both of which propositions Willemen could glean from a perusal of *Scrutiny*. But, Barthes to the contrary (*Pleasure*, 11), we must be concerned with "the integrity of the text" unless we prefer doodling to reading: the text always precedes the reader in a way which Ricoeur's formulation suggests. The desire to avoid (quite rightly) any simple subject/object relation (the myth of "presence") is perpetually in danger of denying the object altogether.

Oedipus and Narrative

Let us turn, then, to Oedipus. Barthes's almost offhand identification of the *process* of narrative as an Oedipal structure concludes with the remark, in parenthesis—"This is written after having seen Murnau's *City Girl* [1930]"—a film which is specifically concerned at a narrative/thematic level with the figure and function of the Father. At the same time, the storytelling/Oedipus analogy is clinched in a generalizing paraphrase which locates in both figure and function "a way of searching for one's origin, speaking one's conflict with the Law, entering into the dialectic of tenderness and hatred." (Barthes, *Pleasure,* 47) Heath appropriates the strategy: films in which an "Oedipal fold" is discernible at the thematic level are felt to jus-tify the union of Oedipus and narrative in terms of "identity, center, perspective, oneness, the vision of the unified and unifying subject." ("Screen Images," 35) The linguistic strategy whereby the stockpiling of appositional clauses is used to establish dubious relations between discrete propositions is a recurrent feature of Heath's style, the verbal flow carrying with it, in this case, the somewhat tendentious suggestion (derived from Barthes) that monocular perspective "constructs" a sort of spiritually monocular spectator. On the abstract level of nar-rative as thing-in-itself, the Oedipal relation has entirely lost its specificity and dwindled into a series of vague assertions about the reader's illusion of a coherent identity which depend for their own coherence on the surreptitious reading-in of the psychoanalytic connotations whose relevance the argument is supposed to establish. On the other hand, the specificity is instantly recuperated by recourse to *particular* narratives.

On inquiry, we discover that what lies beyond the "containment" imposed by narrative is a dream of eternal fluidity, "a flow of images (flashes of movement and energy, sheets of rhythmic multiplicity)" (Heath, "Narrative Space," 102)—the pulsing Heraclitean flux of the Barthesian music-text which narrative "captures and regulates." We are reminded of Kristeva, and Johnston's use of her, and this archetypal romantic vision of anarchic, spontaneous energies liberated from the tyranny of bourgeois form sits rather curiously with *Screen*'s declaration of independence from romantic aesthetics. A brief comparison of Baudelaire, Arthur Rimbaud, and Barthes is sufficient to indicate the decadence of this particular impulse, which—hardly surprisingly—is no longer capable of inspiring anything more valuable than a sort of highbrow camp. The romanticism extends to the use of psychoanalysis. Hence, the enormous attractive-ness of Lacan's description of the drives as "montage"), from which we proceed to the defini-tion of narrative as "film's secondary revision"—that mechanism of censorship which, Freud remarks in *The Interpretation of Dreams*, fills up the gaps in the dream structure with "shreds and patches," imposing a misleading appearance of rationality. Once more, the metaphor is basically the same: narrative as repression.

The problem, then, lies in regarding narrative specifically as the means by which "a film's multiple articulations" are contained as "a single articulation" (Heath, "Screen Images," 35), and the extent to which the containment of the *articulation* is the containment of a process of *meaning*. Thus, (a) if Heath's proposition about "the time of (narrative) film" is applicable to *Meet Me in St. Louis* (1944), it applies equally, at that level of generalization, to any artifact, and (b) both *Taxi Driver* (1976), as an example of "the novelistic (as) the category of the realisation of narrative," and *Numéro deux* (1975), as an example of a film which refuses the novelistic, are "shut in to the return at last of [their] initial images." (Heath, "Contexts," 41) Both are also, very emphatically, "enclosed in a vision"—Travis Bickle's and Jean-Luc Godard's, respectively.

"The title of the novelistic," according to Heath, is the "Family Romance":

> Narrative maps a memory in film from the novelistic as the reimaging of the individu-al as subject, the very representation of identity as the coherence of a past reappropri-ated—the past 'in' the film . . . and 'of' the film (the join of the images, the holding of the spectator as the unifying position of their relation)." ("Screen Images," 35)

We have, then, two propositions: (a) that the thematic material of "the novel" can be analyzed in terms of the family romance; and (b) that the *mode* of "the novel," as distinct from its thematic material, constantly reproduces the reader within the "relations and positions" of the family romance, constantly re-creates an impression of coherent selfhood in terms of a reappropriation of the past. (Heath, "Screen Images," 41) Let us assume for a moment that that last phrase is an adequate description of family romance and that (b) as a whole is true. It immediately becomes rather difficult to distinguish the "novelistic" from the mode of, say, *The Divine Comedy* or *Sir Gawain and the Green Knight*, not to mention that of Chartres Cathedral. This is scarcely surprising, since the "holding of the spectator as the unifying position" of subjectivity and institutions has been a matter with which art has often been concerned. As a description of a specific literary form, the description lays itself open to the charge of facility.

If art *in abstracto*, as social practice, might function in certain instances in terms of the binding-in of individuals and institutions, the extent to which any particular work of art functions in those terms is to be gauged not by the fact that it uses certain conventions but by its use of them—that is, dynamically. Heath's conception of narrative, as argued here, is essentially static and non-dialectical: the mode determines the work. While this is true, of course, it is equally true that the work determines the mode, and that any particular work is the product of a set of complex dialectical tensions between various operative modes and what is done in their realization. There are indeed novels which move toward the achievement of coherent identity in terms of the possession of the past as necessary order and the replacing of the subject in ideology—supremely in, as Robin Wood has argued, *Anna Karenina*. ("Levin and the Jam") But then this procedure is not the prerogative of novels. There are also novels which propose such a movement, but which are structurally too complex and problematic to accommodate it (for example, *Middlemarch*), novels which subvert such a movement by enforcing its arbitrariness (for example, late Dickens), and novels which refuse to confirm whether the movement has been achieved (for example, *Daniel Deronda*). There is also an entire genre of novels (the American novel, from James Fenimore Cooper onward) which is concerned precisely to analyze the impossibility of those achieved unities which Heath feels to be the hallmarks of the "novelistic." This is not to say that the themes, imagery, structure, and iconography of *Pierre* and *The Marble Faun* cannot be read in terms of the family romance, but then, so can *Beowulf*. In fact, the refusal of dialectics extends right down the line: the mode determines the work determines the reader.

Freud and Fiction

I wish to add a word, parenthetically, about the value judgments which the use of psychoanalysis here (and elsewhere in *Screen*) covertly enforces, and about the relation between the "novelistic" and Freud's case histories.

a. "In a sense (therapeutic, efficacious), psychoanalysis replaces one story, this mesh of fantasy, obsession, symptom, with another, which tells the truth of the former, makes up the history of the subject." (Heath, "Contexts," 39) While Heath goes on to balance this claim with the traditional alibi of psychoanalysis (the cure is interminable

417

because of the working of the death instincts), the passage proposes an opposition between (neurotic) fantasy and truth which is uncomfortably puritanical in emphasis. It is quickly confirmed in the use of a quotation from Freud to associate "family romance and the production and use of fictions" with the "correction of actual life," and the claim that "film fiction. . .[invests] in a constant repetition of family romance fantasising." (41) A comparison of the use of the quotation with its context in Freud's "Creative Writers and Daydreaming" makes it clear that Heath is passing a negative value judgment on the "imaginative activity" as a form of escapism, and the claim that the "imaginary" and "objectification" are always alienating is, of course, central to Lacan (despite his repeated repudiation of existentialism, the concept is pure Sartre). In both cases, the suggestion that fictions serve necessarily to "correct actual life" seems to me unhelpful and banal.

One would be more chary about making such a point if *Screen* were less insistent on the "scientific objectivity" of its use of psychoanalysis, but it seems to me hypocritical to deny that the particular way in which *Screen* has associated the pleasure of narrative film with forms of imaginary alienation is based in a rationalist-idealist rather than a Marxist ideology. It is a truism that Hollywood has "invested in fantasizing," and that truism makes a point of major significance, but what is immediately in question is the validity of the conceptual complex of Family Romance/fiction/imaginary alienation—that is, the suggestion that a particular narrative mode re-creates a fictional identity engendered universally by the socialization of individuals. We are brought back, as always, to the Procrustean bed of the Lacanian myth of the Fall into the Imaginary, and the formula fails to account for that very area it is intended to accommodate—the area of ideological contradiction. Thus, according to Heath, *Meet Me in St. Louis* and *The Exorcist* (1973) share an identical mode which re-images the subject in the terms of the family romance. ("Screen Images," 35) Splendid! The links between the two films are profoundly important. But then why are they different? Why does *The Exorcist* exist? Why is Tootie there in Minnelli's film? And what conceivable coherence is constructed in either—in text or in reader? It can scarcely be argued that replacement in the family romance is unproblematic in either.

b. Heath claims that Freud's case histories "as Freud writes them [are] the novel overturned (where 'overturned' indicates a work in and against)." ("Screen Images") While the thesis has a certain validity—consider, for example, Freud's avowed sense of the difficulty of finding an adequate form for the writing up of the Wolf-Man analysis (*From the History of an Infantile Neurosis*)—it seems to me, rather, that the case histories are markedly characterized by that arbitrary closure and that elimination of areas of contradiction with which Freud is unable to deal, which Heath finds characteristic of the novel. Schatzman has analyzed such processes in Freud's reading of the Schreber case. "I parted from him, regarding him as cured . . . Since then the patient has felt normal and behaved unexceptionably," Freud remarks of the Wolf-Man, adding, with the familiar supreme complacency, that his patient's total destitution during World War I has "probably contributed to the consolidation of his recovery by gratifying his sense of guilt." (*Collected Papers*, vol. III, 480) One has to look elsewhere to discover that the Wolf-Man continued to see psychoanalysts to the end of his life and that he wrote in 1963, "the conflicts are still the same." (Gardiner, 372) Freud's case histories read less like the novel overturned than like symbolist dramas (compare, say, the chamber plays of August Strindberg), enacted within condensed, interior landscapes in which institutions, when present, figure as the functions of psychodrama. Clearly, as such they have their efficacy, but no Freudian analysis approaches the complexity of George Eliot's analysis of, say, Gwendolen Harleth, Bulstrode, and Mrs. Transome, in which the construction of neurosis in relation to specific institutions and ideological positions is the focus of attention.

Related to this are those alarming hiatuses which occur repeatedly in Freud's exposition of his cases, of which the following is typical. Dora

> had once again been insisting that Frau K. only loved her father because he was *ein vermögender Mann* ("a man of means"). Certain details of the way in which she expressed herself (which I pass over here, like most other purely technical parts of the analysis) led me to see that behind this phrase its opposite lay concealed; namely, that her father was *ein unvermögender Mann* ("a man without means"). ("Fragment of an Analysis of a Case of Hysteria," *Collected Papers*, vol. III, 58)

("Without means" carries a colloquial second-level meaning of "impotent.") This is precisely the voice of the omniscient narrator, whose ideological position is repressed and who exists outside the contradictions he expounds; indeed, Freud speaks elsewhere of "the network of causes and effects that I shall now proceed to lay bare," for which "I can claim objective validity." ("Psychogenesis," *Collected Papers*, vol. III, 213) As an overturning of "novelistic" devices, this is scarcely impressive. Freud is he-who-sees ("led me to see that . . ."). Before his all-consuming gaze, illusion melts from the real like the snows of spring, and the real is then offered to us as unmediated "truth." That "led me to see" obviates all further comment: the guarantee is in the analytic eye. At its extreme, this produces the sort of analysis contained in the "Psychogenesis" (202–31), which is primarily interesting in terms of the imposition of a male authorial discourse onto a female discourse (the patient as transgressor) which resists it at every point, the resistance producing those internal contradictions which expose the narrative discourse. Freud is confronted by a woman who is not only (as he admits) completely un-neurotic but also proud of her homosexuality, and who also maintains a certain distance from and indifference to the psychoanalytic revelations. Freud's revenge is swift and systematic. The love of women can only be explained by embitterment following the frustration of a desire for men, and the indifference to Freud by the transference to the analyst of her antipathy to her father whom, nevertheless, she *really* desires. This, Freud remarks, is how things are "in reality." (222) So men really come off rather well; instead of being impertinent intruders, Freud and the father are really love objects. What is "overturned"? It is pure Hemingway.

"Transparency"

The "novelistic" is not "the category of the realization of narrative." One can, of course, generalize about the novel, as about any artistic form. It is possible to demonstrate that *Moby Dick*, *Wuthering Heights*, *Les Liaisons dangereuses*, *War and Peace*, and *Doctor Faustus* have certain elements in common. It is even easier to demonstrate that the "realization" of narrative is remarkably different in each case, and that in any discussion of narrative form, it transpires very rapidly that the category of the "novelistic" is, at best, vague, arid and, at worst, actually obstructive. It is conceivable, perhaps, that someone might wish to read Thomas Mann as "bourgeois realism" gone mad, and to interpret the information that Adrian in *Dr. Faustus* "had a view of the square, the medieval City Hall, the Gothic Marienkirche . . . the statue of Roland and the bronze statue of Handel" as items of local color, verifiable by any observant tourist, designed to assure us of the reality of Halle, the reliability of the narrator, the cohesion of the narrative world, and the certainty of our own identity as omniscient readers. (91) We are being offered a transparent image of the world from the perspective of a speaker to whom we give credence, and with whom we identify in such a way that our confidence in our own perception is reinforced. This is what Halle really looks like from Adrian's window. This information about the objective physical world is objectively true. Therefore, it is possible to obtain reliable knowledge through sense perceptions. The reality of the world, and my own ability to know about it, are assured.

While it would be possible to interpret the information in this way, the reader who did so would not simply be misreading the particular passage, but also be failing to perceive the "category of the realization of the narrative." That is, he/she would not be reading the novel in any significant sense, for the point is that the information is *not* transparent. Each detail of the view from Adrian's window has a complex symbolic significance in relation to nonlinear narrative patterns, and the same might be said of, for instance, a passage of "realistic" descriptive prose, such as the first paragraph of *Middlemarch*. To read the information as transparent is not to read it. Work on modes of narrative in the novel—let alone in the cinema—has scarcely begun, but any analysis of "realism" which ignores its status as symbolic, or poetic, drama, or fails to observe the ways in which the modes of the popular novel and the popular cinema relate to those of other narrative forms, such as allegory, is in danger of radically misconstruing the relationship between text and reader. (See, for example, Gay Clifford's *The Transformations of Allegory*.) To reduce "narrative" to something known as "the novel," and then to reduce Hollywood to the "novelistic," is to make all three categories incomprehensible. *Meet Me in St. Louis* has little to do with novels and a great deal to do with the pastoral convention. The complex interrelationship between the conventions of the various genres and their various cultural determinants fails to be contained within the most capacious Platonic form. One should remember also that the narrative forms developed within white American culture are themselves highly idiosyncratic and relate directly to narrative forms which precede the novel. Herman Melville and Nathaniel Hawthorne are not working in the same genre as Flaubert and Stendhal, and while Hollywood forms have more in common with *The Scarlet Letter* than with *Le Rouge et le Noir*, they are also influenced by forms of "low" culture which have nothing to do with the novel at all.

Both *Taxi Driver* and *Numéro deux* are "fixed by writing" which constructs perspectives of reading, and both contain multiple articulations (ramifying, nonlinear structures of meaning) within a single articulation (concrete form). This is not to say that either is "homogeneous" or that either "constructs" a homogeneous spectator. What is of crucial significance is not the myth that any one form of artistic practice imposes homogeneity on heterogeneity to a greater or lesser extent than any other, but in Willemen's phrase, "to have knowledge of the principles by which symbolic codes function" ("Notes," 18)—that is, to have access to the procedures through which structure is articulated, and thus to be able to read the heterogeneity on which any artistic practice imposes a certain formal closure.

Hollywood in Five Easy Lessons

It follows from this, perhaps, that when one looks for convincing analyses of the concrete realization of particular "classical" texts, the record is curiously uneven. Heath's reading of *Touch of Evil*, however much one might wish to disagree with it, is clearly criticism of great distinction. Johnston has produced trenchant and stimulating essays on *Anne of the Indies* (1951) and "The Place of Woman in the Cinema of Raoul Walsh," and Mark Nash has written interestingly on *Vampyr* (1932) and the *fantastique* ("*Vampyr*"), an interest which his recent pamphlet on Carl Dreyer fails to retain. Elsewhere, the prospect is depressing. I have commented already on Willemen's reading of *Pursued* (1947). The "construction" of Jacques Tourneur, though somewhat less fanciful, still inclines incorrigibly toward text forcing, most notably in the amazing attempt to prove that *I Walked with a Zombie* (1943) embodies the "breakdown" of the "classical realism" of *Stars in My Crown* (1950) on no better ground than that Willemen finds the Christian religion unacceptable. Indeed, the uncontrollable impulse to indulge in anti-Christian polemics leads him to describe the complex, qualifying interrelations set up by the latter film's formal symmetry as "the compulsion to repeat"—which means, of course, that it is governed by the death instinct. Like a Mozart symphony, one presumes. Geoffrey Nowell-Smith's ruminations on melodrama conclude with the proposition that ideological contradiction is "studiously closed off [by] most Hollywood forms" but emerges once more in the melodrama, "at least in the versions of it that are due to" a few privileged auteurs—in this case, Ophüls, Minnelli, and Douglas Sirk. ("Minnelli and Melodrama," 118) Alarming as it may be to have to turn for a more radical suggestion to Robin Wood, it seems to me that the thesis that the genres are themselves the product of ideological contradiction, and that such contradiction emerges from the most basic, trans-generic conventions before the simplest narrative has been proposed, is more likely to lead to interesting developments than a surreptitious revamping of the auteur theory. (See, for example, Robin Wood's "Ideology, Genre, Auteur.") Elsewhere, readers of *Emma*, *Daniel Deronda*, *Our Mutual Friend*, and Victorian melodramas may be pleased to discover that "melodrama, like realism, supposes a world of equals . . . a world without the exercise of social power." (Nowell-Smith, "Minnelli and Melodrama," 115)

Mulvey, in "Visual Pleasure and Narrative Cinema" (1975), when she actually gets down to cases after some valuable preliminary generalizations, succeeds in producing a discussion of Alfred Hitchcock which tells one nothing one has not already learned from Jean Douchet (credited) and Robin Wood (uncredited). She also offers an account of *To Have and Have Not*

(1944) which inverts the development, and hence the significance, of the narrative (Lauren Bacall does not cease to be, but becomes, a showgirl, public performance and private sexual invitation meeting in the final song) and misconstrues its ethos (the characteristic emphasis on impermanence—"Maybe it's just for a day"—and the defining tone of Bacall's performance prohibiting a sense of her as the hero's "property"). Finally, Mulvey gives us an analysis of Josef von Sternberg that is all but indistinguishable from the crudities of Paul Rotha and John Grierson, and totally inadequate to the complex poetic structures of *The Devil Is a Woman* (1935) or *The Shanghai Gesture* (1941). MacCabe's discussion of *Klute* (1971) achieves the dubious feat of contradicting itself in the space of a couple of sentences: (a) Bree's "estimation of the situation" at the end of the film is wrong; and (b) "Bree's discourse is more nearly adequate to the truth at the end of the film than at the beginning." ("Realism," 11) He also manages to impose definitive closure on the structured irresolution of the final scene and to suppress the explicit identification, through the imagery, of Klute and the murderer.

Jacqueline Rose's reading of *The Birds* (1963) is also remarkable for its attempts to impose consistency on a text characterized by its systematic ambiguity. (97) Not only are the attacks not wholly interpretable in terms of "the look" (the death of Dan Fawcett is an irritating discrepancy) but also the attempt to limit "the look" to Melanie radically misreads the attack on the children's party, in which the presence of Annie and Mrs. Brenner is crucial. "The oppositions set up by the narrative" are not resolved in any sense (compare Rose's account of the ending with Wood's in *Hitchcock's Films*), and the reading consistently fails to distinguish meanings which are effectively operative in the text from those which are not. (See, for example, Michael Riffaterre's "Describing Poetic Structures.") The suggestion, for instance, that "the relationship between glass and vision is punned constantly throughout the film" has recourse to various images of glass and vision, but it is unable to define what significant relationship links "Michele's cracked glasses" to "the schoolroom windows." Most damagingly, the article takes on board all the impedimenta of paranoia, to the extent of positing, on an analogy with the "primordial aggressivity" of the imaginary relation, a latent aggressivity within the shot/counter-shot convention, and that code's relation, by "an intrinsic property," to the relation between mother and child. The idea of "code" has hardened into an objective entity with "properties," and Rose not only finds herself able to attribute the birds to "the inherent instability of the film's own system"—a sort of symptom of its paranoia—but also to conclude, after Raymond Bellour, that "the camera has to identify" with the positions it assumes, as if it were a consciousness. (97) Doubtless—we have it on Freud's authority—the paranoia of Hollywood movies can be associated with their repressed homosexuality.

Screen has contributed much which it would be foolish to ignore, the measure of which can be expressed by suggesting that Heath, however intensely one might wish to disagree with him, is one of the most stimulating and distinguished minds at present engaged in film criticism. Simply to place him beside Barthes is to separate the serious critic from a writer who has always exhibited those elements of charlatanism which have since established themselves to the exclusion of everything else. But it is necessary to make distinctions, not only within a corpus of work but also between it and others, and while Heath's criticism and the development of feminist analyses by Johnston and others seem to me potentially the most valuable develop-

Paranoia in Alfred Hitchcock's *The Birds*. Personal collection of the editor.

ments to date, disagreement must finally involve itself with the ethos which gives them their context. The ethos is partially explicable in historical terms, in that *Screen* intervened at a moment when the question as to what film studies should be had scarcely been asked (indeed, the answer had been felt to be self-evident), and operated henceforth, as far as confronting the serious issues was concerned, within a film culture characterized largely by the journalistic, the complacent, and the trivial. That is to say that *Screen* had to deal with resistance rather than criticism.

We have *Screen* to thank for making the issues apparent, for concerning itself with the radical transformations in the forms and substance of education which the recognition of those issues necessitates, and for helping, in recent years, to make the Edinburgh Film Festival a significant event. We also have *Screen* to thank for posing the issues in terms of Althusser, Barthes, and Lacan. None of these writers is unusable, but to proceed, like MacCabe, from the mysticism of André Bazin to the mysticism of Lacan, and then to suggest not only that one has got somewhere but that one has performed a scientific operation, is to confuse turning one's head with making a journey. While the seriousness of *Screen*'s political commitment is beyond question, it is to be doubted whether either the materials employed or (inseparably) the manner of their employment are consonant with political radicalism. When one talks about the circumscription of "positions of meaning," one is not talking about the "submission to language" but about the delimitation of language possibilities (the possibilities of conceptual thought) within particular, determinate, analyzable, alterable social conditions. I would accept that psychoanalysis can be made helpful, but not "fixed and founded" as an Althusserian life buoy, nor transfigured as the mystical algebra of the mind of man, let alone as the monstrous birth engendered by marrying the two. While the alliance of "the ideological and the imaginary" through the construction of the subject in language has produced a theory of ideology of very satisfying coherence, it seems to me scarcely adequate to the most elementary social organization. To this extent, the fixity in the concept "signifier"—Saussure's fears for it have proved well-founded—is necessarily reactionary in emphasis, even before Lacan sees fit to infuse it with *l'esprit libre*. Lacan's theory of language need concern itself neither with history nor with change. Indeed, the Lacanian unconscious is the very triumph of Structuralism, the quintessence of its aspiration to "the order of things." To postulate, theoretically, intractable monoliths and then to assert as a political principle that they are, after all, neither intractable nor monolithic may be preferable to the first procedure in isolation, but it scarcely casts a happy light on the claims made for either.[2]

The Philosophy of the Pigeonhole: Wisconsin Formalism and "The Classical Style" (1989)

The following is an extract from a forthcoming book entitled *Reading Hollywood*, and it is offered here as an essay on critical method. The nature of my assumptions will be clear enough from the essay itself, but perhaps it will be as well to begin with a brief statement of principle. I assume, firstly, that all works of art represent an intervention in a culture and that interpretation is a process of defining what the nature of that intervention is. I also assume that the aim of interpretation is to arrive at a judgment of the value of the work. Cultural analysis divorced from an explicit evaluative project leads at best to the accumulation of data which have a potential critical usefulness, and at worst to the rationalization, as objective truth, of an evaluative project which is never presented as such. Evaluation without cultural analysis leads at best to the expression of intelligent opinions and at worst to "I like it because I like it." The critic should aim, to begin with, to understand what Gerard Manley Hopkins called "the sakes" of the work: what do its makers think of the work as being? What do they want to do? What is the significance of their wanting to do this? The critic should proceed then to an account of what the work *does*, which may well be very different from anything grasped by its project. This inquiry is already implicitly evaluative: the critic writes from a point of view, one which ought to be as conscious and as explicit as possible. It should also be relevant, and the only test of its relevance is the work, which is not something simply available to be constituted at will by the discourse of criticism but a historical object to which criticism aspires to be adequate.

It follows that the critic should read without inappropriate bias. We cannot properly object to *The Pilgrim's Progress*, for example, because we think that John Bunyan's theology is false: it is not a valid criticism of a work that it disagrees with the critic. What we judge is the work itself as the material form of a sensibility defined by, and addressing itself to, a culture, and we derive our sense of this form from an analysis of the work both as historical project and realized meaning. Interpretation and evaluation are, in any case, continuous with each other: interpretation necessarily implies, and appeals for the reader's assent to, a judgment. The critic should be aware of this fact and should write accordingly as a person judging in the present, from a given position, that such and such a work is or is not significant and valuable for what s/he takes to be creative cultural life now. The critical enterprise, in other words, is intrinsically—and should be frankly—political. There can be no impartial discourse, and if readers do not know where the critic stands in relation to the work, they have no means of defining or assessing the critic's judgments—which may, of course, be found seriously to misrepresent the work. The generalized point will be seen to have its relevance for the case I discuss below, which seems to me to represent in an extreme form the two most serious of all critical errors: indifference to the concrete historical particularity of works of art, and the subordination of interpretation to judgments of value, derived from *idées reçues*, which precede the act of analysis.

> It is . . . evident that the interrelationships between stylistic procedures are best discovered when one of them is used in particularly outrageous fashion, provoking a reaction in others. That is why the extreme cases give more information than the average. At any rate, the average cannot give one the range of a style—only the extremes can do that, and they alone can endow the average with its true sense. We may say that the extremes give the outline of the style, and the average gives its center of gravity. A middle-point has no significance until we know what it stands between. (Rosen, 163)

The Classical Hollywood Cinema by David Bordwell, Janet Staiger, and Kristin Thompson is the first serious attempt in the history of film criticism to challenge that division of labor between theory and historical scholarship which has been so persistent, characteristic, and unhelpful a feature of Hollywood studies. The magnitude of the authors' ambition is given in their subtitle: "Film Style and Mode of Production to 1960." They offer to define the nature of "a distinct and homogeneous style [which] has dominated American studio filmmaking" between 1917 and 1960—"a style whose principles remain quite constant across decades, genres, studios, and personnel." (Bordwell et al., 3) Further, they offer to demonstrate that every aspect of this style was determined by the Hollywood cinema's "dependence upon a specific economic mode of film production and consumption." (Bordwell et al., 6) This is a very large offer indeed, and it is no doubt the book's daunting art of appearing to account for everything which has inhibited the widespread argument and controversy one would naturally expect to follow from the publication of a work advancing claims of this kind. I say "naturally" because the claims seem to me to be, for all their plausibility, obviously false, and if the authors fail so largely to substantiate them, that is because nothing of the kind could be substantiated: the project, as defined, is unrealizable.

In what follows, I am primarily concerned with the matter of "film style," and I have concentrated, accordingly, on the first of the book's seven parts: "The Classical Hollywood Style, 1917–60." The contents page attributes this section to Bordwell alone, but since he regularly employs the first person plural, and since the function of Part One is to adumbrate the theoretical principles which structure the book as a whole, I have taken it for granted that, though he may not employ a uniform "group style," he speaks nevertheless in a group voice, and I have therefore, where necessary, attributed the particular form of the opinions he expresses to his collaborators as well as to himself.

When I say that Part One is without question the worst part of the book, I should not be taken to mean that in later sections the standard of the criticism improves or that the theory applied to the films becomes less disastrously inappropriate. It is true to say, however, that my criticisms (which are entirely hostile) will be focused on the one part of *The Classical Hollywood Cinema* where the skills in which its authors' qualities manifest themselves most impressively are not called for: Part One is, from first word to last, pure unmitigated Theory. The strictly scholarly parts of the book are on the whole very good, and had Bordwell and his colleagues confined themselves to the tasks which scholarship can properly attempt, one would have been happy to recommend their work, without qualification, as an invaluable reference for all serious students of Hollywood movies. As things stand, however, the recommendation must be very severely qualified indeed, for the scholarship is attached to and serves in its context to rationalize, a critical discourse which is in every respect unacceptable and against which one is bound to protest. The authors tell us that the scholarship and the critical theory are interdependent, each illuminating and drawing sustenance from the other, but it is at least pleasant to report (the theory being what it is) that this is not the case. A divorce is very easily effected, and one can return with profit to the scholarly material even after one has decided that the accompanying attempt to theorize it may remain hereafter unread.

This is not to say that the scholarship should not be read with a critical eye: its limitations are summed up in the phrase "mode of production" in the book's title. Staiger's descriptions of successive forms of management in the Hollywood film industry are useful and important, but they suffer (as Hollywood histories generally do) from the author's assumption that it is possible to extrapolate the object "Hollywood" from the social history of twentieth-century American capitalism as a whole. Staiger takes over the concept of mode of production from Marx, but she does not take over Marx's analytical method, and she treats "the Hollywood mode of production" and its development as if this mode were a thing in itself which can be studied independently of the culture within which the development took place. It is significant that on the one occasion when she sets out to remedy this omission, and discusses the implications for Hollywood studies of various attempts to theorize the logic both of monopoly and of advanced capitalism (Bordwell et al., 314–17), she displays an economism which answers exactly to the formalism characteristic of the book's aesthetics. Momentarily, Hollywood is brought into contact with mode of production in the larger sense, but capitalism itself is construed as a purely economic structure rather than a structure of social relations, and the contact remains purely external. Staiger derives no more from her excursion through Rudolf Hilferding, Ernest Mandel, and Paul M. Sweezy than "new methods for analyzing the film industry" (316): the wider world is acknowledged to exist, but it only confirms the autonomy of the object which has been detached from it.

This is, perhaps, predictable, and although we should be aware of the limitation, it does not detract from the interest of the data which Staiger assembles so cogently. The consequences of the authors' belief in a "distinct and homogeneous" classical style for their exposition of developments in film technology are very much more serious: here, again and again, the book's drastic critical/theoretical shortcomings intrude on the scholarship, to its detriment as scholarship. Consider, for example, Bordwell's account of deep focus cinematography. (Bordwell et al., 341–52) Naturally, the account entails an extensive discussion of the development of new kinds of lenses, arc lamps, and film stock, as well as new techniques in the process of film developing, and Bordwell and his colleagues do this sort of thing very well. In circumstances such as these, they are under no obligation to read or to judge, and they conduct the reader through material which might easily become dull in a lucid and lively manner. It is also an advantage of Bordwell's approach that he shows the reverse of a tendency to indulge the idea that deep focus arrived with a bang in *Citizen Kane* (1941), which he shows to have been, if not typical, yet exemplary of a contemporary preoccupation with the deepening of visual space.

However, when the same approach leads Bordwell to write that "These innovations are not all that drastic. Within the context of the classical style, such depth devices were quickly assigned familiar functions" (345), we begin to feel that he is demanding more of his method than it can properly yield, and the feeling grows as we read through the analysis of the career of Gregg Toland which immediately follows. The career, as Bordwell renders it, is a familiar tale: the story of the innovative and adventurous "creative artist" who "developed too eccentric a style" which was subsequently "modified" (that is, as Bordwell makes plain, recuperated) "to fit classical norms." (348–49) It is taken for granted that the "too eccentric" style of *Citizen Kane* is Toland's, despite the fact that it has much more in common with the style of *The Magnificent Ambersons* (1942) and *Touch of Evil* (1958) than it does with any of the films that Toland made without Orson Welles. But I am less concerned here with questions of authorship (whichever way one looks at it, Toland's influence on *Kane* was decisive) than with the similarity between "the Gregg Toland story" narrated by Bordwell and "the Orson Welles story" narrated so often before. Bordwell admits, of course, that the style of *Citizen Kane*, apart from being "too eccentric," is also remarkably inflexible—"The most famous deep-focus shots in the film . . . are notably rigid and posed, relying greatly upon frontality and narrowly circumscribed figure movement" (347)—and he illustrates the "new flexibility" of later works with the scene of Dana Andrews's phone call from *The Best Years of Our Lives* (1946) which so pleased André Bazin. Yet, while new flexibility might seem to connote "greater expressiveness," Bordwell continues to refer to the development of deep focus cinematography after *Kane* in negative and, at times, explicitly abusive terms: "The ability to execute a shot in depth became one more mark of the expert cinematographer, but the wary professional chose not to call attention to deep focus by making it a personal trademark." (352)

This vision of wary professional experts betraying, while also cashing in on (with what looks like conscious cynicism), the innovations of an "artist" who has rocked the classical boat is offered by Bordwell as a fact, though he brings forward nothing better in support of it than a review of *The Little Foxes* (1941) in *American Cinematographer* which complains that the depth of field makes the action difficult to follow, and another review (from the same periodical) which praises Arthur Miller's "eloquent use of the modern increased-depth technique" in *How Green Was My Valley* (1941) for its avoidance of "the brittle artificiality which has so often accompanied the use" of deep focus. (348–49) How we get from these reviews to the canny journeymen who prefer not to jeopardize their careers "by making deep focus a personal trademark" I do not know. It seems a long way, and one might begin by asking Bordwell whether, in his opinion, the cinematography of Stanley Cortez in *The Magnificent Ambersons* is to be thought of as falling mainly under the heading of "wary professionalism" or that of "new flexibility." That an extended discussion of the use of deep focus in Hollywood should not even mention, once, a work which is by any reckoning central to the topic cannot but strike us as remarkable (especially as the film does turn up later on in the chapter on "widescreen processes and stereophonic sound" [362]), though when we think about it, the explanation is not hard to find. *Ambersons* is, by Bordwell's standard, a perfectly orthodox genre movie which could hardly fail to present itself to him as supremely exemplary of "the assimilation of deep focus to classical norms." (351) He shrinks, however—for indefinable reasons—from suggesting that the film represents a judicious watering down, by Cortez and Welles ("wary professionals" both), of the unorthodox formal audacities of Toland, and solves his dilemma by ignoring the existence of *The Magnificent Ambersons*.

Deep focus, in fact, is a pretty tough nut to crack from Bordwell's point of view. *Citizen Kane*, whatever we may think of it, is hardly notable for its conventionality and formal reticence, and yet it is a "classical Hollywood film" which plainly had a profound influence on other "classical Hollywood films"; the evidence, as Bordwell feelingly says, "seems to be baldly there on the screen." (341) The scholar, therefore, must find a way of showing (a) that *Kane* was a deviant work by virtue of the obtrusiveness of its style; (b) that this style, on the other hand, was not too obtrusive to be absorbed by the "the classical paradigm," which was visibly changed; and (c) that despite this change, nothing changed, for "the classical style promptly assigned the new techniques to already-canonized functions." (339) In the light of this devious project, Welles becomes a major headache, since he went on to make several movies which labor under the triple disadvantage of being classical genre films, having exceptionally flamboyant and obtrusive "styles," and being artistically superior to *Citizen Kane*. Toland, however, recommends himself ideally as the stylistic freebooter who went too far and who, having (of course!) endowed the norms with new flexibility, bowed to peer pressure and went to work for William Wyler.

It turns out after all, then, that *Citizen Kane* has the conventional status for Bordwell that it has for everyone else, and it certainly does not occur to him to ask whether the phrase "brittle artificiality" does not point in the direction of a valid negative criticism of that film's visual "style." Of course, no one will argue that the phrase will do on its own: deep focus does have expressive functions in *Kane*, even if the functions are not very complex and even if the expressed is very often the *superbia* [pride] implicit in Welles's relation to his protagonist. Brittle artificiality is certainly the term, however, for the deep-focus compositions in *Ball of Fire* (1941), which could hardly be more inert and academic, and if one hesitates to describe Toland as a "creative artist," for all his obvious brilliance, that is because the expressiveness of his photography is so intimately bound up with the dramatic context created for it by a particular director. Howard Hawks, as we might expect, is not interested in deep focus one way or the other: the shots are there because Toland has prestige and is shooting the film, but they are patently un-Hawksian, and Hawks neither protests against nor makes use of them; his interests lie elsewhere. The case is very different with John Ford and Welles, and it is no slight to Toland to suggest that *The Grapes of Wrath* (1940) looks so unlike *Citizen Kane* because the compositional style and thematic preoccupations of Ford are very unlike those of Welles. It is even more important to insist that the new flexibility of post-*Kane* deep focus cinematography was precisely that, and that "the assimilation of deep focus to classical norms" both transformed the norms and radically increased the expressive power of deep focus. It can be argued, indeed—as seems to be true, on Bordwell's own showing—that the new flexibility had already been achieved before *Citizen Kane* was made, and that *The Magnificent Ambersons* represents

"Eccentricity" and "obtrusiveness" in the style of Orson Welles's *Citizen Kane*. Personal collection of the editor.

not a retreat into classical conventionality but a recognition of the artistic limitations of what Bordwell calls "the grotesquely monumental depth" of the earlier work. (345) The "eccentricity" and "obtrusiveness" of *Kane*'s style are not in themselves virtues, and while the assimilation of deep focus undoubtedly made it less eccentric, it did not necessarily make it less visible and striking, as a number of Bordwell's examples amply demonstrate (and of course, many more could be found). When depth of field does look eccentric and obtrusive, it also looks like academy art—all the more incongruously in *Ball of Fire* because Hawks is as far from the academy as an artist can reasonably be—and here, perhaps, we glimpse the logic which leads Toland to Wyler: a photographer who dreamed of "perfect[ing] an 'ultimate focus' lens that could stop down to f-64" (Bordwell et al., 351) might well end up, in practice, producing a film which "reeks of the oils" (in Lord Byron's phrase) as strongly as *The Little Foxes* does.

The scholarship of *The Classical Hollywood Cinema* is very often sustained by the kind of assumptions about "the classical style" which obtain here, and it is time now to turn to the first part of the book, where these assumptions are spelled out and thematized. There is a sense in which my epigraph from Charles Rosen's splendid essay on Walter Benjamin, pertinent as it is to the case in hand, also misrepresents it by conceding too much to the method of Bordwell and his collaborators. The "extreme cases" may well give us "more information than the average," but it is not with the average that Bordwell is in fact concerned. What he gives us is the lowest common denominator, which he then construes not merely as the average itself but as the type of the extreme cases as well.

One's doubts begin at once, with Bordwell proposing "the concept of *group* style," and he goes on to suggest that "group styles" are to be thought of as sets of rules or norms which artists know and which they then proceed to obey or apply in their work. (Bordwell et al., 3ff) There is a certain sense, of course, in which this is perfectly true. Jacobean dramatists knew of the existence of a "rule" which stipulated that plays should be written in blank verse and which circumscribed by convention the occasions on which the dramatist might legitimately write in prose or use a metrical unit other than the unrhymed ten-syllable line, and William Shakespeare, Ben Jonson, and Thomas Middleton accordingly refrained from composing plays in couplets or terza rima. It is hardly possible to feel, however, that they understood the group style which they undoubtedly employed in this external and mechanistic kind of way. The whole point about group styles is that they are perceived by artists and their audiences as a significant means of articulating common social experience: the "rules" become rules because they conduce in some way to the exploration of a range of important, and widely shared, assumptions, feelings, and attitudes. This would seem to suggest that such rules leave, and are acknowledged to leave, very considerable leeway, and that they are present to those who submit to them less as constraints than as enabling possibilities. Indeed, when we examine the history of any given group style, we invariably discover that when the sense of constraint becomes paramount, the style begins both to ossify and to generate substantial cultural opposition.

It goes without saying that group styles are historically specific and that they exist in part as a set of formal limits, but we need to be very scrupulous in our definition of what this commonplace means. Franz Joseph Haydn did not wish to write, and could not conceivably have written, either the "Vespro della Beata Vergine" or "Pierrot Lunaire," and it may well seem, from the point of view of late twentieth-century sophistication, that this fact is obviously to be explained in terms of Haydn's "obedience to the rules" of the classical symphony. In fact, Haydn was not following rules at all: he was exploring the possibilities of a culturally significant artistic form, and his work was, and had the effect of being, a development and reinvention of the "norms" from which he started (and which, of course, he played a certain part in inventing in the first place). This work, and its effect, was possible precisely because the norms were continuous with his sensibility, and that working within (or, better, *with*) them allowed him to give material embodiment to that sensibility and to examine its nature and conditions. This sensibility was in no sense private: Haydn was not using a "group style" to express "himself." Artistic norms are cultural norms, and the deployment of them cannot be identified in any simple way with a process of individuation or "self-expression" (for all that this unfashionable idea seems to me to remain important in the discussion of art). To work with such norms is to work on and, in the major cases, to modify and change the terms of a public discourse which structures sensibility and which governs the ways in which art is able to signify, and engage with, the existing social world. No artist who impresses us as having major distinction relates to the norms of an artistic practice as structures external to him- or herself which are there to be appropriated and "applied," and when we come across a work in which it is apparent that the artist is working in a spirit of obedience to rules that have to be followed, we know that a negative judgment will sooner or later be called for.

In that they are social norms, the norms of an art are not "formal" in any sense of that word which is congenial to a formalist, but it does not follow from their determinate social existence that they therefore embody, absolutely and monolithically, the dominant value system of the culture which produced them. Their provenance can and must be referred to that value system, but they no more "reflect" or "express" it than, in any given case, they merely reflect or express the consciousness of the artist who happens to be using them. Further, all highly conventionalized group styles are remarkable for the way in which many of the artists who use them find ways of placing and challenging the values implicit in the norms, even when these values are, in the culture as a whole, very strictly policed and enforced. This fact is often overlooked, especially by cultural scholarship. It was argued for years, for example, that English Renaissance drama promulgated something called "the Elizabethan/Jacobean world-view," and that Shakespeare's tragedies (which were, after all, performed at, and partly sponsored by, the English court) were dedicated to exposing the disastrous consequences of tampering with a "natural" order guaranteed by, and dependent on, the sacred institutions of kingship. Many of the conventions of English Renaissance tragedy do indeed answer to such a description, but the majority of the plays written within those conventions do not. The status of artistic norms is extremely complex, and while they are not available for use in any way that the artist thinks fit, and may be said to foreclose the possibility of certain kinds of utterance completely, they do not necessarily exact a discourse which reproduces the values that they themselves embody.

The authors of *The Classical Hollywood Cinema* admit, of course, that the group style which they deduce from Hollywood movies allows of various kinds of formal choice and "offers a *range* of alternatives" to actual filmmakers (Bordwell et al., 5), but it is not too much to say that, in their description of the nature of these choices, they take it for granted that the films were made in the same spirit in which they offer to read them, with a like disregard for, and innocence of, all those aspects of artistic production which are designated by the concept of "expression." A subject, for whatever reason, suggests itself, and it is then structured according to the known principles of "classical narration": that is the basic argument. Logically enough, the habitual formalism of Hollywood's *artists* is answered by, and can be seen to conduce to, a formalist disposition on the part of the audience. Bordwell argues, to his credit, that what he calls the "illusionist" theory of narrative, which posits a spectator who is passively "constructed" by the classical text, is obviously unacceptable, and that Hollywood movies solicit an activity of reading from their audience, yet this activity—as he conceives it—amounts to little more than the learning and decipherment of the "schemata" in terms of which (we are to believe) the film was structured to begin with. Bordwell imagines that Hollywood's audiences consist of a series of miniature clones of himself, and although we might feel tempted to conclude, at first glance, that this vision is less infelicitous than that to which we have been accustomed by decades of Critical Theory, it turns out, in no very long run, that "miniature" is decidedly the operative word: the activities "called forth" by the classical film are "highly standardized and comparatively easy to learn." (7) For all their imputed "activity," Bordwell's spectators are in no better a position than *Screen*'s or Theodor W. Adorno's to appreciate the superior virtue of the avant-garde.

This virtue being in question, it is time to point out, perhaps, that the particular concept of group style to which Bordwell and his colleagues commit themselves (and which I, for the purposes of argument, have taken up from them) is utterly unintelligible. It is the implicitly—more often than not, explicitly—pejorative counterpart of the "unique internal stylistic norms" which Bordwell discovers "in the work of Dreyer, Bresson, Mizoguchi, Straub/Huillet, Ozu, Resnais, and Godard" (a concatenation of names which, I would say, already portends a serious failure of critical thought) and for the greater glory of which (he supposes) he has concocted his grotesque parody of Hollywood's "classicism." The paradoxical nature of the idea of a "unique norm" (81) should be enough to warn us against it: there is not, never has been, and never will be a work of art whose "style" derives from norms which are unique and internal to itself, and there has not been and cannot be a "group style" of the kind postulated in *The Classical Hollywood Cinema*. All styles are "group styles": that is to say, the style of any given artist is a more or less complex, adventurous, and idiosyncratic inflection of conventional cultural materials which, by definition, precede and create the conditions for the artist's work. Bordwell would like to believe otherwise, but he can only contrive to do so by inflating his norms and schemata into "a distinct and homogeneous" stylistic system in some cases (3) and completely ignoring their existence in others. His work on Yasujiro Ozu and Carl Dreyer—and Thompson's on Sergei Eisenstein—is very notably not characterized by its preoccupation with the traditions, conventions, and cultural circumstances within which these artists produced their films, and one might be forgiven if one failed to realize, from Bordwell's account, that Ozu was a commercial, genre filmmaker, and that he (and Kenji Mizoguchi) flourished under "conditions of production" which were in some ways very similar to Hollywood's. I agree with Bordwell that Ozu's "style" is "unique," and it is rather different from Alfred Hitchcock's. But it is no more sui generis than Hitchcock's (or any significant Hollywood director's) is "an 'unstable equilibrium' of classical norms." (5) When he is talking about Hollywood, Bordwell insists (in his way) on norms, modes of production, and the "bounds of difference" (70), and he inveighs against "the individualist emphases of auteur criticism." (4) But when Bordwell is talking about Ozu, he insists only on what he imagines (wrongly) to be the absolute distinctions between Ozu's procedures and the monolithic classical style he himself has constructed.

The pioneering earnestness, and the single-minded disingenuousness, with which the authors of *The Classical Hollywood Cinema* set about the joyless and laborious task of building their "model of the ordinary film" are staggering, and it cannot but strike us as inevitable that their "formalist approach," coexisting as it does with their foreknowledge of the conclusions they are going to reach, should lead them to take the "unprecedented" step (their own word) of applying "the practice of unbiased sampling" to the "stylistic analysis of the cinema." (10) If this step is indeed "unprecedented" (as I gladly suppose it to be), that is perhaps because it has seemed to earlier critics that the practice is so obviously inappropriate, and the "findings" it is likely to yield are so obviously fatuous, that they have preferred not to run the risk of having their names associated with a precedent of the kind. Moreover, it seems to me to be a telling symptom of the fundamentally primitive character of contemporary film theory (the primitiveness being perfectly compatible with—indeed, portentous of—the sophistication) that Bordwell and his colleagues did not at once eschew this innovation as soon as the thought of it had occurred to them. What serious literary critic, undertaking a theoretical study of the nine-teenth-century bourgeois novel, would proceed on the basis of an "unbiased sample" which might or might not include examples of the work of Jane Austen, Charlotte Brontë, Charles Dickens, George Eliot, Stendhal, Gustave Flaubert, Nathaniel Hawthorne, Herman Melville, Leo Tolstoy, or Henry James, but which might very well be dominated by the collected works of Charlotte Yonge, Bulwer Lytton, and Captain Maryatt? And what information about the nineteenth-century bourgeois novel would such an undertaking, persisted in, be likely to pro-vide? We would certainly discover (as we might, and ought, to have known) that there are large numbers of inferior nineteenth-century novels of varying degrees of documentary interest, but we would learn less than nothing about the novel as a form—for the simple reason that the kind of interest which the inferior works have is only comprehensible in the context of the incomparable artistic achievement excluded by the intrinsic bias of the unbiased sample.

The idea that there is an ideal "normal," "typical," or "representative" film which could be constituted by this or any method is illusory, and it is equally an illusion to suppose that what the unbiased sample gives us is the normal work—as Bordwell and his colleagues, even if their critical sense did not alert them, might readily have deduced from the functions of unbiased sampling in that kind of bourgeois sociology which originated the method. The work of art which is, in the negative sense of the word, "conventional," is interesting not because it is "normal" but because it represents the use of convention at its most inert and unconscious. The conclusion that this use of convention is "the norm" is not a valid deduction but an unsup-ported, and clearly specious, value judgment, the inconsequence of which asserts itself as soon as we admit that the concept of "normality" might be used in a different way. It was "normally" the case, throughout the studio period, that the Hollywood cinema produced large numbers of challenging and distinguished films and a smaller, but very considerable, number of major masterpieces along with the contents of the authors' unbiased sample, but this "norm" is so far from being detectable by their method, or favorable to their assumptions, that they impose a definition of the "normal" which negates it—and which is intended to do so. This definition is supposed to be "scientific," as that word is understood in the circles where the science of unbiased sampling is practiced, but the more assiduously the authors claim that they are in the business of ascertaining an objectively verifiable standard of the "ordinary," the more blatantly obvious does it come to seem that the "ordinary film" is their construction. That they should insist so loudly on the method's "objectivity" is an indication of the strength of their parti pris, and when we consider the banality of their findings—a banality which, in all seriousness and with righteous confidence, they attribute not to their analysis but to its object—we very quickly discover what that parti pris is.

Consider, for example, the opening gambit of Bordwell's disquisition on classical narrative:

> "Plot," writes Frances Patterson in a 1920 manual for aspiring screenwriters, "is a care-ful and logical working out of the laws of cause and effect. The mere sequence of events will not make a plot. Emphasis must be laid upon causality and the action and reaction of the human will." Here, in brief, is the premise of Hollywood story

construction: causality, consequence, psychological motivations, the drive toward overcoming obstacles and achieving goals. Character-centered—i.e., personal or psychological—causality is the armature of the classical story. (13)

"This sounds obvious," Bordwell goes on at once to add, "so obvious that we need to remember that narrative causality could be impersonal as well." (13)

Indeed! Though having remembered this, Bordwell does not perceive that the "i.e." in his penultimate sentence is a non sequitur. Hollywood movies are indeed "obviously" character centered, but it is by no means obvious that "personal or psychological causality" is therefore "the armature of the classical story." Why should character-centered narrative causality necessarily imply personal causality, and why should it be by definition incompatible with that "causality of institutions and group processes" for which Soviet films of the 1920s strike Bordwell as being so supremely remarkable? (13) Curiously, the question is not asked: curiously, because he tells us a few pages later that Hollywood "continues traditions stemming from the chivalric romance, the bourgeois novel and the American melodrama." (16) This is a sufficiently various, and sufficiently complex, set of traditions, and the fact that they date back to the Middle Ages surely has the most unfortunate implications for the claim that "making personal character traits and goals the causes of actions led to a dramatic form fairly specific to Hollywood." (16) And of course we are not even obliged to stop at the *Morte d'Arthur* and *Sir Gawain and the Green Knight*. In that Homer's Ulysses has a number of very striking personal traits, not least among them a "drive toward overcoming obstacles and achieving goals" of an intensity to which John Wayne might defer, it would seem to follow that the dramatic forms specific to Hollywood (or "fairly" so) were invented in ancient Greece.

However that may be, Ulysses, John Wayne—and Captain Ahab, too—would probably have taken their hats off to Bordwell, whose heroic indifference to the obstacles which keep him from his goal is striking by the most exacting standards: only a writer protected by a very obstinate desire to prove his point at all costs could possibly have been convinced by the case Bordwell makes out in defense of it. Narratives have been centered on characters who have set out to accomplish goals since the dawn of time, as Bordwell virtually admits—for the excellent reason that human beings are the only animals who are capable of formulating social projects independent, and often in defiance, of their instinctual drives. It is scarcely astonishing, in the light of this fact (which provides Marx with the basis for his fable of the bee and the architect), that these same human beings are possessed of an insatiable impulse to construct symbolic dramas in which such projects are conceived, impeded, thwarted, and accomplished, and in which feelings about the nature, conditions, limits, and consequences of human action are worked through. Bordwell's assertion that "Hollywood characters, especially protagonists, are goal-oriented" (16), for all that it is couched in the David Shipman idiom, is not in itself exceptionable. On the other hand, however, it is not sufficient to distinguish Ford's Ethan Edwards from Beowulf and Bunyan's pilgrim, and it does not exempt the critic from the business of defining, in a given instance, what the character's goals are and what the film's attitude to them is. That Scottie Ferguson, the hero of *Vertigo* (1958), has goals is indisputable, and he himself remarks, in the final scene, that the struggle to achieve them has been attended by a kind of success, but no one who reads *Vertigo* at all attentively will suppose that the matter can be left there. Both the goals and the success are placed in a complex total context which defines them as something more than actions which have been completed, and it is to this context that we must refer if we wish to distinguish Scottie's goals from those of Siegfried, Coriolanus, Jane Eyre, or Pierre Bezukhov.

The reader's curiosity as to why Bordwell should be so keen to demonstrate that the presence of characters in pursuit of goals tells us anything interesting about American films is satisfied early on: "It is easy to see in the goal-oriented protagonist a reflection of an ideology of American individualism and enterprise, but it is the peculiar accomplishment of the classical cinema to translate this ideology into a rigorous chain of cause and effect." (16)

Bordwell, like all formalists, expels "content" with scorn at the front door only to welcome it home at the back, and I will have reason to return to this aspect of his method later. For the present, it will be enough to say that a "goal-oriented protagonist" and the sequential dramatization of such a protagonist's pursuit of these goals do not in themselves "reflect," let alone (as Bordwell implies) affirm, any ideology whatever. The goals of the protagonists of *Moby Dick* (1956), or of the films *Scarface* (1932), *It's a Wonderful Life* (1946), *Now, Voyager* (1942), and *Blonde Venus* (1932), can and clearly should be referred to the existence of "an ideology of American individualism and enterprise," but they do not reflect it, and the narratives centered on them do not demonstrate its efficacy by virtue of their adherence to the formal rules of linear causality. It is a precondition of heroic status that a protagonist's goals should bear some kind of relation to the culture's dominant ideologies: one cannot imagine a culture which produces narratives with protagonists whose desires and aspirations are culturally irrelevant. Bordwell strategically ignores the possibility that a protagonist might have goals which are sanctioned by the culture but the pursuit and consummation of which turn out to be, in practice, disastrous or, again, that the protagonist might have difficulty in achieving the goals, or in formulating any constructive goals at all, because, for example, she is a woman, and her powers of practical agency are very severely circumscribed. He cannot (and in fact he refuses to) see either that a narrative's judgment of the ideologies implicit in its protagonist's goals can only be deduced from the narrative itself, or that narratives centered on "goal-oriented" protagonists have very often been used, in all historical periods, to test, examine, or criticize a culture's dominant norms by locating them in a protagonist whose goals are in some fundamental way problematic. George Bailey's goals in *It's a Wonderful Life* do (as Bordwell would have it) reflect an ideology of American individualism and enterprise—for the important reason that the film is not a mirror but a complex formal structure which is dedicated to the analysis of the ideology.

The lack of scruple with which Bordwell sets out to impose his thesis is breathtaking. "What would narrative cinema without personalized causation be like?" he pleasantly asks. "We have some examples (in Miklos Jansco, Ozu, Robert Bresson, Soviet films of the 1920s), but we can find others. Erich Von Stroheim's *Greed* (1924) shows that a Naturalist causal scheme is incompatible with the classical model: the characters cannot achieve their goals, and causality is in the hands of nature and not people." (18) The "classical" cinema is littered with protagonists who cannot achieve their goals (melodrama is specifically geared to protagonists of this kind), and with many more who are destroyed by achieving them or who achieve them only to discover that they are worthless, and there could be no clearer indication of the function of the unbiased sample (dominated as it inevitably would be by marginal hackwork) than that it filters out, with predictable efficiency and (for the well-deceived) an appearance of rigorous impartiality, the kind of work that is, like *Greed*, "incompatible with the classical model" concocted by Bordwell and his collaborators. The fact that the protagonists of *Greed* fail to achieve their goals can hardly be said to explain away the evidence of their obsessional investment in them, which demonstrably "causes" the action of *Greed*. And since, *pace* Bordwell, genetic determinism is most certainly not the sole principle of causality in Naturalist fiction (though no one will dispute its importance), I await with interest his demonstration of the sense in which narrative causation in *Greed* (or *Le Débâcle, An American Tragedy, The Octopus*, and *USA*) can be said to be "in the hands of nature." I should also be interested to learn—if it is indeed the case that "psychologically motivated causality in the classical narrative" is a form of determinism, as Bordwell at once goes on to claim (18)—why and how it is that the "Naturalist causal scheme" is incompatible with it at all, in that the question of what the determining principle is is irrelevant to the structure of a determinism.

Before they address these questions, the authors of *The Classical Hollywood Cinema* should probably decide whether they would prefer to have their cake or to eat it. If they wish to object to narratives in which "personal character traits and goals [are] the causes of actions," they should do so consistently, admit that the failure to realize the goals and the determination of the traits by genetic inheritance (or anything else) can have no theoretical significance whatever for persons bent on castigating such narratives, resign themselves to the fact that *Late Spring* (1949), *Pickpocket* (1959), and *Greed* are "compatible with the classical model," and renounce Ozu, Bresson, and von Stroheim and all their works. If they do not wish to object to such narratives, they will have to find some other "dramatic form fairly specific to Hollywood" which can be objected to on some other ground, as well as some more particularized narrative datum than a goal-oriented protagonist to signify a work of art's endorsement of American individualism and enterprise. I do not doubt for a moment that they are capable of formulating such objections, the evidence of their desire to do so being so overwhelming, but Bordwell himself betrays the extreme difficulty of the task when he mentions, in the passage I began by quoting, that it is (to him) "so obvious" that "character-centered" and "personal or psychological" causality are synonymous (13), and then reminds us that "narrative causality could be impersonal as well": "Hollywood films of course include causes of these impersonal types, but they are almost invariably subordinated to psychological causality." (13)

The example he gives is, like the unbiased sample, loaded and unrepresentative, but at least it has the effect of confusing the discussion of what constitutes "impersonal" causality in narratives. It is certainly true that when major historical events are represented in Hollywood films, their causality is ignored, drastically simplified, or attributed to individuals, but on the other hand, this treatment of history is not peculiar to "the classical film," and it tells us nothing about a work's artistic value. *Marie Antoinette* (1938) is a bad film, and it gives a highly tendentious and misleading account of the history of France in the late eighteenth century, but if it is bad *because* "the classical film makes history unknowable apart from its effects on individual characters," then we are surely obliged to conclude that not only *The Scarlet Empress* (1934) but also Tolstoy's *War and Peace, Redgauntlet* (1970 [a television miniseries]), and Shakespeare's history plays are bad classical films. Inaccuracies and simplifications of historical fact in a work of scholarship are very seriously culpable, but in themselves they are not valid criteria for impugning works of art which represent historical events. If *Antony and Cleopatra* makes history unknowable apart from its effects on Antony, Cleopatra, Octavius, Lepidus, and Enobarbus, then the play is to be judged in the light of Shakespeare's realization of these effects, and readers concerned to "know history" in the historian's sense, in which Shakespeare shows not the slightest interest, should seek out material less likely to disappoint them. All cultures, of course, are exceptionally sensitive to the depiction of the past, and the conventions which govern its representation in works of art are often elaborately mystified: Shakespeare's histories, the western, and those "Soviet films of the 1920s" are obvious cases in point. It follows, therefore, that an Elizabethan history play or a western is to be judged not by its reliability, justice, or accuracy as history but by its use of the conventions—which pertain, in any case, not to the past as such but to an ideological construction of the past sanctioned by the dominant culture in which the artist is working. As narratives which make history knowable, *Richard III* and *To Have and Have Not* (1944) are somewhat more than risible: as critical interventions in the convention which mediates the depiction of the history concerned, they are interesting—and even good. I will add (though the news will shock Bordwell) that classical films are by no means exceptional, either for their mystification of historical causality or for their interest in dramatizing the effects of history on individuals, as the work of Mizoguchi, Dreyer, Dziga Vertov, Eisenstein, Robert Bresson, Alain Resnais, and Jean-Luc Godard (among the directors he is known to favor) sufficiently attest. Indeed, *Ivan the Terrible* (1948, 1958) (to which one of Bordwell's collaborators has dedicated a lengthy study) indulges both of these classical vices on an elephantine scale—though Thompson's book has convinced me, and might surely have convinced Bordwell, that *Ivan the Terrible* is not a classical film.

Bordwell's aside on the classical film's betrayal of historical truth strikes us as confusing the issue, not merely because it is in itself nonsensical but because it creates the impression that narratives in which a principle of "personal or psychological" causality can be shown to operate necessarily subordinate "impersonal" causality to it. Unfortunately, this is not the point which his argument proves—though the fact that he takes it to do so is certainly a significant datum for the critical reader of *The Classical Hollywood Cinema*. *Ivan the Terrible* and *The Scarlet Empress* certainly "make history unknowable apart from its effect upon individual characters," but this description throws no light at all on the way in which the characters are conceived, and when we actually examine these works, we find that "personal" and "impersonal" causality are continuous with one another—that the films construe the personal goals and the psychological traits in terms of objective social forces which are neither personal nor psychological. The opposition between personal and impersonal narrative causality is wholly unreal, and while Bordwell is familiar with "the chivalric romance, the bourgeois novel and the American melodrama," the extent to which his study of these forms has failed to enlighten his critical practice is suggested when he informs us that causality might be conceived as "social" rather than "personal" and goes on to adduce the Soviet silent film. What on earth does Bordwell imagine the causality of *Great Expectations* and *Way Down East* (1920) to be? "The bourgeois novel and the American melodrama" are precisely remarkable, in their different ways, for their development of a way of conceptualizing "character" in which personal traits, more or less complexly realized, are perceived as representative social traits, and in which individual feelings and behavior are referred to the objective social world in which the characters live. The protagonists of *Dombey and Son*, *The House of Mirth*, *The Devil Is a Woman* (1935), *While the City Sleeps* (1956), and *Marnie* (1964) are individuals with goals and traits, but if we persist in viewing them as being "individual" in some sense which precludes their being at the same time the focal points of "a causality of institutions and group processes," then we will not understand the works—as *The Classical Hollywood Cinema* so largely demonstrates.

I am not quite sure in what ways, specifically, Hollywood continues the traditions of the chivalric romance, but since Bordwell brings it up, I will take the opportunity he offers of suggesting that what the chivalric romance proves, in this context, is that the impersonal conception of individual character is not in itself very new. The narrative act is, where character is concerned, a dramatic process through which the structures of impersonal causality which bear on "the personal" are defined, and the fact that this is so helps to explain our interest in making, and attending to, stories about people. There has never been a narrative in which private individuals pursued personal goals and exhibited personal tics and idiosyncrasies, and if Bordwell and his colleagues find so many such narratives in "classical" Hollywood, that is because their formalist method banalizes everything it touches. At any given historical moment, a culture offers its inhabitants a certain set of terms with which to make sense of the impersonal determinants of individual feelings and actions, and we must understand narration as an activity of reality testing whereby the nature, content, and adequacy of these terms are examined and reexamined through the histories of representative symbolic figures. It is precisely because narrative poses "character-centered causality" in relation to "causes of impersonal types" that we have narrative, and one of our major criteria in the judgment of a narrative work is our sense of whether the work is exploring (to a greater or lesser degree of profundity) the understandings of impersonal cause which the culture makes available, or merely is reproducing them.

The specificity of bourgeois narrative, as has often been noted, is that the understandings of impersonal cause which it embodies are predominantly social and secular, which is why it has been increasingly difficult since the early nineteenth century (and is now impossible) to produce valid religious art. "Predominant," of course, does not imply "exclusive," still less "uncontradictory." Long before the bourgeois period, we find narratives like *Piers Plowman* and *The Canterbury Tales* in which "character-centered causality" is quite explicitly referred to as a secular causality of social processes and institutions but which also assume the reality of causes which are explicitly metaphysical, and the organization of the latter work as a series of separate, interrelated tales is obviously determined by this fact: the status of the impersonal (social or metaphysical?) is one of the themes of the work. Conversely, we will find many bourgeois narratives in which the characters embody a principle of cause which is not social, or through whom social causality is so thoroughly mystified that it effectively becomes metaphysical, as in much (though not all) Naturalist fiction. The point to be made, however, is that the individual characters in a narrative enact some concept of "supraindividual causality" *by definition* (this is what a narrative is) and that in the great Hollywood movies, which are exemplary bourgeois works, the content of this concept is social: character-centered causality is inseparable from the dramatization (often highly critical) of the impersonal social forces which structure individuality in twentieth-century bourgeois culture.

If Bordwell had read "the bourgeois novel and the American melodrama" more carefully (for it is from these traditions that the Hollywood cinema does indeed stem), he might have reached this conclusion on his own, for it is hard to see how anyone who had paid the most superficial attention to the development of prose fiction in the eighteenth and nineteenth centuries could have failed to grasp that the attempt to analyze character in relation to a "causality of institutions and group processes" is the imaginative drive behind the bourgeois novel. He might also have perceived that the most striking thing about the development of prose fiction in America (and he is supposed, after all, to be analyzing an American form) is the quite extraordinary insistence and explicitness, unparalleled in any other national tradition, with which the novel's status as a symbolic drama about the institutions and value systems of the culture is enforced. There is no equivalent of Tolstoy or George Eliot in the American tradition, and it is significant that when we do find an American novelist who has been deeply influenced both by the complex psychological realism and by the materialist sociology of the author of *Middlemarch*—as we do in Henry James—this influence has been crucially modified by the influence of Hawthorne and the concept of the novel (and tale) as critical, schematic fable which Hawthorne, with Edgar Allan Poe and Melville, established. "Schematic" here should not be taken to connote "the absence of complexity": there is nothing simple or simplifying about *The Scarlet Letter*, *The Golden Bowl*, or *Moby Dick*. I mean only that the central American narrative tradition in the nineteenth century—which derives, as I've noted elsewhere, from the secularization of allegory as Gothic melodrama—is peculiar for the way in which it assimilates the conventions of bourgeois prose fiction to a conception of the fictional action as symbolic process which is very close to allegory, and that within this tradition the fact that character-centered causality is not primarily personal or psychological is emphasized by the narrative form itself. What reader who was even half awake can ever have imagined that s/he had anything to gain by reading such character-centered narratives as "The Fall of the House of Usher," "My Kinsman, Major Molyneux," "Bartleby," *Uncle Tom's Cabin*, *Pudd'nhead Wilson*, and *The Europeans* as studies of the personal traits and goals of their central actors, or that the authors of these works were encouraging the reader to do so? We are told, explicitly and systematically, that the characters, and the dramatic world in which they move, are symbolic, and it is this fictional tradition which feeds into, and becomes the decisive formative influence on, the narrative style of the Hollywood cinema.

Of course, the same tradition produces the dime novel, to which Bordwell would love to reduce it: "The popular short story," he tells us, "acted as a model for narrowing . . . individualized characterization to fixed limits." (Bordwell et al., 14) This may well be true, though its truth is not substantiated by Bordwell. But since the American narrative tradition provided many "models for narrowing individualized characterization to fixed limits," with results more impressive and aims more complex than are to be found in what Bordwell means by "the popular short story," this truth (or assertion) is neither here nor there. The pejorative nature of the intention emerges even more clearly here: "From the nineteenth century melodrama's stock characterizations, Hollywood has borrowed the need for sharply delineated and unambiguous traits." (13–14)

Bordwell shows not the slightest awareness that the American melodramatic tradition also includes Poe, Hawthorne, Melville, Mark Twain, Harriet Beecher Stowe, and James. He assumes, as he assumes throughout, that a tradition can be represented by its most inferior products, and that if it can be shown that a convention has been used meretriciously (as all conventions have), then this in some way disposes of the convention. He also assumes that a tradition, like a child of tainted blood, carries forever the stigma of its origins. Even if it were not the case that the Hollywood cinema had behind it a sophisticated literary tradition which, primarily through D. W. Griffith, came to include Dickens, and which was in general exemplary of the use of popular, melodramatic, and highly schematized symbolic forms for profoundly serious purposes, it would hardly follow from the mere fact of the borrowing of "stock characterizations" from rather unsophisticated traditions that Hollywood did not later transform what it had borrowed. It would be perfectly possible for someone who wished to frame Bordwell's kind of argument to assert that English Renaissance dramatists borrowed stock tropes and rhetorical formulas from the Emblem books, or that eighteenth-century novelists took over stock characterizations and narrative formats from contemporary journalism, or that Giuseppe Verdi and Richard Wagner appropriated stock musical and theatrical structures from academic grand opera. All this is true—but it is not an insult, and such knowledge is worse than useless if it is not accompanied by knowledge of what was later done with the borrowings. Hawthorne's tales, Griffith's *Way Down East*, George Cukor's *Gaslight* (1944), and Douglas Sirk's *Written on the Wind* (1956) have, as American melodramas, a great deal in common with the literary lumpen proletariat adduced by Bordwell, including the reduction of characters to "consistent bundles of a few salient traits." (Bordwell et al., 14) The "salience" is only the critic's primary concern, though Bordwell, of course, ignores it because the *use* of convention is not salient for the formalist approach.

If Bordwell and his colleagues were challenged on this ground, they would no doubt reply that their conclusions were authenticated by the unbiased sample, cornucopia as it is of such deathless monuments of the human spirit as *The Merry Wives of Reno* (1934), *The Three Must-Get-Theres* (1922), *Sh! The Octopus* (1937), *The Speed Spook* (1924), and *The Case of the Lucky Legs* (1935). I should add, in justice to these works, that they may well be masterpieces. The hypothesis is, I admit, unlikely, but the approach to which they and their ilk are submitted in *The Classical Hollywood Cinema* is not such as to allow us to adjudicate the issue. It ought also to be said that an approach, or method, which bases its findings so largely on descriptions of works which few readers are likely to have seen, and which so often rests its case on assertions that the reader is not in a position to check, is both arrogant and, procedurally, highly dubious. I am loathe to consign *Sh! The Octopus* to the dustbin of history on the evidence of authors who find nothing of interest to say about such interesting or considerable works as the sample contains, but I will assume, for the purposes of argument, and until I am blessed with the opportunity to give it the close and undivided attention which it might deserve, that it answers perfectly to the "model of the ordinary film" which the collaborating writers construct. Even if it does so, however (and I concede that the cast—Hugh Herbert, Allen Jenkins, Marcia Ralston—is less than auspicious), it is not a "model" from which one can deduce, or to which one can assimilate, the formal structure of *Tarnished Angels* (1958), or even *Mr. Skeffington* (1944)—one of the many undistinguished works included in the sample which is, nevertheless, of some interest as a document. It is implicit in the authors' much-vaunted approach that a work's "form" is synonymous with the technical "devices" it employs (understood, as we have seen, as mere devices), and that these devices in their turn work in determinate ways according to "the functions" that the stylistic system assigns to them. (Bordwell et al., 6) Their pious faith in this grotesquely mechanical determinism moves the authors to displays of *suffisance* by which, in retrospect, they must surely be embarrassed. "No auteur critic has in practice shown," Bordwell, *en grand seigneur*, announces, "that, say, the shot/reverse shot patterns or the usage of lighting across all of Sirk's films constitute a distinct handling of the classical paradigm; what stands out in an individual film is what stands out in the work as a whole (e.g., a tendency toward blatant symbolism for some purposes)." (80)

It is significant, of course, that at moments such as these (and there are a great many of them) Bordwell and his colleagues should find themselves in the mental world of *TV Guide*, whose language and presumptions come to hand, in that final clause, with such betraying ease. To ask for it to be "shown in practice" that Sirk's handling of the shot/reverse-shot convention is *in itself* distinct is rather like asking for a demonstration of Haydn's "distinct handling" of the convention which divides the classical symphony into four movements. It is the music written in the convention which is distinct, and it is this music, too, which constitutes the form of Haydn's symphonies. Sirk's handling of Hollywood editing conventions is, precisely, a *handling* of them: that is to say, it is inseparable from the specific formal/dramatic context created by a specific work—a context which is defined, not only by the use of cutting, but also by the direction of actors, the use of color, the composition of the frame, shot-length, editing rhythm, and "a tendency toward blatant symbolism for some purposes"—and we cannot analyze the formal properties of Sirk's editing without analyzing this context *as a whole*. When Bordwell takes the "auteur critic" to task for failing to show the distinctness of Sirk's use of a convention which cannot actually be used independently of other conventions—their use, in this particular conjunction, being the form of the work—he intimates no more than that questions of artistic form are not susceptible to discussion by a formalist.

This may seem a harsh conclusion, but it is difficult to read *The Classical Hollywood Cinema* for long (or so it seems to me) without finding fresh evidence of its justice. Consider this, for example:

> At the most abstract level of generality, narrative causality dominates the [Hollywood] film's spatial and temporal systems. We have already seen how genre, spectacle, technical virtuosity, and other factors encourage narrative to slip a bit from prominence, only to allow the narration to compensate for this slip by adjusting its overall structure. In a similar fashion, authorial reshifting of the hierarchy of systems vie for prominence with narrative causality and even override it; Bresson, Tati, Mizoguchi, Ozu, Snow,

Frampton, *et al.*, can in various ways problematize narrative, making overt narration a pervasive presence. But there is little chance in Hollywood of what Burch calls "organic dialectics," the possibility of using purely stylistic parameters to determine the shape of the film (including its narrative). (78–79)

Bordwell is drawn to the phrase "purely stylistic parameters" by the same force which attracts him to the baleful concept of "artistic motivation," one of the stock characterizations which he borrows from the Russian formalists. What are "purely stylistic parameters," and how could they be identified? Style in art only exists as the articulation of materials, and it has no parameters independent of the process of articulating them. It may well be the case, as Bordwell claims, that Joseph Cornell's *Rose Hobart* (1936), which I have not seen, "creates a play of spatial and temporal relations among elements discovered in but freed from a narrational matrix" (Bordwell et al., 79), but it does not follow (insofar as this description of *Rose Hobart* is comprehensible) that "the shape of the film" has been determined by pure style. If the film has a shape, and if it does indeed "create . . . relations among elements," then it is, for the purposes of a discussion of its "style," the structure of elements so related, and our analysis and judgment of the style will be continuous with our analysis of the meaning generated by the structure.

My ungracious suspicion that the description of *Rose Hobart* is not comprehensible arises from the description's contiguity with equivalent assertions about Ozu and Mizoguchi (the other names, I confess, do not greatly concern me), which are demonstrably false. I have never been convinced by Bordwell's account of Ozu's "stylistic systems" (for the reasons I gave many years ago in my essay on "The Ideology of Screen," when he first propounded it), and the passage of time has only confirmed my initial feeling that no one could have had such an account to offer who was not more interested in snatching Ozu, for whatever reason, from the omnivorous maw of "classical narrative" than in the works which Ozu actually made. Bordwell is welcome to the proposition that no Hollywood director could have used space as Ozu uses it. Nor could any English, German, Spanish, or Indian director; if Ozu does belong to "modernism" (a word which, in contemporary polite usage, is on the verge of becoming meaningless except as a term of, according to taste, vague abuse or approbation), then some more convincing proof will have to be found than the extreme unlikeness of his style to the styles of directors working in different cultural traditions who have been arbitrarily lumped together as representatives of "classicism." I am at one with Bordwell in setting a supremely high value on the work of Ozu and Mizoguchi, but I am sure that a writer who puts them in the same company with Michael Snow and Hollis Frampton, as exemplars of "the same kind of thing," has not the faintest notion of what this value is. I am sure, too, that any auteur critic, on any day of the week, could advance exactly the same claims which Bordwell makes for Ozu on behalf of, say, Hawks, by simply following Bordwell's lead and extrapolating Hawks's stylistic systems from the culture and the history in which Hawks arrived at them. It would be hard to think of a director whose style is more deeply rooted in traditional "schemata" (to take up the proffered term) than Ozu's, and this style manifests itself, in his surviving works, as a series of family comedies and family melodramas. It has never seemed to me that the author of *Late Spring* and *An Autumn Afternoon* (1962) (or of *Sisters of the Gion* [1936] and *Ugetsu Monogatari* [1953]) either wished to "free himself from a narrational matrix" or thought of this matrix as a trap, and I find it curious that Bordwell should want to praise so desolating a work as *Tokyo Story* (1953) on the grounds that "its temporal and spatial systems vie for prominence with narrative causality." The fact that they plainly don't suggests that Bordwell and his colleagues share that impulse to keep works of art at a safe distance (the distance necessary to "see through" them), for which so much contemporary bourgeois ratiocination on cultural subjects is remarkable, but the same fact is suggestive of much more than the character of a prevailing *niveau*. Bordwell tells us, of Hitchcock and Otto Preminger, that "both auteurs remain within classical bounds: Hitchcock cannot always keep us aware of his narrational presence, whereas Preminger will often claim his *droit du seigneur* [*sic*] at the end of a film by an overt camera movement." (80)

Who is "us"? If this is the royal prerogative, then I have no quarrel with Bordwell, but on the other hand, if "we" are in possession of the category "Hitchcock-as-narrator," then we will always be aware of his narrational presence and find that it "pervades" *Marnie* as completely as Michael Snow's pervaded *Wavelength* (1967). The significance of Bordwell's weird assumption that narration does or does not pervade, independently of the spectator's having the concepts of "narration" or "Preminger's authorship," emerges when he tells us, apropos *Rear Window* (1954), that "for the viewer, constructing the story takes precedence [over interpretation]; the effects of the text are registered, but its causes go unremarked." (Bordwell, *Narration*, 48) This "viewer," plainly, is the dumb schmuck in the back row of the local fleapit, but it is also Bordwell, who devotes all the powers of strained intellection at his disposal to establish the truth that Frampton's narration is, quite apart from any act of reading, objectively "overt" and that Hitchcock's, except in special circumstances, is not. The "causes" of *Rear Window*, in Bordwell's reading, do indeed "go unremarked," but this is the fault, less of Hitchcock or "the classical style" than of Bordwell himself, who has decided that narrative causality "takes precedence" over the spatial and temporal systems of Hollywood films, and who is therefore unable to read the films—which are only there to be read, alas, inasmuch as these systems organize their narratives. Bordwell's benighted viewer, unless pump-primed by himself and his collaborators, would "construct the stories" of *Ordet* (1955) and *Les Vacances de M. Hulot* (1953) as obstinately as those of *Rear Window* and *Laura* (1944), and the possibility should at least be considered that in doing so, s/he would stand a rather better chance of comprehending the temporal and spatial systems of Hitchcock and Preminger than Bordwell does.

The criterion of "overt narration" which Bordwell employs is extremely exacting: anything which is, in his opinion, "motivated by realism or genre or story causality" (Bordwell et al., 79) is peremptorily disqualified. I do not know what Bordwell means by "realistic motivation," and he does not know either—or so I assume from the fact that the example of it which he gives is a film set in nineteenth-century England in which the actors are dressed in nineteenth-century costumes (19)—but if this criterion is allowed to stand, it is difficult to see what kind of narration is left. The precedent which Bordwell sets surely has the most alarming implications for our judgment of the work of Ozu and Mizoguchi, if only because the characters in their films are invariably dressed in clothes appropriate to the period in which the action takes place: Mizoguchi's narration (at least in the films I have seen) never becomes so overt that he dresses medieval Japanese peasants in tuxedos and crinolines, or obliges his leading actresses to negotiate the streets of nineteenth-century Tokyo beneath a pompadour. Bordwell's blithe indifference to contradictions of this kind is symptomatic of the grim-lipped desperation with which he sticks to his approach, to which the films will and must be made to correspond, even when their failure to do so is, for the reader who cannot share the writer's enthusiasms, most blatant and most ludicrous.

The kind of theoretical misconception (if that's the word) which the approach, or method, of *The Classical Hollywood Cinema* so spectacularly exemplifies is admirably described by Charles Rosen and Henri Zerner in their indispensable book *Romanticism and Realism: The Mythology of Nineteenth-Century Arts*. It is in fact a model of critical writing (or ought to be: I have never met anybody who has heard of it). Recalling Hugh Honour's contention that there is, in Romantic art, "no common language of visual forms and means of expression comparable with the Baroque or Rococo," Rosen and Zerner write:

> This distinction between Romanticism and earlier "styles" is not tenable except with a certain amount of juggling and no little confusion. It works only by a narrow definition of, say, the Baroque and a wide one of Romanticism: . . . A "common language" for Baroque art could be arrived at only by resolutely excluding anything that does not fit, and casting it out as non-Baroque. The problem here is a naive methodology, which defines a style by listing the characteristics that a given number of roughly contemporary works have in common.

"Underlying this method," the authors go on,

> is often an even more naive belief that works that belong to the same style ought to look alike. Anthony Blunt, for example, defined Baroque architecture by the Roman style of Bernini and Borromini; he admitted as Baroque anything that resembled their works or was obviously derived from them, and disqualified everything else. This kind of definition is distinguished by its consistency, rigidity and poverty. It does not stimulate understanding but leads to pigeonholing, to a dead end of classification, of no use as a tool of analysis. Works are disposed of as Baroque or non-Baroque, Romantic or non-Romantic, as if these were categories that had some objective historical reality. But terms like "Baroque" or "Romantic" do not designate well-defined entities or even systems. They are primitive short-hand signs for long-range historical developments that one feels nevertheless to have a certain integrity. (31)

This leaves little more to be said, and its pertinence to the case of *The Classical Hollywood Cinema* is illustrated by Bordwell himself when he refers, in passing, to "the problem . . . of defining 'non-classical' styles." (Bordwell et al., 75) The definition of classical styles poses no problem at all, and Bordwell, armed with this confidence, can then proceed without so much as a blush to castigate critics who take "style terms" such as "Baroque" as a "positive definition and . . . try to find the essential traits of the style." (75) Called on to distinguish between Bordwell and his collaborators and Honour and Blunt, we would find ourselves obliged to say that for the former, the pigeonholing process is an act of aggression, almost of vandalism: it is a method (both more strenuous and more circuitous than the one we are used to) for belittling and demeaning the films, and explaining them definitively *away*.

> The typical thematic interpretation of an auteur film commences by summarizing the story action, moves to a psychological description of the characters and abstract thematic oppositions, and buttresses the reading with a rundown of privileged motifs that reinforce the themes. The very form of such essays confirms the fluctuations of classical narration. In each film, the auteur critic invariably turns up great swatches of the classical style . . . . (Bordwell et al., 80)

The insistence of this vocabulary and this tone (which a responsible critic should not permit him- or herself) and the significance of Bordwell's querulous hostility to a discourse that fails either to coincide with or to confirm the assumptions and conclusions of his own are unmistakable. It is hardly a coincidence, therefore, that when (as I have put it) Bordwell welcomes home at the back door the auteur critic's preoccupation with ideology and thematic interpretation, the features of the now-honored guest should turn out to be so very familiar. "Our examination of classical narration has shown that it accustoms spectators to a limited and highly probable range of expectations. Classical narration's reliability habituates the viewer to accepting regulated impersonality and sourceless authority." (Bordwell et al., 83)

As the triumphant upshot of five hundred pages of scholarly prose, this seems to me to be less than impressive, and nothing suggests more clearly the redundancy of this conclusion than the genuflection to Adorno in the sentence which precedes the passage I have quoted. But of course, Bordwell and his colleagues do not "show" this anymore than they "show" that "Hollywood cinema has been made stringently uniform by its dependence upon a specific economic mode of film production and consumption." (6) In fact, the two halves of the book fail to coincide: the claim to demonstrate the absolute determination of "film style" by "mode of production" remains, inevitably, merely a claim. It is itself a component of the general pejorative intention, and Hollywood films have to be pretty thoroughly worked over by the formalist approach before that "stringent uniformity" can be ascribed to them which the mode of production is supposed to have determined.

Bordwell's quest for uniformity is as stringent as the uniformity itself, and in pursuing it he goes one better than Blunt, who was content merely to exclude from the category of "Baroque architecture" any building that did not resemble the work of Bernini. Bordwell cherishes the loftier ambition of redescribing every film ever made in Hollywood in such a way that it will appear to resemble the work of H. Bruce Humberstone, and chapter seven of the book, "The Bounds of Difference," which deals with the auteur theory, film noir, and Hollywood's assimilation of the European avant-garde, and in which the ambition asserts itself most implacably, seems to me to be, without doubt, the most monumental chutzpah in the history of Hollywood criticism. To call it chutzpah is not to suggest that Bordwell isn't taking it seriously. He is dealing, he knows, with three deadly enemies, any one of whom could seriously undermine the central thesis of the book and who, should they form a united front, would have little difficulty in bringing the whole elaborate edifice tumbling down around his ears. He proceeds, therefore—with the understandable bitterness of a man who has dedicated months of his life to the unholy task of dissecting *Sh! The Octopus*—to screw his courage to the sticking place [limit], to seek and to kill.

Consider, as exemplary, the bloody snuffing out of film noir—an antagonist whose many obnoxious features, grimly enumerated by Bordwell between clenched teeth (the undermining of "classical conventions of logical action," the "assault on psychological causality," the critique of heterosexuality, the repudiation of closure, the challenge to "the neutrality and 'invisibility' of classical style," the "disorientation" of the spectator), foredoomed it, sooner or later, to his undying enmity. It is, indeed, the epitome of everything that a classical film cannot conceivably be. Bordwell appraises the loathsome heretical object with icy contempt for some moments, pondering the most efficient method of attack, and then opts boldly for a vicious surprise assault on its exposed ontologicals: speaking ex-cathedra, he issues a Declaration of Total Oblivion whereby the object shall be deemed henceforth to have no finite existence. "What is film noir?" he scornfully asks: "Not a genre. Producers and consumers both recognize a genre as a distinct entity; nobody set out to make or see a film noir in the sense that people deliberately chose to make a [w]estern, a comedy, or a musical." (Bordwell et al., 75)

Perhaps not, but people did set out to make and to see *The Big Sleep* (1946), *Out of the Past* (1947), *Detour* (1945), *The Lady from Shanghai* (1947), and *Double Indemnity* (1944), and although these pitiful sallies and alarums were not illuminated by the critical concept which has excited Bordwell's wrath, the fact that Hawks and Jacques Tourneur could not have told themselves that they were making "films noirs" does not eradicate the works they produced or the conventions which *The Big Sleep* and *Out of the Past* have in common, both with each other and with *Follow Me Quietly* (1949) and *The Maltese Falcon* (1941). Even Bordwell can hardly suppose that George Eliot sat down at her desk with the aim of writing a "bourgeois realist novel." "Is film noir then a style? Critics have not succeeded in defining specifically noir visual techniques (one [*sic*] that would include, say, *Laura* and *Touch of Evil* [1957]) or narrative structure (one that would include policiers, melodramas, and historical films like *Reign of Terror* [1949])." (Bordwell et al., 75) Bad syntax is often telling, particularly when it passes the proofreading stage, and what it tells us here is that Bordwell's animus against film noir is primarily a matter of its refusal (to borrow a phrase from Rosen and Zerner) to "sit still for its portrait."

"Two respected critics find only twenty-two films noirs; a recent book on the subject lists over two hundred and fifty. Another critic's list includes *High Noon* (1952) and *2001* (1968)." (75) Bordwell is as baffled as any fleapit voyeur confronting the looming prospect of *Gertrud* (1964): he cannot "construct the story"; he does not know how many films noirs there really are; and if he were faced with an examination paper which demanded to know what the "visual techniques" of *Laura* and *Touch of Evil* have in common, he would not be able to give "the right answer." It is even the case that "respected critics" disagree on the subject, and that one of them has gone so far as to procure intimate and immoral contact between film noir and what might have seemed, at first glance, to be a perfectly decent western. *Sh! The Octopus*, stretched on the rack of Bordwell's viewing table, yields up the secrets of its inner life with commendable promptitude, but *Reign of Terror* is stubbornly equivocal: it purports to be a "historical film," but at the same time, it flaunts its perverse knowledge of the narrative structures and visual styles of other genres. Textual miscegenation—the brazen public congress of discrete style terms—is, from the point of view of "the approach," the most abominable of crimes, and film noir has no one but itself to thank if Bordwell at once goes on to pass upon it the film theorist's equivalent of God's judgment of the Cities of the Plains.

The whole shocking mess can be traced back, apparently, to "the summer and fall of 1946," when a group of snotty French intellectuals, concerned "less to define than to differentiate," saw "a new sort of American film for the first time" and, in the innocent conviction that it was new, cooked up the term *film noir* to distinguish it "from the mainstream Hollywood product." Later critics have persistently failed to see that this illusory category, deriving as it does from a criminal addiction to the making of distinctions, is little more than a symptom of chronic culture shock after "years of occupation," and they "have continued to use 'film noir' as a constitutive category, forgetting that it emerged as what Gombrich calls a term of exclusion": "Thus we inherit a category constructed *ex post facto* out of a perceived resemblance between continental crime melodramas and a few Hollywood productions." (Bordwell et al., 75) So much for Buckingham! Its vile pedigree laid bare, and its promiscuous history of critical gang bangs and one-night stands held up for all to see, film noir falls to the ground in agony, clutching its bleeding ontologicals.

But suddenly, Bordwell seems to remind himself that there is more than one way to skin a cat, and with a Jesuitical leer he bends down and offers film noir a Band-Aid™. It can have its ontological status back: "It is not a trivial description of film noir to say that it simply indicates particular patterns of nonconformity within Hollywood." (75) The Declaration of Total Oblivion is generously withdrawn—but only on condition (it rapidly transpires) that film noir should agree to confine its "patterns of nonconformity" within "specific and non-subversive conventions" (76) and that it should accept that it is as miserable as, and essentially indistinguishable from, all other objects of its kind. That is, film noir can be deemed to exist so long as it is prepared to lead a life of chastity from now on.

With this stern injunction on his lips, Bordwell proceeds to "solve the case" (his own phrase) of a thoroughly chastened and humbly grateful film noir, and the solution is both simple and predictable. "Every characteristic narrative device of film noir was already conventional in American crime fiction and drama of the 1930s and 1940s," he tells us, and to drive the point home, he announces twice in the space of a single paragraph that a given literary convention had been "made respectable" long before it came to have an influence on Hollywood. (76) What Bordwell means by this (I presume) is that Raymond Chandler, Dashiell Hammett, Graham Greene, and others were taken to be serious and distinguished writers by an intelligent contemporary public; whether or not we agree with this judgment (which I, in fact, do not), it is critically improper to deduce from it that the convention in question has been domesticated ideologically. I cannot see, either, what sin it is that Bordwell imagines himself to have identified when he points out that a literary convention has demonstrably influenced the narrative conventions of another art form, or that "almost 20 percent of the films noirs made between 1941 and 1948 [are] adaptations of hard-boiled novels" (76);

though that this is a sin for Bordwell certainly indicates that if anyone should ever decide to take out a contract on Shakespeare, Verdi, or Alban Berg, he is the man for the job. In any case, this still leaves 80 percent of the buggers to be accounted for, so Bordwell is obliged to brandish his cutlass at "the psychological thriller," which "underwent rejuvenation during the 1930s, in novels and plays by Frances Iles, Emlyn Williams and Patrick Hamilton." (76) In what sense Cukor's *Gaslight* (1944) can be said to be the "result" of Patrick Hamilton's "successful play *Angel Street*," let alone the novels of Iles, as Bordwell claims, I cannot say. The play is certainly Cukor's starting point, but his film is so utterly different in theme, tone, and structure, so obstinately inseparable from the temporal and spatial systems of his mise-en-scène, and so obviously the bastard progeny of a wild fling between "film noir" and "the woman's movie," that to call it the "result" of either *Angel Street* or its success seems about as helpful and as pertinent as the delightful claim (again, in Leonard Maltin–speak) that *Gaslight* is one of "a series of films stressing abnormal psychology and murder in a middle-class setting." (76) Bordwell intends to say, I suppose, that "not all marriages are like that," and with this sturdy common sense I readily concur: if, in general, things were that bad, we would have had the revolution long ago. There is nothing "abnormal," however, about the "psychology" of the characters, and *Gaslight* is so profoundly disturbing because it takes the logic of the norms to their limit: Paula and Gregory Anton do not represent "the typical," but the power and the very meaning of the film depend on the fact that they do represent the continuation of it.

This, of course, is the kind of consideration which Bordwell disdains to countenance, his business being to specify the objective formal systems which construct the film and the meanings and spectatorial activities objectively determined by them.

> My account of *Rear Window* does not constitute a critical interpretation. I have not labeled Jeff a voyeur, judged his peeping naughty or nice, or sought to establish him as a "castrated" adventurer fantasizing the dismembering of a woman's body. Indeed, my sketch is not even an analysis of the film, since specifying the spectator's activity cannot itself provide that. (*Narration*, 48)

The disingenuousness is total, and one wonders with keen interest how far Bordwell is prepared to go in this direction. If, for example, he ever brought his method to bear on *Triumph of the Will* (1935), would he also refrain (as so many "film critics" have done before him) from judging whether Leni Riefenstahl was "naughty or nice," or whether her film is or is not a celebration of the Nazi Party? It may be thought that he protests a little too much, for it goes without saying that he makes his critical interpretation anyway: "Every fiction film does what *Rear Window* does . . . of course, not every film reinforces such conventional ideological categories (nagging wife, society model, adventurous photographer, lusty newlyweds, old maid) and places such trust in the connection between seeing and understanding. (*Narration*, 46–47) No amount of caution or vigilance can save Bordwell and his colleagues from disasters of this kind, so little conscious are they of the impertinence of their method to the material they are analyzing or of the energy of repudiation which fuels the drive to impose the method.

I do not know, and will not speculate, where that energy comes from, but that the drive behind the book is of this kind seems to me unquestionable, and it always manifests itself with glaring clarity whenever the authors venture, or fail to conceal, a judgment of value. Again and again, their descriptions imply a measure of appreciation: "The Hollywood auteur film offers a particular pleasure and knowledge: the spectator comes to recognize norm and deviation oscillating, perhaps wrestling, within the same art work, that work being actively contained by the pressures of tradition." (Bordwell et al., 82) This is admirably put, and "pleasure and knowledge" would certainly seem to be positive terms. But again and again, too, the impulse to annihilate the pleasure and to deny the knowledge insists on its presence and its dominance. What sort of pleasure in, or knowledge of, the Hollywood auteur film is compatible with that amazing, that scarcely credible, assertion that *Rear Window* (of all films!!) "places such trust in the connection between seeing and understanding"; with those references to Sirk's "blatant symbolism" and "swatches" of classical style; and with the breathless intensity with which Bordwell—in the teeth (hence, the intensity) of the overwhelming evidence to the contrary—sets out to prove that the auteur can do little more than "choose how to be redundant" or that F. W. Murnau, Ernst Lubitsch, Ford, Buster Keaton, and Frank Borzage, for all their "greatness," are to be thought of primarily (or at all), where a discussion of the 1920s is concerned, as having failed to "displace the sovereignty of the story in the classical model"? What sense is it of the imputed greatness of Lubitsch, Murnau, and Keaton which limits their range of expressive action to the choice of redundancy and the momentary "disruption" of classical norms, but which attributes to the authors of Hollywood screenplay manuals an artistic power and influence of what would seem to be all-embracing scope? What critic, having become aware of the existence and distinction of these artists, would want to think that *Sh! The Octopus* is, in any sense, a representative Hollywood film, and then write a lengthy book in which it is shown that Ford "failed to displace the sovereignty of" the paradigm which *Sh! The Octopus* embodies? And for what reader prepared to expend the time and energy required to ingest such a book can the following admonition be intended: "At the same time, however, we cannot denounce the Hollywood style as uniformly suspect." (Bordwell et al., 83) The reader implied by this remark, as its context makes plain, is none other than Bordwell himself, who has just reached the climax of a denunciation which now, apparently, "we" cannot make, and who suddenly finds himself in the embarrassing position of having won a Pyrrhic victory. The field is his, but everyone is dead.

The paradoxical result of these arduous labors is that Bordwell and his colleagues give us almost no idea whatever of what the conventional limits were within which "the classical Hollywood cinema" actually operated: we are no closer to an understanding of "the bounds of difference" when, at the end, we set the book aside, exhausted, than we were when we picked it up, bright-eyed and bushy-tailed, at the beginning. The authors invent constraints where none exist, and the major works through the analysis of which they might have been able to establish the real boundaries of the Hollywood style have to be ruthlessly travestied in the compelling interests of the grand formalist design. "If you are a classical filmmaker, you cannot light a scene in such a way as to obscure the locale entirely (cf. Godard in *Le Gai savoir*); you cannot pan or track without some narrative or generic motivation; you cannot make every shot one second long (cf. certain avant-garde works)." (Bordwell et al., 5)

If the first and the third of these items do indeed constitute "limitations," I cannot in honesty say (despite the single prestigious example offered) that they strike me as being very onerous ones, and I do not understand why Bordwell supposes that they are. Had he said that "if you are a classical filmmaker you cannot stage a shot like the first shot of the Maison Tellier sequence in *Le Plaisir* (1952) or make 'the Raising of the Bridges' in *October* (1928)," I would gladly have agreed with him—while insisting, at the same time, on the critical necessity of comparing these scenes with, say, Hitchcock's long-take camera movements in *Under Capricorn* (1949) and Marnie's riding accident in order to establish why, and to what extent, this is so. The problem with such an exercise, from Bordwell's standpoint, is that the shot from *Le Plaisir* is objectionable on the second of the grounds that he cites above, and it is the unfortunate fact that any element of any film is objectionable on exactly the same ground which disqualifies Bordwell and his colleagues as reliable guides to the boundaries of the Hollywood style. The "classical constraints" are not classical constraints. They are the constraints (or conditions) of cultural production in general, which is always mediated by conventions and which, in the case of narrative, always involves the construction of a causal sequence centered on the actions of persons (whether or not the persons are "individuals" like—to cover the ample range—Achilles or David Copperfield or Norman Bates). If *Sh! The Octopus* has to go, then so does *The Man with a Movie Camera* (1929), and while the authors of *The Classical Hollywood Cinema* may well wish to equivocate on this matter, it remains the case that the principal effect of their hatchet job on Hollywood movies is to hoist them on their own petard.

There could be no more salutary warning than this of the extreme dangers which attend the use of the concept of "Hollywood classicism": I have come to feel, indeed, that the concept may well be more trouble than it's worth. Noting that "it was probably André Bazin who gave the adjective ('classical') the most currency," Bordwell argues that "it seems proper to retain [it] in English" in that "the principles which Hollywood claims as its own rely on notions of decorum, proportion, formal harmony, respect for tradition, mimesis, self-effacing craftsmanship, and cool control of the perceiver's response—canons which critics in any medium usually call 'classical.'" (Bordwell et al., 3–4)

The presence in this list of the word *mimesis* forbodes the elephantiasis to which, in the hands of the authors of *The Classical Hollywood Cinema*, "classicism" will rapidly succumb, but even if mimesis were excised, the sentence would remain ominous. Bordwell assumes that classicism is a thing with a number of stable, clearly defined, and unambiguous characteristics which manifest themselves in statistically verifiable ways and whose meaning is completely self-evident, and the method of himself and his collaborators virtually consists of identifying the imputed features of "the Hollywood style" which correspond to the imputed model of classicism. Our authors know what classicism is—"elegance, unity, rule-governed craftsmanship" (4)—and they proceed to demonstrate the existence of these qualities in the hapless specimens on their operating table. This is building on sand with a vengeance, and while it never occurs to Bordwell to question the adequacy of his notion of "the classical," he does acknowledge, fleetingly, that some of the specimens (which are at this point still alive) are behaving rather oddly: "All of which is not to say that Hollywood's classicism does not have disparate, even 'non-classical', sources. Certainly the Hollywood style seeks effects that owe a good deal to, say, romantic music or nineteenth century melodrama." (4)

The terms in which the doubt is expressed (Hollywood's classicism has nonclassical sources) are themselves a way of overcoming it, but it is as plain to Bordwell as it is to me that no less self-effacing and decorous genre could be imagined than the American melodrama, and that if we wish to offer quintessential examples of "propriety" and "cool control of the perceiver's response," *Broken Blossoms* (1919), *The Wind* (1928), *Duel in the Sun* (1946), *Imitation of Life* (1959), and Vincente Minnelli's *Madame Bovary* (1949) are not the first works of art that spring to mind. Bordwell can do nothing with this inconvenient fact except repress it, and having gestured toward the melodrama, he goes on at once to add, with mind-blowing insouciance: "The point is simply that Hollywood films constitute a fairly coherent aesthetic tradition which sustains individual creation." (Bordwell et al., 83) If *this* is what classicism boils down to, it is hardly surprising that all narratives turn out to be classical—except those which are granted a Declaration of Indulgence (as opposed to Oblivion) by Bordwell.

One is tempted to say, simply, that the book has made the concept of classical Hollywood unusable and to throw it cheerfully in the wastepaper basket, but before one does so, one should consider a set of possibilities which lie beyond the authors' ken.

> A nymph of quality admires our knight;
> He marries, bows at court, and grows polite:
> Leaves the dull cits, and joins (to please the fair)
> The well-bred cuckolds in St. James's air:
> First, for his son a gay commission buys,
> Who drinks, whores, fights, and in a duel, dies:
> His daughter flaunts a viscount's tawdry wife;
> She bears a coronet and pox for life. (Pope, vol. 3, 158)

This—it comes from one of the most astonishing passages in Alexander Pope, the story of Sir Balaam which concludes the moral essay "Of the Use of Riches"—is preeminently "classical": the effect depends on the elegance, precision, and propriety embodied in the convention of the heroic couplet, and on the regularity and predictability with which the formal pattern of the verse repeats itself. At the same time, however, the poetry is clearly highly improper—it borders, indeed, like so much of Pope's verse, on the obscene—and as we read it, we observe that there would be little point in trying to disentangle "propriety" from "impropriety" or to fix the place where one ends and the other begins. When, in the last line, the stress falls with perfect "propriety," as convention dictates, on "pox," the effect is not only elegant and decorous but also jarring and startling—and, of course, witty. Pope's "classical" wit, in all its varieties, is invariably bound up with the creation of "shocks" of this kind: the wit is the shock, which is generated by the collision between the high decorum of Pope's conventions and a use of language which is both immaculately refined and, it might have been thought, incompatible with decorum of any kind. This tension in the verse, while it is certainly focused in words such as "pox," "cuckolds," and "whores," is not confined to them. It is a pervasive presence, and it generates an answering tension in the reader, who is held in a state of continual alert attention to the tone and significance of a speaking voice which is very far from being "self-effacing." The conventions of classical eighteenth-century English verse, as Pope employs them, exist in the form of this speaking voice, which is present as a voice to the reader who knows the conventions. In the context provided by the formalism of Bordwell and his colleagues, it is "proper" to add that Pope's verse is not, for himself or his readership, a sophisticated game involving "the application of devices" or the conventionalized deviation from formal norms which then reassert themselves. The narrative of Sir Balaam is a devastating critical analysis of a representative eighteenth-century bourgeois life.

Or consider this: Pope again—this time the passage from the second of the Moral Essays, "Of the Character of Women," in which he represents the old age to which his culture condemns its fashionable society ladies:

> At last, to follies youth could scarce defend,
> It grows their age's prudence to pretend;
> Ashamed to own they gave delight before,
> Reduced to feign it, when they give no more:
> As hags holds sabbaths less for joy than spite,
> So these their merry, miserable night;
> Still round and round the ghosts of beauty glide,
> And haunt the places where their honor died. (111)

The first three couplets imply a critical distance from the women's "folly," and a fastidious revulsion from the grotesque indignities of their fate, which, by the time we get to "hags" and "spite," have begun to look like misogynistic animus: the women, apparently, have now been firmly placed as "other" by the knowing, superior male narrator. Then, suddenly, the tone changes—with a force the more impressive for the rapidity and completeness of the change. The exquisite cadence of "Still round and round the ghosts of beauty glide" involves the reader in the movement of characters who, only a second before, had been brutally objectified as cackling, raddled harridans, and the effect is completed by the remarkable use of enjambment: both the emphatic end-stopping of the line and the confident, regular pattern of stresses characteristic of Enlightenment prosody are, in this final couplet, completely subdued. The reader (and this is the point) is caught off guard. A distinct imaginative effort is involved in getting from the lurid *Walpurgisnacht* of the penultimate couplet to the quite different, and incompatible, supernatural world of the "ghosts of beauty," who may well be wilis but who are certainly not witches, and this effort is continuous with a radical change in our attitude to the women—a change of which Pope encourages us to become conscious by making it impossible to anticipate the shift of tone. The dance of the ghosts is a *danse macabre*, but unlike the witches' Sabbath, it is neither grotesque nor "other." It has the eerie, elegiac grace of the couplet which describes it, and the verse's movement, as we follow and respond to it, makes us participants in the dance.

The key to this astonishing transition is "delight" in the third line—a word which, given the context, we have probably undervalued but the significance of which now strikes us retrospectively. Delight evokes a positive concept of pleasure, spontaneity, and vitality which is debased and trivialized in the beau monde where the women move, but which is now recalled, as something tragically lost, by the magical ballet of their ghosts. It is this sense of loss and waste—so poignantly realized, and so vividly communicated to the reader, through the couplet's movement, as a process in which s/he is involved—that allows Pope to invest the conventional and (one might think) impossibly bombastic trope of "the death of Honor" with that immense solemnity and power. The "honor" that died here is suggestive of very much more than the term usually connotes, and "died," when it comes, carries its full weight of meaning. Pope has now prepared us for what follows, in which the profound sympathetic involvement with the women created by the final couplet and the savage critical irony of the lines which precede it are, with almost incredible perfection, combined.

> See how the world its veterans rewards!
> A youth of frolics, an old age of cards;
> Fair to no purpose, artful to no end,
> Young without lovers, old without a friend;
> A fop their passion, but their prize a sot,
> Alive, ridiculous; and dead, forgot! (111–12)

Pope's anger and intensity, at once contained and enabled by the extreme rigors of the decorum, have now become a protest on the women's behalf.

The point in invoking Pope here (whose classicism no one will dispute) is, firstly, to suggest that "decorum, proportion, formal harmony, respect for tradition, cool control of the perceiver's response and rule-governed craftsmanship" are tricky concepts, and that Bordwell and his colleagues do not know what they mean. They do not, in fact, mean any one thing, and they are perfectly consonant (as I have tried to show) with the creation of dramatic/poetic effects whose tone and character is very far removed from anything that the word *decorum* ordinarily signifies in conventional usage. We do not know what "classical decorum" means until we have analyzed its use in a given context, and this context is not "purely" formal but dramatic: it is a context of realized meaning. The proprieties of English Enlightenment verse can be listed in the form of a set of rules, but these rules meant very different things to John Dryden, Pope, Samuel Johnson, William Cowper, and George Crabbe. The verse of these writers is governed by a common decorum, but it would be impossible to extract from their poetry a unitary definition or understanding of the rules to which they all adhered, and it would be exceedingly foolish to try.

Pope allows me, secondly, to address myself to Bordwell's claim that

> our account of [the classical] paradigm must also recognize how redundant it is. Not only are individual devices equivalent, but they often appear together. For instance, there are several cues for a flashback in a classical Hollywood film: pensive character

attitude, close-up of face, slow dissolve, voice-over narration, sonic "flashback," music. In any given case, several of these will be used together. (Bordwell et al., 5)

This is about as intelligent as claiming that Pope's paradigm is redundant because the basic metrical unit is signified by five feet and ten syllables and rhyme and end-stopping. These "devices" are, in a sense, "equivalent," and they invariably occur together (enjambment and the occasional alexandrine are the only possible deviations), but the presence of "redundancy," like the significance of decorum, can only be decided, as Bordwell lamely adds, on the evidence of a "given case." His catalogue of "cues for a flashback" is perfectly accurate, but in the given case, a specific selection will be made from among the cues, we will dissolve from something particular to something particular, the voice-over will be speaking words which relate to the images in particular ways, and the "pensive character attitude" will convey a particular set of feelings. It is the given case that matters, and great classical art is remarkable not for its redundancy but for the complete absence of it. Every word in the passages of Pope which I have quoted (and they are fully representative of his mature practice) is intensely significant, and classical conventions, in the hands of a great artist, actively conduce to this kind of density and complexity of realization. The conventions are only redundant to the eye of the formalist.

The comparison between "classical" English verse and "classical" Hollywood has, however, another—rather different—point. Pope's conventions were so much more constricting than Hitchcock's that they were only able to produce one Pope, and when we examine the two traditions, we are immediately struck by the infinitely greater range of the formal possibilities available to the classical filmmaker, and the infinitely greater number both of distinct styles and of distinguished single works which the Hollywood tradition produced. In searching for an explanation of this fact, we could do worse than to glance back at Bordwell's offhanded (and soon-forgotten) admission that Hollywood's "classicism" had sources which were "even" not classical—which were, in fact, vulgar in precisely the kind of way which alarmed the eighteenth century. Pope, too, had his "nonclassical" sources—most crucially, John Donne, who was, by Enlightenment standards, thoroughly "improper"—and it is important to note for the present purpose that the only English poet after Pope who was able to produce consistently distinguished verse in heroic couplets, Crabbe, is also remarkable for the strength of his connections with artistic forms external to the dominant poetic convention of his time (Geoffrey Chaucer on the one hand, and the newly emerging, non-"polite" novel on the other). The conditions in which the classical English poet worked made it extraordinarily difficult to establish connections of this sort, for the reason that the "rules" of Enlightenment poetic decorum are so emphatically and self-consciously the rules of a social class which imagines itself to be creating the first true postclassical civilization. Cultural propriety, for the Enlightenment, is and is felt to be continuous with the bourgeois social project as a whole, and the proprieties are therefore enforced, as Leavis has pointed out (*Revaluation*), with what seems in retrospect to have been an impoverishing rigidity. In order to write good classical verse, Pope and Crabbe had to find a means of being impolite with propriety, and their poetry stands out by virtue of the uniqueness of their success. When we again find major poetry which is rooted in classical forms, as we do in William Wordsworth and Byron, its authors are Romantics who have reinvented the forms and explicitly repudiated Enlightenment propriety.

Classical Hollywood, by contrast, made being impolite with propriety remarkably easy for those who were so disposed, and I do not think that the advantages which Hollywood enjoyed as a result of being considered beneath the contempt of cultivated bourgeois taste—and thus not answerable to its canons—have ever been sufficiently stressed. It has its decorum, but it is the decorum of an art form which was, and was felt to be, intrinsically indecorous, and which was therefore in a position to grab any set of traditions or conventions that came along. While he insists so much on "decorum" and "elegance" and "rule-governed craftsmanship," Bordwell is also offended by these magpie proclivities: the early pickings were, as he virtually says, "low," and when Hollywood moved on to higher things like Expressionism and montage, it was only to debase and recuperate them. (Bordwell et al., 72–74) I have to say that this sounds to me like bourgeois snobbery rationalizing itself, and I have my suspicions of an account of Hollywood's appropriation of montage which has a great deal to say about Slavko Vorkapich and goes on to mention *The Taking of Pelham 123* (1974), but which shows no consciousness of the existence of, say, the final scene of *Notorious* or the death of Mr. Hadley in *Written on the Wind* (1956) or the exposition of *Clash by Night* (1952). However, it is certainly true, as Bordwell fears, that most of the traditions grabbed—the assorted romanticisms and modernisms, psychoanalysis, melodrama, variety and vaudeville, that mongrel form "the bourgeois novel" itself—are not in any significant sense of the word *classical.* On the contrary, they are all, in their different ways, products of that complex cultural process initiated by the Romantic movement in the course of which the notion of cultural decorum established, and so rigorously enforced by the Enlightenment, was progressively undermined, either by conscious program or by the inexorable expansion of the market for cultural products.[1] The decorum of "classical" Hollywood is a decorum, but it also represents the most extreme form of the repudiation of decorum in the Enlightenment's sense which bourgeois culture has produced (and which "postmodern art" is now struggling to reinvent).[2] This is why Hollywood was scandalous to a John Grierson and to an Adorno alike, and why it remains so immensely important: the studio system marks the last point at which it was historically possible for a bourgeois art form to be rigorously and systematically conventional while at the same time subverting, and throwing into confusion, all existing cultural boundaries and proprieties and the ideologies of culture guaranteed by them.

It follows, therefore, that if we are to retain a concept of Hollywood "classicism"—as I suppose we must—we have to define and use it very carefully. The classical Hollywood conventions have been arrived at through the yoking together, by violence, of the most contradictory and heterogeneous formal and ideological materials, and the resulting admixture is both exceptionally elegant and coherent and potentially explosive. We cannot pretend, of course, that the cultural riches at Hollywood's disposal (like those at the disposal of the English Renaissance theater) were not regularly squandered. *Sh! The Octopus* and *The Speed Spook* exist, though I have no intention of talking about them, and they have no more interest for the film critic than the student of opera would discover in the procession of Dafnes and Orfeos who dragged their weary limbs across the stage in the late eighteenth century. The great and the interesting Hollywood films, however, explore their conventions, and their classicism is that of works committed to various kinds of excess and cultural critique under social conditions which include the successive Production Codes.

It is rather like holding a fireworks display in a gunpowder plant: the enterprise is both dangerous in itself and subject to severe penalties. Some works blunder heedlessly into peril and, having become aware of the fact, struggle frantically to extricate themselves without being caught. Others again proceed with sufficient caution to get away with it, but they pay a price in the more or less diminished glory and audacity of the display. A third group of works, however, sets out to raise the roof while also escaping detection, and they are able to do so because Hollywood's "classical" decorum permits the dramatic realization of the compressed, combustible cultural materials which, at the same time, it actively contains. These works can be both "proper" (if not polite) and outrageous: they can be "just a melodrama" and Epic Theater; "just a western" and a critique of American imperialism; "just a screwball comedy" and a celebration of the abolition of bourgeois gender roles; "just swatches of classical style" and exemplary forms of high modernism. The eighteenth century has its own examples of such perverse objects. Pope played both ends against the middle with dazzling expertise, and with the most profound seriousness, and as we listen to the symphonies of Haydn's "Sturm und Drang" period or read *Mansfield Park*, we come to realize that it is perfectly possible—where the spirit is willing—to reconcile the requirements of a decorum very much more stringent than that which weighed on Fritz Lang and Hitchcock with a critical, exploratory artistic project. How does one narrate class conflict and the oppression of women to a polite bourgeois audience? "You don't know?" replies Jane Austen. "You think it can't be done? Watch!"

This is the spirit in which the great classical movies operate.

The Myth of Postmodernism: The Bourgeois Intelligentsia in the Age of Reagan (1988)

Is there never to be an end to petty bourgeois theorists making long-term adjustments to short-term situations?
—Raymond Williams, "The Uses of Cultural Theory"

I remember when we were all reading Adam Smith. There is a book, now. I took in all the new ideas at one time—human perfectibility, now. But some say, history moves in circles; and that may be very well argued; I have argued it myself. The fact is, human reason may carry you a little too far—over the hedge, in fact. It carried me a good way at one time; but I saw it would not do. I pulled up; I pulled up in time. But not too hard. I have always been in favor of a little theory; we must have Thought; else we shall be landed back in the dark ages. But talking of books, there is Southey's *Peninsular War*. I am reading that of a morning. You know Southey?
— Brooke in George Eliot's *Middlemarch*

During the last decade, the concept of the "postmodern" has established itself securely as the reigning bourgeois intellectual fashion. Its empire has expanded as rapidly as Napoleon Bonaparte's and is ruled, indeed, in rather the same manner: one by one, post-Marxism, post-feminism, post-capitalism, post-criticism, post-theory, post-sexuality—a whole tribe of discursive uncles, brothers-in-law, and cousins twice removed of the buccaneering imperial adventurer has clawed its way to a little authority via his coattails. Whatever its philosophical merits, there is little doubt that this spectacular Thermidor "spells boff B.O.," as *Variety* would say if it were in this particular trade (which it very nearly is). Careers, reputations, and money are being made, and the bright graduate student with an eye to professional advancement would be well-advised to commit to paper, as rapidly as possible (fashions being what they are), a learned post-thesis on "the postmodern whatever" or "postmodernism and such-and-such." As the flood of anthologies and special issues of theoretical journals shows no sign of abating, it is certainly sufficiently easy to gain access to an audience, and the criteria for success are sufficiently unexacting. Ever since Fredric Jameson made his tour of the Bonaventura Hotel, the urban picaresque has been much in vogue, and the fresh-faced academic postulant who aspires to work up an addition to his/her curriculum vitae is not called upon to do much more than take a turn or two in the downtown core of the local hyperspace and meditate on the condition of the postmodern city.

Those of my readers who hesitate to believe that a genre has been born will have the pleasure and the profit of disabusing themselves when they dip into a recent issue of *Social Text,* which includes the reports of no less than two such expeditions, the author of one of which describes himself, with a candor which is presumably intended to be disarming, as a "suburban arriviste." (Herron, 75) It is even possible—or so I deduce from the collection of epigrams on the subject of "panic cinema" by Arthur Kroker and Michael Dorland—that the time, the legwork, and the bus fare required in order to research these *crépuscules du soir* represent an expenditure in excess of what is strictly required by the standards of contemporary cultivated discourse: "6. PANIC CINEMA. Filmmakers have only interpreted the world in various ways; the point, however, is to see *through* it." (Kroker and Dorland, 5) I would be very sorry to learn that any moderately ambitious young person with the advantage of a middle-class upbringing could not, in the space of thirty seconds, produce something at least as good.

The secret of this success (which Kroker, who is virtually an industry in himself, exemplifies; he has produced a couple of sizable volumes in exactly the same vein) is less than obscure. Not since the days of "the global village" and "the medium is the message" have thinking persons had at their disposal a reputable vocabulary with quite the same degree of racy glamour— quite the same air of having been coined in an advertising agency to promote the ultimate hamburger or the automobile of the day after tomorrow. "A pioneering attempt to establish a 'postmodernism of resistance' as the new cutting edge," announces Stanley Aronowitz apropos one of the most widely handled collections on postmodern culture, *The Anti-Aesthetic*—an encomium which the book's publishers, taking Aronowitz at his word, have understandably reprinted on the back cover as the ideal puff. "Cutting edge" is itself a Madison Avenue phrase, and it must be especially gratifying to think of oneself as being on, or at, it in an age in which the professional intelligentsia has never been more conspicuously irrelevant to the way in which social life is actually conducted or, as a group, more thoroughly complicit with the values and institutions of the dominant culture.

We may properly begin with the question of what it is that we are supposed to be "post." The suggestions would sometimes seem to be that we are post the so-called modern movement in bourgeois high art, and by this reckoning, I assume that "modernity" can be said to have begun at some point in the second half of the nineteenth century and to have ended during, or shortly after, World War II. There is, however, an alternative chronology which, while it is in general agreement with the first as to the moment when the "modern" stopped, maintains that it started considerably earlier—maintains, in fact, that modernity is roughly synonymous with what was once referred to, in a more primitive age, as "bourgeois culture." According to this argument, artistic "modernism," far from being "the modern" *tout court*, is actually the last fling of a larger "modern project" formulated by the first bourgeois intelligentsia during the Enlightenment—in a spirit which can now be seen to have been excessively sanguine.

This equivocation about what, exactly, modernity was is already sufficiently betraying, but the category is nothing if not elastic, and we discover, as we peruse the relevant literature, that it has, like Topsy in *Uncle Tom's Cabin*, a tendency to grow. Thus, for example, in a paper on "Feminists and Postmodernism" in *The Anti-Aesthetic*, Craig Owens informs us: "As recent analyses of the 'enunciative apparatus' of visual representation . . . confirm, the representational systems of the West admit only one vision—that of the constitutive male subject—or, rather, they posit the subject of representation as absolutely centered, unitary, masculine. The postmodernist work attempts to upset the reassuring stability of that mastering position." (58) For Owens, modernity would appear to consist of the whole of human culture (the obligatory concession to the Eastern Hemisphere is merely prophylactic) prior to the date of his own birth.

We may agree with Jameson that "Every position on postmodernism in culture—whether apologia or stigmatization—is also at one and the same time, and necessarily, an implicitly or explicitly political stance on the nature of multinational capitalism today." ("Postmodernism," 55) The more interesting fact, however, is that it may be deduced from the extraordinary variety and instability of the definitions of "the modern," for which postmodernist theory is supremely remarkable, that one of the things that is crucially at stake in the whole discourse is the contemporary bourgeois intellectual's sense of *the past*. Of course, the account of the past and the "implicitly or explicitly political" judgment of the present go together. In every case, the particular vision which we are offered both of the postmodern condition and of the obligations of the postmodern intellectual is rationalized by reference to a correlated fiction of the homogeneous content of modernity.

While all the theorists of postmodernism with whom I will be concerned in this paper define themselves, often rather assertively, as radicals, they can be divided nonetheless into two quite distinct groups. The writers in the first group, of whom Owens is representative, understand modernity (however defined) to be archaic and reactionary, and their affirmation of the postmodern is continuous with an orgiastic massacre of ancestors by means of which they enroll themselves imaginatively as members of the first true avant-garde. This celebratory postmodern discourse has its origins in French post-structuralism, and its political logic is anti-Marxist: that is to say, the construction of the category of postmodernity subserves the construction of alibis for the repudiation of Marxism. The writers in the second group, of whom Jameson and Jürgen Habermas are no doubt the most familiar, either are Marxists or are sympathetic to certain versions of Marxist ideas, and they propose a more or less nuanced negative critique of postmodern culture, which is perceived as the corollary of the advanced multinational capitalism which emerged, under U.S. hegemony, in the period following World War II. I will argue at a later stage both that the concept of the postmodern is fundamentally incompatible with a Marxist discourse (as the concept's lineage might suggest) and that Marxist appropriations of it do little more than surreptitiously recapitulate the theory of cultural apocalypse which the original Frankfurt School derived from putative features of capitalist culture which predate World War II by some 100 years. It seems to me, indeed, that the very obvious similarities between Theodor W. Adorno's "culture industry" and the postmodern condition analyzed by Jameson (not to say Habermas) reflect a current, and very serious, blockage in Marxist thought about culture in general and the commodity form of culture in particular.

Such considerations may be postponed for a while, however. The numerous promotional agents of postmodernism who regard themselves as the storm troopers of a new, improved Enlightenment have a prior claim to our attention, for they, after all, are the inventors of the talismanic discursive object with which we are concerned.

Postmodernism as Enlightenment

While every major movement in culture and the arts involves a reaction against the conventions, values, and assumptions of the previously dominant culture, the claims that are currently being made for the virtues of postmodernism differ in two crucial respects from, say, the repudiation of the Gothic during the Renaissance or the attack on eighteenth-century norms of decorum and propriety by the artists and theorists of the Romantic movement. The first is the quite remarkable inclusiveness of the disapprobation of the past: the history of (Western) culture from the moment at which modernity is deemed to begin would appear to boil down to a few rather gross, and rather basic, intellectual errors, endlessly remarked under a confusing variety of brand names which has encouraged the innocent to suppose that there are substantive differences between the products. The second is the evident tendentiousness, and the curious lack of clarity and conviction, in the etching of the alternative—ultraradical though it undoubtedly is—which postmodernism is supposed to represent. We find, on inspection, either that there is no alternative at all—and that we are a little foolish (indeed, a little reactionary) to have imagined that there was—or that the account of it which we are given is sustained by nothing better than the conjurer's sleight of hand and a more or less consciously cynical bluff. There seems to be some reason to suppose that these two things are intimately connected.

The postmodern epitaph for history is brief and crushing: Owens, taking his cue from Jean-François Lyotard, needs no more than two sentences to dispose of four or five centuries of political struggle and intellectual labor.

> In fact, Lyotard diagnoses the postmodern condition as one in which the *grands recits* of modernity—the dialectic of spirit, the emancipation of the worker, the accumulation of wealth, the classless society—have all lost credibility. Lyotard defines a discourse as modern when it appeals to one or another of these *grands recits* for its legitimacy; the advent of postmodernity, then, signals a crisis in narrative's legitimizing function, its ability to compel consensus. (64)

Should a dissenting churl, from his/her station in what Geoffrey Chaucer calls "the lewednesse behinde" (a station to which I feel increasingly that I belong), attempt to point out to Owens that the accumulation of wealth and the class struggle, despite the fact that people have written about them, are material social processes rather than narratives, and that it is, moreover, possible (and even desirable) to distinguish politically between the practices and discourses of capitalism and socialism, Owens would have his answer ready.

> *Master narrative*—how else to translate Lyotard's *grand recit*? And in this translation we glimpse the terms of another analysis of modernity's demise, one that speaks not of the incompatibility of the various modern narratives, but instead of their fundamental solidarity. For what made the *grands recits* of modernity master narratives if not the fact that they were all narratives of mastery, of man seeking his telos in the conquest of nature? What function did these narratives play other than to legitimize Western

man's self-appointed mission of transforming the entire planet in his own image? And what form did this mission take if not that of man's placing of his stamp on everything that exists—that is, the transformation of the world into a representation, with man as its subject? In this respect, however, the phrase master narrative seems tautologous, since all narrative, by virtue of "its power to master the dispiriting effects of the corrosive force of the temporal process," may be narrative of mastery. (65–66)

The "fundamental solidarity" of the discourses of modernity—and above all, of capitalism and Marxism—is indeed the leitmotif of the apology for postmodernism, and the significance of Owens's essay is that it shows us very clearly, with the confidence intimated by that astonishing cascade of rhetorical questions, what are the political consequences of the theory of representation-as-oppression which gained such currency in the 1970s and of which Colin MacCabe's articles on "realism" and Laura Mulvey's on "Visual Pleasure and Narrative Cinema" were the most influential examples. For whom, it might be asked, has the master narrative of the accumulation of wealth "lost credibility"? That it has no hold on Lyotard and Owens I will pay them the compliment of believing, but I am convinced that the directors of General Motors, IBM, and AT&T take a quite different view of the matter, and that if the question were put to them, they would be able to explain—with a brevity and passion in direct proportion to their lack of theoretical sophistication—exactly in what ways the ideal of the accumulation of wealth is to be distinguished from that of the classless society. The shattering discovery that capitalism and socialism are the same thing has escaped the notice of the ruling class which, for reasons best known to itself, continues to act on the old-fashioned assumption that one of them is to be preferred to the other. For this obstinate conservatism there is, perhaps, after all, an explanation: the belief that "Western culture" consists of a handful of interchangeable narratives can only be enjoyed in the cloistered seclusion of the library (or its postmodern equivalent). Lyotard and Owens may well feel somewhat jaded about modernity and inclined to give the whole thing up as a bad job, but all the evidence suggests that capitalism is not.

Aronowitz recapitulates Owens's argument, very much more suavely, in a recent article on "postmodernism and politics." One of the "ineluctable features" of postmodern discourse, he tells us, is *the rejection of universal reason as a foundation for human affairs* (italics in the original).

Reason in this sense is a series of rules of thought that any ideal rational person might adopt if his/her purpose was to achieve propositions of universal validity. Postmodern thought, on the contrary, is bound to discourse, literally narratives about the world that are admittedly *partial*. Indeed, one of the crucial features of discourse is the intimate tie between knowledge and interest, the latter being understood as a "standpoint" from which to grasp "reality." Putting these terms in inverted commas signifies the will to abandon scientificity, science as a set of propositions claiming validity by any given competent investigatory. What postmodernists deny is precisely this category of impartial competence. For competence is constituted as a series of exclusions—of women, of people of color, of nature as a historical agent, of the truth value of art. (103)

The most immediately striking thing about this passage is its breathtaking hypocrisy. "The renunciation of foundational thought" is, of course, a key item in the postmodernist sales pitch, but just as Lyotard's anathemas against the very idea of a *grand recit* do not prevent him from advancing one of the grandest ever concocted, so Aronowitz's disavowal of "impartial competence" sits cheek by jowl with a definition of reason, and (charmingly) of the "ineluctable" features of postmodernism, which is agreeable to the very criteria he claims to be rejecting. This contradiction may be unfortunate, but it is hardly surprising. No human being ever uttered a public statement about the world which did not embody an appeal to a conceptual "foundation" independent of the speaker. Such an appeal is implicit in the use of language, and the notion of a form of thought which has renounced foundations is an illusion. This is not to say that every utterance enters an appeal in the court of "universal reason." Universal reason is a bourgeois myth which had no philosophical existence before René Descartes (in whose work it appeared, historically, as a subversive category). Pre-Cartesian philosophies had a variety of different foundations, and as universal reason has come in for a good deal of criticism over the last three hundred years from a number of points of view, Aronowitz's announcement that the cogito has its limitations seems somewhat ill timed.

But then, serious theoretical disputation is not in Aronowitz's line: the proposition that all modern philosophies take their stand on universal reason is so obviously ludicrous that we suspect that Cartesian rationalism is being used as a stalking horse for something else, and so, indeed, it proves to be. Aronowitz's ploy is to identify "foundational thought" with rationalism and then to classify as rationalism the whole corpus of Western philosophy between (at least) Descartes and the postmodernists. Strangely enough, however, having effected this monumental synthesis, Aronowitz shows no great interest in castigating Immanuel Kant or Gottfried Leibnitz or Ludwig Wittgenstein: it is Marxism he is after.

> Fredric Jameson differs, of course, from Habermas in his criticism of post-modernism . . . Yet his critique is actually another version of universal reason. Jameson does not establish the validity of [M]arxism by defending it against postmodernity, but by invoking its categories to explain the phenomenon. Thus he preserves the most stunning element of [M]arxist theory, its explanatory power. (103)

Aronowitz would not be caught dead invoking a category to explain anything. He prefers, as a representative postmodernist, to place "standpoint" and "reality" in quotation marks and to pretend to himself and his readers that he has achieved the Homeric feat of speaking "just for himself" in a public language which he did not invent. His elaborate repudiation of "foundational thought" and his candid admission of his partiality are, in fact, an ingenious way of claiming for himself the very impartial competence which he traduces in the arguments of others. It is the thought of *other people* which has the foundations. Postmodernist thought is sui generis, its objectivity and independence guaranteed by the exposure of the myopic foundational bias of the discourses of which the writer disapproves and the grace with which s/he adverts to the "intimate tie between knowledge and interest"—the intimacy expressing itself, in the most embarrassing cases, as autobiographical sweet talk. The appeal of anti-foundationalism, in other words, is that it gives a new lease on life to one of the most desiccated myths of bourgeois scholarship—the myth of academic impartiality.

The political respectability of postmodernist theory is habitually secured by reference to what Ernesto Laclau and Chantal Mouffe call "the new social movements"("Post-Marxism," 104)—of which it can truly be said that had they not existed, postmodernism would have been obliged to invent them. It is in the name of the disenfranchised—women, "people of color," gays (yes, there is a good word for gays too)—that Aronowitz launches his attack on foundational thought, though why foundationalism should issue automatically in the "exclusion" of these unfortunates is not clear (at least, to me) from Aronowitz's essay. It might even be claimed that the validity of the proposition that "women are not inferior to men" can be established without an appeal to "universal reason as a foundation for human affairs," and I for one remain to be convinced that the political aims of the feminist movement can be realized on the basis of foundational "agnosticism." However this may be, one would have considerably greater sympathy for, and confidence in, the wave of sympathy for women and gays which seems to be sweeping the campuses of Europe and North America if it were not so often accompanied by Red-baiting on the one hand and contempt for the working class on the other.

"Marxism privileges the characteristically masculine activity of production as the definitively human activity (Marx: 'men begin to distinguish themselves from animals as soon as they begin to produce their means of subsistence'); women, historically consigned to the spheres of nonproductive or reproductive labor, are thereby situated outside the society of male producers, in a state of nature." (Owens, 63) In a footnote to this passage, Owens is even clearer: "Marxism's difficulty with feminism is not part of an ideological bias inherited from outside; rather, it is a structural effect of its privileging of production as the definitively human activity." (79) We have reason to be suspicious of a supposedly feminist critique of Marx which rests on the astonishing proposition that women have always been excluded from the process of production as Marx defines it, and one's sense that there is something in Owens's deployment of feminism which can only be called opportunistic is confirmed by his apparent ignorance of, or lack of interest in, the existence of large numbers of women who define themselves as Marxists.

What are such women to deduce from Owens's essay as his explanation of them? No one will deny that there is a "patriarchal bias" in some Marxist text or that Marxism has on occasions had "difficulty" with feminism. Many women and men during the last century have devoted their time and energy to confronting, and attempting to overcome, this "difficulty," and while a univocally anti-Marxist feminism may be useful for the purposes of Owens's essay, it remains a fictional construction of his own, which bears as little resemblance to the forms and contents of women's political struggles and feminist theory in the twentieth century as it does to the existing corpus of Marxist literature. Part of the difficulty Owens mentions is attributable not to the nasty masculinism of Marxism (and Marxists) but to the extreme difficulty of analyzing the way in which, in any given social formation, class and gender inequalities intersect and act on each other. While, as Owens says, "sexual inequality cannot be reduced to an instance of economic exploitation" (63)—an observation that will not come as news to anyone seriously interested in the subject—it is at least equally obvious that the struggle against women's oppression is unlikely to be furthered by the thesis that "economic exploitation" is intrinsically masculine.

Aronowitz and Laclau and Mouffe are also unhappy with Marx's "privileging" of class, especially his privileging of the working class. This unhappiness gives two quite different accounts of itself, and the discrepancy between them is very revealing. Thus, Laclau and Mouffe tell us in the first place, as a matter of theoretical principle, that "there are no *a priori* privileged places in the anti-capitalist struggle," and that Marx was clearly incorrect when he assigned such a place to the proletariat. ("Post-Marxism," 104) Aronowitz, while he admits (in one of my favorite phrases in the whole postmodernist literature) that "power tends to accrue to those possessing superior economic resources," is essentially in agreement. Despite this mysterious incremental "tendency" on power's part, "power distribution . . . does not obey any definite laws," and consequently Marx's conception of "the primacy of the accumulation process with its concomitant class differentiation and struggle" is erroneous. (107) Rather, "There are many points of antagonism between capitalism and various sections of the population (environmental pollution, property development in certain areas, the arms race, the flow of capital from one region to another, etc.), and this means that we will have a variety of anti-capitalist struggles." (Laclau and Mouffe, "Post-Marxism," 104)

Whatever we might think of these arguments—and the fact that Laclau and Mouffe rest their case on a quite outrageous travesty of Marx's analysis of the objectively exploitative nature of the wage form does not inspire confidence—it can at least be said that they do not deny the existence and the political significance of class struggle altogether. However, they coexist with, and are flatly contradicted by, arguments of another kind, the tenor of which can be fairly represented by this:

> The history of the production of "Man" (in the sense of human beings who are bearers of rights in their exclusive human capacity) is a recent history . . . and it has been one of the great achievements of our culture; to outline this history would be to reconstruct the various discursive surfaces where it has taken place—the juridical, educational, economic and other institutions, in which differences based on status, social class or wealth were progressively eliminated. (104)

A page later we are informed that while Eduard Bernstein's projection of "future advances in the democratization of the State and of society . . . was, without any doubt, excessively simplistic and optimistic," he was nevertheless "fundamentally correct" in his intuition that workers were ceasing to be "proletarian" and becoming "citizens." (Laclau and Mouffe, "Post-Marxism," 105)

As descriptions of any observable state, process, or tendency in capitalist society, these remarks are so grotesque as to raise the question of why it is that Laclau and Mouffe—who, when I last heard of them, lived in Margaret Thatcher's Britain—do not immediately join the Conservative Party: the adjective "post-Marxist" seems altogether inadequate to designate a vision of history which might have been promulgated by the Tory Central Office in a pamphlet on the democratic consequences of the sale of council housing. It would seem that the class struggle has been won—though no doubt a little "class discrimination" (betraying phrase!)

continues to "limit the emergence and full validity of humanism" ("Post-Marxism," 102)—and that it is not so much the case that the struggle of the working class is one form of anticapitalist struggle among others as that the material conditions which generate that struggle have been effectively abolished. Since this happy state of affairs appears to have been brought about by "the consolidation and democratic reform" of the capitalist state, and since the solvent of such political inequalities as continue to exist appears to consist of more consolidation and more reform, it is difficult to see in what sense the struggle of the working class (or of anybody) can be thought of actually as being anticapitalist. How is it possible to conduct an anticapitalist struggle through the medium of a state which is itself capitalist? Or, conversely, if the struggle is indeed anticapitalist, is it not reasonable to suppose that capitalism will do some struggling in its turn? Laclau and Mouffe never really address these questions, in part, perhaps, because their conception of "struggle" is so sedate: "Everything depends," apparently, "on a proliferation of public spaces of argumentation and decision whereby social agents are increasingly capable of self-management." ("Post-Marxism," 104)

Laclau and Mouffe seem to think of capitalist society as a sort of extended Senior Combination Room in which free and equal citizens—some of whom, for reasons which remain unclear, are for the time being more free and equal than others—engage in "processes of argumentation which never lead to an ultimate foundation" but, as a result of which, things in general miraculously improve. ("Post-Marxism," 105–6) The basis for this improvement is as mysterious as the fact that any improvement is necessary, for Laclau and Mouffe's denial that the antagonism between capital and labor is intrinsic to the capitalist mode of production does not have the consequences they suppose it to have. They imagine themselves to be proving that the working class, such as it is, has no privileged role in the democratic struggle: what they actually contrive to do is to theorize away the material basis for any form of oppression whatever within capitalist society. They tell us that such oppression exists in a multitude of forms, but they cannot tell us why, for their ingenious scheme of reforming capitalism and consolidating it at the same time obliges them to show—as they do, very effectively—that capitalist social relations are not objectively oppressive.

While Laclau and Mouffe can scarcely contain their enthusiasm for the democratic potential of the capitalist state and its striking contributions to the welfare of the working class, their contempt for Marxism and Marxists knows no bounds, and Norman Geras's assertion—innocent enough, in all conscience—that "it is an axiom that socialism should be democratic"—provokes an outburst of Cold War anticommunism of which the *Sun* would be proud: "Has Geras ever heard of Stalinism, of the one-party system, of press censorship, of the Chinese Cultural Revolution, of the Polish coup d'etat, of the entry of Soviet tanks into Prague and Budapest?" ("Post-Marxism," 101) Laclau and Mouffe have no excuse for failing to be aware that a Marxist critique of Stalinism has existed for as long as Stalinism itself, and this catalogue of specifically socialist atrocities—the addition to which of "press censorship" and, in the age of Reagan, "the one-party system," might be deemed to be tactless—seems especially distasteful in the context of an essay which fails in any way to distance itself from, or even to take cognizance of, the actual conduct of political life at any given moment in the history of capitalist society.

Aronowitz also takes a dim view of the workers (who have "lost their autonomous voice") and a favorable one of the "new social movements," but I would find it difficult to summarize what he wishes to tell us about them. "Postmodern politics, then, takes as its object the pragmatic willingness of ruling groups to accommodate the demands of organized movements which, in turn, frame their own politics in terms set externally by the ruling class." (107) As a description of "the struggle for democratic power" in Latin America and South Africa—which Aronowitz goes on to offer as shining examples of postmodern politics in practice—this seems to be curious, if not bizarre, but I am still more bewildered by the proposition that the South African Union of Mineworkers "does not appeal to traditional class solidarity as its primary line of attack, but addresses *power itself* as an antagonist," or that, in South Africa, race has replaced class as a "detonator" of cultural contradictions. (113, 110) The political significance of race in South Africa consists in the fact that the workers are black and the ruling class white, and the South African Union of Mineworkers is fighting not "*power itself*" (italicized by way of pretending that it means something) but the fascist form of the capitalist state. And what is one to make of Aronowitz's claim that "unlike the bourgeois and socialist revolutions, which involved the marginalization of the Church from centers of power, base Christian communities—especially in Latin America—have placed the Catholic Church in the midst of the struggle for democratic power"? (110) The fact to which this formulation points is that large numbers of Latin American priests are socialists who interpret Christian theology in the light of Marxist politics—at the risk of excommunication by His Holiness, who, on his last South American jaunt, attempted to preach the virtues of chastity and poverty in a packed football stadium and was roundly booed.

Aronowitz might easily have spared himself these intellectual somersaults by ignoring the revolution in the Third World completely: his politics are hardly distinguishable from those of Laclau and Mouffe, who have the good sense, however, to steer clear of subjects which will oblige them to pretend that the class struggle is really something else. In doing so, they also spare themselves the embarrassment of constructing a category of "postmodern politics" which defines every contemporary political struggle from that of the Sao Paolo metalworkers to that of North American ecologists as an example of a new form of resistance from which class has been "displaced" and which demonstrates the superannuation both of the proletariat and of Marxism. For if it is indeed the case that the workers have had their day and that socialism "is to be understood as an extension of the democratic revolution" (that is, as Aronowitz makes plain, a nicer version of capitalism, including, of course, "its parliamentary forms"[111]), then some way must indeed be found of convincing oneself that the anti-imperialist revolution is "nice" too, even at the expense of "displacing" its class character and inventing a progressive role for Catholicism—as opposed to the turbulent revolutionary priests who have so displeased the Vatican. Since Aronowitz seems to be so well disposed toward religious revivals as correctives to the perniciously secular character of "bourgeois and socialist" life, he may yet discover, I suppose, that Protestant fundamentalism has a vital contribution to make to the struggle for democracy in the United States, though I hardly think that even the postmodernist cause would be advanced by such an alliance.

The problem with Aronowitz's reasoning is the self-deception it entails. The revolution in the Third World is not a nice postmodern "democratic" movement "speaking a language of localism and regionalism" (113) but a nasty class struggle of the traditional kind; alas, the workers of North America and Western Europe who appear to Aronowitz to have lost their autonomous voice are fighting the class struggle too. The results may not be as spectacular as he would wish, and it may well seem to him that the local proletariat has failed to come up to "requirements"—a word which, like "standpoint" and "reality," he astutely places in quotation marks. (114) When I last looked, Western workers were fighting tooth and nail—amid mass unemployment, welfare cuts, and confident capitalist *revanchisme*—to preserve those institutions and organizations, "characterized by a whole network of cultural affinities," which seem, from Aronowitz's coign of vantage, to have a merely "instrumental" character (112). Moreover, the spectacle of professional middle-class intellectuals taking the labor movement in the advanced capitalist countries to task for failing to offer them "a vision of a better life," or assuming that because the working class has not produced the revolution on cue it has thereby ceased to "make demands that challenge existing arrangements," seems to me so gross as to virtually defy eloquence. (114)

As a gay man, I am the last person to underestimate the political significance of "the new social movements"—a form of words to which, it is only proper to add, I take the most extreme exception. There is nothing "new" about the political struggle against the oppression of gays, women, and blacks (feminism, in fact, is rather older than socialism), and the phrase is nothing more than an opportunistic rhetorical convenience with the assistance of which a move to the right can be experienced, and promoted, as a new, higher form of radical commitment. The autonomous struggles of gays, women, and blacks are politically crucial: they are not reducible to class struggle, and their goals will not automatically be realized by an anticapitalist revolution, as we have good reason to know. It remains the case, however, that without an anticapitalist revolution, the goals of the gay, women's, and black movements (not to mention the peace and the green movements) will not be achieved, and the ideal of "equal democratic rights within class society," to which the program of "the movements" is now so often reduced, is as banal as its consummation is unlikely. I am correspondingly opposed to the use of these movements as an alibi for McCarthyist jeremiads against Marx, Marxist theory, and the Soviet Union; or as a means of patronizing the labor movement and wishing class struggle away; or as a support for the egregious illusion that, by dint of gradual reform and scrupulous argumentation between right-minded, "self-managing" persons, the inequalities of capitalist society can be transcended in a society which remains capitalist. The most striking feature of the development of the capitalist state in the last twenty years has been a growing repressive administrative centralism on the one hand and a reduction, through "privatization" and cuts, of the state's socioeconomic functions on the other. The effect of this development has been not to promote "democracy" but to fiercely exacerbate the most basic inequalities and the most fundamentally undemocratic aspects of capitalist society. Even if there were any evidence whatever that this trajectory will be reversed, the idea that capitalism would countenance the reform or abolition of those of its characteristics which constitute it as capitalist would remain ridiculous, and persons of goodwill who conspire to believe—in the age of Margaret Thatcher, Oliver North, Clause 28, and the Free Trade Bill—that the existing form of the state can be used to realize the democratic demands of gays, women, workers, or anybody are doomed to yet further disillusionment.

In the 1960s, Isaac Deutscher told an audience of American university students: "You are effervescently active on the margin of social life, and the workers are passive right at the core of it. That is the tragedy of our society. If you do not deal with this contrast you will be defeated." (74) "Passive" seems to me the wrong word—though that the working class in the advanced capitalist countries is profoundly on the defensive and lacks, for understandable reasons, a sense of practical alternatives no one will dispute. Nevertheless, Deutscher's austere judgment retains its force. Faced with the "tragedy" he describes, it is certainly pleasant to cheer oneself up by claiming that the workers are no longer up to it, that they were probably never up to it in the first place, and that the "new social movements" will get the job done in record time by formulating anti-foundationalist democratic demands which the capitalist state will promptly meet. The reason for concerning oneself with this simpleminded fantasy is its catastrophic implications for concrete political strategy—implications which, as it happens, might be construed already: for all the anti-Stalinist invective of its proponents, "postmodern politics" is essentially Stalinist popular frontism under a different name. The new social movements deserve a rather better fate than to be co-opted as propaganda for a thrilling remake of that ill-fated adventure.

The Museum

In the room the women come and go
Talking of Michelangelo.
　　—T. S. Eliot, "The Love Song of J. Alfred Prufrock"

If postmodern politics derive from the knowledge that "modernist political ideology" (that is—insofar as they can be distinguished—liberalism and Marxism) is, like Oscar Wilde's Bunbury, thoroughly exploded, post-art and post-criticism consist of the belief that Western culture is a vast junk heap of miscellaneous objets d'art on the lines of Citizen Kane's cellar—though, as we have renounced foundations, there is, of course, no Rosebud. Here is Eugenio Donato, quoted approvingly by Douglas Crimp in an essay "On the Museum's Ruins":

> The set of objects the Museum contains is sustained only by the fiction that they somehow constitute a coherent representational universe ... Such a fiction is the re-sult of an uncritical belief in the notion that ordering and classifying, that is to say, the spatial juxtaposition of fragments, can produce a representational understand-ing of the world. Should the fiction disappear, there is nothing left of the Museum but "bric-a-brac," a heap of meaningless and valueless fragments of objects which are incapable of substituting themselves either metonymically for the original objects or metaphorically for their representations. (Crimp, 49)

We are not to suppose from Crimp's hostility to the institution of the museum that he has any challenging new criteria of aesthetic or cultural value to propose: on the contrary, what he objects to is the "fiction" allegedly perpetuated by museums that one fragment is of greater (or lesser) consequence than another. It goes without saying that the brisk cancel-lation of the concept of value, like that of the concept of class in the discourse of "radical democracy," is presented to us as a revolutionary achievement, and Crimp begins his essay with an attack on the "moralizing cultural conservatism" of the art critic Milton Kramer, who suggests (in a review which Crimp quotes) that Edouard Manet is a finer painter than William-Adolphe Bouguereau and that there is something anomalous about hanging canvasses by these two artists under the same roof. It is the second of these claims that provides Crimp with his pretext, and one must admit (I suppose) that in this respect he has a point. Bouguereau's paintings, like Alfred, Lord Tennyson's epic poems, are documents in the history of taste which have, as such, certain (not, it seems to me, very great) interest and whose existence certainly deserves to be acknowledged in any comprehensive survey of the art of the period—if only, in the case of Tennyson's "charades from the Middle Ages" (as Gerard Manley Hopkins called them), by brief quotation. What Crimp really objects to, however, is the distinction between "document" and "masterpiece"—a distinction foisted on us, we are told, "throughout the era of modernism" and artificially preserved, in the postmodern era, within the museum's walls. (50)

Crimp's very representative argument rests on two false assumptions: firstly, that it is sufficient to dispose of the concept of artistic value by pointing out that the value of a work of art is not "self-evident"; and secondly, that the art of the past has no order or coherence except that which is arbitrarily imposed upon it by an institution such as the museum or a discourse such as art history. It is so far from being the case that the superiority of Manet's "Olympia" to Bouguereau's "Early Morning" is "self-evident" that a person who knew nothing about painting in general and nineteenth-century French painting in particular would not be in a position to adjudicate the subject, and since a value judgment is a historical action by the person who judges, there will never come a day when Manet's superiority to Bouguereau will have been "proved" in the mathematical sense. Works of art are also historical actions, and the greatness of "Olympia" was certainly not self-evident to the patrons of the Salon of 1865, who regarded it as a disgusting affront to all known moral and aesthetic standards. Inasmuch as it is such action, a work of art cannot be detached from the history in which it intervened, and one's judgment of it will be continuous with one's understanding of what the nature of that intervention was. That museums have the effect of fetishizing art is obvious: in a bourgeois society, they are one of the means by which art is separated off from the public social world in which it originated and defined as "other." It hardly follows, however, that the only difference between a Manet and a Bouguereau is that the value of one of them has been inflated by the museum and the value of the other has not. There are no doubt people in the world who think Manet is great because they have been told that he is or because they have seen his works rather than Bouguereau's when they visited an art gallery, and these things tell us a great deal about the sizable quotient of snobbery in bourgeois philistinism. They do not account for favorable judgments of Manet (Paul Cézanne's, for example) which were arrived at on another basis, and they do not explain away the demonstrable fact that Manet's and Bouguereau's relations to the artistic conventions and cultural values of their time were different. No doubt Manet's paintings have been fetishized by the bourgeois museum—from which we conclude that fetishization is one of the contents of the history of Manet's paintings: other social conditions can produce different conditions of reception—but the bourgeois museum cannot be used to demonstrate either that there is a difference in value between his work and Bouguereau's or that there is not.

The historical interest of "cultural documents" being in question, we can at least pay Crimp the compliment of saying that he has produced an interesting cultural document in his own right: he may not shed much light on the subject of art, but as an example of what I take to be the dominant contemporary taste in these matters, his essay is really indispensable. We have become accustomed to hearing a great deal about the cultural debasement of the working classes—which has been, indeed, since the days in which Adorno lamented the obliviousness of "the common people" (as he called them) to "the wrong that is done them" by jazz and the Hollywood cinema (Horkheimer and Adorno, 121), one of the grand themes of bourgeois critical theory. It puts in a reappearance (under another name) in Louis Althusser's account of "the interpellation of the subject," from whose iron laws the theorist, his epigones, and his readers are miraculously exempt. We hear a good deal less about the cultural debasement of the bourgeoisie, despite the fact that the phenomenon is equally interesting. The postmodern intellectual tourist is a kind of cheerful, cultivated vandal for whom the bourgeois past, construed as "modernity," consists precisely of bric-a-brac—a collection of tacky gimcracks and gewgaws none of which is clearly perceived, all of which are reducible to one another, and to each of which the tourist is in fact profoundly indifferent. S/he—insofar as s/he pays attention to these faded glories at all—finds in them nothing but the endless reiteration of a single, boring, bankrupt myth (representationalism, the myth of presence, phallocentrism) which, with the privilege of hindsight and a superior education, the keen tourist has seen through. In spite of this revelation, however, the tourist cannot conceive of a way of doing anything different: "Few have produced new, 'positive' images of a revised femininity; to do so would simply supply and thereby prolong the life of the existing representational apparatus." (Owens, 71) All that remains, therefore, is to issue public notice of one's disengagement from, and one's knowingness about, the reactionary representational strategies characteristic of the bourgeois hall of fame—which is what postmodern art amounts to.

The existence of a bourgeois intelligentsia which is blind to the most challenging and disturbing artifacts of its own culture, and which derives its conviction that it is a vanguard from displays of pure ironic distance from its own past, is a momentous new social fact, the significance of which asserts itself fairly plainly in this passage from Michel Foucault (quoted, again approvingly, by Crimp):

"Dejeuner sur l'Herbe" and "Olympia" were perhaps the first "museum" paintings, the first paintings in European art that were less a response to the achievement of Giorgione, Raphael and Velázquez than an acknowledgment . . . of the new and substantial relationship of painting to itself, as a manifestation of the existence of museums and the particular reality and interdependence that paintings acquire in museums. In the same period [Flaubert's] *The Temptation* [*of St. Anthony*] was the first literary work to comprehend the greenish institutions where books are accumulated and where the slow and incontrovertible vegetation of learning quietly proliferates. Flaubert is to the library what Manet is to the museum. . . . They erect their art within the archive. . . .

every painting now belongs within the squared and massive surface of painting and all literary works are confined to the indefinite murmur of writing. (Crimp, 47)

Before it could become apparent to Foucault that Manet "erects his art within the archive," "Olympia" caused one of the greatest artistic scandals of the nineteenth century, and Gustave Flaubert was prosecuted in the French courts for publishing *Madame Bovary*, which he conceived from the outset in terms of a critique of the sort of art represented by *The Temptation*. The great advantage of solipsism, by contrast, is that it is unlikely to upset anybody, and the appropriation of Manet and Flaubert (of all people) for the genealogy of the postmodernist enterprise would almost be touching if it were less reprehensible. If the postmodernist aesthetic has been found so attractive, it is because it provides such solipsism with impeccable political credentials and allows the artist and his/her audience (which is in general materially rather comfortable and wishes to remain so) to believe that an object which is to all intents and purposes purely decorative is also a critical intervention in contemporary culture. Anyone who doubts the validity of this diagnosis might well consider the odious General Idea AIDS poster, which is so patently convinced of its political responsibility and which so patently reduces AIDS to an occasion for the production of a piece of tasteful, best-selling middle-class wallpaper. Postmodern art is the program of a class fraction which is no longer capable of expressing significant opposition to the dominant tendencies of capitalist society and which has no pressing interest in doing so, but which continues to spin fantasies of its own radicalism by facetiously debunking an erroneous model of the cultural past and attempting to politicize (without jeopardizing its chances at the box office) the conventions of late twentieth-century fashion magazines and interior decoration.

The Intellectual as Dandy

The role of the postmodern intellectual is explicitly theorized by Jacques Derrida:

> We are today on the eve of Platonism. Which can also, naturally, be thought of as the morning after Hegelianism. At that specific point, the *philosophia*, the *episteme*, are not "overturned," "rejected," "reined in," etc., in the name of something like writing; quite the contrary. But they are, according to a relation that philosophy would call *simulacrum*, according to a more subtle excess of truth, assumed and at the same time displaced into a completely different field, where one can still, but that's all, "mime absolute knowledge." (*Dissemination*, 107–8)

With a happy consciousness of his own casuistry (why not "the after-dinner sleep of historical materialism"?), the post-thinker embraces the necessity of dilettantism. It is all a game, and no more is required of the player than a certain bravura and talent for self-promotion. The dying words of the postmodern intellectual will be, like Cyrano's, "*Mon panache!*"

In his essay on the duties of the post-critic in *The Anti-Aesthetic*, Gregory Ulmer earnestly develops the Master's hint and moves triumphantly toward an analogy between the contemporary intellectual and the saprophyte, which "lives off the decay of dead organisms in a way that makes life possible for living plants."

The point is that if normal critics adhere to the model of the poem as living plant—the critic M. H. Abrams, for example, one of those accusing the deconstructors of being "parasites," whose *Mirror and the Lamp* provides the definitive study of the organic model in poetry—it might be useful to emblematize post-criticism as the saprophyte, growing among the roots of literature, feeding off the decay of tradition. (106)

This is charmingly put: the intellectual is, or ought to be, knowingly bankrupt, but this bankruptcy remains, sub specie aeternitatis, in some unfathomable way useful. I am not quite sure (despite the example he gives) what Ulmer means by a "normal critic"—there being so many critics around who do not subscribe to the view that works of art are, or can properly be compared to, living plants. I will say, however, that there seems to me to be a close correspondence between the pernicious absurdity of the concept of criticism which is normal to him and Crimp's suggestion, elsewhere in the same volume, that Flaubert's *Bouvard et Pécuchet* provides us with the paradigm of "the modernist intellectual," and that this correspondence sums up in itself the latest form of *la trahison des clercs*.

The Poverty of Critical Theory

No one, of course, would think of putting Jameson's work in the same category as that of the Arthur Krokers and the Douglas Crimps. Jameson not only tries to be serious but also wishes to hold on to his Marxism, and in the context of contemporary North American academic life, where polite (and sometimes not so polite) forms of anti-Marxist sentiment are again becoming respectable, if not obligatory, this perverse endeavor commands our admiration and respect. And yet it is difficult not to feel (or so it seems to me) that the conditions in which the professional literary academic is now obliged to work have not taken their toll on Jameson too: who would have thought that the author of *The Prison-House of Language* could ever have written a piece as muddled, as inconsequent, as eclectic, and as question begging as that lengthy disquisition on "the cultural logic of late capitalism"? ("Postmodernism") Jameson spares us Friedrich Nietzsche, but he throws in everything else: Susan Sontag on camp, Edmund Burke and Kant on the sublime, Sigmund Freud on the uncanny, Raymond Williams on the residual and the emergent, Harold Innis on space and time, Jacques Lacan on schizophrenia, Ernest Mandel on late capitalism, Thomas Mann on pastiche, Kevin Lynch on the city, Jean-Paul Sartre on "derealization": there is even what looks like the odd conciliatory gesture toward the Heidegger revival. It is precisely because Jameson is not a dilettante that this sort of dilettantism, when a figure of his distinction is betrayed into it, is hardly readable as a personal idiosyncrasy. He is, as I have said, very different from Kroker, but his writings on postmodernism must be referred to the same *niveau* which encourages Kroker to flit lightly from Marquis de Sade to Margaret Atwood, from Marshall McLuhan to Mary Shelley, from Foucault to Thomas Aquinas, and then dole out the resulting cognitive soup as a Theory. There was a time when Jameson would have been able to resist the temptation to tell us that Vietnam was "the first postmodern war."

One cannot read any of the various versions of Jameson's thesis on postmodernism for long without encountering the feeling that one has read something rather like it before. If

Dialectic of Enlightenment does not suggest itself at once as the obvious model (or precedent), despite some pretty obvious parallels, that is in part because the tone is so very different. Adorno and Max Horkheimer did not feel in the least obliged to institute a search for a utopian moment in downtown Los Angeles, and it is safe to assume that if they had strayed into the lobby of the Bonaventura Hotel, they would have been unable to share Jameson's pleasure in the design of John Portman's elevators. Nevertheless, when Jameson tells us that in the post-modern era "aesthetic production . . . has become integrated into commodity production generally" ("Postmodernism," 56), we recall having been told in *Dialectic* that this process of integration began in the second half of the nineteenth century (for Jameson, the very pinnacle of modernity), and that it was already complete before the outbreak of World War II. Again, while Jameson assures us that "the culture of the simulacrum comes to life in a society where exchange-value has been generalized to the point at which the very memory of use-value is effaced . . ." ("Postmodernism," 66), we have only to turn to "The Fetish Character in Music and the Regression of Listening" to discover that as far as Adorno was concerned, the concerts of the detestable Toscanini (one of his favorite *bêtes noires*) had already effaced the memory of use value as long ago as 1938: "If the commodity in general combines exchange-value and use-value, then the pure use-value, whose illusion the cultural goods must preserve in completely capitalist society, must be replaced by pure exchange-value, which precisely in its capacity as exchange-value deceptively takes over the function of use-value." (Adorno, "On the Fetish Character," 34) see note on p 487

Furthermore, while Jameson is of the opinion that the elimination of "the enclaves of precapitalist organization [which capitalism] had hitherto tolerated and exploited in a tributary way" is one of the signal achievements of "the purer capitalism of our own time" ("Postmodernism," 78), Adorno, inveighing against 1930s hit songs and bikinis, was in a position to announce the disappearance of "the last pre-capitalist residues" in the very same paragraph in which he mourns the extinction of use value. As for "the death of the subject," Jameson's perception that "the liberation, in contemporary society, from the older anomie of the centered subject may also mean, not merely a liberation from anxiety, but a liberation from every other kind of feeling as well, since there is no longer a self present to do the feeling" ("Postmodernism," 64) would scarcely have raised an eyebrow in the Institute of Social Research, which had already recorded the finding that "the culture industry as a whole has molded men as a type unfailingly reproduced in every product." (Horkheimer and Adorno, 127) It is hardly surprising, therefore, that when Jameson ventures a comment on music (and he ventures a comment on every art that he can think of), he avails himself of Adorno's distinction between "Schoenberg's innovative planification [and] Stravinsky's irrational eclecticism" and imparts to his readers the shattering *trouvaille* that "Stravinsky is the true precursor of postmodern cultural production." ("Postmodernism," 64–65)

"Irrational eclecticism" is not a happy phrase in the context of Jameson's essay—though, of course, we are dealing with something rather more interesting than a case of plagiarism, or even of unconscious reminiscence. What that "something" is betrayed here, in the essay's very first paragraph:

The case [for the existence of postmodernism] depends on the hypothesis of some radical break or *coupure*, generally traced back to the end of the 1950s or the early 1960s. As the word itself suggests, this break is most often related to notions of the waning or extinction of the hundred-year-old modern movement (or to its ideological or aesthetic repudiation). Thus, abstract expressionism in painting, existentialism in philosophy, the final forms of representation in the novel, the films of the great auteurs, or the modernist school of poetry ... : all these are now seen as the final, extraordinary flowering of a high modernist impulse which is spent and exhausted with them. ("Postmodernism," 53–54)

If Adorno had been asked to compile a list of the finest flowers of the modern movement, he would not have included "the films of the great auteurs," and he would have greeted with astonishment Jameson's claim that the Beatles and the Rolling Stones represent the "high-modernist moment" of rock (I am astonished myself, though I trust for rather different reasons). Yet now, for Jameson, Hitchcock is a great "modernist" artist whose name one naturally mentions in the same breath as that not only of a respectable European filmmaker like Jean Renoir, but also of a Rainer Maria Rilke or a D. H. Lawrence, or even an Igor Stravinsky—despite his irrational eclecticism (Jameson, "Destructive Element," 113).[1] How Hitchcock exemplifies the "essentially high-modernist" dislocation of "high culture and so-called mass or commercial culture" I am not quite sure, but it is at least apparent that "what has happened" in the course of the half-century that separates Adorno's bilious denunciations of the Hollywood cinema from Jameson's writings on postmodernism is not that "aesthetic production . . . has become integrated into commodity production generally" (Jameson, "Postmodernism," 54), but that the number and the type of cultural commodities which can be deemed to be artistically respectable has increased, and the moment of apocalyptic *coupure* at which the subject died, use value was annihilated, and the precapitalist enclaves ran up the white flag has been correspondingly moved forward. Adorno and Horkheimer, employing Walter Benjamin's terminology but exactly reversing the argument he developed with it, attribute these calamities to "the universal triumph of the rhythms of mechanical production and reproduction" (134), and they state categorically that the effacement of culture by the commodity form, the achievement of cultural "standardization," and the erasure of all distinctions "between the logic of the work and that of the social system" are phenomena of the monopoly phase of capital (121). Jameson, however, who likes Hitchcock and the Beatles, states equally categorically that the monopoly phase of capital and the triumphant rhythms of "machine production of electric and combustion motors since the '90s of the 19th century" were the material basis of artistic modernism, and that the cultural catastrophe which, for some reason, Adorno and Horkheimer derived from the radio, the movie projector, and the Ford assembly line was actually engendered by the multinational phase of capital and "the machine production of electronic and nuclear-powered apparatuses since the '40s of the 20th century." ("Postmodernism," 78).

The only visible difference between Adorno's "culture industry" and Jameson's "postmodernism" is that Jameson makes a tentative concession to the idea of cultural contradiction, and instead of declaring bluntly that "all mass culture is identical" (Adorno and Horkheimer) opts for the more modest claim that postmodernism is only the "cultural dominant . . . or hegemonic norm" of the current period. (Jameson, "Postmodernism," 57) Unfortunately, his only reward for this dialectical gesture is that his argument, unlike Adorno's, ceases to make sense in its own terms. The "culture industry" thesis may be ludicrous, but it is at least consistent: a certain stage in capitalist commodity production is reached; culture is subordinated to it; disaster results. Jameson, on the other hand, aspires to offer us a reflection theory of culture which accommodates (under vague and totally untheorized circumstances) both a certain activity on the part of the mirror and a disaster with bits that are not disastrous. If postmodernism does indeed correspond to the multinational phase of capital, how was it possible for Stravinsky—and, apparently, Gertrude Stein, Albert Roussel, and Marcel Duchamp as well—to be postmodernists *avant la lettre*? Conversely, what business did Hitchcock and the Rolling Stones have to produce modernist art in the 1950s and '60s? And if the individual subject is really dead, might not Jameson have spared us the final pages of his article, in which he meditates on the possibility of equipping this unfortunate zombie with a "cognitive map" of the postmodern world? What good the living dead will derive from their newfound ability (through the Virgilian ministrations of the Marxist intellectual) to successfully negotiate the lobby of the Bonaventura Hotel I am not quite sure, and to judge from the turgid word-spinning for which this section of his article is remarkable, Jameson is not sure either—but it is always nice, I suppose, to end on a note of uplift. No one who reads through these innocent pages will have much trouble resisting the impulse—as they might well do on setting down *Dialectic of Enlightenment*—to run straight to the bathroom and swallow a handful of barbiturates.

Premature announcements of the extinction of the lights of culture by the most recent development in commodity production are a staple feature of bourgeois thought on cultural subjects: since at least the end of the eighteenth century, every new cultural technology and every significant expansion of the audience interested in consuming cultural products has been greeted by somebody as a harbinger of the imminent triumph of barbarism. Samuel Taylor Coleridge was a great radical artist and one of the most intelligent men of his time, but his radicalism and his intelligence did not prevent him from writing this:

> For as to the devotees of the circulating libraries, I dare not compliment their *pass-time*, or rather *kill-time*, with the name of *reading*. Call it rather a sort of beggarly day-dreaming, during which the mind of the dreamer furnishes for itself nothing but laziness and a little mawkish sensibility; while the whole *material* and imagery of the doze is supplied *ab extra* by a sort of mental *camera obscura* manufactured at the printing office, which *pro tempore* fixes, reflects, and transmits the moving phantasms of one man's delirium, so as to people the barrenness of a hundred other brains afflicted with the same trance or suspension of common sense and all definite purpose. (*Biographia Literaria,* vol. 7, pt. 1, 48)

Coleridge's account of the novel and its readers is identical to Adorno's of Hollywood and its audience, and he is even a Lacanian film theorist—avant la lettre. The trouble with such edicts is that they require constant revision as bourgeois taste—perpetually between 50 and

100 years in arrears of the significant work which is actually being produced—gradually reconciles itself to the cultural products which embody the commodity form before last. Far from challenging the notion that the commodity form is the negation of culture, Marxist aestheticians have often tended to give it a new lease on life, and the philosophy of art with which we associate the Frankfurt School consists, explicitly, of an apology of the imputed autonomy of *Kultur*. It might have been hoped that the discovery that many Hollywood directors and many jazz musicians were geniuses would lead in its turn to the discovery that the lapsarian theory of cultural commodification stands in need of revision—but no. Instead, the films of Hitchcock and the music of Louis Armstrong, purged by time of the taint of the market, are elevated to the canon, and more recent commodities take their place.

The transition is easy, and the nature of the rhetoric which rationalizes it could be guessed in advance by an intelligent five-year-old. Here, for instance, is part of an exemplary postmodern Marxist discourse on "the political economy of music":

> Music did not really become a commodity until a broad market for popular music was created. Such a market did not exist when Edison invented the phonograph; it was produced by the colonization of black music by the American industrial apparatus. The history of this commodity expansion is exemplary. A music of revolt is transformed into a repetitive commodity. An explosion of youth—a hint of economic crisis in the middle of the great postwar economic boom—rapidly domesticated into consumption. From Jazz to Rock. Continuations of the same effort, always resumed and renewed, to alienate a liberatory will in order to produce a market, that is, supply and demand at the same time. . . . A music of the body, played and composed by all, jazz expressed the alienation of blacks. Whites would steal from them this creativity horn of labor and the elementary forms of industrialization, and then turn around and sell it back. . . . (Attali, 103–4)

Capital's effort, "always resumed and renewed," to alienate art's emancipatory potential on the market is as nothing to the effort expended by Marxist theoreticians in shifting around the date at which art "really" became a commodity. Students of the economic structure of the concert hall and the opera house in the eighteenth and nineteenth centuries (not to mention the Victorian evening around the pianoforte) will find Jacques Attali's chronology no more convincing, and no less arbitrary, than Adorno's, and they may also feel— despite, or perhaps because of it, his disingenuous recuperation of jazz at rock's expense—that if he had been writing in the 1930s, Attali would have produced something very similar to "The Fetish Character in Music and the Regression of Listening." The lesson to be drawn, both from Attali's piece and from Jameson's tortuous theorization of "the cultural logic of late" (rather than, as we had hitherto supposed, monopoly) capitalism, is that the time has very definitely come for Marxist cultural analysis to abandon the idea that there was ever a moment of seismic rupture when culture became a mere function of the reproduction of the capitalist economy. Such ideas are perfectly at home in those devastating indictments of the appalling effects of the media which find their way periodically into the nonfiction best seller lists, but Marxism can surely come up with something better. As a matter of fact, we have an excellent model to hand in the work of Raymond Williams, which seems to be sufficient in itself to dispose of the Frankfurt thesis for ever.

Pastiche, High Art, and "Mass" Culture

It is perhaps because I am at least as unfavorably disposed as Jameson to much of what passes as "postmodern culture" that I find myself objecting so strongly to his account of it. Consider, for example, that concept of "pastiche" which he has put into circulation:

> The disappearance of the individual subject, along with its formal consequence, the increasing unavailability of the personal style, engender the well-nigh universal practice today of what may be called pastiche. . . . Pastiche is, like parody, the imitation of a peculiar mask, speech in a dead language: but it is a neutral practice of such mimicry, without any of parody's ulterior motives, amputated of the satiric impulse, devoid of laughter and of any conviction that alongside the abnormal tongue you have momentarily borrowed, some healthy linguistic normality still exists. . . . For with the collapse of the high-modernist ideology of style—what is as unique and unmistakable as your own fingerprints, as incomparable as your own body . . . —the producers of culture have nowhere to turn but to the past: the imitation of dead styles, speech through all the masks and voices stored up in the imaginary museum of a now global culture. ("Postmodernism," 64–65)

This is a little too neat to be true. Once upon a time, so the story goes, there was a group of individuals—Marcel Proust, Pablo Picasso, Alfred Hitchcock, Gustav Mahler, T. S. Eliot, and so on—who had "unique private worlds" to express. The "centered subject," having died from complications following the onset of multinational capitalism, there is nothing for the contemporary artist to do but to imitate the distinctive styles of the past (in another version of his essay included in *The Anti-Aesthetic*, Jameson even goes so far as to suggest that the Mahlers and the Prousts have used all the distinctive styles up), and cultural producers who, all other things being equal, would be painting "Les Demoiselles d'Avignon" or directing *Vertigo* or writing *A la Recherche du Temps Perdu* find themselves, instead, painting the collected works of Gilbert and George, directing *Blue Velvet*, and writing *Writing for the Second Time through Finnegan's Wake*.

The first point to make about this astonishing argument is that no artist, "modernist" or other, has ever had a "unique private world" to express, and "unique private worlds" were not what Mahler, Hitchcock, and Proust were expressing. A great artist's "style" is not, and is not like, a "fingerprint": it is an instrument for the critical interrogation of the existing social world—the world which includes and which shaped the artist's sensibility—and it is arrived at through a critical engagement with the existing conventions of representation and the structures of feeling and value which they embody. There may well have been a "high-modernist ideology of style," but this does not mean that "inimitable" artistic styles are somehow a prerogative of the modern movement—or for that matter, "the autonomous bourgeois monad." Is

William Faulkner's "style" any more or less inimitable or distinctive than Chaucer's? Obviously not. No monad or "autonomous" ego (if such a quantity can be imagined) would be able to produce an artistic style at all, for the simple reason that such styles are not private dialects but inflections and developments, more or less radical, of historical discursive or representational norms which by definition precede any given representational act, and the various artistic styles of the modern movement can no more be referred to the hegemony of the monad than their disappearance can be referred to its death. In any case, the styles of Philip Glass and John Cage, or Gilbert and George and Andy Warhol, or Philippe Sollers and William Burroughs, seem to me quite as distinctive as those of any given "modernists," if immensely inferior, and Jameson is wholly mistaken if he believes (as he clearly does) that either the styles or the inferiority can be explained by postulating a social world in which distinctive utterance is objectively impossible. Gilbert and George do what they do not because no one any longer has the kind of idiosyncratic personal consciousness which produces an *Olympia*, but from their own unembarrassed volition—and with the encouragement of a substantial public.

The bourgeois subject, of course, has not died at all; though on the other hand, the bourgeoisie as a class has undergone a very noticeable change, the nature of which can be suggested with the help of Adorno, who remarks (in that essay on "The Fetish Character in Music") that Arnold Schoenberg, as a representative "advanced" artist, has "renounced consumption." This form of words is typically misleading: Schoenberg did not "renounce consumption" and could not conceivably have done so. What he renounced was the only audience for the musical tradition in which he composed, which is a very different thing; it should also be added that the renunciation was mutual. We have become accustomed to think of the modern movement in the arts as "progressive" in relation to a dominant bourgeois culture which was "conservative," and while this opposition is attractive—and even, in a sense, accurate—we ought to be aware that it can also be construed as an antagonism—internal to the bourgeois tradition—between two conservatisms, the content of which is determined by two radically different understandings of what the tradition is and of what the necessary measures are to preserve its integrity and its dominance. Schoenberg thought that the logic of the tradition entailed the invention of serialism, which (as he himself puts it) would guarantee the supremacy of German music for a thousand years. The German bourgeoisie thought that it entailed the comic operas of Richard Strauss, which it eagerly consumed as fast as Strauss could churn them out, each more fatuous than the last. The condition of existence of "the modern movement" is the eruption of this class tension which had been developing since at least the end of the eighteenth century and which, by the end of the nineteenth, frequently amounted to open war between a certain kind of bourgeois artist and the bourgeois audience, each voicing rival and incompatible claims to the stewardship of the culture of the class as a whole. In some cases, though by no means all (a point to which I'll return), the "advanced" artist and the "conservative" audience were united in their contemptuous hostility to those forms of cultural production which the bourgeois tradition could not countenance. Conventional literary taste deplored "The Waste Land" and F. R. Leavis's passionate advocacy of the "new bearings in English poetry," but Eliot and Leavis were at once deploring capitalist commercial culture and the debasement of the audiences who enjoyed it.

The difference between bourgeois high culture in the late nineteenth and early twenti-eth centuries and bourgeois high culture now is that any similar ideological tension between professional artist and bourgeois audience is utterly inconceivable. On the one hand, the con-temporary moneymaking middle classes—yuppies of all ages—cannot be imagined as giving a two-penny damn about music, literature, painting, or any other form of cultural activity, and they show no interest whatever in guarding the integrity of the bourgeois tradition, of which they are massively ignorant. On the other hand, contemporary bourgeois artists are conspicu-ously unwilling to commit themselves to the political positions which, in the late twentieth century, are the indispensable prerequisites of significant opposition to capitalist society. If we have no Schoenberg in 1988, it is not because the subject has died but because this kind of cultural intervention absolutely depends on the presence of an audience which is passionately concerned to hear something else and which is prepared to stage a riot when it is disappointed. For Schoenberg—who was not only a great artist and a hero but also a political reactionary, like so many of the major modernists—the production of important oppositional art did not entail articulate political opposition to capitalism because bourgeois culture was itself a battle-ground, and Schoenberg's "conservative" audience experienced the formal innovations of his music as political dissent—which, of course, in the given conditions, they effectively were, though they have in themselves no political content. The bourgeoisie will never again produce an audience for bourgeois high culture which is even remotely comparable to the audience whose fury stopped the first concert of dodecaphonic music halfway through, and if World War II and its immediate aftermath do represent some sort of turning point in this respect, the thing that they mark is the moment at which the bourgeois cultural tradition ceased to have any political significance for, and (therefore) ceased to play any appreciable part in the emo-tional life of, the bourgeoisie as a class.

High culture is no longer a contested terrain—not because "the avant-garde was won," as is sometimes suggested, but because the bourgeoisie understands (quite correctly, from the point of view of its own immediate interests) that it is the culture of the marketplace which mat-ters. It is hardly an accident that the transition to the characteristic postwar cultural forms was signaled by the destruction, through state action, of the economic base of the internally capital-ized Hollywood studio system, in the context of a political purge of its artistic personnel and the introduction of sponsored television. The battleground now—as we might have gathered from the state's preoccupation in recent years with the censorship of pornography and "video nasties," the proscription of "positive images" of homosexuals, the banning of memoirs which cast an unfortunate light on the activities of the capitalist secret police, and the troublesome corporate autonomy of nonsponsored broadcasting institutions—is not the concert hall but the inventory of the local newsagent and, in general, the vulgar cultural life of the average front room.

Where matters of taste are concerned, the most striking consequence of this develop-ment is the contemporary bourgeoisie's loathsome philistine indifference to its own cultural past—an indifference which large sections of its current intelligentsia share, reflect, and per-petuate while experiencing it, at the same time, as the very latest thing in cultivated sophisti-cation. Even if the theory of culture were in the least advanced by Jameson's contention that Stravinsky's neoclassical ballets, Stein's *The Making of Americans*, and the artwork of Andy

Warhol are representative of a single phenomenon, "pastiche" is a quite inadequate word to describe the kind of art for which, in *The Anti-Aesthetic*, Crimp and Owens advance themselves as propagandists. We have had pastiche before—in the Elizabethan lyric, in Jacobean tragedy, in the nineteenth-century string serenade, even (let it be said) in the serial compositions of Schoenberg, which are, perhaps, not so completely the antithesis of "Stravinsky's irrational eclecticism" as Jameson (on Adorno's less than reliable advice) supposes. What we have certainly not had is a professional cultural elite which constitutes itself as the vanguard of a culture to whose values it is incapable of offering the most feeble substantive challenge by the simple expedient of declaring to all who will listen that it knows all about them. What Jameson calls pastiche consists in fact of a flattering exchange of signals between the bourgeois artist and an audience that is only too happy to receive them and return them in kind—signals which enact some variant of the proposition "We can see through that, can't we?" or "We've heard that one before, haven't we?" or "That's a signifying practice that's had its day, isn't it?" or "We weren't found under a gooseberry bush, were we?" The examples of the work of Barbara Kruger, Cindy Sherman, and Martha Rosler with which Owens illustrates his article on "Feminists and Postmodernism" are classically exemplary of this simple semaphore, the function of which in these cases is to confirm the spectator's conviction that s/he already knows everything that there is to be known about the representation of women, Hollywood B movies, and the iniquities of capitalism. Bourgeois high cultural production is now virtually synonymous with this sort of exercise, which is the artistic equivalent of what Derrida means—in his philosopher's way—by the "miming of absolute knowledge." (*Dissemination*)

I will defer so far to my subject matter as to illustrate my point with an autobiographical anecdote: it concerns the screening, last September at 9:30 in the morning, of Jean-Luc Godard's *King Lear* (1987) at the Varsity Cinemas in Toronto, in the course of the Toronto Festival of Festivals. Despite the early hour, the cinema was packed almost to overflowing with persons whom I take to have been representative of the postmodern educated public—a public very different from the one I am accustomed to encounter in that auditorium—and it was apparent from the very first scenes, which are dedicated to exposing the stupidity of Norman Mailer and those well-known capitalist barbarians, producers Menahem Golan and Yoram Globus, that Godard had another winner. In the publicity which preceded the unveiling of his masterpiece, Godard was careful to make a great point of the fact not only that the film had been "stabbed in the back" by the truculent egotism of his collaborators but also that he had never read Shakespeare's play and that he had seen it performed only once—and that in French. It is continuous with one's sense of the Godardian case that one should be in some doubt as to whether or not this latter claim is true. I suspect myself that it is not true—the film suggests that Godard's knowledge of the play is adequate to his purposes, but its veracity is not, in fact, the point. What matters is Godard's evident conviction that this is what his audience would like to hear, and his audience's evident satisfaction at being told (and by a great artist too) that one does not really need to have read *King Lear* (since one was obliged to do so in high school) in order to reach the conclusion that the play, its author, and the sanctimonious notions of Great Art, High Seriousness, and Creative Genius which (of course) they represent are a load of the old malarkey.

In the foyer afterward there was a great deal of predictable talk about "Brecht," whose name was ready to hand in explanation of the film's ragweed humor—ready to hand, in large part, because of the earlier work of Godard and of his more influential critics, which have had their role to play in the fascinating process by which the distantiation effect has been progressively reduced to a gratifying testimonial to the middle-class spectator's *suffisance*. The parties to the conversation in which I took a (minor) part were quite unable to give a satisfactory account of what it was they thought they were being distanced from, to what end—and of why, in particular, being "distanced" from *King Lear* should be felt in itself to be desirable. It was the distance they had come for, and it was the distance which, as usual and on cue, Godard provided: though as the days of '68 are long gone, he is no longer advising us, as he did in *Vent d'Est* (1970), to adopt the degree of distance required to blow up civilians in shopping malls (*autres temps, autres mœurs*) and has settled down, with every appearance of extreme contentment, in what may be called, following Ulmer, his "saprophyte" period. (Ulmer, 105) The only dissonant note in this orgy of bourgeois self-conceit was introduced, significantly enough, by two intruders from the world of mass culture—Burgess Meredith and, above all, Molly Ringwald—who were presumably too simpleminded to appreciate the nature of Godard's undertaking. Ringwald's remarkable account of her role as Cordelia—or of what is left of it after Godard has finished alienating us by introducing characters who wonder (to the audience's delight) why the reconciliation scene was not scored by Miklos Rosza—suffices to remind us of those aspects of Shakespeare's text which must be thoroughly disavowed before Godard and his clientele can aggrandize themselves at Shakespeare's expense. And it is peculiarly fitting that such moments of contradiction as disfigure this seamless, complacent, trivial, and utterly useless *Kunstwerk* are generated by the discredited and oft-deconstructed capitalist institution of the star system.

"Tradition," declared Mahler, "is mere slovenliness," and in the sense of the word *tradition* which Mahler here intends (the Margaret Thatcher sense, we might say), he is clearly right. Yet Mahler knew that he belonged to a tradition, and indeed, he explicitly said that just as Wagner had "appropriated the means of expression" of the Beethoven symphony for the purposes of reinventing opera, so he now availed himself of "the expressive power gained for music by the achievement of Wagner." Schoenberg's attitude toward Mahler was very similar. Neither Mahler nor Schoenberg could have believed—as the representative producer of bourgeois high culture now conspires (the word seems appropriate) to believe—that they were objectively external to the cultural traditions to which they belonged, and it was the fact that he knew that his own radical transformation of the musical language had, as its necessary precondition, the work of his great predecessors in the past that Mahler had a right to the expression, "tradition is mere slovenliness." The welcome feeling that one's relation to the cultural past is that of an amused spectator on the top of Mount Olympus is illusory, and in signifying that feeling Godard (to make him exemplary) does no more than to signify his incomprehension of what he sees and his blindness to the necessity of his own involvement with it—unless we concede that the sense of involvement manifests itself, through a return of the repressed, as self-disgust: Godard clearly despises himself, his film, and the audience he flatters at least as much as he despises Shakespeare.

Similarly, when Theory tells us that all "realist" novels, by virtue of being "realist," homogenize and mystify the social worlds they represent, or that Western painting since the Renaissance is governed by one or two invariant structures which immerse the spectator in the patriarchal imaginary, it merely reproduces—for a reader who "does not know *King Lear*"— the sense of the past we can indulge any day, without Theory's help, by settling down to a game of Trivial Pursuit. Indeed, the discourse of postmodernism as a whole reminds one of nothing so much as a game of Trivial Pursuit for highbrows.

As we have seen, Jameson makes a great deal of the fact (or assertion) that postmodernism has effaced "the older (essentially high-modernist) frontier between high culture and so-called mass or commercial culture." ("Postmodernism," 54) Nothing could be further from the truth: what is called "postmodern art" derives, on the contrary, from a concerted and systematic reinforcement of the category of bourgeois high culture, which is, in the 1980s, as wholly parasitic on capitalist commercial culture as it is on the high bourgeois tradition. Andy Warhol's artworks of, or on, Marilyn Monroe appropriate a figure who, in her work, embodied in the most complex and moving way some of the most profound contradictions of the culture which produced her, and transform her, with bland insolence, into a piece of *Kunst* which may be read, at the spectator's convenience, as a searing critique of the objectification of women or as a pleasant addition to the condominium wall.

If Jameson is really interested in art which challenges the distinction between "high" and popular, or commercial, culture, he should turn his attention not to "postmodernism"—which is in this respect quite plainly reactionary—but to certain tendencies in the modern movement and in the earlier Romantic tradition with which the modern movement is continuous. The critique of bourgeois poetic diction by the early Romantic poets in favor of a poetry which, in Wordsworth's phrase, "addresses men in the language of men" and which draws on popular forms like the ballad and the folk lyric; the interest of so many nineteenth-century composers in popular dance and song; the key Romantic art of book illustration, so directly tied to developments in capitalist technology and the expansion of the cultural market; the nineteenth-century operatic tradition in Italy; the novels of Charles Dickens; the paintings of Gustave Courbet, part of the scandal of which was generated by Courbet's deployment of popular imagery; the music of Mahler, in whose "Third Symphony" that most prosaic of instruments, the posthorn (pointedly not included in the bourgeois symphony orchestra), becomes, in one of the most magical moments of Western music, the vehicle of the Sublime, and whose work as a whole suggests an attempt to abolish the boundary between high and popular culture by an act of will; the tales and novels of Joseph Conrad, in which the detective story and the nautical yarn are yoked together by violence with the Flaubertian conception of the art of the novel; the work of Bertolt Brecht in the 1920s, and of the composers who collaborated with him—in none of these cases can we speak of a frontier between "high" and "popular/commercial" culture having been erected or jealously guarded or viewed as anything other than a nuisance and an impediment. The idea that from the end of the eighteenth century onward an ever-widening gulf opens up between "serious" culture and the culture of the market is a figment of Adorno's imagination, which has had the very serious effect of obscuring the fact that one of the major impulses in a great deal of nineteenth-century bourgeois art is to undermine the rules of decorum and propriety through which Enlightenment culture had sought to constitute art as a specialized practice with as few external contacts as possible.

This does not mean that Mahler and Conrad were not bourgeois artists producing bourgeois art, and it certainly does not mean that we cannot point to Romantic and "modernist" artists who despised the culture of the market. What it does mean is that the bourgeois tradition is, from this point of view, profoundly contradictory, and we can neither invent an emancipatory role for nor—alternatively—abuse "postmodern" artists for resisting categories which so many artists have resisted before them. As for the alleged incompatibility of "high modernism" and the capitalist media, we have only to turn to the classical Hollywood cinema and consider (for instance) *Psycho* (1960), *Written on the Wind* (1956), *While the City Sleeps* (1956), *Blonde Venus* (1932), *Now, Voyager* (1942), *Bonjour Tristesse* (1958), *Letter from an Unknown Woman* (1948), and *Gaslight* (1944) to provide ourselves with the evidence that high modernism could, and once did, exist as a viable popular commercial culture.

Contemporary bourgeois cultural production, by contrast, suggests to me the resurrection of a pre-modernist, and pre-Romantic, concept of culture as a privileged realm of knowing experts. If I, for one (offered the choice), would prefer to spend the evening watching reruns of "Falconcrest" and "The Price Is Right" than reading Derrida, looking at recent Godard, or listening to Philip Glass, it is because the popular television shows, ghastly as they are, do at least make contact with the way in which the majority of human beings in the North America of the 1980s actually lead their lives. "The Price Is Right" may be awful, but it is, for better or worse, alive, whereas *Spurs: Nietzsche's Styles: Untitled Film Still 1980* (1980), *Je vous salue, Marie* (*Hail Mary* [1985]), *The Decline of the American Empire* (1986), *Wavelength* (1967), and *Einstein on the Beach* (1986), which are fittingly representative of what bourgeois high culture has come down to, seem to me to have about as much vitality as a row of dead fish on a slab.

No one will suppose me to be undertaking a defense of game shows or of the majority of contemporary media culture, which is also jaded, impoverished, and solipsistic: I have discussed the phenomenon in an article on "Reaganite entertainment." Many of the points which are most frequently made in this connection—the fragmentation of attention; the symbiosis of entertainment and sales promotion; the proliferation of "a world of media images"; and so on—are accurate, and it is clearly true that North American commercial television represents something specific to the new phase of multinational capital produced by the last war. We should be very clear, however, about what follows from these facts, and what most certainly does not follow is that monolithic Kafkaesque "hyperspace," at once unreadably fragmented and perfectly coherent, conjured up by Jameson and by the breathless prose poems of Kroker and Jean Baudrillard. The derivative nature of these visions of the obscene delirium of communication, universal psychic burnout, and "panic" this, that, and the other should be sufficient to warn us against them: Jameson, as we have seen, is a less rebarbative (and correspondingly more inconsistent) Adorno, and the Kroker/Baudrillard act is merely a dystopian version of the equally popular, and equally inane, turn which McLuhan took on the road a few years back under the catchy rubric "the global village"—a phrase of which Kroker's "the absolute domination of parasitism-plus" is the disillusioned, and somewhat more cumbersome, equivalent. Insofar as these arguments, at their worst (of which, I repeat, Jameson is not exemplary) signify anything more than the reduction of critical thought to a display of tail feathers, they reflect a querulous, snobbish disdain for the plebeian which seems to me most unfortunate: people live in the media world, and they are not, perhaps, so much its abject slaves as we sometimes like to think. Popular culture is in no sense reducible to the capitalist media, and even contemporary commercial entertainment—though it is difficult to think of it, given the nature of the economic conditions, as producing the equivalent of a Hitchcock—retains a greater energy and a greater potential for generating contradiction and resistance than the airless world of bourgeois art described by Crimp.

It is for such a world—the world of an allegedly autonomous bourgeois culture—that Habermas, as the most distinguished living representative of the Frankfurt tradition, continues to apologize in his notes on "the incomplete project" of modernity in *The Anti-Aesthetic*: "When the containers of an autonomously developed cultural sphere are shattered, the contents get dispersed. Nothing remains from a desublimated meaning or a destructured form; an emancipatory effect does not follow." (11) This view of culture as a container with contents which can or cannot be dispersed seems to me curious in itself, but it is merely paradoxical that culture in this sense is what a staunch opponent of postmodernism should feel himself called upon to reaffirm.

Conclusion

The discourse of postmodernism offers us a number of visions of contemporary capitalism, ranging from the glorious new birth of difference posited (in their different ways) by Owens and Mouffe and Laclau to the incomprehensible horror show deducible from the streams of consciousness of Kroker and Baudrillard. All the visionaries have one thing in common: their complete inability to propose an intelligible strategy of cultural/political resistance to the social conditions they describe. They are unable to do so because the description is wrong. Late twentieth-century capitalism is neither a golden opportunity for democratic pluralism and bourgeois renaissance nor a phantasmagoric total system peopled by gray somnambulists in thrall to the culture of the simulacrum. It is a form of capitalism which continues to be analyzable as such, and which is no more likely than capitalism has ever been either to realize the state of things in which its own objective contradictions and inequities can be transcended or to reduce its inhabitants to tractable mobiles who simply embody its own values and priorities.

The triumphant reemergence of the most antiquated ideologies of bourgeois reformism and intellectual vanguardism on the one hand, and of yet another version of the determinism of capitalist cultural technology on the other, may well tell us a great deal about the material situation, and the intellectual exhaustion, of the thinking classes, but they tell us nothing at all about the actually existing social world and how to change it. The function of the concept of postmodernism is to define this world as unprecedented (for good or ill, according to taste) and then to deduce from it that it has an objective tendency to become democratic, that it has an objective tendency to rational authoritarian closure, or that the whole of the past from which it has been extrapolated was a mistake or a joke or a confidence trick which has at last been exposed. In other words, the concept is both un- or (better) anti-historical and, despite being the latest thing, rather *passé*: there is nothing here that we have not heard before apropos conditions which had also been carefully dehistoricized and which were similarly perceived to be the *via reggia* to Heaven or to Hell. Such new elements as there are—the tendency to conscious casuistry and charlatanism, and the readiness, under certain circumstances, to appropriate (for radical purposes) the odd rhetorical trope or demagogic formula from the dominant culture—can hardly be regarded as a great stride forward in human affairs.

I myself remain convinced that Marxist Socialism provides us with the best tools that we have both for analyzing capitalist society in concrete detail and (therefore) for devising practical ways to eliminate the structural impediments to an authentic democracy which capitalism embodies. But whether or not one agrees with this proposition, it can only be obvious (I would say) that the discourse of postmodernism represents the smoked-out butt end of the kind of theory we have been required to think of as "progressive" for the last twenty years or so. In the space of two decades the Western intelligentsia has—as George Eliot's Mr. Brooke would have put it—"gone into" everything: one by one, every conceivable hermeneutic and every conceivable subject—Hollywood and historical materialism, psychoanalysis and representational painting, the novel and Prague linguistics, feminism and Brecht, structuralism and textual pleasure, the higher mathematics and the lower television—has been taken down, dusted off, toyed with, and used up. "Postmodernism" is the name for the state of bloated stupefaction which has very naturally followed from this glutton's feast, and if contemporary intellectuals feel themselves to be "post," it is for the excellent reason that they have consumed too much rich aliment in too short a time and the table is now bare. No single item on the menu was ever really tasted, let alone enjoyed, and in the retrospective, surfeited postprandial haze, the *épigrammes de Saussure* and the *macédoine* of historical materialism *à la mode*, the realist novel Valencia and the fillets of Lévi-Strauss *en cocotte*, all blur together to constitute the single category "Western food." We may or we may not sympathize with the victims of this epidemic of discursive indigestion, but we are probably ill-advised to take them at their own word. Such extremities are notoriously incompatible with sober reflection.

Consuming Culture: The Development of a Theoretical Orthodoxy (1990)

In my article on postmodernism, I argued that the analysis of contemporary Western culture advanced by postmodern theorists who think of themselves, and wish to be thought of, as being "on the left" does nothing more than recapitulate, in a fashionable new vocabulary, an argument about the commodity form of culture which was first propounded by the Frankfurt School in the 1930s. The argument is no more acceptable now than it was then, and the present essay is a critique of the work of its most influential advocate, Theodor W. Adorno: the nature and the scale of the influence in socialist cultural studies are one's principal excuse for discussing ideas which, in themselves, are strikingly incompatible with a socialist theory of culture. Walter Benjamin, a colleague of Adorno's and, to such a marked degree, the more distinguished mind, contested these ideas. I shall also be concerned in what follows with what seems to me to be the solipsistic character of the Adorno/Benjamin debate, which ends in a stalemate that has yet to be properly resolved.

Adorno accepts Marx's proposition that "the commodity in general combines exchange-value and use-value," and he then proceeds to argue that "in completely capitalist society" cultural products cease to exist as use values at all; their use value, in fact, is "replaced by pure exchange value." ("On the Fetish Character," 34) It follows, therefore—inasmuch as commodities can be defined in terms of the realization of use value as exchange value—that the commodification of cultural products is, in itself, the negation of culture. As soon as a work becomes a commodity, any "distinction between the logic of the work and the logic of the social system" (Horkheimer and Adorno, 121) disappears: from this point onward, the logic of the work is, and can only be, the logic of the capitalist market. We are now in a position to conclude that "under monopoly all mass culture is identical," in that all cultural practices and all works are uniform embodiments of the principles and interests of exchange. There may well appear to be distinct differences between cultural products, but these differences are merely cosmetic: indeed, they are a necessary function of the "classification, organization and labelling" of consumer groups. (121)

> How formalized the procedure is can be seen when the mechanically differentiated products prove to be all alike in the end. That the difference between the Chrysler range and General Motors products is basically illusory strikes every child with a keen interest in varieties. What connoisseurs discuss as good or bad points serve only to perpetuate the semblance of competition and range of choice. The same applies to the Warner Brothers and Metro Goldwyn Mayer productions. (121)

The differences, in other words, are both illusory and strategic: while they are not, in essence, differences at all, they serve nevertheless in their capacity as mechanical differences to create a false sense of the abundance and freedom of the market. Thus, from the theoretical point of view it is as absurd to differentiate film A from film B as it would be to distinguish between two brands of soap powder, for the distinctions are themselves only functions of the market which has destroyed the very possibility of cultural difference. The conclusion is as terrible as it is inescapable: as soon as culture becomes "subject to the law of exchange . . . it amalgamates with advertising." (161) The commodity form, in reducing works to exchange values, co-opts them at the same time for the promotion of exchange. They become advertisements for the social logic which they embody.

This striking argument creates a number of conceptual problems by which a Marxist writer might have been expected to be particularly embarrassed. As we have seen, cultural products have been appearing on the market since the second half of the sixteenth century. If it is really the case, then, that it is in the nature of the commodity form as such to reduce cultural products to pure exchange values, how are we to explain the fact that the lamentable state of affairs which Adorno describes so feelingly did not materialize before the first half of the twentieth century? Adorno does not address this question at any point, for the purposes of his argument are better served by a very careful delimitation of the kinds of work which it is legitimate to think of as being commodities. It turns out, in fact, that where culture is concerned, commodification can be attributed to, and identified with, certain technologies which we are invited to think of as quintessentially "modern": "For only the universal triumph of the rhythm of mechanical production and reproduction promises that nothing changes and nothing unsuitable will appear." (Horkheimer and Adorno, 134) Naturally, Adorno is sufficiently sophisticated to anticipate and preempt (to his own satisfaction) the charge of technological determinism, and he goes out of his way to emphasize that the "standardization" of culture is an effect, not of the technology itself, but of its subordination to the interests of capital. Unfortunately, however, Adorno's appeal to "technique" and to the class interests which control it only compounds the problem which the technique has been invoked to solve in the first place: for Adorno is still not in a position to explain why films, radio, and magazines, in particular, should have played the historical role which he ascribes to them. The technologies which enable the "mechanical production and reproduction" of works of literature, sheet music, and certain kinds of visual and plastic art were invented and largely subordinated to "the interests of capital" several centuries before Adorno's critique of the culture industry was either written or (we might add) published. Although he never ventures to commit himself on the matter, it is probably safe to assume that even Adorno would hesitate before dismissing the whole of bourgeois literature as a reflection of the logic of the social system.

In assuming this, we are paying Adorno the reverse of a compliment, for we are saying, in effect, that the argument about the "culture industry" which he wishes to advance presupposes a patently spurious use of the concepts on which, at every point, the argument depends. Adorno claims, repeatedly, that he is describing a cultural situation which is specific to contemporary capitalism, and he draws on crucial Marxist categories to substantiate the description. But the categories have the practical effect of demonstrating not only that the description is false but also that it has been arrived at on the basis of assumptions which are actually incompatible with the use of the categories. It would certainly be possible for some kind of Marxist to argue that bourgeois culture expresses the interests of the bourgeoisie and is therefore deplorable: such an argument would be neither intelligible nor Marxist, but it would at least make sense in its own terms. It cannot be argued, however, that the culture industry is uniquely deplorable because capitalist ownership of the reproduction processes on which the industry depends has the unprecedented effect of reducing cultural products to pure exchange values. The alleged "effect" cannot be derived from the alleged "cause": indeed, cause and effect fail even to make contact with each other.

The discrepancy is profoundly betraying, and it tells us two things. In the first place, Adorno can only sustain his account of the culture industry by willfully refusing to acknowledge that cultural products with a commodity form had ever existed before the fateful advent of films, radio, and magazines, and by identifying particular historical modalities of the commodity form of culture with commodification *tout court*. His is a theoretical error, but it is an error which has a function in Adorno's argument, for the ideologies of culture and, above all, of "Art" to which he subscribes oblige him ingeniously to rewrite the history of bourgeois society in such a way as to suggest that certain of its artifacts and cultural traditions had no connection with the market. I will return to this point a little later.

It is clear, in the second place, that for all the freedom with which he deploys a materialist vocabulary, Adorno never analyzes twentieth-century American culture in materialist terms, and he shows no interest whatever in doing so. Indeed, read in its proper context in *Dialectic of Enlightenment*, the chapter on the culture industry serves the interests of a theory which is plainly antimaterialist. The theme of the book is the way in which Enlightenment rationality, because of its alleged inability to reflect on the "destructive aspects" of the social progress to which it is committed, inevitably degenerates to the point at which rationality is entirely geared to the planning, realization, and maintenance of authoritarian forms of social control. "The curse of irresistible progress," Horkheimer and Adorno announce grandly, "is irresistible regression," and the dialectic of Enlightenment rationality, working itself inexorably through, leads us not to utopia but to the barbarism of the totally planned and ruthlessly homogenized repressive society, governed by "the rationale of domination itself." (36) The culture industry and German Fascism represent the necessary outcome of this logic—and it is a sufficient comment on Adorno's materialism that he considers these two phenomena to be virtually indistinguishable and that he undertakes to explain both of them in terms not of specific historical processes but of the "self-destruction" of a single ideology. The Marxist terms ("monopoly," "exchange-value," "commodity fetishism") serve a purely forensic purpose: they give an appearance of theoretical substance to what might otherwise seem to be an ad hoc collection of empirical details and bald assertions, and they carry, to Adorno's mind, an impressive weight of moral disapprobation, by virtue of which vitriolic outbursts of spleen and animus appear to be granted a kind of impersonal warrant.

Unfortunately, the various components of the Enlightenment thesis—the notion of historical change as "irresistible regression"; the conviction that this regression is induced by the inability of rational thought to reflect upon itself; the belief that an absolutely homogeneous class society is theoretically conceivable, let alone realizable in practice—unanimously repudi-ate the Marxist idioms in which they are couched. Adorno's culture industry, and, for that mat-ter, his "Nazism," are not historical entities at all. They are logical abstractions of mathematical purity—the forgone conclusion of the theory of history which is then invoked to denounce them. In that they are, as Adorno describes them, mere postulates of the theory, the denuncia-tion is always correspondingly complacent and self-serving, and the extreme unpleasantness of Adorno's writing is inseparable from the tendentious and inauthentic nature of the displays of savage indignation which are so strikingly characteristic of it. The intensity of the indigna-tion only serves to emphasize the degree to which its objects have been conceived with a view to indulging it, and while the results are no doubt especially distasteful where anti-Semitism is concerned, they are hardly less so when Adorno takes it upon himself to deplore "the mis-placed love of the common people" (telling phrase!) for "the wrong that is done them" by jazz and the Hollywood cinema. (Horkheimer and Adorno, 121)

Many persons who have no notion of a dialectic of Enlightenment—or a dialectic of anything—have reached the Frankfurt School's conclusions without its assistance, and even the most cursory perusal of the available literature on the media will disclose the fact that arguments identical to Adorno's flow very readily from the pens of authors who could never be accused of a sympathy for Marxism, and who are even actively hostile to it. Jean Baudrillard's "requiem for the media," for example, effectively rehearses the culture industry thesis in order precisely to demonstrate the total bankruptcy of dialectical materialism which, we are told (in something like Adorno's tone), is wholly incapable of theorizing a social situation from which the very possibility of contradiction has been banished, and in which "the media" function, with irresistible efficiency and impeccable precision, to perpetuate a system of "decentralized totalitarianism." (Horkheimer and Adorno, 134) Baudrillard differs from Adorno only in his substitution of the term *the media* for the culture industry and in his propensity for an etio-lated form of individualist anarchism: he feels that "the media system" is homogeneous and impermeable, and he is opposed to organized political action by what Adorno would call "the common people" because it only serves to strengthen the system, but he is willing to proclaim that "graffiti is transgressive [because] . . . it simply smashes the code" which the media unilat-erally impose on every other form of cultural practice. (Baudrillard, 181)

This is less than impressive, and Baudrillard's slick, dandified postmodernity may seem merely disreputable, but it has at least the virtue of demonstrating where the "total system" argument leads us. Whether we base our account of this system on the inexorable laws of exchange and the commodity form, in Adorno's manner, or decide that in the end the media embody and perpetuate "the terrorism of the code," in Baudrillard's manner (176)—the tyr-anny of Language itself—we will only succeed in the end in rationalizing what we describe. Both Adorno and Baudrillard, in their different ways, set up a formalized model of media culture for a stinging indictment which turns, by degrees, into an apology. It is an unfortu-nate consequence of this line that it entails an attitude toward "the common people" which is uncomfortably close to what can be imagined to be Madison Avenue's attitude toward them, though no doubt the average advertising executive is less sensitive on the subject of their oppression.

"The culture industry as a whole has moulded men as a type unfailingly reproduced in every product. All the agents of this process, from the producer to the women's clubs, take good care that the simple reproduction of this mental state is not nuanced or extended in any way." (Baudrillard, 179) Thus, materialism; meanwhile, in the opposite corner: "There is no need to imagine [television] as a state periscope spying on everyone's private life—the situation as it stands is more efficient than that: it is the certainty that people are no longer speaking to each other, that they are definitively isolated in the face of a speech without response." (Horkheimer and Adorno, 127)

Any element of truth which these passages may contain is negated by their writers' ulterior commitment to a model of the world in which the common people cannot but appear as the drugged and stupid victims of a successful confidence trick: where there is a deceiver, there must be a gull. Adorno is even prepared to risk an entire psychology of the commodity form by means of which it can be proved that the stupidity of "consumers" is an objective corollary of relations of exchange. He starts out from a grotesque paraphrase of Marx's theory of commodity fetishism, which is boiled down to the proposition that consumers venerate things made by themselves, even as they are alienated from these things by the exchange form. Undeterred by the fact that consumer is not a Marxist category, and blithely ignoring the omission from this precis of the theory's most crucial element (the class relationship between labor and capital),

Adorno continues:

> This is the real secret of success. It is the mere reflection of what one pays in the market for the product. The consumer is really worshipping the money that he himself has paid for the ticket to the Toscanini concert. He has literally "made" the success which he reifies and accepts as an objective criterion, without recognizing himself in it. But he has not "made" it by liking the concert, but rather by buying the ticket. ("On the Fetish Character," 34)

It may be granted that the Toscanini concert is a commodity, the purchase of a ticket to which by a consumer may contribute to its success. This concert commodity, however, is in no sense a product of the consumer's labor, and the analogy with the theory of commodity fetishism can only be sustained by displacing the commodity form of the concert onto the success which, with the help of those disarming quotation marks, the consumer can then be said to have "made." The analogy depends, in other words, on the suggestion that the success of the commodity is itself a commodity—from which it can be deduced that the "making" of this success by the unfortunate consumer is an act of labor. The reader who is prepared to go along with this sort of conceptual jiggery-pokery will have no difficulty in agreeing with Adorno that since the consumer has had to buy a ticket in order to make the success which then rebounds to the greater glory of the appalling Toscanini, s/he has therefore been alienated from the product of his/her labor by the commodity form.

Had anyone bothered to ask Adorno how he knew that the person who attended the concert was "really worshipping the money" he paid for the ticket, he would no doubt have replied that this imputed reality can simply be read off the political economy of the event:

it is objectively given, like the worker's relation to capital. But alas, Marx's theory does not require us to infer feelings, motives, and emotional states from the behavior of members of the working class as they go about their daily business, still less does it presuppose that when they buy something they are "really" venerating the money that changes hands in the course of the transaction. The whole ramshackle concoction is sustained by nothing better than an apocryphal pejorative psychology of "consumers," the validity of which is rationalized by reference to prior assumptions which are equally arbitrary and equally unsubstantiated. If it is true that "exchange-values destroy use-values for human beings," as Adorno has assured us that it is, then it follows, as the night the day, that individual acts of consumption must represent the consumer's veneration of the commodity as exchange value. "Where they react at all, it no longer makes any difference whether it is to Beethoven's Seventh Symphony or to a bikini." (Adorno, "On the Fetish Character," 33) In the Adorno epigram, theoretical acumen is essentially a matter of the promulgation of alibis for contempt.

It is not the least of the disadvantages of such lines of reasoning (which are, in this respect, the progenitors of Althusser's theory of ideology) that they leave the subtle consciousness of the theorist unaccounted for. Had Adorno attended the Toscanini concert, would he have worshiped the money he paid for the ticket—and would he have mistaken its success for an "objective criterion" of its value? The cascades of bile which Adorno showers on Toscanini at every available opportunity seem to suggest that he would not, but he never explains how it is that he has been exempted from the common lot, and while Adorno is ready to assure Walter Benjamin that the proletariat "needs us for knowledge as much as we need the proletariat to make the revolution," he is quite unable to show us how, consistently with his theory, this saving knowledge is to be achieved. (Adorno, "Letters," 125) Adorno simply assumes that all men except Adorno are molded as a single type which is unfailingly reproduced in every product of the cultural industry; just as, twenty years later, Althusser and his innumerable epigones would assume that a mysterious providence had granted them a dispensation from the iron law of "interpellation of the subject." In a work whose declared theme is the failure of enlightened thought to reflect upon itself, this theoretical black hole looms with an especially portentous largeness, but all accounts of social orders which are supposed to depend, for their own reproduction, on their power to replicate their own practices and priorities in the minds of their inhabitants must eventually be engulfed in some such form of question-begging hypocrisy. The theory can explain everything except its own conditions of possibility. Conversely, if Adorno and Althusser have contrived to escape, why should not another? That is, in accounting for everything but itself, the theory accounts for nothing at all: its existence is the tacit contradiction of its contents.

Theoretical inconsequence in these matters goes hand in hand with reactionary politics. The world of Adorno's culture industry can no more be changed than it can be intelligibly derived from any previously existing state of affairs. It is only monolithically and intractably itself, at once alpha and omega, suspended in a historical void without conceivable precedent, origin or issue. Nothing is left for its creator but to express his scorn for the gray somnambulists with whom he has peopled it. But it remains for Baudrillard, who has divested himself of Adorno's vestigial socialistic piety, to adumbrate a "media world" which not only cannot but also should not be resisted—unless, perhaps, through occasional "wildcat strikes" which, though easily defeated, remain sufficiently romantic to generate a frisson in the jaded chronicler of *faits divers*. (176)

"The media"—those who cling to the idea of progress—are at least in a position to report that with the passage of time Adorno's culture industry has at last found an appropriate lodging in the discourse of common sense. The point at which common sense and left-Hegelian High Theory meet can be exemplified by these extracts from a representative piece of "media sociology."

> For the world market Hollywood performed an impressive publicity conjuring trick. Although the American film industry was run by a cartel—which largely kept out foreign competition—on the world scene Hollywood was the apostle of free trade and no-holds-barred competition. Its ability to perform this dazzling conjuring trick was partly dependent on Hollywood's location in Hollywood—remote from New York beyond the shimmering desert, cocooned behind the mountains in a large and growing smog of publicity, stardom and illusion. (Tunstall, 70)

And again:

> T. W. Adorno at one time claimed that even a symphony concert when broadcast on radio was drained of significance; many mass culture critics also had very harsh things to say about the large audiences which went to western and crime films in the 1930s— films which yet other cultural experts have subsequently decided were masterpieces after all. Even more bizarre, however, is the western intellectual who switches off the baseball game, turns down the hi-fi or pushes aside the Sunday magazine and pens a terse instruction to the developing world to get back to its tribal harvest ceremonials or funeral music. (Tunstall, 59)

Tunstall, of course, lacks Adorno's inwardness with the dialectic, and these hearty, bracing judgments suggest that he has not taken the immanent extinction of the lights of culture quite so much to heart. He even seems prepared to hedge his bets, for he clearly has no intention of relinquishing his long-playing records or advocating a return to Nature on the off chance that some "[w]estern intellectual" will turn out to be right about Toscanini. It may be said, nevertheless, that this is where *Dialectic of Enlightenment* gets us: the brutal confidence and the philistinism (if not the joviality) are already there, after all, in Adorno's text, and his assumptions and rhetorical strategies turn out to be perfectly congenial to the sort of middlebrow "serious reading" which he would presumably have despised. That Tunstall has employed the tabloid adjective "bizarre" to do the tabloid's work we know from that reference to "cultural experts" and "intellectuals" (*pace* Adorno); yet, these "experts" are the same people as Adorno's "connoisseurs," quibbling over the "good or bad points" of artifacts which "every child with a keen interest in varieties could show to be identical." (Horkheimer and Adorno, 123) The appeal to "every child" is an appeal to a sense of the obvious which Adorno shares with Tunstall, who is similarly disposed to chastise the recalcitrant highbrow with shafts of withering irony, and who is only to be distinguished from Adorno by his eagerness, as a good sociologist, to authenticate his instinctual aversions with the charts, statistics, and mountains of miscellaneous hard facts which Adorno thought, quite rightly, that it was not worth his time and energy to compile.

Despite himself, however, Tunstall makes a valid point; for in assuming that what was once obvious to Adorno and is now obvious to him is also obvious to us, he is actually assuming that the concept of the culture industry is already included in his readers' habitual mental furniture. We imbibe Tunstall's convictions about the Hollywood cinema with our mother's milk, and the term *the media* is most ardently canvassed not by sociologists of culture (though they come a close second) but by the institutions designated in the term. It is, as a term, an invitation not to pay attention, and "critical" appropriations of it are prone to the kind of slippage that takes place here: "The United States media emerged from, and reflect the assumptions of, American politics. The US media do not merely 'fit' neatly into the US political system, the US media are an important, indeed essential, part of that system." (172) It would be foolish (and it is, in any case, not necessary) to deny that these sentences point in the direction of something important, but the phrase "the assumptions of American politics" and the assertion that "the media" emerge from and reflect them ought, it seems to me, to give us pause. What are these unitary "assumptions?"—and in what sense can the distinct cultural practices of journalism, advertising, television, and movies be said to "reflect" them in a unitary way? The conclusion that the media operate in identical ways, and produce identical or mutually compatible effects, is not only preordained by the concept in terms of which the conclusion is reached; it corresponds to an experience of "media products" which we all spontaneously have.

Moreover, we need look no further than the body of work in which the existence of the media was first proclaimed to discover that they lend themselves as readily to celebrations of the advent of a "global village" as to jeremiads against the triumph of barbarism. Marshall McLuhan's hymn to a world made one by the expansion of international communications carefully omits to mention the economic and political interests which the communications systems embody, as Raymond Williams has pointed out with admirable trenchancy. (Williams, *Television*, 127–28) There is, however, a great deal more than that to complain of. "The medium is the message is not a critical proposition," says Baudrillard, "but in its paradoxical form it has analytic value" (172)—and Adorno might well have agreed. Its "analytic value" (it might be better to say "convenience") consists in the fact that it is one of the statements which can be appropriated, without modification, by any political position whatever: like Caesar's wife, it is all things to all men. To say that "the medium is the message" is to assert that the nature of a work can be deduced from the technology of the medium or, alternatively, from the interests which control that technology, and one has only to decide what the technology in itself is, or what the interests are that regulate it, in order to have a general theory of contemporary culture ready-made. The medium/message can be a good or a bad thing, and it can tell a tale: now of apocalypse and now of the Second Coming; now of sex and violence and now of monopoly capital; now of the brotherhood of Man and now of the terrorism of the Code. In every case the analysis comes precooked, as it were, leaving nothing to the discretion of the chef but the spice of value judgment.

If the fastidious scrupulosity of the "cultural expert" or "connoisseur" seems misguided for the purposes of the given accounts of "media" or "culture industry," that may well be, however, because the accounts will not do, and I would certainly be unwilling to assume in advance that an interest in discriminating between one artifact and another is in itself incompatible with a radical position.

Art

If you defend the kitsch film against the "quality" film, no one could be more in agreement with you than I am: but *l'art pour l'art* is just as much in need of a defense, and the united front which exists against it and which to my knowledge extends from Brecht to the Youth Movement, would be encouragement enough to undertake a rescue.

—T. W. Adorno in a letter to Walter Benjamin

For all its pseudo-Marxist ornamentation, if Adorno's concept of the culture industry has been readily assimilated by an anti-Marxist post-semiotics on the one hand and a breezy empiricist sociology on the other, it has a specific function in Adorno's work of which no trace remains in its progeny: here alone it is inseparable from, and may be said actually to subserve, the promotion of an ideology of "Art." This ideology is important, not because it is in the least degree acceptable but because it is a strenuous version of ideas about art which we all take for granted. Two hundred years ago we could not have done so, but these ideas are now a very serious impediment to thought, and we will make no progress until we have confronted them.

The central category of Adorno's aesthetics is "the autonomous work of art," the bearing of which for his discussion of the culture industry Adorno himself indicates when he calls the products of the latter "dependent art" by comparison. The two contrasting adjectives incite to questions which are never answered, or even acknowledged, at any point in Adorno's work. Of what, precisely, does the "autonomy" of the autonomous work consist—and what is it supposed to be "autonomous" of? Adorno is as clear as he ever is in this passage from a private letter to Walter Benjamin criticizing Benjamin's famous essay, "The Work of Art in the Age of Mechanical Reproduction":

> Dialectical though your essay may be, it is not so in the case of the autonomous work of art itself; it disregards an elementary experience which becomes more evident to me every day in my own musical experience—that precisely the uttermost consistency in the pursuit of the technical laws of autonomous art changes this art and instead of rendering it into a taboo or fetish, brings it close to the state of freedom, of something that can be consciously produced and made. I know of no better materialistic programme than that statement by Mallarmé in which he defines works of literature as something not inspired but made out of words; and the greatest figures of reaction, such as Valery and Borchardt, . . . have this explosive power in their innermost cells. ("Letters," 122)

Adorno's reference, in the phrase "taboo or fetish," to Benjamin's concept of "aura" may be set aside for a moment: his own attempt to define the characteristic features of autonomous art has the prior claim on our attention. The definition labors under the double disadvantage that the content of its main component is ambiguous, and that, whichever meaning we chose, we end up with a tautology. It is quite unclear whether the autonomy of art derives from the autonomy of its "technical laws" or from the consistency with which these laws are pursued, and no matter what the answer to this conundrum may be, we are no nearer to knowing than we were in knowing how, and in relation to what, the laws achieved their autonomy. And what, in any case, are these technical laws? Is technique, or the use of technique, in art subject to anything that could be described as a "law"? Artists certainly use techniques, and in doing so they are working with and on conventions—conventions which can he thought of, in Williams's phrase, both as "limits" defining the boundaries of artistic activity and as "possibilities" enabling it. A number of artists working over time within the limits of a given set of conventions and exploring their "possibilities" constitutes a tradition. It is far from being the case, however, that the formation of a tradition can be construed as the "pursuit of a law" by the artists within the tradition. On the contrary, the great cultural traditions are remarkable not for the "consistency" with which "technical laws" are pursued but for the extraordinary diversity and heterogeneity of utterance which is achieved within the tradition's conventional limits. Herman Melville, Charlotte Brontë, Henry Fielding, and Virginia Woolf all employed the conventions of the novel; John Dos Passos, Gertrude Stein, Edith Wharton, and Ernest Hemingway were all American novelists variously employing the novel's conventions at a particular stage in the evolution of the form. But if we try to think of these artists as being in consistent pursuit of a law, we may well come to the conclusion that there were no conventions at all.

This, in fact, is more or less the conclusion that Adorno does reach—though, naturally, he does not put the thing in quite that way. "Conventions" tend to have an obstinately material character: they are formed under specific historical conditions through the agency of persons who inhabit those conditions, and their subsequent development in the hands of other persons is deeply rooted in other conditions which are likewise historically specific. The persistence of conventions over long periods of time does not lift them out of history for the simple reason that this persistence can only ever be realized through the work of successive historical individuals who use them. In other words, it is a necessary condition of the persistence of a convention across historical time that all uses of a convention are defined by their historical particularity, and the elements of the novel which have persisted from Fielding to Stein have only done so on the basis of a series of material social actions.

The pursuit of the technical laws of autonomous art, on the other hand, takes place on an altogether loftier plane. Adorno feels, as we have seen, that the unfolding of the dialectic in the actually existing social world has reached a highly unsatisfactory conclusion. Although a Marxist, he continues to hold to the teleological view of human history which Marx, in his innocence, supposed himself to have refuted, but the "great end" of the historical process is less than it was once cracked up to be.[1] Far from fulfilling their revolutionary task, the common people (whose superannuation—latterly a favorite theme both of Eurocommunism and of the truculently red-baiting postmodern Left Bank—Adorno was the first to proclaim) have surrendered to the siren lure of capital, and with their abdication from the political scene, history can now be said to have stopped. But if it is no longer possible to believe that the promise of happiness will ever be redeemed on earth, the dialectic continues to perform its progressive functions in the realm of the spirit from which Marx so mischievously removed it. It lives on in "the technical laws of autonomous art"—that is, in Hegel's *Geist*, now identified exclusively with the aesthetic and decked with a Marxist fig leaf ("the state of freedom") for the sake of political respectability. Although it is worn with an air, the fig leaf serves only to draw attention to the nakedness it covers: the existence of an ideology to the effect that works of literature are "inspired" scarcely entitles us to discover a "materialistic programme" in the statement that they are, after all, "made out of words." In that all artifacts are "consciously produced and made," whatever their makers may think about them, it is not in the least surprising that "the greatest figures of reaction" should turn out to have an "explosive" radical potential—though on the other hand, the claim that one work can be closer to, or further from, the state of freedom than another seems to have lost something of its force. Readers of *Screen* in its Althusserian period will be familiar with this ploy, and with the end that it serves: having identified an artistic preoccupation with "material form" with materialism in the Marxist sense, Adorno goes on to insist that this preoccupation is exclusively the property of a putative avant-garde in the name of which it is possible—nay, one's revolutionary duty—to trounce "dependent art."

Adorno's belief that art has "laws," and that he knows what they are, has the result that one would expect: his work is peppered with, and seems at times virtually to consist of, apoplectic denunciations of "the recidivist element." Artists who are alleged to have departed from, stood athwart, or otherwise impeded the forward march of artistic progress are subjected to merciless ritual humiliation and harassment, and they are found guilty of some form of complicity with or indebtedness to the culture industry. The lengths to which Adorno is prepared to go are astonishing.

> In the opinion of this writer—and he is prepared to back it by concrete technical analysis—the work of Sibelius is not only incredibly overrated, but it fundamentally lacks any good qualities. It would be interesting to show: first, to what extent Sibelius is played over the radio, and second, to what influences his popularity is due.
>
> . . . If his great success is really a fact, and not some sort of manufactured popularity (which is still the writer's opinion), this probably would indicate a total state of musical consciousness which ought to give rise to even graver apprehension than the lack of understanding for great modern music or the preference for cheap light music . . . If Sibelius' music is good music, then all the categories by which musical standards can be measured . . . must be completely abolished. (Adorno quoted in Horowitz, 240)[2]

Needless to say, after these brave words, the "concrete technical analysis" either of Jean Sibelius's music or of the sources of his popularity is not forthcoming: it never is. The value judgment is obviously ludicrous, but the procedure is exemplary of the Adorno anathema.

The Hegelian dialectic, of course, has a nationalistic coloration, and it is perhaps the most deplorable paradox of Adorno's work that a Marxist Jew formed by Weimar Germany should have devoted himself with indefatigable energy to theorizing the supremacy of *Kultur*. If he contrives to remain unaware of the fact—as he clearly does—that is because the field in which his confidence is most lavishly enjoyed is the field of music, where he is entitled to the assumption that the Austro-German tradition is not only by far the most influential but also (work for work, and composer for composer) the most distinguished national tradition in bourgeois culture. Music for Adorno means German music (or selected features of it) from Johann Sebastian Bach to Arnold Schoenberg, understood in scarcely modified Hegelian terms as the self-creation of autonomous art through the pursuit of its own formal logic. As we might expect, this line proves to be quite extraordinarily difficult to hold, on both political and aesthetic grounds. The Hegelian dialectic and the concept of Kultur remain intransigently reactionary, and Adorno can only accommodate them to a Marxist position at all by reminding us periodically, in moments of embarrassment, that "progress" is, after all, dialectical and contains elements of "regression." This allows him to resolve, after a fashion, the particularly thorny problems raised by that bane of German philosophy, "the case of Wagner," which can now be seen actually to epitomize the dialectic's devious tendency to incorporate "the recidivist element" within itself.[3] It permits him, too, to argue at one and the same time that the logic of autonomous art has led inexorably to modern German music, and that Schoenberg and Anton Webern are to be valued precisely because "their work is nothing but a single dialogue with the powers that destroy individuality"—that is, modern German politics.[4]

In his attempt to establish the ideal preeminence of a culture which he perceives, in practice, to be degenerate, Adorno was not alone: he has a precedent in the case of Richard Wagner, and he himself provided Thomas Mann with the recipe for *Doctor Faustus*, in which the tortuous "dialogue" of the German genius and the Nazi is reenacted, at interminable length, around a fictionalized representation of Schoenberg. Schoenberg, who loathed Adorno ("my privy councillor," in Mann's phrase), was appalled, and violently repudiated the novel; yet, he was sufficiently susceptible to the mystique it elaborates to have proclaimed, in a chilling and painful phrase, that the invention of serialism would guarantee the hegemony of German music for a thousand years. He most certainly could not have said that he, his pupils, and (of course) Adorno were the only individuals capable of consciously representing the aims of collectivity in the field of culture, and that every other development in modern music had abandoned the dialogue with the forces of darkness in order to collude with them. The objects of Adorno's familiar fury—the Russian romantics, Sibelius, Igor Stravinsky, George Gershwin, jazz—have nothing in common except the fact that they are not German. Furthermore, it must have been especially galling that the man who prostituted Beethoven and Mozart on the American airwaves was an Italian. Toscanini's debasement of Kultur is certainly epistemologically convenient: since it is "not for nothing [that] the rule of the established conductor reminds one of that of the totalitarian Führer," it provides the perfect theoretical link between the hell of fascism and the hell of the culture industry. (Adorno, ("On the Fetish Character," 39)

It is perfectly natural, then, in the light of these priorities, that Adorno should have taken umbrage at Benjamin's essay "The Work of Art of Mechanical Reproduction," which aspires to show that "the liquidation of the traditional value of the cultural heritage" by contemporary developments in the technology of cultural production is a progressive development. (Benjamin, 223) When one considers the Adorno/Benjamin debate (if it can be called that—it amounts to an exchange of letters), there can be no doubt, it seems to me, of where one's sympathies lie. Benjamin's modesty and disinterestedness compare only favorably with the brutality and lack of scruple of his interlocutor, and his readiness, in the age of darkness that weighed so much more heavily on him than on Adorno, to perceive and try to comprehend the creative elements of the culture of his time is all the more astonishing for Adorno's scornful acceptance of apocalypse as High Theory's Benjamin's development (so tragically abbreviated) out of an arcane romantic mysticism to the work on Bertolt Brecht and Charles Baudelaire is a heroic achievement which must be honored by any Marxist.

And yet the ironic paradox of his disagreement with Adorno is that there is no conceptual disagreement at all, as the vagueness and concessiveness of his brief response to Adorno's criticisms demonstrates: the two mens' value judgments are absolutely incompatible with each other, but they are arrived at on the basis of a common theoretical framework which deprives them of their substance. Benjamin's age of mechanical reproduction is merely the inverted mirror image of Adorno's culture industry, and it is arbitrary in exactly the same way: both concepts depend on the assumption that the mechanical reproduction of works of art begins with the invention of film and photography, and that as a result of their invention, "the total function of art [has been] reversed." (Benjamin, 226) Benjamin wishes to take a favorable view of "the tremendous shattering of tradition" (223) which follows, and he does so by arguing that the new cultural technologies objectively embody the political interests of the working class. The argument is excruciatingly willed and tenuous, and it obliges Benjamin to work up a Brechtianized version of the reflection theory of realism. For, it appears that film and photography, by virtue of their technology, are in essence "realistic": they "pry an object from its shell" and show us what is actually there, and in doing so they "manifest in the field of perception" the general contemporary political process by which reality is gradually adjusted to the masses and the masses to reality. (225) By virtue of the same technology, film and photography are inherently "critical" in the Brechtian sense: a banalizing appropriation of Brecht's theory of distantiation allows Benjamin to suggest that the technology of mechanical reproduction, in and of itself, generates the critical distance between the spectator and the representation of the real which Brecht attributed to a specific, systematic practice of performance.

Adorno, with his antipathy to Brecht to help him, has no difficulty in showing that this is mumbo jumbo, though Theory and common sense unite to protect him from the perception that his own thesis is only Benjamin's turned back to front. Moreover, he has the advantage over Benjamin at every point that his negative attitude to film does not require him to explain why the cinema which actually exists, and which the masses actually like, bears not the slightest resemblance to its imputed essence. Benjamin's explanation takes the predictable form:

> In Western Europe the capitalistic exploitation of the film denies consideration to modern man's legitimate claim to being reproduced. Under these circumstances the film industry is trying hard to spur the interest of the masses through illusion-

promoting spectacles and dubious speculations. . . . The film responds to the shriveling of the aura with an artificial build-up of the "personality" outside the studio. The cult of the movie star, fostered by the money of the film industry, preserves not the unique aura of the person but the spell of the personality, the phony spell of a commodity. (223)

Given the terms in which the debate is conducted, Adorno's victory is a fait accompli. Benjamin's attempt to maintain that capitalist technical innovation can embody the essential interests of a subordinate class is doomed to incoherence, and when Adorno trumps his hand by insisting that it must embody the interests of capital, Benjamin can make no better riposte than that capital has alienated the essence of film. Even if this reply were less implausible than it is, it is tantamount to a withdrawal from the field, and Benjamin is eventually compelled to retreat to the equally implausible, and utterly unsubstantiated, notion that the development of the sound film was an industrial operation designed to break the revolutionary primacy of the silent film, which generated reactions that were hard to control and therefore dangerous politically. Benjamin offers this sentence as a "dialectical mediation" between Adorno's and his own, but what it proves is the impossibility of mediating, dialectically or otherwise, between rival versions of the same determinism. One can only yield to the other.

By the same token, the assumptions which Benjamin shares with Adorno give the latter an intrinsic advantage in the parallel disagreement about the value of "art." For Benjamin, as for Adorno, art is *Kunst*, and the only service which the famous concept of "aura" performs is that of projecting across the whole of human history—from the cave to the invention of photography—the aesthete's definition of art as thing in itself which is in fact a product of the very conditions of late nineteenth-century capitalism to which Benjamin wishes to attribute the aura's decay. In fact, the whole structure of the essay rests on an initial definition of art as an object with "a unique existence in time and space" which excludes—among the "traditional" arts—literature, theater, dance, and music, and which cannot even be sustained in the fields of graphic art and sculpture, where it might seem, at half a glance, to be most plausible. Benjamin is able to overlook the fact that his definition is patently false because he takes for granted the attitude to art which he betrays here in drawing an analogy between the aura of art and the aura of Nature: "We define the aura of the latter as the unique phenomenon of a distance, however close it may be. If, while resting on a summer afternoon, you follow with your eyes a mountain range on the horizon or a branch which casts its shadow over you, you experience the aura of those mountains, of that branch." (Benjamin, 224–25) The feelings Benjamin is describing are always most appropriately enjoyed in the horizontal plane, and while no one would have dreamed of adopting a semi-recumbent posture before a work of art until a few decades before Benjamin was born, the essay invites us to think of it as a historical universal: culturally speaking, people have always been prone "and, as it were, convalescent." The explanation of this endemic lassitude in the face of cultural products is that the products themselves have always invited it: the Paleolithic mural, the medieval Madonna, and "the secular cult of beauty" which has, apparently, "prevailed" in Western art since the Renaissance, are all alike embodiments of a "cult value" to which prostration has been the traditional response and which bespeaks art's "parasitical dependence on ritual" throughout its history. (226)

Benjamin claims to object to art in this sense—as who would not?—but his failure to recognize either its historical sources or his own surreptitious allegiance to it draws him implacably to the conclusion that human culture to date consists of a collection of mystified fetish objects whose value must be "liquidated" if culture is to be renewed. Benjamin felt constrained to approve, and it was his unfortunate fate that there was no one on hand to disabuse him but an aesthete who was made of considerably sterner stuff. Adorno objects, quite rightly, that art is not in itself "a taboo or fetish," but he does so precisely in the name of "art for art's sake," now refurbished as the sine qua non of a materialist aesthetics and prescribed to Benjamin as the antidote to Brecht.

Before art for art's sake could recommend itself to Adorno as a Marxist slogan, it had to be invented by the bourgeoisie for use in a quite different connection. The phrase embodies a view of art which D. H. Lawrence, in *Women in Love*, ascribes to, and repudiates in, the sculptor Loerke.

> Ursula wavered, baffled. Then her words came. "But why does he have this idea of a horse?" she said. "I know it is his idea. I know it is a picture of himself, really—"
>
> Loerke snorted with rage.
>
> "A picture of myself!" he repeated in derision. "*Wissen Sie, gnädige Frau*, that is a Kunstwerk, a work of art. It is a work of art, it is a picture of nothing, of absolutely nothing. It has nothing to do with anything but itself, it has no reflection with the everyday world of this and other, there is no connexion between them, absolutely none, they are two different and distinct planes of existence, and to translate one into the other is worse than foolish, it is a darkening of all counsel, a making confusion everywhere. Do you see, you must not confuse the relative world of action with the absolute world of art. That you must not do. (421)

Here, very plainly, is Adorno's "autonomous work of art," which is even defined in terms of an opposition between the kingdom of necessity (known to Loerke, who was not a Marxist, as "the relative world of action") and the state of freedom. It is implicit in the opposition that "the absolute world of art" is not only autonomous of, but superior to, the other world, and Adorno expresses his sense of its superiority in his own distinctive way: "The history of serious music since Mozart" is a "flight from the banal." ("On the Fetish Character," 275) Adorno is speaking from his "own musical experience" (a subject on which Schoenberg, in his bitter way, was wont to indulge his skepticism), and "serious music" here is to be equated with "serious art." "The power of the street ballad, the catchy tune and all the swarming forms of the banal has made itself felt since the beginning of the bourgeois era." ("On the Fetish Character," 275) We may ignore "the beginning of the bourgeois era," just as Adorno did: for the man to whom Homer's *Odyssey* is "one of the earliest representative testimonies of Western bourgeois civilization," the "bourgeois era" is plainly synonymous with "life." (Horkheimer and Adorno, xvi)

Notes

CARY GRANT: COMEDY AND MALE DESIRE

1. I would like to thank Robin Wood and Richard Lippe, who provided me with hospitality while I was writing this essay and who read the first draft and made a number of very helpful suggestions. I dedicate the essay to them.

2. Farce and wit coexist in other sophisticated comedies, but it is not the case, of course, that the sophisticated couple always acquires the meaning that it does in *The Awful Truth*, *Bringing Up Baby* and *Holiday*. In *It Happened One Night* (1934) and *My Man Godfrey* (1936), the hero presides over the heroine's democratic education, as does the Grant character in *Once Upon a Honeymoon* (1942). In *Holiday* and its two predecessors, we have a mutually enabling encounter among stars, director, and genre, in which the radical possibilities of each are realized.

3. *An Affair to Remember* is a close remake of McCarey's own *Love Affair* (1939), in which Nickie had been played by Charles Boyer, and there are evident affinities between the Grant characters in *Gaslight* and *Notorious* and the Boyer characters in *Gaslight*, *A Woman's Vengeance* (1947), and *The Thirteenth Letter* (1951), or between Grant in *Indiscreet* and Boyer in *Back Street* (1941). In Boyer, too, the charisma of the romantic lover has often been continuous with the vicious, the corrupt, and the cynical; yet the difference between the two personae appears in the fact that while RKO compelled Hitchcock to tack on a happy ending to *Suspicion* to protect Grant's image, no such scruple was allowed to impair the dramatic logic of *Gaslight*, in which Boyer, playing a variant of the same melodramatic type, remains unambiguously the villain.

   In accounting for the difference we may note, to begin with, that if Grant rarely plays action heroes and Boyer doesn't play them at all, Grant appears even less frequently in woman's pictures (*An Affair to Remember* and *Penny Serenade* [1941] are the major exceptions) and Boyer appears in them all the time. Given the thematic of the woman's film, and the privilege accorded by the genre to the exhaustive intensity of the heroine's passion—an intensity that comes to be synonymous with emotional integrity and disinterestedness—the withholding of intimacy and of full reciprocal engagement which Boyer shares with Grant are inflected in another direction.

   In, say, *The Garden of Allah* (1935) or *All This and Heaven Too* (1940), where the Boyer character's refusal to commit himself to "love" is associated with a tragic moral dilemma, and the claims of passion are contested not by those of egotistic self-assertion but by those of self-abnegating duty (to religious vocation and family, respectively), Boyer is presented sympathetically. In *Back Street* and, supremely, *Conquest* (1937), Boyer embodies a ruthless male ambition which withdraws from love to achieve power and position in a public world from which the heroine is excluded: in both cases, the heroine is reduced to the ignominious role of "mistress" and finds herself in an indeterminate hinterland between public and domestic life, without a secure and recognized position in either. The theme of a woman's exploitation by a love to which her "destiny" as a woman commits her but which the man, though he has appeared to share it, does not return, is taken to an extreme in *Gaslight*, in which the lover's charisma and allure are, from the outset, weapons in a confidence trick.

Significantly, while Grant can still be cast as a desirable romantic male until virtually the end of his career, a number of Boyer's later performances, such as those for Vincente Minnelli in *The Cobweb* (1955) and *The Four Horsemen of the Apocalypse* (1961), emphasize the dessication of aging charm and associate the strained, insinuating facility which are all that remain of it with the character's moral bankruptcy. Here, the feeling that the Boyer character's ambitions are worthless (already clear enough in *Conquest*) is compounded by the evident meretriciousness of the manner which once made him plausible.

It is crucial here that the suggestion of Boyer's "Europeanness" is very different from Grant's. As the French lover, Boyer inherits the bad connotations of Europe along with its glamour, and in that he does so, he can be used to dramatize with particular cogency the suspicion, implicit in the woman's film, that a woman's destiny can very easily become her oppression. Grant's "Europeanness," by contrast, is hardly an issue at all. Even when he plays British characters, the emphasis falls on their class position rather than their national origins, and in American settings we are invited to read him as American. In this he can be distinguished not only from Boyer but also from, say, Ronald Colman, whose romantic attractiveness is inseparable from his being an English gentleman and whose persona has no suggestion either of insincerity or of sexual manipulativeness.

4. During the lull in his career in the early '50s, Grant was in fact offered the part of the fading movie star Norman Maine (eventually played by Mason) in George Cukor's remake of *A Star Is Born* (1954), but he turned it down because he thought it might harm his image.

5. Compare *Mr. Lucky* with *The Philadelphia Story* (1940) in this respect. The animus against Tracy Lord (Katharine Hepburn) in Cukor's film (or Barry's play—it might be argued that Cukor qualifies it) is so intense, and the commitment to transform her into "a first-class human being" so relentless, that we can be asked to write off the moral weakness of Dexter Haven (Grant) as a mere by-product of his ex-wife's intransigence. At the same time, Haven's unfitness to be the hero is tacitly acknowledged in the presence of Mike (James Stewart), who undertakes Tracy's democratization in his stead before returning her to her ex-husband. *The Philadelphia Story* manages to give the Grant persona an entirely negative content (his "femininity" becomes castration and his "irresponsibility" dissoluteness) while also requiring us to see it, in the light of Tracy's aberrations, sympathetically. In this, and as a reactionary comedy of remarriage, the film also invites comparison with *The Awful Truth* and *His Girl Friday* (the second of which is also disturbed by an uncertainty as to what our attitude to the Grant figure is to be).

A NEW SERVITUDE

1. The influence of *Rebecca* on *Citizen Kane* has not, I think, been noticed, though the derivation of the opening and closing sequences of Orson Welles's film is surely obvious enough. The influence is presumably unconscious, and it is inseparable from a reactionary inversion of Hitchcock's themes. *Kane* is, in effect, the Freudian-feminist melodrama from the husband's point of view, and to compare what Welles makes of "the second marriage" (to Susan Alexander) with either *Rebecca* or *Jane Eyre* (1944) is very revealing.

2. I should probably add that I do not accept Lacan's account of female sexuality, and that my use of the concept of Woman is entirely opportunistic.

3. The lover may cease to be merely Phallus and become a dramatically significant figure on the one condition that he is represented as being capable of recognizing that his own investment in masculinity entails the suffering of the heroine. The classical case is *Letter from an Unknown Woman*.

4. *The Little Foxes* (1941), of course, is also about a mother/daughter relationship, but it is not a part of the "motherhood" cycle initiated by *The Old Maid*. Davis's work with Wyler is very strikingly unlike the work with Edmund Goulding and/or Casey Robinson which is exactly contemporary with it. Indeed, the William Wyler films may be thought of as a conservative counterpart to, or commentary on, the motherhood cycle.

5. *Jezebel* (1938), in which the heroine is obliged to expiate her sins by accompanying her stricken lover to a colony for the victims of yellow fever, is an obvious example from Davis's own work, but such endings, when they occur, cannot simply be derived from the nature of the genre. The punitive aspects of *Jezebel* tell us more about Wyler than about the woman's film, and it is relevant to point out in this connection that two of the most famous cases of affirmed female self-sacrifice, *Casablanca* (1942) and *Brief Encounter* (1945), must be referred to as the crossing of the woman's movie with the commitment film and to a specifically British petit bourgeois addiction to the virtues of quotidian joylessness, respectively.

6. One doubts that such a film could be made now. Margaretha von Trotta's *Marianne and Juliane* (1981), which one can almost imagine as a Warner Brothers melodrama starring Davis and Mary Astor, comes closest, but with all its beauties—it is one of the few really great European films of the last decade—it does not get very much further than *Now, Voyager*.

BLISSING OUT: THE POLITICS OF REAGANITE ENTERTAINMENT

1. Another excellent article on Reaganism in the same issue of the *New Left Review* is Mike Davis, "The New Right's Road to Power," 128 (July/August 1981): 28–49.

DETOUR

1. Elsewhere in this book [*The Movie Book of Film Noir,* where this essay originally appeared], Douglas Pye discusses a rather different use of unreliable narration in the work of Fritz Lang.

THE EXORCIST

1. I am indebted to Tony Williams for this information.

SEXUALITY AND POWER, OR THE TWO OTHERS

1. It should be added that women are, intermittently and momentarily, shown to be present in the Bolshevik ranks. This presence is so insubstantial, however, that it scarcely affects the argument, which is concerned with the extent to which women are functional in the narrative.

2. See Yon Barna's *Eisenstein*, Marie Seton's *Sergei M. Eisenstein*, and the introduction to the indispensable shot-by-shot breakdown of the script (Lorrimer). For an alternative reading of Eisenstein's project, see the introduction to the translation of the screenplay by Ivor Montagu and Herbert Marshall, and Ivor Montagu's *With Eisenstein in Hollywood*. Montagu asserts authoritatively that Eisenstein "intended no criticism" of Stalinism in *Ivan the Terrible* (he appears to consider suggestions to the contrary as a sort of insult to Eisenstein's "integrity as an artist") and "was solely intent on fathoming and vividly representing the true essence of a past patriotic glory, spots and all." (Montagu, 117) Unfortunately, the whole of Part II and the last third of Part I appear to consist of nothing but spots, and the usefulness of interpreting the film as a documentary reconstruction of life and times in the Middle Ages seems somewhat more than dubious.

3. Purdon writes that Eisenstein "explained the creation of the Crown Prince Dimitri [*sic*] in *Ivan*, for example, as a direct working-out of a homosexual mother-fixation, thus accepting the insulting masterstroke of psychiatry in which 'queer' and 'motherfucker' reached identity." "Psychiatry" stands here, as a subsequent sentence makes clear, for "psychoanalysis." It is clear, I think, that the theorization of gayness both by Freud and by various post-Freudian developments of psychoanalysis is riddled with tensions and contradictions. Equally, it is crucial to distinguish not only between psychoanalysis and psychiatry (that all-purpose monolith) but also between reactionary and scientific elements in Freud. This is not the place for the extensive and rigorous analysis that this matter demands, but it is proper to remark that the Freud who asserted, in a note added in 1915 to the discussion of "inversion" in *Three Essays on the Theory of Sexuality*, that homosexuality and heterosexuality can both be seen as "a result of restriction in one direction or the other" of an original bisexuality and that in consequence, heterosexuality "is also a problem that needs elucidating," is a crucial figure for Gay Liberation. (Vol. VIII, 145–46)

4. In narrative and imagery, *Macbeth* is preoccupied with the concept of infanticide—the massacre of the innocent—to which the murder of Duncan is symbolically assimilated and of which the import emerges most explicitly, perhaps, in the murder of Lady Macduff and her son ("You egg!"): that is, the crimes of the Macbeths become crimes against the substance of life and "natural process." *The Boyars' Plot* shares this preoccupation and lends itself to an analysis proceeding from the complex interrelationships set up between the various children in the narrative. One can relate this not only to *Bezhin Meadow* but also to other elements of Eisenstein's work and to the crucial theoretical concepts of "pathos," subsequently informed by his interest in the Victorian novel. Consider, for example, the film on abortion Eisenstein made in Switzerland; the double murder of Roberta and her unborn child in the script of *An American Tragedy*; the Odessa Steps in *Potemkin*, where the plunging baby carriage and the desolate mother with her slaughtered child have a function analogous to that of the girl in the Raising of the Bridges. Crucial here is Eisenstein's extraordinary essay on Chaplin, "Charlie the Kid," in which he defines the "task" of the Soviet state as that of making "the children's paradise of the past accessible to every grown-up, to every citizen of the Soviet Union." The revolution has realized, in its "very practice . . . a wonderful resurrection, on a newly perfected—the most perfect—phase of human evolution, of just that premise, which at the very dawn, the Childhood of Mankind, in the past Golden Age seemed to man in his primeval, natural, and simple condition to be the natural conception of work and the rights and obligations involved therein." (121) This suggests very pointedly the means by which "innocents" (women, children) can come to be "pathetic" emblems of the revolution. One notes that it is characteristic of "innocence" (indeed, the raison d'être of the concept), to be pre-sexual, pre-lapsarian and that if Eisenstein is able to disavow the consciousness of the sexuality of the Bolsheviks in *October* as completely as he does, it is because they can be thought of, in some sense, as children. Hence the ending of the film, in which the "new man" is, literally, a child. Hence, also, the possibility of interpreting the film as an exhilarated hymn to the anarchism of children liberating themselves from the restrictions imposed by their parents and taking their revenge on them. (Compare, for instance, *The Exorcist* [1973]!) The theme of infanticide obtains its force in this context, Ivan's crime—or rather, the crimes perpetrated within the dominating ideological structures outlined by the film—being similar to Macbeth's.

5. Note throughout, and particularly in connection with the chess metaphor and the concept of retribution-through-the-masquerade, the influence of Eisenstein's interest in Jacobean tragedy (Tourneur, Middleton, Webster).

6. Crucial—and radical—in this context is Max Ophüls's penultimate American film, *Caught* (1948), which poses the link between the oppression of women and the oppression of gays with extraordinary explicitness, through the wife and male secretary of Smith Ohlrig, the Robert Ryan character (the gayness, obviously, cannot be "named" in a 1940s film, but is coded by a familiar stereotype which the film proceeds to subvert). In both cases, the oppression has been partially internalized, emerging in the woman (Barbara Bel Geddes) as surrender to capitalist dream (creating herself as sex object to catch a rich husband) and in the homosexual as a veneer of cultivated indifference ("Tough, darling, tough!"). The oppressor is the successful American male, whose neurosis (assimilated, through his obsessively repeated games, to the death drive) is itself placed in terms of defining ideological structures, and the film moves toward the point at which wife and secretary liberate themselves from him.

THE IDEOLOGY OF *SCREEN*

1. Page references to *Ecrits* are to the French edition. [All translations are by the author.]

2. I have been conscious of a general debt to *Beyond Curriculum* by the Marxist educator Douglas Holly, while acknowledging that his positions (derived from Lev Vygotsky and Jerome Bruner) require considerable qualification and redefinition. I have discussed many of the ideas argued above with John Fletcher who, while he should not be blamed for their final appearance, has been generally invaluable.

THE PHILOSOPHY OF THE PIGEONHOLE

1. "Perhaps an even better definition of Romanticism than the progressive destruction of centrality would be a progressive destruction of decorum—not, we must emphasize, the absence of decorum but the process of its destruction." (Rosen and Zerner, 38)

2. "Postmodern classicism" is no doubt the grossest example. Commenting on the Venturi design for the new Sainsbury Wing of the National Gallery in London, Honour remarks that the projected building "defers to its setting in a city where past versions of classicism are prevalent," and he adds, charmingly, that the design "is, above all, an example of architectural tact." (27–33) The decorum of postmodern art is always "tactful" in this sense, though the setting deferred to is not primarily geographical.

THE MYTH OF POSTMODERNISM

1. Between the writing of this piece in 1981 and the appearance of the "Postmodernism" essay in *New Left Review* in 1984, Stravinsky appears to have been downgraded from an exemplary modernist to a postmodernist *avant la lettre*.

CONSUMING CULTURE

1. In the period when he was working on *Capital*, Marx noted, and praised, Charles Darwin's repudiation of teleology in the field of the natural sciences, and his own non-teleological account of the development of class society represents a crucial break with the tradition of utopian socialism.

2. Joseph Horowitz's book, which is in essence an obsessively extended recapitulation (across no less than five hundred pages) of Adorno's fulminations against this great musician, provides further striking evidence of the inexhaustible appeal of the Frankfurt version of Marxism for bourgeois letters.

3. Adorno's refusal, or inability, to provide any basis for his critical judgments in the analysis of actual works is one of the most characteristic features of his writings on "the culture industry."

4. Adorno addresses himself at length to the embarrassment of Wagnerian opera in *In Search of Wagner*, trans. Rodney Livingstone (London: New Left Books, 1981).

Bibliography

Adair, Gilbert. "E.T.cetera." *Sight and Sound* 52, no. 1 (Winter 1982/83): 63.

———. "The Critical Faculty." *Sight and Sound* 51, no. 4 (Autumn 1982): 248–57.

Adorno, Theodor W. "On the Fetish Character in Music and the Regression of Listening." In *The Culture Industry*, ed. J. M. Bernstein, pp. 26–52. London: Routledge, 1991.

———. "Letters to Walter Benjamin." In *Aesthetics and Politics*, by Ernest Bloch, George Lukács, Bertolt Brecht, Walter Benjamin, and Theodor Adorno, pp. 110–33. London: New Left Books, 1977.

———. *In Search of Wagner*, trans. Rodney Livingstone. London: New Left Books, 1981.

Althusser, Louis. *Essays in Self-Criticism*, trans. Ben Brewster. London: New Left Books, 1976.

———. "Ideology and the Ideological State Apparatus." *Essays in Ideology*, pp. 1–60. London: Verso, 1984.

———. *Lenin and Philosophy and Other Essays*, trans. Ben Brewster. London: New Left Books, 1971.

———. *Reading Capital*, trans. Ben Brewster. London: New Left Books, 1975.

Anger, Kenneth. *Hollywood Babylon*. New York: Dell, 1981.

Aronowitz, Stanley. "Postmodernism and Politics." *Social Text* 18 (Winter 1987/88): 99–115.

Attali, Jacques. *Noise: The Political Enemy of Music*. Minneapolis: University of Minnesota Press, 1985.

Austen, Jane. *Emma*, ed. David Lodge. London: Oxford University Press, 1971.

Auty, Chris. "The Complete Spielberg." *Sight and Sound* 51, no. 4 (Autumn 1982): 275–79.

Babuscio, Jack. "Camp and the Gay Sensibility." In *Gays and Film*, ed. Richard Dyer, pp. 40–57. London: British Film Institute, 1977.

Barna, Yon. *Eisenstein*. Bloomington: Indiana University Press, 1973.

Barnouw, Eric. *Documentary: A History of the Non-Fiction Film*. New York: Oxford University Press, 1983.

Barthes, Roland. *Image-Music-Text*, ed. and trans. Stephen Heath. New York: Hill & Wang, 1977.

———. *Mythologies*, ed. and trans. Annette Lavers. New York: Hill & Wang, 1977.

———. *The Pleasure of the Text*, trans. Richard Miller. New York: Hill & Wang, 1975.

———. *Sade/Fourier/Loyola*, trans. Richard Miller. New York: Hill & Wang, 1976.

———. *S/Z*, trans. Richard Miller. New York: Hill & Wang, 1974.

Bateson, F. W. "Correspondence: The Responsible Critic." *Scrutiny* XIX, no. 4 (1953): 317–21.

Baudrillard, Jean. *For a Critique of the Political Economy of the Sign*. St. Louis: Telos Press, 1981.

Belton, John. *The Cinema Stylists*. Metuchen, NJ: Scarecrow Press, 1983.

Benchley, Peter. *Jaws*. New York: Doubleday, 1974.

Benjamin, Walter. "The Work of Art in the Age of Mechanical Reproduction." In *Illuminations*, ed. Hannah Arendt and trans. Harry Zohn, pp. 219–53. New York: Harcourt, Brace & World, 1968.

Bertolucci, Bernardo. "Interview with Bernardo Bertolucci." *Bananas*, no. 4 (Spring 1976).

———. *Last Tango in Paris*. New York: Dell, 1973.

Bhaskar, Roy. *The Possibility of Naturalism: A Philosophical Critique of the Contemporary Human Sciences*. London: Routledge, 1998.

Blake, William. *The Poems of William Blake*, ed. W. H. Stevenson and David V. Erdman. London: Longman, 1972.

———. *The Poetry and Prose of William Blake*, ed. David V. Erdman. Garden City, NY: Doubleday, 1965.

Blatty, William Peter. *The Exorcist*. New York: Harper and Row, 1971.

Blumer, Herbert. *Movies and Conduct*. New York: Arno Press, 1970.

Bordwell, David. *Narration in the Fiction Film*. Madison: University of Wisconsin Press, 1985.

———, Janet Staiger, and Kristin Thompson. *The Classic Hollywood Cinema: Film Style and Mode of Production to 1960*. New York: Columbia University Press, 1985.

Brecht, Bertolt. *Brecht on Theatre: The Development of an Aesthetic*, ed. and trans. John Willett. New York: Hill & Wang, 1992.

Brewster, Ben, et al. "Reply." *Screen* 17, no. 2 (Summer 1976): 110–16.

———, Stephen Heath, and Colin MacCabe. "Comment." *Screen* 16, no. 2 (Summer 1975): 83–90.

Britton, Andew. *Katharine Hepburn: The Thirties and After*. London: Tyneside Cinema, 1984. Reprinted as *Katharine Hepburn: Star as Feminist*. New York: Continuum, 1984, and New York: Columbia University Press, 2003.

Brontë, Charlotte. *Jane Eyre*, ed. Mark Schorer. Boston: Houghton Mifflin, 1959.

Brown, Geoff. "*Mandingo*." *Monthly Film Bulletin* (August 1975): 178.

Brown, Norman O. *Hermes, the Thief: The Evolution of a Trickster*. New York: Vintage, 1969.

———. *Life Against Death: The Psychoanalytic Meaning of History*. New York: Vintage, 1959.

———. *Love's Body*. New York: Random House, 1966.

Burch, Noel. "Narrative/Diegesis—Threshold, Limits." *Screen* 23, no. 2 (July/August 1982): 16–33.

———, and Jorge Dana. "Propositions." *Afterimage* 5 (Spring 1974): 40–65.

Buscombe, Edward, Christine Gledhill, Alan Lovell, and Christopher Williams. "Statement: Psychoanalysis and Film." *Screen* 16, no. 4 (Winter 1975/76): 119–30.

Cameron, Ian, ed. *The Movie Book of Film Noir*. New York: Continuum, 1993.

Cant, Bob. "Fassbinder's *Fox*." *Jump Cut* 16 (1997): 22.

Clarke, Simon, et al. *One-Dimensional Marxism*. London: Allison & Busby, 1980.

Clifford, Gay. *The Transformations of Allegory*. London and Boston: Routledge and Kegan Paul, 1974.

Coleridge, Samuel Taylor. *The Collected Works of Samuel Taylor Coleridge*. Vol. 7, *Biographia Literaria*, ed. James Engell and W. Jackson Bate. Princeton, NJ: Princeton University Press, 1983.

Conrad, Joseph. "Heart of Darkness." In *Tales of Land and Sea*, pp. 33–104. Garden City, NY: Hanover House, 1953.

Cook, Pam, and Claire Johnston, eds. *Jacques Tourneur*. Edinburgh: Edinburgh Film Festival, 1975.

Cooper, James Fenimore. *The Pioneers*. New York: New American Library, 1964.

Coward, Rosalind. "Class, Culture, and the Social Formation." *Screen* 18, no. 1 (Spring 1977): 75–105.

———, and John Ellis. *Language and Materialism*. London: Routledge and Kegan Paul, 1977.

Cowie, Peter. *International Film Guide 1976*. London: Tantivy/New York: A. S. Barnes, 1972.

Crèvecoeur, Hector St. John de. *Letters from an American Farmer*. New York: Dutton, 1957.

Crimp, Douglas. "On the Museum's Ruins." In *The Anti-Aesthetic*, ed. Hal Foster, pp. 43–56. Port Townsend, WA: Bay Press, 1983.

Crofts, Stephen. "Debate: Psychoanalysis and Film (1)." *Framework* 4 (1976): 15–16.

Davis, Mike. "The New Right's Road to Power." *New Left Review* 128 (July/August 1981): 28–49.

———. "Urban Renaissance and the Spirit of Postmodernism." *New Left Review* 151 (May/June 1985): 106–13.

Derrida, Jacques. *Dissemination*. Chicago: University of Chicago Press, 1981.

———. *Writing and Difference*. Chicago: University of Chicago Press, 1978.

Descartes, René. "Rules for the Direction of the Mind." In *The Philosophical Writings of Descartes*, trans. John Cottingham, Robert Stoothoff, and Dugald Murdoch, pp. 7–78. Cambridge and New York: Columbia University Press, 1985.

Deutscher, Isaac. *Marxism in Our Time*. Berkeley: Ramparts Press, 1971.

Dickens, Charles. *A Tale of Two Cities*. Oxford: Oxford University Press, 1988.

Durgnat, Raymond. *Greta Garbo*. London: Studio Vista, 1965.

Dyer, Richard. "Entertainment and Utopia." *Movie* 24 (Spring 1977): 2–13.

———. "Gays in Film." *Jump Cut* 18 (1978): 15–17.

———. "It's Being So Camp as Keeps Us Going." *The Culture of Queers*, pp. 49–62. London and New York: Routledge, 2002.

———. "Pasolini and Homosexuality." In *Pier Paolo Pasolini*, ed. Paul Willemen. London: British Film Institute, 1977.

Editors of *Cahiers du cinéma*. "John Ford's *Young Mr. Lincoln*." In *Movies and Methods*. Vol. 2, ed. Bill Nichols, pp. 493–529. Berkeley: University of California Press, 1976.

Eisenstein, Sergei. "Charlie the Kid." In *Film Essays and a Lecture*, ed. Jay Leyda and trans. Herbert Marshall, pp. 108–139. Princeton, NJ: Princeton University Press, 1982.

———. *Ivan the Terrible*. London: Faber and Faber, 1989.

———. "Mr. Lincoln by Mr. Ford." In *Film Essays and a Lecture*, ibid. pp. 139–49.

———. *October and Alexander Nevsky*, ed. Jay Leyda. London: Lorrimer, 1984.

———. "Word and Image." In *The Film Sense*, ed. and trans. Jay Leyda, pp. 3–65. New York: Harcourt, Brace & World, 1947.

Eliot, George. *Daniel Deronda*. London: Dent, 1964.

———. *Middlemarch*, ed. Bert G. Hornback. New York: Norton, 1977.

Eliot, T. S. "Shakespeare and the Stoicism of Seneca." *Elizabethan Essays*, pp. 33–54. New York: Haskell House, 1964.

Ellis, John, and Rosalind Coward. *Language and Materialism*. London: Routledge and Kegan Paul, 1978.

Elsaesser, Thomas. "Tales of Sound and Fury: Observations on the Family Melodrama." *Monogram* 4 (1972): 2–15.

Engels, Frederick. *The Origins of the Family, Private Property and the State: In Light of the Researches of Lewis H. Morgan*. New York: International Publishers, 1972.

Faulkner, William. *The Sound and the Fury*. New York: Vintage, 1956.

Fiedler, Leslie. *Love and Death in the American Novel*, rev. ed. New York: Dell, 1967.

Firestone, Shulamith. *The Dialectic of Sex: The Case for Feminist Revolution*. New York: Morrow, 1974.

Fitzgerald, F. Scott. *Tender Is the Night*. New York: Charles Scribner's Sons, 1962.

Foster, Hal, ed. *The Anti-Aesthetic: Essays on Postmodern Culture*. Port Townsend, WA: Bay Press, 1983.

Foucault, Michel. *The Order of Things*. London: Tavistock Press, 1970.

Fox, Robin. *Kinship and Marriage: An Anthropological Perspective*. Harmondsworth, UK: Penguin, 1967. Reprinted Cambridge and New York: Cambridge University Press, 1983.

Franklin, Benjamin, "Information for Those Who Would Remove to America." In *Autobiography Selected Writings,* ed. Larzer Ziff, pp. 256–263. San Francisco: Rinehart Press, 1969.

———. *Poor Richard's Almanac*. In *The Autobiography and Other Writings of Benjamin Franklin*, ed. Frank Donovan. New York: Dodd, Mead, 1963.

Freeman, Rosemary. *English Emblem Books*. London: Chatto & Windus, 1948.

Freud, Sigmund. "A Case of Paranoia Running Counter to the Psychoanalytical Theory of the Disease." In *The Standard Edition of the Complete Psychological Works of Sigmund Freud,* ed. and trans. James Strachey. Vol. XIV, *On the History of the Psycho-Analytic Movement: Papers on Metapsychology and Other Works*, pp. 261–72. London: Hogarth Press and Institute of Psycho-Analysis, 1955.

———. *Collected Papers*, 4 vols., trans. Joan Riviere. London: Hogarth Press, 1953.

———. "Creative Writers and Day Dreaming." In *The Standard Edition*, ibid. Vol. IX, *Jensen's "Gravida" and Other Works*, pp. 141–54.

———. "From the History of an Infantile Neurosis." In *The Standard Edition*, ibid. Vol. XVII, *An Infantile Neurosis and Other Works*, pp. 3–123.

———. "Letter to an American Mother." *American Journal of Psychiatry* 107 (1951): 787.

———. "On Narcissism: An Introduction." In *The Standard Edition*, ibid. Vol. XIV, *On the History of the Psycho-Analytic Movement*, pp. 67–102.

———. *The Standard Edition*, ibid. Vol. XX, *An Autobiographical Study, Inhibitions, Symptoms and Anxiety, and the Question of Lay Analysis*, pp. 75–176.

———. *The Standard Edition*, ibid. Vol. XVIII, *Beyond the Pleasure Principle: Group Psychology and Other Works*, pp. 3–64.

———. *The Standard Edition*, ibid. Vol. VII, *A Case of Hysteria, Three Essays on the Theory of Sexuality, and Other Works*, pp. 123–245.

———. *The Standard Edition*, ibid. Vol. XXI, *The Future of an Illusion and Civilization and Its Discontents, pp. 59–145.*

———. *The Standard Edition*, ibid. Vol. IV, *The Interpretation of Dreams*, and Vol. V, *The Interpretation of Dreams, Part 2, and On Dreams.*

———. In *The Standard Edition,* ibid. Vol. XV, *Introductory Lectures on Psycho-Analysis*, pp. 123–34.

———. *The Standard Edition*, ibid. Vol. VIII, *Jokes and Their Relation to the Unconscious.*

———. "Thoughts for the Times on War and Death." In *The Standard Edition*, ibid. Vol. XIV, *On the History of the Psycho-Analytic Movement*, pp. 273–300.

———. "Types of Onset of Neurosis." In *The Standard Edition*, ibid. Vol. XII, *The Case of Schreber, Papers on Technique, and Other Works*, pp. 227–38.

Gardiner, Muriel, ed. *The Wolf-Man and Sigmund Freud*. London: Hogarth Press, 1972.

Gaskell, Elizabeth Cleghorn. *The Life of Charlotte Brontë*. New York: Dutton, 1960.

Gramsci, Antonio. *Selections from Cultural Writings*, ed. David Forgacs and Geoffrey Nowell-Smith and trans. William Boehlower. Cambridge, MA: Harvard University Press, 1985.

Grene, Marjorie Glicksman. *The Knower and the Known*. London: Faber and Faber, 1966.

Guthrie, Lee. *The Life and Loves of Cary Grant*. New York: Drake Publishers, 1977.

Habermas, Jürgen. "Modernity—An Incomplete Project." In *The Anti-Aesthetic*, ed. Hal Foster, pp. 3–15. Port Townsend, WA: Bay Press, 1983.

———. "A Philosophico-Political Profile." *New Left Review* 151 (May/June 1985): 75–105.

Hawthorne, Nathaniel. *The House of the Seven Gables*, ed. Hyatt J. Waggoner. Boston: Houghton Mifflin, 1964.

———. *The Marble Faun*. New York: New American Library, 1961.

———. *The Scarlet Letter*, ed. Sculley Bradley, Richmond Croom Beatty, and E. Hudson Long. New York: Norton, 1962.

Heath, Stephen. "*Anata Mo.*" *Screen* 17, no. 4 (Winter 1976/77): 49–66.

———. "Contexts." *Edinburgh '77 Magazine* (1977): 36–43.

———. "Film and System, Terms of Analysis," Pt. 1. *Screen* 16, no. 1 (Spring 1975): 7–77; Pt. 2. *Screen* 16, no. 2 (Summer 1975): 91–113.

———. "*Jaws*, Ideology and Film Theory." In *Movies and Methods*. Vol. 2, ed. Bill Nichols, pp. 509–14. Berkeley: University of California Press, 1985.

———. "Lessons from Brecht." *Screen* 15, no. 2 (Summer 1974): 103–28.

———. "Narrative Space." *Screen* 17, no. 3 (Autumn 1976): 68–112.

———. "Notes on Suture." *Screen* 17, no. 4 (Winter 1977/78): 48–76.

———. "Screen Images, Film Memory." *Edinburgh '76 Magazine* (1976): 33–43.

Herron, Jerry. "Postmodern Ground Zero, or Going to the Movies at Grand Circus Park." *Social Text* 18 (Winter 1987–88): 61–77.

Hillier, Jim. "Humphrey Jennings." In *Studies in Documentary* by Alan Lovell and Jim Hillier. New York: Viking Press, 1972.

Hobbes, Thomas. *Leviathan, or the Matter, Forme and Power of a Commonwealth Ecclesiastical and Civil*, ed. Michael Oakshott. New York: Collier, 1962.

Holly, Douglas. *Beyond Curriculum*. London: Hart-Davis MacGibbon, 1973.

Honour, Hugh. "The Battle over Post-Modern Buildings." *New York Review of Books* (29 September 1988): 27–33.

Horkheimer, Max, and Theodor Adorno. *Dialectic of Enlightenment*. New York: Continuum, 1972.

Horowitz, Joseph. *Understanding Toscanini*. New York: Knopf, 1987.

James, Henry. *The Ambassadors*, ed. S. P. Rosenbaum. New York: Norton, 1994.

———. "The Beast in the Jungle." In *Henry James: Selected Fiction*, ed. Leon Edel, pp. 482–535. New York: Dutton, 1964.

———. "Crapy Cornelia." In *The New York Stories of Henry James*, ed. Colm Toibin. New York: New York Review Books, 2006.

———. *The Portrait of a Lady*, ed. Leon Edel. Boston: Houghton Mifflin, 1963.

———. *The Sacred Fount. Novels, 1901–1902*. New York: Library of America, 2006.

———. "The Turn of the Screw." In *Ghostly Tales of Henry James*, ed. Leon Edel, pp. 212–337. New York: Grosset & Dunlap, 1963.

———. *Washington Square*. In *Selected Fiction*, ed. Leon Edel, pp. 80–288. New York: Dutton, 1964.

Jameson, Fredric. "'In the Destructive Element Immerse': Hans-Jürgen Syberberg and Cultural Revolution." *October* 17 (Summer 1981): 99–118.

———. "Postmodernism, or the Cultural Logic of Late Capitalism." *New Left Review* 146 (July/August 1984): 53–92.

———. *The Prison-House of Language*. Princeton, NJ: Princeton University Press, 1974.

Johnston, Claire. "Femininity and the Masquerade: *Anne of the Indies*." In *Jacques Tourneur*, ed. Paul Willemen and Claire Johnnston, pp. 36–44. Edinburgh: Edinburgh Film Festival, 1975.

———. "Towards a Feminist Film Practice: Some Theses." In *Movies and Methods*. Vol. 2, ed. Bill Nichols, pp. 315–26. Berkeley: University of California Press, 1985.

———, and Paul Willemen. "Penthesilea, Queen of the Amazons—Interview with Laura Mulvey and Peter Wollen." *Screen* 15, no. 3 (Autumn 1974): 120–34.

Jones, John. *John Keats's Dream of Truth*. London: Chatto & Windus, 1969.

Kael, Pauline. "The Man from Dream City: Cary Grant." *When the Lights Go Down, pp.* 3–32. New York: Holt, Rinehart & Winston, 1980.

———. "The Pure and the Impure." *Taking It All In*, pp. 347–55. New York: Holt, Rinehart & Winston, 1984.

Kroker, Arthur, and Michael Dorland. "Panic Cinema: Sex in the Age of the Hyperreal." *CineAction* 10 (Fall 1987): 2–5.

Lacan, Jacques. *Ecrits*. Paris: Les Editions du Seuil, 1966. (*Ecrits: The First Complete Edition in English*, trans. Bruce Fink. New York: Norton, 2006.)

———. "God and the Jouissance of Woman." In *Feminine Sexuality: Jacques Lacan and the Ecole Freudienne*, ed. Juliet Mitchell and Jacqueline Rose, pp. 137–49. London: Macmillan 1982.

———. *The Language of the Self: The Function of Language in Psychoanalysis*, ed. and trans. Anthony Wilden. Baltimore: Johns Hopkins University Press, 1968.

———. *Le Séminaire de Jacques Lacan*, ed. Jacques-Alain Miller. Paris: Editions du seuil, 1975.

Laclau, Ernesto, and Chantal Mouffe. *Hegemony and Socialist Strategy: Towards a Radical Democratic Politics*. London: Verso, 1985.

———. "Post-Marxism Without Apologies." *New Left Review* 166 (November/December 1987): 79–106.

Lawrence, D. H. *Studies in Classic American Literature*. New York: Penguin, 1971.

———. *Women in Love*. New York: Viking, 1964.

Leavis, F. R. *Anna Karenina and Other Essays*. London: Chatto & Windus, 1973.

———. *D. H. Lawrence: Novelist*. New York: Knopf, 1956.

———. *English Literature in Our Time and the University*. London: Chatto & Windus, 1969.

———. *The Great Tradition*. Harmondsworth, Middlesex: Penguin, 1962.

———. *The Living Principle*. London: Chatto & Windus, 1975.

———. *Nor Shall My Sword: Discourses on Pluralism, Compassion and Social Hope*. London: Chatto & Windus, 1971.

———. *Revaluation: Tradition and Development in English Poetry*. New York: Norton, 1947.

———. "Reply." *Scrutiny* XIX, no. 4 (1953): 321–28.

———. "The Responsible Critic or the Function of Criticism at Any Time." *Scrutiny* XIX, no. 3 (1953): 162–83.

Lévi-Strauss, Claude. *The Raw and the Cooked: Introduction to a Science of Mythology—I*, trans. John Weightman and Doreen Weightman. New York and Evanston: Harper & Row, 1969.

———. *Structural Anthropology*, trans. Claire Jacobson and Brooke Grundfest Schoepf. New York: Doubleday, 1967.

Lewis, Sinclair. *Elmer Gantry*. New York: Signet, 1970.

Lovell, Terry. *Pictures of Reality: Aesthetics, Politics, Pleasure*. London: British Film Institute, 1980.

Macbean, James Roy. "*Vent d'est* or Godard and Rocha at the Crossroads." In *Movies and Methods*. Vol. 1, ed. Bill Nichols, pp. 91–106. Berkeley: University of California Press, 1976.

MacCabe, Colin. "Presentation of 'The Imaginary Signifier.'" *Screen* 16, no. 2 (Summer 1975): 7–13.

———. "Realism and the Cinema: Notes on Some Brechtian Theses." *Screen* 15, no. 2 (Summer 1974): 7–27.

———. "Theory and Film: Principles of Realism and Pleasure." *Screen* 17, no. 3 (Autumn 1976): 7–28.

Mailer, Norman. *Advertisements for Myself*. New York: Putnam, 1959.

Mandel, Ernest. "The Threat of Nuclear War and the Struggle for Socialism." *New Left Review* 141 (September/October 1983): 23–50.

Mann, Thomas. *Dr. Faustus*, trans. H. T. Lowe-Porter. London: Secker & Warburg, 1959.

Marcuse, Herbert. *The Aesthetic Dimension: Towards a Critique of Marxist Aesthetics*. Boston: Beacon Press, 1978.

Marx, Karl. *Capital: A Critique of Political Economy*, ed. Frederick Engels. New York: International Publishers, 1967.

——. *Outlines of the Critique of Political Economy*, trans. Martin Nicolaus. New York: Penguin, 1973.

McCarthy, Todd. "Sand Castles." *Film Comment* 18, no. 3 (May/June 1982): 53–59.

Melville, Herman. "Benito Cerino." In *Selected Tales and Poems*, ed. Richard Chase, pp. 3–91. New York: Holt, Rinehart & Winston, 1950.

——. *Billy Budd, Sailor (An Inside Narrative)*, ed. Harrison Hayford and Merton M. Sealts Jr. Chicago and London: University of Chicago Press, 1962.

——. *The Confidence-Man*, ed. Herschell Parker. New York: Norton, 1971.

——. "I and My Chimney." In *Selected Tales and Poems*, ed. Richard Chase, pp. 159–89. New York: Holt, Rinehart & Winston, 1950.

——. *Moby Dick; or, The Whale*, ed. Harrison Hayford and Hershel Parker. New York: Norton, 1967.

——. "The Paradise of Bachelors and the Tartarus of Maids." In *Selected Tales and Poems*, ed. Richard Chase, pp. 206–29. New York: Holt, Rinehart, & Winston, 1950.

——. *Pierre, or The Ambiguities*. New York: Grove Press, 1957.

Middleton, Thomas, and William Rowley. *The Changeling*, ed. N. W. Bawcutt. London: Methuen, 1970.

Miller, Jacques-Alain. "Suture: Elements of the Logic of the Signifier." *Screen* 18, no. 4 (Winter 1977–78): 24–34.

Mitchell, Juliet. *Psychoanalysis and Feminism*. London: Penguin, 1975.

——. *Woman's Estate*. Harmondsworth, Middlesex: Penguin, 1971.

Montagu, Ivor. *With Eisenstein in Hollywood*. New York: International Publishers, 1969.

Mulvey, Laura. "Visual Pleasure and Narrative Cinema." *Screen* 16, no. 3 (Autumn 1975): 6–18.

Nash, Mark. *Dreyer*. London: British Film Institute, 1977.

——. "*Vampyr* and the Fantastic." *Screen* 17, no. 3 (Autumn 1976): 29–67.

Neale, Steve. "*Personal Views*." *Screen* 17, no. 3 (Autumn 1976): 120–22.

Nowell-Smith, Geoffrey. "Editorial." *Screen* 18, no. 1 (Spring 1977): 5–7.

——. "Minnelli and Melodrama." *Screen* 18, no. 2 (Summer 1977): 113–18.

Orwell, George. "Inside the Whale." *The Collected Essays, Journalism and Letters of George Orwell*. Vol. 1, *An Age Like This: 1920–1940*, pp. 493–526. London: Secker and Warburg, 1968.

Owens, Craig. "Feminists and Postmodernism." In *The Anti-Aesthetic*, ed. Hal Foster, pp. 57–82. Port Townsend, WA: Bay Press, 1983.

Poe, Edgar Allan. *The Complete Stories and Poems of Edgar Allan Poe*. Garden City, New York: Doubleday, 1966.

Pope, Alexander. *The Works of Alexander Pope*, 10 vols., ed. Whitwell Elwin and William John Courthope. London: John Murray, 1881.

Propp, Vladimir. *Morphology of the Folktale*, ed. Luis A. Wagner and trans. Laurence Scott. Austin and London: University of Texas Press, 1975.

Ricoeur, Paul. *The Rule of Metaphor*. Toronto: University of Toronto Press, 1977.

———. "Structure-Word-Event." *Philosophy Today* 12, nos. 2/4 (1968): 114–29.

———. "What Is a Text?" In *Hermeneutics and the Human Sciences: Essays on Language, Action and Interpretation*, ed. John B. Thompson, pp. 145–64. Cambridge: Cambridge University Press, 1981.

Riffaterre, Michael. "Describing Poetic Structures: Two Approaches to Baudelaire's Les Chats." *Yale French Studies* 36–37 (1966): 200–242.

Robinson, David. "A Matter of Life and Death." *London Times* (12 September 1975): 10.

Robinson, Kenneth. "Black Comedy: *Mandingo*." *The Spectator* (20 September 1975): 387.

Rose, Jacqueline. "Paranoia and the Film System." *Screen* 17, no. 4 (Winter 1976/77): 85–104.

Rosen, Charles. "The Ruins of Walter Benjamin." In *On Walter Benjamin: Critical Essays and Reflections*, ed. Gary Smith, pp. 129–75. Cambridge, MA: MIT Press, 1988.

———, and Henri Zerner. *Romanticism and Realism: The Mythology of Nineteenth-Century Art*. New York: Norton, 1984.

Roud, Richard. *Max Ophüls—An Index*. London: British Film Institute, 1958.

Rubin, Isaak Il'lich. *Essays on Marx's Theory of Value*, trans. Miloš Samard-zija and Fredy Perlman. Detroit: Black and Red, 1972.

Russell, Bertrand. *History of Western Philosophy*. London: Allen & Unwin, 1967.

Sartre, Jean-Paul. *Saint Genet: Actor and Martyr*, trans. Bernard Frechtman. New York: Mentor, 1964.

Saussure, Ferdinand de. *Course in General Linguistics*, ed. Charles Bally and Albert Sechehaye and trans. Wade Baskin. New York: McGraw-Hill, 1959.

Schatzman, Morton. *Soul Murder: Persecution in the Family*. London: Allen Lane, 1973 and New York: Random House, 1973.

Scheib, Ronnie. "Charlie's Uncle." *Film Comment* 12, no. 2 (March/April 1976): 55–62.

Seaton, Marie. *Sergei M. Eisenstein: A Biography*. London: D. Dobson, 1978.

Shipman, David. *The Great Movie Stars: The Golden Years*. New York: Bonanza Books, 1970.

Sontag, Susan. "Notes on Camp." *Against Interpretation*, pp. 275–92. New York: Dell, 1966.

Sragow, Michael. "A Conversation with Steven Spielberg." In *Steven Spielberg Interviews*, ed. Lester D. Friedman and Bret Notbohm, pp. 107–13. Jackson: University Press of Mississippi, 2002.

Stowe, Harriet Beecher. *Uncle Tom's Cabin, or Life Among the Lowly*. New York: Signet, 1966.

Suid, Lawrence. "Hollywood and Vietnam." *Film Comment* 15, no. 5 (September/October 1979): 20–25.

Sweezy, Paul M., Leo Huberman, and Harry Magdoff. *Vietnam: The Endless War, from Monthly Review*. New York: Monthly Review Press, 1970.

Thompson, Edward. *The Poverty of Theory and Other Essays*. London: Merlin Press, 1978.

Thompson, Kristin, and David Bordwell. "Space and Narrative in the Films of Ozu." *Screen* 17, no. 2 (Summer 1976): 41–73.

Thompson, Kristin. *Ivan the Terrible: A Neoformalist Analysis*. Princeton, NJ: Princeton University Press, 1981

Thompson, Richard. "Screenwriter: *Taxi Driver*'s Paul Schrader." *Film Comment* 12, no. 2 (March/April 1976): 6–11.

Timpanero, Sebastiano. *On Materialism*. London: New Left Books, 1976.

Trotsky, Leon. *Literature and Revolution*, trans. Rose Strumsky. New York: International, 1925.

Truffaut, Francois. *Hitchcock*. New York: Simon and Schuster, 1967.

Tunstall, Jeremy. *The Media Are American: Anglo-american Media in the World*. New York: Columbia University Press, 1977.

Twain, Mark. *The Adventures of Huckleberry Finn*, ed. Thomas Cooley. New York: Norton, 1999.

———. *Puddn'head Wilson*. London: Penguin, 1986.

Ulmer, Gregory. "The Object of Post Criticism." In *The Anti-Aesthetic*, ed. Hal Foster, 83–110. Port Townsend, WA: Bay Press, 1983.

Unger, Steven. "Deutscher and the New Left in America." In *Isaac Deutscher: The Man and His Work*, ed. David Horowitz, pp. 211–25. London: Macdonald, 1971.

Walton, James. "Caleb Williams and the Novel Form." *Salzburg Studies in English Literature* No. 47, Institut für Englische Sprache and Literatur (1975).

White, Morton, and Lucia White. *The Intellectual Versus the City*. Cambridge, MA: Harvard University Press and MIT Press, 1962.

Whitman, Walt. *Leaves of Grass*, ed. Sculley Bradley and Harold W. Blodgett. New York: Norton, 1973.

Willemen, Paul. "Notes Towards the Construction of Readings of Jacques Tourneur." In *Jacques Tourneur*, ed. Claire Johnston and Paul Willemen, pp. 16–35. Edinburgh Film Festival, 1975.

———, ed. *Ophüls*. London: British Film Institute, 1978.

Williams, Raymond. *Marxism and Literature*. New York and Oxford: Oxford University Press, 1978.

———. "The Road to Vitebsk: The Uses of Cultural Theory." *New Left Review* 158 (July/August 1986): 19–31.

———. *Television: Technology and Cultural Form*. New York: Schocken Books, 1975.

———. "The Uses of Cultural Theory." *New Left Review* 158 (July/August 1986): 19–31.

Williams, William Carlos. *In the American Grain*. New York: New Directions Books, 1956.

Wolfe, Alan. "Sociology, Liberalism and the Radical Right." *New Left Review* 128 (July/August 1981): 3–27.

Wollen, Peter. "Godard and Counter-Cinema." In *Movies and Methods*. Vol. 2, ed. Bill Nichols, pp. 500–509. Berkeley: University of California Press, 1985.

———. "Ontology and Materialism in Film." *Screen* 17, no. 1 (Spring 1976): 7–25.

———. *Signs and Meaning in the Cinema*, 3rd ed. Bloomington: Indiana University Press, 1972.

Wood, Robin. "Democracy and Shpontanuity: Leo McCarey and the Hollywood Tradition." *Film Comment* 12, no. 1 (January/February 1976): 6–15.

———. *Hitchcock's Films Revisited*. New York: Columbia University Press, 1986.

———. *Hollywood from Vietnam to Reagan*. New York: Columbia University Press, 1986.

———. *Howard Hawks*. London: British Film Institute, 1981. Reprinted Detroit: Wayne State University Press, 2006.

———. "Ideology, Genre, Auteur." In *Film Genre Reader 3*, ed. Barry Keith Grant, pp. 60–74. Austin: University of Texas Press, 2003.

———. "Introduction to the American Horror Film." In *The American Nightmare*, eds. Andrew Britton, Richard Lippe, Tony Williams, and Robin Wood, pp. 7–32. Toronto: Festival of Festivals, 1979.

———. *Personal Views*, rev. ed. Detroit: Wayne State University Press, 2006.

———. "The Shadow Worlds of Jacques Tourneur." *Film Comment* 8, no. 2 (Summer 1972): 64–70.

———, and Richard Lippe, ed. *The American Nightmare: Essays on the Horror Film*. Toronto: Festival of Festivals, 1979.

Zaretsky, Eli. *Capitalism: The Family, and Personal Life*. London: Pluto Press, 1976.

Index

Page numbers in boldface refer to photographs.

Designed by David Alcorn, Alcorn Publication Design
Typeset by Alcorn Publication Design
Composed in the Minion Pro family of fonts by Adobe, with
display type set in the Futura Std family of Open Type by Adobe